THE W.E.A. EDUCATION YEAR BOOK 1918

THE W.E.A.
EDUCATION YEAR BOOK
1918

Reprinted

with

introductory essays

by

HERBERT DELAUNEY HUGHES

and

GEOFFREY FREDERICK BROWN

I.S.B.N.: 0 902031 57 0

Printed by Barnes & Humby Ltd., Nottingham.

THE W.E.A. EDUCATION YEAR BOOK 1918

Introductory Essays

1.   A General Introduction to the Year Book—H. D. Hughes   5

2.   The Workers' Educational Association and Educational
     Reform—G. F. Brown   13

The W.E.A. Education Year Book 1918   27

THE W.E.A. EDUCATION YEAR BOOK 1918

A General Introduction to the Year Book

H. D. (Bill) HUGHES
Former Principal of Ruskin College Oxford
and
Former President of the Workers' Educational Association

A GENERAL INTRODUCTION TO THE YEAR BOOK

1918/19, like 1944/45, were years of hope for educational advance. The Fisher Act, while falling far short of the recommendations submitted to the Reconstruction Committee by the WEA and other progressive bodies, nevertheless marked a considerable advance, including permissive powers to LEA's to introduce compulsory part time education for the 14-16 age group. The 1919 Report of the Adult Education Committee became the blue-print for advance in the much neglected area of 'life-long' education.[1]

The WEA, founded in 1903, had emerged from the trials of the war in remarkably good shape. It saw itself as a federation of working class and progressive bodies aiming at educational and social reform. 'It becomes more and more plain that education is the way to power', wrote the Rev. Temple, President. 'Education becomes more and more necessary to the realisation of anything like true democracy.[2]

Linked with the Association, at national, district and branch level, were over 2,700 organisations, including over 1,000 trade unions, trades councils and trade union branches, 465 Co-operative societies and committees, 189 adult schools and brotherhoods, 96 working men's clubs and institutes, and 629 'various societies, mainly of workpeople'. Educational partners included 199 teachers' associations, 77 educational and literacy societies, 8 Universities and 12 LEAs.

Tutorial classes had risen to 121 in 1917-18, with 3,000 students; half of them concerned with economics, industrial and social history. Of equal importance were 238 one year classes and study circles, and 402 short courses.[3]

'The interests of the great majority of students naturally turn to those subjects which are directly related to those social and industrial problems which constitute the issues raised by political parties (J. M. Mactavish, General Secretary).[4] 69 conferences, mainly on educational reconstruction, were convened in 1918, campaigning on the basis of the Association's memorandum on educational reconstruction, some of the planks of which are of considerable contemporary interest today. Some districts were paying special attention to women's classes, with a wide spread including singing, elocution, home nursing, infant welfare, business correspondence and shorthand. There was a special committee on adult rural education, and gardening classes (? dig for victory) were being promoted in the North East, Western and London districts. (London also noted the increasing popularity of Literature.)

Individual membership rose by nearly 50% in 1917/18 to 14,697; but the branches consisted mainly of their affiliated bodies. Grants from the Board of Education increased to £45 per tutorial class and some LEAs 'enable branches to pay small tuition fees to many tutors . . . a considerable number, however, render voluntary service . . . tutorial classes must aim at inspiring and equipping their students to become teachers and leaders of classes and study groups (Mactavish).[5]

---

1. *The 1919 Report, The Final and Interim Reports of the Adult Education Committee of the Ministry of Reconstruction 1918-1919.* Reprinted by Department of Adult Education, University of Nottingham 1980.

2. See this volume *'Leading Facts in the History of the WEA'* (p. 325).

3. *W.E.A. Annual Report 1918.*

4. See this volume *The WEA 'Its Propaganda, Organisation and Method'* (p. 330).

5. Ibid. (p. 332).

The leaders of the Association saw the termination of hostilities as providing the country with 'the greatest educational opportunity in its history'. Seeing the WEA as having an important role to play in achieving this, they produced this ambitious Year Book, which seems to combine the functions now performed by the National Institute of Adult Education Report and Journal, UCAE and DES statistical reports, and other educational publications all rolled into one.

What a galaxy of talent it assembles! It would be difficult today to find a team comparable with Shaw, Galsworthy, J. A. Hobson, S. G. Hobson, G. D. H. Cole, H. G. Wells, Margaret McMillan, Sidney Webb, Beatrice Webb, and Lord Haldane, to single out only those names whose records have survived the test of time, not to mention the High Master of Manchester Grammar School, the late Chief Inspector of Elementary Schools, and the Reader in Education of Oxford University!

The total result is perhaps somewhat confused. There are brilliant individual contributions on educational philosophy, mainly directed at the schools. There is an analysis of the existing school system with brief comparative studies. There is the WEA manifesto on educational reconstruction. There is a descriptive picture of the WEA and its related bodies, notably the Universities. (It is significant that little attention, if any, is paid to the role of LEAs in further and adult education.) Perhaps because of the imminence of the 1919 Report of the Ministry of Reconstruction, there is no real development of the case for adult and continuing education. A firm editorial hand seems to have been lacking. Nevertheless, the volume gives a fascinating picture of the educational system as it was and as it was hoped it might become. It is a pity that the effort to produce a year book was not repeated in later years.

Over half a century later, the Russell Report described the WEA as 'unique among the voluntary bodies . . . for many years a pioneer not only in bringing university quality adult education to a wider public but also in the teaching methods it has fostered and the degree and kind of student participation it has encouraged.'[6] Unique also, surely in the partnership it has established between labour and learning, bringing working class organisations like trade unions, co-operatives and working men's clubs into direct partnership with the universities and the state. The alternative is described in J. F. Horrabin's brief section on the Plebs League—where are they now?[7]

Mactavish faces the issue squarely. 'The prevailing opinion that the study of controversial questions is not a fit object for grant aid is in no small measure due to . . . the problem of denominational teaching . . . No matter whether the teacher be a follower of Marx or Marshall, so long as he does not seek to proselytize his students aids them to select, arrange and sift the facts of the problems, and tests the value of what he has achieved by the amount of independent thought existing in the class, his services ought to be enlisted . . . To encourage the study of technical subjects by the payment of grants, while refusing to assist the study of other subjects that are equally vital to the mental and spiritual well-being of the community on the ground that they are controversial, is enthroning Philistinism and damning back the finest qualities of our people.'[8] Fortunately the liberal approach to adult

6. *Adult Education: A Plan for Development*. HMSO 1973 para. 226.

7. See this volume Plebs League (p. 390)

8. See this volume (pp. 332-3).

education has long been accepted by our educational authorities, and enabled the WEA to continue to expand.

What then was the essential role of the WEA as seen in 1918, and to what extent has it changed in the ensuing sixty years?

In 1918, despite the extravagances of the Plebs League, the WEA was clearly an educational instrument of the working class movement, as the federal nature of its branch structure and the content of its classes, outlined at the beginning of this article, clearly shows. It was in the business of 'education with a social purpose'. As Professor Bernard Jennings has said, 'The Branches were at first federations of working class and educational bodies rather than individual members. The WEA was set up not to *reach* the workers, but to *be* the workers, to *unite* the workers . . . the WEA succeeded because, although it did not secure the support of the entire working class movement, enough co-operative, trade union, political and educational societies identified with it to guarantee its genuinely working class character.'[9]

In the post war period, as J. H. Matthews has written 'workers education was beginning to change slowly into adult education.'[10] By 1923/4, literature (78 tutorial classes) was pressing hotly on the heels of economics (81). The major occupational groups of students were 'clerks, secretaries, etc. 1446, teachers 1382, housewives and domestics 972, followed by colliery workers 538, engineers 513, metal workers 479, civil servants 362'. The attempt of the TUC to amalgamate the various organisations catering for workers' education had founded. But the WETUC continued to provide for trade union needs, with 'no falling off' even during the general strike.

The 1924 Adult Education Regulations, raising the standards of class work, and improving tutors' salaries 'marked an important stage in the development of the WEA's relations with the Board of Education' (Mary Stocks).[11] LEAs were brought into the picture as grant-aiding bodies. The future trends were evident.[12]

Reporting in 1973, the Russell Committee said 'the WEA's original purpose remains its profession, which is still 'to stimulate and satisfy the demands of adults, in particular members of workers' movements, for education.'[13]

In its evidence to Russell, the Association had indicated four priority areas of work

—education for the socially and culturally deprived
—work in an industrial context
—political and social education
—courses of liberal and academic study below the level of university work.

Given limited resources, it had been most successful in developing the fourth of these, which had become regarded as its traditional work, and the influx of individual members many of them white-collar and professional people, into its branches, had stimulated this type of programme.

9. 'Looking backwards and forwards.' Text of lecture to WEA National Council, June 1978. *WEA News No. 15* Autumn 1978.
10. Unpublished letter to E. Mooney, author of thesis on J. A. Mactavish (Liverpool).
11. *The WEA: the first 50 years.* Mary Stocks (1953).
12. *WEA Annual Report 1924.*
13. *Adult Education: A Plan for Development* para 111.

But side by side with this, through its trade union affiliations, there was developing a considerable volume of individual work in partnership with the TUC education department, with its own core of specialist tutors. Interesting experimental work in education for the socially and culturally deprived was being pioneered in a number of districts. 'Unfinished Business'[14] had reaffirmed the WEA's belief in 'education with a social purpose.'

In its belated response to the Russell Report, the Department of Education and Science took the Association at its word. Increased grant aid would be considered if the Association was prepared to commit itself to developing work in the first three priority areas. The fourth, which the Association regarded as its essential base, would have to suffer some temporary diminution—indeed Russell had suggested that much of it might be taken over by the LEAs, with the WEA being mainly a promotional body.

By 1981, the Association, though not relinquishing its hold on the 'traditional work' which the bulk of its individual membership holds dear, had accepted growth targets in the priority areas, and in most areas had made the 'substantial effort of reorientation' indicated by the Russell Committee as necessary if a better balance was to be achieved. About a quarter of its work was in trade union education, and one fifth each in education for the deprived, and in social and political education. The problem facing the Districts is to fuse the new work, largely professionally promoted, with the broader liberal adult education which forms the core of the branch programmes. In some areas, new industrial branches are coming into existence side by side with the traditional branches. Elsewhere, special industrial committees are being formed within the branch structure. 'Workers' education' and 'adult education' are uneasy bedfellows, but each has much to offer the other, and the tension, properly handled, is a constructive one.[15]

University tutorial classes are now a far smaller proportion of the work of the WEA, and of the University extra-mural departments, concerned as they are with 'post-experience' work of various kinds. There is a much closer partnership with the adult education work of LEAs, which though temporarily cut-back by cuts in public expenditure should grow in the long run with the establishment of Local Development Councils on Russell lines.

Though still active as an educational pressure group, the Association no longer holds the central position in this respect that was indicated in the 1918 Year Book. The Council for Educational Advance is now dominated by the educational trade unions, all affiliated to the TUC. The National Institute of Adult Education brings together the LEAs, the Universities, and a wide range of voluntary and statutory bodies. The new Advisory Council on Adult and Continuing Education is charged with the task of promoting the development of future policies and priorities, with full regard to the concept of education as a process continuing throughout life. The Save Adult Education Campaign is endeavouring to fight the battle of the cuts and campaigning for a new statutory basis for adult education. WEA people are prominent in all these bodies, but the Association is no longer a still small voice, crying alone in the wilderness, as it must often have seemed in the early days.

---

14. '*Unfinished Business*' WEA.

15. See, for example *WEA News* No. 16 Spring 1979. Article on 'Policies for the Future' by P. Caldwell, P. Gerhardt and Ray Kohn.

Tawney wrote half-a-century ago 'the hereditary curse upon English education is its organisation upon lines of social class'. 'As Professor Halsey and Goldthorpe have recently shown in their analyses of the Nuffield Social Mobility project, recent evidence holds no comfort for those who believe that inequalities of educational opportunity have been eradicated, particularly in access to higher education. Some 60% of the adult population parted company with the educational system at the age of 16 or less. The priority task of adult and continuing education must be to seek to cater for their needs, at all levels from basic education to academic study for those so motivated. The task of the WEA remains to promote and provide for this to the limits of its own resources, and to pressurise the public educational system to co-operate in the development of a comprehensive network combining the respective strengths of statutory and voluntary bodies, professionals and volunteers.'[16]

The 1918 Year Book had as its contemporary the seminal Reports of the Adult Education Committee of the Ministry of Reconstruction, which paved the way for so many of the post war developments. In the view of many, we are now approaching a period in which adult and continuing education will soon have to be fully recognised, in the words of the 1919 Report, as a permanent national necessity. Social and technological changes are making it clear that initial education, to the age of 16 or through college and university to 21 or 25, cannot alone meet the requirements of education for democracy, which requires mature minds constantly exercised on problems of social concern. We need a comprehensive system of adult and continuing education to cater for the vocational, individual and social needs of men and women of all ages. To achieve this we need a firm legislative base making it clear that it is the duty of the public educational system to secure such provision, in partnership with the voluntary bodies old and new.

This is even clearer today than it was to the contributors of the 1918 Year Book. It is to be hoped, however, that the re-publication of this remarkable symposium will stimulate still further discussion and understanding of the history and purpose of the adult education movement which has made such a significant contribution to society in the twentieth century, and has yet a greater one to make, in the future.

---

16. Presidential Address to the WEA Conference, Harrogate, 1981, by H. D. Hughes.

11

THE W.E.A. EDUCATION YEAR BOOK 1918

The Workers' Educational Association and Educational Reform

GEOFFREY F. BROWN

Lecturer in Modern Social History
Department of Adult Education, University of Nottingham

THE WORKERS' EDUCATIONAL ASSOCIATION AND EDUCATIONAL REFORM

From its inception the WEA had educational reform as one of its objectives. The third object of the Association decided upon at the founding conference in 1903 was : "The development of an efficient School Continuation System"—and to this was added the statement that "The time might not be far distant when the Association might well commit itself to an attempt to secure compulsory Evening School education up to the age of 17, but such a step would at the present probably be premature".[1] For the next forty years the WEA was to be concerned in trying to bring about the establishment of a more extensive provision of post-elementary education, or secondary education as it soon came to be called.

The WEA began its work as an educational pressure group in a modest way by carrying out a small enquiry into attendance at Evening Schools. The findings of this were presented to a conference at Oxford in August 1905, one of the Association's activities on the fringe of the Extension Movement's summer meeting.[2] On 22nd November, 1905 a WEA deputation led by Will Crooks, Labour MP for Woolwich, lobbied the Board of Education demanding the bringing about of compulsory attendance at continuation schools, and urging the Board to ask Local Education Authorities whether employers and employees in their areas would welcome legislation to bring about compulsory attendance at Evening Schools.[3] Mansbridge later claimed that this deputation to the Board was the first "entirely composed of working-class representatives."[4] The Board's response was to refer the question to its Consultative Committee which reported on Continuation Schools in 1909. The Committee estimated that there were at any one time 170,000 children between 12 and 14 years old who had left school and who were not attending any weekday classes, and that added to this there were large numbers of other children who were still at day school who were "engaged in wage-earning occupations which injure their physical development and prevent them from deriving full benefit from such education as they receive." Only one in four of the two million children between 14 and 17 received any continued education.[5]

The outbreak of war in 1914 led to a considerable intensification of the WEA's concern with educational reform. The labour shortage and the drive to maximise war production tended to draw children into the labour market in an even more important way and to the great detriment of their education. The WEA's paper, *The Highway*, from the end of 1914 gave increasingly more attention to the question of child labour. In the May 1915 issue, for instance, it carried a detailed article on the subject. Shortly afterwards the WEA's national office produced a widely circulated pamphlet on the issue, and representations were made to the Board of Education.[6] This pattern—careful enquiry, modest demands, and polite

1. Quoted in W. H. Draper, *University Extension. A Survey of Fifty Years, 1873-1923* (Cambridge 1923) pp. 67-68.

2. T. W. Price, *The Story of the WEA, 1903-1924* (London 1924) p. 27.

3. B. Simon *Education and the Labour Movement, 1870-1920* (London 1965) p. 308 and WEA publication No. 7 *Attendance at Evening Schools* (London 1906).

4. A. Mansbridge, *An Adventure in Working-Class Education* (London 1920) p. 17.

5. Extracts from Board of Education Report on Continuation Schools 1909, quoted in W. Van Der Eyken *Education, the Child and Society: a documentary history 1900-1973* (Harmondsworth 1973) p. 163.

6. *WEA Annual Report 1915*, p. 20, see also T. W. Price, op. cit., pp. 60-61.

lobbying—seemed to be well established. But, from 1916, the WEA pursued educational reform with considerably more vigour, made larger demands, and, wherever possible, sought to mobilise mass support. This new approach was not initially welcomed by the WEA's national officers. Rather it was an approach which was forced upon them.

The origins of it seem to have been a delegate conference organised by the WEA at the Memorial Hall, Farringdon Street, London, on 22nd January, 1916, to discuss the decision made by the London County Council, in the interests of wartime economies, to cut £360,000 off the education budget. A WEA head office sponsored resolution was put to the meeting of delegates from trade union branches, local labour parties, co-operative organisations and other working class organisations. The resolution recognised that some cuts were inevitable in the circumstances, but sought to pledge the WEA and its affiliated organisations to resist those cuts which might have "an effect prejudicial to the mental development of the children in London," and finally to work for the improvement of the education service in London. The resolution was moved by the WEA's president, the Rev. William Temple, and seconded by Margaret McMillan. Both of them said that the LCC had made the best of a bad job. A dissenting note quickly emerged with Marion Phillips of the Women's Labour League disagreeing about the LCC's efforts while still supporting the resolution. Even this was not enough for some of the delegates. Herbert Morrison (representing the National Union of Clerks) and Susan Lawrence put forward an amendment to the resolution which some delegates welcomed as an attempt to put "some backbone" into the original resolution. Temple and McMillan were forced to accept the amendment—which substituted for the original preamble of "Whilst recognising that some changes detrimental to the efficiency of education were unavoidable during the present crisis," a new one which read "Recognising the policy of educational reaction, decided upon by the leaders of the two official parties on the London County Council at its meeting of 9th November last, as opposed to the true interests of the workers and the nation as a whole, the meeting calls upon" etc. Two other leading figures in the London Labour Party, J. S. Whybrew of the Workmen's National Housing Council, and John Stokes, a member of the SDF and chairman of the London Trades Council, then moved a resolution which went even further. It said that if the LCC did not rescind the cuts, then the conference should pledge itself "to use every influence to prevent the re-election of every member of the LCC who, by speech or vote, has indicated, or may indicate, approval of economy in education prejudicial to the future of the children of London." Since Susan Lawrence was the only member of the LCC who was speaking out against the cuts, and also was the only Labour member of the Council, there seemed to be the danger that this resolution, if approved, would commit the WEA to work against the Conservative and Progressive Parties on the LCC. Such a possibility clearly worried the WEA platform since it was an obvious departure from the association's customary "non-political" stance. A way round the problem was found by the chairman ruling that the resolution would not commit the WEA as such, but that it was up to the 399 organisations represented at the meeting to interpret the resolution in their own ways. With that point cleared up the resolution was passed by an overwhelming majority.[7]

---

7. *The Highway*, February 1916.

The WEA was clearly influenced by the events of this conference for in an editorial in the same issue of *The Highway* which carried the report of the London conference it was stated that the time had now come for the WEA to have "a clearly defined policy" on the education cuts. The development of a clearly defined policy on education cuts necessitated also having a clearly defined policy on education in general. In developing such a policy the WEA inevitably (given its membership and affiliations) began to line up, though not completely, with the Labour movement. A new note of urgency began to show itself. *The Highway* editorial of February 1916 argued that it was the duty of education authorities to save money in every other available way before any cuts were made in expenditure on education, and that any such cuts on education should be temporary. WEA branches and districts were urged "to conduct such enquiries as may justify their taking reasonable action wherever it may be necessary to do so". In a major article in *The Highway* called "Economy and Education" it was noted that copies of a resolution criticising reduction of expenditure on education had been sent to all LEAs, all organisations affiliated to the WEA and to all branches of the National Union of Railwaymen with over 200 members. A large number of replies had been received to the resolution, all of them, apparently, in favour of the policy. A pamphlet, *Fair Play for the Children,* which summarised these views had been, it was reported, "especially useful in rousing labour opinion to the urgency of our campaign. Our largest sales have been to the branches of the National Union of Railwaymen and to the Workers' Union."

This move towards more active engagement with labour movement organisations was a general feature of WEA activity at this time. Mansbridge had resigned as general secretary in November 1915 and had been replaced by J. M. Mactavish, the maker of the radical speech at Oxford in 1907, who had an authentic claim to activity in the labour movement. One of Mactavish's first major tasks was in August 1916 to write a pamphlet called *What Labour Wants from Education,* thousands of copies of which were distributed and sold to working class organisations throughout the country.[8] The pamphlet contained as an appendix a series of questions on education which it was hoped would be discussed by these organisations, and the answer sent back to the WEA in order that it could "put forward a programme of educational reconstruction that would meet with universal working class approval and support"[9]. At the same time the objects of the association were widened to include pressing for

"the development of a national system of education which shall ensure to all children, adolescents and adults such education as is essential for their complete development as individuals and citizens."[10]

By November 1916 the WEA had prepared a full scheme for educational reform which it submitted to the Government's Reconstruction Committee. As Arthur Marwick puts it "Reconstruction" was a word "which, from the summer of 1916, was on every politician's lips."[11] Grandiose claims were made about how society would be re-made after the inevitable military victory and the Reconstruction

---

8. J. M. Mactavish in a letter to the Secretary of the Reconstruction Committee, 24th November 1916 claimed that 25,000 copies were distributed and 45,000 copies were sold: see this volume, p. 341.

9. T. W. Price, op. cit., p. 61.

10. Quoted in Price, loc. cit.

11. A. Marwick, *The Deluge* (Harmondsworth 1967) pp. 258-259.

Committee was up-graded into a full Ministry. Education was singled out as a major area for reconstruction activity and the new Prime Minister, David Lloyd George, appointed as his reforming President of the Board of Education, H. A. L. Fisher, vice-chancellor of Sheffield University.[12]

The WEA's scheme (printed on pp. 342-349 of the present volume) talked of a "broad highway" of education and advocated a list of measures, as follows:
1. Nursery schools from 2 to 6 years.
2. The gradual increase in the school leaving age to 16.
3. Half-time education from 16 to 18.
4. Reduction in class size to a maximum of 30.
5. Better facilities for teacher training, and improved salaries and conditions for teachers.
6. School medical and dental services.
7. Open-air schools, playing fields, school meals, physical training, swimming baths, etc.
8. The provision of 75 per cent of the costs of education from the Treasury.

In this respect the WEA's programme was very much in line with the educational policy which was adopted by both the Labour Party and the TUC in 1917. In one important respect, however, the WEA's programme differed from that of the organised labour movement at this time. Resolution 3 of the WEA programme, "Universal Full-Time Education," expressed a belief in raising the school leaving age to 16 and proposed a time-table for achieving it as follows: first, that LEAs should be compelled to raise the leaving age to 15 within five years, and that second, they should be granted powers which enabled (but did not compel) them to raise it to 16 thereafter. The Labour Movement, adopting as it did the "Bradford Charter" called on the other hand for universal, free, compulsory Secondary Education and by implication a "common school."[13] The WEA's policy involved what Brian Simon has called "the Achilles Heel of Labour's post-war educational policy."[14] This involved a belief that there should be an expansion of what the WEA called "Full Secondary Education." This would not be available for all pupils but only for a proportion selected on academic grounds. All other children were merely to continue their education in an elementary school. The relevant clause of the programme reads (p. 344) as follows: "That all children admitted to a Secondary School should have reached an approved standard of education, the ground of transfer being the fitness of the scholar for the broader curriculum."

A few years later when the WEA and the Labour Party, linked by one of the editors of this Year Book, R. H. Tawney, came to advocate "secondary education for all," there was still the fatally ambiguous emphasis on different types of school for different types of pupil.

It was not that the WEA had not been warned. In this Year Book published as part of the WEA's campaign for improvements in Fisher's Education Bill, William Leach, one of the chief architects of the "Bradford Charter" spells out the dangers in no uncertain terms. Leach was a former member of Bradford Education

---

12. See for example Gerald Bernbaum, *Social Change and the Schools 1918-1944* (London 1967), Chapter 2 for the background.

13. B. Simon, op. cit., p. 348.

14. Ibid., p. 362.

Authority and leading figure in the Independent Labour Party in Bradford. The ILP in the town had by 1918 carried out years of militant activity as minority members of the School Boards in attempting to use the 1902 Education Act in the best interests of the working class.[15] Leach had proposed the Bradford programme to the Labour Party Conference in 1917, arguing that "no longer ought education to be administered on the assumption that only a minority are fit to be educated, or that education is for the few."[16] In his article in the Year Book, "A Suggested Labour Education Programme," Leach begins by welcoming the fact that the WEA had at last become serious about its role as an educational pressure group. He gives us an unusual but justifiable perspective on the early years of the WEA:

"The W.E.A., in publishing its programme of education reform, has at last come out in the open to justify its title. Gone, let us hope for ever, is the limitation it foolishly imposed upon itself in existing merely to secure for working men and women, after a hard day in field or factory, the nearest cheap imitation of university training that was to be had. It is now a fighting organisation, with a real fighting charter upon which to question Parliamentary candidates, harass Ministers, and make itself thoroughly disagreeable to the enemy and a live force in the army of those who work for wages."

After making relatively minor criticisms of the WEA's programme, he moves on to make his major criticism of it. The section of his article headed "A Real Point of Difference" (p. 65) is a small masterpiece of polemical writing and a strong indictment of the WEA's emerging thinking on public education.

But, for all its faults, the WEA's programme was considerably in advance of that being prepared by H. A. L. Fisher. From the end of 1916 to August 1918 when a new Education Act finally arrived on the statute book the WEA worked hard at national, district and branch level initially to bring about improvements in it, and later, owing to considerable opposition from organised capital, to get even the unsatisfactory end product on to the statute book.

In September 1916, for instance, the WEA branch in Blackburn decided to organise a conference on "What Labour Wants from Education" in the town and on 25th November a number of resolutions to go to the conference had been prepared. These included the following items: "effectual provision for the physical well-being of children"; "an extension of the school leaving age with the abolition of the present half-time system"; "the establishment of a system of compulsory part-time Education for all adolescents to be given during the normal working day"; and "that in the interests alike of Education + of Economic efficiency, a sound general Education in childhood + adolescence is the necessary foundation for any course of technical or professional training." In Rotherham to cite another case, on 9th November, 1916 the WEA branch there also considered the question of Educational Reconstruction, and it mandated its delegates to the special meeting of the Yorkshire District Council to be held in Sheffield to vote, amongst other things, for a resolution from the Bradford Branch which stated "That education should be entirely free to all classes without distinction." Education policy was discussed at many other meetings of the branch throughout 1917. If

---

15. For the Bradford ILP's battle on child feeding see J. H. Palin, "The Feeding of School Children: Bradford's Experience" in *Socialist Review*, March 1908, reprinted in W. Van Der Eyken, op. cit., pp. 150-155.

16. Quoted in B. Simon, op. cit., p. 348.

anything the continuing discussion on education was more vigorous in Blackburn than in Rotherham. The Blackburn branch set up its own Education Reconstruction Sub-Committee and through it sent many deputations to meetings of the organisations affiliated to the branch. At one meeting of the committee on 5th February, 1917 it was decided to send deputations to explain the WEA's education proposals at meetings of the Trades Council, two working men's clubs, the town's two NUR branches, the two Carpenters' and Joiners' branches, the Weavers' and Overlockers' unions, the Men's Brotherhood, the James Street Young Men's Class and the Independent Labour Party. The Branch also played its part at conferences demanding educational reform organised by the WEA at national and district level. The branch also sent a delegate to the large and influential national conference on Educational Reconstruction that was held in London on 3rd May, 1917.[17]

By the time this conference took place Fisher had already submitted his Bill to the Cabinet. It had been approved at the end of February 1917. In April 1917 a high powered deputation from the WEA, including Temple and Ernest Bevin, had lobbied the Minister.[18] All this activity had little effect, for the Bill which Fisher brought before Parliament in August 1917 left much to be desired as far as the WEA was concerned. It contained two main proposals. First, that all children should stay at school until the age of 14, "implying," as Brian Simon puts it, "an end to all exemptions below this age and abolition of the half-time system", and second, for those whose full-time education finished at 14 there should be part-time education of 320 hours a year up to the age of 16.[19] Other provisions permitted nursery schools for children under 5, improvements in the school meals service, baths, playing fields, and games centres. Delegates from the Blackburn branch were at the special meeting of the North Western District of the WEA held in Manchester at the end of September 1917 at which the following resolution was passed unanimously: "that the Association, while welcoming the Education Bill as an advance on pre-war educational standards, regrets to record its profound dissatisfaction that the Bill does not meet the demands set forth in the WEA recommendations." The objections were then listed.[20] The Bill was no better received in Yorkshire. The special meeting on the Bill called by the Yorkshire District of the WEA in Leeds, was, according to the report in *The Highway* of October 1917 "mainly critical in tone."

Although the WEA was far from happy with the Bill, regarding it as being merely "really a measure abolishing half-time"[21], it was prepared to do what it could to press for improvements in it. The WEA Central Council at its meeting on 25th September, 1917 passed a resolution which read as follows:

"That the WEA, while recognising that the Education Bill represents a considerable advance on pre-war conditions, re-affirms its own recommendations as the minimum that is adequate to the needs of the country and the opportunity before it, and demands that the Bill be improved and extended in

---

17. The accounts of activity in Rotherham and Blackburn are based on the Minute Books of the WEA branches in those towns.

18. B. Simon, op. cit., pp. 350-351.

19. Ibid., p. 352. I have relied heavily on Brian Simon's work for this account of the passage of the 1918 Act.

20. *Times Educational Supplement*, 27th September, 1917.

21. *The Highway*, September 1917.

such a way as to conform to these recommendations."[22]

Before long, however, the fight was not one for improvement in the Bill but rather for the existence of the Bill at all. Not only was it strongly attacked by local education authorities fearful of the increased power it would give to the Board of Education, but it was (more sinisterly) attacked by organised capital, most notably those employers who felt that their profits depended on the retention of the half-time system.[23] This combined hostility was indeed so influential that the Bill was withdrawn at the end of October 1917, allegedly due to lack of time in that parliamentary session. Such, however, was the public outcry at what looked suspiciously like acquiescence to business interests that the Government agreed to introduce a revised Education Bill (No. 2) directly the new session of parliament began on 14th January, 1918. The new Bill was very little different from the previous one, though it did reassure the local education authorities about their autonomy from the Board. The organised employers, through the Federation of British Industries were, however, far from happy and issued a notorious memorandum in January 1918 in which they particularly attacked the Bill's provision for compulsory continuation schooling up to 18 years of age.[24]

The WEA's reply to this incredibly reactionary document was not only the famous and brilliantly scathing article by R. H. Tawney, which appeared in the *Daily News* on 14th February, 1918,[25] but also the great number of rallies, protest meetings and the like held by WEA branches and districts up and down the country. Before the No. 2 Bill emerged the WEA was busily mobilising opinion in favour of Educational Reconstruction. In December 1917, for instance, amongst the WEA's activities in this direction are the following: North Western District executive passed resolution calling on the Government to proceed with the Education Bill; Western District, large meeting at Frome in favour of educational reform; North Eastern District, meeting on the Educational Bill at Middlesbrough; Eastern District, educational reconstruction campaign meetings at Berkhamsted, Letchworth and Luton; Midland District, course of lectures on "Education and Democracy" at Coventry, and lecture by Master of Balliol at Stafford; and London District, conference on the Educational Bill at Grays.[26]

As the new Bill began to move through Parliament pressure of this sort intensified. Conferences held, for example, at Kendal and Maryport during January and at Peterborough in April were sponsored jointly with the local Trades Councils, the Co-operative Societies and the National Union of Teachers. Liaison with the labour movement from now on increasingly characterised the WEA's campaign: a conference in February on the Education Bill organised by the WEA in the North West at which Tawney gave an "inspiring address" was attended by three hundred delegates representing over half a million members; and at a similar

---

22. See this volume pp. 342ff. for the WEA's recommendations and the annotations concerning the content of the Bill.

23. B. Simon, op. cit., pp. 352-353.

24. B. Simon, op. cit., p. 355. For another account of industrialists' objections to the Bill see G. Bernbaum, op. cit., pp. 21-24.

25. Reprinted under the title "Keep the Workers' Children in their place", in R. H. Tawney, *The Radical Tradition* ed. R. Hinden (Harmondsworth 1966).

26. *The Highway*, January 1918. See also the reports of District activities on educational reconstruction in this volume: pp. 354-358.

venture organised by the North Eastern District in March there were three hundred and forty delegates.[27] Following the passing of the second reading of the Bill in the House of Commons on 19th March, the editorial in *The Highway's* April issue noted that forces were marshalling against the Bill. It continued: "It is imperative, therefore, that every member of the WEA, every student in our classes, and every believer in education should do all in his power to demonstrate to Parliament the strength and earnestness of popular feeling... On this question we will witness the first great battle between the forces of reaction and the forces of progress for the possession of the future. We must be up and doing."

There was again considerable activity to report, especially in the enemy's main heartland, the cotton areas of Lancashire and Cheshire. Alongside the many meetings a pamphlet, *Will Continued Education Ruin the Cotton Industry?* had been published, with the WEA claiming that it "effectively answers the recent pamphlet of the Master Cotton Spinners."[28] As the Bill continued its progress the WEA maintained its pressure. The enemy, not surprisingly, did likewise; with the result that Fisher was forced to accept an amendment postponing for seven years the continued education provision for 16 to 18 year olds. On 8th August, 1918 the much flawed, largely permissive Education Act was passed—the school leaving age was raised to 14, without exemptions and there was to be part-time education for 14 to 16 year olds.[29]

In its editorial in September 1918, *The Highway* began generously by calling the Act "another step towards that equality of educational opportunity, without which our visions of a true democracy are but idle dreams." But, it continued with a more guarded and realistic tone, the Act was not

"all that we desire, or yet all that is needed. Like all Acts of Parliament, it is a compromise between those who want things done and those who don't. If the former had been stronger, or the latter weaker, we should have been given a more generous measure. It may therefore be regarded as a rough test of the contending forces making for reaction or progress, not only in education, but in the task of social reconstruction that awaits us."

The Act was in some respects weaker than the 1917 Bill, notably because of the concessions Fisher had been forced to make to save the continued education principle. In other respects it was stronger: child labour on Sundays and school days had been restricted to a maximum of two hours a day; and the autonomy of the local education authorities had been retained and strengthened (there were some progressive local authorities) while at the same time the Board of Education had more powers "to deal with backward authorities." The 1918 Act was a very long way from secondary education for all in any form. Good practice, within the sharp parameters of the Act, was all that would be possible: the "national system, locally administered" could be made to provide good practice if there was adequate local, political pressure. *The Highway's* editorial correctly indicated what would be the continuing work by the WEA to implement at the local level the many permissive elements of the Act. It wrote:

27. *The Highway*, February-May 1918.

28. *The Highway*, April 1918.

29. G. Bernbaum, op. cit., p. 24, and B. Simon, op. cit., p. 356.

". . . the value of the Act depends very largely on the initiative and enthusiasm of local authorities . . . But since we cannot convert reactionary local authorities by Act of Parliament, we must help to give them wider vision by the judicious pressure of public opinion. In this work our movement had played, and must continue to play, a large part."

In the economically bouyant years immediately after the war WEA Districts and branches, often acting as the central organising points for the whole of a local labour movement on educational matters, worked diligently to secure the implementation of the 1918 Act at local level. In Rotherham, for instance, at its Annual Meeting on 17th March, 1919 the WEA set in train a joint campaign with the Trades Council "with a view to pushing the workers' demands in Rotherham's educational system and to get the best possible results from the Act." The Education Committee was lobbied with its singularly unhelpful Secretary rejecting the pressure exerted on him by making much of what he called the distinction between educational idealism and educational practicability. In Blackburn, to give another example, in February 1920 the WEA branch set up an Education Advisory Committee and at its first meeting, attended by delegates from numerous local working class organisations, the North Western District Secretary, Eli Bibby, called on the organisations represented there to press the local education authority to make operative the permissive clauses of the Act.

Before the end of the year in which Bibby spoke, however, the sharp downturn in the national economic situation allied to a vigorous press campaign against increased government expenditure led to the Cabinet announcing that expenditure on education should be cut. The implementation of Fisher's Act was obviously going to be a costly enterprise, so if, in effect, its implementation was impeded considerable savings would be made. The Board of Education issued a circular which clearly stated that "Except with fresh Cabinet authority, schemes involving expenditure not yet in operation are to remain in abeyance."[30] This, however, was only the start. Before long demands were being made for cuts in existing, rather than merely potential, expenditure. In short, it was not long before Sir Eric Geddes wielded his notorious axe, with education being a particular target for its intentions.[31] Savings of about £6½ million were made on education. As Gerald Bernbaum puts it: "The main effect of the economy drive was that all plans for major reconstruction on the lines suggested by the 1918 Act were discarded. Nationally the Act remained virtually inoperative as far as nursery schools, day continuation classes and the raising of the school leaving age . . . were concerned."[32]

The WEA now began a new phase in its educational campaigning. It was a phase which lasted throughout the inter-war years and was, of necessity, more about trying to retain such glimmers of progress that existed in the educational system, than about trying to bring about wholesale reform. From the Spring of 1922, with the first protest meetings against the Geddes cuts, there was a constant stream of national, district and local initiatives (conferences, meetings, leaflets, deputations) by the WEA and its affiliated organisations against continued Government retrenchment on education. The chief campaigns were those against

---

30. Quoted in G. Bernbaum, op. cit., pp. 28-29.
31. See W. Van Der Eyken, op. cit., pp. 276ff.
32. G. Bernbaum, op. cit., p. 30.

Circular 1371 of 1925 (further general money saving, the 1922 cuts not having been large enough); against Circular 1421 of 1932 (parents of school children given secondary school places now invariably had to pay fees, thus destroying the embryonic systems of free secondary education for some working class children which had been developed in the more progressive local education authority areas like Durham, Bradford and Manchester) against the disappointments of the 1936 Education Act, shot through with exemptions on the crucial question of the raising of the school leaving age.[33]

Such was the volume of activity generated by the WEA over educational reform, or at least against educational reaction, that in 1927-28 the National Office created a Bureau of Public Education, and in the 1934-35 session appointed Harold C. Shearman as its full-time Education Officer. Shearman did much to orchestrate and stimulate the protests, petitions and meetings throughout all the WEA districts and, along with figures like Tawney, Laski and Lady Simon, spoke and wrote extensively on all aspects of education.[34] Increasingly, given the complexion of the vast majority of the Governments of these years a close connection began to emerge between WEA educational policy and that of the Labour Party. Indeed, Tawney's *Secondary Education for All: a policy for Labour* (1922) contained little that was different from the WEA's policy on that issue. The WEA's policy statement of the late 1930s, *Education for Freedom*, included, for instance, the same fatal ambiguities about secondary education (the three types of secondary school favoured by Tawney rather than the common school favoured by the redoubtable William Leach in his remarkable contribution to this Year Book).

In general, however, the WEA had to carefully eschew too direct a connection with the Labour Party on educational reform. Rather it worked more often with such organisations as the National Union of Teachers and the Nursery Schools Association and the Co-operative Union. This process culminated in the formation of the Council for Educational Advance in 1942. Shearman was its Honorary Secretary and Tawney was its Chairman and its member organisations were the WEA, the TUC, the Co-operative Union and the NUT. Seizing on the reconstructionist consensus and the popular radicalism that, as in the previous war, emerged during the "People's War" the WEA, both with and without the Council, again mobilised support in favour of educational reform. In September 1942 the WEA published its *Plan for Education: a programme for Educational Reconstruction*, a direct successor to "The Highway of Education" submitted by the WEA to the Reconstruction Committee in 1916. In his preface to *Plan for Education*, J. H. Nicholson correctly pointed out that the WEA had been involved in educational policy issues for many years, and recalled the agitation which "helped to put steam behind the Fisher Education Bill." He went on by recalling the dismal years between the wars when the WEA "found itself obliged to use its influence in successive campaigns against policies of educational restriction and parsimony— miscalled "economy". The latest of a long series of disappointments," he went on, "was the Education Act of 1936 in which the object of raising the school-leaving

---

33. For full details on the politics of education in these years see Brian Simon, *The Politics of Educational Reform 1920-1940* (London 1974), though Simon, in my view, underestimates the WEA's contribution to the resistance to Government reaction. For the "free-place" and scholarship system, see K. Lindsay, *Social Progress and Educational Waste*, (London 1926).

34. Something of the scope of the WEA's National Office work on educational reform can be found in *WEA Retrospect 1903-1953* (London 1953), pp. 17-23.

age was frustrated by provisions for exemptions." The suspension of the Act on the outbreak of the war should not, he felt, be regarded as a defeat but rather as "a new opportunity for real advance". The demands for a scheme of educational reconstruction included the following: equal educational opportunities; lifelong education; service to the community rather than competition as the main principle of school life; the abolition of the old elementary/"secondary" system; the raising of the school leaving age to 16 years; free education, free medical and dental services, free school meals; nursery education and the regulation of juvenile employment. The "Common School" was also advocated as a system in which "social distinctions and privileges no longer play any part", yet when this is elaborated in a section on Secondary Education things begin to look rather different. The *Plan* stated:

> "The purpose of secondary education should be to develop to the full the varied capacities of all children from the age of eleven to sixteen or eighteen. To do so it is necessary to place the emphasis on different studies and activities for different pupils. This may necessitate, if only for practical convenience in particular cases, the establishment or continuance of separate schools or departments for the more literary or scientific (or Grammar school), the more practical (or Modern school) and the more technical type of course . . . It is, however, of the greatest importance that no sharp cleavages should be allowed to reappear within the new secondary system. The multilateral school in which all these types of courses are comprised in a single school on the same "campus", so that they can share and interchange many of their activities, may be the best way to insure against such divisions."[35]

How comforting these words must have appeared to the wartime Education Minister, R. A. Butler, when even the pressure from the main educational arm of the working-class movement justified the "equal but different" rationale of the 1944 Act with, in practice, its three types of secondary school for the three types of young mind which could be discerned by examination and IQ test at eleven plus! William Leach probably turned in his grave, but Sir Cyril Norwood probably nodded his agreement![36]

When R. H. Tawney, during his presidential address to the WEA Conference in October 1943 reviewed the 40 years since the WEA had been founded, he not only pointed to the great growth of WEA classes since 1903 but also

> "Equally important, our long struggle to convert a class-ridden educational system, under-staffed, under-housed and perpetually suffering from financial anaemia, into something more worthy of a self-respecting democracy, though it has not yet attained its goal, has at least defined a goal at which to aim."[37]

This was a quite correct assessment. During and between the two bursts of enthusiasm for educational reconstruction in the two world wars, the WEA was an extremely important educational pressure group and probably the most persistent advocate of educational reform in the working class movement. The popular agitation for educational reform (the early years of which are indicated in this

---

35. WEA Educational Pamphlets No. 1 (new series) *Plan for Education: a programme of Educational Reconstruction*, (September 1942, reprinted June 1943) p. 26.

36. For the Norwood Report, 1943 see David Rubinstein and Brian Simon, *The Evolution of the Comprehensive School, 1926-1966* (London 1969) pp. 27ff.

37. R. H. Tawney, *Education: The Task Before Us* (London 1944) p. 3.

volume) which the WEA generated and sustained amongst ordinary people was a remarkable phenomenon. It is a pity that so many of the egalitarian aspirations, no more elegantly expressed than by people like Tawney, should in the end have come to so little other than a replication, under new names, of the old class-ridden education system.[38]

---

38. For a contemporary advocacy of the Common or Multilateral School system, see Lady Simon, *Three Schools or One?* (London 1948); and for evidence of the discussion on this matter in the WEA see WEA Educational Pamphlet No. 12 (new series) *Secondary Education for All: Some Problems Discussed* (1947), esp. pp. 34-36.

THE W.E.A.
EDUCATION YEAR BOOK
1918

The following pages are a photographic
reproduction of the original
W.E.A. Education Year Book, 1918

" There will always of necessity be large bodies of students who from unfavourable circumstances of locality, means, time, age, or for other special reason cannot avail themselves of the opportunites of oral instruction. To those a well-organised Correspondence College, such as that which flourishes under the direction of Dr. Briggs, with its highly qualified and expert teachers, its clerical staff and well-devised machinery, is a help of the most valuable kind "—THE SCHOOLMASTER.

SELF EDUCATION COURSES

FOR THE SAKE OF SELF-IMPROVEMENT
AND WITHOUT ANY EXAMINATION IN VIEW.

University Correspondence College

PROVIDES 75 DIFFERENT COURSES OF VARIOUS GRADES OF DIFFICULTY AT FEES FROM ONE GUINEA. PROSPECTUS POST FREE ON APPLICATION TO THE DIRECTOR OF STUDIES,

No. 46, BURLINGTON HOUSE, CAMBRIDGE.

RECOMMENDED FOR USE IN STUDY CIRCLES.

A PRIMER OF ENGLISH CITIZENSHIP,
BY
Frederic Swann, B.A.; B.Sc. (Lond.),

*Scholar of King's College, London ;   Of the Inner Temple, Barrister-at-Law ;
Formerly Headmaster of the Grammar School, Ilkley.*

OF this work "*THE TIMES*" says: "The book is a model of clear statement and arrangement. . . . . The first chapter defines the position of the King in the State and the next four the procedure of Parliament, after which everything bearing on local government and the collection and disposal of rates and taxes, together with the judical, the naval and military, and the educational systems of the country, are carefully considered and explained from the point of view of the citizen who wishes to take an intelligent and possibly an active interest in public affairs. . . . . Mr. Swann has not only observed the correct historical sequence of events, but has by so doing made an exceedingly difficult subject appear both easy to understand and a really interesting study. Few people who read the book—and we hope many will do so—will lay it down without having learnt something, and in most cases a great deal that they did not know before. "The object of the last five chapters is to present an account of the social reforms of recent years, particularly with regard to the status of children and the relations between capital and labour, and between the Mother Country and the Empire. In these, too, the ordinary reader will find : first, that the author helps him to formulate his previous ideas and knowledge with greater lucidity ; and secondly, that any predisposition he may have had to view with proper seriousness his duties as a citizen will be materially strengthened."

LONGMANS, GREEN & CO.   2nd Edn.   pp. 268+XX.   Price 2/6.

BY THE SAME AUTHOR:—
A PRIMER OF LONDON CITIZENSHIP,
WITH A PREFACE BY THE LATE
Sir Laurence Gomme.

WITH SEVERAL MAPS AND ILLUSTRATIONS.

OF this book "*THE TIMES*" says: "In his new volume Mr. Swann handles with equal success the more restricted but also more complicated subject of what it means to be a citizen of London."

P. S. KING & SON.   Price 2/-

CURWEN'S MUSIC

RUDIMENTS OF MUSIC (Curwen's Edition, 5766)
——— By EVELYN F. KIRKALDY. ———

A set of Twelve Theoretical Cards on the elements of music specially arranged for the music section of the W.E.A.

——— PRICE : ONE SHILLING. ———

CHORAL MUSIC (Latest Issues)

GRANVILLE BANTOCK :

MIXED VOICES.	No.	Staff.	Solfa.
Annie Laurie (Arrangement)	60863	2d.	1d.
Dumbarton's Drums (Arrangement) ...	61021	4d.	1½d.
Music, When Soft Voices Die... ...	60991	3d.	1½d.
Song of Liberty	61023	2d.	
MEN'S VOICES.	No.		
Down Among the Dead Men ...	50497	4d.	2d.
Good King Wu	50546	3d.	1½d.
My Luve is Like	50499	2d.	1d.
Wilt Thou be My Dearie	50500	2d.	1d.

CYRIL JENKINS :

MIXED VOICES.	No.		
O Little Snowflake	61050	3d.	2d.
Echo's Lament	61068	3d.	2d.
MEN'S VOICES.	No.		
Excelsior...	50551	4d.	2d.
The Lee Shore...	50547	3d.	2d.

S. COLERIDGE TAYLOR :

MIXED VOICES.	No.		
The Sea Shell	60974	3d.	1d.
Summer is Gone	60973	2d.	1d.
The Viking Song	60982	2d.	1d.
MEN'S VOICES.	No.		
Drake's Drum	50533	4d.	2d.
Loud Sang the Spanish Cavalier ...	50461	2d.	1d.
O Mariners Out of the Sunlight ...	50462	3d.	1½d.

Messrs. Curwen issue Text-Books on all Musical Subjects, Music for Schools, Choirs, Entertainments, and Concerts, and will gladly send full Catalogues on receipt of postcard.

LONDON: J. CURWEN & SONS, LTD.,
24, Berners Street, W. 1.

POETRY AND LIFE SERIES.

General Editor: — — — Professor WILLIAM H. HUDSON,
*Staff Lecturer in Literature to the University
Extension Board of the University of London.*

The series is printed in a beautifully clear type on deckled-edged rag paper. With Photogravure Frontispiece, 1s. 6d. net.

VOLUMES NOW READY :—

1. **KEATS AND HIS POETRY.** By WILLIAM HENRY HUDSON.
2. **JOHNSON AND GOLDSMITH AND THEIR POETRY.** By WILLIAM HENRY HUDSON.
3. **GRAY AND HIS POETRY.** By WILLIAM HENRY HUDSON.
4. **SHELLEY AND HIS POETRY.** By E. W. EDMUNDS, M.A.
5. **COLERIDGE AND HIS POETRY.** By KATHLEEN E. ROYDS.
6. **MATTHEW ARNOLD & HIS POETRY.** By FRANCIS BICKLEY.
7. **LOWELL AND HIS POETRY.** By WILLIAM HENRY HUDSON.
8. **BURNS AND HIS POETRY.** By H. A. KELLOW, M.A.
9. **SPENSER AND HIS POETRY.** By S. E. WINBOLT, M.A.
10. **MRS. BROWNING & HER POETRY.** By KATHLEEN E. ROYDS.
11. **MILTON AND HIS POETRY.** By WILLIAM HENRY HUDSON.
12. **SCOTT AND HIS POETRY.** By A. E. MORGAN, B.A.
13. **ELIZABETHAN LYRISTS AND THEIR POETRY.** By AMY CRUSE.
14. **TENNYSON AND HIS POETRY.** BY R. BRIMLEY JOHNSON, B.A.
15. **BYRON AND HIS POETRY.** By WM. DICK, M.A.
16. **LONGFELLOW AND HIS POETRY.** By OLIPHANT SMEATON, M.A.
17. **POE AND HIS POETRY.** By LEWIS N. CHASE.
18. **HORACE AND HIS POETRY.** By J. B. CHAPMAN, M.A. (The Quotations are in Latin).
18A. **COMPANION TO HORACE AND HIS POETRY.** By J. B. CHAPMAN, M.A. Full Notes on the Latin Quotations, with Glossary, Schemes of Metres and Conditions, and Two Maps.
19. **POPE AND HIS POETRY.** By E. W. EDMUNDS, M.A.
20. **BROWNING AND HIS POETRY.** By ERNEST RHYS, M.A.
21. **WORDSWORTH AND HIS POETRY.** By WM. H. HUDSON.
22. **SCHILLER AND HIS POETRY.** By WILLIAM H. HUDSON.
23. **ROSSETTI AND HIS POETRY.** By Mrs. F. S. BOAS.
24. **COWPER AND HIS POETRY.** By JAMES A. ROY.
25. **MARLOWE AND HIS POETRY.** By JOHN H. INGRAM.
26. **CHAUCER AND HIS POETRY.** By E. W. EDMUNDS, M.A.
27. **WALT WHITMAN AND HIS POETRY.** By H. BRYAN BINNS.
28. **CHATTERTON AND HIS POETRY.** By JOHN H. INGRAM.
29. **WHITTIER AND HIS POETRY.** By W. H. HUDSON.
30. **VICTOR HUGO AND HIS POETRY.** By W. H. HUDSON.

LONDON: GEORGE G. HARRAP & CO., Ltd.
Directors: **GEORGE G. HARRAP, G. OLIVER ANDERSON.**
2 & 3, Portsmouth Street, Kingsway, London, W.C. 2.

Oxford University Press

EDUCATION TO-DAY AND TO-MORROW.
Addresses by P. E. MATHESON.   2s. 6d. net.

EDUCATIONAL SYSTEMS OF GREAT BRITAIN
AND IRELAND. By SIR G. BALFOUR.   7s. 6d. net.

A HISTORY OF SECONDARY EDUCATION IN
SCOTLAND. By J. STRONG.   7s. 6d. net.

EDUCATIONAL VALUES AND METHODS.
By W. G. SLEIGHT.   5s. net.

AN ADDRESS to the Swindon Branch of the Workers'
Educational Association, given on October 28th, 1916, by R. BRIDGES,
Poet Laureate.   Paper cover, 9d. net.

ESSAYS ON SECONDARY EDUCATION. Edited by
C. COOKSON.   4s. 6d.

THE RUDIMENTS OF CRITICISM. A general study of
poetic form for young students. By E. A. GREENING LAMBORN. 3s. net.

MECHANISM OF EXCHANGE. By J. A. TODD.
A Handbook of Currency, Banking, and Trade in Peace & War. 5s. net.

THE LIVING PAST. A Sketch of Western Europe.
By F. S. MARVIN. Third Edition revised.   4s. net.

THE GREEK COMMONWEALTH. Politics and
Economics in Fifth-Century Athens. By A. E. ZIMMERN. Second
edition, revised and reset.   8s. 6d. net.

THE GREEK GENIUS and its Meaning to Us.
By R. W. LIVINGSTONE. Second edition, revised and reset. 6s. net.

FOUR STAGES OF GREEK RELIGION.
By GILBERT MURRAY. Columbia University Lectures. *Columbia
University Press.*   6s. net.

THE PAGEANT OF ENGLISH POETRY, being
eleven hundred and fifty poems or parts of poems arranged in the
alphabetical order of the Poets' names (Chaucer to Henley, excluding
living poets), with a subject-index.   2s. 6d. net.

THE CONCISE OXFORD DICTIONARY, adapted by
H. W. FOWLER and F. G. FOWLER from The Oxford Dictionary.
Fourth impression.   From 4s. 6d. net.

THE ADVANCED ATLAS OF PHYSICAL AND
POLITICAL GEOGRAPHY. A new Series of Maps, specially
designed for Schools, Colleges, and Private Students. By J. G.
BARTHOLOMEW.   Crown Folio, 10s. 6d. net.

LONDON: HUMPHREY MILFORD, Oxford University Press, AMEN CORNER, E.C. 4.

The W.E.A.

Education Year Book

1918

LONDON:
The Workers' Educational Association, 16, Harpur Street,
Theobald's Road, W.C. 1.

Canada and the United States:
Ginn and Company, Boston and New York.

Printed by the Co-operative Printing Society Limited, Tudor
Street, E.C.; and at Manchester and Newcastle.

CONTENTS.

PART I.—INTRODUCTION.

PAGE

Preface. G. B. Shaw 13
Two Views of Society and Education. A. Clutton-Brock 33
The Balance Sheet of the Soldier-Workman. J. Galsworthy .. 39
Thoughts on Working-class Education. J. A. Hobson 51
Why the Worker should Demand Education. G. D. H. Cole and
    Arnold Freeman 56
Technical Training in the Social Structure. S. G. Hobson.. .. 59
A Suggested Labour Education Programme. W. Leach 63
The War and the Workers. H. G. Wells 66

PART II.—THE EDUCATIONAL SYSTEM.

England and Wales (Statistical Introduction) 67
The Education System of Ireland. A. J. Rahilly 120
The Education System of Scotland. W. Boyd 127
The Training of Teachers. M. W. Keatinge 131
Eugenics and Education. C. W. Saleeby 139
Day Nurseries and Nursery Schools. Grace Owen 143
Treatment versus Training. Margaret McMillan 149
The Foundations of Democracy. Edmond Holmes 155
The Ideal Number of Pupils in a Class. Miss M. L. V. Hughes .. 159
A Spiritual Purpose in the Schools. T. H. Hayward & A. Freeman 164
Educational Self-Government. C. H. C. Osborne 167
The Little Commonwealth. Earl Sandwich 171
The Expansion of Secondary Education. J. L. Paton 174
The Neglect of Adolescence. Arnold Freeman 178
How to Pay for Education. Sidney Webb 181
Our Old Educational Endowments. J. A. Fallows 192
Education and the Organisation of Research. Viscount Haldane .. 197
Education by Music. Miss Beryl de Zoete 200
Libraries. B. M. Headicar 205

PART III.—EDUCATION IN OTHER COUNTRIES.

Preface. Miss T. M. Browne 211
Education in America. V. Seldes 213
Danish High Schools. Miss A. C. Heath 217
Education in France. Miss T. M. Browne 220
Education in the Far East. P. M. Roxby 223
Education in India. R. M. Joshi 229
Switzerland (p. 234), Belgium (p. 234), Holland (p. 235), Sweden
    (p. 236), Italy (p. 237), Canada (p. 237), South Africa (p. 238),
    Australia (p. 238), New Zealand 239

PART IV.—THE UNIVERSITIES AND THE WORKERS.

The Universities and Public Opinion. A. E. Zimmern 240
The Problems of University Government. H. A. Grimshaw .. 245
The Tutorial Class Movement. Winifred Beaton 253
The University Tutorial Class: A Student's View. Miss Scruton.. 262
Bangor Summer School 263

University Tutorial Classes : Tutors' Conference 265
Association of Tutorial Class Tutors of the University of London .. 273
University Education for Women. Miss A. M. A. H. Rogers .. 275
Settlements. Miss H. Cashmore 278
University Representation in Parliament 283
The Universities : Birmingham (p. 286), Bristol (p. 288), Cambridge
(p. 290), Durham (p. 292), Leeds (p. 295), Liverpool (p. 297),
London (p. 298), Manchester (p. 301), Oxford (p. 304), Sheffield
(p. 309). University Colleges : Exeter (p. 311), Nottingham
(p. 311), Reading (p. 311), Southampton (p. 312). **Scotland :**
St. Andrews (p. 312), Glasgow (p. 313), Aberdeen (p. 314),
Edinburgh 314
The Scottish Universities and the W.E.A. 314
Ireland : The National University of Ireland (p. 317), Queen's
University in Ireland (p. 317), Belfast (p. 318), Dublin 318
The Irish University and the W.E.A. M. W. Robieson 318
Wales : University of Wales (p. 321), University College of Wales
(p. 321), University College of South Wales and Monmouthshire
(p. 321), The University College of North Wales.. 321
The University College of Wales and the Workers. J. Thomas .. 323

PART V.—THE WORKERS' EDUCATIONAL ASSOCIATION.

Leading Facts in the History of the W.E.A. Rev. W. Temple .. 324
The W.E.A. : Its Propaganda, Organisation, and Method. J. M.
Mactavish 328
The W.E.A. in Australasia. F. A. Bland 335
A Junior Fellowship of the W.E.A. W. E. Simnett 339
Educational Reconstruction 341
The W.E.A. : Its Constitution and Activities 350
W.E.A. Directory 362

PART VI.—EDUCATIONAL MOVEMENTS.

Trade Unionism and Education. G. D. H. Cole 370
The Co-operative Movement and Education. G. Stanton 374
The Adult School Movement. G. Peverett 377
The Y.M.C.A. in Wartime. The Rev. B. Yeaxlee 380
The Club Union and Education. A. Temple 383
North Staffordshire Miners' Higher Education Movement. 386
Ruskin College 388
The Plebs League 390
Directory of Education Associations 392

PART VII.—THE ORGANISATION OF THE TEACHING
PROFESSION

Introduction. Mrs. Sidney Webb 433
The Need for the Organisation of the Teaching Profession. W. G.
Pincombe 438
The Teachers' Registration Council. F. B. Jevons 443
The National Union of Teachers 445
The Sheffield Teachers' Education Campaign, 1917. W. H. Robinson 447
Directory of Teachers' Organisations 449
Directory of Education Authorities :—
England (p. 466), Wales (p. 474), Scotland 475
Indices, General (p. 497), Names (p. 502), Organisations 504

EDITORIAL PREFACE.

THE aim of the initial issue of the W.E.A. Education Year Book is not so much to supply information as to set people thinking about educational questions and to increase the desire for educational progress. In future issues, when paper is cheaper and stimulation less imperative, we hope to extend the scope of the Year Book as a work of reference. As things are, it seems to us that our business is to appeal to the imagination of the reading public and to make it feel what we hold to be indubitable—that no phase of Reconstruction so much demands attention as Education. In order that such an appeal might be effectively made we approached leading educationists, asked them for contributions, and gave them entire freedom to say what they pleased. As the reader will see, they have responded chivalrously. The orthodoxy of their views—if there is such a thing as educational orthodoxy —is no concern of ours. Each writer is alone accountable for his or her own opinions. Our responsibility ends with making it possible for the public to know what the thinkers and experts have to say.

As we go to press the fate of the Education Bill is undecided. In many respects the Bill as it stands does not conform to W.E.A. ideals of what the next Education Act ought to be. Nevertheless, it is a most valuable Bill, containing many provisions that will mean health and capacity and happiness to the country. Upon the enthusiasm and energy of the friends of education its successful enactment depends.

G. D. H. COLE,
ARNOLD FREEMAN,
J. M. MACTAVISH, } *Editors.*
R. H. TAWNEY,
W. TEMPLE,
A. E. ZIMMERN,

A. C. STEWART, *Secretary.*

Information for future issues of the Year Book will be welcome, and should be addressed to the W.E.A., 16, Harpur Street, Holborn, W.C. 1.

PART I.

INTRODUCTION.

PREFACE.

By Bernard Shaw

(Author of " Parents and Children," etc.).

Some years ago, in an essay entitled Parents and Children, published, according to my custom, as a preface to a play, I gave a fairly exhaustive account of my view of the process commonly called education. Returning to the subject by way of a careful perusal of the essays by other hands which make up this book, I can assure the reader that all the facts that are fit for publication are here, all the hopes are here, all the failures are here, all the finance is here, set forth at worst readably, and at best with rare knowledge, penetration, and literary skill. There is nothing left for me to say except the very simple things that stand as mountains in the path of the writer on education, and that he must usually ignore if he is to get to his subject at all. And I have said most of them before.

First, there is the fact that education is mostly a pretext under cover of which parents get rid of the trouble, the vigilance, the noise, the unconscious chaperonage, the perpetual questioning of children. By performing this service, Churchmen and sectarians are enabled to proselytize the rising generations, classes to segregate and corrupt them, and schoolmasters to make money. The tense silence in which my exposure of this radical imposture has been received, in contrast with the garrulous discussions of minor points, shows how deeply guilty our society is on this score. Yet the guilt, as I have insisted, does not lie in the parents' quite natural and socially wholesome desire to escape from the intolerable inroads made by the continual presence of children on their privacy, their quiet, their pursuits, and their pleasures, but in our callous indifference to the methods by which the schoolmaster relieves us for so much a year cash.

What does the schoolmaster do with the child when the parent delivers it over with a sigh of relief, having nothing more to dread until the holidays come round? He simply imprisons it, and hires a body of minor masters to act as warders and turnkeys. An admirable essay in this volume by Mr. Edmond Holmes deals with the essential slavery of school life, and concludes that we must " defeudalize " education. But strong and deeply felt as Mr. Holmes's condemnation is, he flatters our school system in comparing its child victims to feudal serfs. Serfs had rights and a status. School children have neither one nor the other : they are treated as outlaws pure and simple. And their condition is not improving in this respect. One of the contributors to this book, a man not yet past middle age, tells me that during his last two years at Eton he did what he liked. Recent biographies of Etonians (for example, Mr. Gosse's Life of Swinburne) shew that the public schoolboy was once left to himself sufficiently to enable him to cultivate tastes of his own and approach and commune with Nature in his own way. Compare this picture of Eton life with the recent ones written by young men, especially those young men who are so proud of having been at a public school that they delight in describing how they were thrashed because they tried to botanize, or naturalize, or take country walks, or read instead of drudging at compulsory games. In our socially pretentious preparatory schools the boys who are too young to play games are actually forced to stand and watch their seniors playing. Is anyone imposed on by the pretence of liking this and believing that it was good for them with which our eager climbers of the social ladder present their credentials as " public school men " ? Yet this modern invasion and enslavement of every moment of a child's waking life is represented as a development of education. The most impressive documentary novel of recent years is Mr. Alec Waugh's Loom of Youth, which is almost a diary of life at Sherborne. Compared with the medieval public school curriculum, in which the wretched scholar rose at six and learned Latin for nearly twelve hours without any play at all, it exhibits the complete capture of the school by the athletic schoolboy and the athletic schoolmaster, the medieval system being almost completely restored with the substitution of football and cricket for Latin and Greek. Soon a schoolboy caught reading or looking at pictures or listening to music will be thrashed as he once was when caught playing.

Meanwhile the schoolmaster is not yet merely a shameless boy farmer : he has to make his prisoners learn certain things, whether games or murdered languages. Now there are, unfortunately, two ways of doing this. One way is teaching : a process which requires some natural vocation, a good deal of skill and experience, and an honorable character. The other way is open to any fool or blackguard. You do not teach : you set the pupil a task, and beat him, bully him, ridicule him, or torture him in any other way that may be convenient to you unless he is able to perform it. To naturally cruel men, the Creakles and Murdstones and Squeerses, this makes schoolkeeping a delightful occupation. The old cries of " See, Udal, see," and " The schoolmaster's delight is to flog " are still stifled in the breasts of many inarticulate victims of much worse men than Creakle or Squeers; for Dickens never told the worst of the orgiast-pseudo-pedagogue, though he need have gone no further than the boasted records of Bell and Lancaster for evidence of them.

This fact has to be faced if the profession of teaching is to be lifted from the abyss of popular dislike and contempt into which it has fallen. Of all men the most naturally reverenced are teachers. Of all men the most naturally despised are executioners. And as long as the schoolmaster is paid, not for teaching, but for saying to the growing child " Learn this, you little devil, or I will cane you until you will not be able to sleep for terror of me," the schoolmaster will be classed with the executioner in popular esteem. That, and that alone, is the secret of the shameful poverty and low social status of the schoolmaster.

If this were merely an abuse in practice such as must arise in all professions when the practitioner is a scoundrel, there would be no disgrace in it. Most unfortunately, it is the accepted and legalized theory of schoolmastering; and, although the practice is seldom as vile as the theory, it is by the theory that the status of the practitioner is determined. The reader of this book may ask me how I can maintain such a proposition in spite of the spirit informing the essays of Mr. C. H. C. Osborne on The George Junior Republic and The Little Commonwealth, of Miss M. L. V. Hughes with her admirable Two Decalogues, of Mr. Edmond Holmes already quoted, and of Lord Haldane with his claim that even the technical formula for calculating the strain on a girder should not be taught without relating it, not to the fear of a caning, but to the Cartesian mathematic which is part of a philosophy. I shall be asked if I have ever read Goethe's Wilhelm Meister; heard of Dr. Montessori; or met a pupil from President Pearse's Sgoil Eanna.

I will, therefore, mention something that I have read quite recently and that everyone who takes in a newspaper has read. A schoolboy, with an unusually manly mind, summoned his schoolmaster for assaulting him. The schoolmaster's defence was that he was " teaching " the boy geography. The process, as described by himself, was asking the boy questions in geography and hitting him with a cane when the boy was unable to answer them. The magistrate at once accepted this as the normal and proper business of a schoolmaster; reproved the boy for being (of all things) unmanly; and dismissed the summons. There was no protest either in editorial or correspondence columns. The Press agreed with the magistrate. The parental public agreed with him. That is what education means at present, both in law and public opinion, in spite of the few genuine teachers, who are regarded simply as cranks.

I recommend this case to Dr. F. B. Jevons and the other writers who are very justly concerned about the inferior status and wretched pay of schoolmasters as a class. I am a professional man, paid, when I am in luck, 200 times as much for my work as the poorest schoolmaster is for his, and perhaps 30 times as much as many an envied headmaster. I am invited to feel indignation because this police-court hero, with his cane and his geography lesson, is not placed on my level as to social esteem and income. I admit the claim as to income because I am a Socialist, and because I am perfectly well aware that my income has no reference whatever to my merit. But as to social esteem I must really ask whether I, who am, for good or evil, a genuine teacher by a highly skilled method, am to admit as my equal a person whose " profession " it is to hit a boy half his size with a cane hard enough to make him wince with pain. The schoolmaster's gardener, who could probably hit harder than the schoolmaster, and can at least plead that he produces vegetables without assaulting people, makes no such claim. My feeling is that 30s. a week, and the status of a trainer of performing dogs, is as much as a schoolmaster can reasonably expect until he learns to teach. He would probably think this quite good enough for me if my success as a playwright were obtained by imprisoning my audiences in the theatre and caning them when they omitted to applaud, or whispered, or coughed, or shuffled their feet.

I am not for the moment dealing with the question whether it is possible to make all our children learn in any other way, having regard to the multitudes of them and the dearth of teachers of genuine vocation. And I am certainly not proposing that children, any more than adults, should be artificially exempted from physical coercion, or even from summary natural personal vengeance, to the extent of making them imagine that they are living in a moral vacuum and can do as they like without regard to the feelings and convenience of others. I am simply insisting that the forcing children to learn by beating them is unskilled labor of an unedifying and repulsive character. I call it unskilled advisedly. I am aware that it would break down in practice if the curriculum were not planned with some skilled knowledge of the cane's possibilities, and that you cannot teach the infinitesimal calculus to a child of 3 by any amount of flogging. But the ordinary schoolmaster does not devise the curriculum : he simply carries out a pre-arranged routine like the school charwoman; and if some practical joker were to slip the calculus into the junior time-table most of the masters would try to whack it into their youngest pupils as solemnly as they used to try to whack the very difficult subject of grammar. While this state of things lasts they will rebel in vain against the tendency of public commonsense to keep them in their proper places.

The remedy is not to give professional pay and status to unskilled men who cannot even pronounce the alphabet presentably, but to exact genuine professional qualifications from the schoolmaster and pay him their market value. His status will then take care of itself. I have not noticed that genuine teachers who now undertake the care of children are at any disadvantage pecuniarily or socially in ordinary professional society. They have, comparatively, a good time of it; for, I repeat, the true teacher can leave the doctor, the lawyer, and even the parson nowhere in the rapidity with which he can gain respect and liking both in his school and out of it, and that, too, without being by any means an absolute angel in point of temper. Most real teachers probably have occasionally to pretend to be rather shorter tempered than they really are lest they should mollycoddle their charges. But they do not appear in police-courts to explain that in their schools the pupils have to learn without being taught on pain of being beaten, the schoolmaster's department being confined to the beating. They try to make the teaching half of the transaction interesting enough to induce the pupil to do the learning half either for its own sake or for theirs.

The modern tendency is to relieve the caning system for the masters in two ways. One is to confine the use of the cane to the headmaster. That is to say, the head, who ought to be the moral centre of the school, is made a sort of Lord High Executioner, and spends his time between doing the dirty work of his assistants and the making out of the school bills. The other plan, started by Arnold, is to get the boys to do their own caning by the prefect system. This was a natural move enough; for whereas under the old system the masters, if they did not teach, at least had to cane, under the prefect system they neither teach nor cane; and it becomes possible for a comparatively easygoing, lazy, unauthoritative, donnish sort of person to hang on to a mastership. Also the boy who is caned can look forward to the time when he will cane other boys, and can form a taste in that direction, just as he forms a habit of treating servants as fags. But these alleviations of the schoolmaster's lot do not entitle him to call himself a teacher, or to claim the respect and emolument considered proper to a professional man. He still has to depend for any credit he enjoys on such incidentals as holy orders or a University degree. The common schoolmaster who has neither of these qualifications is still in the most embarrassing of all social positions. The gentry inexorably refuse to accept him as a gentleman; and the common people refuse to accept him as a fellow creature. And they will both be entirely justified in their attitude as long as his profession of teaching is only a cloak for the practice of a turnkey and an executioner carrying out a law which is purely lynch law.

Under such circumstances it is not surprising to find that when an educationist is also a statesman, like Sir Robert Morant, he will not support the schoolmaster's claim to be organized and recognized as the medical profession is organized and recognized : that is, as a monstrous tyranny with legal powers of coercion over the rest of the community, and with unlimited power to dictate its own qualifications; to prevent anyone practising as a teacher without its authority; and to set all lay power at defiance. The schoolmasters are not even aware of the fact that the inevitable operation of these powers has brought the medical profession into such disrepute and open conflict with the public interest that nothing but the gross ignorance and superstition of Parliament in regard to political and hygienic science stands between the General Medical Council and the deprivation of its worst privileges, accompanied by a resolute exercise of the powers already possessed by the Government and the Universities to secure a majority of laymen on it. One of the very first things a true teacher should teach is that such bodies as the General Medical Council, and the ideal at which the National Union of Teachers (so-called) brazenly aims, should be resisted as Star Chambers and Bastilles should be resisted. To Sir Robert Morant's refusal to allow the teachers themselves to be the judges of their own success and the prescribers of their own qualifications, so that they can ruin any teacher who dares to criticize their methods, the Registration Council opposes a simple assumption that a body of men whose notion of teaching is to beat the children for not learning, is omniscient, infallible, and infinitely virtuous, and should, therefore, at once be entrusted with powers which this country made two revolutions sooner than entrust to the Throne and the Church. Those who advance such a demand are not only incapable of teaching, but incapable of learning. By all means let us have a register of teachers; but let the learners keep the key of it.

It must never be forgotten that education is such a dangerous thing that it is very doubtful whether the invention of printing would have been tolerated if more than a very few people had been able to read. The Roman Catholic Church has not to this day consented to place the Scriptures in the hands of the laity. We must either go through with education or let it alone. A state of things like the present, in which everybody knows how to read and nobody knows what to read, and in which the crudest, darkest, poorest minds are allowed to propagate their crudity, darkness, and poverty through the Press for a pittance which leaves them no chance of culture, is disastrous : the war is only one of its disasters, and not the worst of them. For it must be added that the richer classes which have gone through the entire routine of schooling, as established at our public

B

schools and Universities, are, except as experts in athletics, sport, and drawing-room accomplishments, as crude and ignorant as the journalists from the elementary school, who have become journalists because they are so incorrigibly inaccurate that they could not keep situations as clerks for a fortnight. The newspapers which cater specially for public schoolmen and University graduates, for the country house and the rectory : that is, for the classes which represent our education untempered by the teaching which men of business or professional men get from their daily pursuits, are frankly organs of savagery and snobbery. The war has revealed an astounding ignorance in the classes that actually govern us : one wonders sometimes how any human beings with so much interest in their own ambitions and amusements could possibly be so void of intellectual interests and curiosities as not to have learnt something by merely walking about with their eyes open, nor have reasoned enough about what they see to become capable of a few simple syllogisms.

Take an actual specimen of their powers of reasoning upon what is one of the main interests of their lives : pheasant shooting. They want pheasants to shoot; therefore nobody must be allowed to kill pheasants except gentlemen with guns. Nevertheless, as we shall lose the war by starvation unless we economise food, we must not feed the pheasants. And there the matter was left. The pheasants were strictly preserved; and their food was cut off. The country houses of England apparently did not contain a single representative person with intelligence enough to argue to the result that followed, which was, that the pheasants, not being fed as usual by the gamekeeper, ate the farmer's crops; and the farmer, being forbidden to shoot them, quarrelled fiercely with his landlord, their proprietor. In the same way, when the war imposed a need for economy, we had, instead of the educated man's conception of economy as a facilitation of production, the miser's conception of it as mere abstinence. The first thing we were to abstain from was education, which was sacrificed not merely with indifference to its economic value, but positive malice against its superiorities. The next thing was locomotion, the very circulation of the productive organism. Even communication was restricted to such a degree that the penny post is now a thing of the past. We have seen, even as I write, a gentleman who was appointed to control the Air Service because his brother is a rich newspaper proprietor beginning by making a speech in which he described his own official business as murder, like any poor woman in a slum who has seen her child killed by a bomb, and following this up by demanding that the British Museum be cleared out to make room for him and his staff. He did not ask for Westminster Abbey to store petrol in; but it can hardly have been any cultural consideration that hindered him. And the working classes can hardly reproach him after handing over Ruskin College for war purposes with an alacrity which suggested that they were glad of an excuse to get rid of it.

All this means not only that the people we send to school at great expense are ignorant, but that their minds are of very limited use to themselves, and worse than no use to the nation : nay, positively injurious to it. The stupendous blunders made by the Germans, most fortunately for us, shew that their school methods are no better than ours; but they respect education, having an intellectual conception of it, whereas we, having no such conception, dislike and despise it, and actually prefer the ignorant and insolent young barbarians who keep up the reputation of certain Oxford and Cambridge Colleges for rowdiness to those whose civilized instincts and naturally refined tastes lead them to behave like grown-up people with some sense of their duty to their neighbors.

I might say a good deal more about this fundamental vice and error of imposing as education a system of imprisonment and " breaking in " which has no reference to education at all, and is intended only to secure a livelihood for schoolmasters by saving parents trouble and making children quiet and submissive : that is, unfit to be free citizens in a democracy. Suffice it to say here, that the curse of a prison is that by its very nature it reverses every law and aspiration of Christian conduct, being violent, revengeful, coercive, and deliberately planned to destroy happiness. In these pages the essays of Mr. Osborne, of Miss McMillan, of Mr. J. L. Paton, of Miss M. L. V. Hughes, of Dr. Keatinge, and of Mr. Holmes are penetrated with a sense of struggle against the prison morality of our schools; but they do not seem to me to grasp the fact that what they are in revolt against is not fundamentally a bad method of education, but a selfish and evil purpose of which neither the parents nor the masters are in the least ashamed. That is why I have felt bound to harp on it.

I need hardly add that the fact that at this moment the majority of schoolmasters are schoolmistresses does not affect my argument. They are quite as handy with the cane as the men. What is more important is that as it is possible to make a case for the statement that " corporal punishment is disappearing," we should bear jealously in mind that corporal punishment is only one of many available methods of intimidation and coercion, and by no means the most cruel and injurious. There are worse tortures, both physical and moral, in actual use (I shall not propagate them by giving particulars) in schools where " corporal punishment is not permitted."

I pass on to the controversy as to technical and liberal education which occupies the contributions of Mr. S. G. Hobson and Lord Haldane. I do not think that liberal education, which is really recreation, can ever be made the subject of compulsory instruction. Until English literature was made a school subject the Shakespear nausea which is now common among the secondarily educated did not exist, though already schoolgirls had learned to loathe Beethoven. Now no adult loathes the multiplication table; nor indeed would any have loathed it in childhood had it been made clear then that a child who knows it can enjoy money and liberty to an extent impossible to one who cannot change a sixpence to buy a tram ticket or visit a picture palace. Technical education is a qualification for living in society. Being necessary to life, it justifies itself by its results even to those who acquire it with difficulty and repugnance, and exercise its accomplishments without pleasure for ulterior objects. But a liberal education cannot be acquired without interest and pleasure. Compulsory Shakespear only provides a public for books written to prove that Shakespear was Bacon by people who lack the literary and dramatic sense to know that the fact that Shakespear was not Bacon is not a matter of evidence or argument, but of the direct evidence of the literary and dramatic sense, just as the fact that

Bacon's statue at St. Albans does not represent the same man as the Stratford bust is a simple matter of eyesight, and the fact that Wagner was not Brahms is a simple matter of listening to their music. It does not provide audiences for Shakespeare's plays : on the contrary, it keeps them away. A liberal education, in short, cannot be imposed : all that can be given is access : water should be provided for the horse ; but it must not be injected with a stomach pump submitted to under threat of the whip.

But the acceptance of this distinction between liberal and technical education will force us to recognize that the scope of technical education is wider than most schoolmasters think. It includes civic education, for instance. Calvin, I take it, though he would perhaps have admitted that the children of Geneva could not be taught to appreciate and enjoy the music of Orlandus Lassus and Josquin Deprès and Van Sweelinck as they could be taught to navigate a ship or amputate a limb, would have maintained that his Institutes should be taught in order to qualify the children technically to become citizens of " the perfect city of God." And I think he would have been right. To live in Geneva in Calvin's time, or in Scotland in the 16th and 17th centuries, as in Ulster to-day, without intolerable social friction, a knowledge of the Calvinistic scheme of salvation and damnation was as necessary to the man who abhorred it as to the man who accepted it. Dante's scheme of Catholicism was equally a technical subject for the diplomatists of the Holy Roman Empire. What is the matter with civilization at present is that Calvinism and the Holy Roman Empire having become incredible, and the Church Catechism and the Thirty-Nine Articles in great part unthinkable, chiefly through the discovery of Evolution, there is a void left in our technical education. Now, as Nature abhors a vacuum, the void is being filled by demoralizing pseudo-scientific stupidities like Weismannism and Mechanism on one side, and a mess of crude sentimentalities on the other ; whilst the creed of Creative Evolution, obviously the coming religion, has not been formulated and popularized. But it will have to be. The symphonies of Beethoven will never be possible as text books ; but the treaties of Bergson certainly will if we are to have a society as genuinely organized as the Protestant and Catholic societies of the pre-evolutionary times. There must be a common technical theory of the goal of Evolution to replace the old common technical theory of the will of God. Those who do not believe it will at least know where society stands, which no man knows at present.

Science, admittedly a technical subject, must include political science, not only in its elementary branch of law, but in its later developments as industrial democracy and Socialism, which subjects, in a modern democratic State, should be as compulsory, up to the limit of the scholar's capacity for them, as the multiplication table. At least a conception of them should be inculcated : such a conception, for instance, as I have of mathematics, though I cannot do the simplest sum in algebra. And it may very well follow that a good deal of the most helpful teaching will still be done by academic persons who know the nature of the science without special skill in its operations : indeed, without any skill except skill in thought. This, by the way, is the best answer to my famous gibe, " He who can, does : he who cannot, teaches." I do not know whether that utterance of mine ever led a dyspeptic man to ask a man of sound stomach to teach him how to digest; but it is a simple fact that when men do things consummately well they do them as they breathe, automatically, without intellectual consciousness, and can give no account of how they do them, being therefore useless as teachers. Socialism will certainly not be taught in schools by successful Prime Ministers. Lord Haldane might have pointed out in his essay, if it had been relevant, that Descartes himself did not build bridges, though an engineer without Cartesian consciousness is not a liberally educated man. " He who can do, does : he who can think, teaches " is just as true as the other formula.

Education will never really flourish without a system of rights and privileges entirely dissociated from money. The makeshift of prizes and punishments now in use is, as Mr. C. H. C. Osborne points out, more corruption. It is odd that though we will not allow a barrister to practise, or a doctor to call himself a doctor and sign death certificates, or a clergyman to hold a living, unless they undergo a test of technical qualification, anybody may practise political science as voter, or even as Cabinet Minister, without knowing how to read and write. What is worse, anyone may practise abortion and poisoning on the nation's mind and spirit as a journalist or newspaper proprietor with complete impunity and even huge profit, though if he did the same with a mechanical instrument on an unborn baby he would go unpitied to penal servitude. It is even proposed that legislation shall be initiated and imposed, or defeated and cancelled, without discussion or information, by the man in the street acting through a referendum : indeed, this can already be done in some States. The consequences under modern democratic conditions are so appalling that we are in visible danger of that revulsion against democracy which, instead of saving Athens, hastened its ruin. The people will either throw over democracy altogether in disgust at its disastrous ignorance, and fall back on the hopeless expedient of thrusting dictatorial powers on the nearest adventurer whom they may romantically imagine, at his own silly suggestion, to be an Earthly Providence, or else they will demand some sort of scientific evidence of political capacity as a qualification for election or office. Already the public services are protected from absolute imbecility and illiteracy by examinations; and sooner or later we shall see the absurdity of demanding educational qualifications from the clerk and none from the Secretary of State, with the result that we have Secretaries of State for Foreign Affairs who cannot speak French at the head of an office in which a knowledge of French is obligatory on everyone else. The difficulty is that though a knowledge of French and drawing-room dancing may qualify a man to be an attaché, it does not qualify him to be a Foreign Minister. The late President Kruger, who would not have been accepted by the Foreign Office as a hall porter, outwitted all the diplomatists of Britain and Germany until he was in his dotage. People who have a positive genius for passing examinations, and who learn languages with extraordinary facility, are often quite impossible as chiefs of staff, to say nothing of Ministers; and for this reason it has never been possible to apply the examination system throughout the whole public service, the necessary exceptions becoming excuses for a good deal of jobbery. Also, examinations can be manipulated so as to favor or exclude classes; and the shameless resort of our own ruling classes to this device has cooled the enthusiasm with which the examination system was formerly hailed as a democratic reform.

In short, we still lack a trustworthy anthropometric method for high purposes of State. Poets, like other observant people, notice "the straitened forehead of a fool," often in the highest offices or in feudal command of a county; but we have not yet invented the callipers, ascertained the measurements, or discovered the reagents which should test the Prime Minister and the Commander-in-Chief as the tape round the chest and the height measurer test the rank and file of the police and the Army. I remember once being much flattered by a speaker in a discussion following a political harangue of mine, who said, " I did not understand the lecturer's arguments, because, as you will see if you observe the shape of my head, I have not the requisite faculty; but as a professional phrenologist I can assure you that you may trust to his judgment." I followed up this clue far enough to convince myself that the analysis of human faculty made by the phrenologists has not yet carried them beyond classifications so crude and ambiguous as to verge on positive illiteracy here and there, the results being far too imprecise to be of any practical value for political purposes. Nevertheless, the need for some method of measuring personal capacity which shall be as completely beyond the control of the operator or the subject as the measurement of a yard of cloth is beyond the control of the cloth or of the yardstick, is becoming more conscious. I have myself been tested with contrivances designed to ascertain how quickly I can respond to a sensory stimulus, or how long I can distinguish between two colors when they are being substituted for one another with increasing rapidity. The inferences from these tests vary from the simplest statement of the result to a certificate classing you with a Fuegian or with Plato or Shakespear : that is to say, from cautious fact to extravagant romance; but if these contrivances be taken with the various tests used in the Army and other public services, they will appear as part of a growing body of anthropometric devices ranging from the shoemaker's rule to attempts at psychometric machines. These things should not be passed over lightly because some of them are obviously cranky, and none have superseded the experienced college tutor who tells an undergraduate what honors it is worth his while to read for in view of his natural capacity. But tutorial measurement is founded on a degree of intimacy and familiarity which is not practicable for general public purposes. We seem far from the day when persons classed by natural capacity as distinguished from acquirements will be disqualified or conscribed for public work according to their degree ;· when Class A 1 will be compelled on incorruptible evidence to elect representative peers to undertake the highest duties of the State, and Class Z 17, however self-assertive and noisily popular, will be absolutely debarred from voting at elections, contesting Parliamentary seats, or running newspapers.

In making this rough suggestion I am not forgetting that one of the uses of democracy is to save people from being intolerably well governed, and, in fact, discouraged out of existence as savages are by civilized men. I would give Class A 1 rights of counsel and criticism, but no vote. The mass of men coming between J and K should neither be dragged in the mud by Z nor dragged up to the clouds by A to share the fate of Phaeton; and my old proposal that Parliament should contain 50 aldermen elected by proportional representation under the original Hare scheme, the whole nation voting as one constituency, should be safeguarded by the proviso that their rights of speech in the Assembly should not include access to the voting lobbies. But even with such safeguards, which would not exclude the popular actor of the day and the popular general, however incapable they might be politically, a wise electorate would still ask for some scientific, bias-proof test of capacity, taking capacity in its widest sense to include intellectual integrity and social instinct, and giving no more than its due value to that power of working for 16 hours a day every day for 30 years which at present enables the stupidest routineers to oust from important posts men of much higher faculty, whose real work cannot be sustained except in emergencies for more than two or three hours, and even at that imposes extensive periods of total recreation.

Now secondary education, as we have it to-day, wholly fails to supply such a test.

Mr. J. L. Paton points out how very little secondary education we actually give. People who have attended a secondary school are in an absurd minority. These two propositions are not, however, the same. There is, fortunately, a great deal of secondary self-education : indeed civilization would not hold together if its culture depended on its schools instead of on its bookshops and lectures and summer schools and general currency of intellectual intercourse. Many of our most cultivated people owe absolutely nothing to their schooling; and some of them, especially among the women, have never been to school at all. Though Ruskin took an Oxford degree, he was never a schoolboy; and he differed from his Etonian and Harrovian fellow graduates only in being, not worse educated (conspicuously the contrary, in fact), but much much less of a blackguard. I can lay my hand on my heart and say that nothing that I know was taught me at school except a collection of foul jests on the very subjects that ought to be kept cleanest in a boy's mind; and even these were not in the curriculum. The place where I was imprisoned for half the day, and which was called a school, kept me from the books, the great public picture gallery, the music, and the intercourse with Nature which really educated me; and admirable as the spirit and insight of Mr. Paton's plea for more secondary education seem to me, I am not sure that the extension of what is now called secondary education to the age of 18 or 20 for all classes would not abolish the little culture we have, and produce a generation of young Goths and Vandals which would reduce all Europe to the intellectual level of a mess table. The experiment has actually been tried through Eton and Harrow, Oxford and Cambridge; and the result is that the young gentlemen trained in this way are conspicuously absent from the learned societies, political societies, artistic societies and other cultural organizations, whilst the hunts, shoots, dances, and dinners which enable men to endure the crushing dullness of the drawing-room and the tedium of church on Sunday are recognized as their special provinces.

Even in these enlightened pages it is remarkable (though I doubt whether anyone will remark it) that with the single exception of a passing reference by Mr. Sidney Webb to " subjects requiring exceptional provision," and a paper on Eurythmics by Miss Beryl de Zoete which is too special to save the situation, there is not a word about music, painting, sculpture, literature, or to any other department of that education of the senses and refinement of the imagination without which the inevitable division of a life's activity into work and play, or business and pleasure, means nothing but its division between compulsory necessary money-making and voluntary intemperance in eating, drinking, and sexual sensuality. The appalling fact that nobody in this country seems to know that intellect is a passion, and that its exercise produces happiness, satisfaction, and a desirable quality of life, shews that we do not yet know even our crude bodily appetites in their higher aspects as passions : a passion being, I take it, an overwhelming impulse towards a more abundant life. We all have to admit that the greatest poets and dramatists, though great because of their philosophic power and biologic instinct, have been artists, because there is no denying that Euripides and Shakespeare and Goethe and Ibsen were artists by profession. But we talk of professional philosophers as if they were only half men, having brains without eyes or ears or souls. Yet the philosophers who have most deeply moved the world, whether for good or evil, are those who have been artist-philosophers : Plato, Schopenhauer, Nietzsche, Croce, and Bergson, for instance.

I have already insisted on the fact that the fine arts cannot be taught by school methods : the attempts at it end only in trying to make a boy appreciate Venetian painting by asking him the date of Tintoretto's birth, and hitting him if he cannot give the correct answer. What is needed is plenty of books, plenty of picture postcards of masterpieces of design, plenty of good performance of the best plays and the best music obtainable (not necessarily always in the heaviest *genres*, remember), and plenty of rambles in the country. But of what use will these be if the growing boy and girl is always reading that unreadable imposture, a schoolbook, or imprisoned in a school or in a cricket or football field when the music is going on, or the galleries are open, or the view from the mountain is at its best. Ask any schoolmaster to provide for this method of culture ; and he will first demand that the manifestations of fine art shall be changed into school lessons ; and when they are thus turned into a deadly seed of hatred of all art, and even of Nature, he will sulk furiously over having to find a place for them in his time-table, first declaring it to be utterly impossible, and then grudgingly squeezing them into half-an-hour a week, perhaps by sacrificing that *bête noir* of his, the drawing lesson. The moment we come down from pompous phrases about education and fine art to the actual facts of the school and the schoolmaster we are in danger of being driven beyond all patience into a simple declaration that the first step must be the utter annihilation of both, as of Sodom and Gomorrah.

We have, however, admitted that civic education is a technical subject and, therefore, a school subject. Now no real civic education is possible without discussion and controversy. The dogmatic schoolmaster, with his authoritative text book and his argument of the cane, or the imposition, or the keeping in, will not do here. Mr. J. M. Mactavish speaks in these pages of the difficulty of asking for grants of public money for instruction in controversial questions. But no difficulty is ever made provided only one

side is taken in the controversy : provided, that is, that the controversial question is falsely taught as a closed question. It is
quite true that there is a certain difficulty in obtaining grants of
public money to teach that baptism and the Supper of the Lord are
necessary to salvation; but you can get any amount of public
money to teach that vaccination is necessary to escape a horrible
death from smallpox. No human being could believe either
statement if he had all the arguments for and against presented to
him fairly : that is, by hearing them, not from one humbug pretending to be an omniscient and impartial judge, but from two
well-informed but strongly partial advocates. Both methods have been
amply tried ; and over and over again the dogmatically schooled
professions, on the very questions which concern their own work,
have been proved wrong where the laity, especially the unschooled
laity, has been proved right. The doctors, the lawyers, the clergy, have
been converted again and again, after the most uppish resistance, by
movements conducted by self-educated men. At last a superstition
has arisen that popular ignorance has some mystic sanction which
makes it more trustworthy than science and knowledge. This is
pestilent nonsense : the truth is that the popular movements are
educated by open discussion and vehement controversy, and know all
the facts and have balanced all the considerations more thoroughly
than the professionals. It is not ignorance shaming education : it is
controversial education shaming dogmatic cramming. In every street
you may find a doctor who is ignorant of a wide range of fact and
discovery concerning his own art that is familiar to every member of
the debating class in the nearest Young Men's Christian Association,
just as any frequenter of Secularist meetings can knock an average
curate into a cocked hat in a religious discussion, though he may
drop next day to the gun of a Jesuit who has had to defend his
intellectual position against continual challenge in Protestant England.

This point is the more vital because, as far as our philosophic basis
is concerned, we have changed the forms of our civilization, and with
them the conditions of social intercourse, without revising it, with
the result that, though our social structure has reached a degree
of complexity, and secured a degree of State protection for married
women and children at which it is far more important that every
adult should be a good citizen than a pious parent or spouse, we are
still teaching a code of personal righteousness, and denouncing
Socialism and loyalty to the State, which are now simple necessities of
life, as abominable German inventions. And when any man takes us
at our word and, on the authority of his personal righteousness, denies
all obligation to accept any State decision of which his individual
conscience does not approve, we first admit this anarchic right in
the Act of Parliament which imposes the State decision on him,
and then, in defiance of that Act, persecute him with murderous
ferocity for exercising it. At this moment the most opprobrious
epithet that can be levelled at an Englishman is " conscientious." The
controversy is really the old one between the Holy Roman Empire of
Dante and Calvin's Perfect City of God, of which our modern
Nonconformity and Anglicanism are only muddled, corrupt, and very
Laodicean versions. Now both these formulas of the whole duty of
man have, I repeat, been made as incredible and unthinkable by the
discovery of Evolution as they have been made impracticable by the

industrial revolution. Yet the moment anyone proposes to teach children anything else in public schools he is told that public money cannot be spent on controversial subjects. This ends in the children not being seriously taught anything at all on the plane of philosophy, religion, and political science : they are taught scraps of Dante and Calvin with the tongue in the cheek, and learn from their parents that such doctrines are " rot." In consequence we have such a generation of atheists and anarchists as never existed before. In the 18th century Frederick the Great, Catherine the Great, and a handful of financiers and philosophers were atheists, with Voltaire defending God and Rousseau defending Jesus Christ against them on modern Free Church Deistic lines ; but the common people were Catholic or Lutheran, and men could be and were broken on the wheel for not kneeling down when the Host was carried past them in the street. But to-day Fred Smith and Kitty Jones are too utterly godless to be even conscious that they are atheists ; and the Voltaireans and Rousseauites are classed as ultra-pious chapel folk. Ignorant parsons who used to excite the indignation of Carlyle by absurdly describing Voltaire and Rousseau as atheists are succeeded by the far more dangerously ignorant laymen who imagine that Charles Darwin discovered Evolution and that Natural Selection is an explanation of the universe.

Consider the dilemma that we are thus landed in. Nobody who knows what contemporary Governments are would dream for a moment of trusting even the best of them to impose a creed on the children of the nation through the schools. Yet nobody who understands how vitally necessary a common faith is to a common civilization dares persist in the attempt to muddle through as we are. Well, suppose a Minister of Education, Mr. Fisher or another, proposed to adopt Natural Selection or " neo-Darwinism " as the creed of the Empire, with Weismann for its prophet ! Instantly he would provoke a raging opposition that would bring any Government to the ground. Calvinist and Catholic alike would declare that they would fight to the last drop of their blood to save their children from the lake of fire and brimstone. The Creative Evolutionists, with Butler and Bergson for their prophets, would offer to swallow the Bible ten times over sooner than the doctrine with which Darwin " banished mind from the universe " and hope from the soul of man. In vain would the Minister of Education exclaim, " My good people : what are you making all this fuss about? Don't you know that the scientific sides of our schools and Universities have been teaching nothing else but Natural Selection and purely mechanical Tyndallic-Lucretian physics for the last half century, and that it would be harder for a teacher who taught anything else to hold a professorship than for Mr. Edward Clodd to hold the pulpit of the City Temple or the Deanery of Westminster? " The reply would be that the people had not known it and would not have stood it if they had, and that all the professors on the scientific side must immediately sign either the Thirty-Nine Articles or the Westminster Confession, or else be thrown out of their chairs.

The Australian way out of this difficulty is secular education, meaning total exclusion of religious and philosophic teaching. But it does not mean the exclusion of scientific teaching. Now to teach science without any reference to philosophy and religion is to present the world to the child as an automatic machine worked by soulless mechanical forces and energies without purpose or scruple : the organism called Man going through a course of action as an avalanche does when it rolls down a hill or a hydrogen balloon when it rises through the air. The children may not be interested enough or intelligent enough to question this view spontaneously; but as there will be plenty of theologians at hand to prompt them the teacher will soon be asked whether Will and Conscience are not powers as real as gravitation or magnetism, and where they come in under his scheme of things. He must reply, " Oh, that is the science of psychology : we shall come to that presently." But the moment he comes to it he must overleap his non-controversial limit and plunge into metaphysics ; for he cannot enter the domain of Aristotle without poaching on St. Thomas Aquinas, nor combine the science of mind and motive with Weismann's dismissal of a butterfly's flight from the sweep of the entymologist's net (and presumably also the movement by which I dodge a motor bus in the Strand) as mere reflex action responding to a purely sensory stimulus of the retina, without presently having to discuss the pre-Weismannic version of Predestination put forward by Calvin, which at least had the mind of God behind it. Once the question of free will is thus raised you are in the controversy about Determinism, to which there is no answer but Bergson's answer. When purpose is once admitted in the course of a psychology lesson the question whether the existence of evil does not prove an evil purpose behind evolution cannot be staved off ; and there is no answer to that except, if I may so, *my* answer.

Now if secular education thus leads inevitably to the discussion of St. Thomas Aquinas, Calvin, Darwin, Bergson, and Shaw, what is the use of pretending that it is non-controversial or that it can steer clear of religion ? You can no more draw a line and put a barrier between the temporal and spiritual in education than you can in the soul of man. You may forbid a teacher to mention the Bible or the Koran, to refer to the Pope or the Archbishop of Canterbury as an authority. But what sense is there in that when you are thrusting on the scholar little text books reeking with the crudest theories of creation, destination, and predestination, and claiming an authority for the rites of Jenner and Pasteur that St. John the Baptist himself would have regarded as blasphemous?

The only solution of the difficulty is controversial education. That is what all the real education we have at present is. The student must be informed that there is, for example, a controversy between neo-Darwinic Weismannism and Butler-Bergsonism ; and if he feels interested he must hear champions of the opposed views fighting it out in debate and be encouraged to take part himself. He had better be warned that he must not hope to be able to dodge his moral responsibilities by any nonsense about Agnosticism : the world cannot be run on evasion and paralysis ; and where knowledge stops intuitions and dogmas must come to the rescue. England cannot expect every man to do his duty until she makes up her mind as to what his duty is ; and she will find when it comes to the point that his duty consists to a great extent of doing what everybody else does, and not what he think right; for it is necessary in managing the human traffic called society to insist that under certain common circumstances everybody shall do the same thing and thus create that confident expectation of how other people will behave, which, though irritating to reformers and improvers and victims of the Tolstoyan Weltverbesserungswahn generally, is, nevertheless, a first condition of civilization. The child must be taught, in direct contradiction to the current cult of salvation by personal righteousness, that men in society must reform society before they can reform themselves. The individual may see a better line for the main road; but he should be educated to understand that his business is to persuade his fellows to make the new road and plough up the old, and not immediately to trample and trespass along his new line as if the business concerned himself alone.

Yet who will dare to say that this is the last word as to civic education? " Do as everybody else does; and never disappoint expectation " is as necessary a rule in business and general conduct as at a dinner party or when driving a motor car down a crowded street; but it is none the less a law of stagnation and not of evolution. There are departments of the greatest importance in which it will be fatal to set up a rule of perfect expectedness until we were all trained to expect and tolerate and even demand the unexpected. Not only are individuality, originality, initiative, moral courage, and a bold preference of the inner light to the neighboring example vital in society, but mere novelty, change for the sake of change, is needed to make human activity endurable. The schoolmaster or parent who teaches a child the occasionally very necessary lesson that it must not do what it likes, presently finds that a child who is not engaged mostly in doing what it likes is the worst sort of spoilt child. All kinds of conflicting rules arise. " Act according to your conscience " is a rule no sooner applied than we find that its validity depends altogether on what sort of conscience you have. Do what you like except when there are good reasons to the contrary is a rule which would forbid most of us to refrain from immediate suicide; for none of the " natural rights " on the recognition of which all stable society must be built are reasonable; and, if they were, nine people out of ten would be unable to state the reasons for them. Pearse founded a school of romantic heroism, teaching boys to throw away their lives for their ideals, and sealed his teaching with his blood by throwing away his own life. But is it not clear that these boys of Pearse's, stuffed as they were with legends of the Fianna and of Cuchullain, should have heard the other side from Professors Falstaff, Sganarelle, and Sancho Panza, and been encouraged to perform The Wild Duck and A Phenomenon In A Smock Frock as well as The Coming of Fionn and so forth? Is a man who does not know the uses of perversity, of paradox, of derision, an educated man? Is it desirable that one person in every million should be a hero and a martyr, or that every unit in the million should be taught Toleration sufficiently to relieve our unfortunate pioneers from the unwholesome strain of being heroes at the excessive risk of becoming martyrs?

Toleration, Liberty of Conscience, Freedom of Speech and of the Press are all dogmas; consequently no person ignorant of history will accept them; for they are against all reason. It is for want of historical knowledge that they are not accepted at present. No doubt we all profess the deepest regard for liberty; but no sooner does anyone claim to exercise it than we declare with horror that we are in favour of liberty but not of licence, and demand indignantly whether true freedom can ever mean freedom to do wrong, to preach sedition and immorality, to utter blasphemy. Yet this is exactly what liberty does mean. He who remarks that it is a fine morning is not taking a liberty. Galileo took a XVII. century liberty when he said that the earth moved round the sun; but the most abject slave may say that in the XX. century. It is from history alone that we learn that the obvious and immediate evils of allowing individuals and newspapers to utter and publish revolting propositions and to deny sacred beliefs are not so dangerous as the stagnation and retrogression which follow the enforcement of conformity, and that even in the crises of a war the consequences of deceiving the enemy, involving as they do the consequences of deceiving the nation, may easily be more disastrous than fighting strictly on the facts and discarding bluff. Now there is no sign that this lesson has been effectively taught to our educated classes, or even taught at all. It is the received opinion and practice among us that heresy should be persecuted and " bad taste " punished. There is, it is true, a benefit of clergy and of class and of income allowed in time of peace; and party invective and vulgar abuse are always privileged; but this is not Toleration : we do not tolerate suttee in India, nor did the United States tolerate the cult of nakedness introduced by the Doukhobors.

These two examples bring home to us at once that Toleration is no golden rule : in fact, all laws act in restraint of toleration, even when they are laws to enforce toleration. In decently conducted churches a quaker is allowed to walk to a pew before taking off his hat; but if he were to put his heels up on the back of the pew in front of him, and light a cigar, he would assuredly be thrown out and charged with brawling; and no plea of an imperative inner light would secure his acquittal. Toleration is a matter of degree : we all draw the line somewhere; and nothing will shift that line except education. In a rude village a stranger may be stoned for wearing his hair two inches longer than usual, though on the great bridge across the Golden Horn men and women of every race, class, color, fashion, costume or no costume on earth jostle one another without even looking round, the reason being that the Turks have been educated by experience to believe that a long-haired man may be as honest a neighbor as a short-haired one, improbable as that may seem to a British islander. Yet in matters which depend on historical education, the Turk is as intolerant as any other equally ignorant person. One of the main objects of education is to prevent people from defeating their own civilization by refusing to tolerate novelties and heresies which history proves that they had better tolerate. Therefore it is of extraordinary importance that all citizens should be educated in liberty, toleration, and the theory of natural rights. At present they are taught nothing but an idiotic demonstration that natural rights are a fiction of the vulgar imagination, because, forsooth, natural rights *are* natural, and not derived or acquired : in short, not logical.

When we turn from the toleration of acts to the toleration of doctrine, we become immediately conscious that we are not prepared to allow any doctrine which we believe to be pernicious to be taught to young persons dogmatically. For example, I am not prepared to allow Calvinism to be taught to any infant under any circumstances, nor to older children otherwise than controversially. I have never suffered from the fear of ghosts, because when I was a child, and the servants tried to frighten me with ghost stories, my father assured me that there are no such things as ghosts, and I believed him; but I know people who to this day are afraid to be alone in the dark because their parents were not as careful as my father. Now the dread of ghosts is a trifle compared to the dread of hell; and though there are stages of civilization, like that of the Arabs in Mahomet's time, in which men can be kept under moral restraint only by threatening them with a horribly tortured immortality, yet Mahomet never defeated his own expedient by complicating it and indeed demoralizing it by a doctrine of election and predestination as the Calvinists do. I have enjoyed the friendship and conversation of a gentleman who holds that the two greatest scoundrels who ever lived were Calvin and Robespierre; and though I am not prepared without further consideration to subscribe to this refreshingly vigorous estimate, I should insist that no Calvinist be allowed to proselytize in a school except through controversies with other zealots of the complexion of my friend, and with a sound Nazarene Christian or two as well. This involves, of course, my conceding to the Calvinist in the nominally Christian countries that he should have his say against Creative Evolution in the schools. Calvinism and Paulinism cannot be ignored. The Atonement religions are all much older than Christianity, and have captured it to such a degree that no one can possibly understand human nature or history, even to the very limited extent to which they can be understood at all, without a knowledge of these religions, especially the modern forms of them established by the Reformation.

We are driven to conclude then that technical elementary education and civic education must be compulsory, but that the latter must be controversial, whilst liberal education must be voluntary, though the community must provide the material and conditions for it. The compulsion can only take the form of political or social disability involved by failure to qualify for benefit of clergy. If people have no civic interest or capacity, and therefore cannot be civically educated, it is as absurd to give them votes or admit them to responsible public offices as it would be to give money to a child incapable of counting it. However we may be tempted to say that the only qualification the voter needs is the power of suffering from misgovernment, a moment's reflection will convince us that a baby might claim a vote on this ground. The one thing that is certainly worse than the suffering of a political imbecile is his notion of a remedy for it.

For born fools, civilized public education can do nothing. We cannot teach Voodoo to a beach comber merely because he is capable of nothing better. And to men of genius public education will do harm as well as good by inculcating errors into which they, left to themselves, would not fall. But as long as what we do teach is controversially taught, even erroneous teaching will educate us in the use of our minds, and in good manners.

Our manners at present, when we have any at all, are at best amiable but not admirable. Amiable because we have a horror of being disagreeable; not admirable because in deference to susceptibilities which should not exist, they consist in talking about the weather instead of about religion and politics, which, in one department or another, would be the normal subjects of conversation between strangers in any really educated community.

I am fully aware of the difficulties which my suggestions raise, and how impossible it is to accept them save as part of a social synthesis which involves the reconstruction of many other institutions besides our schools. Reforming our educational system may end like what is called " restoring " a medieval cathedral : we talk of numbering each stone, and replacing carefully and reverently those which are not too far gone to be saved; but in practice the edifice crumbles to pieces at the first touch of the pick and leaves us contemplating a heap of fragments which have miraculously lost all the shape they had a moment before, and now have neither head nor tail, top nor bottom. The schoolmaster as we know him may, like the cathedral stones, be numbered and registered ever so carefully; but when child slavery is abolished, and a new constitutional edifice of children's rights is set up, he will not fit into it. Genuine born teachers will hold their own, and indeed come to their own; but there will not be enough of them to go round; and the teachers who are not born but made by training will have to be a new generation. Still, the change has to come; for democracy without democrats : that is, without civically educated voters and representatives and officials, means, as we now see, red ruin. And civic education does not mean education in blind obedience to authority, but education in controversy and in liberty, in manners and in courage, in scepticism, in discontent and better-ment, tempered by the fear, not of artificially manufactured punishments, but of genuine natural consequences, to be faced or funked, as the case may be, in the light of kindness, humor, and common sense.

The human result will probably be much more like the so-called self-educated man of to-day than the public school man and the university graduate whose cloistered ignorance and inculcated error have made such a mess of things as they are. Yet what self-educated man, if he can afford to send his son to the public school and university, dares let him run wild? He knows too well that even in the matter of schooling it is a questionable kindness to take a child too far out of the common groove. If, like Romulus or Mowgli, it has to live the life of a wolf, it had better be brought up as a wolf. The good school is now, unfortunately, the crank school : the problem is to make the common school a good school. And good schools are not easily tolerated by bad civilizations. The parent may wish in his soul that his son could be taught that honesty is the best policy; but he has to consider that if he is led to take that precept seriously as a practical rule of life in competitive commerce he may starve for it. All our conventional schools at present teach false ethics, false science, false history, and false hygiene. And if there were sufficient vested interests in false geography and false arithmetic they would teach these too. Truth is a guilty secret, heavily punishable on discovery; and the parent who allows his child to be taught truth without also leaving him an independent income must be prepared to hear his child curse him. This, I think, is the real reason why we dare not embark on controversial education. It would tear away the camouflage from commercial civilization.

For the rest, I can only repeat that if the advance of education is to mean nothing more than the widening of the net of the child prison and boy farm until not one of us can escape it we had better abolish it altogether. Our main disqualifications for citizenship now are ignorance, unsociability, and terrorism. And the government of the world by people who have been longest at school has been so far an organization of ignorance, unsociability, and terrorism, exploding from time to time in such monstrous smashes as the present war, which the belligerents can bear only by persuading themselves that it is a crusade, though it has really no more ethical character than a railway collision.

TWO VIEWS OF SOCIETY—AND EDUCATION.

By A. Clutton Brock.

Behind all educational theory there must be social theory. We must know what we wish society to be before we can know what we wish education to be; and all ideas about education are based on ideas about society, even where no social theory is consciously expressed. Thus, there is a view of society âs a machine existing for some material purpose, either for national survival or for the survival of the human race, and of every individual as a part of that machine. Where that view of society is held, education is conceived as a means of discovering what part each individual is by nature suited to play in the machine, and of training them all for their parts when their fitness has been discovered. Thus, according to the Prussian theory of society and of education, the Prussian society is a machine for maintaining and increasing the national strength, and the aim of Prussian education is to discover and train every individual to play his part in that machine, and, in particular, to pick out the individuals fit to direct the machine and to train them very thoroughly for their task. This view is held also by many people in England who hate Prussia and all her ways; but they believe that it could not make England like Prussia, since Englishmen are born better than Prussians.

With this theory of education is commonly associated the idea of the educational ladder, which many people in England believe to be democratic. By means of the educational ladder ability is discovered in all classes, and an able boy has his chance of becoming a member of the governing class, no matter who his parents may have been. The educational ladder existed, in some form, in the Roman Empire and in the Catholic Church of the Middle Ages. It still exists, to some extent, in the Roman Church, so that a peasant may become a Pope. But the educational ladder, while it may raise an able boy out of his class, does not necessarily improve the circumstances of those who remain in the class of their birth, and, according to all mechanical theories of society, that improvement is not, in itself, to be aimed at. Society is, in the first place, a machine, and the first necessity is to train all to play their part in the machine. If it is a lowly part, then the more narrow and specialised their training the better. It would be folly to educate them so that they might become discontented with the functions they have to perform. For the good of the machine they are necessarily sacrificed, as human beings, to their mechanical efficiency. They are broken in like domestic animals and trained to expect only the amount of happiness compatible with the proper performance of their functions.

It is to be noted that the Prussian higher education professes to be entirely humanistic. It is from first to last general, not vocational, for the Prussians have found that a general education is the best for a governing class. But, though humanistic in its content, it is not humanistic in spirit, since the struggle for life runs all through it from the first. The future of the boy, his income, his status, are determined by the place he takes in periodical examinations, and it is likely that in all he learns he will think rather of this place than of learning for the love of his subject. The Prussian boy works very hard, but for the sake of his own future, not for the sake of what he learns, and this is likely to happen wherever the mechanical theory of education prevails.

To those who desire a full humanistic education for all the ladder system is at best a *pis aller*. It may be necessary, but it is necessary only because we are on earth and not in Heaven. For the essence of humanistic education is, not merely that it shall not be vocational—in some cases it might be vocational—but that what is learned shall be learned for the love of the subject, or at least as a means of arousing that love in the learner. In humanistic education all thought of the struggle for life is banished, and humanistic education seems desirable only to those who believe that the universe is so happily constituted that an individual, and a society, can be fitted for the struggle for life by an education which ignores it. It is based, therefore, upon a certain faith, a faith contrary to the belief that society is a machine constructed for success in some form of the struggle for life. According to that faith a society so constructed will not in the long run win the success it aims at. He that would save his life shall lose it. Rather the proper aim of society is to sacrifice no one individual, either to other individuals or to a general efficiency, and that aim is not accomplished until there is no such sacrifice of any one of its members.

Needless to say, all existing societies are far from such an achievement. But the aim may exist, even though it can never be completely achieved, and, if it exists, it must necessarily control the whole education of the society in which it exists. It does not control our education at present because we have not consciously or unanimously accepted it; but neither have we consciously or unanimously accepted the other notion of society as a machine, or the theory of education based on it. My object, therefore, is, in the most general terms, to expound the humanistic theory of education and its social implications.

It is called humanistic because it is based on the belief that men are, first of all, men, not animals, servants, or tools. This belief we all profess to hold in so far as we accept the Christian view of life; but in practice most of us are a little afraid of it, and our fear betrays itself in our views about the education of the poor. Let us, however, for the moment, forget our fears and consider merely the belief that men are men, not animals, servants, or tools. Where that belief is held, the mechanical theory of society must be rejected. Society must be regarded, not as a machine planned and constructed for some definite material purpose, but as an association of human beings and as itself alive, being composed of human beings. Being alive, then, it is not fully conscious of its purpose. All living things discover the purpose of their life, in so far as they do discover it, by living. It is not made for them as for a machine. They grow in consciousness as in other things, and always there is before them a goal of which they are never fully conscious. So society has before it a goal of which it is not fully conscious, and to regard it as a machine is to be misled by a metaphor. It is not a machine, for its purpose has to be discovered and willed by itself, and it is mere error to train individuals to be part of this machine which does not exist.

Society then, being composed of human beings, exists for them, for all and each of them in the present. Its test is their happiness, the happiness of all and each of them, which is not to be sacrificed to any theory about the future of society or to any hard and fast definition of its aim. For, while we confess that we have not the prophetic power to know exactly what its aim ought to be or will be in the future, we know this at least—that that aim is to be discovered, so far as it is discoverable, by all the members of society, and not by any select body of men scientifically observing society as if it were a foreign and inferior object. And the members of society have the best chance of discovering its aim, and of achieving it if they are themselves happy, if they are all living well without iniquities to poison their relations with each other, if all have opportunity for the development and exercise of their highest faculties. For, since society is itself a living thing, its life is the life of all its members. None of them can be unhappy or unwise without communicating unhappiness and unwisdom to the whole. It is a body not a machine, as in the old Roman fable, and the stomach, if out of order, will poison the brain, will make it think as badly as the stomach digests. But even this metaphor has error in it, for in society the thinking must be done by all; functions cannot be separated as in the body, and that society is the best and healthiest in which the higher functions are most generally distributed, and in which all men are educated with a view to their exercise of those higher functions. That, I need hardly say, is the democratic theory. It is based on the conception of society as a living thing, not as a machine, and we may judge all theories and measures which profess to be democratic by this test : Are they based on a conception of society as a living thing or as a machine? If on the latter, they are not democratic, whatever they may call themselves, or whatever arguments are used in support of them.

Now, if we apply the democratic theory, the conception of society as a living thing to education, we shall find that we are led to certain difficult and dangerous conclusions. For the educator, every child will be not the raw material out of which a part of the social machine can be made, but a human being whose life is to be part of the life of society. And to the educator all these children, being human beings, will be equal. His business is not to fit them for a certain mechanical function, not to see them from the first as subordinate parts in a general mechanical process, but to develop them as human beings without regard to the particular stations which they may have to occupy when they are grown up. To him these differences of station and of function will be evils, even if necessary evils. His business is not to consent to them in his method of teaching but to act as if they did not exist, and to regard all the limitations which they impose on him not as natural laws but as mere hindrances against which he will rebel to the best of his power.

Thus, if people tell him that the children of the poor ought not to be taught music, since music will be of no use to them in the field or in the factory, his answer will be that to him they are not the children of the poor, but children, and that children should be taught music. If our present society is of such a nature that music is of no use to the poor, then, by learning music in their childhood, the poor will become aware of the defects of our society, will see that it treats them as parts of a machine, not as living human beings with the higher human desires. And, if they are aware of these defects, they may themselves attempt to remove them. That is, of course, a dangerous doctrine, at least to those who conceive of society as a machine. For a machine does not work well if the parts of it are discontented; of a machine we do not say that its parts are discontented, but that it is out of order. And certainly a society in which the poor are aware of higher desires unsatisfied, is not likely to work with mechanical smoothness. We have, therefore, to choose at present between a society in which the poor are aware of higher desires unsatisfied and one in which they are not aware of higher desires at all. It is a choice of evils, but the question is—which choice will lead to greater evils?

The educator who holds the humanistic theory of education will not ask himself whether his teaching is likely to produce discontent, for he does not see society as a machine or education as a means of making the machine work smoothly. If he arouses discontent in his pupils by arousing their higher desires, then it is the business of society, including his pupils, to remove the causes of discontent. Such discontent is to him divine. It is to the spirit what pain is to the body, a warning that something is wrong and needs to be put right. He would not train his pupils to feel no pain where the highest mind would feel it, for his aim is to exalt the minds of all his pupils, because to him they are all human beings. But here, when I speak of the educator, I mean really all of us, for we are all educators in that we all have some say in the education of the poor. It is our common will that decides how they are to be educated, because of our greater knowledge as well as our greater wealth. The parents of poor children are often so ignorant themselves, so unused to thought through pressure of hard work, that they are not aware of the educational aims of the board schools, which are decided by those who have time to think. We then, who have time to think, may decide that we will educate the children of the poor to be parts of a social machine—in which case the social machine will perhaps work with some smoothness in our time—or we may decide that we will educate the children of the poor to be human beings, without fearing lest the demands of their humanity will derange the machine. But we shall free ourselves of that fear only if society is not a machine to us but a living thing, having the quality of life that is in all its members.

One talks glibly of educating the children of the poor to be human beings, but any teacher of them will be provoked, with a bitter smile, to speak of the difficulties, the impossibilities, of that vague programme. A humanistic education takes many years, and the children of the poor begin to work in their childhood. It is expensive, and their schools are stinted of money. It must ignore the struggle for life, and they are subject to the pressure of that struggle always. All that is true, but if we really desire them to be educated as human beings, these facts will become more and more intolerable to us. We ourselves shall know the divine discontent, the wholesome pain, which a humanistic education must arouse in them; we shall feel ourselves thwarted in that task which is the true task of society, the enrichment and heightening of its own life. We shall see suddenly what is the real evil and impotence of our society, its grinding poverty; and by that I mean, not the poverty of poor people but the poverty of all society, its lack of money, of power, to do any of the things that, for a society, are best worth doing. We are able now, or before the war we were able, to spend money on ourselves; but before the war we were not able to spend it on any great common object, whether of education, of art, of science, or of religion. As a community we were miserably poor; and yet the war surprised us with the discovery of our riches as a community, with the vast amount of labour we found it possible suddenly to spend on a common cause without suffering want ourselves. How many of us now are wondering what we spent all that labour on before? The answer is quite simple. We wasted it in the making of innumerable things, both for rich and poor, that no one really needed or desired. And that waste was the cause of our grinding common poverty, of the fact that the great mass of people in the country worked too hard and yet had nothing to spare for great common objects, although our powers of production have increased more than tenfold in a century.

The war has taught us this at least, that we have an enormous superfluous energy, as a community, if only we choose, as a community, to use it, and not to waste it privately in the production of trash. More and more we have been forced to cease from that production. We make munitions where we used to make rubbish. Will it not, therefore, be possible for us, when peace comes, to continue making something better than rubbish, better also than munitions? We were too poor before the war to afford the necessary time or money for the education of the children of the poor, and yet, in the war we can afford the labour and time of millions of men and women for the purposes of the war, because we have learned to do without the trash which that labour used to produce for us. And we have practised this abstinence willingly, because we have seen our society as a living whole in conflict with another society. Will it not be possible for us to see our society as a living whole, not merely for purposes of conflict, but also for purposes of life? At this moment we deny ourselves, and take a pride in doing so, in the hope, the narrow and immediate hope, of victory. Can we not rise to a larger hope, in peace time, of a society always waxing in riches, in happiness, in life? We shall realise it only if we deny ourselves for the purposes of peace as willingly as we have denied ourselves for the purposes of war. And among the chief of those purposes is education, the education of every child in the country to be a complete human being and not part of a machine for the production of rubbish. Education is not everything. Besides, we need a world fit for those who are educated, a world in which they can exercise all those higher faculties which education has trained for them. But if we ourselves learn to do without trash in our passion for education, as we have learned to do without it in our passion for victory, we shall not set the children, when they are educated, to the production of trash. We shall be able to afford worthy things for them to do, and they will be able to do them. The prosperity of a country, material and spiritual alike, depends on the quality of its labour and the nature of the tasks to which that labour is applied; and ultimately the quality of the labour depends upon the nature of the tasks to which it is applied.

That is the fact behind all political struggles, which are always them-selves merely symptoms of a misapplication and a low quality ot labour. If we educate masses of our people so that they are fit only for a low quality of labour, we train them also to a misapplication of labour, and so to an inevitable war of class against class, carried on by them with a blindness equal to our own. There is no way out of it except to see them in their childhood just as we see our own children, to see them as members of our own family, and to deny ourselves for their education as we should deny ourselves for the education of our own children. For if we, as a society, are not a machine for the turning out of trash and the fomenting of a class war, we are a family, which is the type of all living societies, and the happiness of the family depends on the education of all its members. You cannot turn some of them into tools or drudges, without making the life of the rest duller and poorer and less happy. You cannot escape from your poor relations, how-ever much you may try to forget them. At least, the more you suc-ceed in forgetting them, the more, and the more bitterly, they will remember you.

THE BALANCE SHEET OF THE SOLDIER WORKMAN.

By John Galsworthy.

Let the reader take what follows with more than a grain of salt. No one can foretell—surely not this writer—with anything approaching certainty what will be the final effect of this war on the soldier-workman. One can but marshal some of the more obvious and general liabilities and assets, and try to strike a balance. The whole thing is in flux. Metals are going into the crucible at every temperature; and who shall say at all precisely what will come out, or what conditions the product issuing will meet with, though they obviously cannot be the same as before the war? For in considering this question, one must run into the account on either side not only the various effects of the war on the soldier-workman, but the difference his life will encounter in the future, so far as one can foresee; and this is all navigation in uncharted waters.

Talking with and observing French soldiers during the whole of last winter, and often putting to them this very question : How is the war going to affect the soldier-workman? I noticed that their answers followed very much the trend of class and politics. An adjutant, or sergeant, or a Catholic, would consider that men would be improved, gain self-command and respect for law and order, under prolonged discipline and daily sacrifice. A freethinker of the educated class, or a private of Socialistic tendencies, on the other hand, would insist that the strain must make men restless, irritable, more eager for their rights, less tolerant of control. Each imagined that the war would further the chances of the future as they dreamed of it. If I had talked with capitalists—there are none among the *poilus*—they would doubtless have insisted that after-war conditions were going to be easier, just as the *sans-sous* maintained that they were going to be harder, and provocative of revolution. In a word, the wish was father to the thought.

Having observed this so strongly, the writer of these speculations says to himself : " Let me, at all events, try to eliminate any bias, and see the whole thing as should an umpire—one of those pure beings in white coats, purged of all the prejudices, passions, and predilections of mankind. Let me have no temperament for the time being, for I have to set down—not what would be the effect on me if I were in their place, or what would happen to the future if I could have my way, but what would happen all the same if I were not alive. Only from an impersonal point of view, if there be such a thing, am I going to get even approximately at the truth."

Impersonally, then, I note the credit facts and probabilities towards the future's greater well-being; and those on the debit side, of retrogression from the state of well-being, such as it was, that prevailed when war was declared.

First, what will be the physical effect of the war on the soldier-workman? Military training, open-air life, and plentiful food are of such obvious physical advantage in the vast majority of cases as to need no pointing out. And how much improvement was wanted is patent to anyone who has a remnant left of the old Greek worship of the body. It has made one almost despair of industralised England, to see the great Australians pass the streets of London. We English cannot afford to neglect the body any longer; we are, or are becoming— I know not which—a warped, stunted, intensely plain people. On that point I refuse to speak with diffidence, for it is my business to know something about beauty, and in our masters and pastors I see no sign of knowledge and little inkling of concern, since there is no public opinion to drive them forward to respect beauty. One-half of us regard good looks as dangerous and savouring of immorality; the other half look upon them as " swank," or at least superfluous. Any interest manifested in such a subject is confined to a few women and a handful of artists. Let anyone who has an eye for looks take the trouble to observe the people who pass in the streets of any of our big towns, he will count perhaps one in five—not beautiful—but with some pretensions to being not absolutely plain; and one can say this without fear of hurting any feelings, for all will think themselves swans. Frivolity apart, there is a dismal lack of good looks and good physique in our population; and it will be all to the good to have had this physical training. If that training had stopped short of the fighting line, it would be physically entirely beneficial; as it is, one has unfortunately to set against its advantages—leaving out wounds and mutilation altogether—a considerable number of over-strained hearts, and nerves, not amounting to actual disablement; and a great deal of developed rheumatism.

Peace will send back to their work very many men better set up and hardier; but many also obviously or secretly weakened. Hardly any can go back as they were. But, while training will but have brought out strength that was always latent, and which, unless relapse be guarded against, must rapidly decline, cases of strain and rheumatism will for the most part be permanent, and such as would not have taken place under peace conditions. Then there is the matter of venereal disease, which the conditions of military life are undoubtedly fostering—no negligible factor on the debit side; we must write off the health of many hundreds on that score. To credit, again, must be placed increased personal cleanliness, much greater handiness and resource in the small ways of life, and an even more complete endurance and contempt of illness than already characterised the British workman, if that be possible. On the whole, I think that, physically, the scales will balance pretty evenly.

Next, what will be the effect of the war on the mental powers of the soldier-workman? Unlike the French (60 per cent. of whose army are men working on the land), our Army must contain at least 90 per cent. of town workers, whose minds in time of peace are kept rather more active than those of workers on the land by the ceaseless friction and small decisions of town life. To gauge the result of two to five years' military life on the minds of these town workers is a complicated and stubborn problem. Here we have the exact converse of the physical case. If the army life of the soldier-workman stopped short of service at the front one might say at once that the effect on his mind would be far more disastrous than it is. The opportunity for initiative, and decision, the mental stir of camp and depôt life is nil compared with that of service in the fighting line. And for one month at the front, most men spend many at the rear. Military life, on its negative side, is more or less a suspension of the usual channels of mental activity. By barrack and camp life the normal civilian intellect is, as it were, marooned. On that desert island it finds, no doubt, certain new and very definite forms of activity, but anyone who has watched old soldiers must have been struck by the " arrested " look that is stamped on most of them—by a kind of remoteness, of concentrated emptiness, as of men who by the conditions of their lives have long been prevented from thinking of anything outside a ring fence. Two to five years' service will not be.long enough to set the old soldier's stamp on a mind, but one can see the process beginning; and it will be quite long enough to encourage laziness, in minds already disposed to lying fallow. Far be it from this pen to libel the English, but a feverish mental activity has never been their vice; intellect, especially in what is known as the working class, is leisurely; it does not require to be encouraged to take its ease. Someone has asked me : " *Can* the ordinary worker think less in the army than when he wasn't in the army? " In other words : " Did he ever think at all? " The British worker is, of course, deceptive; he does not look as if he were thinking. Whence exactly does he get his stolidity—from climate, self-consciousness, or his competitive spirit? All the same, thought does go on in him, shrewd and " near-the-bone "; life-made rather than book-made thought. Its range is limited by his vocabulary; it starts from different premises, reaches different conclusions from those of the " pundit "; and so is liable to seem to the latter non-existent. But let a worker and an educated man sit opposite each other in a railway carriage without exchanging a word, as is the fashion with the English, and which of their two silent judgments on the other will be superior? I am not sure, but I rather think the worker's. It will have a kind of deadly realism. In camp and depôt life the mind standing-at-ease from many civilian frictions and needs for decision, however petty—and shaken away from civilian ruts, will do a good deal of thinking of a sort, be widened and probably re-value many things—especially when its owner goes abroad and sees fresh types, fresh manners, and the world; but actual physical exertion, and the inertia which follows it, bulk large in military service, and many who " never thought at all " before they became soldiers will think still less after ! I may be cynical, but it seems to me that the chief stimulus to thought in the ordinary mind is money, the getting and the spending thereof; that what we call " politics," those social interests, which form at least half the staple of the ordinary worker's thought, are made up of concern as to the wherewithal to live. In the army money is a fixed quantity that demands no thought, neither in the getting nor the spending; and the constant mental activity that in normal life circles round money of necessity dries up.

But against this indefinite general rusting of mind machinery in the soldier-workman's life away from the fighting line certain definite considerations must be set. Many soldiers will form a habit of reading —in the new armies the demand for books is great; some in sheer boredom will have begun an all-round cultivation of their minds; others, again, will be chafing continually against this prolonged holding-up of their habitual mental traffic—and when a man chafes he does not exactly rust; so that, while the naturally lazy will have been made more lazy, the naturally eager may be made very eager.

A lecturer for the Y.M.C.A. in France, being asked whether he thought our soldiers were losing the power of concentrating their thoughts, answered : " Not in my experience. On the contrary, they'll sit through an hour's lecture without the least sign of inattention." But that again may only be natural reaction from having nothing much else to think about, or perhaps a tribute to the particular lecturer. Besides, does not military life impart to the face and figure a certain immobility even out of military hours ? It is not a question of whether the worker had good and useful thoughts before he became a soldier— whether he kept his mind active in a satisfactory way ; but of whether civil life does not necessarily jog the liver of his mind more constantly than military life. I think it must.

The matter of age, too, is not unimportant. A soldier of 20, 25, even up to 30, probably seldom feels that the mode of life from which he has been taken is set and permanent. He may be destined to do that work all his days, but the knowledge of this has not so far bitten him ; he is not yet in the swing and current of his career, and feels no great sense of dislocation. But a man of 35 or 40, taken from an occupation which has got grip on him, feels that his life has had a slice carved out of it. He may realise the necessity better than the younger man, take his duty more seriously, but he must have a sense as if his springs were let down flat. The knowledge that he has to resume his occupation again in real middle age, with all the steam escaped, must be profoundly discouraging ; therefore, I think his mental activity will suffer more than that of the younger man. The recuperative powers of youth are so great that very many of our younger soldiers will unrust quickly, and at a bound regain all the activity lost. Besides, a very great many of the younger men will not go back to the old job. But older men, though they will go back to what they were doing before, more readily than their juniors, will go back with diminished hope and energy, and a sort of fatalism. At 40, even at 35, every year begins to seem important, and several years will have been wrenched clean out of their working lives just, perhaps, when they were beginning to make good.

But at the front there will be no rusting,—the novelty of sensation, the demand for initiative and adaptability are too great. An officer said to me : " My two years in depôt and camp were absolutely deadening ; that eight weeks at the front before I was knocked over were the best eight weeks I ever had." Spells at the front must wipe out all or nearly all the rust ; but against them must be set the deadening spells of hospital that too often follow, the deadening spells of training that have gone before ; and the more considerable though not very permanent factor—that laziness and dislocation left on the minds of many who have been much in the firing line. As the young man put it : " I can't concentrate now as I could on a bit of work—it takes me longer ; all the same, where I used to chuck it when I found it hard, I set my teeth now." In other words, less mental but more moral grip.

On the whole, then, so far as mental effect goes, I believe the balance must come out on the debit side.

And, now, what will be the spiritual effect of the war on the soldier-workman ? And by " spiritual " I mean the effect of his new life and emotional experience, neither on his intellect nor exactly on his " soul "—for few have such a rarefied thing—but on his disposition and character.

Has anyone the right to discuss this who has not fought? It is with the greatest diffidence that I hazard any view. On the other hand, the effects are so various, and so intensely individual that perhaps only such a one has a chance of forming a general judgment unbiassed by personal experience, and his own temperament. What thousands of strange and poignant feelings must pass through even the least impressionable soldier who runs the gamut of this war's " experience." And there will not be too many of our soldier-workmen returning to civil life without having had at least a taste of everything. The embryo Guardsman who sticks his bayonet into a sack, be he never so unimaginative, with each jab of that bayonet pictures dimly the body of a Hun, and gets used to the sensation of spitting it. On every long march there comes a time that may last hours, when the recruit feels done up, and yet has to go on " sticking it." Never a day passes, all through his service, without some moment when he would give his soul to be out of it all and back in some little elysium of the past; but he has to grit his teeth and try to forget. Hardly a man who, when he first comes under fire, has not a struggle with himself that amounts to a spiritual victory. Not many who do not arrive at a " Don't care " state of mind that is almost equal to a spiritual defeat. No soldier who does not rub shoulders during his service with count-less comrades strange to him and get a wider understanding and a fuller tolerance. Not a soul in the trenches, one would think, who is not caught up into a mood of comradeship and self-suppression that amounts almost to exaltation. Not one but has to fight through moods almost reaching extinction of the very love of life. And shall all this —and the many hard disappointments, and the long yearning for home and those he loves, and the chafing against continual restraints, and the welling-up of secret satisfaction in the " bit done," the know-ledge that fate is not beating, cannot beat him; and the sight of death all round, and the looking into death's eyes—staring those eyes down; and the long bearing of pain; and the pity for his comrades bearing pain—shall all this pass his nature by without marking it for life? When all is over, and the soldier-workman back in civil life, will his character be enlarged or shrunken? The nature of a man is never really changed, no more than a leopard's skin, it is but developed or dwarfed. The influences of the war will have as many little forms as there are soldiers, and to attempt precision of summary is clearly vain. It is something of a truism to suggest that the war will ennoble and make more serious those who before the war took a noble and serious view of life; and that on those who took life callously it will have a callousing effect. The problem is rather to discover what effect, if any, will be made on that medium material that was neither definitely serious nor obviously callous. And for this we must go to considera-tion of main national characteristics. It is—for one thing—very much the nature of the Briton to look on life as a game with victory or defeat at the end of it, and to feel it impossible that he can be defeated. He is not so much concerned to "live" as to win this life match. He is combative from one minute to the next, reacts instantly against any attempt to down him. The war for him is a round in this great personal match of his with Fate, and he is completely caught up in the idea of winning it. He is spared that double consciousness of the French soldier who wants to " live," who goes on indeed superbly fighting " *pour la France* " out of love for his country, but all the time cannot help saying to himself : " What a fool I am—what sort of life is this? " I have heard it said by one who ought to know, if anyone can, that the British soldier hardly seems to have a sense of patriotism, but goes through it all as a sort of private " scrap " in which he does not mean to be beaten, and out of loyalty to his regiment, his " team," so to speak. This is partly true, but the Briton is very deep, and there are feelings at the bottom of his well that never see the light. If the British soldier were fighting on a line that ran from Lowestoft through York to Sunderland, he might show very different symptoms. Still, at bottom, he would always, I think, feel the business to be first in the nature of a contest with a force that was trying to down him personally. In this contest he is being stretched and steeled—that is, confirmed in the very quality of stubborn combativeness which was already his first characteristic.

Take another main feature of the national character—the Briton is ironic. Well, the war is deepening his irony. It must, for it is a monstrously ironic business, only to be faced out by the sort of comic courage that makes him sing :—

> " O, death, where is thy sting-a-ling-a-ling,
> Where, grave, thy victoree?
> The bells of hell go ting-a-ling-a-ling,
> For you, but not for me."

Some—especially those who wish to—believe in a religious revival among the soldiers. There's an authentic story of two convalescent soldiers describing a battle. The first finished thus : " I tell you it makes you think of God." The second—a thoughtful type—ended with a pause, and then these words : " Who could believe in God after that? " Like all else in human life, it depends on temperament. The war speeds up " belief " in some, " disbelief " in others. But comic courage flouts orthodoxy—and comic courage rules out there.

The religious movement that I think *is* going on is of a subtler and a deeper sort altogether. Men are discovering that human beings are finer than they had supposed. A young man said to me : " Well, I don't know about religion, but I know that my opinion of human nature is about 50 per cent. better than it was." That conclusion has been arrived at by countless thousands. It is a great factor—seeing that the belief of the future will be belief in the God within ; and a frank agnosticism concerning the great " Why " of things. Religion will become the exaltation of self-respect, of what we call the divine in man. " The Kingdom of God is within you." That belief, old as the hills, and reincarnated by Tolstoi years ago, has come into its own in the war ; for it has been clearly proved the real faith of modern man, underneath all verbal attempts to assert the contrary. This—the white side of war—is an extraordinarily heartening phenomenon ; and if it sent every formal creed in the world packing there would still be a gain to religion.

Another main characteristic of the Briton, especially of the " working " Briton, is improvidence—he likes, unconsciously, to live from hand to mouth, careless of the morrow. The war is deepening that characteristic, too—it must, for who could endure if he fretted over what was going to happen to him, with death so in the wind?

Thus the average soldier-workman will return from the war confirmed and deepened in at least three main national characteristics : His combative hardihood, his ironic humour, and his improvidence. I think he will have more of what is called " character " ; whether for good or evil depends, I take it, on what you connote by those terms, and in what context you use them. I may look on " character " as an asset, but I can well imagine politicians and Trade Union leaders regarding it with profound suspicion. He was not exactly a lamb before the war ; and after the war he will be a restive fellow, knowing his own mind better, and possibly his real interests less well ; he will play less for safety, since safety will have become to him a civilian sort of thing rather contemptible. He will have at once a more interesting and a less reliable character from the social and political point of view.

And what about his humanity? Can he go through all this hell of slaughter and violence untouched in his gentler instincts? There will —there must be—a good deal of brutalisation. But old soldiers are not usually inhumane—on the contrary, they are often very gentle beings. I distrust the influence of the war on those who merely write and read about it. I think editors, writers, old gentlemen, and women will be brutalised quite as much as our soldiers. , An intelligent French soldier said to me, of his own countrymen : " After six months of civil life you won't know they ever had to ' clean up ' trenches and that sort of thing." If this is true of the Frenchman, it will presumably be true of the less impressionable Briton. If I must sum up at all on what, for want of a better word, I have called the " spiritual " count, I can only say that there will be a distinct increase of " character," and leave it to the reader to decide whether that falls on the debit or the credit side.

On the whole, then, an increase of " character," a slight loss of mental activity, and neither gain nor loss, to speak of, physically.

We have now to consider the rather deadly matter of demobilisation. One hears the suggestion that not more than 30,000 men shall be disbanded per week ; this means two years at least. Conceive millions of men whose sense of sacrifice has been stretched to the full for a definite object which has been gained—conceive them held in a weary, and, as it seems to them, unnecessary state of suspense. Kept back from all they long for, long months after the reality of service has departed ! If this does not undermine them, I do not know what will. Demobilisation—they say—must be slow and cautious. " No man should be released till a place in the industrial machine is ready waiting for him " ! So, in a counsel of perfection, speak the wise who have not been deprived of home life, civil liberty, and what not for a dismal length of two, three, and perhaps four years. No ! Demobilisation should be as swift as possible, and risks be run to make it swift. The soldier-workman who goes back to civil life within two or three months after peace is signed goes back with a glow still in his heart. But he who returns with a rankling sense of unmerited, unintelligible delay— most prudently, of course, ordained—goes back with " cold feet " and a sullen or revolting spirit. What men will stand under the shadow of a great danger from a sense of imminent duty they will furiously chafe at when that danger and sense of duty are no more. The duty will then be to their families and to themselves. There is no getting away from this, and the country will be well advised not to be too coldly cautious. Everyone, of course, must wish to ease to the utmost the unprecedented economic and industrial confusion which the signing of peace will bring, but it will be better to risk a good deal of momentary unemployment and discontent rather than neglect the human factor and keep men back long months in a service of which they will be deadly sick. How sick they will be may perhaps be guessed at from the words of a certain soldier: "After the war! You'll *have* to have conscription. You won't get a man to go into the army without!" What is there to prevent the Government from beginning now to take stock of the demands of industry, from having a great land settlement scheme cut and dried, and devising means for the swiftest possible demobilisation? The moment peace is signed the process of re-absorption into civil life should begin at once and go on without interruption as swiftly as the actual difficulties of transport permit. They, of themselves, will hold up demobilisation quite long enough. The soldier-workman will recognise and bear with the necessary physical delays, but he will not tolerate for a moment any others for his so-called benefit.

And what sort of civil life will it be that awaits the soldier-workman? I suppose, if anything is certain, a plenitude, nay, a plethora, of work is assured for some time after the war. Capital has piled up in hands that will control a vast amount of improved and convertible machinery. Purchasing power has piled up in the shape of savings out of the increased national income. Granted that income will at once begin to drop all round, shrinking perhaps fast to below the pre-war figures, still at first there must be a rolling river of demand and the wherewithal to satisfy it. For years no one has built houses, or had their houses done up, no one has bought furniture, clothes, or a thousand other articles which they propose buying the moment the war stops. Railways and rolling stock, roads, housing, public works of all sorts, private motor-cars, and pleasure requirements of every kind have been let down and starved. Huge quantities of shipping must be replaced; vast renovations of destroyed country must be undertaken; numberless repairs to damaged property; the tremendous process of converting or re-converting machinery to civil uses must be put through; State schemes to deal with the land, housing, and other problems will be in full blast; a fierce industrial competition will commence; and, above all, we must positively grow our own food in the future. Besides all this, we shall have lost at least a million workers through death, disablement, and emigration; indeed, unless we have some really attractive land scheme ready we may lose a million by emigration alone. In a word, the demand for labour, at the moment, will be overwhelming, and the vital question only one of readjustment. In numberless directions women, boys, and older men have replaced the soldier-workman. Hundreds of thousands of soldiers, especially among the first three million, have been guaranteed reinstatement. Hundreds of thousands of substitutes will, therefore, be thrown out of work. With the exception of the skilled men who have had to be retained in their places all through, and the men who step back into places kept for them, the whole working population will have to be refitted with jobs. The question of women's labour will not be grave at first because there will be work for all and more than all, but the jigsaw puzzle that Industry will have to put together will try the nerves and temper of the whole community. In the French army the peasant soldier is jealous and sore with the mechanic, because he has had to bear the chief burden of the fighting, while the latter has to a great extent been kept for munition making, transport, and essential civil industry. With us it is, if anything, the other way. In the French army, too, the feeling runs high against the " *embusqué*," the man who—often unjustly—is supposed to have avoided service. I do not know to what extent the same feeling prevails in our Army, but there is certainly an element of it, which will not make for content or quietude.

Another burning question after the war will be wages. We are assured they are going to keep up. Well, we shall see. Certain special rates will, of course, come down at once. And if, in general, wages keep up it will not, I think, be for very long. Still, times will be good at first for employers and employed. At first—and then!

Some thinkers insist that the war has to an appreciable extent been financed out of savings that would otherwise have been spent on luxury. But the amount thus saved can easily be exaggerated—the luxury class is not really large, and against their saving must be set the spending by the working classes, out of increased wages, on what in peace years were not necessities of their existence. In other words, the luxury or investing class has cut off its peace time fripperies, saved and lent to the Government; the Government has paid the bulk of this money to the working class, who have spent most of it in what to them would be fripperies in time of peace. It may be, it *is*, all to the good that luxurious tastes should be clipped from the wealthy, and a higher standard of living secured to the workers, but this is rather a matter of distribution and social health than of economics in relation to the financing of the war.

There are those who argue that because the general productive effort of the country during the war has been speeded up to half as much again as that of normal times, by tapping women's labour, by longer hours, and general improvement in machinery and industrial ideas, the war will not result in any great economic loss, and that we may with care and effort avoid the coming of bad times after the first boom. The fact remains, and anybody can test it for themselves, that there is a growing shortage of practically everything except—as they say—cheap jewellery and pianos. I am no economist, but that does seem to indicate that this extra production has not in any way compensated for the enormous application of labour and material resources to the quick-wasting ends of war instead of to the slow-wasting ends of civil life. In other words, an enormous amount of productive energy and material is being shot away. Now, this, I suppose, would not matter, in fact, might be beneficial to trade by increasing demand, if the purchasing power of the public remained what it was before the war. But in all the great countries of the world, even America, the peoples will be faced with taxation that will soak up anything from one-fifth to one-third of their incomes, and, even allowing for a large swelling of those incomes from war savings, so that a great deal of what the State takes with one hand she will return to the investing public with the other, the diminution of purchasing power is bound to make itself increasingly felt. Moreover, the levy on capital is bound to come. When the reconversion of machinery to civil ends has been completed, the immediate arrears of demand supplied, shipping and rolling-stock replaced, houses built, repairs made good, and so forth, this slow shrinkage of purchasing power in publics, British and foreign, will go hand in hand with shrinkage of demand, decline of trade and wages, and unemployment, in a slow process, till they culminate in what one fears may be the worst " times " we have ever known. Whether those " times " will set in, one, two, four, or even six years after the war is, of course, the question. A certain school of thought insists that this tremendous taxation after the war, and the consequent impoverishment of enterprise and industry, can be avoided, or at all events greatly relieved, by national schemes for the development of the Empire's latent resources; in other words, that the State should even borrow more money to avoid high taxation and pay the interests on existing loans, should acquire the lands of native races, and develop swiftly mineral and other potentialities. I hope there may be something in this, but I am a little afraid that the wish is father to the thought here, that the proposition contains an element akin to the attempt to lift oneself up by the hair of one's own head; and I suspect many of its disciples are recruited from those who in old days were opposed to the State development of any thing, on the ground that individual energy in free competition is a still greater driving power.

However we may wriggle in our skins and juggle with the chances of the future, we shall certainly have to pay the piper. We have, without doubt, during the war, been living to a great extent on our capital. Our national income has gone up, *out of capital*, from twenty-four hundred to, they say, thirty-six hundred millions, and will shrink to an appropriate figure. Wealth may, I admit, recover much more quickly than deductions from the past would lead us to expect. Under the war's pressure, secrets have been discovered, machinery improved, men's energies and knowledge brightened and toned up. The Prime Minister, not long ago, said: " If you insist on going back to pre-war conditions, then God help this country." A wise warning. If the country could be got to pull together in an effort to cope with peace, as strenuous as our effort to cope with the war has been, I should not view the economic future with disquietude. But one is bound to point out that, if the war has proved anything, it has proved that the British people require a maximum of danger dangled in front of their very noses before they can be roused to any serious effort, and that danger in time of peace has not the poster-like quality of danger in time of war; it does not hit men in the eye, it does not still differences of opinion, and party struggles, by its scarlet insistence. I hope for, but frankly do not see, the coming of an united national effort demanding extra energy, extra organising skill, extra patience, and extra self-sacrifice at a time when the whole nation will feel that it has earned a rest, and when the lid has once more been taken off the political cauldron. I fancy, dismally, that people and a Press who have become so used to combat and excitement will demand and seek further combat and excitement, and will take out this itch amongst themselves in a fashion even more strenuous than before the war. I am not here concerned to try to cheer or depress for some immediate and excellent result, as we have all got into the habit of doing during the war, but to try to conjure truth out of the darkness of the future. The vast reconstructive process which ought to be, and perhaps is, beginning now, will, I think, go ahead with vigour while the war is on, and for some little time after; but I fear it will then split into pro and con, see-saw, and come to something of a standstill.

These, so sketchily set down, are a few of the probable items—credit and debit—in the industrial situation which will await the soldier-workman emerging from the war. A situation agitated, cross-currented, bewildering, but busy, and by no means economically tight at first, slowly becoming less bewildering, gradually growing less and less busy, till it reaches ultimately a bad era of unemployment and social struggle. The soldier-workman will go back, I believe, to two or three years at least of good wages and plentiful work. But when, after that, the pinch begins to come it will encounter the quicker, more resentful blood of men who in the constant facing of great danger have left behind them all fear of consequences; of men who in the survival of one great dislocation to their lives have lost the dread of other dislocations. The war will have implanted a curious deep restlessness in the great majority of soldier souls. Can the workmen of the future possibly be as patient and law-abiding as they were before the war, in the face of what seems to them injustice? I don't think so. The enemy will again be Fate—this time in the form of Capital trying to down them; and the victory they were conscious of gaining over Fate in the war will have strengthened and quickened their fibre to another fight and another conquest. The seeds of revolution are supposed to lie in war. They lie there, because war generally brings in the long run economic stress, but also because of the recklessness or "character"—call it which you will—which the habitual facing of danger develops. The self-control and self-respect which military service under war conditions will have brought to the soldier-workman will be an added force in civil life; but it is a fallacy, I think, to suppose, as some do, that it will be a force on the side of established order. It is all a question of allegiance, and the allegiance of the workman in time of peace is not rendered to the State but to himself and his own class. To the service of that class and the defence of its "rights" this new force will be given. In measuring the possibilities of revolution the question of class rides paramount. Many hold that the war is breaking down social barriers and establishing comradeship, through hardship and danger shared. For the moment this, perhaps, is true. But whether that new comradeship will stand great pressure of economic stress after direct regimental relationship between officer and man has ceased, and the war is becoming a painful memory, is to me very doubtful. But suppose that to some extent it does stand, we have still the fact that the control of industry and capital, even as long as ten years after the war, will be mainly in the hands of men who have not fought, of business men spared from service either by age or by their too precious commercial skill. Towards these the soldier-workman will have no tender feelings, no sense of comradeship. On the contrary—for somewhere back of the mind of every workman there is, even during his country's danger, a certain doubt whether all war is not somehow hatched by the aristocrats and plutocrats of one side, or both. Other feelings obscure this instinct during the struggle, but it is never quite lost, and will spring up again the more confirmed for its repression. That we can avoid a straitened and serious time a few years hence I believe impossible. Straitened times dismally divide the classes. The war investments of the working class may ease things a little, but war savings will not affect the outlook of the soldier-workman, for he will have no war savings, except his life, and it is from him that revolution or disorder will come, if it come at all.

C

Must it come? I think most certainly, unless between now and then means be found of persuading Capital and Labour that their interests and their troubles are identical, and of overcoming secrecy and suspicion between them. There are many signs already that Capital and Labour are becoming alive to this necessity. But to talk of unity is an amiable distraction in which we all indulge these days. To find a method by which that talk may be translated into fact within a few years is perhaps more difficult. One does not change human nature; and unless the interests of Capital and Labour are *in reality* made one—and factory conditions all over the country transformed on the lines of the welfare system—no talk of unity will prevent capitalist and workingman from claiming what seem to them their rights. The Labour world is now, and for some time to come will be, at sixes and sevens in matters of leadership and responsibility; and this just when sagacious leadership and loyal following will be most needed. The soldier-workman was already restive under leadership before the war; returned to civil life he will be far more restive. Yet, without leadership, what hope is there of co-operation with Capital; what chance of finding a golden mean of agreement? But assume that the problems of leadership are solved, and councils of Capital and Labour established, whose decisions will be followed—one thing is still certain—no half-measures will do; no seeming cordialities with mental reservations; no simulated generosity that spills out on the first test; nothing but genuine friendliness and desire to pull together. Those hard business heads which distrust all sentiment as if it were a poison are the most short-sighted heads in the world. There *is* a human factor in this affair, as both sides will find to their cost if they neglect it. Extremists must be sent to Coventry, " caste " feeling dropped on the one hand, and suspicion dropped on the other; managers, directors, and Labour leaders, all must learn that they are not simply trustees for their shareholders or for Labour, but trustees of a national interest that embraces them all—or worse will come of it.

But I am not presumptuous enough to try and teach these cooks how to make their broth, neither would it come within the scope of these speculations, which conclude thus: The soldier-workman, physically unchanged, mentally a little weakened, but more " characterful " and restive, will step out through a demobilisation—that, heaven send, be swift, even at some risk—into an industrial world, confused and busy as a beehive, that will hum and throb and flourish for two or three years, and then slowly chill and thin away into, may be, the winter ghost of itself, or at best an autumn hive. There, unless he be convinced, not by words but facts, that his employer is standing side by side with him in true comradeship, facing the deluge, he will be quick to rise, and, with his newly found self-confidence, take things into his own hands. Whether, if he does, he will make those things better for himself, would be another inquiry.

June, 1917.

THOUGHTS ON WORKING-CLASS EDUCATION.

By J. A. Hobson

(Author of " Democracy After the War," etc.).

The workers constantly tell themselves that one of the chief goods denied to them and monopolised by the well-to-do classes is education. They are coming to realise that they want education for three purposes. Two of these purposes are primarily of individual value to them, one is of collective value. A worker needs education in order that he may make the best use of any special aptitude, or skill, or trade opportunities that he possesses, so as to " get on " in his particular calling. This does not merely signify some technical or business training with an immediate bearing on the work he undertakes, but also some general education to " improve his mind " and " broaden his outlook." But the purpose of this education is to help him as a wage-earner, or possibly to help him to get out of wage-earning into some more independent but still a special business career. It is education " for the shop."

But as far as a worker realises the value of education, not only for his economic work, but for his manhood, another broader purpose actuates him, viz., the demand for personal cultivation. He wants the opportunity for an all-round development of his body and mind. This purpose is often related to the desire to " get on " in his special work. But when the life of knowledge and ideas gets a grip of anyone and becomes valued for its own sake, the sort of education that is wanted gets further away from the more obviously " paying " qualities of the polytechnic or the ordinary continuation school.

Though it will be personal culture that such a man or woman is primarily after, they will be brought ever more clearly to recognise that the full manhood or womanhood they seek is not attainable by living to themselves alone, and that for popular education there must be a collective purpose. In other words, a main purpose of education must be to secure that collective self-government in industry, politics, and the other forms of co-operation which we call " democracy." The necessity for the spread of higher, broader, and more disinterested education, in order to achieve democracy, receives formal recognition among all intelligent workmen. They recognise that without such education they are liable to be the dupes of vague, abstract notions and grandiose phrases, or else to commit themselves to enthusiastic and impassioned waves of energy which lead nowhere because they are not directed by thought and clear purpose. Education is needed to supply direction to democratic force.

My object in stressing these three " purposes " is to put workers on their guard, lest they should rush into educational grooves prepared for them by those who are not true friends of democracy and working-class culture, but who will use education to divide, divert, and render innocuous the democratic movement. By these " educational " grooves I signify not only the whole apparatus of school and college training, but also the newspaper and the printing press in general, the drama, and the other arts of recreative suggestion. If the ruling and possessing classes, whose powers and privileges are threatened by democracy, can provide from their own intellectual factories the mental paliatives of higher education to the aspiring young men and women of the working classes, they will, by infecting the " people " with tastes, ideas, and valuations, which are the decorative luxuries of a leisure and a parasitic class, poison the moral and intellectual springs of democracy. The danger is a very real one. It is only natural that the workers to whom education has been hitherto denied should be eager to take it when it is offered by those who have got it. When, therefore, it will be proposed to pass their sons and daughters through secondary and technical schools and to open up to them fully and freely the new local colleges and even the older seats of university culture, they will be tempted to seize the proffered opportunities and not to look a gift horse in the mouth.

But, if they are wise, they will exercise some self-restraint in this thirst for knowledge, and inquire why it is that the well-to-do are now tumbling over one another in their anxiety to give educational facilities to the workers. There is an illuminating phrase of a Mid-Victorian statesman, Mr. Lowe, when the first wide extension of the franchise to the working classes took place. " We must educate our masters." Note the mockery of the word " masters." The keener witted rulers have always been aware that the vote did not give real power, so long as " we " were in control of the apparatus of education and could withhold it, dole it out and dope it to suit " our" ends. For half a century " we " did next to nothing towards educating " our masters," beyond teaching them in a slovenly way the three R codes, with some worthless fragments of geography, history, and Scripture, adding later on bits of technical instruction for town workers. Intelligent workers have always been suspicious of upper class zeal for education, which they have thought was designed to turn out cheap clerks and give the bare modicum of general instruction needed for a competent workman in any calling. This suspicion has not been misplaced. For, though plenty of well-meaning folk in the " upper " classes genuinely desired that the workers should get education and the opportunities it gave, the prevalent feeling among the " master" class has been against any education which " puts ideas " into the minds of working-class children. They felt that any education which " elevated " the mind would be " dangerous." By " dangerous " they really meant (though they did not formulate this meaning) that any free eating of the tree of knowledge of good and evil might stimulate them to revolt against the inequalities of life and to make " dangerous " attacks on power, privilege, and property. They did not think this out, they felt it in their bones, and so they were generally against any education with " ideas " in it.

They now perceive that this obstruction to education was overdone. Even before the war there was a growing recognition that more working-class education was desirable for two reasons. The first was the growing importance of more scientific industries, demanding qualities of skill and knowledge of a higher kind for considerable numbers of employees, in order that " we " might compete success-fully in the world with the better educated nations of the Continent. The failure of experiments in technical education conducted on the low basis of general education in our primary schools had taught the necessity of doing something to raise the general standard of popular instruction. Along with this worked the fear lest the workers should be getting " out of hand " and should be misled into revolutionary ways. After all, knowledge might have a sobering and steadying effect if properly administered. It should be understood that these motives seldom stood out in the clear consciousness of the master class, who may well repudiate with indignation the suggestion that they play any appreciative part in the new-born zeal for popular education. And it is true that many of the active promoters of this higher education are consciously motived by other more genuinely liberal sentiments. But none the less the other side must be taken into full account. The class politician, the charitable donor, the college don, and the expert bureaucrat, who between them supply the money and the machinery of higher education for the people, will make every effort to ensure that this education shall be conducted on " safe " lines.

This is done in two ways. The first is by selection and rejection of subjects, teachers, and methods. If the curriculum and studies of the universities and public schools, at which the sons of the master class get their learning and culture, can be imposed with certain slight modifications upon the sons of the workers, all will be well. Orthodox class culture, falsely figuring as " humanities," with a scientific, historical, and philosophic teaching selected and imposed by its clerical, pedagogic, and official classes, would help to do for " the people " what it has done for the classes, viz., keep things of the mind in a properly subordinate place, chill intellectual enthusiasm, and destroy the essentially revolutionary power of thought. This education has made our " classes " the worst informed and least intellectual of all the aristocracies and bourgeoisies of Europe, and it would have the same depressing and dulling influence upon the minds of eager young men and women of the working classes if they were put into its atmosphere My positive charge against this education is that it omits, selects, or castrates the subjects and treatments which, because they contain strong appeals to living human interests and feelings, are disturbing in their tendency. It should belong to the education of every man and citizen not merely to understand what is known and thought of the nature of his body and his mind, and of the physical world in which he is sent, but to study in a fearless, disinterested way the origins, structure, and potentialities of the human institutions which constitute society. Some genuine teaching in biology, economics, and politics, conveyed largely through an amplified and humanised " history," should play a great, perhaps a dominant, part in popular education. But if class culture is let down upon the workers there will be no such teaching. For these subjects vitally handled everywhere would generate disturbing scepticism and inconvenient demands. " We " simply dare not teach " our masters " subjects which will certainly make them not content to live in that state of life to which it shall please God (our class God) to call them. The fight our classes put up to stop these essential reforms in popular education, they will pretend to be a fight against letting down the higher and severer standards of accepted culture, in favour of lower, speculative, and inexact studies which would not really " train " the mind.

The workers who are after education must try to be alive to these dangers, and not permit their vital intellectual needs to be starved by the authoritative regimen of our unreformed upper class education. The teaching of history is a test issue. Our standard books and modes of teaching are in large part fraudulent pretences of disinterested research, concealing everywhere a selection and suppression of subject and events, and accompanied by interpretations that are mere class or personal prejudice. To put such history upon our workers is worse than giving them a stone for bread.

To keep out " dangerous " influences is one form of the educational policy of the masters. The other is to insert motives and atmospheres positively serviceable to their cause. In our schools this process has always been going on, but recently with more impudent obstrusiveness. For the most part it consists in thimble-rigging education with three P's—Patriotism, Piety, and Productivity. It is needless to dwell upon the attempts still maintained to keep clerical control over education. Every church wants to " capture " the mind while it is open to suggestion and incapable of intellectual resistance. It is a really wicked thing to do. The only extenuating circumstance is that it is usually done so clumsily and so dully that it fails. There are three educational and social injuries which it inflicts.

First, it purports to teach as facts what are not facts. Theology is not a branch of knowledge.

Secondly, it does not train, but injures the thinking powers, by imposing unreasonable authority as a ground for beliefs and fostering credulity.

Thirdly, it is used and intended as other worldliness to keep men quiet and submissive in this world.

One need not, however, suppose that any distinctively religious influence of the British Christian order would play much part in the higher education that we are discussing. The old piety is yielding place in our schools and colleges to a new piety, mis-called patriotism, with a rubric, a mysticism, and a mythology of its own. The war period has seen conspicuous advances along this road—military drill, flag worship, and fresh falsification of history. Imperialism is deliberately exploited as an inflammatory emotion in the teaching of geography and history. A large inevitable part of this project is to stress the exclusive virtues of our nation, to glorify our Empire in terms of size, strength, and number, and to misrepresent the essential relations of our nation to other nations as those of hostile opposition, thus sapping the moral sentiment of humanity which is the true salvation of the world.

A closer analysis, however, would show that both the old and the new piety are essentially the tools of productivity. For by that term we express the direct influence of capitalism upon education. The workers must be kept quiet, submissive, and instructed so that they may become more productive. So the quietism of class culture will be crossed by a distinct strain of utilitarianism. Local millionaires who endow chairs in their university will want something tangible for their money. The prosperity of local industry they will call it. But it will be secretly visualised as abounding profits. After the war, the need for " economic efficiency " will be more clearly realised in order to turn out well trained and disciplined workers.

These are the three deadly sins against human education for the furtherance of personal liberty and progress. The workers must beware of them. Their case is a difficult one. They cannot refuse to make themselves more efficient producers for fear their masters, and not they, should get the good of their increased productivity. For, even if they avoid the snares of a superimposed education and get a modern culture accommodated to their needs, they will, in fact, become not only better educated but more productive workers. Thus they have two problems of pre-eminent importance to solve. The first is how to secure the higher human education they require. The difficulty here is that they must, to some extent, rely upon aid from persons themselves belonging to the better-to-do and better educated classes. Fortunately, class-cleavages in this country are not so absolute as to break all free contact and communications between workers and bourgeoisie. There exists here, as elsewhere, what is called an intellectual proletariat, which, though reared to some extent upon vitiated pabulum and methods, is relatively free thinking.

The other problem is how to keep for themselves and the people the improved economic productivity which any higher education, however incomplete, will surely bring. This is not itself an educational but a political economic problem, nothing less than establishment of democracy.

A final word. The Press is probably a more potent instrument for "influencing" the popular mind than the school. Nominally the workers are alive to the dangers of a capitalist Press. But they have at present no escape. Better school education may abate some of its worst hypnotic tyranny. But the capitalist Press will still continue to select, reject, and distort news and views to suit the policy of its owners and the propertied classes who advertise. How to secure a genuinely "popular" Press, self-governing at least in the sense that the reader or consumer and not hidden hands behind the producing machines control the contents, is of more urgent importance than ever. Leave the capitalistic forces in control of the Press, no better schooling or college education will give a real security for democracy. A single newspaper may undo the good of a thousand schools. Our present Press is the most immoral of our institutions. For it relies mainly upon appeals to fear, suspicion, envy, hate, and the passions which divide men and nations and corrode mutual goodwill and confidence. An educated democracy must own and control the newspapers it reads or it will be educated to little purpose.

WHY THE WORKERS SHOULD DEMAND EDUCATION.

By G. D. H. Cole and Arnold Freeman.

To-day the question of education is not simply, or even mainly, a question for the educationist and the expert, but one for the whole people. With our educational system are bound up the fundamental realities of the social order in industry, in politics, and in every aspect of our national life. If the workers desire a revolution in industry and in politics they must wish also for a revolution in education. They must ask for more education, and for more education for all, for the ungrudging expenditure of public money and public ability on training the people of to-morrow. But they must not confine their demand to quantity in education; they must also demand, and insist upon, the sort of education that harmonises with their social ideals. We might open countless new schools and train count-less new teachers; we might raise the school-leaving age to 18 and provide efficient tuition up to that date, and still we might be no nearer to an educational system such as Labour requires. For, if our education is to be in tune with our social ideals, it must be a free education. Its aims must be, not training for the profit-making work of the world, but the development of the will, understanding, and initiative of the whole people. It must not be subordinated to the making of efficient wage-earners or salary-earners; and still less must it be imbued with the idea of social status. It must not seek to fit each man and woman for the place in the world to which it has pleased man to call them; it must seek to fit every man and woman to take their share in the world's work and in the shaping of the world's future.

Our education to-day is a class education. We have one educational system for the rich man and another for the poor. Not only do we isolate their bodies in different places and under very different material conditions, we also teach quite different ideals to rich and poor. There is discipline in the schools of the rich, but there are also freedom and initiative, and the attempt is made to train our " better-class " youth in self-reliance and capacity for power. The class-room is not even the centre of his education; the atmosphere and the common life of school and university count for far more in his upbringing. The ideal behind this training of a governing class may be fundamentally wrong, but there is no doubt that the thing is as a rule done effectively enough to supply the necessary leaders for the governing class. The desired types are produced; the governing class is maintained; and Whitehall, the Services, and the Empire are equipped with administrators who, however ignorant they may be of the world they rule, at least do not hesitate to undertake the work of ruling.

Our State schools, on the other hand, provide a very different kind of education. For them the class-room is everything, or almost everything, because it is too expensive to create for the children of the poor the social environment with which alone the rich are satisfied for their own children. Almost without exception, the teachers are over-worked and underpaid; and the classes are far too large for the children to receive any individual attention. The curriculum inevitably, if to a slightly decreasing extent, tends to be a thing of cast-iron rules and lifeless formulæ : the most devoted teacher finds it difficult to struggle on in face of discouragement, and in the knowledge that, at the best, the school life is too short to admit of satisfactory results. The leaving age reached, the children are flung upon the world with an utterly inadequate equipment of knowledge and power of thought, and—in proof of the complete failure of what has been achieved—with no conception of the meaning of education except a gladness that it is over and done with. Even our secondary scholars receive, in too many cases, only a narrow training for their professions of teacher or clerk, and carry away from their schooling neither desire nor capacity for responsibility and power.

Yet, unless every man and woman is able to understand the nature of government and to criticise its administration and accept a measure of responsibility, it is impossible for us ever to be a democratic community of free men and women. Throughout the working classes of all countries there has been passing of recent years a growing conscious-ness of potential strength, which, rightly used, might make them masters of their fate in industry, in politics, and in society. Nor is it difficult to see what stands in the way of making this potential strength actual. It is the lack of understanding, leadership, self-reliance, of just those qualities which our schools tend rather to crush than to encourage. We have built our industrial system on a servile pattern, so that, as a rule, it calls for no more than obedience from the ordinary worker. And, in our education, we have created a system to train men for a society in which the few command and the many obey.

It is clear, then, why the working class must demand education—and not simply more education, but education better directed to the making of free men. The workers cannot be content with an educational system, however " improved " and enlarged, in which there is still one education for the rich and another for the poor, and in which both types of education are animated largely by anti-democratic purposes. Labour must set out to destroy the class basis of education, and if it can succeed in this it will be likely to destroy the class basis of society also.

Educational reconstruction, to be worth anything to Labour, must rest upon a changed conception of the purpose of education. We know that we shall get more education after the war, but we do not know that we shall get education of the right kind. Already we are being told of the need to remodel our educational system with a view to our industrial requirements, and the interest of the great capitalists is being sought for these purposes. We fear such helpers, as we fear those whose spiritual home in educational matters is Germany. For we do not believe that men whose conceptions of industry and politics are undemocratic are likely to be a whit more democratic in their educational ideas. Men who believe that industry must continue to be controlled by the possessing class, and that the ordinary worker is forever incapable of playing any real part in its control, will scarcely believe in an educational system that will train the few to power and the many to subordination. Those who believe in the democratisation of industry, on the other hand, must believe in the democratisation of education, because by no other means can they get a people capable of controlling industry. The education demanded must be one which remembers that the child's " educability " depends upon its heredity, its ante-natal environment, and the conditions under which it develops during infancy; it must be an education continued not only through childhood and adolescence, but approving itself to the growing citizen sufficiently to induce him .to pursue it voluntarily into adult life—and certainly of as long duration for the less gifted as for those more fortunately endowed by Nature; it must above all be an education not designed for any small or specialised end in industry, or the home, but for the spiritual enrichment, the awakening, the freeing, the drawing out of the individual in order that his life may be a life worthy of his humanity.

Educational ideals, then, are inseparably bound up with all other social ideals, and our choice in education will be different according as we prefer the rule of the many or of the few. Unless they are satisfied with the economic and political conditions of the 19th century the workers must demand a revolution in education; for such a revolution is a necessary part, and no mean part, of the coming revolution in our social order, and when it comes it will affect no less the purpose and the quality than the quantity of education. As the workers awake to a desire for power and self-expression they are beginning to realise that the educational system holds them down ; that its ideals are not their ideals, but those of the class under which they are held in subjection ; and that, to fit their new ideals, a new method in education must be devised. When they realise this they will demand at once more and better education, but they will also demand that every child, irrespective of social position or of any other superficial circumstance, shall have the same educational opportunity. Then at last we shall create a system of which the fundamental purpose will be not the training of industrial or military recruits, but the creation of a manhood and womanhood capable of controlling together their own destinies in a free and democratic community.

TECHNICAL TRAINING IN THE SOCIAL STRUCTURE.

By S. G. HOBSON

(Author of " National Guilds " (with A. R. Orage), " Letters to My Nephew," and " Guild Principles in War and Peace).

No subject so fascinates the non-professional mind as does education. There are obviously many reasons for it. We are all of us conscious of defects in our own—and particularly of others'—education, defects which we feel are, at least in part, due to the system. We say to ourselves that did we control education we would change the system root and branch. And the more ignorant we are of the technique the more definite and absolute are our opinions. When we become parents we sooner or later observe developments in our children's characters which we rightly or wrongly ascribe to their training at school. The less we know of the teacher's difficulties the more dogmatic our condemnation, the more insistent our demands for reform. But it is the propagandist who becomes most urgent and censorious. Everybody who pioneers ideas inevitably falls back upon education. Wearied of the struggle, he at length says that the prospects are hopeless until we have a better system and more of it. " Educate, agitate, organise !" The words began with the Chartists.

In my younger, infallible days, like so many others, educational theory lured me to heights of cocksureness never equalled by young propagandists of any school. After some study of the orthodox text-books and heterodox theorists, I thought I saw a splendidly symmetrical system of education guaranteed to open the portals of the future. I even lectured upon it, casting fine scorn alike upon Whitehall, School Boards, teachers. They were all blind to my brilliant visions, all wedded to the old ways. I ultimately found that I was guilty of a little omission : I had overlooked the diabolical tricks of the English schoolboy ! Nowadays I am very shy of uttering *obiter dicta* upon education. I am frightened lest that confounded schoolboy should make me a mock and a scorn. If only the young rascal would fall in with my theories. . . . .

Nevertheless, an amateur may draw certain broad generalisations without making a fool of himself. It does not require a large experience of life to discover that middle-class and working-class education are different in atmosphere and purpose. From the very beginning they are taught to look to very different futures ; the one to a professional or commercial career, the other to join the ranks of the wage-earners. Our vocabulary unconsciously betrays the facts. Middle-class fathers habitually speak of their son's " career "—something brilliant, masterful, scintillating. Working-class fathers humbly and vaguely speak of their son's " future," or of " putting him to a trade." A middle-class school that failed to foster the idea of a career would speedily find its desks empty, its playground deserted. Now a career presupposes some conventional culture, some touch with the classics and a modern language or two. What, in fact, we call education. However inadequate or biased, in some degree, it is education. Not so with the wage-earner's child. He is destined to be an artisan; so we give him, at the cost of the community and to the profit of the capitalist, the necessary instruction. We politely call it education; it is really instruction. In these distinctions there is abundant matter for the satirist, Henry Straker, for example, in " Man and Superman," or Sylvanus Wilkins in " Letters to My Nephew."

Whilst we are thankful that there are many men who have successfully resisted the grinding of the machine and remain genuine pedagogues (I bear one gratefully in mind), sending out into the world a stream of cultured citizens, I fear we must reluctantly agree that education in all its stages is really little more than technical education, properly so called. For what is technical education? It is a training for one's livelihood. If our middle and upper-class schools deliberately train their boys for their careers, if our working-class schools equally deliberately train their boys for a proletarian life, they are both fundamentally " technical " in character and aim. The only conscious purpose of pure education should be to produce good citizens. It may be objected that, after all, men who have been trained to be competent and diligent in business make good citizens. They may; but they may become bad citizens.' And there are many incompetent business men who also make good citizens. The foundation of good citizenship is pure education. The conclusion, as it seems to me, is that pure and technical education should be separated and their different purposes defined. The way of good citizenship is through the humanities. It is a national responsibility; and it must be opened, without implication of trespass, to every child of every class. But is technical training equally the burden of the community, or is it properly the charge of the professions and industries concerned? Before we can answer that question we must glance at recent social and economic developments.

The pressure of the war has set in motion two contrary tendencies : an extension of bureaucratic power in one direction; in another direction a consciousness and concentration of industry towards autonomy. The growing interference of the Government officials in industry has induced a reaction amongst capitalists and managers against bureaucracy, and a claim, gradually growing clearer and more defined, for some form of industrial autonomy in which the co-operation of Labour is invited. The present situation would seem to be this : Employers are irritated and alarmed by the intervention of an untrained amateurish bureaucracy, and would be glad, if it were possible, to buy off Labour by offering it some form of workshop control and then standing four-square against Government interference. But they certainly do not intend to antagonise the State unless assured that they can retain their control of Labour. If, however, Labour proves recalcitrant, refusing any kind of industrial truce, then the employers must rely upon the State for protection and support. Altogether an unpleasant dilemma.

It can hardly be doubted, in the light of experience, that the bureaucracy is extraordinarily incompetent in its management of industry. Its blundering would make a classic comedy were it not a gigantic tragedy, for which we have paid in thousands of precious lives and millions of money. It has committed the fatal blunder of assuming responsibility without technical capacity. The skilled men have been deprived of responsibility and have seen their technical knowledge flouted or cynically exploited. In other words, function and responsibility have been divorced when they should have been married. We cannot tell how our industry will be reconstructed after the war; all schemes, however attractive, are merely guess-work; but this I take to be imperative : skill, craftsmanship, technique, must be accorded more power and direction.

However dissatisfied Management may be with its present dilemma, it is certain that Labour is far more dissatisfied. Apart from the commodity valuation placed upon labour-power, morally and socially degrading, Labour has spent itself on war production and, horrified, has seen vast fortunes made out of its patriotism. Its cry is, " Never again !" Like Management, Labour, too, demands a growing share in industrial control. The propaganda of the " New Age " and the National Guilds League is falling on fruitful soil. We can now almost set a term to wage servitude.

Out of this welter of contending interests two facts emerge : (*a*) That technical efficiency will in the future acquire much greater economic power; and (*b*) craft unionism is gradually being merged into industrial unionism, with Labour monopoly in view—the blackleg-proof union. It follows that both Management and Labour will seek to control technique. Labour monopoly *plus* technique means ultimately National Guilds; capitalist management controlling technique means the prolongation of the wage-system. Here, as else where, battle is joined, none the less deadly because disguised in calm, academic terms.

It was, therefore, to be expected that in preparing for post-war reconstruction the employers should seize technical instruction and regard it as their own preserve. The " Times' " writers on recon-struction sounded the first alarm; but we find a more considered judgment in the " Garton Memorandum." The " Garton " writers visualise the same organisation for general and technical education. Very properly, they do not urge, as have previous short-sighted generations, that the primary schools should concern themselves with technical instruction, beyond showing a preference for eye and hand training over book learning, to which I personally have no particular objection. Indeed, they take a liberal view of continuation and secondary schools, recognising the value of civic education and the cultivation of the " public-school spirit "—a spirit, however, that cannot be evoked in an atmosphere of wagery. So far, so good. " The true period for specialisation and the perfecting of industrial, as of professional training," they say, " is after the age of 18; for it is only then that most young people become fixed in what is most likely to be a life-long occupation." The culminating proposal is that employers' associations should subsidise technical colleges and municipal laboratories mainly for research purposes. I see in these suggestions a humane desire to improve proletarian efficiency inside the wage-system. But some criticism is called for.

Firstly, Labour will be caught napping if it permit the employers to subsidise industrial research. In education, as in our other national activities, they who pay the piper call the tune. It is evident that the commercial benefits from subsidised research will accrue to the subsidisers. It will not be done crudely, we may be sure; but the profiteers will claim the results, and it will be difficult to resist them when they remind us that they paid for them. In this way we shall have technique more effectually bound to capital, and the wage-system more definitely stereotyped. But we must remember that the employers will establish their claim if they can truthfully assert that they stepped into the breach when nobody else would. Pending, therefore, a more definite democratic industrial control of technical instruction and research, it is more prudent for the community in general and the municipalities in particular to control the work. A municipally trained chemist or engineer, free from any monetary obligation to the employers, will feel himself at greater liberty to serve the industrial democracy than if he had acquired his knowledge from capitalist subsidies. He would, in fact, have worked in a freer atmosphere. There are doubtless many creditable exceptions, but capitalist subsidies are generally Greek gifts.

The vital objection, however, to present suggestions for improved technical instruction is that they postulate the same educational machinery both for general or pure education and technical. But we are now rapidly moving towards some form of industrial autonomy, possibly the precursor of National Guilds. This, in effect, means the growing differentiation of the political or civic from the economic functions. Inasmuch as civic education is properly the concern of the community, and as technical training is properly an industrial responsibility, the time now seems ripe to release the civic from the technical, and so put an end to the three-legged race to which they have hitherto been condemned.

If no questions of industrial policy were affected, if Capital and Labour had coalesced or signed a truce, if economic emancipation were an accomplished fact, every theoretical and practical considera-tion would still dictate the separation of general from technical educa-tion. The one does not thrive in the atmosphere of the other; linked together, as they are to-day, each impedes and nullifies the work of the other. I might almost go further and assert that the introduction of the technical spirit into civic education has a vitiating effect, which soon declares itself in a baser politics, whilst the interjection of the civic into the technical confuses the mind and impairs technical efficiency. But I am free to admit that I want the definite, physical separation of the two divisions, not merely on its academic merits, but because a realisation of the true functions of civic and technical education substantially carries us towards a similar differentiation of civic from industrial activities. As in education, so it is in the larger life that follows; the economic pull in politics has a deadly effect upon the national spirit, crushing every spiritual impulse and degrading our conception of citizenship.

I look forward to the day, not far distant, let us hope, when our national life shall be so organised that the worker shall be free to produce wealth as his creative instincts shall dictate—a freedom only possible under the strong protection of National Guilds, with wagery an evil thing of the past, when our civic life shall be equally free to blossom into fruitful ways unhampered by the "interests" which to-day find their protection in an educational system distracted by confused conceptions of civic and industrial functions. When we finally open the door of the humanities to the wage-earning popula-tion, leaving technical training to the National Guilds, or their fore-runners, we shall be in a fair way to grasp the substance of that co-operative commonwealth which, since the days of Owen, has coloured our dreams and informed our ambitions.

A SUGGESTED LABOUR EDUCATION PROGRAMME.

By William Leach
(Ex-Member, Bradford Education Authority).

The W.E.A., in publishing its programme of education reform, has at last come out into the open to justify its title. Gone, let us hope for ever, is the limitation it foolishly imposed upon itself in existing merely to secure for workingmen and women, after a hard day in field or factory, the nearest cheap imitation of university training that was to be had. It is now a fighting organisation, with a real fighting charter upon which to question Parliamentary candidates, harass Ministers, and make itself thoroughly disagreeable to the enemy and a live force in the army of those who work for wages.

Labour's Blindness.

Organised Labour has consistently failed in this country to be interested in education. The subject is supposed to be very dull and not very important. If Labour knew that it was intimately concerned with the whole subject of wages and conditions perhaps it would then become more important in Labour's eyes. As yet, however, Labour has not found this out, and the possession of the secret still continues to profit Labour's enemies.

The publication of the Workers' Educational Association's charter may help to open Labour's eyes. Labour's cardinal defect is, and always has been, a shocking submissiveness. When its " betters " spoke patronisingly of a " ladder " to be provided for the child of the workman reaching from the elementary school to the university Labour was at once disgustingly grateful. The idea that for the workman's child all real education could only be had by hard climbing up a ladder from which 95 per cent. were barred because there was no room on it for them, and in the case of the 5 per cent. who started a very infinitesimal proportion ever reached the top was not regarded as insulting as it should have been. The misplaced gratitude with which the reversal of the Cockerton judgment by the Balfour Act of 1902 was received by Labour was very pathetic. Labour's attitude should have been that of grim acceptance of the bone thrown, coupled with an equally grim demand for the meat to follow.

The Broad Highway.

The W.E.A. has done with ladders. Hence its opening demand for all education to be free strikes the true note of revolution. There is no stipulation that the rich parent who wants exclusiveness and can pay for it for his offspring, in addition to meeting his proper share of education taxes, shall be prohibited from having it. It's a free country. Toney Oxford and Cambridge, refusing direct public money, may still be left to him. But it is to be feared the fees there will become still heavier, because your national free scholars will all be going to the really public universities run by the nation. However, even if exclusiveness becomes dearer it may still be his and we need not complain.

Let us now tick off with grateful approval the foundation items of the W.E.A.'s broad highway of education :—

1. Nursery schools from two to six years.
2. Gradual increase of leaving age to 16 years.
3. Half-time education from 16 to 18.
4. Reduction in maximum size of classes to 30.
5. Better provision of facilities for those who intend to become teachers, with adequate salaries and pensions.
6. School medical and dental service for all scholars.
7. A great scheme of open-air schools, playing fields, school meals, physical training, baths, swimming, and all that makes for health.
8. Seventy-five per cent. of education costs to come from the Treasury.

OMISSIONS OF THE W.E.A.

In the charter there is a solitary reference of three lines to school buildings, which are to be designed with an eye to beauty of structure. Now all those who have ever been concerned with education on the administrative side are painfully aware that the 1902 Act left us with a ridiculous and irritating problem concerned with what are called provided and non-provided schools. The non-provided schools, which are run so that a church atmosphere may be given to the teaching of arithmetic and geography, still represent private interests in education. The " fabric " of the building has still to be maintained by charity. Starved of public money these schools, which comprise somewhere about half the elementary schools of the kingdom, are for the most part models of how schools should not be built. They are the monuments standing for the idiotic quarrel between church and chapel. Most of them could profitably be burnt. Until new legislation abolishes all private interests in publicly endowed schools hygienic and healthy school buildings will not be universally possible.

The W.E.A. charter demands a properly equipped medical service for school children. But should it not also ask that such a service be given jurisdiction over, or at least be co-ordinated with, schemes for the well-being of nursing and expectant mothers? If the child coming to the nursery school at 2 be already " damaged goods " it is a matter of some concern to the Education Authority, which has then to take in hand the work of repair. There is at once involved an expenditure of public money which earlier attention might have rendered unnecessary. Education law, which at last has ceased to differentiate between the mind and the body when marking out its sphere of influence, should also do the same in the matter of age. The education net must henceforth be spread to take in the expectant and nursing mother and the infant. The W.E.A. must see to this. The missing item must go on to its charter. It cannot in logic be kept off so important a document.

PUBLIC HEALTH.

I know from administrative experience the impossibility of defining the exact spot where a Health Committee must leave off and an Education Committee begin. It may be that all medical service should be managed by the Health Authority. It may be that school dentists should be under the same jurisdiction. Your Education and Health Authorities may fall out about this. The honour of doing the work **is a temptation that** keen chairmen and first-class officials can never resist. But do not trouble about that. You have got dentists and doctors and nurses on your programme. Let the demand be made that no uncovered part of their work is left to hamper and even destroy that which you give them to do.

A REAL POINT OF DIFFERENCE.

I have left my only real quarrel with the W.E.A. charter to the last. It concerns the important question of what is vaguely called " secondary " education. " Secondary " education seems to be a term invented by superior people to prove to the workman that after reaching a certain point his child need not really go further because all after that is more or less unnecessary luxury—a mere process of mind ornamentation and polishing, and quite unimportant to all that is really vital in equipment. The W.E.A. actually lends colour to this monstrous gospel by framing its demand as follows :—

" That all children admitted to a secondary schoool should have reached an approved standard of education, the ground of transfer being the fitness of the scholar for the broader curriculum."

Oh, I could lecture my friends and drub them for twelve more pages about this wrong-headed docility to accepted but wretchedly false dogmas. The well-to-do parent never asks about his child's " fitness " for the broader curriculum. He just sees that he gets it, and he pays the fees for it. If he decided that the youngster was scarcely fit to go through it his class would properly ostracise him as unfit to be a parent. Grammar schools don't differentiate between elementary and secondary. They have no use for the words at all. Neither should the W.E.A. There is not one argument on earth in favour of universal compulsory " elementary " education which does not apply still more forcibly to universal, compulsory, " secondary " education. Have done with this stupid call for " fitness." The system is still uninvented, the professor is still unborn, to tell us what is the " fitness " of a child of 10 or 11 or 14. Not until a groundwork in languages, sciences, literature, and the arts is the common heritage of all the population should we tolerate the idea of specialising for anything at all. Already the British Labour Party has approved the demand for free compulsory universal secondary education.* The W.E.A. must back that wise demand in the interests of a better Britain. There is now no discussion as to the " fitness " of a child for the elementary course. There used to be. It arose from stingy tax-payers when Forster proposed 47 years ago to make elementary instruction a public charge in a limited way. In time it died. The same silly point in respect of all instruction beyond the three R's and their allied subjects will also die. Let us help towards its overdue demise.

REFERENCES.—S. G. Moore, M.B. : " Infantile Mortality, with an Account of some French and German Preventive Measures "; " Minority Report of Poor Law Commission "; " Annual Reports of Chief Medical Officer of Board of Education." R. H. Crowley, M.D. : " The Hygiene of School Life." Margaret McMillan : " The Child and the State."

THE WAR AND THE WORKERS.

By H. G. Wells.

Mr. Wells has written us a letter from which we make the following extracts :—

"You. ask me to write what I think the effects of the war will be on the workingman-soldier. Well, I don't know. The workingman is a perplexing person, and the army tradition is a remarkable influence, but my hope is that the workingman-soldier will come back a revolutionary, resolved to end for ever the dominion of the game-preserving, horse-riding, park-owning army people who have stuck like leeches to the staff and higher positions of the British Army throughout this war, who have used the censorship chiefly to save their faces, and whose incapacity and class-conceit are responsible for the disasters of 1915, of July, 1916, and of 1917 (at Monchy), and for the wasting of countless thousands of British lives. These are the same people who plotted the Gough treason that broke our faith with Ireland, and who are the curse of India. All my life I have been an active Socialist and a promoter of social reconstruction, but this war has convinced me that a political spring-cleaning is a necessary preliminary to any hopeful economic readjustment. We must clear out the ' Anglicans ' before we can have a free England. . . . Will the workingman-soldier come back a clear-minded republican, resolved to end the established church with its fatal grip upon our higher education, and to break up the tacit class conspiracy that makes our political life futile? Or will he just come back to get drunk and earn a poor week's wages for a poor week's work and vote for his ' betters ' in the good old style? "

PART II.

THE EDUCATIONAL SYSTEM.

THE EDUCATION SYSTEM OF ENGLAND AND WALES.

STATISTICAL INTRODUCTION.

ELEMENTARY EDUCATION.

The following table gives in detail the various kinds of schools recognised by the Board of Education in 1914, with the accommodation of each class of school :—

England and Wales.

NUMBER OF SCHOOLS RECOGNISED ON 31ST JULY, 1914, WITH THEIR ACCOMMODATION.

Number of Schools and Accommodation.

	Council Schools.		Voluntary Schools.		Total.	
	Number.	Accommodation.	Number.	Accommodation.	Number.	Accommodation.
1.	*2.*	*3.*	*4.*	*5.*	*6.*	*7.*
1. ORDINARY PUBLIC ELEMENTARY SCHOOLS :—						
(a) Maintained by Local Education Authorities - - - -	8,510	4,239,724	12,443*	2,747,325*	20,953	6,987,049
(b) Not maintained by Local Education Authorities -	—	—	64	16,958	64	16,958
2. HIGHER ELEMENTARY SCHOOLS	46	13,161	1	240	47	13,401
3. "CERTIFIED EFFICIENT" SCHOOLS - - - -	—	—	59	7,173	59	7,173
4. CERTIFIED SCHOOLS FOR BLIND CHILDREN - - -	24	1,008	17	1,465	41	2,473
5. CERTIFIED SCHOOLS FOR DEAF CHILDREN - - -	37	2,285	13	2,209	50	4,494
6. CERTIFIED SCHOOLS FOR MENTALLY DEFECTIVE CHILDREN:—						
(a) Certified Day Schools - -	171	13,202	—	—	171	13,202
(b) Certified Boarding Schools -	1	32	9	733	10	765
7. CERTIFIED SCHOOLS FOR PHYSICALLY DEFECTIVE CHILDREN :—						
(a) Certified Day Schools - -	74	5,968	1	65	75	6,033
(b) Certified Boarding Schools -	5	250	17	1,357	22	1,607
8. CERTIFIED BOARDING SCHOOLS FOR EPILEPTIC CHILDREN -	1	100	5	396	6	496
TOTAL - - -	8,869	4,275,730	12,629	2,777,921	21,498	7,053,651

* The denominations of the Voluntary Schools which are included in these figures, according to the nature of the Religious Instruction given, were as follows :—

	Church of England Schools.	Wesleyan Schools.	Roman Catholic Schools.	Jewish Schools.	Undenominational and other Schools.
Number of Schools - - - -	10,734	189	1,091	12	417
Accommodation - - - -	2,291,784	57,279	388,213	9,863	90,186

NUMBER OF SCHOOLS 1915-16.—England and Wales.

	England.	Wales.	Total.
1. Ordinary Public Elementary Schools .	19 081	1,888	20,969
2. Higher Elementary Schools . . .	33	14	47
3. Special Schools	391	10	401
4. Certified Efficient Schools . . .	57	2	50
Totals	19,562	1,914	21,476

In the table given below the growth in the number and accommodation of schools during the last 47 years is shown. It will be noticed that during the last few years there has been a steady rise of about 200 per annum in the number of schools until 1915; when, owing to the effects of the war—lack of teachers, buildings, etc.—the numbers declined. In the first year of the war 97 new schools were opened, while in 1915-16 the number only amounted to six. As contributing to the serious decline in educational facilities must be reckoned the commandeering, especially in the East and North-East of England, of large numbers of schools for hospitals or for billeting troops. In these cases emergency arrangements for the continuance of the school work elsewhere have been made, and accepted by the Board of Education as "fairly adequate." Yet in spite of the loss of these buildings there has still been an increase in the number of schools during the war period, slight though it appears to be.

In the following table it is interesting to note the steady decline in the number of voluntary schools. These reached their zenith in 1889-90, since when a decline of about 100 per annum has taken place :—

England and Wales.

SCHOOLS AND ACCOMMODATION (COMPARATIVE TABLE).

Ordinary Public Elementary Schools and "Certified Efficient" Schools.

Alternate Statistic Year, or Date.	Ordinary Public Elementary Schools.						"Certified Efficient" Schools.	
	Council Schools.		Voluntary Schools.		Total.			
	Number.	Accommo-dation.	Number.	Accommo-dation.	Number.	Accommo-dation.	Number.	Accommo-dation.
1.	2.	3.	4.	5.	6.	7.	8.	9.
1869–70	—	—	8,281	1,878,584	8,281	1,878,584	—	—
1871–2	82	17,156	9,772	2,278,738	9,854	2,295,894	—	—
1873–4	838	245,508	11,329	2,615,811	12,167	2,861,319	--	—
1875–6	1,596	556,150	12,677	2,870,168	14,273	3,426,318	—	—
1877–8	2,682	890,164	13,611	3,052,173	16,293	3,942,337	290	18,496
1879–80	3,433	1,082,634	14,181	3,158,119	17,614	4,240,753	425	34,793
1881–2	3,868	1,298,746	14,421	3,239,574	18,289	4,538,320	386	34,365
1883–4	4,181	1,490,174	14,580	3,336,564	18,761	4,826,738	347	28,462
1885–6	4,402	1,692.505	14,620	3,452,787	19 022	5,145,292	352	30,597
1887–8	4,562	1,809,481	14,659	3,547,073	19 221	5,356,554	312	26,937
1889–90	4,676	1,915,182	14,743	3,624,103	19,419	5,539,285	277	25.048
1891–2	4,831	2,041,464	14,684	3,651,511	19,515	5,692,975	206	20,439
1893–4	5,081	2,199,111	14,628	3,633,833	19,709	5,832,944	164	15,743
1895–6	5,432	2,433,411	14,416	3,638,963	19,848	6,072,374	136	13,101
1897–8	5,555	2,625,879	14,382	3,690,987	19,937	6,316,866	133	12,278
1899–1900	5,691	2,785,801	14,409	3,723,810	20,100	6,509.611	108	9,516
1901–2	5,878	2,957,966	14,275	3,723,329	20,153	6,681,295	117	11,046
1903–4	6,162	3,178,541	14,150	3,706,282	20,312	6,884,823	93	9,953
31st July, 1906	6,990	3,552,674	13,537	3,506,588	20,527	7,059,262	79	10,951
1907	7,231	3,674,857	13,365	3,407,078	20,596	7,081,935	74	9,710
1908	7,426	3,772,421	13,196	3,315,995	20,622	7,088,416	76	9,965
1909	7,651	3,871,827	13,048	3,246,411	20,699	7,118,238	77	9,739
1910	7,841	3,923,320	12,924	3,093,307	20,765	7,016.627	71	9,314
1911	8,052	3,982.989	12,795	2,825,399	20,847	6,808,188	65	7,598
1912	8,200	4,065,316	12,703	2,797,508	20,903	6,862,824	63	7,100
1913	8,362	4,162,001	12,606	2,778,002	20,968	6,940,003	58	6,866
1914	8,510	4,239,724	12,507	2,764,283	21,017	7,004,007	59	7,173
1915	8,603	4,289,134	12,439	2,750.472	21,042	7,039,606	—	—
1916	8,609	4,312,756	12,360	2,742,036	20 969	7,054,792	—	—

HIGHER ELEMENTARY SCHOOLS.—The numbers of higher elementary schools remained unaltered between 1911 and 1914. In 1912-13 it will be seen that, whereas the number of men full-time teachers increased from 287 in the previcus year to 309, the number of boys had only increased by 172.

In 1913-14 the number of men teachers fell to only one more than in 1911-12, while the boys numbered 302 less than in 1911-12. But, even in the year when the number of men teachers was at its highest, the average number of boys to one teacher was about 17, a number none too small for one teacher in a school where individual attention is more necessary than in the ordinary elementary school, or, at any rate, more to be expected.

One of the few good effects of the war on education has been that the increased prosperity of a section of the working classes has resulted in an increase in the number of pupils entering the higher elementary and secondary schools, and it may be hoped that this will result in a better supply of young teachers, as it is from such schools that they are mostly recruited.

England and Wales.

HIGHER ELEMENTARY SCHOOLS.

Summary (Schools, Teachers, Scholars).

	1913-14.	1912-13.	1911-12.
1. NUMBER OF SCHOOLS ON LAST DAY OF SCHOOL YEAR :—			
(a) For Boys only · · · · · · ·	7	7	7
(b) For Girls only · · · · · ·	2	2	2
(c) For Boys and Girls · · · · · ·	38	43	42
(d) Total ? · · · · · · ·	47	52 ·	51
2. NUMBER OF FULL-TIME TEACHERS ON STAFF OF SCHOOLS ON LAST DAY OF SCHOOL YEAR :—			
(a) Men · · · · · · · ·	283	309	287
(b) Women · · · · · · ·	192	196	177
(c) Total · · · · · · · ·	480	505	464
3 NUMBER OF PART-TIME* TEACHERS ON STAFF OF SCHOOLS ON LAST DAY OF SCHOOL YEAR · · ·	68	64	78
4. SCHOLARS :—			
(a) Number of Scholars on the Registers on last day of school year :—			
(i) Boys · · · · · ·	4,993	5,295	5,123
(ii) Girls · · · · · ·	4,525	4,906	4,612
(iii) Total · · · · · ·	9,518	10,201	9,735
(b) Average Number of Scholars on the Registers during the school year · · · · ·	10,877	11,475	10,818
(c) Average Number of Scholars in Attendance during the school year · · · · ·	9,955	10,454	9,724

* Part-time Teachers are counted once for each School in which they served.

NUMBER OF SCHOLARS ON SCHOOL REGISTERS.—In the table giving the numbers and ages of children attending school over a period of 40 years one of the most significant facts is the large number of children under 3 years of age who were sent to school in 1873-4. The ordinary elementary school that could provide suitable education for such very young children would be remarkable at any time, and it cannot be regretted that in 1913-14 no children under 3 years of age were attending school. One of the best features of the Education Bill at present before the House of Commons* is the proposal to transform the present infant departments of the elementary schools, to which children may not be sent until they are 5 years of age, into " nursery schools " quite distinct from the elementary schools, for children from 2 to 6 years of age.

The figures for children of 15 and over are very low in all the years recorded. This may be due in recent years to two causes : either to the hurrying of children into employment at the lowest possible age, or to the fact that, through more careful medical inspection and general care of health, together with school meals, a greater number of children have, at a younger age, attained the standard required for leaving school.

More particulars as regards juvenile employment will be found in another section.

England and Wales.

NUMBER OF SCHOLARS OF VARIOUS AGES ON THE SCHOOL REGISTERS (COMPARATIVE TABLE).

Statistical Year.	Number of Scholars on the Registers on last day of School Year.*						
	Under 3.	3 and under 5	5 and under 7	7 and under 12	12 and under 15	15 and over	Total
1.	2.	3	4	5	6	7	8
1873-4	19,002	322,025	575,564	1,351,352	229,659	x	2,497,602
1883-4	10,176	412,388	934,659	2,477,715	520,188	x	4,355,126
1893-4	3,917	522,976	1,111,426	2,895,322	666,391	6,362	5,206,394
1903-4	1,460	608,389	1,249,057	3,177,419	1,010,025	7,335	6,053,685
1913-14	—	316,148	1,311,626	3,364,741	1,112,802	5,711	6,111,028

x In these years scholars at the age of 15 and over are included in Column 6.

* For years prior to 1903-4 the figures included in respect of Certified Schools for Blind and Deaf Children are the numbers of scholars on account of whom grant was claimed.

NUMBER OF SCHOLARS AND ATTENDANCE.—England and Wales.

The subjoined table, which gives the number of scholars on the books on 31st January for each of the five years 1912 to 1916, relates to Ordinary Public Elementary Schools, Higher Elementary Schools, Special Schools, and Certified Efficient Schools.

Year.	Number of Scholars on the books on January 31st.				Net Increase or Decrease.
	Under 5.	5 and under 12.	12 and over.	Total.	
1912 . .	320,889	4,636 926	1,088,710	6,046,585	—
1913 . .	301,150	4 644,678	1,111,589	6,057,417	+ 10,832
1914 . .	289,757	4,672,753	1,116,385	6,078,895	+ 21,478
1915 . .	283,200	4,689,298	1,136,167	6,108,665	+ 29,770
1916 . .	269,400	4,690,675	1,110,237	6,070,312	— 38,353

NUMBER OF TEACHERS.—The supply of elementary school teachers has, during the ten years given in the table below, been greatly improved in the most important direction, that is to say, on the whole the number of certificated teachers has gone up, while the number of uncertificated, and consequently not so highly skilled, teachers has gone down. But when the total number of teachers is compared with the total number of pupils it will be seen that the average number of pupils in any one class is much higher than it should be. Sixty is the maximum limit allowed by Article 14 of the Board of Education Code. This is, of course, some improvement on the classes of 80 to 90 common up to 1880, but it is feared that the shortage of teachers which has resulted from the Military Service Acts and the various appeals for women for work of what is considered of more " national importance " than education has resulted in larger classes to be dealt with by the remaining teachers.

In the section dealing with the supply of teachers more particulars on this subject will be found.

England and Wales.

NUMBER OF FULL-TIME TEACHERS AND STUDENT-TEACHERS ON STAFF OF SCHOOLS ON LAST DAY OF SCHOOL YEAR (COMPARATIVE TABLE).

Statistical Year.	Certificated Teachers.				Uncertificated* Teachers.		Supplementary † Teachers.		Student-Teachers.		Total.	
	Trained.		Others.									
	Men.	Women.	Men.	Women.	Men.	Women.	Men.	Women.	Men.	Women.	Men.	Women.
1	2	3	4	5	6	7	8	9	10	11	12	13
1904– 5	19,922	22,972	8,358	27,485	5,530	36,816	46	19,090	—	—	33,856	106,363
1905– 6	20,476	24,074	8,938	30,787	4,928	35,821	560	22,554	—	—	34,902	113,236
1906– 7	21,174	25,329	9,339	33,627	4,751	35,882	632	21,395	—	—	35,896	116,233
1907– 8	22,024	26,752	9,181	33,171	5,320	38,947	546	19,968	1	—	37,072	118,838
1908– 9	22,639	28,035	9,386	34,712	5,670	38,714	314	18,069	563	1,085	38,572	120,615
1909–10	23,381	29,950	9,424	34,641	6,005	39,550	149	16,239	842	1,623	39,801	122,003
1910–11	24,412	32,252	9,601	34,731	6,131	39,506	10	14,408	755	1,517	40,909	122,614
1911–12	25,402	34,429	9,503	34,181	5,830	38,632	—	13,865	572	12,69	41,307	122,376
1912–13	26,497	36,731	9,493	33,306	5,303	37,590	—	13,477	542	12,13	41,835	122,317
1913–14	**27,573**	**38,964**	**9,393**	**32,802**	**4,654**	**36,750**	**—**	**13,367**	**485**	**1,486**	**42,105**	**123,369**

* Including retired Army Schoolmasters, and also, up to the year 1907-8 inclusive Provisionally Certificated Teachers.

† Including, up to the year 1909-10 inclusive, Provisional Assistant Teachers.

Instruction in Special Subjects.—Educational authorities have generally recognised that the present need for economy in food has made it specially necessary that girls should be taught domestic work of all kinds; and in 1914-15 there was a good increase in the number of centres where such subjects were taught. The decrease in the figures for 1915-16 is probably due to the penny wisdom and pound foolishness of parents who have sent their daughters into factories where their earnings may, in some cases, be high, but are probably more than counteracted by the increased cost of living. It is unfortunate that in 1915-16 there should have been a decrease of 13 in the number of centres giving instruction in dairy-work, and this just when the national need for all possible help in that work is most serious.

With regard to instruction in handicraft for boys the demands of the Army and munitions works have seriously reduced the number of instructors, as well as of pupils, and the Board of Education reports that the amount of instruction will probably be less still in the present year.

England and Wales.

INSTRUCTION IN SPECIAL SUBJECTS.

Subject.	Number of Schools and Centres in which instruction was given.					Number of Registered Scholars.			
	1915-16.	1914-15.	1913-14.	1912-13	1911-12.	1913-14.	1912-13.	1911-12.	Sex.
						379,095	380,977	333 ,88	Girls
						387	283	291	Boys
Cookery . . .	3,276	3,284	3,150	3,008	2,857	379 482	381,260	334,079	Total
Laundry Work .	1,251	1,264	1,137	999	900	182,342	168,537	168,830	Girls
Housewifery . .	597	503	403	327	277	55,490	49,072	34,393	Girls
Mixed Courses in DomesticSubjects	214	172	139	93	x	6,152	4,253	x	Girls
Combined Domestic Subjects . .	252	239	210	186	155	15,446	14,415	10,850	Girls
Dairy Work . .	9	22	17	20	19	180	203	196	Girls
						56,577	51,681	46,057	Boys
						3 179	2,877	2,218	Girls
Gardening . .	3,406	3,362	3,189	2,949	2,641	59,756	54,558	48,275	Total
Handicraft other than light Wood-work . . .	1,715	1,735	1,607	1,467	1,315	328,034	302,772	266,353	Boys
Light Wood-work.	395	393	325	226	144	10,476	6,873	4,434	Boys

x Mixed courses in Domestic Subjects were not recognised before the year 1912-13.

POOR LAW SCHOOLS.— No very remarkable changes in. the figures for Poor Law schools are found in the following table. It is to be hoped that this table will soon disappear from the Education Statistics by the complete abolition of this type of school, and its merging into the general educational system :—

England and Wales.

STATISTICS FOR YEARS ENDING 31ST MARCH OF POOR LAW SCHOOLS INSPECTED BY THE BOARD OF EDUCATION.

	Details for 1913-14.						
	Union Schools		District Schools	Schools under the administration of the Metropolitan Asylums Board.	1913-14.	1912-13.	1911-12.
	Forming parts of Work-houses.	Separate from Work-houses.					
1	*2*	*3*	*4*	*5*	*6*	*7*	*8*
NUMBER OF SCHOOLS .	11	40	8	9	68	71	70
NUMBER OF TEACHERS ON STAFF OF SCHOOLS ON 31st March:—							
(*a*) School Teachers:—							
(i) Certificated Teachers Men . .	—	79	31	8	118	112	110
Women . .	4	106	42	13	165	174	168
(ii) Other Teachers Men . .	1	11	1	, 3	16	27	23
Women . .	8	64	9	14	95	98	95
(iii) Total Men . .	1	90	32	11	134	139	133
Women . .	12	170	51	27	260	272	263
(*b*) Industrial Instructors Men . .	1	168	35	44	248	247	253
Women . .	—	70	17	4	91	97	84
Total	1	238	52	48	339	344	337
NUMBER OF SCHOLARS ON THE REGISTERS ON 31ST MARCH . . .	3 3	9,155	3,312	1,895	14,675	15,205	15,478

SECONDARY EDUCATION.

The number of secondary schools in England and Wales, as shown by the following table, is deplorably small, when it is considered that these schools afford the chief means by which elementary school pupils can develop and continue their education. Secondary schools are not merely places where the well-to-do artisan can send his children after they leave the elementary school, for a year or two's "finishing" : they are open to children up to 18 years and over, and they offer a much more liberal education in all branches than can be crowded into the curriculum of the elementary schools. As the entry is to some extent competitive, or by recommendation from the teacher, this makes for a high standard of intelligence among the pupils.

The regulations with regard to grants from the Board of Education require that a percentage of free places must be provided in each school, and this varies from 10 per cent. to 25 per cent.

There is unfortunately a great lack of correlation between the elementary and secondary schools. Large centres are found without a secondary school in any shape or form, while an older and less important centre may have as many as four.

The first months of the war showed a decrease of 1,069 pupils of all ages in secondary schools, the decline applying to children of all ages, except those between 10 and 12. This decrease, however, was, during the end of 1914 and throughout 1915, not only made good, but converted into an increase of 1,568. In October, 1915, there was an increase of 3,363, nearly two-thirds of which was among pupils under 12, and including many under 10 years of age.

Summary Table showing for the Year 1911 the Approximate Numbers and Percentages of Children and Young Persons in England and Wales, at each Year of Age from 12 to 18, known to be under Full-Time or Part-Time Instruction.

Pupils Classified according to the Nature of Instruction and Type of Institution.	Aged 12 and under 13.		Aged 13 and under 14.		Aged 14 and under 15.		Aged 15 and under 16.		Aged 16 and under 17.		Aged 17 and under 18.	
	No.	Per Cent.	No.	Per Cent.	No.	Per Cent.	No.	Per Cent.	No.	Per Cent.	No.	Per Cent.
(a) Under half-time instruction in Public Elementary Schools.	25,231	3·61	8,921	1·29	—	—	—	—	—	—	—	—
(b) Under full-time instruction in Public and other Elementary Schools	597,612	85·43	421,869	61·08	48,378	7·05	7,243	1·08	747	0·1	200	0·03
(c) Under full-time instruction in State-aided and other Secondary Schools recognised by the Board of Education.	32,709	4·68	36,455	5·28	30,722	4·47	20,628	3·08	11,522	1·71	4,905	0·74
(d) Under full-time instruction in schools working under the regulations for Technical Schools and Schools of Art, etc.	419	0·06	1,225	0·18	3,016	0·44	1,958	0·29	1,318	0·20	811	0·12
(e) Under part-time instruction in Schools working under the regulations for Technical Schools and Schools of Art, etc.	6,009	0·86	51,967	7·52	112,270	16·34	93,717	13·99	82,592	12·27	65,312	9·8
(f) Pupil Teachers and Student Teachers.	—	—	—	—	—	—	4	0·00	1,727	0·26	4,603	0·69
(g) Under instruction in Universities	—	—	—	—	—	—	2	0·00	167	0·02	431	0·07
(h) Total of above	661,980	94·64	520,487	75·35	194,386	28·30	123,552	18·44	98,073	14·56	76,345	11·45
(i) Difference between the total above and the number of persons enumerated in the Census of 1911.	37,531	5·36	170,295	24·65	492,869	71·7	546,419	81·56	574,896	85·44	589,890	88·55
(j) Total of persons enumerated in the Census of 1911.	699,511	100·00	690,732	100·00	687,255	100·00	669,971	100·00	672,969	100·00	666,235	100·00

England and Wales.

SECONDARY SCHOOLS ON THE GRANT LIST.

Summary (Schools, Teachers, Pupils).

——	1913-14.	1912-13.	1911-12.
1. NUMBER OF SCHOOLS ON LAST DAY OF SCHOOL YEAR :—			
(a) For Boys	397	390	383
(b) For Girls	349	339	335
(c) For Boys and Girls	281	281	277
(d) Total	1,027	1,010	995

	31st January,		
	1914.	1913.	1912.
2. NUMBER OF FULL-TIME TEACHERS :—			
(a) Men	5,447	5,241	5,100
(b) Women	5,377.	5,157	4,988
(c) Total	10,824	10,398	10,088
3. NUMBER OF PART-TIME* TEACHERS	3,418	3,392	3,360
4. NUMBER OF FULL-TIME PUPILS, CLASSIFIED ACCORDING TO AGE ON 31ST JANUARY :—			
(a) Boys :—			
(i) Under 12 years of age	19,583	17,689	
(ii) 12 and under 16 years of age	70,096	66,138	
(iii) 16 and under 18 years of age	8,651	8,196	†
(iv) 18 years of age and over	841	900	
(v) Total	99,171	92,923	88,973
(b) Girls :—			
(i) Under 12 years of age	16,083	14,710	
(ii) 12 and under 16 years of age	57,644	53,157	
(iii) 16 and under 18 years of age	12,786	11,941	†
(iv) 18 years of age and over	1,523	1,692	
(v) Total	88,036	81,500	76,597
(c) Total of (a) and (b) :—			
(i) Under 12 years of age	35,666	32,399	
(ii) 12 and under 16 years of age	127,740	119,295	
(iii) 16 and under 18 years of age	21,437	20,137	†
(iv) 18 years of age and over	2,364	2,592	
(v) Total	187,207	174,423	165,570

	1st October,		
	1913.	1912.	1911.
5. NUMBER OF PART-TIME PUPILS :—			
(a) Student-Teachers	2,727	2,601	2,439
(b) Pupil-Teachers	2,545	2,764	3,582
(c) Other Part-time Pupils	530	465	524
(d) Total	5,802	5,830	6,545

* Part-time Teachers are counted once for each School in which they served.
† Figures for 1912 on the same basis are not available.

England and Wales.

SECONDARY SCHOOLS ON THE GRANT LIST.

Tuition Fees.

Council Schools	Roman Catholic Schools.	Foundation and other Schools.	Welsh Inter-mediate Schools.		1913-14.	1912-13.	1911-12.
1	*2*	*3*	*4*	*5*	*6*	*7*	*8*
				NUMBER OF SECONDARY SCHOOLS CLASSIFIED ACCORDING TO THE TUITION FEE NORMALLY CHARGED PER ANNUM TO PUPILS OF 12 YEARS OF AGE :—			
6	—	—	—	No Fees charged	6	5	1
6	—	—	—	Not over 1 guinea	6	6	6
6	—	1	—	Over 1, but not over 2 guineas . .	7	9	12
26	—	1	11	,, 2, ,, ,, 3 ,, . .	38	35	41
47	1	7	25	,, 3, ,, ,, 4 ,, . .	81	72	68
50	6	22	32	,, 4, ,, ,, 5 ,, . .	110	114	109
81	18	53†	17	,, 5, ,, ,, 6 ,, . .	169†	168†	164†
62	5	52	5	,, 6, ,, ,, 7 ,, . .	124	120	122
52	7	64	2	,, 7, ,, ,, 8 ,, . .	125	123	111
47	5	66	6	,, 8, ,, ,, 9 ,, . .	124	121	122
25	1	55‡	—	,, 9, ,, ,, 10 ,, . .	81‡	81‡	81‡
9	—	24	—	,, 10, ,, ,, 11 ,, . .	33	32	34
11	1	25	—	,, 11, ,, , 12 ,, . .	37	37	35
1	—	6	—	,, 12, ,, ,, 13 ,, . .	7	8	9
—	—	11	—	,, 13, ,, ,, 14 ,, . .	11	12	13
1	1	17	—	,, 14, ,, ,, 15 ,, . .	19	16	15
1	—	9	—	,, 15, ,, , 16 ,, . .	10	9	8
2	—	4	—	,, 16, ,, ,, 17 ,, . .	6	5	6
—	—	20	—	,, 17, ,, ,, 18 ,, . .	20	22	23
—	—	4	—	,, 18, ,, ,, 19 ,, . .	4	4	4
—	—	4	—	,, 19, ,, ,, 20 ,, . .	4	6	6
—	—	3	—	,, 20 guineas	3	3	3
427	45	448	99	Total	1,019	1,003	992

* Two Schools which take boarders only, and have no separate tuition fee, have not been taken into account for the purposes of this table.

† In one of the Schools shown under *Head 2 (f)* the Tuition Fee is 5*l* 9*s*. 6*d*. for the Boys and 5 guineas for the Girls.

‡ One of the Schools shown under *Head 2 (k)*, has also a "Mercantile" or "Modern" side, in which the Tuition Fee charged is 6*l* per annum.

England and Wales.

SECONDARY SCHOOLS ON GRANT LIST.

——	1913-14.	1914-15.	1915-16.
Council Schools	427	448	450
Endowed Schools	448	429	429
Girls' Public Day School Trust	—	25	25
Roman Catholic	45	45	45
Welsh Intermediate Schools	99	100	100
Total Number of Schools	1,019	1,047	1,049
Pupils: Boys	99,997	105,096	108,354
,, Girls	87,650	93,788	100,336
Total Number of Pupils	187,647	198,884	208,690

SCHOOLS NOT ON THE GRANT LIST.

In addition to the 1,049 schools on the Grant List there were 129 other schools, the same number as in the previous year, recognised by the Board as efficient during 1915-16. Of these, one was provided by the Local Authority and one was a Welsh Intermediate School, 104 were Endowed Schools or schools of a similar type, two were controlled by Roman Catholic Orders, and 21 were Private Schools. In these schools there were, in 1914-15, 23,438 pupils (14,185 boys and 9,253 girls). No figures are available for 1915-16, but it is probable that the number of pupils was about the same as before.

TEACHERS ON STAFF OF SECONDARY SCHOOLS.—The supply of secondary school teachers is better than that in elementary schools in proportion to the numbers of pupils, in addition to which a higher standard is required in the subjects to be taught.

England and Wales.

SECONDARY SCHOOLS ON THE GRANT LIST.

Teachers on Staff of Schools.

31st January.				1914.			
1912.	1913.	1914.		Council Schools.	Roman Catholic Schools.	Foundtn. & other Schools.	Welsh Intmdte. Schools.
1	*2*	*3*	*4*	*5*	*6*	*7*	*8*
			I.—FULL-TIME TEACHERS :—				
			1. Head Teachers :—				
			(a) Men—				
605	616	630	. . (i) Gradua es . . .	232	8	314	76
43	41	38	. . (ii) Non-Graduates . .	20	3	15	—
648	657	668	. . (iii) Tota¹ . . .	252	11	329	76
			(b) Women—				
227	240	258	. . (i) Graduates . . .	147	4	86	21
104	99	91	. . (ii) Non-Graduates . .	25	30	34	2
331	339	349	. . (iii) Total . . .	172	34	120	23
			(c) Men and Women—				
832	856	888	. . (i) Gradua'es . .	379	12	400	97
147	140	129	. . (ii) Non Graduates . .	45	33	49	2
979	996	1,017	. . (iii) Total . . .	424	45	449	99
			2. Assistant Teachers :—				
			(a) Men—				
2,948	3,110	3,308	. . (i) Graduates . . .	1,352	37	1,638	281
1,504	1,474	1,471	. . (ii) Non-Graduates .	632	68	690	81
4,452	4,584	4,779	. . (iii) Total . . .	1,984	105	2,328	362
			(b) Women—				
2,333	2,482	2,633	. . (i) Graduates . .	1,497	68	825	243
2.324	2,336	2,395	. . (ii) Non-Graduates .	1,083	301	921	90
4,657	4,818	5,028	. . (iii) Total . . .	2,580	369	1,746	333
			(c) Men and Women—				
5,281	5,592	5,941	. . (i) Graduates . .	2,849	105	2,463	524
3,828	3,810	3,866	. . (ii) Non-Graduates .	1,715	369	1,611	171
9,109	9,402	9,807	. . (iii) Total . . .	4,564	474	4,074	695
10,088	10,398	10,824	3. Total of Head and Assistant Teachers	4,988	519	4,523	794
			II.—PART-TIME TEACHERS* :—				
1,808	1,833	1,830	. . 1. Men	752	34	919	125
1,552	1,559	1,588	. . 2. Women	691	67	712	118
3,360	3;392	3,418	. . 3. Total	1,443	101	1,631	243

* Part time teachers are counted once for *each* school in which they served. The figures include certain teachers who served for the remainder of their time in other Institutions organically connected with the Secondary Schools, viz.: 158 in 1914, 168 in 1913, and 158 in 1912. Of these, 7 in 1914, 8 in 1913, and 7 in 1912 were Head Teachers.

D

MEDICAL AND HEALTH.

ORGANISATION FOR MEDICAL TREATMENT.—The following tables of those Local Education Authorities which have or have not made some provision for medical treatment explain themselves, though attention should be called to the fact that there is still so large a proportion where no provision of any such kind has been made. The rise in this number in 1916 is probably due to the shortage of doctors and other health officers in that year. It appears that the war is responsible for a decline of about 28 per cent. in the number of children medically examined, and, though no figures are available for 1917, it is feared that medical inspection of schools can hardly be on the increase :—

LOCAL EDUCATION AUTHORITIES : ORGANISATION FOR MEDICAL TREATMENT.

Year.	Made some arrangements for Medical Treatment.	Number of Authorities which have made no provision for Medical Treatment of any kind.	Provided School Clinics.	Contributed to Hospitals.	Made Provision for supplying Spectacles.
1908	55	264	7	8	21
1912	167	152	97	37	101
1913	241	78	139	53	125
1914	266	53	179	75	165
1915	279	40	212	78	210
1916	276	43	219	87	216

The number of Local Education Authorities which used their arrangements during 1916 for the treatment of certain conditions :—

Condition.	Counties.	County Boroughs	Boroughs	Urban Districts.	Total.	Number for 1915.
Minor ailments	27	72	88	29	216	213
Dental defects	22	52	50	22	146	147
Defective vision	42	65	83	31	221	211
Provision of spectacles	29	56	68	36	189	179
Enlarged tonsils and adenoids	20	26	42	14	102	93
Ringworm (X-rays)	12	32	15	14	73	71
Number of Authorities in England & Wales	63	82	126	48	319	

DEFECTIVES.—Medical inspection has brought to light the fact that many children, though not specifically " feeble-minded," are so dull and backward as to be unable to derive the full benefit from schooling ; while over 10 per cent. of the whole are unclean, and 10 per cent. are insufficiently nourished. As regards disease, by far the most common is dental disease, which handicaps children almost as much as adolescents and adults. It is computed that not less than half of the 6,000,000 children in schools in England and Wales are in need of dental treatment. More than half-a-million children are defective in eyesight, and another quarter of a million are in a relatively serious condition with ear, throat, and gland disease.

THE INSPECTION OF SCHOOL CHILDREN AND THE TREATMENT OF DEFECTIVES (TYPICAL AREAS) 1916.

Type of Area.	Average Attendance.	Children Medically Inspected.		Children found Defective.		Children Medically Treated.	
		No.	Percentage on Average Attendance.	No.	Percentage on Children Inspected.	No.	Percentage on Children Defective.
Counties (22)	534,922	135,454	25·3	37,954	28·0	20,755	54·6
County Boroughs(34)	705,780	216,212	30·6	78,475	36·2	45,572	58·0
Boroughs (55)	209,411	70,273	33·5	27,501	39·1	17,372	63·1
Urban Districts (22)	173,388	50,872	29·3	19,847	39·0	12,701	63·9
Totals (133)	1,623,501	472,811	29·1	163,777	34·6	96,400	58·8

TABLE SHOWING PROPORTION OF TOTAL DEFECTIVES TREATED.

Local Education Authority.	No. needing Treat-ment.	No. for which no Report is avail-able.	No. Treated.	Results of Treatment.			No. not Treated.	Per-centage Treated.
				Re-medied.	Im-proved.	Un-changed.		
Bacup - - -	1,045	98	858	718	85	55	89	82·11
Barry - - -	4,156	—	2,784	2,310	176	298	1,372	66·99
Batley - - -	639	114	319	198	83	38	206	49·92
Berkshire - -	2,151	893	573	316	223	34	685	26·64
Beverley - - -	247	20	174	70	101	3	53	70·45
Bolton - - -	2,483	117	1,915	1,380	349	186	451	77·12
Bournemouth ↵	1,737	569	763	572	191	—	405	43·93
Brecknockshire -	1,508	527	375	306	59	10	606	24·86
Burton-on-Trent -	1,824	199	1,443	590	574	279	182	79·12
Cambridge - -	355	19	270	261	· 9	—	66	76·05
Carlisle - - -	1,499	189	1,033	371	391	271	277	68·91
Carmarthen - *	371	22	115	53	46	16	234	31·0
Gillingham - -	419	—	217	111	102	4	202	51·79
Gloucester - -	557	40	475	251	151	73	42	85·28
Gloucestefshire*	3,369	—	2,651	887	1,246	518	718	78·69
Grantham - -	1,474	829	451	153	298	—	194	30·59
Gravesend - -	2,960	304	1,758	780	896	82	898	59·39
Guildford - -	354	16	228	171	43	14	110	64·41
Halifax - - -	2,891	869	1,868	1,646	205	17	154	64·61
Hartlepool - -	1,276	55	707	599	102	6	514	55·41
Heywood - -	801	51	515	191	188	136	235	64·29
Hindley - - -	2,184	70	1,105	425	653	27	1,009	50·59
Hove - - -	2,556	422	1,585	1,538	43	4	549	62·01
Huntingdonshire -	1,279	213	865	225	462	178	201	67·68
Isle of Wight - -	1,558	258	712	516	164	32	588	45 7
Keighley - -	2.638	330	1,939	795	937	207	369	73·5
Kendal - -	333	37	220	86	127	7	76	66·06
King's Lynn - -	253		170	110	56	4	83	67·19
Lincolnshire (parts of Lindsey).	4,189	136	1,912	1,321	472	119	2,141	45 64
Maidenhead -	712	152	386	205	91	90	174	54·21
Mansfield - -	947	501	394	165	188	41	52	41·61
Middleton - -	2,941	2,104	461	361	94	6	376	15·67
Mossley - -	216	5	152	133	17	2	59	70·37
Mountain Ash -	3,219	125	2,887	2,315	465	107	207	89·6
Newport (Mou.) -	1,599	* 358	926	222	587	117	315	57·91
Northumberland -	9.592	1,606	6,767	2,434	3,045	1,288	1,219	70·55
Richmond - -	984	46	222	152	64	6	716	22·5
Rochester - -	958	—	748	548	166	34	210	78·08
Rutland - -	2.714	648	573	291	268	14	1,493	21·11
Stalybridge -	522	—	426	362	49	15	96	81 61
Stoke-on-Trent -	11,729	—	9,800	5,041	·4,030	729	1,929	83·55
Swinton and Pendle-bury	670	2	642	378	135	129	26	95·82
Wallsend - -	690	18	433	281	109	43	239	62 75
Westmorland - -	871	139	440	277	163	0	292	50·52
Wolverhampton -	1,890	271	702	92	493	117	917	37·14
Worcestershire -	864	18	678	228	377	73	168	78·47
Yorks (E.R.) - -	3,389	877	1.466	838	566	62	1,046	43·37
„ (N.R.) - -	1,261	301	532	276	210	46	428	42·19
Total - -	92,874	13,568	56,635	31,549	19,549	5,537	22,671	60 98

The following table shows the percentages of certain defects amongst all children inspected (routine inspections only) in 1915 as indicated in the School Medical Officers' reports for 90 areas, except in the case of vision, the figures for which are based on the inspections in 34 areas :—

Defect.	Number Inspected.	Number Defective.	Percentage Defective.
Clothing defective	335,796	17,640	5˙25
Footgear defective	335,796	36,003	10˙72
Uncleanliness of head	335,796	47,638	14˙19
Uncleanliness of body	335,796	20,845	6˙21
Malnutrition	333,395	44,176	13˙25
Disease of nose and throat	335,812	69,614	20˙73
External eye disease	335,824	8,134	2˙42
Ear disease	435,822	8,535	2˙54
Dental disease	302,409	209,010	69˙12
Disease of heart and circulation . . .	335,814	12,016	3˙58
Disease of the lungs	335,814	12,138	3˙61
Nervous disease	335,814	1,839	˙55
Skin disease	335,814	6,081	1˙81
Rickets	335,814	14,151	4˙21
Deformities	331,770	6,465	1˙95
Tuberculosis (non-pulmonary) . . .	331,797	1,283	˙39
Speech defects	335,305	4,462	1˙33
Mental condition	307,282	15,656	5˙09
Defective hearing	238,129	26,373	11˙08
Defective vision	71,128	12,221*	17˙20

* In addition, there were 11,535 children whose vision was less than 6/6 but not less than 6/9 in one or both eyes.

The following Table shows the net expenditure on the School Medical Service for the past three years and the amount of grant paid in respect thereof.

Local Education Authority.	Expenditure for Year ending 31 July, 1913.	Grant.	Expenditure for Year ending 31 March, 1914.	Grant.	Expenditure for Year ending 31 March, 1915.	Grant.	Expenditure for Year ending 31 March, 1916.	Grant.
	£	£	£	£	£	£	£	£
Counties . . .	95,435	39,511	107,049	45,538	137,078	61,360	122,630	55,430
Urban Districts.	18,382	7,971	21,255	9,591	25,133	11,643	29,171	13,517
Municipal Boroughs.	30,325	13,001	33,965	15,098	39,293	17,935	42,684	19,738
County Boroughs .	76,868	34,154	91,167	42,052	115,567	54,297	127,907	60,471
London . . .	64,981	31,191	72,298	36,149	94,355	47,177	95,472	47,736
* Total . .	285,993	125,830	325,735	148,429	411,428	192,414	417,870	196,893

* These totals include the cast of the shillings and pence omitted in the table.

Analysis of the Main Heads of Expenditure on the School Medical Service.

	1912-13.	1913-14.	1914-15.	1915-16.
Salaries of Medical Officers and Specialists	£ 139,774	£ 151,339	£ 180,377	£ 179,579
Nurses' salaries	37,119	43,212	57,586	66,439
Travelling expenses of Medical Officers and Nurses . .	15,258	16,779	21,052	17,579
Drugs, materials, and apparatus .	7,378	9,808	14,069	11,440
Provision of Spectacles . . .	1,650	2,155	3,681	4,023
Contributions to external Bodies (hospitals, infirmaries, nursing associations, etc.) . . .	23,629	27,459	39,315	43,403
Provision of clerical assistance, premises, stationery, printing, postage, and miscellaneous objects	61,135	74,983	95,348	95,407
Total . . .	285,993	325,735	411,428	417,870

The following table shows the number of routine medical inspections during the years ending on the 31st March, 1913, 1914, and 1915.

	1912-13.	1913-14.	1914-15.
Entrants	712,310	732,797	706,142
Leavers	548,028	600,372	651,189
Intermediate age group . .	218,357	373,212	357,067
	1,478,695	1,706,381	1,714,398

MEDICAL STAFF.—The effect of the war in withdrawing so many school medical officers has been to add greatly to the value of the work done by school nurses and school attendance officers. These officers are able to pick out the children most obviously in need of examination, and see to it that, however short the supply of medical officers may be, those children, at any rate, receive attention. They are thus able to prevent the actual increase in defects in some children, and that is as much as can be looked for at the present time.

SUMMARY OF PARTICULARS OF THE MEDICAL STAFF AND NURSES EMPLOYED BY LOCAL EDUCATION AUTHORITIES, together with the Average Attendance of Children in Public Elementary Schools for 1913-14, and the Number of Entrants and Leavers inspected during the Year ending 31st December, 1915, as shown by the School Medical Officers' Reports for 1915.

AREA	No. of Areas	School Medical Officers — Whole-time: also M.O.H.	WT: not M.O.H.	WT: undertake Specialist Work	Part-time: also M.O.H.	PT: not M.O.H.	PT: undertake Specialist Work	Total Number	Assistant S.M.O. — No. of Areas	ASMO WT: also M.O.H. or Asst.	ASMO WT: not M.O.H. or Asst.	ASMO WT: undertake Specialist	ASMO PT: also M.O.H. or Asst.	ASMO PT: not M.O.H. or Asst.	ASMO PT: undertake Specialist	Total Number	Specialist — No. of Areas	WT Ophthalmic Surgeons	WT Dental Surgeons	PT Ophthalmic Surgeons	PT Dental Surgeons	PT Aural Surgeons	PT Anæsthetists	PT X-ray Operators	Total Number	Nurses — No. of Areas	Total No.	WT giving Whole Time to Sch. Med. Service	Part-time Public Officers	Total Number	Average Attendance, 1913-14	No. of Children in Code Groups inspected
ENGLAND.																																
Counties	49	40	3	3	5	1	–	49	41	49	105	45	41	39	5	234	23	5	16	31	11	–	–	3	66	42	306	81	344	650	1,878,764	389,683
Urban Districts	40	18	1	6	18	3	2	40	16	7	3	5	1	11	–	22	23	–	4	15	13	5	4	9	50	34	63	28	2	65	274,090	87,505
Boroughs	49	49	3	13	50	17	4	119	28	5	4	5	2	24	9	35	65	–	2	37	55	9	9	12	114	111	122	67	24	146	454,571	148,270
County Boroughs	78	57	16	11	1	4	1	78	66	34	82	40	1	38	1	144	57	–	28	44	42	17	6	1	149	76	293	234	8	301	1,721,041	461,961
London	1	1	1	–	–	–	–	1	1	–	45	6	–	30	4	65	1	–	–	–	30	–	–	–	30	1	140	140	–	140	644,320	258,386
Total, England	287	165	23	33	74	25	7	287	150	95	239	101	44	122	19	500	169	5	50	127	151	31	19	25	409	264	924	560	378	1,302	4,972,996	1,345,805
WALES.																																
Counties	13	12	–	2	1	–	1	13	7	3	9	4	11	4	–	27	10	–	4	7	2	3	–	2	18	11	30	21	108	138	243,163	57,290
Urban Districts	7	6	–	2	1	–	–	7	3	3	1	4	1	–	–	4	5	–	–	2	5	–	–	1	8	7	15	4	1	16	74,138	21,933
Boroughs	5	2	–	1	1	1	–	5	2	–	–	–	–	2	2	2	1	–	–	1	2	–	–	–	3	5	4	2	1	5	15,512	5,976
County Borough	4	3	1	2	1	–	–	4	4	2	3	2	–	1	–	6	3	–	1	2	2	1	1	–	7	4	23	9	–	23	75,670	17,201
Total, Wales	29	23	1	7	4	1	1	29	16	8	13	10	11	7	2	39	19	–	5	12	11	4	1	3	36	27	72	36	110	182	408,483	102,310
Total, England and Wales	316	188	24	40	78	26	8	316	166	103	252	111	55	129	21	539	188	5	55	139	162	35	20	29	445	291	996	586	488	1,484	5,381,479	1,448,115

These totals do not include the 215 medical officers who undertake treatment at the London Treatment Centres.

TREATMENT.—The value of school clinics can best be estimated by the fact that in 1908 there existed seven of them; in 1916 there were 480, and the number of attendances at the clinics has increased with very great rapidity. At Nottingham, for instance, the attendances rose from 48,000 in 1915 to 63,000 in 1916, and these figures are not exceptional.

In addition to the figures given below for hospitals who have provided special facilities for the treatment of school children, a large number of hospitals have co-operated in treating defects of children without any organised arrangement with a Local Education Authority.

PLACES WHERE TREATMENT IS CARRIED OUT, 1916.

Looal Education Authority.	Place where Treatment is carried out.			Total No. of Areas.
	School Clinic.	Homes or Schools.	Hospital.	
Counties	14	17	1	27
County Boroughs . . .	70	7	4	72
Boroughs	79	12	1	88
Urban Districts . . .	29	2	—	29
Total	192	38	6	216

EXCEPTIONAL CHILDREN.—The two following tables should be taken together as showing the proportion of special schools to exceptional children :—

Number of Exceptional Children, England and Wales, 1915.*

Physically Defective Children.	34,500
Mentally Deficient Children (excluding imbeciles and idiots, but including a number of ineducable low-grade feeble-minded children)	30,800
Deaf and Dumb Children (including partially deaf)	5,5 0
Blind Children (including partially blind)	4,250
	75,100

* Statistics not quite complete.

SPECIAL SCHOOLS, 1916.

Showing the provision made for exceptional children.

	No. of Schools.				Present Accommodation.	Average No. of Scholars on Registers in 1915-16 (England and Wales).
	In England.	In Wales.	Provided.	Voluntary.		
Blind	48	2	33	17	2,791	2,392
Deaf	49	2	37	14	4,676	3,918
Mentally defective . . .	186	5	178	13	15,068	14,405
Physically defective . . .	64*	—	55	9	5,623	5,649
Tubercular	34†	—	15	19	1,935	1,388
Epileptic	6	—	1	5	496	476
Open-air Schools . . .	26	1	18	9	1,843	1,375
Total . . .	413	10	337	86	32,432	29,603

* Including two Ophthalmic Schools.
† Including four Hospital Schools.

SPECIAL SCHOOLS.—During the last seven years a remarkable development has taken place in the number, character, and scope of the special schools provided for abnormal children. New types of school have come into existence, and the number of children in attendance has increased by 50 per cent. This growth is largely due to the development of the School Medical Service.

England and Wales.

SPECIAL SCHOOLS.

	Schools.			Number on Registers.			Teachers (Full Time).					
							Men.			Women.		
	†A	‡B	§C	†A	‡B	§ C	†A	‡B	§C	†A	‡B	§C
For Blind Children .	41	40	38	2,138	2,074	1,871	63	69	66	144	141	142
For Deaf Children .	50	50	49	3,905	3,796	3,681	150	149	150	277	272	264
For Mentally Defective . . .	179	177	171	13,651	13,226	12,767	89	89	86	608	580	546
For Physically Defective . . .	91	74	68	7,326	6,167	5,560	23	18	15	303	262	234
For Epileptic Children	6	6	6	474	441	395	7	5	6	17	15	13
Total . . .	367	347	332	27,494	25,704	24,274	332	330	323	1,349	1,270	1,199
* Part time teachers . .							135	121	104	153	131	140

* Part time teachers are counted one for each school in which they served
† A. 1913-4.   ‡ B. 1912-3.   § C. 1911-2.

OPEN-AIR SCHOOLS.—Those who chiefly need open-air schools are the 600,000 dull, backward, or weakly children who form over 10 per cent. of the total number of children in schools at the present time. School medical officers constantly testify to the increased physical and mental vigour that results in children who are able to spend the greater part of the school hours in the open air. The following figures give the number of special open-air schools, but in addition to this large numbers of schools hold classes in their playgrounds or in public parks or open spaces, though these classes are often not for the whole school, but for specially weakly children :—

DAY OPEN-AIR SCHOOLS.

Day Open-Air Schools recognised under the Regulations for Special Schools were open during 1916 in the following places :—

Local Education Authority or Area. Name of School. Date of Certification.	Age of Children at the School.	Accommodation.	Average No. on Books during period in which School was opened.
(1) London, Lewisham, Birley House, 10th June, 1908	7-15	110	84
(2) London, Plumstead, Shooter's Hill, 10th June, 1908	7-14	100	111
(3) Halifax, Bermerside, 20th July, 1908	6-13	100	92
(4) Bradford, Thackley, 31st August, 1908	5-14	190*	240
(5) Sheffield, Whiteley Wood, 31st June, 1909	6-13	100	107
(6) Norwich, Colman Road, 23rd May, 1911	7-13	100	93
(7) Birmingham, Uffculme, 18th September, 1911	6-14	120	125
(8) Kettering, 15th September, 1913	5-13	40	41
(9) Lincoln, 14th October, 1913	7-13	40	44
(10) Bristol, Knowle, 20th October, 1913	7-14	90	88
(11) Bristol, Barton Hill, 15th October, 1914	7-12	20	25
(12) Aberdare, Park Lane, 26th October, 1914	7-14	75	68
(13) Nottingham, Arboretum. 22nd May, 1916	4-14	60	70
(14) Cambridge, 24th July, 1916	8-14	20	23
(15) Salford, 28th August, 1916	7-13	60	53
Total		1,225	1,264

* Including 50 temporary places.

SCHOOLS FOR MOTHERS.—Schools for mothers should become less necessary as the teaching of mothercraft to the elder girls in schools is developed. At the present time, however, the need for such schools is urgent, and the figures given below for 1916, though they show an improvement on 1915, are still hopelessly inadequate. There are probably, however, a number of schools for mothers and day nurseries carried on by voluntary committees, which do not necessarily obtain a grant from the Board of Education :—

Grants paid to Schools for Mothers and Day Nurseries under the Regulations of the Board.

	Year ending 31st March, 1915.	Year ending 31st March, 1916.
	£ s. d.	£ s. d.
Schools for Mothers	5,869 14 5	8,938 10 9
Day Nurseries	4,960 14 11	6,395 7 3
Total	10,830 9 4	15,333 18 0

SCHOOL FEEDING.—The Education (Provision of Meals) Act of 1906 empowered the Local Education Authority to take such steps as they think fit for feeding the children attending public elementary schools in their area. They may provide the meals free of charge, or require payment from the parents. Under the Amending Act of 1914 meals may be provided on holidays as well as school days, and a grant-in-aid not exceeding half the cost may be provided by the Exchequer.

The following table gives the number of local authorities which have or have not provided meals since the outbreak of war. It will be seen that the problem has been met most fully in the county boroughs, whereas in the counties, excluding London, only 13, with an average attendance of 804,379, have used the Act, while 49, with an average attendance of 1,276,969, have not done so.

Shortly after the outbreak of war the number of children fed daily reached its maximum, namely, 195,000; but when this is compared with the number of children in average attendance (5,400,000) it will be seen to yield a percentage of less than 4, and less than a third of the number of malnourished children.

In 1915-16 the decline in school feeding was remarkable. Before the war the average number of children fed per annum was about 150,000. In 1915 it was 422,000, and in 1916 it was 117,000. The causes for the decline are obvious. The great increase in employment and wages has resulted to a large extent in the better feeding and clothing of children at home, and the demand for school feeding has diminished proportionately.

FEEDING OF SCHOOL CHILDREN.

—	No. of Authorities which *have* provided Meals, 1914-1917.	Average Attendance of Children in Public Elementary Schools in those Areas.	No. of Authorities which *have not* provided Meals, 1914-1917.	Average Attendance of Children in Public Elementary Schools in those Areas.
England and Wales.				
Counties (including London)	14	1,489,278	49	1,276,969
County Boroughs	68	1,695,900	14	100,811
Boroughs	36	154,989	90	315,394
Urban Districts	32	273,868	16	74,270
Total	150	3,614,035	169	1,767,444

Year.	Number of Authorities which fed under the Act.	Total Number of Children fed in the Year.	Total Number of Meals provided in the Year,	Total Expenditure.	Cost per Meal.	Amount of Exchequer Grants.*
				£	d.	£
1907-8	32	‡	2,751,326†	Information not available.	—	—
1908-9	113	‡	14,218,560	72,333	1·22	—
1909-10	126	‡	16,102,104	134,105	2·0	—
1910-11	128	‡	16,872,997	153,568	2·18	—
1911-12	131	‡	16,122,219	157,127	2·34	—
1912-13	137	§358,306	19,001,729	183,805	2·32	—
1913-14	98	156,531	14,525,593	147,519	2·43	71,383
1914-15	134	422,401‖	29,560,316	304,583	2·47	148,753
1915-16	115	117,901	9,930,074	169,677	4·1	77,985
1916-17	93	63,939	5,781,584	132,010	5·48	¶

* Grants-in-aid were first paid by the Exchequer in the financial years 1914-15, based on the work done in the year 1913-14.

† Excludes London.

‡ Number cannot be stated, as many Authorities did not supply full particulars previously to receiving grants-in-aid.

§ This large number was partly accounted for by the Coal Strike of 1912.

‖ This increase is due to the need arising on the outbreak of war.

¶ Grants in process of payment.

EXEMPLIONS AND EMPLOYMENT.

PARTIAL EXEMPTIONS.—Concurrently with factory legislation a series of Education Acts, beginning in 1870, have been passed which has made the employment of children of school age, except (a) under "labour" or attendance certificates, (b) under partial exemption, and (c) by employment out of school hours. Thus, a child between 12 and 14 may not be employed whole-time unless he has satisfied the requirements of the local bye-laws. These bye-laws almost invariably require a certificate of proficiency as a condition of full-time exemption below 13, and above that age prescribe, in about half the areas in England and Wales, a certificate of proficiency and, in the remaining half, a certificate of previous due attendance. Thus it comes about that there are, broadly speaking, five groups of employed children, partially or wholly exempt from school attendance :—

1. Young persons over 14 years of age.

2. Children under 14 (but above 12) wholly employed, as possessing an exemption certificate.

3. Children under 14 (but above 12) partially exempted (so-called "half-timers"), excluding a small number of children under 12 employed under the agricultural bye-laws.

4. Children aged 12-14 employed under the Coal and Metalliferous Mines Acts.

5. Children in attendance at school, but employed out of school hours.

The great majority of the " half-timers," as shown in the following table, are employed in Lancashire and Yorkshire, in the cotton and woollen industries.

Speaking generally, it is estimated that some 400,000 children annually pass out of the State schools at or about the age of 14. The number who pass out possessing labour or attendance certificates is about 200,000; the number of " half-timers " is estimated at upwards of 30,000; and the number of school children employed out of school hours is, in normal circumstances, about a quarter of a million. Under war conditions this figure has, of course, increased greatly, but it is impossible to estimate the number of children so employed. Such children work from five to 30 hours or more per week, in addition to $27\frac{1}{2}$ hours of schooling, bringing up their total hours of work every week to the adult standard, in addition to time and energy spent in coming and going.

PARTIAL EXEMPTION SCHOLARS.

	1913-14.	1912-13.	1911-12.
1.—Number of Departments which claimed Additional Attendance on account of Partial Exemption Scholars. . .	2,196	2,353	2,456
2.—Number of Scholars on the Partial Exemption Registers at any time during the School Year :—			
(a) Number removed from the Registers during the school year	35,758	36,070	34,977
(b) Number on the Registers on last day of school year :—			
11 and under 12 years of age	23	25	27
12 ,, ,, 13 ,, ,, ...	27,143	27,161	26,003
13 ,, ,, 14 ,, ,, ...	8,513	8,539	9,112
Total	35.679	35,725	35,142
(c) Total of (a) and (b)	71,437	71,795	70,119
3.—Additional Average Attendance Allowed	8,720	8,616	8,352

From 1907-8 to 1914-15 there was a continuous decrease in the number of departments in England in which additional attendances were claimed for Partial Exemption scholars. The figures for 1915-16, however, show an increase over those for 1914-15.

The figures for a series of years are as follows :—

	1909-10.	1910-11.	1911-12.	1912-13.	1913-14.	1914-15.	1915-16.
Departments where claimed.	2,905	2,606	2,439	2,340	2,183	2,041	2,067
Scholars for whom claimed.	75,699	71,419	70,074	71,719	71,382	69,555	72,630

The two following tables, which show the effect of employment on the health of school children, speak for themselves; but it should be pointed out that a great deal of the harm done to children is so insidious as to escape observation, and cannot, therefore, be estimated by available figures :—

THE EFFECT OF THE EMPLOYMENT OF SCHOOL CHILDREN ON HEALTH (HOURS WORKED).

Hours worked Weekly (in addition to school hours).	Actual number of Boys.	Fatigue signs.	Anæmia.	Severe Nerve Signs.	Deformities.	Severe Heart signs.
All school boys of district (workers and non-workers) .	3,700	—	25	24	8	8
Working 20 or less hours . . .	163	50	34	28	15	11
Working 20-30 hours	86	81	47	44	21	15
Working over 30 hours . . .	95	83	45	50	22	20

Fatigue signs included general reduction of muscular tone, relaxed orbiculares, head balance impaired, touch, attitude, alteration or loss of voice.

Severe nerve signs included excessive tremor, stammering, incoordinations, chorea, altered reflexes.

Deformities included wry neck, flat foot, spinal curvature, tilting of pelvis, unsymmetrical development.

THE EFFECT OF THE EMPLOYMENT OF SCHOOL CHILDREN ON HEALTH (TRADES).

Trade.	No. of Boys.	Anæmia.	Nervous.	Deformities.	Heart Disease.
All	330	40	40	17	16
Milk . . .	63	41	46	19	21
Shop . . .	134	38	44	26	21
Newsboys . .	52	35	27	6	8
Barbers . . .	11	72	63	9	27

TEACHERS.

Supply of Intending Teachers.—For some years past the Board of Education has been concerned with the serious deficiency of candidates for the teaching profession. Various causes have contributed to the shortage, chief among which is the economic cause. Salaries, it is true, have been increased, but not in proportion to the rise in the cost of living even before the war, while the fact that the teacher does not begin to earn money until 19 years of age, or later, and during the years between 16 and 19 not only contributes nothing, but is a charge upon the family, has acted largely as a deterrent. Maintenance grants offered by Local Education Authorities to intending teachers while at the secondary school are usually very small, while the expenses of the education of candidates have increased.

Such was the state of affairs before the war, and the withdrawal of men candidates for the Army and other work, and the better financial attractions of other forms of employment for girls and women, have brought the Educational Authorities to realise that no minor improvements in the status of teachers will suffice to meet the dangerous shortage.

England and Wales.

SUPPLY OF RECOGNISED INTENDING TEACHERS: SUMMARY BY TYPES

(*A*)—Number of intending Teachers recognised for the first time during the year, and proportion which that number bore to the number of posts for Certificated and Uncertificated Teachers in Public Elementary Schools.

(*A*)

Type of Local Authority.	Number of Bursars, Pupil-Teachers, and Student-Teachers who had not been Bursars, recognised for the first time during the year.									Number of Posts on 31st January, 1914.		Percentage of Col. 10 to total of Cols. 11 and 12.
	Bursars.		Pupil-Teachers.				Student Teachers who had not been Bursars		Total.	For Certificated Teachers.	For Uncertificated Teachers.	
			Instructed in Centres.		Not in Centres							
	Boys.	Girls.	Boys.	Girls.	Boys.	Girls.	Boys.	Girls.				
1	*2*	*3*	*4*	*5*	*6*	*7*	*8*	*9*	*10*	*11*	*12*	*13*
ENGLAND AND WALES.												
1. County Councils (other than London C.C.)	296	895	219	755	50	346	43	76	2,680	35,629	25,493	4'38
(*a*) Borough Councils	68	283	25	119	—	—	7	26	528	9,574	5,011	3'62
(*b*) Urban District Councils	41	107	32	99	—	—	12	19	310	7,142	2,536	3'20
Total of above	405	1,285	276	973	50	346	62	121	3,518	52,345	33,040	4'12
2. London County Council	24	315	—	—	—	—	13	60	412	18,060	197	2'25
3. County Borough Councils	253	998	45	415	—	—	23	111	1,845	37,050	11,091	3'83
Total for Urban Authorities [1 (*a*) and (*b*), 2, and 3]	386	1,703	102	633	—	—	55	216	3,095	71,826	18,835	3'41
4. Total for England and Wales	682	2,598	321	1,388	50	346	98	292	5,775	107,455	44,328	3'80

*In addition one Pupil Teacher was recognised in a Public Elementary School not

† In addition one ex-Pupil-Teacher entered a Training College after serving as an Education Authority.

England and Wales.

OF LOCAL AUTHORITY FOR THE YEAR ENDING 31ST JULY, 1914.

(*B*)—Total number of recognised intending Teachers.

(*C*)—Number of persons from each type of area previously recognised as intending Teachers who during the year entered Training Colleges, or took up service as Uncertificated Teachers.

(*B*)							(*C*)					
Total number of recognised Bursars Pupil-Teachers, and Student-Teachers in each type of area during the year.							Number of persons who had been Bursars, Pupil-Teachers, or Student Teachers, and who during the year—					
							became Uncertificated Teachers.		entered a Training College—			
Bursars.		Pupil-Teachers.		Student-Teachers.					after serving as Uncertificated Teachers.		without serving as Uncertificated Teachers.	
						Total.						
Boys.	Girls.	Boys.	Girls.	Boys.	Girls.		Men.	Women	Men.	Women	Men.	Women
14	*15*	*16*	*17*	*18*	*19*	*20*	*21*	*22*	*23*	*24*	*25*	*26*
296	899	494	1,809	365	890	4,753	249	767	415	227	371	729
68	283	53	239	62	253	958	37	165	75	51	52	203
41	107	63	200	52	181	644	27	111	65	51	51	91
405	1,289	610	2,248	479	1,324	6,355	313	1,043	555	329	474	1,023
24	317	—	—	38	322	701	—	4	1	6	91	156
253	1,003	120	889	248	992	3,505	95	442	187	192	280	1,064
386	1,710	236	1,328	400	1,748	5,808	159	722	328	300	474	1,514
682	2,609	730*	3,`37	765	2,638	10,561	408	1,489	743	527†	845	2,243

maintained by a Local Education Authority.

Uncertificated Teacher in a Public Elementary School not maintained by a Local

TRAINING FOR ELEMENTARY EDUCATION SCHOOLS.—The following tables show the facilities for training students as elementary school teachers. The men's colleges have suffered severely through the withdrawal of many teachers and students for military service, and the women's colleges are in some cases in occupation by the military authorities. The number of women students applying to enter training colleges has not fallen off to any great extent; but, though the War Office has not taken over women's colleges for military purposes except as a last resort, this has happened in some cases, and also it has been quite impossible to continue any schemes for the building of hostels or new buildings of any kind through shortage both of building labour and materials and of money :—

Type of College.	1913-14.		1914-15.		1915-16.		1916-17.	
	No.	Accommodation.	No.	Accommodation.	No.	Accommodation.	No.	Accommodation.
University Training Colleges . . .	20	3,466	20	3,466	19	3,462	18	3,387
Council Training Colleges . . .	20	3,918	22	4,168	19	3,541	19	3,530
Voluntary Training Colleges . . .	47	5,709	47	5,722	40	5,136	35	4,561
Total . .	87	13,093	89	13,356	78	12,139	72	11,478

CANDIDATES OF VARIOUS KINDS RECOGNISED IN ENGLAND AND WALES, 1912-16.

Year beginn'g 1st · August.	Pupil Teachers commencing				Bursars.		Student-Teachers who have not been Bursars.		Total Entrants.
	in Centres.		not in Centres.						
	Boys.	Girls.	Boys.	Girls.	Boys.	Girls.	Boys.	Girls.	
1912	367	1376	17	73	722	2391	70	227	5270
1913	321	1389	54	363	682	2598	98	392	5797
1914	353	1556	50	432	756	2764	92	365	6368
1915	377	1777	45	426	797	3133	85	407	7047
1916	299	1615	25	228	675	3006	64	379	*5291

* In addition there were 156 applications under consideration.

NUMBER OF STUDENTS AT THE COLLEGES.

The following table shows the number of men and women students who were following courses of training under the Regulations for the Training of Teachers for Elementary Schools at the beginning of 1915-16, as compared with the numbers for the two preceding years :—

	1913-14.	1914-15.	1915-16.
Men	4,242	3,245	2,217
Women	7,545	7,703	7,943
Total	11,787	10,948	10,160

4,044 students completed their training satisfactorily in 1916.

The ordinary grants to training colleges, which are based on the number of students in residence or attendance in the year, did not prove adequate to meet the needs of the colleges during the past two years under war conditions, as the number of students was subject to sudden reductions owing to causes connected with the war. The Board of Education accordingly gave, in addition to the ordinary grant, a supplementary grant to training colleges or hostels in certain cases, and under various conditions. In 1914-15 these supplementary grants amounted to £15,767.

England and Wales.

ACCOUNTS OF INSTITUTIONS FOR HIGHER EDUCATION.

(a) CURRENT ACCOUNTS OF SECONDARY SCHOOLS ON THE GRANT LIST.

Summary (Receipts and Payments).

	1912-13.				
	Council Schools.	Roman Catholic Schools.	Foundation and other Schools.	Welsh Intermediate Schools.	Total,
1	2	3	4	5	6
RECEIPTS:—	£	£	£	£	£
(a) Grants from the Board of Education	336,865	25,275	254,808	60,569	677,519
(b) Welsh Intermediate Education Fund . . .	—	—	100	60,419	60,519
(c) Contributions from Local Authorities . . .	382,114	4,703	165,435	13,928	566,180
(d) Fees	351,263	44,932	657,075	46,974	1,100,245
(e) Net income from Endowments	6,013	—	169,329	1,242	176,585
(f) Other Receipts . . .	4,467	17,921	58,414*	1,805	82,610
(g) Total	1,080,725	92,832	1,305,163	184,939	2,663,661
PAYMENTS IN RESPECT OF MAINTENANCE :—					
(a) Salaries of Teachers . .	797,415	55,110	891,150	136,702	1,880,378
(b) Provision for Pensions .	601	2	17,744	—	18,348
(c) Maintenance of Premises .	165,084	19,675	200,837	20,535	406,132
(d) Administration . . .	31,419	2,054	55,735	6,676	95,886
(e) Other Payments . . .	82,026	13,932	122,934	13,104	231,998
(f) Total	1,076,548	90,775	1,288,402	177,018	2,632,744

* Includes £40,690 received by a single School.

England and Wales.

ACCOUNTS OF INSTITUTIONS FOR HIGHER EDUCATION.

(b) CURRENT ACCOUNTS OF PUPIL TEACHER CENTRES.

Summary (Receipts and Payments).

			Details for 1912-13.			
			Separately organised Centres—		Centres attached to Higher Elementary Schools—	
1911-12.	1912-13.		for Girls.	for Boys and Girls.	for Girls.	for Boys and Girls.
1	2	3	4	5	6	7
£	£	RECEIPTS :—	£	£	£	£
11,650	8,550	(a) Grants from the Board of Education	3,196	4,493	237	624
13,931	11,915	(b) Contributions from Local Authorities	4,448	6,126	370	970
1,996	1,557	(c) Fees	682	870	—	4
109	322	(d) Other Receipts	272	44	—	5
27,687	22,345	(e) Total	8,599	11,534	607	1,603
		PAYMENTS IN RESPECT OF MAINTENANCE :—				
21,812	17,318	(a) Salaries of Teachers	6,542	9,181	494	1,099
—	—	(b) Provision for Pensions	—	—	—	—
3,848	2,930	(c) Maintenance of Premises	1,289	1,337	110	192
600	508	(d) Administration	207	273	—	27
1,638	1,523	(e) Other Payments	494	742	2	283
27,899	22,280	(f) Total	8,534	11,534	607	1,603

England and Wales.

ACCOUNTS OF INSTITUTIONS FOR HIGHER EDUCATION.

(c) CURRENT ACCOUNTS OF TRAINING COLLEGES AND HOSTELS FOR ELEMENTARY SCHOOL TEACHERS.

Summary (Receipts and Payments).

———	1912-13.	1911-12.	1910-11.
RECEIPTS OF COLLEGES AND HOSTELS :—			
(a) Grants from the Board of Education [excluding Personal Grants—*see (f)* below] :—	£	£	£
(i) Grants on account of Recognised Students	366,245	357,099	351,756
(ii) Grants for Payment of University Fees of Four Year Students	16,452	4,379	—
(iii) Grants in aid for renting temporary premises	3,198	2,153	3,238
(iv) Total	385,896	363,633	354,994
(b) Fees of Recognised Students	125,513	124,679	121,252
(c) Fees of other Students (including Private Students)	13,873	14,236	15,536
(d) Other Receipts	71,665	76,132	62,574
(e) Total Receipts [excluding Personal Grants—*see (f)* below]	596,949	578,681	554,358
(f) Personal grants from the Board of Education paid to Day Students	99,217	109,169	117,631
PAYMENTS BY COLLEGES AND HOSTELS.			
(a) Payments in respect of Maintenance	530,225	523,411	507,975
(b) Payments in respect of Premises (other than Maintenance of Premises)	47,386	54,191	49,945
(c) Other Payments not in respect of Maintenance	19,494	6,674	3,263
(d) Total Payments	597,106	584,277	561,184

TEACHERS' SALARIES AND PENSIONS.—When the following tables are examined any uncertainty as to the main cause for the shortage of teachers is removed. It will be seen that the average salary of an uncertificated man head teacher was £77 7s. in 1912-13, and that of a woman head teacher £67 17s. It should be noted that the figures quoted apply to *uncertificated* teachers, the salaries of certificated teachers ranging from £147 to £290 for men and £103 to £209 for women head teachers; while men assistant teachers' salaries range from £103 to £160 and women's from £83 to £118. It does not appear from these figures that national appreciation of the teaching profession goes very far. Moreover, though there have been increases during the war, they have not been such as to make any substantial change in the teachers' standard of life. So far the teaching profession continues to live on the promise of a better time that is coming.

England and Wales.

TEACHERS' SALARIES AND PENSIONS.

SALARIES OF FULL-TIME UNCERTIFICATED TEACHERS ON STAFF OF TEACHERS IN ORDINARY PUBLIC ELEMENTARY SCHOOLS ON LAST DAY OF SCHOOL YEAR, FOR THE STATISTICAL YEAR 1912-13.

Salary per Annum.	Number and percentage of Teachers in receipt of Salary stated in *Column 1.*											
	Men.						Women					
	Head Teachers.			Assistant Teachers.			Head Teachers.			Assistant Teachers.		
	No.	%	*	No.	%	*	No.	%	*	No.	%	*
1.	2.	3.	4.	5.	6.	7.	8.	9.	10.	11.	12.	13.
Under £40	—	—		64	1 21		—	—		512	1·38	
£40 and under £45	—	—		36	69	98 79	—	—		1,095	2·94	98·62
£45 „ „ £50	—	—		85	1·61	98 10	—	—		4,467	12·02	95·68
£50 „ „ £55	—	—		304	5·77	96·49	7	1·72	100·00	7,621	20·50	83·66
£55 „ „ £60	—	—		719	13·65	90·72	13	3·18	98·28	6,785	18·25	63·16
£60 „ „ £65	4	11·76	100·00	869	16·50	77·07	89	21·82	95·10	11,709	31·50	44·91
£65 „ „ £70	9	26·48	88·24	907	17·21	60·57	117	28·67	73·28	3,471	9·34	13·41
£70 „ „ £75	3	8·82	61·76	913	17·33	43·36	96	23·53	44·61	1,274	3 42	4·07
£75 „ „ £80	4	11·76	52·94	673	12·78	26·03	52	12 75	21 08	147	40	65
£80 „ „ £85	6	17·65	41·18	468	8·88	13·25	25	6 12	8 33	32	09	25
£85 „ „ £90	4	11·77	23·53	78	1·48	4·37	4	98	2·21	20	05	16
£90 „ „ £95	1	2·94	11·76	49	93	2·89	5	25	1·23	10	03	11
£95 „ „ £100	1	2·94	8·82	17	33	1·96	3	73	98	3	·00	08
£100 „ „ £110	—	—		46	87	1 63	1	25	25	7	02	08
£110 „ „ £120	—	—		20	38	76	—	—	—	8	03	06
£120 „ „ £130	1	2·94	5·88	6	11	38	—	—	—	6	} 01 {	03
£130 „ „ £140	—	—		4	08	27	—	—	—	6		02
£140 „ „ £150	—	—		4	08	19	—	—	—	—		
£150 and over	1‡	2·94	2·94	6§	·11	11	—	—	—	1‖	00	·00
Total · · ·	34	100·00		5,208	100·00		408	100·00		37,174	100·00	
Average Salary	£ 77	s. 7		£ 66	s. 9		£ 67	s. 17		£ 55	s. 16	
Teachers whose Salaries were included with those of other Teachers	—			1			—			8		

* Percentage of Teachers in receipt of Salary at or above the lesser of the two limits mentioned in *Column 1.*
‡ Viz., 1 at £150.
§ Viz., 1 at £150, 1 at £157, 1 at £182, 1 at £190, 2 at £200.
‖ Viz., 1 at £150.

England and Wales.

SALARIES OF FULL-TIME CERTIFICATED TEACHERS ON STAFF OF ORDINARY PUBLIC ELEMENTARY SCHOOLS ON LAST DAY OF SCHOOL YEAR, FOR THE STATISTICAL YEAR 1912-13.

Salaries up to £300, arranged in groups of £10 from £50 to £200, in groups of £25 from £200 to £300, and in groups of £50 from £300 upwards.

Salary per Annum.	Men.						Women.					
	Head Teachers.			Assistant Teachers.			Head Teachers.			Assistant Teachers.		
'1.	No. 2.	%† 3.	• 4.	No. 5.	%† 6.	• 7.	No. 8.	%† 9.	• 10.	No. 11.	%† 12.	• 13.
Under £50	2	·01		1	·00		1	01		218	42	
£50 and under £60	3	}·05{	99·99	36	·17	100·00	14	·07	99·99	902	1·73	99·58
£60 „ „ £70	·3		99·96	270	1·22	99·83	176	·99	99·92	3,237	6·24	97·85
£70 „ „ £80	17	·12	99·94	426	1·94	98·61	80	4·51	98·93	7,647	14·67	91·61
£80 „ „ £90	109	·78	99·82	1,640	7·44	96·67	1,616	9·04	94·42	9,517	18·25	76·94
£90 „ „ £100	334	2·41	99·04	2,410	10·94	89·23	2,235	12 51	85·38	10,472	20·09	58·69
£50 and under £100	466	3·36		4,782	21·71		4,846	27·12		31,795	60·98	
£100 and under £110	660	4·75	96·63	2,518	11·43	78·29	2,422	13·56	72·87	8,140	15·61	38·60
£110 „ „ £120	898	6·46	91·88	2,308	10·48	66·86	2,008	11·24	59·31	5,646	10·83	22·99
£120 „ „ £130	1,088	7·83	85 42	2,169	9·80	56·38	1,795	10·05	48·07	2,160	4·14	12·16
£130 „ „ £140	1,460	10·51	77·59	2,008	9·11	46·58	1,694	9 49	38·02	1,656	3·18	8·02
£140 „ „ £150	977	7·03	67·08	1,816	8·38	37·47	1,077	6·03	28·53	980	1·88	4·84
£100 and under £150	5,083	36·58		10,839	49·20		8,996	50·37		18 582	35·64	
£150 and under £160	1,079	7·76	60·05	2,118	9·61	29·09	1,241	6·94	22·50	1,526	2·92	2·96
£160 „ „ £170	898	6·46	52·29	1,206	5·48	19·48	709	3·97	15·56	15	03	·04
£170 „ „ £180	714	5·14	45·83	695	3·15	14·00	385	2·16	11·59	1	·00	·01
£180 „ „ £190	671	4·83	40·69	587	2·67	10·85	339	1·89	9·43	2	01	·01
£190 „ „ £200	612	4·40	35·86	250	1·31	8·18	170	·96	7·54	1	00	00
£150 and under £200	3,974	28 59		4,896	22·22		2,844	15·92		1,545	2·96	
£200 and under £225	1,691	12 17	31·46	1,508	6·85	6·87	434	2·43	6·58	—	—	—
£225 „ „ £250	916	6·60	19·29	1	·00	02	453	2 53	4·15	—	—	—
£200 and under £250	2,607	18·77		1,509	6·85		887	4·96		—	—	
£250 and under £275	769	5·53	12·69	4	02	·02	113	63	·62	—		
£275 „ „ £300	333	2·40	7·16	—	—	—	59	34	99	—		
£250 and under £300	1,102	7·93		4	02		172	·97		—		
£300 „ „ £350	434	3·12	4·76	—	—	—	117	65	·65	—	—	—
£350 „ „ £400	121	87	1·64	—			—			—		
£400 „ „ £450	99	71	·77	—			—			—		
£450 „ „ £500	7	05	·c6	—			—			—		
£500 and over	1†	01	01	—			—			—		
£300 and over	662	4·76		—	—		117	65		—	—	
Total	13,896	100·00		22,031	100·00		17,863	100·00		52,140	100·00	
Average Salary	£ s. 175 4			£ s. 128 7			£ s. 124 11			£ s. 94 7		
Teachers whose Salaries were included with those of other Teachers	63			—			3			29		

Percentage of Teachers in receipt of Salary at or above the lesser of the two limits mentioned in *Column 1.* Viz., 1 at £600,

The salaries given to teachers in higher elementary schools show very little improvement on those of elementary schools, particularly when it is considered that a higher degree of knowledge is expected in schools of this kind than in the ordinary elementary schools. Many of the future teachers are to be found in higher schools, and the future education of the nation to a large extent depends on them and on the education they receive.

England and Wales.

SALARIES OF FULL-TIME CERTIFICATED TEACHERS ON STAFF OF HIGHER ELEMENTARY SCHOOLS ON LAST DAY OF SCHOOL YEAR, FOR THE STATISTICAL YEAR 1912-13.

Salary per Annum. 1.	Number of Teachers in receipt of Salary stated in *Column 1.*			
	Men.		Women.	
	Head Teachers. 2.	Assistant Teachers. 3.	Head Teachers. 4.	Assistant Teachers. 5.
Under £50 -	—	—	—	—
£50 and under £75 -	—	—	—	2
£75 „ £100 -	—	3	—	36
£100 „ £125 -	—	57	—	79
£125 „ £150 -	—	70	—	41
£150 „ £175 -	—	59	—	6
£175 „ £200 -	—	32	1	—
£200 „ £250 -	15	8	3	4
£250 „ £300 -	17	—	1	—
£300 „ £350 -	15	—	—	—
£350 „ £400 -	2	—	—	—
£400 and over -	1*	—	—	—
Total - -	50	229	5	168
Average Salary -	£272	£145	£216	£114

There were 4 full-time Uncertificated Assistant Teachers on the Staff of Higher Elementary Schools on the last day of the school year, for the statistical year 1912-13, viz. :— 2 Men with salaries of £62 and £75 per annum respectively, and 2 Women with salaries of £100 and £120 per annum respectively.

* Viz., 1 at £400.

The salaries to teachers in secondary schools are rather more creditable in the case of Council Schools, particularly where head teachers are concerned, but in the Roman Catholic Schools, and perhaps more so in other religious schools the salaries are lower.

England and Wales.

SALARIES OF FULL-TIME TEACHERS ON STAFF OF SECONDARY SCHOOLS.

Reference Number.	Salary per Annum.	Council Schools.		Roman Catholic Schools.		Foundation and other Schools.		Welsh Intermediate Schools.	
		Men.	Women.	Men.	Women.	Men.	Women.	Men.	Women.
	I.	2.	3.	4.	5.	6.	7.	8.	9.
	1. HEAD TEACHERS:—								
1	Under £160	—	—	4	21	—	1	—	—
2	£160 and under £180	—	1	—	8	—	2	—	—
3	£180 " " £200	1	2	2	2	—	1	—	1
4	£200 " " £220	1	13	1	1	—	3	1	—
5	£220 " " £240	3	22	1	—	7	1	2	2
6	£240 " " £260	11	24	—	1	10	10	4	4
7	£260 " " £280	12	12	—	—	6	5	6	2
8	£280 " " £300	3	11	—	—	10	8	7	2
9	Under £300	31	85	8	33	33	31	20	11
10	£300 and under £350	66	42	2	1	38	22	17	1
11	£350 " " £400	45	23	—	1	49	19	13	1
12	£300 and under £400	111	65	2	2	87	41	30	2
13	£400 and under £450	44	8	1	—	46	13	11	2
14	£450 " " £500	18	4	—	—	28	11	8	3
15	£400 and under £500	62	12	1	—	74	24	19	5
16	£500 and under £600	19	1	—	—	54	13	2	1
17	£600 " " £700	9	—	—	—	33	10	4	—
18	£700 " " £800	6	—	—	—	18	1	1	—
19	£800 " " £900	2	—	—	—	17	1	—	—
20	£900 " " £1,000	—	—	—	—	3	1	—	—
21	£1,000 and over	2	—	—	—	10	—	—	—
22	£500 and over	38	1	—	—	135	26	7	1
23	Total - -	242	163	11	35	329	122	76	19
24	Average Salary -	£393	£292	£215	£163	£500	£396	£373	£331
	2. ASSISTANT TEACHERS:—								
25	Under £60	1	10	—	39	4	31	—	—
26	£60 and under £80	7	19	1	73	11	42	—	—
27	£80 " " £100	17	114	8	106	43	121	3	25
28	£100 " " £120	69	668	18	122	135	476	27	97
29	Under £120	94	811	27	340	193	670	30	122
30	£120 and under £140	230	783	41	27	233	606	60	131
31	£140 " " £160	369	446	15	8	397	263	104	39
32	£120 and under £160	599	1,229	56	35	630	869	164	170
33	£160 and under £180	409	183	7	3	410	105	83	24
34	£180 " " £200	331	85	3	—	296	53	48	9
35	£160 and under £200	740	268	10	3	706	158	131	33
36	£200 and under £220	250	43	1	—	314	27	21	3
37	£220 " " £240	69	20	3	—	162	7	8	1
38	£200 and under £240	319	63	4	—	476	34	29	4
39	£240 and under £260	36	4	1	1	155	4	3	—
40	£260 " " £280	19	—	—	—	52	—	—	—
41	£280 " " £300	8	—	—	—	22	—	—	—
42	£300 " " £350	10	—	—	—	51	1	—	—
43	£350 " " £400	1	—	—	—	16	—	—	—
44	£400 " " £450	2	—	—	—	2	—	—	—
45	£450 " " £500	—	—	—	—	1	—	—	—
46	£500 and over	—	—	—	—	1	—	—	—
47	£240 and over	76	4	1	1	300	5	3	—
48	Total - -	1,828	2,375	98	379	2,305	1,736	357	329
49	Average Salary -	£169	£129	£130	£89	£179	£125	£155	£126

In the following table, showing allowances and pensions to teachers, it is curious to note the fact that so much larger a number of women than men have claimed disablement allowances, while the difference in the numbers of annuities is so small. No pension has yet exceeded £69 6s. 4d. for a man (allowance £60 15s. in respect of 45 years' service, annuity £8 11s. 4d.) or £59 0s. 4d. for a woman (allowance £53 18s. in respect of 44 years' service, annuity £5 2s. 4d.) The average amounts of the retiring allowances beginning in 1916-17 were £60 for men on an average service of 40 years, and £49 for women on an average service of 38 years. No provision is made for the dependents of a teacher in the case of his or her death. Thus, at present, teachers in most areas have to save out of their salaries to provide to a large extent for their old age, or their dependents in the case of their own death.

England and Wales.

ANNUITIES, ALLOWANCES, AND PENSIONS FOR CERTIFICATED TEACHERS.

Summary (Disablement and Superannuation Allowances and Annuities).

	Year ending 31st March, 1914.		Year ending 31st March, 1913.		Year ending 31st March, 1912.	
	Men.	Women.	Men.	Women.	Men.	Women.
1.	2.	3.	4.	5.	6.	7.
1. DISABLEMENT ALLOWANCES :—						
(a) Number of Allowances commencing during the year	97	195	77	179	66	149
(b) Total Number of Allowances in force at the end of the year	587	1,754	531	1,635	496	1,526
(c) Annual Amount of Allowances commencing during the year	£5,031	£6,472	£3,733	£5,677	£2,477	£3,830
(d) Annual Amount of Allowances in force at the end of the year	£23,664	£47,151	£20,329	£42,668	£18,235	£38,880
(e) Total Amount of Allowances paid during the year :—						
(i) Out of the Deferred Annuity Fund	£336	£410	£267	£286	£221	£209
(ii) Out of the Imperial Exchequer	£20,638	£42,796	£18,142	£38,628	£17,101	£36,574
2. ANNUITIES AND SUPERANNUATION ALLOWANCES.—						
(a) Number of Annuities { and } { or } Allowances commencing during the year	160	168	186	189	196	214
(b) Total Number of Annuities { and } { or } Allowances in force at the end of the year	1,533	1,428	1,459	1,312	1,344	1,168
(c) Annual Amount of Annuities and Allowances commencing during the year	£9,366	£7,957	£10,350	£8,558	£7,632	£6,379
(d) Annual Amount of Annuities and Allowances in force at the end of the year	£64,532	£46,982	£58,476	£40,655	£50,674	£33,444
(e) Total Amount of Annuities and Allowances paid during the year :—						
(i) Annuities (out of the Deferred Annuity Fund)	£4,842	£2,788	£3,991	£2,281	£3,234	£1,792
(ii) Allowances (out of the Imperial Exchequer)	£55,114	£39,013	£48,029	£32,638	£43,223	£27,864

FINANCE.

The following tables show the latest financial figures available. It will be seen that the total net expenditure on public elementary education in 1912-1913 was £14,332,018 from national funds and £13,221,371 from local funds. This excludes loan accounts. The corresponding figures for higher education are £1,224,753 from national and £2,315,310 from local sources.

EXPENDITURE OF THE BOARD OF EDUCATION.

	1913-14.	1912-13.	1911-12.
	£	£	£
1. ADMINISTRATION, INSPECTION, AND EXAMINATION	439,093	*431,006	438,368
2. PUBLIC ELEMENTARY SCHOOLS, &C. :—			
(a) Aid Grants to Local Education Authorities for Elementary Education	2,452,112	2,454,481	2,472,599
(b) Special Grants in aid of certain Local Education Authorities for Elementary Education	350,000	350,000	350,000
(c) Other Grants to meet expenditure in respect of Elementary Education :—			
(i) Grants for Ordinary Public Elementary Schools	8,538,584	8,614,616	8,693,935
(ii) Grants for Higher Elementary Schools	27,050	23,301	22,621
(iii) Grants for Certified Schools for Blind, Deaf, Defective, and Epileptic Children	99,683	98,282	90,013
(d) Grants for Medical Treatment and Care of Children	129,829	50,344	—
(e) Allowances and Pensions for Certificated Teachers	176,005	156,883	145,849
(f) Total	11,773,266	11,747,910	11,775,017
3. SECONDARY SCHOOLS, PUPIL-TEACHERS, BURSARS, &C. :—			
(a) Grants for Secondary Schools	704,486	668,437	656,722
(b) Grants on account of Pupils in Preparatory Classes and Pupil-Teachers	32,022	41,295	54,374
(c) Grants on account of Bursars	40,269	39,626	47,420
(d) Total	776,779	749,359	758,518
4. TECHNICAL, ART, AND EVENING AND SIMILAR SCHOOLS AND CLASSES :—			
(a) Technical Institution Courses	10,093	10,429	32,882*
(b) Day Technical Classes	29,577	27,127	24,762*
(c) Schools of Art	68,200	64,640	65,935
(d) Art Classes	2,705	2,977	3,032
(e) Evening and similar Schools	471,964	480,627	460,587
(f) Total	582,540	585,802	587,200
5. TRAINING OF TEACHERS :—			
(a) Maintenance Grants for Training Colleges, &c. :—			
(i) Training of Teachers for Elementary Schools	476,810	479,087	470,895
(ii) Training of Teachers for Secondary Schools	2,657	2,800	2,305
(iii) Training of Teachers of Domestic Subjects	4,787	4,407	4,386
(b) Grants for provision of Training Colleges and Hostels :—			
(i) Building Grants	95,102	93,313	91,343
(ii) Grants in aid for renting temporary premises	1,738	3,198	2,153
(c) Total	581,095	582,806	571,084
6. GRANTS TO UNIVERSITY INSTITUTIONS IN RESPECT OF TECHNOLOGICAL WORK	44,623	41,647	
7. GRANTS TOWARDS EXPENDITURE UNDER THE EDUCATION (CHOICE OF EMPLOYMENT) ACT, 1910	2,809	925	—
8. SCHOLARSHIPS, EXHIBITIONS, AWARDS, AND PRIZES	27,321	29,251	29,066
9. IMPERIAL COLLEGE OF SCIENCE AND TECHNOLOGY, AND CHELSEA PHYSIC GARDEN :—			
(a) Imperial College of Science and Technology	30,000	35,000	20,000
(b) Chelsea Physic Garden	150	150	150
10. ROYAL COLLEGE OF ART	9,722	9,506	8,996
11. VICTORIA AND ALBERT MUSEUM	77,800	76,199	78,924
12. SCIENCE MUSEUM	19,150	17,814	17,297
13. BETHNAL GREEN MUSEUM	5,044	5,169	4,937
14. GEOLOGICAL MUSEUM AND GEOLOGICAL SURVEY	20,561	20,590	20,350
15. COMMITTEE ON SOLAR PHYSICS	—	2,202	2,230
16. REFUND TO TEACHERS OF FEES PAID FOR REGISTRATION	—	6,450	—
17. TOTAL	14,389,959	14,341,793	14,312,142
18. Deduct—APPROPRIATIONS IN AID	21,164	9,775	9,282
19. NET TOTAL EXPENDITURE	14,368,794	14,332,018	14,302,859

* The grants paid in 1911-12 for work similar to that to which Head 6 for 1912-13 and 1913-14 relates form part of the entries under Heads 4 (a) and (b) for 1911-12 ; these entries include grants in respect of Medical Schools for which the corresponding educational statistics are not included.

England and Wales.

ACCOUNTS OF LOCAL EDUCATION

Summary of Loan

(A)—Summary of

RECEIPTS.	Financial year from 1st April to 31st March.		
	1912-13.	1911-12.	1910-11.
	£	£	£
1. LOANS RAISED - - - - - - - - -	2,173,171	2,118,250	2,180,346
2 ADVANCES FROM CAPITAL FUNDS - - - -	25,462	69,464	41,213
3. OTHER RECEIPTS - - - - - - - -	18,754	4,197	3,492
4. TOTAL RECEIPTS - - - - - - - -	2,217,387	2,191,912	2,225,053

(B)—Summary of

RECEIPTS.	Financial year from 1st April to 31st March.		
	1912-13.	1911-12.	1910-11.
1. PARLIAMENTARY GRANTS:—	£	£	£
(a) Grants under the Agricultural Rates Act, 1896, &c. -	114,788	114,750	114,717
(b) Grants other than for Industrial and Special Schools	11,529,763	11,512,719	11,309,534*
(c) Grants for Industrial and Special Schools - -	116,484	107,970	105,880
(d) Total - - - - - - - - -	11,761,036	11,735,440	11,530,132
2. RATES AND BOROUGH FUNDS - - - - - -	13,221,371	12,750,115	12,216,898
3. IN RESPECT OF INDUSTRIAL AND SPECIAL SCHOOLS :—			
(a) Contributions from Local Authorities and Boards of Guardians - - - - - - -	42,262	41,866	38,614
(b) Contributions from Parents - - - - -	15,143	14,046	13,508
(c) From sale of Goods and Work done - - - -	8,451	8,459	7,900
(d) Other Receipts (excluding Grants) - - - -	7,526	955	1,247
(e) Total - - - - - - - - -	73,383	65,329	61,271
4. OTHER RECEIPTS FROM LOCAL AUTHORITIES - -	62,983	63,416	69,605
5. SCHOOL FEES (less amounts paid to Managers of Voluntary Schools) ; AND SALE OF BOOKS AND OTHER ARTICLES (Public Elementary Schools) - -	138,305	129,508	126,903
6. ENDOWMENTS - - - - - - - - -	21,401	22,004	21,335
7. OTHER RECEIPTS :—			
(a) From Teachers for Rent of Houses - - - -	13,770	14,238	13,177
(b) Miscellaneous - - - - - - -	111,705	78,186	90,283
8. TOTAL RECEIPTS - - - - - - -	25,403,958	24,858,238	24,129,608

* Includes £6,242 Building Grants in aid of the provision of Public Elementary Schools.

England and Wales.

AUTHORITIES (ELEMENTARY EDUCATION).

and Current Accounts.

Loan Accounts.

PAYMENTS.	Financial year from 1st April to 31st March.		
	1912-13.	1911-12.	1910-11.
	£	£	£
1. PURCHASE OF LAND; AND ERECTION, ENLARGEMENT, OR ALTERATION OF SCHOOL BUILDINGS - - -	2,147,706	1,830,998	2,137,078
2. FURNISHING OF SCHOOL BUILDINGS - - - -	67,520	69,414	86,049
3 OTHER PAYMENTS - - - - - - - -	74,367	62,134	75,827
4. TOTAL PAYMENTS - - - - - - -	2,289,594	1,962,547	2,298,955

Current Accounts.

PAYMENTS.	Financial year from 1st April to 31st March.		
	1912-13.	1911-12.	1910-11.
1. IN RESPECT OF ORDINARY PUBLIC ELEMENTARY SCHOOLS (excluding Loan Charges):—	£	£	£
(a) Purchase of Land; and erection, enlargement, or alteration of School Buildings - - -	237,034	207,767	230,241
(b) Maintenance of Land, Buildings, and Furniture (including purchase of Furniture) - -	679,702	644,106	614,050
(c) Salaries of Teachers - - - - -	16,062,078	15,663,827	15,241,202
(d) Other Expenses of Maintenance - - -	2,979,250	2,837,571	2,756,239
(e) Contributions to Local Education Authorities - -	60,087	58,086	58,733
(f) Total - - - - - - -	20,018,153	19,411,360	18,900,466
2. IN RESPECT OF HIGHER ELEMENTARY SCHOOLS (excluding Loan Charges):—			
(a) Purchase of Land, and erection, enlargement, or alteration of School Buildings - - -	763	1,571	2,170
(b) Maintenance of Land, Buildings, and Furniture (including purchase of Furniture) - -	3,593	3,592	4,569
(c) Salaries of Teachers - - - - -	74,651	83,855	95,763
(d) Other Expenses of Maintenance - - -	20,997	21,397	23,719
(e) Contributions to Local Education Authorities -	356	146	293
(f) Total - - - - - - -	100,362	110,564	126,517
3. IN RESPECT OF INDUSTRIAL AND SPECIAL SCHOOLS (excluding Loan Charges):—			
(a) Schools under the management of the Council -	401,450	365,137	349,169
(b) Contributions to other Schools, and other Expenses -	230,798	223,312	217,306
(c) Total - - - - - - -	632,249	588,449	566,476
4. ADMINISTRATION :—			
(a) For enforcement of School Attendance - - -	301,131	312,839	310,241
(b) Administration other than School Attendance (including Loan Charges for Offices) - - -	1,040,808	970,368	901,580
(c) Total - - - - - - -	1,341,940	1,283,207	1,211,821
5. LOAN CHARGES (PRINCIPAL AND INTEREST) other than for Offices - - - - - - - -	3,039,972	2,932,466	2,859,439
6. SCHOOL MEDICAL SERVICE - - - - - -	216,499	197,128	187,000
7. EXPENSES UNDER THE EDUCATION (PROVISION OF MEALS) ACT, 1906 - - - - - -	168,369	143,486	153,874
8. OTHER PAYMENTS (excluding proportion of Fees paid to Managers of Voluntary Schools) - -	39,898	38,174	32,516
9. TOTAL PAYMENTS - - - - - - -	25,557,356	24,704,837	24,038,113

England and Wales.

DETAILS OF CURRENT ACCOUNTS FOR THE YEAR ENDING

of Local Education Authority

Reference Number.	Type of area of Local Education Authority for Elementary Education.	RECEIPTS.				
		Parliamentary Grants.				Rates and Borough Funds.
		Grants under the Agricultural Rates Act, 1896, &c.	Grants other than for Industrial and Special Schools.	Grants for Industrial Schools.	Grants for Special Schools.	
	1.	2.	3.	4.	5.	6.
1	1. ADMINISTRATIVE COUNTIES (other than LONDON): (a) Areas under COUNTY COUNCILS · · ·	£ 102,065	£ 4,495,529	£ 7,165	£ 488	£ 4,008,264
2	(b) BOROUGHS · · · ·	2,981	1,149,024	—	906	1,082,346
3	(c) URBAN DISTRICTS · · ·	2,626	855,305	—	1,398	834,191
4	Total of above · · · ·	107,673	6,499,860	7,165	2,793	5,924,801
5	2. LONDON · · · · ·	702	1,290,807	8,355	42,222	3,448,906
6	3. COUNTY BOROUGHS · · ·	6,413	3,739,096	19,879	29,799	3,847,664
7	Total for Urban Authorities [1 (b) and (c), 2, and 3] · · ·	12,723	7,034,233	28,235	74,327	9,213,107
8	4. JOINT AUTHORITIES · · · ·	—	—	5,292	975	—
9	Total · · · · ·	114,788	11,529,763	40,692	75,791	13,221,371

Reference Number.	Type of area of Local Education Authority for Elementary Education.	RECEIPTS—continued.				
		Special Schools.				
		Contributions from Local Education Authorities.	Contributions from Boards of Guardians.	Contributions from Parents.	Sale of Goods and Work done.	Other Receipts (excluding Grants).
	12.	13.	14.	15.	16.	17.
10	1. ADMINISTRATIVE COUNTIES (other than LONDON): (a) Areas under COUNTY COUNCILS · · ·	£ 93	£ 70	£ 4,589	£ —	£ · 112
11	(b) BOROUGHS · · · ·	167	6	1,323	31	9
12	(c) URBAN DISTRICTS · · ·	257	—	619	13	—
13	Total of above · · · ·	517	77	6,532	45	121
14	2. LONDON · · · · · ·	916	72	1,142	1,427	—
15	3. COUNTY BOROUGHS · · ·	7,291	284	6,051	1,164	1,512
16	Total for Urban Authorities [1 (b) and (c), 2, and 3] · · ·	8,632	363	9,137	2,637	1,522
17	4. JOINT AUTHORITIES · · · ·	8,218	127	28	1	25
18	Total · · · · ·	16,944	561	13,755	2,639	1,660

England and Wales.

31ST MARCH, 1913, ANALYSED UNDER DIFFERENT TYPES (Elementary Education).

RECEIPTS—continued.

Reference Number.	Industrial Schools.				
	Contributions from Local Education Authorities.	Contributions from Boards of Guardians and other Local Authorities.	Contributions from Parents.	Sale of Goods and Work done.	Other Receipts (excluding Grants).
	7.	8.	9.	10.	11.
	£	£	£	£	£
1	6,321	722	—	1,491	5,668
2	—	23	9	—	—
3	200	—	—	—	13
4	6,521	746	9	1,401	5,681
5	186	—	190	460	—
6	5,505	198	1,184	3,569	71
7	5,891	222	1,383	4,029	84
8	11,362	236	3	291	113
9	23,575	1,180	1,387	5,812	5,865

RECEIPTS—continued.

	Other Receipts from Local Authorities (excluding contributions from Local Authorities and Guardians in respect of Industrial and Special Schools).		School Fees (less amounts paid to Managers of Voluntary Schools); and sale of Books and other Articles (Public Elementary Schools).	Endowments.	From Teachers for Rent of Houses.	Transfers from Loan Account.	Other Receipts.	Total Receipts.	Rate in £ calculated on amount in Column 6.
	Local Education Authorities.	Other Authorities.							
	18.	19.	20.	21.	22.	23.	24.	25.	26.
	£	£	£	£	£	£	£	£	d.
10	14,205	1,273	31,878	17,453	12,578	4,458	19,846	8,734,276	13·0
11	9,308	1,222	18,560	2,046	454	2,392	8,819	2,279,633	13·7
12	10,840	1,373	7,149	258	472	2,743	7,078	1,724,542	20·8
13	34,354	3,869	57,588	19,758	13,505	9,594	35,744	12,738,452	13·9
14	11,279	—	21,459	155	—	—	12,477	4,840,760	19·6
15	12,773	706	59,258	1,488	265	30,661	23,227	7,798,068	17·5
16	44,201	3,302	106,427	3,948	1,192	35,797	51,603	16,643,005	17·9
17	—	—	—	—	—	—	—	26,676	—
18	58,407	4,575	138,305	21,401	13,770	40,256	71,449	25,403,258	16·1

England and Wales.

DETAILS OF CURRENT ACCOUNTS FOR THE YEAR ENDING

of Local Education Authority

Reference Number	Type of area of Local Education Authority for Elementary Education 27	PAYMENTS.						
		In respect of Ordinary Public Elementary Schools (excluding Loan Charges).						
		Purchase of Land: and erection, enlargement, or alteration of School Buildings. 28.	Maintenance of Land and Buildings (including Repairs) 29.	Furniture for Schools (including Repairs). 30.	Salaries of Teachers. 31.	Other Expenses.		Contributions to other Local Education Authorities. 34.
						Books, Apparatus, Stationery, and other Materials for purposes of instruction. 32.	Miscellaneous. 33.	
		£	£	£	£	£	£	£
1	1 ADMINISTRATIVE COUNTIES (other than LONDON): (a) Areas under COUNTY COUNCILS -	90,814	153,198	77,762	5,793,646	343,003	734,966	30,551
2	(b) BOROUGHS -	4,938	38,312	15,430	1,534,637	89,863	177,461	5,305
3	(c) URBAN DISTRICTS -	16,804	37,899	10,371	1,079,149	59,899	131,218	15,629
4	Total of above	112,557	229,410	103,564	8,407,433	492,766	1,043,646	51,486
5	2 LONDON -	74,972	128,612	31,654	2,729,565	136,290	447,860	1,717
6	3. COUNTY BOROUGHS -	49,503	145,189	41,271	4,925,078	243,106	615,579	6,882
7	Total for Urban Authorities [1(b) and (c), 2, and 3] -	146,219	350,014	98,728	10,268,431	529,159	1,372,120	29,535
8	4. JOINT AUTHORITIES -	—	—	—	—	—	—	—
9	Total -	237,034	503,212	176,490	16,062,078	872,163	2,107,086	60,087

Reference Number	Type of area of Local Education Authority for Elementary Education. 43.	PAYMENTS—continued.						
		In respect of Special Schools (excluding Loan Charges).						
		Schools under the management of the Council.				Contributions to Schools under—		Other Expenses. 50.
		Purchase of Land; and erection, enlargement, or alteration of School Buildings. 44.	Maintenance of Land, Buildings, and Furniture (including purchase of Furniture) 45.	Salaries of Teachers. 46.	Other Expenses. 47.	other Local Education Authorities. 48.	other Bodies or Persons. 49.	
		£	£	£	£	£	£	£
10	1 ADMINISTRATIVE COUNTIES (other than LONDON): (a) Areas under COUNTY COUNCILS -	1,846	34	984	484	8,437	38,908	780
11	(b) BOROUGHS -	36	141	1,799	743	1,841	8,426	318
12	(c) URBAN DISTRICTS -	—	127	3,724	1,645	1,260	5,250	219
13	Total of above -	1,883	303	6,508	2,873	11,539	51,685	1,318
14	2. LONDON -	3,142	4,974	85,858	64,189	62	6,168	—
15	3. COUNTY BOROUGHS -	2,067	4,757	50,118	39,668	5,125	33,548	673
16	Total for Urban Authorities [1(b) and (c), 2, and 3] -	5,246	9,999	141,500	106,247	8,289	53,393	1,211
17	4. JOINT AUTHORITIES -	2,015	1,033	2,247	5,406	—	—	—
18	Total -	9,108	11,068	144,733	112,138	16,727	91,402	1,992

England and Wales.

31ST MARCH, 1913, ANALYSED UNDER DIFFERENT TYPES (Elementary Education)—*continued.*

PAYMENTS—*continued.*

Reference Number.	In respect of Higher Elementary Schools (excluding Loan Charges).	In respect of Industrial Schools (excluding Loan Charges).						
		Schools under the management of the Council.				Contributions to Schools under—		Other Expenses.
		Purchase of Land; and erection, enlargement, or alteration of School Buildings.	Maintenance of Land, Buildings, and Furniture (including purchase of Furniture).	Salaries of Teachers	Other Expenses	other Local Authorities.	other Bodies or Persons.	
	35.	36.	37.	38.	39.	40.	41.	42.
	£	£	£	£	£	£	£	£
1	35,292	356	1,902	1,309	15,362	2,802	7,710	451
2	12,018	—	—	—	—	3,387	3,246	98
3	11,693	—	—	—	—	2,684	1,163	3
4	59,004	356	1,902	1,309	15,362	8,874	12,120	553
5	—	1,426	3,309	3,530	22,015	4,100	45,132	2,008
6	41,357	1,420	5,939	12,429	39,406	6,938	40,481	380
7	65,069	2,847	9,248	15,959	61,421	17,110	90,024	2,490
8	—	130	1,529	2,626	11,707	—	87	—
9	100,362	3,334	12,681	19,895	88,491	19,912	97,822	2,942

PAYMENTS—*continued.*

Ref.	Administration.				Loan Charges (Principal and Interest) other than for Offices.			School Medical Service.	Expenses under the Education (Provision of Meals) Act, 1906.	Transfers to Loan Account.	Other Payments (excluding proportion of Fees paid to Managers of Voluntary Schools).	Total Payments.
	For enforcement of School Attendance.		Administration other than School Attendance.		Interest and Dividends.	Principal.						
	Salaries of Officers other than Teachers.	Legal and other Expenses of Administration.	Salaries of Officers other than Teachers.	Legal and other Expenses of Administration (including Loan Charges for Offices).		Repaid otherwise than out of invested Sinking Funds.	Paid into Sinking Funds.					
	51.	52.	53.	54.	55.	56.	57.	58.	59.	60.	61.	62.
	£	£	£	£	£	£	£	£	£	£	£	£
10	99,324	10,107	228,156	136,919	362,909	469,237	9,660	77,255	6,133	434	13,389	8,753,238
11	22,277	2,292	47,056	25,646	121,616	120,221	6,171	25,324	4,896	303	1,621	2,275,435
12	17,505	1,229	31,561	17,932	123,685	126,042	1,537	14,707	9,588	479	1,434	1,724,451
13	139,108	13,629	306,775	180,498	608,212	715,501	17,368	117,287	20,618	1,217	16,445	12,753,124
14	42,209	2,172	199,638	94,366	342,855	—	392,491	38,269	86,473	—	6,649	5,001,720
15	93,868	10,143	168,506	89,207	470,158	453,175	39,232	60,399	61,277	6	15,579	7,772,481
16	175,861	15,838	446,763	227,153	1,058,315	699,439	439,432	138,701	162,235	789	25,285	16,774,088
17	—	—	1,048	766	363	613	—	452	—	—	—	30,029
18	275,185	25,946	675,968	364,839	1,421,588	1,169,290	449,092	216,409	168,369	1,223	38,674	25,557,356

E

England and Wales.

FINANCIAL STATISTICS

(c) ACCOUNTS OF LOCAL

Summary of Loan

(A)—Summary of

RECEIPTS.	Financial year from 1st April to 31st March.		
	1912-13.	1911-12.	1910-11.
	£	£	£
1. LOANS RAISED - - - - - - -	731,529	849,182	966,394
2. ADVANCES FROM CAPITAL FUNDS - - -	1,170	1,815	5,746
3. OTHER RECEIPTS - - - - - - ,	11,362	26,869	17,427
4. TOTAL RECEIPTS - - - - - - , -	744,062	877,867	989,568

(B)—Summary of

RECEIPTS.	Financial year from 1st April to 31st March.		
	1912-13.	1911-12.	1910-11.
	£	£	£
1. RESIDUE GRANTS - - - - - - -	807,985	1,220,755	635,258
2. PARLIAMENTARY GRANTS :—			
(a) Grants for Secondary Schools, Preparatory Classes, Pupil-Teachers, and Bursars - - -	413,100	430,473	465,034
(b) Grants for Technical, Art, and Evening , and similar Schools and Classes - - - - -	567,502	531,841	510,221
(c) Grants for the Training of Teachers other than Pupil-Teachers - - - - - -	215,629*	204,062*	176,983*
(d) Grants from the Treasury under the Welsh Intermediate Education Act, 1889 - - -	25,567	25,149	25,195
(e) Grants under the Agricultural Rates Act, 1896, &c.	2,952	2,941	3,094
(f) Total - - - - - - - -	1,224,753	1,194,466	1,180,531
3 RATES AND BOROUGH FUNDS - - - -	2,094,114	1,923,784	1,973,894
4. RECEIPTS FROM LOCAL AUTHORITIES - -	221,196	219,916	195,450
5. FEES ; AND SALE OF BOOKS AND OTHER ARTICLES -	594,500	532,109	490,084
6. OTHER RECEIPTS - - - - - - -	120,034	151,044	185,002
7 TOTAL RECEIPTS - - - - - - -	5,062,584	5,242,077	4,660,222

* Including Building Grants in respect of Training Colleges and Hostels (Training of Teachers for Elementary Schools), viz., £91,884 in 1912-13, £84,949 in 1911-12, and £57,809 in 1910-11. Also including Grant in aid for renting temporary premises for Training Colleges and Hostels, viz., £3,198 in 1912-13, £2,153 in 1911-12, and £3,238 in 1910-11.

England and Wales.

(Higher Education).

AUTHORITIES (HIGHER EDUCATION).

and Current Accounts.

Loan Accounts.

PAYMENTS.	Financial year from 1st April to 31st March.		
	1912-13.	1911-12.	1910-11.
1. PURCHASE OF LAND; AND ERECTION, ENLARGEMENT, OR ALTERATION OF SCHOOL BUILDINGS	£ 739,291	£ 719,775	£ 837,481
2. FURNISHING OF SCHOOL BUILDINGS	68,776	65,112	51,592
3. OTHER PAYMENTS	35,984	86,145	85,642
4. TOTAL PAYMENTS	844,053	871,032	974,717

Current Accounts.

PAYMENTS.	Financial year from 1st April to 31st March.		
	1912-13.	1911-12.	1910-11.
1. IN RESPECT of SECONDARY SCHOOLS, PREPARATORY CLASSES, AND PUPIL-TEACHER CENTRES (excluding Loan Charges and Payments to Local Authorities) :—	£	£	£
(a) Schools, Classes, and Centres maintained by the Council :—			
(i) Buildings and Equipment	39,551	46,012	45,832
(ii) Apparatus, Stationery, and other Materials	77,907	73,757	67,862
(iii) Salaries of Teachers	820,597	772,851	704,529
(iv) Other Expenses of Maintenance	199,729	187,494	175,773
(b) Schools, Classes, and Centres not maintained by any Council	365,989	319,598	335,731
(c) Aid to Students	384,296	388,457	408.548
(d) Total	1,888,070	1,788,171	1,738,277
2. IN RESPECT OF TECHNICAL, ART, AND EVENING AND SIMILAR SCHOOLS AND CLASSES (excluding Loan Charges and Payments to Local Authorities) :—			
(a) Schools and Classes maintained by the Council :—			
(i) Buildings and Equipment	49,818	48,707	44,668
(ii) Apparatus, Stationery, and other Materials	104,095	100,555	94,338
(iii) Salaries of Teachers	967,535	933,353	837,797
(iv) Other Expenses of Maintenance	330,995	307,199	284,714
(b) Schools and Classes not maintained by any Council	387,173	383,249	352,062
(c) Aid to Students	136,842	131,270	125,088
(d) Total	1,976,460	1,904,336	1,738,670
3. IN RESPECT OF THE TRAINING OF TEACHERS OTHER THAN PUPIL-TEACHERS (excluding Loan Charges and Payments to Local Authorities) :—			
(a) Maintenance of, or aid to, Institutions	152,019	178,756	165,841
(b) Aid to Students	56,867	28,202	29,249
(c) Total	208,887	206,958	195,091
4. PAYMENTS TO LOCAL AUTHORITIES	216,097	225,323	197,033
5. ADMINISTRATION (including Loan Charges for Offices)	270,224	256,534	240,930
6. LOAN CHARGES (PRINCIPAL AND INTEREST) IN RESPECT OF—			
(a) Secondary Schools, Preparatory Classes, and Pupil-Teacher Centres	294,257	263,119	214,754
(b) Technical, Art, and Evening and similar Schools and Classes	162,200	148,901	132,146
(c) the Training of Teachers other than Pupil-Teachers (Training Colleges, Hostels, etc.)	46,200	59,959	30,134
(d) Total	502,659	471,979	377,034
7. OTHER PAYMENTS	186,072	182,702	165,839
8. TOTAL PAYMENTS	5,248,471	5.036,004	4,652,878

England and Wales.

DETAILS OF LOAN ACCOUNTS FOR THE YEAR ENDING
OF LOCAL AUTHORITY

Reference Number.	Type of area of Local Authority.	Number of Local Authorities.		RECEIPTS.				
		Number in existence at any time during the year.	Number to whom the Statistics relate.	Loans Raised.	Advances from Capital Funds.	Transfers from Current Account.	Other Receipts.	Total Receipts.
	1.	2.	3.	4.	5.	6.	7.	8.
1	1. ADMINISTRATIVE COUNTIES (other than LONDON)	62†	46	£ 329,772	£ 1,170	£ 499	£ 5,346	£ 336,788
2	(a) BOROUGHS— (i) with population* over 10,000	139	25	45,695	—	35	438	46,169
3	(ii) with population* not over 10,000	110	—	—	—	—	—	—
4	(iii) Total	249	25	45,695	—	35	438	46,169
5	(b) URBAN DISTRICTS— (i) with population* over 20,000	49	12	31,843	—	—	—	31,843
6	(ii) with population* not over 20,000	760	5	889	—	—	—	889
7	(iii) Total	809	17	32,732	—	—	—	32,732
8	Total for above	1,120	88	408,199	1,170	534	5,784	415,689
9	2. LONDON	1	1	157,556	—	—	—	157,556
10	3. COUNTY BOROUGHS	75	46	165,773	—	4,898	145	170,816
11	Total for Urban Authorities [1 (a) (iii) and (b) (iii), 2, and 3]	1,134	89	401,757	—	4,933	583	407,274
12	Total	1,196	135	731,529	1,170	5,432	5,929	744,062

DETAILS OF CURRENT ACCOUNTS, FOR THE YEAR
OF LOCAL AUTHORITY

Reference Number.	Type of area of Local Authority.	Number of Local Authorities.		RECEIPTS.			
		Number in existence at any time during the year.	Number to whom the Statistics relate.	Residue Grants	Parliamentary		
					Grants for Secondary Schools, Preparatory Classes, Pupil-Teachers, and Bursars.	Grants for Technical, Art, and Evening and similar Schools and Classes.	Grants for the Training of Teachers other than Pupil-Teachers.
	1.	2.	3.	4.	5.	6.	7.
1	1. ADMINISTRATIVE COUNTIES (other than LONDON)	62†	62†	£ 427,435	£ 175,770	£ 200,738	£ 32,414
2	(a) BOROUGHS— (i) with population* over 10,000	139	115	—	14,256	607	4
3	(ii) with population* not over 10,000	110	31	—	1,058	55	—
4	(iii) Total	249	146	—	15,314	663	4
5	(b) URBAN DISTRICTS— (i) with population* over 20,000	49	43	—	4,003	12	—
6	(ii) with population* not over 20,000	760	249	—	809	257	..
7	(iii) Total	809	292	—	4,812	270	—
8	Total for above	1,120	500	427,435	195,897	201,672	32,419
9	2. LONDON	1	1	176,993	24,837	109,038	63,536
10	3. COUNTY BOROUGHS	75	75	203,556	192,365	256,791	119,674
11	Total for Urban Authorities [1 (a) (iii) and (b) (iii), 2, and 3]	1,134	514	380,550	237,329	366,763	183,215
12	Total	1,196	576	807,985	413,100	567,502	215,629

* Population at date of Census of 1901.   † This number includes the Council of the Isles of Scilly.

England and Wales.

31ST MARCH, 1913, ANALYSED UNDER DIFFERENT TYPES (HIGHER EDUCATION).

Reference Number.	PAYMENTS.					
	Purchase, &c., of Land and Buildings. 9.	Furnishing of School Buildings. 10.	Transfers to Current Account. 11.	Repayments of Unexpended Balances. 12.	Other Payments. 13.	Total Payments. 14.
	£	£	£	£	£	£
1	291,708	35,818	6,097	2,421	7,361	343,408
2	36,940	1,968	280	—	3,000	42,190
3	—	—	—	—	—	—
4	36,940	1,968	280	—	3,000	42,190
5	28,169	2,236	7	458	4,903	35,774
6	5,543	135	440	—	—	6,118.
7	33,712	2,371	447	458	4,903	41,896
8	362,361	40,159	6,825	2,879	15,264	427,491
9	156,754	802	—	—	—	157,556
10	220,175	27,815	2,313	—	8,701	259,003
11	447,583	32,957	3,041	458	16,604	500,644
12	739,291	68,776	9,139	2,879	23,965	844,053

ENDING 31ST MARCH, 1913, ANALYSED UNDER DIFFERENT TYPES (HIGHER EDUCATION).

Reference Number.	RECEIPTS—continued.							
	Grants.							
	Grants from the Treasury under the Welsh Intermediate Education Act, 1889. 7 (a).	Grants under the Agricultural Rates Act, 1896, &c. 7 (b).	From Rates, or (if a Borough) from Borough Fund or Rate. 8.	Receipts from Local Authorities. 9.	Fees; and sale of Books and other Articles. 10.	Transfers from Loan Account. 11.	Other Receipts. 12.	Total Receipts. 13.
	£	£	£	£	£	£	£	£
1	20,756	2,942	741,130	23,555	236,739	6,097	41,802	1,009,383
2	—	—	52,990	122,118	28,326	280	6,590	225,174
3	—	—	2,034	2,396	1,490	—	77	7,113
4	—	—	55,024	124,515	29,816	280	6,668	232,887
5	—	—	22,273	15,801	3,341	7	4,013	49,452
6	—	—	22,269	88,321	5,527	440	1,430	69,056
7	—	—	44,542	54,123	8,869	447	5,443	118,509
8	20,756	2,942	840,697	202,194	275,425	6,825	53,914	2,260,180
9	—	—	512,675	—	38,423	—	4,415	929,920
10	4,811	10	740,741	19,002	280,651	2,313	52,564	1,872,483
11	4,811	10	1,352,984	197,640	357,761	3,041	69,092	3,153,200
12	25,567	2,952	2,094,114	221,196	594,500	9,139	110,394	5,062,584

England and Wales.

DETAILS OF CURRENT ACCOUNTS FOR THE YEAR

TYPES OF LOCAL AUTHORITY

Reference Number.	Type of area of Local Authority. 14.	School Population (Secondary Schools, Preparatory Classes, and Pupil-Teacher Centres) on 31st January, 1913. 15.	PAYMENTS.				
			Payments (excluding Loan Charges) in respect of Secondary Schools—				not maintained by any Council. 20.
			maintained by the Council.				
			Buildings and Equipment. 16.	Apparatus, Stationery, and other Materials. 17.	Salaries of Teachers. 18.	Other Expenses. 19.	
1	1. ADMINISTRATIVE COUNTIES (other than LONDON) · · ·	100,023	£ 16,192	£ 33,482	£ 292,307	£ 80,697	£ 231,411
2	(a) BOROUGHS— (i) with population* over 10,000		1,844	3,758	47,392	9,936*	3,710
3	(ii) with population* not over 10,000 · ·		50	230	2,284	290	284
4	(iii) Total · · · ·		1,895	3,989	49,677	10,227	3,994
5	(b) URBAN DISTRICTS— (i) with population* over 20,000		347	532	5,470	1,574	1,280
6	(ii) with population* not over 20,000 · ·		534	559	4,247	632	1,679
7	(iii) Total · · ·		882	1,092	9,717	2,207	2,960
8	Total for above · ⸴		18,970	38,563	351,702	93,131	238,366
9	2. LONDON · · ·	25,649	2,473	3,875	63,646	19,054	105,014
10	3. COUNTY BOROUGHS · ·	74,316	17,320	33,713	387,768	83,045	21,642
11	Total for Urban Authorities[1(a) (iii) and (b) (iii), 2, and 3] ·		22,571	42,670	509,810	114,534	133,611
12	Total · ·	199,988	38,764	76,152	802,118	195,231	365,023

Reference Number.	Type of area of Local Authority. 28.	School Population (Technical, Art, and Evening and similar Schools and Classes). 29.	PAYMENTS—continued.						
			Payments in respect of Technical, Art, and Evening and similar Schools and Classes—					Aid to Students. 35.	Loan Charges (Principal and Interest). 36.
			maintained by the Council.				not maintained by any Council. 34.		
			Buildings and Equipment. 30.	Apparatus, Stationery, and other Materials. 31.	Salaries of Teachers. 32.	Other Expenses. 33.			
13	1. ADMINISTRATIVE COUNTIES (other than LONDON) · · ·	371,088	£ 13,426	£ 30,960	£ 245,591	£ 108,856	£ 107,701	£ 74,236	£ 14,731
14	(a) BOROUGHS— (i) with population* over 10,000		3,307	5,723	60,886	18,169	2,123	920	18,003
15	(ii) with population* not over 10,000 · ·		52	158	1,481	330	87	1	201
16	(iii) Total · · ·		3,360	5,882	62,368	18,500	2,210	922	18,205
17	(b) URBAN DISTRICTS— (i) with population* over 20,000		976	1,002	11,145	3,023	93	409	2,937
18	(ii) with population* not over 20,000 · ·		1,273	2,664	28,175	7,735	1,927	1,279	6,107
19	(iii) Total · · ·		2,250	3,666	39,320	10,758	2,021	1,688	9,045
20	Total for above ·		12,037	40,509	347,281	138,115	111,933	76,847	41,982
21	2. LONDON · · · ·	194,209	4,012	17,523	175,684	62,501	190,311	26,040	20,218
22	3. COUNTY BOROUGHS · ·	292,251	26,768	46,062	444,589	130,378	84,928	33,954	99,999
23	Total for Urban Authorities[1(a) (iii) and (b) (iii), 2, and 3] ·		36,391	73,135	721,943	222,139	279,471	62,606	147,468
24	Total · · ·	857,548	49,818	104,095	967,535	330,995	387,173	136,842	162,200

* Population at date of Census of 1901.

England and Wales.

ENDING 31ST MARCH, 1913, UNDER DIFFERENT
(HIGHER EDUCATION).—*Continued.*

Reference Number.	PAYMENTS—*continued.*						
	Payments (excluding Loan Charges) in respect of Preparatory Classes and Pupil-Teacher Centres, other than those provided in Secondary Schools—					Payments in respect of Secondary Schools, Preparatory Classes, and Pupil-Teacher Centres.	
	maintained by the Council.				not maintained by any Council.	Aid to Students.	Loan Charges (Principal and Interest).
	Buildings and Equipment.	Apparatus, Stationery, and other Materials.	Salaries of Teachers.	Other Expenses.			
	21.	22.	23.	24.	25.	26.	27.
	£	£	£	£	£	£	£
1	558	950	8,436	1,993	144	164,348	128,618
2	5	116	789	108	—	3,526	15,191
3	—	—	—	—	—	86	283
4	5	116	789	108	—	3,612	15,474
5	90	38	766	57•	—	1,463	9,330
6	—	—	—	—	—	365	1,896
7	90	38	766	57	—	1,828	11,227
8	654	1,106	9,982	2,159	144	169,789	155,320
9	—	—	—	—	—	129,140	24,005
10	132	648	8,495	2,338	821	85,366	114,931
11	228	803	10,052	2,504	821	219,948	165,638
12	786	1,754	18,478	4,497	965	384,296	294,257

	PAYMENTS—*continued.*										
	Payments in respect of the Training of Teachers other than Pupil-Teachers.			Payments to Local Authorities.				Administration (including Loan Charges for Offices).	Transfers to Loan Account.	Other Payments.	Total Payments.
	Maintenance of, or aid to, Institutions (excluding Loan Charges).	Aid to Students.	Loan Charges for Training Colleges and Hostels (Principal and Interest).	In respect of—							
				Secondary Schools, Preparatory Classes, and Pupil-Teacher Centres.	Technical, Art, and Evening and similar Schools and Classes.	the Training of Teachers other than Pupil-Teachers.	Other Payments, not classified.				
	37.	38.	39.	40.	41.	42.	43.	44.	45.	46.	47.
	£	£	£	£	£	£	£	£	£	£	£
13	26,841	18,172	3,116	55,360	131,661	1,870	6,201	108,024	499	80,189	1,986,575
14	54	144	—	4,001	5,333	—	3,218	10,381	35	7,737	226,513
15	30	—	—	100	641	—	—	461	—	17	7,075
16	84	144	—	4,191	5,975	—	3,218	10,843	35	7,754	233,589
17	—	1,060	—	868	1,082	—	—	2,342	—	2,871	48,766
18	—	—	—	1,019	1,810	—	274	4,491	—	2,401	69,076
19	—	1,060	—	1,887	2,893	—	274	6,833	—	5,273	117,843
20	26,925	19,378	3,116	61,439	140,529	1,870	9,694	125,700	534	93,216	2,338,007
21	46,471	25,407	9,526	—	—	—	—	69,158	—	26,863	1,919,931
22	78,621	12,082	33,558	1,612	439	504	6	75,365	4,898	60,558	1,890,532
23	125,177	38,694	43,084	7,692	9,308	504	3,499	162,200	4,933	100,450	3,261,896
24	152,019	56,867	46,200	63,052	140,969	2,374	9,701	270,224	5,432	180,639	5,248,471

THE EDUCATIONAL SYSTEM OF IRELAND.

By Professor Alfred Rahilly, M.A., B.Sc.

The Board System.

Autocracy is the keynote to Irish government and education. Apart from the three Universities, all administrative authority in education is vested in a number of small Boards nominated by the English Government—the Board of National Education, the Intermediate Board, the Department of Agriculture and Technical Instruction, the Commissioners of Education for our few educational endowments, the Local Government Board for workhouse, industrial, and reformatory schools, and the Board of Works for school buildings. Such a redundancy of authorities is financially very wasteful; in the Intermediate Board, for instance, the expenses of administration, inspection, and examination exceed 50 per cent. of the entire school grant. It also accounts for the overlapping, the want of co-ordination, the unadaptability, the discontinuous stratification of Irish educational systems. Moreover, the concentration of all real authority and initiative in the hands of unelected, unrepresentative Boards has resulted in widespread apathy in educational matters among the public and the teachers; there is everywhere an oppressive sense of the futility of striving to effect any reform by suggestion or agitation. No doubt there is much to be said for the benevolent despotism of experts even in a country which professes democracy. But in Ireland it is notorious that the real educationists and educators have no voice; the teachers, for instance, are never consulted, they have become drilled into implicit acceptance of any system imposed from above at short notice. And the Boards which thus usurp the administration of all publicly financed education are responsible to no one; as at present constituted they are decidedly out of touch with the educational ideals of the country—witness the National Board's recent undignified doctoring of Irish History. In any review of Irish education, however brief, it is necessary thus to emphasise this un-national, unrepresentative, and undemocratic basis as its fundamental defect.

The National Schools.

The National Board was established in 1831 to replace the earlier proselytizing institutions. Since 1860 it consists of 20 members—ten Catholics and ten Protestants—appointed by the Lord Lieutenant, all unpaid except the Resident Commissioner. On paper the system of elementary education aims at providing combined instruction in secular subjects and separate instruction in religion; but in reality only about 50 religiously mixed (chiefly inter-Protestant) schools exist in Ireland. This denominational character—without which the system would never have succeeded—is secured by the appointment of a local clergyman as Manager. The Manager's right to appoint and remove teachers is not limited by any appeal to civil authority, though in the case of Catholic managers appointments and removals require the approval of the Bishop. The Board pays all salaries through the Manager and provides at least two-thirds of the cost of new buildings.

The Manager transacts all official school business with the Board and its inspectors. He can determine the curriculum, choose the text-books, arrange the religious instruction—subject to the regulations of the Board. These regulations are skilfully and effectively designed to make the secular instruction absolutely colourless on all national and religious questions. As a result of these official restrictions, the fine primary schools of the Christian Brothers have secured freedom by remaining entirely outside the system of the National Board. In spite of these drawbacks the present *de facto* denominationalism of education has insured the acceptance of the Board scheme. At the same time there seems to be a growing feeling that some modifications of the present managerial system are necessary. The difficulty is to combine therewith securer status for the teachers and more local interest in, and responsibility for, education. The development will probably be on the lines of the English system of six Managers administering the school under a deed of trust.

Owing to the apathy, or rather the powerlessness, of the public there are many obvious defects in our elementary school system. The buildings in many cases are quite unfit and even insanitary; there is practically no provision of playgrounds and play-centres and no medical inspection—the grants for dental clinics have remained largely unused; only two county boroughs and nine urban districts have provided meals for school children.* The attendance at school is very deficient. In Dublin alone there are well over 8,000 children of school age who are attending no school. There are 39 urban and 109 rural districts without any School Attendance Committee. But, indeed, the law of compulsory attendance, as it now exists in Ireland, is a mere sham. It requires attendance on only 150 out of the 220 school days, and the means provided for securing this, minimum are ludicrously cumbrous and inadequate. Education should be made really compulsory until 16, with exemptions only to those over 14; and the local authorities should be obliged to adopt the Children's Employment Act of 1903.

Intermediate Education.

Secondary education is controlled by the Intermediate Education Board, established in 1878, which consists of twelve unpaid members (six Catholic and six Protestant). The entire function of the Board consists in distributing money grants to schools and their pupils who have been subjected to examination and inspection in the secular subjects of education. Last year this school grant amounted to £41,996, or an average of £6 16s. 9d. per pupil passed; there was also an inspection grant of £8,013. The Department also inspects the science teaching in secondary schools—which the other Board examines!—and last year made therefor a grant of £29,000, averaging £2 1s. 9d. per pupil. Apart from these subventions, Irish secondary education is in private hands; it is denominational in ownership and management; no State secondary school has ever existed in Ireland. Anyone can anywhere establish an intermediate school, if he secures the legal quorum of " seven students eligible as regards age for the Board's examinations," and he will receive result fees for any pupils

---

* Since this was written the Treasury has at last promised a grant in aid as is given in Great Britain.

who happen to pass. There is no power to deal with schools which under any system ought not to exist; and there is no means of helping small and struggling schools. The corresponding Welsh Board raise to £400 the grants earned by small schools, and in England the minimum grant to any recognised secondary school is £300. Last year the average grant (examination and inspection) to an Irish school was less than £147; 177 schools received less than £100 each; 68 schools presented each less than ten pupils. In addition to such grant Irish secondary schools are supported by the pupils' fees and by funds provided by religious orders and diocesan organizations. In Ireland very little is contributed to education by wealthy individuals; and there are no richly endowed " public schools," at least no Catholic. Hence most of the secondary schools are financially unsound, many being run at an actual loss; most of them survive only by having wholly unpaid religious teachers and greatly underpaid lay teachers.

It should be noted that the word " intermediate " is really a misnomer, for it is the final education of the vast majority of the students. Of every 100 who pass the Junior Grade only 43 pass the Middle, and of these only 25 pass the Senior Grade, and a fraction of these survivors pass to the Universities. These figures are a sufficient indication that our present system of secondary education is not adapted to the needs of the country. In addition to the colourless cosmopolitan neutrality which seems to be the official ideal of Irish culture, the whole education is bookish and lifeless; religion, civics, art, music, speaking, deportment, hygiene, being entirely " outside the course." This narrow, deadening uniformity, which suffers no individual or national initiative, is attributed to the examination system on which the result fees are largely based. But it is not really inherent in a properly conducted scheme of curricula and examinations; it is due to the concentration of all power into the hands of a dozen Commissioners appointed to secure a religious equipoise and amenable to no criticism. Doubtless, the present method of result fees is unsatisfactory; it has led, for instance, to competitive advertising and to touting for exhibitioners. But with the Board as at present constituted it is the only method which can secure public confidence.

FINANCE.

For the financial shortcomings of Irish education the responsibility lies not with the Boards but with the English Treasury. It is with Scotland rather than with England that Irish conditions are comparable. If since 1903 educational grants to Ireland had been on the same scale (per head of population) as the Scottish, we should have received about seven and a-half millions more than we did; even adopting the English scale, our deficit for the same period would be over two and a-half millions. In Great Britain secondary education secures £1,211,000 from the Treasury and about £3,282,000 from local taxation and rates. The total income of the Irish Intermediate Board for 1916 was £83,913, exclusive of the Teachers' Salaries' Grant. Not a penny of this really comes from the English Treasury; it consists mainly of interest on portion of the Irish Church Fund Surplus and an allocation from the Local Taxation Account. While in 1900 there were 7,608 pupils examined by the Intermediate Board and £19,313 distributed in rewards, in 1917 there were 11,415 pupils examined and about 6,000 inspected, but the rewards were only £6,526.

Only when the Board unanimously threatened to resign in 1908 after six years of fruitless appeals was it allowed by the Treasury to satisfy its statutory obligation to appoint inspectors. The income of the Intermediate Board is now partly fixed and independent of the Treasury, but it is stationary and inelastic. The English and Scotch Departments usually have Supplementary Estimates, and more than once have been allowed to retain unexpended balances and to spend them under other heads of vote. In Ireland they are always surrendered by the National Board; for example, the five thousand a year saved by the abolition of the book department automatically went back to England. It is typical of the Government's attitude towards Irish education that no special grant analogous to that for Great Britain should be allocated this year to Ireland. The Government just waits to see if there will be an outcry! And when the grant is grudgingly promised, it is, of course, a mere fraction of Ireland's proportional share.

Though there is in Ireland no local rate towards primary education, it must not be forgotten that a very substantial sum is annually contributed. It was the Government which withdrew the local rating of Boards of Guardians and abolished the school fees. The Managers undertake gratuitously very onerous duties. Many of the best and largest schools are built wholly by local generosity; one-third of the cost of most State-aided schools is borne by the parishioners. All the furnishing and books, half the heating and cleaning, all the school prizes, are locally provided. In many cases food and clothing are provided by the people for poor children.* Altogether it has been estimated that on an average £50 is collected yearly for educational purposes in every Catholic parish in Ireland by the clerical Managers.

It is unfortunate that the most keenly debated problems of Irish education are not so much educational as financial. This is most prominent in the case of the teachers whose energies seem to be largely absorbed in efforts to secure a living wage. The following table of salaries of elementary school teachers will probably help to explain the grievance† :—

	Principals.		Assistants.	
	Men.	Women.	Men.	Women.
	£	£	£	£
England	176 ...	126	129 ...	95
Scotland	192 ...	97	142 ...	85
Ireland	116 ...	92	83 ...	70

In fact, over 10,000 fully certificated teachers in Ireland (*i.e.*, about 75 per cent. of the whole) receive less than £2 a week. And in the above table no account has been taken of 2,300 adult whole-time women teachers whose salaries range from £24 to £28 a year. This

---

* " In one school alone in this parish up to £100 a year is spent on food and clothes for the poor children in attendance."—MGR. RYAN, Cashel, 26th May, 1917.

† The meagre grant recently promised has coupled with it conditions which seem designed to split the teachers' organisation into rival civic and rural leagues. The whole proceedings present an exhibition of bureaucratic bullying and squabbling on the part of the Treasury, Chief Secretary, and National Board —an attempt to reduce the Irish teachers to the status of foreign beggars. Ireland is in no mood to tolerate much more of this tyranny.

extraordinary disparity between the incomes of teachers in Ireland and England—in spite of the fact that a much larger percentage of our teachers are trained—is part of the general economic policy of withholding Irish money from developing Irish resources. And there is some evidence that in this case the specific purpose is to attract competent Irish teachers over to England and Scotland. It is small wonder that the Irish National Teachers have come to the conclusion that resolutions, speeches, and appeals are waste of time; it is indicative of the new spirit that the Central Executive Committee has applied for affiliation to the Trades Union Congress.

The condition of lay secondary teachers is even worse than that of the National Teachers. In its last report the Intermediate Board declares that " no improvement in the secondary education of the country can be anticipated until steps are taken to ameliorate the condition of the teachers." According to this report, out of a total of 1,142 lay teachers (1) less than 35 per cent. have salaries (men £140, women £90) and security of tenure (guarantee of three months' notice), satisfying the very modest requirements of the Grant for Teachers' Salaries; (2) considerably over 35 per cent. are non-resident and in receipt of a salary of less than £100; (3) not 40 assistant teachers enjoy an annual salary of £200 or over. The average salary is well under £2 a week, and everyone knows cases of graduates teaching for less than £1 a week. Even the Birrell grant of £40,000, which is given " to improve the position of assistant lay teachers in Irish secondary schools and for no other purpose,"* has only partially improved matters, for in very many cases, especially in the smaller schools, the teachers receive nothing at all from the grant. The lay secondary teacher is, in Mr. Birrell's words, " the victim of the excellent cheap system now prevailing in Ireland "; his most pressing need is to form a strong union or organisation. But, indeed, the whole position of Irish secondary education is financially most precarious; were it not for the self-sacrifice of religious monks and nuns it would long since have collapsed.

TECHNICAL AND AGRICULTURAL EDUCATION.

Technical instruction under local authorities has been very successful in Ireland. In 1915-16 there were 44,185 students, practically all in evening classes; but there are also about a dozen Day Trades Preparatory Schools. Schemes of technical education must be approved by the local authority and by the Department; the contribution of a local rate, generally 1d. in the £, is essential. The limitation of all such technical instruction—as also of technological research—in Ireland lies in the fact that the resources of the country are largely undeveloped and under present conditions largely undevelopable. But apart from this, technical instruction is greatly impeded by the unfitness of the boys leaving the national schools— often before reaching the third standard. There is great need for supplementary evening schools, the only condition for their establishment under the National Board being the provision of a lighted, heated, and equipped school-room. Yet while in 1905-6 there were 631 evening schools, there were only 323 in 1912-13; and since 1904

---

* Mr. Birrell, 19th February, 1914.

£144,000 voted for the purpose has actually been unspent. The Catholic Working Boys' Technical Aid Association has put forward an excellent scheme for establishing continuation classes in connection with each national school. There is only one difficulty : widespread irresponsibility and apathy.

It must never be forgotten that Ireland is primarily agricultural, not industrial. All the more surprising seems the wide cleavage between our elementary education and the main occupation of the people. This was intelligible enough in the near past when the people had a very precarious and uncertain tenure of the land and when consequently parents and children regarded schooling as a preliminary to life elsewhere. In recent years there were half-hearted attempts to teach agriculture out of books and even to, add demonstration plots; but the efforts were mostly misplaced and unreal. Of all the " practical " subjects added to the primary school course only a few (such as gardening and cookery) survive. The teaching of such subjects may be possible in densely populated districts, but in the ordinary one- or two-teacher school they are a mere divagation. Their appearance in Irish schools has coincided with, or resulted in, a deterioration in systematic training in reading, writing, spelling, and calculation. What rural Ireland really needs is primary continuation schools to supersede the sixth standard in the present schools and to carry the instruction into practical agriculture. At present we have only tinkering at the problem by way of casual or itinerant lecturers and a few agricultural " stations." In a country like Ireland our present type of secondary education is positively dangerous, for it simply declasses and unfits youths for the greatest industry of the nation. The Universities merely accentuate the danger, for, if we except a laudable beginning in Belfast, they have no connection, by way of guidance or research, with the vital processes of the nation's economic life.

Adult Education.

It may surprise English readers to be told that in no country is adult education so flourishing as in Ireland. The Gaelic League and related activities are really the Irish equivalent of the Workers' Educational Association. The greatest educational achievement of Ireland is to be found in the Gaelic Movement, which is entirely voluntary—the educational grants altogether amount only to a few thousands pounds. The students are practically all adult, and are chiefly drawn from the ranks of office clerks, shop assistants, teachers, and such like. In most towns there is a branch of the Gaelic League, with evening classes. In the *Gaeltacht*, or Irish-speaking districts, there are much frequented summer schools; and permanent colleges are open during the year in Dublin, Cork, and Belfast. The education is not merely linguistic, but includes Irish history, literature, music, and art. The movement has had a very important social influence and has helped to provide healthy and ennobling recreation—hurling and *camóg*, *céilidhthe*, which are a unique combination of singing, dancing, and storytelling. There is an annual *Oireachtas* at which large prizes are offered for collections of Irish folktales and oral traditions, composition of Irish dramas and poetry, Irish music and dancing; besides there are numerous similar local *Feiseanna*. Altogether this thoroughly spontaneous national movement has helped to counteract the evil influence of the artificially imposed official education. But it is as yet defective inasmuch as it is disjoined from social and economic study, and, with the possible exception of some of the Transport Workers, is out of touch with the Irish Labour Movement. The study of the social, civic, and economic problems of Ireland is absolutely excluded from Irish elementary and secondary education and receives only a meagre and cursory treatment in the Universities. The backward condition of the Irish workers' education is, therefore, not to be wondered at. In an experiment undertaken by two professors of Cork University College it has been conclusively shown that Irish manual workers quite readily appreciate higher education in social and economic subjects when properly brought within their reach. As a result of these very successful " Economic Conferences " (which were affiliated to the W.E.A.), Cork Corporation voted a grant of £150 for University Extension. This is the first occasion on which this power, conferred by the Irish Universities Act (1908), has been availed of. It remains to be seen whether the National University will prove itself really national by making higher education available to the Irish working class. Since 1910 there have been tutorial classes in the Queen's University, Belfast. It has been the custom for the Lecturer in Economic History to give one or two courses for the W.E.A. each winter, but the teaching is purely voluntary and the Corporation of Belfast contributes nothing.* Without such financial help the incipient movement can hardly succeed. Yet at the moment there is a widespread interest in Irish social and economic problems. The chief hindrance to any attempt at study or action lies in the utter lack of any organisation and in the difficulty of securing suitable tutors. If the problem could be solved in any one place—say, Belfast, or Dublin, or Cork—the example would probably prove infectious. Anyway, the Irish workers are one of the most thoughtful elements of the nation; they are increasing in self-consciousness, discipline, and organisation. It will not be long before they will claim to share, as a class, in the privilege of higher education.

---

* In spite of assertions to the contrary, it has legal power to contribute to the amount of 1d. in the £, or more with the consent of the L.G.B. " The Council of any county or county borough in Ireland . . . may place any sums at the disposal of any University in Ireland, or any college thereof, to be applied for any educational purposes which the Council may consider will benefit their county or borough."—Irish Universities Act (1908), s 10, § 2.

THE EDUCATIONAL SYSTEM OF SCOTLAND.

By Dr. William Boyd
(Lecturer in Education, Glasgow University).

The Education Act of 1872, which brought the present educational system of Scotland into being, differed in some significant respects from its English predecessor of 1870. Following the old Scottish tradition, according to which even the parish schools might give a higher education that would take their best scholars up to the Universities, it made provision not only for elementary, but for secondary education as well. The parish schools under the control of the two great Presbyterian churches and the burgh grammar schools under the control of the Town Councils were both transferred to the School Boards, which were established throughout the country as the local educational authorities. At the head of the system was put an Education Department, exercising jurisdiction of some kind on behalf of the State over all schools. On these foundations the existing system has gradually been reared. Its distinctive features are : (1) the absence of any serious sectarian divisions; (2) a fairly simple method of administration, affecting directly or indirectly practically all education in Scotland except that of the Universities; (3) an organisation of the various types of schools, which makes it comparatively easy for the capable pupil in the smallest village school to reach any of the institutions of higher learning.

1. The " religious " difficulty is scarcely felt in Scotland because the great majority of the people are Presbyterians, and have no objection to their children attending the Board schools, where they will generally be taught the Bible and the Shorter Catechism under the safeguard of a conscience clause. The only dissenters in an educational sense are the Episcopalians and the Catholics, the latter of whom constitute a large section of the population in the S.W. of Scotland. These have schools under the management of their own clergy, which draw grants from the National Exchequer like all schools under the inspection of the Education Department, but receive no share of the money raised by local rates. In the Scottish Education Bill now before the country, provision is made for putting these schools on the same footing as the others if they are prepared to accept local control in all matters except the appointment of teachers and the supervision of religious instruction. ·

2. The administration of Scottish education is in the hands of School Boards, Secondary Education Committees, and the Scotch Education Department. (a) There are 971 School Boards over the country, some with only a single school under their care, most of them with several, one with about a hundred. Their primary duty is to make provision for the education of all children up to the leaving age of 14, but they have also charge of a large number of the schools which go beyond the elementary stage as well as of the continuation classes. Their most important business is the appointment and remuneration of teachers, besides which they have the responsibility

for school time-tables, religious instruction, medical inspection, etc. The members of the Boards are elected triennially by a method of cumulative voting intended for the protection of minorities, which has had the effect of giving clergymen an unduly large proportion of seats. (*b*) There are 39 Secondary Education Committees, for the most part County Committees, charged with the administration of an Education Fund, meant in the first instance for special expenditures on secondary education (the inspection and examination of secondary schools, the provision of bursaries for pupils attending central schools, the supplementing of local contributions for the maintenance of schools serving a wide area, etc.), but extending also to other forms of educational work beyond the compass of parochial Boards. The Committees consist of representatives from various local bodies concerned with education, some co-opted members, and an inspector or other representative of the Education Department. Their constitution makes them rather colourless, ineffective bodies. (*c*) The Education Department is the real master of Scottish education. In virtue of its statutory right of framing the annual Codes for primary and continuation education and of administering the grants for all classes of schools, it exercises an overwhelming influence on the School Boards and Secondary Committees; and its conduct of the leaving certificate, which is conferred at the end of a complete course of secondary instruction, extends its power over the curriculum and work of the endowed higher class schools which are not in receipt of grants. Nominally it acts on behalf of a Committee of the Privy Council, and it has the Secretary for Scotland as its spokesman in Parliament. In actual fact the power behind the throne is the Permanent Secretary. Under the very capable direction of Sir John Struthers, the present Secretary, its formidable bureaucratic powers have been employed with a wisdom and restraint that have done much to raise the standard of Scottish education.

3. Three and a-half centuries ago John Knox planned a sequence of schools that would enable any boy with the necessary ability, irrespective of social rank, to pass by graded steps from the parish school right up to the University. To-day that democratic ideal is more completely realised in Scotland than in any country in the world. The general character of the Scottish school system can perhaps be most easily grasped by following the career of a typical pupil—whether boy or girl is immaterial, since co-education is practically universal from the infant-room to the University except in a few schools in the large cities. Let us suppose that this pupil begins his education in a village or small town school at the age of 5. His teachers will all be trained and certificated : some of them may even be University graduates. Given ordinary ability he goes through infant, junior, and senior divisions of the primary school; and about the age of 12 he passes the qualifying examination—the only individual examination in the primary school—in the various subjects of his previous course, and is ready to go on to the next stage. If he is likely to leave at 14, which (apart from carefully restricted exemptions) is the statutory leaving age, he enters the Supplementary Course, and continues his primary work with the addition of certain commercial, industrial, rural or domestic subjects, as the case may be. On the satisfactory completion of this course he receives a merit certificate, which is the

passport to the continuation classes and possibly through them to a technical college. If, on the other hand, he is willing to spend at least three years at secondary work he will enter an Intermediate Course, where the teachers all hold a higher qualification than the primary teachers. If the school he has hitherto attended has been a higher grade school, either with a three years' course beyond the primary stage, or with a full secondary course of at least five years, as many of the board schools have become, he will not need to leave. Otherwise, he must go to some central school, probably with the help of a county bursary. This will be either a higher grade school or one of the old burgh schools now officially known as a higher class public school. Here he will either pay no fees, or at the most very moderate fees : if he is a boy of any capacity at all poverty will certainly not bar his way to a secondary education anywhere in Scotland. The Intermediate Course he begins now is a uniform course, including English, history, geography, at least one foreign language, science, and drawing. The successful completion of the course is marked by the receipt of the intermediate certificate. As the pupil by this time is 15 or 16, it is not improbable that he will elect to leave school to take up some trade or business, and in the larger towns at least he will have plenty of facilities for preparing himself for his future work by attendance at the higher continuation classes, etc. If, however, he still continues to attend school a variety of courses is open to him. Not improbably he may think of becoming a teacher, teaching being the profession most easily entered by youths of limited means. In that case he will become a junior student, and, in addition to the ordinary secondary work, will take up some semi-professional subjects and get a little experience of teaching under the supervision of a master of method. If, however, he thinks of going on to the University or to some other institution of higher learning, or even if his parents wish no more for him than a good general education, he will spend two or more years at the form of secondary work most likely to be of use to him in the future. He must take English, another language, and mathematics (or science); beyond that he can specialise in classics, modern languages, science, etc., according to his predilections or needs. If at the end he passes the necessary examinations he receives the leaving certificate, which, with certain restrictions regarding the subjects included, qualifies for entrance to the Universities.

4. It is not possible to do more than mention the various central institutions of advanced learning. There are four Provincial Committees for the Training of Teachers, with colleges in the University towns; technical colleges in Glasgow, Edinburgh, Aberdeen, and Dundee, the first two of which are affiliated with the Universities, and have courses qualifying for the B.Sc. degree; agricultural colleges in Aberdeen, Edinburgh, and Glasgow, with diploma courses and courses in conjunction with the Universities qualifying for the B.Sc. in agriculture; three schools of art, two veterinary colleges, a commercial college, a college of physical training, and a nautical college. The four Universities—St. Andrews, Glasgow, Aberdeen, and Edinburgh—though differing from all the others in being autonomous corporations quite without the jurisdiction of the Education Department, are the crown of the whole system. There,

instruction is given in Arts and Science and the several groups of professional subjects; and if in certain respects they are inferior to the older English Universities and to the Universities of Germany, in others they need fear comparison with no Universities in the world. Their Arts course, for example, being based on the conception of a broad culture as the preliminary to specialised professional study, has preserved the best features of the mediæval tradition more completely than has been done in the continental Universities, and has provided a model for the newer English Universities. But perhaps their greatest glory is their democratic character. The cost of attendance at them, even before the benefaction of Andrew Carnegie removed the burden of fees from the capable student, has always been so moderate that they have been readily accessible to aspiring youths of every social rank. This, with the zeal of all classes for education, has made them the Universities of the whole people.

NOTE.—The best short account of the educational system of Scotland is that given by Mr. John Strong, the Rector of the Royal High School of Edinburgh, in Monroe's " Cyclopedia of Education." A more detailed account will be found in Mr. Strong's " History of Secondary Education in Scotland " (Oxford, 1909) and Dr. J. Kerr's " Scottish Education " (Cambridge, 1910). The annual reports of the Scotch Education Department, and the annual Code (of which Nelson's " Annotated Code " is the most useful edition) may also be consulted. The admirable report on " Reform in Scottish Education," recently issued by the Scottish Education Reform Committee, presents the ideals of teachers in Scotland.

THE TRAINING OF TEACHERS.

By M. W. Keatinge, M.A., D.Sc.

(Reader in Education in the University of Oxford).

It is difficult to confine within narrow limits remarks on the training of teachers for elementary and secondary schools. For the topic is a central one and a consideration of the supply of teachers leads on to all the other vital problems that now confront us—the salaries of teachers, the esteem in which their profession is held, the proper scheme of school studies, and the right person to direct them. That it is difficult to disentangle the topic from these other issues indicates surely that here we have the master problem, that this above all other matters should receive attention if that frail babe, democratic education, is not to be stifled by syllabuses and crushed by inspectors.

It will be easier to establish the paramount importance of the teacher if we consider the view that hitherto has held the field. A glance at our school system shows the system on which it is built up. It is this : To have a costly central department, some fairly expensive local officials, a staff of not inadequately remunerated inspectors, and some well-built schools, in which are placed a number of ill-paid and often overworked teachers. Unaided, so the scheme supposes, these teachers cannot be trusted, but under the guidance of instructions and the stimulus of inspectors it is imagined that they can do good work. A staff of mediocre drudges is thus to serve as the mechanical conduit by which a course of instruction determined by a committee and a syllabus is to be distributed. How ignorant the Central Authority considers the teachers in our schools may be seen by anyone who takes the trouble to purchase for a few pence the suggestions issued to teachers in elementary and secondary schools on the teaching of subjects, such as history, or arithmetic, or English literature, or modern languages. While reading them he will rub his eyes and wonder for what kind of teacher they can be intended ; for the advice they give is of such an elementary kind that if translated into terms of, say, medicine, they are about equivalent to telling a panel doctor that it is occasionally desirable to use a clinical thermometer, that cleanliness is a recognised therapeutic agent, and that a cheerful manner in a sick-room conduces to a patient's recovery. Imagine instructions of this kind to be issued to panel doctors by a central authority, and further imagine that inspectors are sent round to the dispensaries to see that patients are not dosed with morphia instead of quinine, and you will have some idea of the place that the teacher occupies in the scheme of education. Unfortunately it cannot be maintained that these suggestions are unnecessary, and it is true that in many businesses the work done by a number of drudges under the control of a vigorous hustler produce results which if not the best possible are, at any rate, sufficient for trade purposes. The clerks in a counting house are probably little the worse as clerks because they would not have the ability to find fresh business if they were at the head of the firm or the skill to organise it economically when they had got it. They do their routine work efficiently under the directions given them and the business asks no more from them. This is the situation that the business man has in view when as a member, say, of a County Council Committee he is satisfied with the poor salaries and status and often with the poor qualifications of the teachers in his district.

But this situation should not be found in a well-organised system of education. Except when the contents of a text-book are being tested by a mechanical examination (so much perhaps may be conceded to the teacher-drudge theory) the personality of the teacher, his grip of his subject, his originality in handling it, his knowledge of the various methods possible, and his skill in combining them, these are the important factors, these are the things that count, and inspectors and headmasters cannot command them at will if they are not there. In the Hindoo cosmology the world is supported by an elephant, and the elephant stands on a tortoise. The tortoise, however, is poised in mid-air, and thus the situation is one of unstable equilibrium. An educational system that poises its Board of Education on a syllabus, and its syllabus on the back of an inspector, is doomed to collapse unless the inspector can place his two feet firmly on the shoulders of a first-class man and teacher. It must, of course, be conceded that mechanical teaching is good up to a point. The New Army has been confronted with the necessity of teaching the nature and use of a complicated rifle to 5,000,000 men, and it solves the problem, and solves it well, by the use of sergeant-instructors, who can be multiplied with ease and speed. But the sergeant-instructor is useful only so long as the matter to be explained or detailed is of a mechanical nature, and in so far as instruction can be given in set forms and with unvarying phraseology. In all teaching there is a little, a very little, work of this kind to be done; but beyond a certain point such teaching is for educational purposes useless, and indeed is harmful to the mental progress of a nation. It is not from teaching of this type that will spring the army of alert technical workers and researchers of whom the industrial reformer dreams; for nothing will produce these but inventive teachers, and if a teacher has not the mental vigour to be inventive no syllabus and no system of inspection can make him so. The position is even more evident where humanity is concerned. If a teacher without any literary taste or insight has to teach literature, of what value can be a syllabus drawn up by the best committee or inspection by the best inspectors? In short, the system that we have outlined, in no sense a distortion of the facts, means this, that the public is paying for an expensive system of organisation and control, but gets poor value for its money because the one essential feature, the alert teacher, has not been provided. If this vital element is neglected the public must understand clearly that the talk about education, the letters to the papers and the conferences of which we read, have little more meaning, as far as education is concerned, than the chattering of monkeys in the tree tops or the chirruping of bats at twilight. These things serve as an eyewash, which makes the nation believe that all is well when in reality much is ill. They give that false appearance of activity and progress which has brought many movements and institutions to ruin.

It may be contended that this picture is overdrawn, and that there are teaching in our schools and training colleges a number of good teachers who have all the qualities of originality and vigour that can be desired. This statement, however, is only partially true, for the number of such teachers is very small. Certainly there is in our schools a small company of gifted men who love teaching for its own sake, quite independently of the rewards and status of their profession, and whose innate talents compensate for their lack of adequate professional training. These men are volunteers in whose persons the nation has made an extremely good bargain. But big businesses cannot be run by a staff of gifted but untrained volunteers, neither can they avoid bankruptcy by making a few good bargains. Nor is this the way in which well-established sciences like medicine have developed. Medicine has reached its present position as a result of careful experiment, of hard thought, and the careful training of generations of doctors to apply in their practice what they have learned in their years of professional training, and these doctors, it may be added, have been attracted to their profession by the promise of adequate remuneration. In education these things are not to be found, and unless the essential machinery can be provided we had better cease to talk about education. What folly it is to demand that no child shall leave school before the age of 15, or that a much larger number of secondary schools shall be provided, while the conduct of our present schools is mediocre and the provision of a teaching staff so uncertain. If in the struggle of wits which follows the conclusion of this war, victory will in the long run fall to the best educated nation, what prospect can there be for a people which refuses to pay and equip its teachers? It has been bad enough to wake to find ourselves in the day of need without an army, without a reserve of rifles and ammunition, and without the means of producing munitions of war. Yet these material things have been supplied with only a moderate delay, though we have had to pay a terrible price, the price of our dead on the battlefields. A system of education which depends for its efficacy not on material buildings, but on the spiritual factor of the men who teach in them, cannot be improvised in a hurry, but needs years of careful preparation. Are we later on to have a still ruder awakening when we find that in the stress and economies of a great war and the period that succeeded it, we neglected to supply the chief condition of success in education and, therefore, of our future prosperity?

If the salaries paid to teachers are so small that only the feebler members of the community enter the profession the preparation of teachers for their work will still be important, for while no training can make a fool into a competent professional man, it can still do something to mitigate his folly. Here, however, we shall assume that no training will be of great use unless the raw material of students is of good quality. We shall also assume (though the assumption is a bold one) that in the near future adequate salaries will attract sturdy men and women, and that on the whole the intending teacher will be a little abler than his fellows, instead of, as now is sometimes the case, a little weaker. Under these conditions what should be the nature of the training given? A very brief outline of the development of teacher-training during the 19th century will serve to show the origin of some of the weaknesses both of theory and practice still to be found in our present system, and will also indicate the direction in which deliverance from them will be found. When Lancaster trained his students at Borough Road he undertook to show them a safe and economical method of teaching reading, writing and arithmetic. The method was a mechanical one and presupposed in the students little more than an acquaintance with the three R's. The course of instruction lasted but a few weeks, and chiefly consisted in being present for a short period at each of the classes in the Lancasterian school. Such a course could produce only mechanical teachers, but it must be confessed that in the state of English education at the time even mechanical teachers were better than none. Lancaster's efforts were followed by a long period during which (1) the pupil-teacher system prevailed, and the students who went to training colleges had been pupil teachers in elementary schools; (2) the subjects taught in these schools were still restricted in scope. The first meant that the students engaged in part-time teaching had little leisure for study and little or no stimulating guidance or instruction. As a result of this when at the training college they had to spend most of their time in acquiring the rudiments of education which should have been learned at a good secondary school. The second meant that in our training colleges and among officials there grew up a wholly erroneous conception of method and of professional training. It was looked upon as being a semi-mechanical method of arranging a very limited stock of knowledge so that it might more easily be grasped by a stupid pupil, and of conducting " mass " lessons with classes far too large to admit of really educational modes of teaching.

In comparison with the mid-19th-century, the situation at the present time embodies three very important changes :—

1. The students entering training colleges have generally been through a secondary school course.

2. The period for which they reside at a training college is in the case of non-graduates in no case less than two years, in many three, and in some cases four.

3. The subjects taught in elementary schools have increased in number and in scope.

Of these the first brings with it this advantage that even during the most restricted training college course less time need be given to teaching the rudiments of literature or science and more is available for educational theory. The longer the intending teacher can be kept at school and the better the school which he has attended the greater the attention that can be given to this subject.

The second in providing three and four-year courses makes it possible for intending teachers to qualify at a university training college as a schoolmaster and at the same time to take a degree course, or (in the case of four-year students) to take their degrees at the end of three years and then to devote the fourth year to the study of education. It is impossible to over-estimate the importance of the opportunities thus offered to teachers, and these opportunities give rise to new questions. If teachers, while pursuing their professional training, are at the same time enabled to qualify for a degree will it not be possible to break down the distinction, often an arbitrary one, that exists between the teachers in elementary and in secondary schools? While we cannot here discuss this important matter, the consideration of the training to be given to all teachers will throw some light on it.

The third change—the increase in the number and scope of the subjects taught in schools—is perhaps for our purpose the most important. The two others deal with machinery and opportunities; this one deals with education itself. It is astonishing to one who looks back on the elementary school in England of 40 years ago, or in Ireland of 20 years since, to find that the subjects which we rightly consider the most cultural were not taught at all. Geography, the newer science that has revivified much of the curriculum, was not in existence. History, which should be the centre of all instruction on social subjects, was, when taught at all, confined to the barest political outlines. English literature was neglected. The nearest approach to natural science was the old-fashioned object-lesson. Manual training did not exist. Singing was little thought of, neither was drawing. The elementary school existed for the formal ends of teaching the mechanism of reading, writing, and arithmetic, and the secondary school was not much better. The chief part of its curriculum was the Latin and Greek classics, and these were taught as formally and in many cases with as little reference to the subject matter as were the linguistic studies of the elementary school. A complete change has now taken place in the spirit in which the curriculum is considered. Though in some schools it is still limited and mechanical, in the best schools, both elementary and secondary, it gets into close touch with life. A more detailed consideration of some subjects will make this clear. History is no longer treated as a series of reigns, battles, and statutes : it is taught from the economic standpoint. It deals with the life and struggle of the people rather than with the intrigues of their rulers. It busies itself with work and wages, with yeomen voters and burgess Members of Parliament. It has become a history of social progress, and there are few parts of it that do not touch our lives at some point. There is scarcely a topic in history that can be taught without at the same time discussing some vital problem of modern social politics.

In the same manner geography, from being a list of capes and bays, or imports and exports, has become the scientific treatment of the conditions of life on this planet. It is impossible to exclude from it such topics as Imperialism, the rights of weaker nations, and our duties towards backward races; while the great problems connected with the production and distribution of goods bring us face to face with modern politics. In discussing the natural and artificial boundaries of Europe or the geographcial distribution of minerals the teacher will not find it possible to avoid treating of the causes of the present war and the future conditions of peace. Literature, from being the reading of a few disconnected extracts from traditional masterpieces, is becoming the introduction to a world of feeling and expression. Indeed, pupils are with great success being encouraged to express their own feelings in their own verses, and this is recognised as of great importance. Science, which so often used to mean a formal process of test-tubing in the chemical laboratory, of little value except to those who in some form or other were going to handle acids and salts, is now getting into closer touch with the world around us. Biology, developing out of nature study, introduces our pupils to problems of evolution and life and makes it easier to discuss matters of sexual ethics; chemistry throws light on agriculture and domestic economy; the history of science emphasises the debt that humanity owes to thinkers and the need of encouraging and aiding them now. Mathematics, which once, for junior forms, consisted of nothing but long sums in addition or division or dreary evaluations, is now, even in the elementary school, treated as a branch of science. Even the beginner is now led to understand how the world around him is pervaded by applied mathematics.

Now it would be untrue to say that all schools conduct their teaching in this way. Such efforts are confined to the gifted volunteers whom we mentioned above. Headmasters now and then try to do so, but often cannot obtain a staff equal to the task. We are talking of ideals which could be realised if the men were there to realise them, but which in their absence remain ideals. To produce teachers who can teach in this spirit is the business of training colleges and courses of professional instruction, but to do so they need many additions and alterations. And the first thing they need is men : first-class men, the best and most inspiring teachers that can by any means be obtained. Given students of good quality (and this depends largely on the promise of adequate salaries) there is no reason why they should not leave the training college able or at least anxious to teach up to the newest lights. But for this the colleges must have teachers who are really inspiring, who have a comprehensive outlook on life and a good knowledge of the subjects they teach and, what is at least as important as the other desirables, have studied educational theory. Those acquainted with our training colleges have no illusions; they know that these first-class teachers and these first-class students are but seldom to be found in them. The reasons are three : (1) the reluctance of the best pupils from our secondary schools to enter the teaching profession, some causes of which we have already discussed; (2) the low salaries paid to training colleges; (3) the unsatisfactory treatment of educational theory and the attitude of the Board towards this subject, the most important element in the professional training of the teacher. The two last are so closely connected that it is difficult to separate them, and here they will be discussed together. Yet they differ in this respect that while the first is the result of tradition and not wholly the fault of the Board, the second is directly traceable to prejudice, the result of lack of insight and of knowledge on the part of our authorities, against what is generally known as educational theory. No disaster to our Armies in the field was ever more directly due to the mistakes of the responsible authorities than is the worthlessness of much of our educational efforts due to the ignorance of those who have guided the policy of the Board in this matter. It is always an ungracious task to criticise a body of hard-working officials, and the object of these remarks is to make suggestions for the future rather than to condemn the past. It will be the task of the historian of English education during the early years of the 20th century to comment on the careless cynicism which has characterised the attitude of the Board towards educational theory and towards the Register of Teachers, the chief object of which, in the minds of its promoters, is to insure that all teachers shall have some knowledge of the aims and methods of education.

The reform of training colleges is so closely interwoven with the position of educational theory that a brief account of what is covered by this phrase will not be out of place. Educational theory deals with the aims of education and with the means by which they can be attained. In so far as it has to do with aims, it is a branch of social ethics and comprises a consideration of the defects of our social system, an ideal of society with reference to which society may be improved and a treatment of the immediate steps that can be taken towards the attainment of the less remote ideals. It is in the light of their meaning for society and their place in the social fabric of the near future that all the subjects taught in a training college must be taught by the teachers and studied by the students. It is not sufficient for the teacher to be an expert in mathematics and natural science, though this is part of his outfit : he must also have considered them from the standpoint of their meaning for the welfare of society and of the individuals who study them. More evidently is this true of the more humane studies, such as history, geography, and literature. The treatment of these apart from their human reference makes them of little value for educational purposes. It is, of course, right that every subject should be studied scientifically in and for itself, but the future teacher, while a student, needs more than this. He needs first to know his subject and then to study it again, up to his standard of knowledge, from the educational or human standpoint. This should form a considerable part of the training of teachers when the training follows on a degree course, and when the degree course is pursued side by side with the course of professional training this human reference must be given while the subjects are being studied, a practice which will not injure, but rather promote, the study of them in their more scientific and detached aspect.

In so far as educational theory deals with means, it has to draw upon and take account of a mass of relevant knowledge contributed by logic, psychology, and hygiene. These subjects are very wide and extremely progressive. The manner in which they are being developed makes their assistance daily of more direct value to education. On both sides, that of ends and that of means, educational theory is baffling in its scope and in the number of elements that come together to form the background of progressive educational practice. This scope and width brings with it its dangers. Educational theory, whether of ends or means, cannot be compressed into a small manual and taught from this by teachers who have only six months' start of their pupils. It needs teachers with a standpoint which can be attained only by considerable study of the separate branches of knowledge that contribute to education, and who have at the same time that interest in bringing them to bear on educational practice that characterises the man of educational insight. Such teachers can be procured if the proper steps are taken to attract them, but they certainly cannot be procured by the salaries offered in our training colleges.

It is on the training college, whether it is designed for a two, three, or four years' course, and whether it is connected with a university or not, that the future of our school education depends. If the teachers are masters of their subjects and have a real love for them, if each training college has on its staff a first-class historian, musician, artist, mathematician, geographer, and the rest, and if these have all studied their subjects from the standpoint of educational " theory," if the principal or the lecturers on education are real authorities on their subject, with a first-hand knowledge of logic, psychology, and social ethics, if in addition all these teachers are good and vigorous human beings, then, and not till then there is some chance that the training college will prove a source of inspiration to the young men and young women who pass through it, and that our schools in the near future will be staffed by live teachers with sufficient imagination to imagine new aims, sufficient enterprise to try new methods, and enough commonsense to make them practical men as well as idealists.

Alas ! the actual is far removed from the ideal. We have training colleges staffed with teachers of whom few have ever studied education and who have failed to obtain the posts in other institutions that carry higher salaries; educational science taught from dull cram-books (they are now being produced to meet the demand for them) by teachers of insufficient insight and equipment; here and there a few good teachers miserably paid and unrecognised; even at our greatest universities no teachers with leisure to undertake educational research and experiment; an Educational Authority that gives no proper guidance or stimulus to the study of education, that still thinks " that elementary teachers need method and secondary teachers a knowledge of their subject," a fatuous phrase, which indicates complete ignorance of what both method and knowledge of a subject should be.

Is there a cure for this? Certainly there is. The disease is not incurable, but the two remedies are unfortunately those that are always the most difficult to obtain. They are money and knowledge on the part of the Central Authority. Sufficient money to insure that posts on the staffs of training colleges, whether of university standing or not, shall be among the most coveted for emolument and for standing, and sufficient knowledge in the Educational Authority to insure that educational thought and research shall be encouraged and guided by inspectors who have themselves made a profound study of educational theory, and that members of training college staffs and, of teachers outside training colleges, at least all headmasters and headmistresses of elementary and secondary schools, shall have been through a course of professional training. The mechanism of education is now being provided; it is for the training college to supply the spirit that will vivify the mechanism. Unless this is done there will be always with us the teacher-drudge, working mechanically to satisfy the demands of a syllabus, and the nation will not get, indeed, cannot get, from education what it has a right to expect. The training college is the one portion of our educational system which will with certainty make a return of an hundredfold in educational value for any money that is spent upon it. It is for democracy to demand that this, the weakest point in our educational armour, shall be strengthened, and to persist in its demands until a proper response is made by those who guide our educational destinies.

EUGENICS AND EDUCATION

(With especial reference to Antenatal Nurture).

BY C. W. SALEEBY, M.D., F.R.S. (EDIN.).

The founder of modern eugenics was the late Sir Francis Galton (1822-1911). A cousin of Charles Darwin and student of the idea of selection, Galton published in 1869 a volume badly called "Hereditary Genius," in which he sought to show that many kinds of human ability are inherited, and to draw certain practical principles therefrom. After being many years out of print this work has at last been republished, at a small price, by the publishers, Messrs. Macmillan, yielding to the writer's reiterated request, and it should be consulted by the reader; but the following paragraph contains its substance, and embodies what the writer regards as the teaching of contemporary eugenics, with one immense omission :—

"The best form of civilisation in respect to the improvement of the race would be one in which society was not costly; where incomes were chiefly derived from professional sources, and not much through inheritance; where every lad had a chance of showing his abilities, and, if highly gifted, was enabled to achieve a first-class education and entrance into professional life by the liberal help of the exhibitions and scholarships which he had gained in his early youth; where marriage was held in as high honour as in ancient Jewish times; where the pride of race was encouraged (of course, I do not refer to the nonsensical sentiment of the present day that goes under that name); where the weak could find a welcome and a refuge in celibate monasteries or sisterhoods; and, lastly, where the better sort of emigrants and refugees from other lands were invited and welcomed and their descendants naturalised."

In 1883, in his "Inquiries into Human Faculty," Galton introduced the now familiar word "eugenics," to which he added the following footnote :—

"That is, with questions bearing on what is termed in Greek *eugenes*, namely, good in stock, hereditarily endowed with noble qualities. This and the allied words *eugeneia*, etc., are equally applicable to men, brutes, and plants. We greatly want a brief word to express the science of improving stock, which is by no means confined to questions of judicious mating, but which, especially in the case of man, takes cognisance of all influences that tend in however remote a degree to give to the more suitable races or strains of blood a better chance of prevailing speedily over the less suitable than they otherwise would have had. The word *eugenics* would sufficiently express the idea; it is, at least, a neater word and a more generalised one than *viriculture*, which I once ventured to use."

As Galton explains in his delightful "Memories of My Life," public interest was not aroused, and he turned to other work; but when the Sociological Society was founded we asked him to use it as his platform for public presentation of the idea of what he loved to call National Eugenics. This he did in May, 1904, and devoted the rest of his life to the subject. The whole of the writings of these latter memorable years are to be found in his "Essays in Eugenics," published by the Eugenics Education Society. At one time the writer nearly persuaded him to pen a volume on eugenics, but advancing years made the task seem too heavy. It was accordingly undertaken by the writer, with Galton's consent, help, and suggestion, in a volume published in 1909. This was specially noticed in the United States, and led to the formation there, in the following year, of the American Eugenics Record Office, which has since done much valuable work, mostly on Mendelian lines. At his death in 1911 Galton left practically all his fortune for the endowment of the Chair of National Eugenics in the University of London, where he had already for some years maintained a scholarship in the subject. In the following year the First International Eugenics Congress was held in London, with remarkable success of various kinds, and an international committee was formed for its continuance, interrupted by the great war. In this enterprise the lead was taken by the Eugenics Education Society, of which Major Leonard Darwin has now for some years been the president, and which has published the "Eugenics Review" since April, 1909. Other eugenic societies now exist in many parts of this country, though a valuable German society is older than any of them; and in France there is now the "Société Française d'Eugénique," which publishes the journal "Eugénique." Other societies exist in various parts of the British Empire and the Continent of Europe.

It could not be otherwise than that floods of nonsense should have been spoken and published on this subject, the development and course of which have almost wholly been in the hands of amateurs, thanks not least to the deplorable attitude of hostility to the medical profession adopted by some advocates of Galton's ideas. Probably much less harm has been done by opponents than by ill-advised friends of contemporary eugenics, including those who have wished to coerce society at its dictates, and those who have opposed social reform and public medicine on the ground that they involve racial degeneracy by keeping alive those whom "natural selection" would have deleted— the slum and the public-house being regarded as natural in this surprising perversion of Darwinism. Now, therefore, after more than a decade of modern eugenics, and in the presence of the appalling and unprecedented racial injury involved in the great war, one may attempt to state the forms and aims and methods of eugenics in the light of experience and criticism, and, above all, of certain discoveries in medicine which were unknown to Galton, and are still ignored by those many eugenists of to-day who have had no training in either the biological or the medical sciences. Hereafter the writer will follow the development of the subject as presented especially in his lectures before the Sociological Society during several years, and at the Royal Institution in 1907, 1908, 1914, and 1917.

If our object be the making of noble individuals, we must first of all ask ourselves : What are the factors that make the individual noble or base, healthy or diseased, wise or foolish, clever or stupid, kind or cruel? The answer is clear. Every attribute and character of every living being is the product of what, following Prospero, we may conveniently call "nature" and "nurture." Nature includes the substance and all the characteristics of the male and female gametes whose union constituted the new zygote or individual, and nurture includes all nutrition from that moment—not from birth—onwards, all environment, physical, social, spiritual, all education, in the widest sense of that term. These two cover between them, if they be properly understood, the whole of the forces that make us, or that make any living being, past, present, or to come. And we recognise that both are essential, for if there be no nature, nurture is impotent; and if there be no nurture, nature comes to nothing. Here we shall ignore, with overt contempt, the endless, jejune, imbecile controversy as to the relative importance of nature and nurture, which occupies all the time at meetings of eugenic societies, and has been the subject of so many meaningless mathematical memoirs. When Prospero, in the lines used by Galton for his terminology, says of Caliban that he is " a born devil, on whose nature nurture will never stick," he exactly expresses the essentially false idea, shared only by those who have not yet grasped at all the essence of life, that part of the creature is given by nature and part added or apposed or stuck thereto by nurture. In fact, every living character, unless a foreign body embedded in the tissues be so-called, is the *product*, not the *sum*, of nature and nurture, including in the latter term both the education of the environment and education in its formal sense. The concept of multiplication, not that of addition, is the true one. Here, therefore, the last of the " nature *versus* nurture " nonsense.

For true eugenics, not merely the mating of fine germ-cells but the making of fine people, we need both nature and nurture. We shall do well, also, to distinguish between bad nature or heredity, and antenatal malnutrition, which have always been and still constantly are confounded by those champions of infant mortality whom, with convenient ambiguity, we may call the better-dead school of eugenists. Since we are determined to be content with neither half of the truth, and since we shall later discover that, as by microscopic demonstration, certain forms of individual malnutrition produce defects of nature in his or her subsequently shed germ-cells, we must henceforward recognise a natural or primary and a nurtural or educational or secondary eugenics, the numerical adjectives being used to indicate order in logic and not in importance.

With Galton's approval, we may reserve the adjective positive for the more abundant breeding of worth which he desired on national grounds, and apply the adjective negative to the complementary process of discouraging the breeding of, for instance, the victims of Mendelian and genuinely genetic, forms of deaf-mutism, epilepsy, mental deficiency, insanity, paralysis, hæmophilia, night-blindness, or what not. And, in fact by far the most important of all, we must take cognisance of what Galton entirely ignored from first to last, those agencies which may damage racial qualities, and to which the writer has given the name, now in general use, of racial poisons. It may, on the other hand, yet be shown that certain agents, acting upon the individual, directly improve his subsequently conceived offspring, by changing for the better the germ-cells which he bears. That is the popular belief regarding education and good nutrition in general. But at present, notwithstanding the possibilities still inherent in Lamarckian theory, science knows nothing of any such definite agents, and therefore what might be called a constructive eugenics must be left for the future, if possible, to practise. Meanwhile, we may exhaust and comprehend the possibilities and consequent duties of eugenics in tabular and systematic form as follows :—

NATURAL OR PRIMARY EUGENICS.

1. Positive : The encouragement of worthy parenthood.

2. Negative : The discouragement of unworthy parenthood.

3. Preventive : The protection of parenthood from the racial poisons.

NURTURAL OR EDUCATIONAL OR SECONDARY EUGENICS.

The nurture and education of every individual from conception onwards.

For a statement of the progress which has so far been made with regard to Natural or Primary Eugenics the student is referred to the article by the present writer in the recently published (1916) edition of the " Encyclopædia Medica." At the request of the editors of this Year Book, the writer will confine himself in this place to a brief note upon the present position of that part of eugenics which might well be regarded as coming within the province of a generously conceived educational system. Some educationists may indeed claim that what the writer terms " Nurtural Eugenics " is not strictly eugenics at all, but education. The writer is not unaware of their arguments. Like them, he desires not fine germ-cells, but fine human beings. But, speaking as a eugenist, he cannot for two excellent reasons consent to any such narrowing of the science. The first and historical reason is that Galton expressly included nurture in his original definition of eugenics given to the Sociological Society in 1904, which ran as follows (italics not in original) : " Eugenics is the science which deals with all influences that improve the inborn qualities of a race, *also with those that develop them to the utmost advantage.*" The second clause admits the whole of nurture within the scope of eugenics, as any useful or logical definition must. The second and scientific reason is that the nurture of the immature individual is the nurture of a future parent, and hence of the whole future of the race. *If it can be shown, as it can, that the nurture or malnutrition of future parents may affect the quality of their offspring*, as in Stockard's experiments, then attention to such nurture is fundamental eugenics if anything is; and none the less so though it has hitherto been ignored altogether by professing eugenists.

Eugenic nurture will begin at the beginning and go on to the end ; or, perhaps, we may regard the province of eugenics as ending with the reproductive career of the individual. The woman of 60 may be regarded as beyond our concern, but so long as the future may flow from any individual, he or she is our concern, as, for instance, to ensure protection from the racial poisons. It was in order to emphasise the eugenic consequences of individual nurture that the writer gave to his lecture to the National Conference on Infant Mortality in 1914 the title of " The Nurture of the Race,"* insisting that, for instance,

---

* Report published by National Association for the Prevention of Infant Mortality, 4, Tavistock Square, London, W.C. 1.

the nurture of the individual involves the nurture of the germ-plasm within the individual body, and hence of the race. Until all the laws of life are abrogated, this will be eugenics.

Its stages may briefly be noted, not that they are not obvious, but because of the singular anomalies in our national attention to them. The first is antenatal. The second is the year of infancy, approximately the period of breast-feeding. Third is the period one to five, almost utterly neglected hitherto by the State. The child at this stage should have a distinctive name. It may be called the *home-child* to indicate its proper environment. The fourth stage is that of the school-child, ending with adolescence and the beginning of the reproductive period. At this point, at any rate in England, if not north of the Tweed, the State, supremely foolish, regards education as finished. After a disastrous gap of two years, some cognisance may be taken of the boy, under the Insurance Act, at 16; but the nation has yet to discover the value of its adolescence, and the immense importance of care at this time for the sake of the future of the individual and the race. In the whole history of idolatry there is nothing more sinister than our present abandonment of the child at 14, of all ages, to the unholy Trinity of cities—Mammon, Bacchus, and Priapus.

The latter stages will be sufficiently treated elsewhere in this volume. Special reference need here be made only to the first stage —that of antenatal nurture. The time has really come when, once and for all, the medical profession and the public must cease to confound antenatal nurture with heredity—to say nothing of antenatal infection. It is, as Dr. Ballantyne has said, " an insult to heredity " to speak of syphilis as part of it. The medical use of such a term as " congenital " is a reproach to a scientific profession. The use of such words as nurture, heredity, and infection must be made more accurate, and the writer has elsewhere argued that the term " congenital " should be omitted from scientific discussions henceforth. When we think of heredity we are dealing with qualities of the germ-cells, and to such qualities the adjective genetic may well be applied. Nothing else is hereditary or genetic, or to be called so.

The popular assumption, shared by too many eugenists, that all the characteristics of the infant at birth are genetic or hereditary, is a monstrous error, and the direct begetter of many monstrosities. No representation can be found in the germ-cells for any but a minute fraction of the defects and diseases which have been called hereditary. So much the greater is the importance of antenatal nurture. The writer, as a pupil of Dr. Ballantyne, and resident in the Royal Maternity Hospital in Edinburgh when the first antenatal bed was founded in 1901, cannot be counted guilty of any disrespect to antenatal hygiene if he insists that, in logic and in experimental fact, this must be counted a part of eugenics. Verily, it is a part which threatens to swallow up the whole. The recent observations upon parental alcoholism, the recent findings of the Wassermann test, and such observations as those of Whitridge Williams in the United States, taken with the extension of genuinely genetic knowledge, all conspire to show what is now overwhelmingly proved, that from its foundation eugenics has been persistently assuming the genetic character of defects and diseases which were no more genetic than scurvy, rickets, or barber's itch. But the malnutrition or the infection, instead of occurring after birth and being obviously non-genetic, happens to have occured before it, and advocates to whom obstetrics, embryology, and antenatal pathology are mere names, if so much, have proceeded to talk about the " multiplication of the unfit," the " degeneracy of the stock," and so forth until the ratepayers, at any rate, have believed them.

The truth, on the contrary, is that, alike for positive eugenics, which the racial poisons can so easily arrest; for negative eugenics, largely dealing with genetic morbidities probably traceable to mal-nurture or infection in past generations; for preventive eugenics obviously, and for the nurture of the individual and future parent, antenatal hygiene is alike fundamental and indispensable. After many years, Dr. Ballantyne has assuredly come into his own. What the nation now needs, for its future welfare and the maintenance of the race in adequate numbers and quality, is a general recognition of the truth that nothing will avail us if we neglect the expectant mother, through and in whom alone can antenatal hygiene, the first stage of nurtural eugenics, be practised. The deplorable failure of the eugenic societies to realise their immediate duty in this respect may be attributed to many causes—historical and other—but our present concern must be to rectify it. Not in a year or two can the record be obliterated that " maternity benefit " was actually opposed by the principal eugenic society in this country, on the manifoldly con-temptible assumption that if superior people are taxed to pay for the proliferation of their inferiors, no more superior babies can be hoped for.

The rescue of eugenics from its present state as too often a class movement, a biological excuse for snobbery, a cover for selfish opposition to social reform, an excuse for the neglect of preventive medicine, is a task which ought to be undertaken jointly by the teaching and the medical professions. Future generations will be to an ever-increasing extent not what our politicians and ministers of religion, but what our school teachers and our medical men make them. In the literal sense, the doctor is a teacher; no less is the teacher a doctor. And the social function of each is so to teach the community as to prevent the waste and misuse of physical, mental, and moral life. Above all, it is the duty of both professions to teach the nation how to preserve, not merely its present health but, by a revival of mother and child worship, the health of the innumerable unborn, who shall inherit from us, if we be wise, the health of body and of mind wherewith to discharge their incomparably difficult but incomparably glorious task of building the great, free, democratic state of the future.

LITERATURE.—1. Ballantyne, " Antenatal Pathology and Hygiene," and " A Petition from the Unborn," British Medical Journal, 1899, i. 889-893. 2. Galton, " Hereditary Genius," 1869, second edition, 1892; reprinted cheap edition, 1914; " Memories of My Life," 1908; " Essays in Eugenics," 1909. 3. Saleeby, " Parenthood and Race Culture : an Outline of Eugenics," 1909; " The Progress of Eugenics," 1914; " The Dysgenics of War," Contemporary Review, March, 1915; " Eugenics," Encyclopædia Medica, second edition, 1916, Volume IV.

DAY NURSERIES AND NURSERY SCHOOLS.

By Grace Owen

(Department of Nursery School Teachers, the Mother Training College, Manchester).

The day nursery and the nursery school are two institutions, both concerned with the welfare of children under 5 or, possibly, 6 years of age. Each has a twofold aim with reference to mother and child.

The day nursery exists to relieve the mother who is obliged to go out to work and to rescue babies and little children from the extreme dangers of neglect and unhealthy home conditions. The nursery school seeks to assist the parents in the education of their children from 2 to 3 years old and onwards, by providing a perfectly healthy environment during the ordinary school hours and a careful training of mind and body. The day nursery is a natural development of the school for mothers. The nursery school involves the transformation of the lower classes of the infants' school. Since, however, both deal with children passing through the same period of life, and living in similar conditions, there can be· no hard lines‎ of demarcation. A good day nursery, which takes in children from a few weeks old up to the age of 5, from 5-30 in the morning till 6 at night, or even keeps them in residence from Monday morning till Saturday night, may have on its staff a nurse trained in kindergarten teaching, or may employ a visiting kindergarten teacher to take charge of the children as soon as they can walk and talk, thus virtually including within itself a nursery school. On the other hand, the nursery school may extend its daily period beyond the usual school hours, for the sake of the convenience of mothers who go out to work—providing meals also for the children, and thus approximating closely to a day nursery.

Till the present time, however, it has been true to say, that the day nursery has been primarily concerned with the physical care of the child in a happy, healthy environment. The nursery school, closely related as it is to the " free kindergarten," has always professed educational aims of a broader character.

In a nursery school, besides careful training in right physical habits and provision for sleep and fresh air, etc., much attention is paid to the development of speech and the use of language. Other means of expression also are afforded, _e.g._, clay modelling, drawing, etc. Besides the miscellaneous toys of childhood, there is a provision for a well-thought-out training of the senses—by means of toys selected for their educational value—for example, the Montessori apparatus. Singing games are used. The children are given opportunity to watch growing plants and animals. They are encouraged to notice the happenings of daily life in the home or the neighbourhood, and are told stories as soon as they are ready for them. In simple ways also, they are taught self-reliance and care for one another ; and time is given every day to training them to look after their own room and make it as beautiful as may be, to manage their own chairs and tables, to take out and put away toys, to dress themselves, to lay lunch and clear away, and thus to meet the demands of their everyday life. The elder children

F

are encouraged to help the younger ones without being asked, and gradually a community consciousness develops.

It is hardly necessary to emphasise the fact that children can only be educated in this way in small groups. The nursery school idea involves the abandonment of the class system and the big school for young children. Each little community, to deserve the name, has to be considered as a whole by itself, and within it children of all ages up to school age must be allowed to mix freely together as they do in a large family. The aim to instruct must give way to the aim to provide the most favourable conditions for the development of personality, including training in self-control. In particular, it is to be noticed that in a good nursery school there are no prescribed requirements in the three R.'s. If they are taught at all there is no attempt to make the children reach a uniform standard, and it is found that many children make better progress if allowed to begin these subjects after the nursery school period is over. It is indeed, most desirable, to defend the nursery school from the condition which has injured so much of the work of the more progressive infants' schools hitherto,—namely, the obligation to impose a prescribed standard in achievement in reading and arithmetic on all the children before they are promoted. Without complete independence in this respect, the broader educational aims of the nursery, and its very character as a nursery rather than a school, are likely, before long, to disappear.

Both day nurseries and nursery schools pay close attention to hygienic conditions. While great variety of equipment may be found, plenty of open-air is considered essential. Miss Margaret Macmillan's experiments have shown that open-air nurseries give the best health records even in winter, and there seems to be no doubt that, ideally, day nurseries and nursery schools are housed in the open-air type of building. Simple cots are provided for each child and the daily sleep is part of the regular routine. Successful nurseries are also carried on in good-sized houses standing in their own constantly used gardens, and another possible plan is to knock several cottages and yards into one. It is being debated whether nursery schools can be carried on efficiently in existing infants' school buildings. While the necessary hygienic conditions and independent organisation could doubtless be secured in some places, it is to be feared that in most cases the result would be an unfortunate compromise in regard to matters quite essential. Moreover, in case the school period is extended and the size of classes reduced throughout the school, more accommodation must necessarily be found, and could probably well be effected at the lower end of the present school.

The influence of a separate organisation for the education of children under 6 years of age would doubtless tend to bring about the junior school from 6 to 10 years of age, and the senior school from 10 to 14.

It is undeniable that numerous little nursery schools would be more expensive than the present babies' classes of 50 in the infants' schools. This fact, however, is one to be faced rather than avoided, in the interest of good citizenship.

The co-operation of the school above is of vital importance if continuity in education is to be secured, and it has been suggested that this would be assisted if nursery school teachers were trained in such a way as to fit them to teach in the lower standards as well as in the nursery school. Some infants' school teachers may also serve as managers for the nearest nursery, and thus make intimate connections between the nursery and the school. Important, however, as the continuity with the elementary school is for the children in the nursery, still more important is the connection with the home. An outstanding feature of the work of the nursery school teacher is her constant intercourse with the parents, and a successful nursery school is felt to be invaluable both to the life of the home and that of the neighbourhood.

It seems also probable, that more co-ordination between various agencies for the benefit of children under 5 than has hitherto existed may be looked for in the future. Schools for mothers, day nurseries, nursery schools, and infants' schools are in their nature essentially connected with one another, and in many a neighbourhood all are needed within the same area and should serve the same homes.

For the sake of true continuity of purpose and method in the education of the child, it is greatly to be hoped that such co-ordination will not be delayed in the numerous districts in town and country which so obviously call for it.

Hitherto the nursery school or free kindergarten has received no grant from the Board of Education, while day nurseries have received grants since 1914. This apparently curious position may be attributed to the fact that in many places children are received into the infants' school at the age of 3. It may also be remembered that the predominant influence in this matter has been the medical side of the Board of Education, and the day nursery ranks first, as a means for the preservation of infant life.

The amount of grant obtainable by a day nursery is 4d. an attendance for each child, provided the whole grant does not exceed half the expense. The usual payment by the mother ranges from 3d. to 10d. an attendance in different nurseries. The average cost per child per attendance has been estimated as anywhere between 1s. and 2s. 6d. according to the accommodation provided. A day and night nursery for munitions workers can claim 75 per cent. grant on the cost of equipment and 7d. an attendance on the running expenses; so that in cases where a high scale of mothers' payments is adopted such a nursery becomes almost or quite self-supporting. At the end of the war such nurseries are to be at the disposal of the Government.

The future of the day nursery is much disputed. To some it is merely an emergency measure taken to meet the abnormal conditions of war time. Some feel that even so it is a doubtful blessing, seeing that it may serve to bolster up conditions of housing and women's work, which ought to be brought to an end as speedily as possible. Moreover, the influence of the habit of leaving the baby to be cared for in an institution every day, is possibly dangerous, as tending to weaken the ties between mother and child. On the other hand, the present neglected conditions of thousands of children left to take care of each other, makes the day nursery an imperative need; these children cannot wait while a larger policy is slowly developed. It is thought also that the day nursery will always have its place, seeing that every mother needs relief from the care of her children sometimes. Sickness, housework, occasional holidays, cause this need to be plainly felt. The work which the nursemaid does in the more comfortable home is better done in a good nursery, with its space and fresh air and its ready, skilled nurses. Moreover, the nursery is a channel of information for mothers as to the best ways of rearing children, and it can hardly be expected that the need for this information will not exist for a long time.

Nevertheless, few people would dispute that the day nursery is best considered in its relation to a wide policy of child welfare, rather than by itself. It has its place between the school for mothers and the nursery school, and in many ways it can be adapted to the needs of the particular district which it serves.

With the passing of Mr. Fisher's Education Bill the nursery school becomes a part of the national system of education, and may be expected to take a permanent place, for it is not necessarily merely the substitute for an unfavourable home, but also the natural assistant to the good one.

Opinion seems to be generally in favour of a non-compulsory policy. No mother is to be forced to part with her child under 5, and attendance can be safely left to the attractive power of the nursery itself. Vigilance, however, will be needed to ensure that opportunities of attendance at a nursery school shall be provided in all districts, rich and poor alike, whether highly respectable or not. Only so will the nursery school take its rightful place in the national system of education.

Both day nursery and nursery school call for a type of training for matrons and teachers not hitherto completely worked out. The nursery school teachers need the essentials of a nurse's training, besides the preparation usually given to the kindergarten teacher. The day nursery matron needs some knowledge of education. In addition to such training and considerable experience, the head of an institution for child welfare will need the equipment of the social worker.

New courses of training to meet the new needs are being started, and such experiments are being encouraged by the recognition of the Board of Education.

REFERENCES.—Dr. Janet Campbell : " Physical Welfare of Mothers and Children " ; Margaret McMillan : " The Camp School " ; Reports of the Chief Medical Inspector of the Board of Education for 1914 and 1916.

"TREATMENT" VERSUS "TRAINING."

BY MARGARET MCMILLAN.

The hour is one which dwarfs every question and weakens every interest save those that have a direct bearing on the war. When the young life of a nation is poured out like wine and the fate of unborn millions is in the balance, all questions involving life and death appear, however, in new and close relations to one another. Their relation may be ignored or treated as insignificant in time of peace and ease. But against the war cloud they appear as parts of a great whole. They are seen to be one, if at no other time, then in the moment of dismemberment. And so now in the midst of great issues the treatment of ailing children does not vanish into nothingness. It is part of the whole question of conservation, of survival, and of progress, the thing for which surely all travail and all warfare is undergone blindly or with vision. An article on this question is not out of place then, surely, but pertinent now as it never was in former days.

For over seven years the children of this country have been receiving medical treatment in school clinics and health centres, and the results —or rather some of the results—have been set forth in Annual Reports sent out by Whitehall. The largest of these centres (in point of numbers and staff) is the health centre at Deptford, now financed by the L.C.C. It receives from the London Authority £1,400 for medical and dental work, and its experience may be said to extend over nearly nine years, since the work (financed by Mr. Joseph Fels in the first three years) was begun in a Poplar school in 1908 with the sanction of the L.C.C., which was not, however, at that time fully convinced of the need for health centres or clinics.

From 6,000 to 7,000 children pass yearly through the treatment-room of the Deptford Health Centre. This represents a large amount of work, and some of it is, of course, preventive as well as curative. Years ago, ere any experiment of the kind was made, it was natural enough to hope that work of this kind, conducted on such a great scale, would give great results not only in the health of school children, but in the uplift of neighbourhoods. In point of fact these vivid hopes have not been realised. Some of the work done seems as important as ever—indeed, more necessary and important than ever (a child's health and life may, for example, be saved by an operation for adenoids or by a few visits to a good dentist)—and yet the effect of working or even observing the work of a big clinic for years is not reassuring in the sense of making one feel that the clinic as such can deal with the problem of early disease and wastage of life. Let the whole truth be said. The waiting-room and streets are crowded year in, year out, with hosts of suffering and neglected children. The clinic staff does it work well—not in vain so far as the well-to-do are concerned—but almost in vain in so far as it affects the life of the great masses of the poor. It is not a small weapon nor a primitive one, this clinic with its trained staff. It is rather like a small part of a great machine gun which has to be fitted and fashioned in many and all its parts ere it can be turned with effect on the enemies of race construction and development. Isolated it is too like a highly finished fragment.

It would be easy to paint glowing and effective word pictures of things that take place in any clinic. It is much more difficult to state the facts of the case so that readers may not only know them, but see their trend and interpret their real meaning. It is this latter task that I am attempting, and at the outset it is well to feel that thorny as the path may be the goal is not doubtful. The mere closing up of byways is making the real paths clearer every day.

There is a very large class of patients, known as " minor ailment cases," which, in spite of the term " minor," make up the bulk of the children who attend the clinic. " Minor," indeed, they are not as regards numbers, nor, for the most part, as regards their diseases. They suffer from " blight," " impetigo " (this last disease is on the increase, and we have to open a centre to treat it alone, as it is infectious and the scabies clinic nurse dare not touch it), broken chilblains, wounds, septic and otherwise, skin diseases of all kinds, also nervous troubles. These diseases are, for the most part, confined to poor areas. But nearly all areas are poor. These children are found in large numbers in *every* Medical Officer's report. The L.C.C. gives a grant of 4d. per head for them. They often cost in drugs alone 20 or 30 times that sum per annum. They suffer a great deal of pain, pain through the ailment and pain through the treatment. It is amazing to see how bravely even the little ones sit in the treatment chair and endure what has to be endured. The stinging pain of a biting nitrate placed on raw eyelids, the probing of bad wounds. Nurse treated 927 of these cases in ten weeks and cured them all. What an ordeal ! And what a splendid thing to cure such miseries ! No one grudges the drugs. Only it should be added that within these ten weeks over 700 of these children had to be treated all over again ! Same misery, same anguish, same labour, same expense. But within ten months all this would have to be undergone not once or twice, but five or six times. That is to say, in one clinic *thousands* of children are treated over and over again for diseases that depress the vitality, that hold back the waking mind, that are costly to cure, *and are, above all, entirely unnecessary.*

How busy they keep everyone—the children who have medical treatment, because they can have little or no hygienic treatment, no nurture. The dentist who often has well-to-do children, sometimes has a spare hour, a slack day. The well-to-do adenoid cases fall off at last. We do not get half the number we used to have in earlier years at the Evelyn Home. And there is no doubt that the run on the eye clinic will be less and less as time goes on and as better methods of eye-work are popular. But the minor ailment cases do not fail nor show signs of failing. They are more numerous than they were five or six years ago. When nurse goes away in the holiday another must take her place to stem the futile anguish of the streets. When school hours are over and other workers rest *she* sees a suffering crowd at her door and does not turn it away. And not only nurses, but clerks and organisers and doctors have to busy themselves in more or less vain work. Organisation is a fine thing, but it is just as efficient and wonderful when it is used to grind chaff as when it is perfected in order to grind corn. There is a kind of nervous trouble that is formed, I believer, by the forming of waste products in the tissues.

151

The living organisms which are, in effect, this waste, not only live but grow in the once healthy body. They evolve a regular system of blood vessels for their own use and nourishment. Something of a like nature is taking place already in the medical service of the people's schools. It is forming a vascular system for a thing that should be taken clear out of the life of a nation's children. If the means taken for dealing with this situation are costly (but they are not costly) that cannot be a reason for turning back, since the life and productive powers of the whole nation is at stake. No Government (whatever its politics) which had any real grasp of the situation would hesitate. No authority who knew could put off or let things go on as they are. When the Easterns got to know the *feel* of evil life in the tissues they made short work of its food transport systems. Their masseurs soon moved the colonies and all their works with strong fingers out of the body. Neither would it occur to any patriot to go paying for drugs and lotions that do no permanent good. Modern people are already willing to give a great deal of time and money to the relief of suffering. The danger lies in this— that people will not early see clearly enough below the surface of things to carry out great reforms without further wastage and delay.

In the second year of the Deptford Centre's existence a rude kind of school was opened at its doors—that is to say, in the heart of a very poor neighbourhood. It was an open-air school, but of a new type. For it did not remove children from their environment,* but accepted the task of changing the environment rather than of transporting children away from it. And it was open, not for six or eight, but for 22 hours out of the 24. The scholars were anæmic, and many had minor ailments, too. But as a matter of fact they were not in a much worse case than are most of the children in any poor area. The funds for the new venture were not large. Mr. Fels and the Ogilvie Trustees were its mainstay, but I saved between £200 and £300 in the last years from the grants paid to the Deptford Clinic. The cost of building was certainly not more than £3 per school place, and the cost of keeping a child in camp did not quite average £10 per annum.

The children slept in an open pavilion (a model of which can be seen at the Sanitary Institute). Nearly every child had a hot bath and cold shower daily, and each had two meals—breakfast and supper—in camp. They went home for dinner and some had a very slight midday meal in consequence, but a great many had a better dinner than they could look for in former days. Practically all were children from the neighbourhood, many from the homes round our doors. The results were very striking.

The campers became clean. " Minor ailments " became things of the past for them. The remedial drill now began to have some value, to take some effect. With regular bathing, regular and good meals, fresh air by night and day, early going to bed, and a new standard in hygiene and habits all the campers leaped with another life. A great gulf separated them from the crowds in the waiting-room. *As long as we refused to admit strangers* from distant places

---

* After the war it admitted children from a distance—a blunder which will not be repeated.

our school compared very favourably with a good kind of secondary school as regards hygiene.

In December, 1912, a group of camp girls was photographed. Impossible to find lovelier and more graceful specimens of English girlhood.

The Medical Officers of the L.C.C. themselves noted all this, pointing out the fact that these graceful, beautiful girls could not be ignored, presenting as they did such startling contrasts to all around them, and being recognisable everywhere as Camp and Evelyn Home girls. Moreover, there is something more to follow which would make any hesitation in telling the whole truth criminal.

The year 1914 was a dark one for all social workers. And it struck more than one staggering blow at the Deptford Centre. At first we admitted strangers from distant areas. That was a mistake, for the vigorous training of months cannot be given in a day. Our resources, too, were heavily drawn on, while the gifts and subscriptions dried up suddenly. We did not after Christmas attempt to keep the night camps open, nor could the salary of the teacher of hygiene and remedial drill be paid any longer. In order to keep the camp school open at all it was necessary to make it, for the time being, a mere day school. Even the daily hot bath was stopped !

All the old evils reappeared. Many of the campers became what they had been in earlier days before the new life came to them. They joined the army of children who crowd the waiting-room daily and are treated at the clinic for the old, preventible ailments. Five members of the baby camp even returned after the April holiday with " blight," and some of the children, who lived under good conditions at home, caught the infection at once. In short, the campers plunged back into the old sea of miseries from which they had entirely risen. One thing, however, was proved. The camp school can make war on evil home conditions with success.

" How with success since the children fall back? " it may be asked. The answer cannot be given in a sentence, nor even in a paragraph, for, as nearly always happens, success is not only gradual, but also it appears to followed by reaction, and is very dependent, as we never thought it could be, on rallying powers. It is something like the fight of healthy organisms with disease germs as seen on a photographic film or plate. At first there is a general change of position as it were, and much movement. Then the colonies gather in dark masses where the movement seems faster, and later clear but small places are seen in this warring darkness. At last a new order is visibly born where the health-giving, living things have fought and routed the enemy.

Something a little like this happened, and is still happening with us. At first there was a great deal of movement around us. Even now at our doors mothers look on without sympathy and even with some rancour. Fathers, who for the most part know nothing of the work or its aims, were opposed and leant their weight against the new-fangled kind of methods. And yet the camp school went on, summer and winter, and a nucleus of very hopeful, rewarding cases was never lacking. They grew in number these bright-eyed, gracious, hopeful ones ; they passed out after two and three years well grown and gentle mannered. On mild evenings mothers gathered on our open space to see their boys and girls to bed. Some of them, and others perhaps who did not come, made a stand in their homes. They held convictions that grew very robust roots at last, and were not to be shaken by flying censure or slight. "What I know is this," said one mother, "my boys were always ill, and now they are well. (Dramatic illustrations are not wanting either, and these clear a bright space with their course on our troubled social plate or film. A boy was treated five months in the clinics for wounds that would not heal. Nine days' feeding and sleeping in camp put him, literally, on his feet.)

The site is a bad one. It is much improved, however, by the existence of an L.C.C. recreation ground in front of the camp enclosure. For, happily, the L.C.C. is not logical. It does not approve of camp schools in bad areas. But it is altogether in favour of recreation grounds and parks in bad areas. It does not sanction our rude shelters and grass plots and flower beds; but it puts up large stone buildings as schools and clears playgrounds for them in the worst sites. It shakes its head at the camp school, but it is going to help us to put up a scabies centre. The fine school building and the asphalt make no pretty inroads on the grime and huddle of mean streets, but the recreation ground makes an inroad. It sends a fair green ribbon of grass, if nothing more, between two dark spaces, breaking and scattering the gloom till it looks a broken thing already and easy of conquest. A few adventurous camp schools would go far to complete the inrush of new life. But nearly all local authorities are still in favour of migration rather than transformation when it comes to dealing with children. We are a race of colonists, travellers, and the minor form of travel, excursioning, is also in favour. Daily excursions from home to schools in pine woods and country fields are charming. But they are excursions; they do not change these old surroundings. They leave parents, and dark streets, and also crowded bed-rooms out of account. The weary child turning home-ward at eventide loves home best, and takes overcrowding and bad air as necessary things after all, since they are an integral part of home. Bathing and frolics on the grass, evening prayer and quiet starlight, free-blowing night winds and the good-night of mothers, all in sight of home are a better preparation for changes that will make the old sites new. Excursions are fine things, but as everyday events they are a runaway kind of method.

In short, the elementary school cannot leave homes out of account on pain of seeing all its work damaged, or even wrecked, by this closing of the eyes. Even to-day it sends out visitors and nurses and (having regard to some homes) refuses to send out lotions and drugs and treats children in clinics. The day of saving piecemeal is over, because every day it becomes clearer that children cannot be saved in this way, that, for example, it is of little use to save a child's teeth if his lungs are diseased, and of even less use to teach him the three R's if he is going to be a night worker at 14. The " saving by inches " epoch is nearly over. It was costly, and, above all, wasteful in its methods. To quit it once and for all is probably the boldest but surest form of economy, but it is a kind of economy that only large communities, or rather the nation, can practice. It is not within the scope of any individual effort.

All our failures hitherto have come from this—that we had to carry out our work by inches : by the splitting up of work that depends for success on the integrity and close union of all its parts. For years we have been tacking about, as it were, in the Deptford Health Centre, dealing with babies, with boys and girls of school age, with the question of clothing, with remedial drill, with outdoor sleeping, feeding, and education, taking up phases of education and abandoning some of them later, not because they were unpromising or unsuccessful, but only because money was wanted for the breaking of new ground, and realising all the while more and more fully that not by one reform, but by the working out of many, will any permanent improvement on a large scale be hoped for. But that such improvement on a large scale would follow any well organised and inclusive work such as has been outlined is no longer in doubt. It is a thing already proved, albeit it has been proved in a piecemeal way. By piecemeal reforms we have shown that children cannot be saved by inches, and also that from the poorest quarters what seems the poorest material is capable of a wonderful and even dazzling evolution.

LAYING IN OUR SCHOOLS THE FOUNDATIONS OF DEMOCRACY.*

BY EDMOND HOLMES

(Late Chief Inspector of Elementary Schools in England).

Education, as it is conducted to-day in most civilised countries, seems to be at open war with the democratic ideal of liberty, equality, fraternity. The children who attend school are despotically governed and compulsorily disciplined, instead of being helped to govern and discipline themselves. In this way violence is done to their natural and quite legitimate desire for liberty, a desire which is generated by their inborn instinct for self-development. They are compulsorily instructed instead of being helped to instruct themselves. A cut-and-dried curriculum is imposed on them, with or without their consent, and no attempt is made to discover, or help them to discover, in what directions their talents really lie. The result is that an arbitrary standard of intellectual worth is applied to them, by reference to which glaring inequalities among them speedily reveal themselves, inequalities which are accepted by both teachers and taught as congenital and inherent, and therefore as ultimately decisive of destiny, and which are duly registered by the teacher, and even numerically appraised. In this way violence is done to the sense of equality which is latent in all children and is ready to assert itself whenever it is given fair play. And as the regime of compulsory discipline and compulsory instruction is distasteful to the healthy child, in order to induce children to exert themselves they are urged and even compelled to compete against one another for prizes and other marks of distinction, and are thus taught to regard their class-mates as rivals instead of as fellow workers and friends. In this way violence is done to the nascent spirit of fraternity—the spirit of comradeship, of co-operation, which has made possible the communal life of man.

The reform of education, then, in the direction of relaxing unnecessary pressure, removing unnecessary restrictions and, in general, giving the child space to grow in and fresh air to breathe, must precede that diffusion of the democratic spirit which is to prepare the way for the advent of democracy. Feudalised education leads of inner necessity to the ascendancy of the feudal spirit in society; and so long as that spirit is in the ascendant it will either thwart or misdirect whatever movements we may make towards the realisation of the democratic ideal. Therefore, if we are really devoted to the cause of political and social reform, our first aim must be to defeudalise education. How is this to be done? We must begin by recognising that the ultimate source of authority in education is not the will of the teacher, but the unfolding spirit of the child. Let this fundamental truth be realised, and reforms which embody it will follow of their own accord and in their own good time. Instead of basing our whole educational system on profound distrust of the child's nature, we shall

---

* Mr. Holmes has now published this article in expanded form in the "Nineteenth Century and After." We are, therefore, called upon to acknowledge the kindness of the Editor of that periodical in allowing us to reprint.—ED.

gradually learn to base it on faith in the inherent sanity of the great forces which are at work in his expanding life, in the limitlessness of his unrealised reserves of capacity, and in the general orientation of his nature towards good. We shall then relax the rigour of a discipline which takes for granted that the child is a potential rebel and criminal, and which therefore does its best to crush his spirit and mechanicalise his life. And we shall relax the rigidity and formality of a system of instruction which takes for granted that the child is as stupid and helpless as he is ignorant, and which, by forcibly cramming him with information, does its best to starve his desire to win knowledge for himself. And in general we shall relax the dogmatic and dictatorial attitude which reflects our traditional conviction that the mind of the child is at best a blank page waiting to be written on, and that his character is at best unkneaded clay.

If we will make the experiment of giving freedom to the child, and persevere in it in spite of inevitable mistakes and failures, results will follow in due season which will surprise us. Relieved from the deadly pressure which was paralysing his natural activities, and therefore either arresting or distorting his expansive tendencies, free at last to obey the laws of his own being rather than the arbitrary commands of his teacher, the child will begin to make healthy and harmonious growth; and his consequent sense of well-being will be realised by him as joy. In the vitalising atmosphere of joy his deeper nature will begin to reveal itself. His secret desire for liberty having been gratified, the sense of equality will begin to awake in him. By this I mean that his competitive instinct, which we, his seniors, have so basely exploited, will be gradually swamped, and at last wholly submerged, by the rising tide of fellow feeling and goodwill. Instead of measuring himself against his class-mates and either envying their prowess or priding himself on surpassing them, he will learn to regard them as his fellow workers and comrades, as sharers with him in the life and well-being of a social community, and will therefore learn at last to take as great a pride in their achievements as in his own. This is no mere dream of what might be. It is a prophecy based on experience of what has actually happened in more schools than one. In the village school which I have already mentioned, prizes, marks of distinction, orders of merit, and all their pernicious kindred were entirely unknown, and any attempt to introduce them into the school would have been strongly resented by the children themselves. If a child had a special gift for drawing or any other subject his reward for doing good work at it was to be allowed to help those who were less proficient than himself and, if possible, raise them to his own level. And as no artificial standard of measurement prevailed in the school, and as all the children were encouraged to cultivate their natural tastes and aptitudes, the clever draughtsman— let us say—was free to remind himself that if he was strong where some of his class-mates were weak he might well be weak where some of his class-mates were strong.

Looking back to the days which I spent in that school, I can say, without hesitation, that it was a perfect social community, in which the spirit of liberty, equality, fraternity was fully realised, in which each lived for all and all for each, in which the development of the children was in the highest degree healthy, vigorous, and many sided, in which the prevailing atmosphere was one of sympathy, goodwill, and joy. I have visited other schools in which the same spirit was producing similar results. If schools of that type were the rule instead of the rare exceptions, the social kingdom of heaven, which is also the spiritual kingdom of heaven, would be at hand.

The spread of the democratic spirit among the young is not the only preparation of democracy which the reform of education may be expected to make. It may be that actually, though not congenitally, the upper classes have a greater capacity for self-realisation than the lower. I do not think they owe this superiority, such as it is, to their school education. At any rate, they owe it in a far higher degree to the general advantages of their environment, especially in the days of childhood and adolescence, to their homes, their surroundings, their friends, their opportunities for travel and self-improvement, and, above all, to the leisure which makes it possible for them, through the medium of books and periodicals, to get into touch with all the ages and with all parts of the world. Taken as a whole, their environment is larger, more varied, more stimulating, and therefore more educational, in the deeper and truer sense of the word. If the poor cannot secure these advantages for their children there is the more reason why the education given in our elementary schools should be of such a character as to keep alive and even foster the child's natural capacity for realising his latent possibilities. Now, as it happens, the type of education which will best secure this end coincides at every point with the type of education which will best promote the growth of the democratic spirit in the rising generation. Give a child freedom for self-development, release him from the cramping and deadening pressure of autocratic authority, rigid discipline, and mechanical instruction, and two things will happen. The spirit of liberty, equality, and fraternity will begin to germinate in his heart, and his capacity for realising capacity, for making the most of his natural aptitudes and inclinations, will at least be kept alive. With such a school life behind him, he will be animated, when he grows up, by the true spirit of democracy, and he will also be ready to play his part as a useful and efficient member of the community, and to take a hand in the great work of governing the community, and the still greater work of governing himself.

The psychology from which I deduce my political philosophy may seem to some of my readers fantastic and even paradoxical. Yet it ought to be familiar to all who call themselves Christians. For I do but take seriously two of the leading tenets of the Christian faith. The doctrine of the Incarnation and the doctrine of the Holy Spirit proclaim, each in its own way, the potential divinity of men. The essence of the doctrine of the Incarnation is that Very Man is Very God. The essence of the doctrine of the Holy Spirit is that the indwelling spirit of God is the life of our life and the soul of our soul. The seers and sages of Ancient India proclaimed the same truth in other words when they taught that the soul of the Universe, the " unbeholden essence " of all things, is the true self of each of us. We do not take this great truth seriously. We give a formal assent to the doctrines which enshrine it, and then leave these for the theologians to deal with, while we devote ourselves to secular pursuits. The doctrines may have a meaning for us—so we seem to think—between certain hours on Sunday and for our children during the first half-hour of morning school on week-days. But they do not otherwise concern us, and we take good care that they shall not enter into and dominate our daily lives. The consequent loss to our daily lives is immeasurable. If the true self of each of us is infinite and even divine, ought not self-development—the unfolding of our latent powers, the realising of our limitless possibilities, the opening of our hearts to the creative spirit of God—to be the central purpose of our lives, the basis of our culture, the basis of our morals, the basis of our social organisation, the basis of our political aims? In the light of this master-principle, should not we who believe in democracy see a deeper meaning in *liberty*, without which self-development is impossible, in *equality*, which reflects the presence of the Infinite in our souls, in *fraternity*, which is the natural outcome of our oneness with and oneness in God. I ask that we shall take this truth, if it is a truth, away from the theologians and bring it into our daily lives. When once the leaven of it has begun to work in our hearts, new vistas will·open before us, and ideals which we had thought impracticable will come within the compass of our forethought and our will. I am no prophet, and I will not pry into the future, but I must be allowed to dream that one of the ideals which will then begin to materialise will be the reconstruction of society on a genuinely democratic foundation.

But even in our dream of that possible millennium we must remind ourselves again, and yet again, that without the democratic spirit no democratic institution can serve its purpose or endure. If the theoretical basis of democracy is recognition, the practical basis of it is realisation, of the divine element in man. The kingdom of heaven is a community as well as an inward state; but if we are to realise it as a community we must also realise it as an inward state.

REFERENCES.—Mrs. D. Fisher: " Mothers and Children "; " A Montessori Mother." Edmond Holmes : " What Is and What Might Be "; " In Defence of What Might Be "; " The Tragedy of Education "; " The Problem of the Soul : A Tract for Teachers." Miss M. L. V. Hughes : " Citizens to Be." N. MacMunn : " A Path to Freedom in the School."

THE IDEAL NUMBER OF PUPILS IN A CLASS.

By M. L. V. Hughes

(Late Classical Exhibitioner of Somerville College, Oxford).

For the purposes of this article " the large class " means one with more than 30 pupils, that being the upper limit for secondary schools; " the small class " means one with less than 30. They may be visualised throughout the argument as classes of 60 and 15 respectively, 60 being the elementary school limit and a prevailing figure in town schools, though often exceeded during the war.

UNDERLYING THEORY.

The large class presupposes the uniformity of human nature. This is a half-truth which, taken alone and made the whole basis of educational theory, is the most deadly lie. Further, it presupposes that this uniformity is desirable, and seeks to maintain it as an end. This, by all evolutionary law, is the method of atrophy and death. On individual variation and experiment the life of the species depends. But the uniformity ideal is condemned by ethical theory also. The essence of ethical theory, as of practical morality, lies in the will and in acts of choice which are meaningless on the assumption of uniformity. External acts may be uniform, but these are not morality. Inner choices are always new and individual; these are morality.

The small class rejects the uniformity ideal in favour of the ideal of social individuality. Not individualism. Rousseau's Emile needs the small class to make him tolerable. Individuality is injured as deeply by loneliness as by crowding. It must have fellowship as well as freedom. In practice, whether for adults or children, this double ideal is best attained in the small group. In adopting the small class, education is obeying not only sound ethical theory, but the best results of experimental psychology.*

THE ARGUMENTS FROM EXPERIENCE.

In favour of the large class it is urged :—

I. That in the hands of a good and well-trained teacher it is a fine instrument, and the fact that it demands training is all to the good, tending to weed out the inefficient and slipshod who would abound if easier conditions enabled them to survive.

II. That on grounds of economy the large class is both necessary and desirable, from the point of view of (a) staffing; (b) buildings; (c) time.

In answer to these :—

I. The large class does indeed necessitate training—of drill-sergeants—to the grave detriment of education.

---

* See Valentine, " Experimental Psychology"; and Thorndike, " Principles of Teaching," etc.

II. The economic argument can scarcely ask for a serious hearing from teachers or educationists henceforth. War Budgets should have shamed it into silence. Yet, since even to-day the additional £3,000,000 secured by the Minister of Education—the price of half-a-day's warfare—seems to be accounted a great thing, the argument must be met, however briefly, on its three grounds.

(a) ECONOMY IN STAFFING.—By changed organisation and free discipline the small class is possible even with the ordinary staffing, though this is, of course, very inadequate. The change in organisation means :—

(1) Increased use of private study and work with partners or small groups.

(2) Increased use of the lecture method for upper school, when classes may be combined up to 100 or 200.

(3) Increased use of the playgrounds by separate small classes all through the school day (instead of the prevailing custom of 15 minutes' Bedlam, for the whole school, and hours in which the playground space is wasted).

Thus, instead of eight lessons a day in a class of 60, the elder boy or girl would have perhaps three periods of silent study, three lessons in small groups, one lecture in the hall, and one playground period. This plan is in some respects that adopted by the Gary Schools, U.S.A., under the management of Mr. Wirt, whose peculiar triumph is the combination of individual teaching of large numbers with economy.

(b) BUILDING.—The class-rooms of new schools can be built for small classes. Existing large class-rooms can be sub-divided. Failing both these, the method of sectional teaching, with plenty of private study, is a makeshift to be tolerated only in preference to the monotonous large-class method.

(c) TIME.—The glory of Bell and Lancaster and the monitorial schools was their time economy, achieved by mass methods. It was the factory system applied to human material, relying utterly on the uniformity fallacy. It turned out a generation of readers, writers, and calculators, and if this were now a sufficient ideal our improved apparatus might enable us to realise it, in a shorter time and for greater numbers, than did Bell and Lancaster. But with our changed and greater ideal the economy argument is transformed. Wastage for us is found to arise through mass methods, which, though they teach the three R's, do not educate. So much time goes to organisation and to discipline, to filling of forms and registers, that too little is left for education. To the truth of this, all actual teachers of large classes will testify. But if the evidence from inside the schools as to the wastefulness of large classes is not sufficiently available, he who runs may read it in the outside world. The present inmates of hospitals, workhouses, asylums, prisons, reformatories, the slum dwellers, and the factory drudges—the vast majority of these have had, perhaps for nine years, education by mass methods, the education that relied on uniformity. But they were *not* uniform, and it did not educate them.

The further arguments for the small class must be enumerated briefly :—

III. HEALTH.—In the class of 60 eye-strain, ear-strain, nerve-strain are inevitable. The " back row " is bound to suffer. The teacher cannot possibly do all that is needed in the way of observation. The latest School Health Report of Sir George Newman, with its record of 1,000,000 mentally or physically defective, is itself a sufficiently powerful argument to demand the immediate abolition of the large class.

IV. INTELLECTUAL PROGRESS.—In general the large class tends to a dull average, and is unfair both to the most intelligent and to the least intelligent in the class. Also, in the various subjects many resources are available for the teacher of the small class which are impossible or unhelpful for a class of 60. Of this self-evident fact a few examples must suffice where thousands might be given :—

ENGLISH, HISTORY, ETC.—Many more books of reference can be made use of in a small class. When only one copy is available it can be read aloud, shared, or passed round. *Small* pictures and illustrations are available in the same way. " Conversation " lessons are genuine, not artificial.

GEOGRAPHY, NATURE-STUDY, ETC.—Excursions, nature walks, gardening, surveying, etc., are all more possible and more fruitful with a small class. A nature walk for more than 30 is quite possible, but quite incongruous.

NEEDLEWORK.—The use of specimens, now generally condemned, is hard to avoid altogether with a large class. It is the natural resort of the teacher who desires to avoid waste of material. With a small class there is no need for it.

ARITHMETIC.—The practical work in mensuration, etc., is far more possible to arrange for 20 than for 60. Hence the largest class is the least able to fulfil the requirements of the Board and of commonsense in this respect.

MANUAL WORK.—This has been found almost to necessitate the small class, individual teaching, and the co-operative method. Hence its peculiar value in schools which have suffered from mass methods and uniformity.

SOCIAL AND CIVIC EDUCATION.—The formal class lesson in this subject may be the most pitiful of futilities, especially when a set syllabus is enforced. But civic education in small groups, through vital, honest discussion, through first-hand acquaintance with the topics (through school visits if necessary), and through actual service rendered to the town or village by the groups, contains the best hope of future civilisation.

V. MORAL EDUCATION.—The last " subject " has outstepped the intellectual category more definitely than the others, though, of course, there is nowhere any sheer sundering of moral and intellectual. We come now to the question of—

DISCIPLINE.—Briefly, the evil of the large class in this respect is its enforcement of an artificial code of school ethics which is radically, not only superficially, different from the Christian code. Allowing for great modifications of the evil by the best teachers, the following summary of differences in the two codes seems borne out by common experience in the schools :—

SCHOOL CODE.	CHRISTIAN CODE.
1. Obey.	1. Be interested.
2. Imitate.	2. Be yourself.
3. Don't move without orders.	3. Be free. Explore.
4. Don't speak without orders.	4. Discuss.
5. Don't laugh without orders.	5. Delight in your work.
6. Try to be top.	6. Try to do it excellently.
7. Try to beat the others.	7. Try to help on the whole class.
8. Don't help your neighbour.	8. Help the weaker specially.
9. Don't get help from him (Both these are cheating.)	9. Get help from the stronger.
10. Don't break any school rule.	10. Do as much for the school as you possibly can.

THE SANCTION.	THE SANCTION.
I. Else you will be punished. II. If you work hard and keep the rules you will get your marks now and good wages afterwards.	Then you will be a fit scholar of Christ, ready for the harder lessons, ready to offer God and your country " no maimed or worthless sacrifice."*

Summed up, the difference of the two Decalogues is that the first appeals to the extrinsic interests of fear and personal ambition; the second to intrinsic interest—love of the work and love of the community, which the school is to foster till it becomes " love to all men 'neath the sun."* The first is the fit and proper school code for an industrial system which rests on competition and a society which has in it all the seeds of war. The second is the fit and proper school code for a Christian state and a co-operative industrialism. Teachers who would deliberately prefer the first would be hard to find. Yet the great majority in the elementary schools use it because it is easier to apply to the large class.

VI. THE TEACHER'S SCALE OF VALUES.—(This and the following arguments deal with the teacher's point of view, which hitherto has been subordinated to that of the child.) The large class forces the teacher to have an inordinate regard for externals of organisation, registration, forms, examination results, verbal accuracy, and outward discipline ; and a corresponding disregard of the greater educational factors—self-government, vital interest, originality, truth of meaning, application, joy. With rare exceptions, the teacher of the large class cannot put first things first.

VII. THE TEACHER'S HEALTH AND WELFARE.—" By Friday night we are all nervous wrecks." " I don't live, I exist." These are testimonies of two teachers of big classes, who might speak for

---

* " The Children's Song " (Kipling).

thousands. They are not likely to give the education we need, however much they wish to.

VIII. TEACHERS AND SOCIAL WELFARE.—The big class renders impossible that full and friendly intercourse between teachers and the homes of the children which might be a most potent means of social amelioration. With the present system of big classes we cannot attempt the Gary plan, which entrusts each teacher with the visiting of a certain number of blocks where the scholars live and with the care of those children's general well-being. But the teachers of small classes could undertake this with infinite gain to the work of the school and the welfare of the neighbourhood.

IX. All these arguments point to one final argument : The type of teacher who is most needed for the elementary schools to-day is exactly the type which *will not apply unless the classes are reduced.* Those who are content with the drill-sergeant methods and the uniformity ideal will more and more have the monopoly, since only these can find their vocation in the class of 60. But if now, in the hour of great changes, this greatest of all reforms were carried through, there is reason to expect strong reinforcement for the teaching profession from the application of teachers of the most liberal type, whose ideal for education is as high as it is genuine.

X.—SUMMARY.—These reservations are to be kept in mind :—

1. That for a few subjects, e.g., singing, and for occasional lectures, etc., the large class is not only tolerable, but desirable.

2. That good teachers may get better results from 60 than bad teachers from 15.

Admitting these things, the evidence of theory and of experience is overwhelmingly in favour of the small class.

Therefore the present proposal of the Workers' Educational Association for the reduction of all classes to 30, and the withholding of the grant from classes over 40, seems the least that any educationist can accept. With an upper limit of 30 we may hope for the realisation of the remaining reforms. But the number to be advocated for most of the ordinary school teaching is probably between 15 and 20.

REFERENCES.—Board of Education : Special Reports, e.g., No. 28 (on Gary Schools). Education Reform Council : Report, 1917. Hughes : " Citizens to Be." Key : " The Century of the Child." McMunn : " A Path to Freedom in the Schools." Thorndyke : " Principles of Teaching." Valentine : " Experimental Psychology."

A SPIRITUAL PURPOSE IN THE SCHOOLS.

By F. H. Hayward and Arnold Freeman.

The people of this country desire fervently that the coming peace may bring (i.) " A League of Nations " and (ii.) " An Industrial and Social Order Based upon Co-operation." But it does not seem to be clearly recognised that the extent to which these two objects can be attained depends not upon cunningly devised machinery, but upon the quality of the human nature involved in each scheme of reconstruction. It seems to us that no League of Nations can achieve the purposes for which we are establishing it unless it is based solidly upon international understanding and goodwill. Nor does it seem probable that any magical social harmony will spontaneously arise after the war as a result of the " brotherhood of the trenches " and the co-operation of all ranks of society to withstand the aggression of the Central Empires.

Is it not, in fact, plain that if we want a fundamental unification of the world and a fundamental social integration, we must achieve them by manufacturing in the schools a spirit of goodwill to other nations and a spirit of service to one another? For the one purpose as for the other, we need citizens who at school have been taught to believe intensely in moral responsibility; who have learned instinctively to " glorify God " (we use the old phrase) in every relation of life; whose constant purpose is the ennoblement of their own country in order that it may in its turn ennoble the commonwealth of nations? The very life of civilised humanity depends, as the war has taught us at last, upon the production of self-controlled and socially-minded, or—as we should prefer to put it—of spiritual human beings.

We contend that at present the schools of this country have no such spiritual purpose in view and that their present methods and curricula are not media through which the culture we postulate can be transmitted.

Our proposal is that there should be compiled for use in the public elementary schools a national school liturgy or formulary consisting of the noblest passages, sacred and secular, from our own and other literature—and selected very largely, of course, from the Bible; of pieces of the finest music the world has produced; and of certain ceremonial features. This liturgy would be utilised for the assembled school at the opening of every school day. Morning by morning, the child would hear the most beautiful passages from the Bible impressively read; he would listen daily to magnificent poetry and prose; he would be familiarised with many hundreds of elevating pieces of music; once a week, perhaps, he would take part in some piece of ceremonial or pageantry in honour of a great man—sometimes of this, sometimes of another country—or of a great idea. (Shakespeare Day, Empire Day, and—in Welsh schools—St. David's Day are already annual celebrations. What could bind the world more effectually together after the war than a League of Nations Day? How could we better inculcate a reverence for Democracy or Science or Agriculture or Co-operation than through appropriate celebrations in the schools?)

The reader who is interested in the scheme will find each point of it more fully elaborated in Dr. Hayward's pamphlet, " The Religious Difficulty in Schools " (6d., post free, from the author).* It is not possible here to develop the scheme fully, nor to meet (except again by reference to the pamphlet) all the criticisms and interrogations that will arise in even a sympathetic person's mind. We can only hope that what has been indicated is sufficient to enable an interested student to grasp what the scheme would mean. We believe that anyone who will think it over, *provided he is not determined at all costs to have his own particular doctrines rammed down the throats of as many children as he can lay hold of*, will see in it an approach to a solution not of the religious difficulty only, but of those two far greater " difficulties " which we noted at the opening of this article : the difficulty of unifying the world and the difficulty of achieving a fine social order.

We add the following notes by way of answer to some of the more substantial of the queries likely to be formulated :—

(i.) In the present divided state of theological and philosophical opinion the nation cannot go further towards " religious education " than a scheme of this character. One step more and we should be trespassing into regions where the State has no right to intrude. In this form, the scheme contains little or nothing unacceptable to any sincere individual, whatever his belief. At the same time, we are certain that an overwhelming majority of thoughtful and high-minded men and women, whether in the churches or out of them, would welcome it for its positive contributions to the enrichment of the spiritual nature of the child.

(ii.) In Roman Catholic, Anglican, Dissenting and Jewish schools the managers insist upon a certain theological atmosphere as an essential to a true education. We do not pretend that this scheme of ours can supply this. Further, we hold that the State can only apply this scheme in such schools in so far as the managers, teachers and parents are themselves consenting parties. We believe, however, that the State might well insist upon such celebrations as " League of Nations Day " in every school, and insist also that every child should have the right to hear frequently the best literature and music the world has produced. In the child's ample leisure, parents and churches will have full opportunity—if they desire to use it—for the inculcation of particular dogmas. The scheme suggested will make the boy or girl far more responsive to explicit religious teaching; it will make him or her in every desirable way a better Anglican, a better Roman Catholic, a better Baptist, or what not; it will thwart no religious instruction except that conveyed in such a hideous narrowness of doctrine as no one has any right to impose upon a child.

(iii.) The stumbling-block to the framing of any such scheme as this is that each particular religious body believes that it has a "corner in Truth" and can produce results compared with which those produced by other bodies are quite inferior or altogether worthless. But those who hold such conceptions in their old intolerant, dogmatic

---

* In this pamphlet will be found also three other proposals supplementary to that here elaborated, and important, as we believe, in genuine education.

form are now few, though, unfortunately, they still have a powerful grip upon the educational system. Unless we democratically admit that Truth is not the monopoly of any one body or party, that we are all learning, that we are all liable to error, that in any case the points we agree on are numberless compared with the points we disagree on, we shall never spiritualise education. The things for the Churchman or the Dissenter to ask himself are : (*a*) Whether it is not finer to strive for an England of cultured and noble men and women than for those articles of doctrine on which he differs from his fellow creatures; (*b*) whether, if the churches cannot bring themselves to accept a scheme of this kind, there is not a danger that the State will decide upon the secular solution of the religious difficulty, or, at any rate, that education will remain the materialistic, uninspiring, dead thing that it has so long been.

(iv.) This scheme would familiarise every child with all the greatest passages of the Bible. With the methods we propose, the child could not but absorb up to the full limit of his capacity the spirit of Christianity. The Bible would as a consequence become what it ought to be, the inspiration of the nation's life.

(v.) Doubt exists among educationists as to the wisdom of the direct teaching of poetry, music, and even civics and morals. The fact is that such subjects—apart from their technical and superficial aspects—should be *imbibed* rather than systematically taught. We hold that the proposal we have put forward does, in fact, suggest the psychologically appropriate method in which true culture should be imparted to the school children.

(vi.) We make no claim to originality. Fragments of this scheme and approximations to it, of a thousand different varieties, are already in operation all over the country. But in many public elementary schools, if not in most, religious teaching is a farce. What is wanted is the conscious national adoption of a scheme which subserves wholeheartedly the spiritual purposes which we set before ourselves as a people.

(vii.) The liturgy might be compiled, and from time to time modified by a Consultative Committee to the Board of Education, consisting of our leading ministers of religion, thinkers, artists, writers, and musicians. (The dignity attaching to membership of this body ought to be the highest honour offered by the State.)

(viii.) The scheme might be introduced at one stroke by the Minister for Education. We believe that if Mr. Fisher were to insist upon its adoption forthwith in the provided schools he would have behind him a majority of voters and a majority of educationists and teachers.

EDUCATIONAL SELF-GOVERNMENT.

By C. H. C. Osborne

(History Master at Gresham's School, Holt).

The belief in the educational value of self-government, which has resulted in a number of experiments during the last 20 years, is part of the wider movement towards freedom in education, to which many causes and persons have contributed. The Montessori System, in particular, is based, not on the traditional methods of repression and adult domination of the child's activities, but on respect for the child and systematic encouragement of his natural efforts at self-expression. This new attitude of mind has become familiar to the English public, chiefly owing to the enthusiastic support given it by Mr. Edmond Holmes in "What Is and What Might Be" and subsequent writings.*

The first experiments in giving children responsibility for the management of their own affairs began, however, independently and somewhat earlier, in America. It is true that Thomas Arnold had long before, by his adoption of the prefect system at Rugby, established what is sometimes known as the self-government of the public schools. But it is important to realise that this is not really self-government at all. However much power may be delegated to prefects, their functions are at present administrative rather than legislative. They are chosen by and responsible to an external authority, not to the organised public opinion of their fellows. Their motive is either loyalty to an individual or at the best the desire to maintain the reputation of the school. Above all, the prefect system provides training in responsibility only for the few. True self-government is democratically organised and entrusts the group of children with autonomy for the determining and carrying out of the group's objects.

In 1895, Mr. W. R. George founded what was afterwards called the George Junior Republic at Freeville, New York, in order to reclaim the waste material of the city's adolescents.† In his previous work among children Mr. George had adopted a semi-military organisation and discipline, in which he was then a great believer. The only result was anarchy, and he was led to see that laws would not be obeyed unless each individual could be made to realise in an immediate and practical manner how his welfare was affected by their being broken. The children were, therefore, given the power of making and administering the laws of their society, and a legislative assembly, courts, judges, and other officials arose, modelled upon the government of the United States. The Junior Republic rested on an economic basis. The citizens could seek employment from the community or set up in business on their own. With the proceeds of their labour they paid for their food and lodging, while taxes were raised by the Republic for common objects. Laws were soon passed for the protection of property, and these were always readily enforced. The citizen who supported himself by his labour acquired a new self-respect as well as a new sense of responsibility for carrying out the laws. Many interesting developments followed, and as a result of this success, by 1912 eleven other Republics had been founded. In

---

* Edmond Holmes, "What Is and What Might Be" (Constable, 4s. 6d.); "The Tragedy of Education" (Constable, 2s. 6d.).

† W. R. George and L. B. Stowe, "Citizens Made and Remade" (Constable, 5s.).

addition to these communities organised upon an economic basis, there are over a hundred schools in the United States, where the public opinion of the children is apparently sufficient, even without an economic basis, to secure effective self-government.*

The experience gained of the value of self-government in reclaiming children of anti-social habits led to the establishment in 1913 at Evershot, Dorset, of the Little Commonwealth.† An account of the Little Commonwealth is given elsewhere in this book, and here it is only necessary to note that it has in many ways improved upon any of the Republics in the United States, and that while started as a reformatory, and challenging comparison with other reformatories, its success is of much wider significance. The Little Commonwealth is now recognised as an educational experiment of the greatest interest, and it is rightly claimed that the principles which underlie it are capable of application to education generally. It has already inspired experiment in this direction.

The unit of self-government may be either the whole community —a school, for example—or some well-defined group within the community—a house, form, society, or club. Similarly the children may be free to regulate autonomously the whole or only a part of their lives and interests. At the Little Commonwealth the citizens are bound by no rules (other than the laws of England) which they have not made themselves. Every requirement of community life— economic, social, political—is regulated by them. If self-government were given to a house in a boarding school, where decentralisation by houses is the practice, an almost equally wide sphere of legislative, administrative, and judicial action might be secured. Although such complete independence has not yet been granted in England, outside the Little Commonwealth, at least three promising experiments have been made. At Hele's School, Exeter, each form is a self-governing unit, and matters concerning the whole school are dealt with by a representative body—the School Committee—elected by the forms. A strong public opinion in favour of work and order has grown up. Mr. F. G. Snowball, the Head Master, writes that " respect for public opinion seems to produce greater self-restraint in many who under the old conditions were always in trouble," while from the stage of self-restraint from wrong-doing many pass into the stage of active public service. A similar quickening of the instinct for service is seen at the Grammar School, Newbury. Here prefects are chosen by the boys themselves, the school prefects being elected by the two top forms, while each form chooses one or more form prefects. There are " no marks, form orders, or prizes, and rewards and punishments, except such as the boys allot, are practically non-existent. Class teaching as such is rapidly dying out—the boys work in small groups or individually." As an instance of the readiness of the boys to assume responsibility, Mr. Sharwood Smith, the Head Master, writes that when the school porter and cleaner volunteered for national service, the boys offered to do the whole work themselves. They under-took the sweeping, cleaning, looking after the school fields, mowing, rolling, managing the heating apparatus, etc., and the result is that

---

* W. R. George and L. B. Stowe, "Citizens Made and Remade " (Constable, 5s.)

† "Annual Reports of the Little Commonwealth," 1914, 1915, 1916 (the three 1s. 6d.), and Homer Lane in the " Reports of the Conference on New Ideals in Education," 1914, 1915 (the Secretary, 24, Royal Avenue, Chelsea, S.W. 3, 1s. 6d., 1s. 3d.).

"the school is better looked after than ever before." The experiment described by Mr. J. H. Simpson* is noteworthy as a successful attempt to introduce self-government into the somewhat rigid and conservative framework of one of the great public schools. The unit of the experiment was one of the lower forms. At this school, classification by forms is for teaching purposes only, and with terminal promotions involving a constantly changing membership, the form could not hope to develop the corporate feeling, which might be created in a day school, where promotion is yearly, and the form organisation utilised for games and other activities besides work. Yet sufficient scope for legislative and judicial action was found to make the experiment a success, and an earnest of what may be accomplished with a more suitable unit. The boys became responsible not merely for form routine and discipline, but for industry and to some extent for the organisation of their work. Something was done to replace the narrow competitive atmosphere of the public school by a social motive for learning; for, while at any rate lip-service is done to co-operation and social service in the government of our schools, the class-room too often remains purely individualistic in its organisation and ideals. This discrepancy has been more fully realised in America than here. Mr. C. A. Scott, of the Boston Normal School, describes how the children are given time to form free self-organised groups within the class to carry out work chosen and planned by themselves. In this way in several schools, groups have been formed for printing, cooking, photographing, building, play-writing and acting, etc.†

Self-government offers a valuable field of experiment to teachers, but perhaps more than for any other kind of experiment a belief and understanding of the system is essential. To grant liberty in small doses—to grant liberty and at the same time to try and retain a measure of control, is dangerous. The independence of the group must, within the sphere of self-government, be complete. This does not mean, of course, that the individual member enjoys absolute liberty, but his freedom is limited and controlled only by the environment and laws which he helps to create. It must be possible for the children to make mistakes—for the society to break up, if the efforts of the children to learn by experience and their endeavour to hold the group together are to develop true responsibility and self-control. There is no analogy, as Mr. MacMunn urges, between the effects of complete and partial freedom from external control.‡ It is again fatal to mistake the machinery of self-government—the right of electing their own governors, the power of punishing their fellows—for the co-operative spirit, which is the motive power of any healthy society. The very simple constitution of the Little Commonwealth was not framed or imposed by the superintendent; it is entirely the outcome of the needs of the community. "To legislate," says the last annual report, "first in the interests of the community, and, secondly, for the reforming of the individual, is the aim which is supplementing the old idea of the law as a protector of self and property." If self-government is to be a reality, if it is to avoid legalism or merely "playing at it" and to promote a higher social ideal, there must be

---

* J. H. Simpson, "An Adventure in Education." (Sidgwick and Jackson, 2s. 6d.)

† C. A. Scott, "Social Education" (Ginn, 5s.).

‡ N. MacMunn, "A Path to Freedom in the School" (Bell, 2s.).

consciously or unconsciously realised a common end to which each feels he is himself actively contributing and in which each is vitally interested in the contribution of others.

It is impossible in the space available to give any idea of the educational value of self-government. Indeed, the system must be observed in the working. What appear at first sight to be miracles of moral restoration are normal occurrences in the Junior Republics and the Little Commonwealth. That moral education must be social is a well-established psychological fact, and social education has lately received much attention, especially in America. "An individual can no more feel responsibility," says Scott, "without some social motive than a fish can breathe without water." Complaint is often made that the school does not effectively prepare for life. "The particular things which are done at the school do not cultivate even a working majority of the habits of action which are used in the world at large." Still less does the school prepare for citizenship; to remedy this it has been proposed that a new "subject," civics, should be introduced into the curriculum. But no scheme of class study can approach the practical civic training given by membership of a self-governing school or group. Only thus do simple and fundamental political conceptions become part of the living experience of the child. Law then ceases to be an abstraction, or to represent the arbitrary will of a superior. It is understood to be the necessary basis for the working out of the group's interests and ideals. Above all, the citizen of a self-governing school receives the most fundamental social and civic education through the substitution of a co-operative for a competitive ideal. His individuality is not stunted by external authority, nor distorted by a herd instinct which has been driven by repression into an attitude of defiance to all law. In the simpler environment of the school it is possible to effect a reconciliation between the claims of society and the individual which will be a valuable preparation for the more complex circumstances of a wider environment.

A society which aims at being progressive, must encourage the greatest possible development of individuality, if the process of improvement is not to be arrested. A democratic society depends for its survival upon the initiative, adaptability, and social consciousness of all its members. Not only knowledge but the development and guidance of the social impulses is necessary, if democratic government is to be free from the dangers of manipulation by political wirepullers, or if it is to be extended to the workshop. The movement towards self-government in education is, therefore, of great importance to the workers. The prefect system has recently been introduced into some of the elementary schools with the hope of developing in the older children a sense of responsibility. Is there not a danger that it may create in the elementary school the aristocratic or oligarchic traditions of the public schools; or that, in the hands of teachers who do not understand the principles of self-government, it may degenerate into a glorified form of tale-bearing, morally weakening rather than strengthening to the character of the children, and without any social value? Not only in the elementary school, but in connection with the coming national organisation of continued education, emphasis is being laid on the importance of moral and social education, and, self-government being especially suited to adolescents, there is room for the most interesting and fruitful experiment.

THE LITTLE COMMONWEALTH.

By Earl Sandwich.

The Little Commonwealth is based on life principles, and in miniature contains practically all the simpler functions of the State. The objects of those who were responsible for founding it were to demonstrate that, given proper self-expression, the adolescent delinquent boy or girl under the changed atmosphere of a healthy environment tends towards what is right rather than towards what is bad.. The early days of Little Commonwealth history show that order came out of chaos simply as a result of natural conditions. The most readily obeyed of all the laws of the Little Commonwealth is that which forbids a boy or girl to go upstairs into the girl's or boy's side of the cottage, or vice versa, on any pretext whatsoever. This originated from the fact of a boy making a girl an apple-pie bed; a form of amusement which was stoutly resented by the girl, and on the matter being discussed in meeting the rule, as stated, was made. Psychologists will perceive in this case the extraordinary value of taking advantage of circumstances, thus enabling a vital law to be established without even so much as a mention being made of sex relationship.

The Little Commonwealth was founded in 1913 on a farm of some 180 acres, and lies immediately at the foot of a beautiful range of hills known as the Dorset Heights, about nine miles south of Sherborne and four miles from the village of Evershot. The existing farmhouse and adjoining farmyard have been converted gradually into a group of buildings containing a large cottage, a carpenter's shop, steam laundry, and shop (at which the house-mothers of the different cottages buy their supplies), a dairy, and an assembly hall; these surround a paved yard. Three cottages and a farm building, which is being extended to meet the growing requirements of the stock, have been added.

At the outset the cottages were presided over by a member of the staff—house-mothers as they were called—but during the last two years some of the older girl citizens have been placed on a small salary and given charge of a cottage, or the management of the steam laundry, shop, kitchen garden, etc. This change has been undoubtedly of great value. It has been found that the citizen helpers as they are called, being nearer in age and in closer touch with the problems of the citizens, are able to keep the social life of the cottages running more smoothly.

Boys and girls of the same ages as are sent to the ordinary reformatory have been admitted from the children's courts, on a term of probation varying from one to three years. A certain number of other cases have been taken from guardians and parents of children who have not passed through the courts; though some of these have been sent for incorrigibility, the large majority have been committed for theft. Recently a certificate has been obtained from the Home Office placing the Little Commonwealth on the same basis as other reform schools, so that in future cases will be committed for three years, and grants will be obtainable from the Home Office and the

Education Authority which will relieve the strain on the demand for voluntary support.

A great assistance, in adopting as far as possible natural conditions, has been the inclusion of a certain number of small children obtained from the Children's Aid Association or other societies and private sources who are being educated on extended Montessori lines— extended because opportunity is given in such an environment for the Montessori principles to be applied to the home as well as school life; the making of beds, cleaning of rooms, laying of tables, and gardening, etc., form additional modes of expression for these children of equal, if not greater, value than those provided in the class-room. One of the cottages of the Little Commonwealth is set apart for the children.

Cottage life is one of the principal features of the Little Commonwealth; the typical institutional building is conspicuous by its absence. Perfect freedom of intercourse as regards workaday and social life is allowed. Space does not permit of a full discussion of the extraordinary value of no restrictions being placed on intercourse between the sexes in such a community as this. In the Republics in America the boys and girls live apart in separate cottages. At the Little Commonwealth they live together, the provision of separate sleeping accommodation alone excepted. The absence of barriers in itself nullifies the difficulties which many have experienced in co-educational boarding schools. Further, here, owing to the continuous environment, the daily break and change of atmosphere from school to home and home to school, the problem of co-educational day schools, has not to be reckoned with. Further, the girls at the Little Commonwealth have equal rights with the boys, execute the same tasks, as, for example, working on the land that the boys do, receive equal wages for equal work, and perform no servile tasks, such as cleaning the boys' rooms. These conditions, added to the daily rubbing of shoulders and the clash of economic and social interests, tend to place the value of sex relationship on a higher plane than is usual in ordinary life. Employment has in many respects followed the vicissitudes of work in the outside world to-day. Working on the land has to a considerable extent displaced the building which was carried out in the second and third year since the Little Commonwealth was founded. In this connection it may be said that a great part of the skilled work in building, plastering, etc., was done by the boys themselves. In the present extension of the farm building, for instance, the cutting down and sawing up of timber is being carried out by the boys under the supervision of a carpenter who is a member of the staff.

Perhaps the greatest asset in the formation of character at the Little Commonwealth is the economic system. A wage of 3d. to 4d. an hour, or more if of greater value, is paid to the citizens in aluminium coin. If a boy is unable to earn sufficient for his keep he either has to go short of an occasional meal, or, if the deficiency is more serious, a tax has to be raised for his maintenance, which is divided amongst the whole community. This, it need scarcely be said, brings a great pressure to bear upon the slacker, and not a few characters owe their birth to the refusal to become pauperised.

It may be as well here to take stock of the psychological process which takes place from the time when the delinquent starts his career to his gradual development under the new environment. Many of these boys and girls come from homes of bad repute. In some there is a quality of courage which refuses to submit to the brutality of the parent, and an adventurous spirit which is not satisfied with the life of the ordinary school. Truancy and sleeping out follows as a natural result. The delinquent's only experience of authority is one of hardship and intolerance. It cannot be wondered, therefore, that in seeking fresh adventure on the street the policeman is solely regarded by him as the opponent of his activities; he even becomes an incentive to daring, and supplies the means by which success can be achieved. On arrival at the Little Commonwealth our new citizen, an adept perhaps by this time at thieving or swearing, endeavours to achieve the success that he has experienced in the past by these or other anti-social attainments, only to find himself brought up sharply by the lack of response to these achievements. He quickly perceives—after all he is out for success in whatever field may be presented to him— that some other goal must be pursued, and searching for what will bring him success in the eyes of the new group in which he finds himself, finds that they are interested in work, economics, government, and the social life of the small community. At first work comes hardly to him, but after a period of correction or punishment by his fellow citizens he gradually becomes interested and learns to like work for its own sake. That, roughly speaking, in all its variety is the process that takes place.

Perhaps the most interesting feature of self-government at the Little Commonwealth is the court. This is held every week, and is a court of approbation as well as correction. The judge, who is elected by the citizens, fixes the penalty according to laws made in the legislative meeting from week to week, or if no law exists to cover the case formulates one. This, as well as all other decisions, are passed by the majority of the citizens. In this way there is no delegation of power to a jury, as in the case of the Junior Republics in America, and a stronger expression of public sentiment in consequence is formed. Executive power lies in the hands of the citizens whose duty it is to report misdemeanours to the court. Every citizen is, in fact, a peace officer.

Apart from the self-government and economic system, the fundamental difference between the Little Commonwealth and other reform schools lies in the fact that, apart from such adult control over work, as exists in the outer world, in the former there is no organised supervision. One of the leading errors, it seems, of all branches of the penal system, whether prison or reformatory, is that the inmate is expected, for example, to learn not to steal while all opportunity of stealing is removed. In the ordinary world a man is not expected to overcome his weakness, or gain strength of character, by eliminating the temptation, but by overcoming it. This principle of life is followed at the Little Commonwealth; no bolt is put upon the storeroom door, and beyond such supervision as is customary by the foreman over the gang during work hours no other is in vogue. Thus does the Little Commonwealth rely for educational value and the formation of character upon the natural processes of labour, economic independence, and the pressure of public opinion.

THE EXPANSION OF SECONDARY EDUCATION.

By J. L. PATON

(Highmaster of Manchester Grammar School).

The backwardness of England in secondary education was clearly illustrated by Lord Bryce's Commission. No exact figures were available at that time. That fact in itself was a proof of our lack of system in this, the most important branch of national progress. But it was abundantly clear that the proportion of boys and girls receiving secondary education in England was painfully inadequate when compared with the number in any other European country that could claim to be progressive. The contrast was quite as marked, whether one took Germany and Switzerland on one hand, or Denmark and Norway on the other. The figures of Wales, and still more of Scotland, were a silent rebuke to our backwardness. The wealthiest country in Europe was among the most backward to spend on the higher education of its boys and girls. That was the indictment. Our plea was "guilty." There were no extenuating circumstances.

There were men and women ready to argue that the lack of supply was due to lack of demand. Now, it is always fallacious to argue from bales of cotton to human souls. Commercial law does not necessarily hold for the spiritual world, and as a matter of fact, in the history of education, supply has always preceded and evoked and fostered the demand. That this is true also for our own country has been amply demonstrated since the beginning of the present century. 1902 saw the first attempt to put within the reach of every home the opportunity for secondary education. The supply at once evoked the demand ; the demand grew and grew so fast that supply has never succeeded in catching up with it. Even in war time, with a clamant demand for juvenile labour, and a scale of remuneration which is out of all proportion to what was in vogue before, with boys and girls under 16 able to command a wage of 35s. per week—even under these conditions, the number in our secondary schools has steadily grown, the figures for 1915-16 showing an increase of over 6 per cent. That rate of increase would certainly be higher if the schools were able to accommodate the pupils who present themselves for entrance, but with the war all building has been stopped, and a good many schools in big towns have been dispossessed of their premises. The consequence is that at the present moment the supply is definitely inadequate to the demand, and many boys and girls are being excluded from the advantages of higher education, whose parents are willing to pay for it. Not only so, but the buildings are overcrowded, and the classes are becoming unwieldily large, also owing to the men of military age being called up, the teachers in day schools are predominantly feminine.

In laying plans for the expansion of secondary education, we are therefore working along the line of spontaneous growth. What happened in Scotland many years ago, what happened in Wales at the end of last century, is happening in England now. At last she has caught the contagion, and is awake to the fact that she must take the flood on the rise or the rest of her national life will be bound in shallows and in miseries.

What do these lines of growth appear to be? It is to be noted that it is the day school, and not the boarding school, that is growing. This is a sign of health. Only the day school can cover the ground and meet the national need. The day school is the only way of opening up education to those social strata of our popula tion with whom the hope of the future resides—the better-paid artisans, the worse-paid professional classes, and that increasing proportion of the population which works under the management of large joint-stock concerns. But Nature does not confine ability to any social stratum, and wherever nature provides the brains, it is for the nation to provide the training—the best training of which those brains are capable. The best brain in the Army, the brain on which the whole well-being of our Army depends, was born in a charwoman's home. First and foremost, then, an enlightened national policy means that we must open up the way for the lad of parts, and equally for the girl of parts, to climb to the highest positions which they are capable of filling, and to render the highest service they are capable of rendering not only in our Government administration, but also in the universities, in commerce, in industry, and in the professions.

Not only so, but the whole level of our national education must be raised. Social progress is not the progress of select individuals here and there, it is the progress of the whole body politic. The gifted few must find their chance, but the ungifted many must not be shut out from the kingdom of light, the treasure house of knowledge and all the things that are more excellent. Until that is done, our democratic government remains democratic only in name, and the basis of our democratic government is insecure because it is un-enlightened. The lines of our advance must be determined mainly by our national needs. These are only too plain at the present time.

1. Our land produces, on the mildest computation, only half the foodstuffs which it should produce. Many causes, legislative and economic, contribute to this, with which we have not now to deal, but the chief cause is, after all, educational. Land cultivation needs not only the sweat of the brow but sweat of the brain. The allotment which the cultivator must assiduously till is the allotment that lies within the walls of his own skull. The educational curriculum of the country school must be related vitally to the science of the garden, the field, and the hedgerow, with which the pupil is daily familiar. It must train his hand to execute the purpose or the invention of his mind. It must open up the way without let or hindrance for the pupil who has brains to learn all that the best agricultural science has to teach him about the management of cattle and crops.

Owing to the scattered nature of the population, this will inevitably mean hostels with free board and tuition in connection with well-placed and well-equipped secondary schools.

The town boy who has aptitude for the land must not be forgotten, and urban authorities which provide all manner of technical and university scholarships must not forget to provide for the higher education of the boy or girl whose bent is agricultural.

In this sphere one may almost say that everything has yet to be done. The yield of the ground in Belgium is five times per acre what it is in England. In Germany, where the soil is far poorer, the yield is twice as great. In other countries the annual yield shows increase; in England it shows shrinkage. There is a much-quoted saying which cries blessing on the head of him who makes two blades of grass grow where one grew before. The saying is foolish. Men and women cannot live on grass. Not grass but corn must be the *leit motif*.

2. The second need is industrial. The war has opened the eyes of the nation as never before to the weaknesses of our industrial position. It has made us see how America, Germany, Austria, and Switzerland, by the study of electricity and applied science in all its branches, have been able to wrest from us whole provinces of production, even when the invention which made these new productions possible was of English origin. What has always been clear to a few is now patent to all, viz., that without a higher standard and a wider range of scientific knowledge our nation stands to lose not only its industrial position, but even its power of self-defence. In this matter we have been too eager for immediate results. We have not taken the long view. We have acted individually when we should have co-operated in our several trades. We have been blind to the industrial value of science.

Our new system must provide for a far closer association between our universities and the work of our staple industries. This implies, in the first place, a less donnish attitude on the part of dons, and appreciation on the part of the manufacturer of the value of that theoretical study of science which hitherto he has set down as academic and unpractical. It will not be a case of quick returns. The call is for prolonged study, concentration, patient endeavour, and a fixing of the eye on distant consequences; in a word, what Benjamin Kidd calls " projected efficiency."

The call is, further, for a new spirit of co-ordination and co-opera- tion on the part of manufacturers and traders of all kinds. Hitherto, competition has been between firm and firm; in the future competition will be between nation and nation, and the nation whose forces are not marshalled and organised will go under. This spirit of co-operation, which is needed as much in agriculture as in industry and commerce, is, like the power of waiting for distant results, a moral quality. And for these moral qualities the school must prepare; in all school societies a healthy corporate spirit is as much needed for national efficiency as sound and strenuous intellectual work.

3. It is, therefore, clear that there must be not only secondary education for the man who is to take up higher directive work, but there must be a higher standard of civic education and intelligence on the part of all the workers in the different trades. The Junior Technical Schools, though few in number, show clearly on what lines progress can be made. Secondary education must not be exclusively bookish; many an English lad is intelligent without being intellectual, just as many are intellectual without being intelligent. At present we put perhaps too much premium on the boy who is intellectual. A secondary curriculum which shall be focussed on practical constructive work, and get its problems for thinking out of the needs of practical occupation, has yet to be thought out. There is no doubt that it will appeal very strongly to a large proportion of English boyhood who have the instinct for things but do not respond to the appeal of words and literary form. American experience shows us how such a scheme of practical secondary education can be infused with a generous and inspiring interest in poetry and literature.

4. For many years the nation has felt that her secondary education was not as effective as it might be for the purposes of commercial efficiency. Its dissatisfaction has not been very articulate, and to meet

it there has grown up a type of " commercial education " which has brought deserved discredit on the term. Shorthand, typewriting, long-tots and cross-tots may be necessary, but they do not call into play the higher activities of the mind. Many of these processes of drudgery will before long be replaced by mechanical contrivance. What we need is a new type of school which shall teach languages as living things, with practical application from the first to the needs of everyday existence, which shall develop in connection with geography the study of products and trade routes, and in connection with history the study of economic law, and so lead on to the intelligent study of economic science as a whole. In this connection it is relevant to point out that in all our universities, and especially in our ancient universities, the study of modern languages lags far behind every other faculty. It is safe to say that at the present time there is next to no organic connection between the highest modern language work in our secondary schools and the universities. This lack of upward development has reacted most prejudicially upon the development of modern language teaching in the schools.

Nothing has been said so far about what are called the learned professions. The reason is that there is no evidence of serious national deficiency in connection with these professions except in the profession of teaching. Indeed, it is evident that a large number of unemployed barristers might have found a much more useful employment of their gifts on the lines of national industry and commerce. But it must not be forgotten that the learned professions, being scientific, must necessarily also be progressive, and in developing on the lines indicated we cannot afford to weaken the provision for these professions or for the higher branches of our civil service. Whether the Civil Service in its lower branches is not absorbing an undue proportion of high-class intellect, and finding for it employment which is by no means commensurate with its intellectual quality, is a question well worthy of consideration by the directors of our national educational policy.

Clearly the position calls for strong handling and a mind that shall be not only synoptic but able to plan on a big comprehensive scale for the future. It must provide machinery which shall not be static but ready equipped for progress in any required direction, which shall not be centralised and bureaucratic, but in touch with local needs, appealing to local patriotism, and adapted to local needs. Above all, our national system must not be laid down in rigid horizontal strata; it must provide for upward mobility on every line, and in order to secure that there shall be no waste of that most precious of all material—human souls, it must exercise educational control and guidance over every boy and girl up to the age of 18. And the need is immediate.

> " Build to-day, then, strong and sure,
>   With a firm and ample base,
>   And ascending and secure
>   Shall to-morrow find its place."

REFERENCES.—A. P. Fleming : " Training of Apprentices." " Interim Report of Consultative Committee on Scholarships." Norwood and Hope : " Higher Education of Boys."

G

THE NEGLECT OF ADOLESCENCE.

By Arnold Freeman.

"It is impossible now to estimate how much of the intellectual and physical energy of the world was wasted in military preparation and equipment, but it was an enormous proportion. Great Britain spent upon Army and Navy money and capacity that, directed into the channels of physical culture and education, would have made the British the aristocracy of the world. Her rulers could have kept the whole population learning and exercising up to the age of 18, and made a broad-chested and intelligent man of every Bert Smallways in the island, had they given the resources they spent in war material to the making of men. Instead of which they waggled flags at him until he was 14, incited him to cheer, and then turned him out of school to begin that career of private enterprise we have compactly recorded. France achieved similar imbecilities; Germany was, if possible, worse; Russia, under the waste and stresses of militarism, festered towards bankruptcy and decay. All Europe was producing big guns and countless swarms of little Smallways."—H. G. Wells, "The War in the Air."

The onset of puberty marks the commencement of adolescence. Manhood or womanhood marks its close. In the interim, as the term itself signifies, we *grow*. Nature's ordinance is, that during this period the child shall put away childish things and learn to be a man. This is what adolescence is *for*. Upon this fundamental fact this article is based.

Nature's purpose for youth is manifest in all the various phases of adolescent growth. Underlying them all—to take first, the most compelling illustration—is the development of the sex instinct. Heralding a myriad terrors and glories, fraught with inexaggerable consequences for the individual and the race, the sex instinct now first asserts itself, and ere long ends by dominating the consciousness. Upon the understanding and control of this instinct, more than upon any other achievement in life, depend the happiness of the individual and the well-being of the race. The most patent external sign of adolescence is the growth in height and weight—the boy or girl suddenly "shoots up." So considerable is this development that nature finds it difficult to co-ordinate one with another all the numberless local growths. That is why children are so awkward at this age and suffer unduly from physical and mental disorders. That is why it is of supreme importance that we should supplement nature's efforts by giving the adolescents their fill of wholesome food, clean air, boisterous exercise, and sound sleep.

To the boys and girls themselves—as anyone, by shutting his eyes may recall from his own past—this period is one of intense sensation, soul-stirring emotions, and endless braggart dreams. In our youth we were all of us poets and artists, lovers and heroes. What man worth his salt has not rescued beauteous virgins from wicked robbers? Has not made orations to applauding multitudes? And while we young men saw visions, the young maidens also, for all their silence, were dreaming dreams. The world was an oyster to us then, as it is now; but in those days we had a magic sword with which to open it, and lo! we discovered a pearl.

During early adolescence, however, reason and will, Nature's sovereign gifts, are imperfectly developed. At this stage of growth Nature bares the soul to the universe, allowing impressions from the outer world to pour in unrestrained; and not till the later teens does she give the power of self-control, which will enable the young man or woman to utilise wisely their accumulated wealth of ideas. Never are we so impressionable, so plastic, so teachable, as in early youth. In each case, for the same reason, this is the age when churches win their converts, and the age at which most criminal careers begin. During early adolescence surroundings determine our destiny; we become what external influences make us.

It is plain that in an ideal civilisation this plastic period would be monopolised for education. The statesmen of Utopia would see in the young men and women committed to their charge one thing only— the future. They would see in them the splendid possibilities of citizenship of which the adolescents are themselves dreaming. Recognising that the one end of statecraft should be the building up of a community of fine and capable human creatures, they would make the utmost of every boy and girl.

But what do we do now?

In future ages they will scarce believe it of us. Our neglect of adolescence will be looked back upon as the consummate instance of the communal crimes for which we shall be despised. At the very hour when that all-important sex instinct is beginning to obtrude itself upon consciousness, we release boys and girls from school discipline and allow them to sally forth unprotected and uninstructed into the world. They spend the bulk of their time in dreary, uneducative, and often demoralising labour, working, as a rule, longer hours than the grown-ups. During these twelve hours or so their keen senses and eager emotions are cheated. The reaction in leisure time is therefore inevitable.

Your fagged juvenile workers, seeing the church or the institute, pass by on the other side. They are too jaded for religion or education; too tired, perhaps, even for exercise. Their thwarted instincts demand abnormal excitement. And in lounging about the streets, in watching football matches, in reading "comics" and "bloods," in frequenting music halls, and, above all, in patronising picture palaces, they find what they seek.

These pursuits provide them their training for adult life. By such influences the mass of our citizens are being shaped into men and women. "During early adolescence surroundings determine our destiny; we become what external influences make us." It cannot be stated too emphatically that "England" is, on the whole, what cheap literature, music halls, and picture palaces make her. Two boys and girls out of three get the greater part of their philosophy of life from these sources—their everyday wisdom, their politics, their religion.

And my own belief—supported by not a little first-hand investigation—is that these influences are almost altogether debasing. The growing boy and girl find all the most sacred and serious things in life treated superficially, flippantly, coarsely. Marriage and children are a joke; politics are a joke; religion is a superlative joke. Sexual irregularities, drunkenness, gambling, and all such terrible evils are the stock humours of songs, papers, and films. The mind of the young man or woman is filled year after year—during this fatally impressionable   period—with   unreal,   frivolous,   and   degrading suggestions.

Thus the work of the elementary school is undone. And the final result of our social neglect of adolescence is that we have growing up about us an enormous population of workers who do not know how to work, of voters who do not know how to vote, and of parents who are not capable of rearing healthy and intelligent families. Largely in consequence of this general incapacity, we have that which we proudly call "Our Country"—low wages, slums, disease, dirt, vice, wretchedness.

In the Introduction to the official Elementary School Code we have long been informed that : "The purpose of the public elementary school is to make the best use of the school years available in assisting boys and girls, according to their different needs, to fit themselves, practically as well as intelligently, for the work of life." That the elementary school fails to do this is generally admitted. Why does it fail?

It fails because it is attempting an impossible task. As hopefully try to teach a caterpillar to fly as attempt to fit a whipster of 13 or 14 for the "work of life." For the man the "work of life" consists in duties to his employer, to his wife and children, and to the State. The woman's duties are for the most part embraced in her manifold activities in the home. Because its control ends prematurely, the elementary school cannot, for either sex, do what the official code requires of it. How can an urchin in knickerbockers learn— "practically as well as intelligently"—his duties as a worker, as the head of a household, as a citizen? How can a little girl learn to bring up a baby (to say nothing of keeping a husband in order)? Even if by some supernatural jugglery such knowledge could be given, is it not obvious that the child would forget it long before it reached the age when it could make use of it? The thing is too ridiculous to need elaboration. Is it at 14 that richer-class schooling ends?

If we are ever to build a State worthy of our loyalty, we must give to the poor, no less than to the rich, an education adequate to the industrial, political, social, and spiritual demands of adult life. It is not sufficient to supplement elementary schooling with a beggarly eight hours a week during the first few years of youth. Such a reform will be no more than a rather shameful beginning.

The people of this country must be entirely freed from profit-making during the whole period of their adolescence. Until that is done there will be no Utopia built—except upon paper.

[NOTE.—For suggestions upon the sort of education we largely want during adolescence see a pamphlet by Dr. F. H. Hayward, entitled "The Religious Difficulty in Schools" (6d., post free of the author, 87, Benthal Road, N. 16). Dr. Hayward has his eyes upon scholars of the elementary schools, but his proposals (*e.g.*, for a national liturgy of Bible, literature and music, and for the controversial treatment of civic problems) seem to me to be more fruitfully applicable to adolescent education.]

REFERENCES.—For an exhaustive bibliography consult "Boy Life and Labour," by Arnold Freeman.

HOW TO PAY FOR EDUCATION.

By Sidney Webb

(Professor of Public Administration in the University of London, School of Economics and Political Science).

We talk of free education, meaning that we should like it to be gratuitous, or without cost. But education, like other human contrivances, cannot ever be without cost, and the question has to be considered how it can be best paid for. There is some thing very attractive in the Hindoo idea that all tuition ought to be gratuitously given by the teacher—that those who have acquired wisdom are under a moral obligation to impart it freely to those willing to be instructed. Auguste Comte insisted on the same principle, which we all feel to be imperative when there is a question of any discovery in the medical art or in physical science being withheld from the world. But even the Hindoo *guru* needs to be provided with subsistence whilst he is teaching, as the medical or scientific investigator does whilst he is discovering; and what seems a small item when we think only of the bowl of rice given to a single wandering prophet becomes in itself a considerable matter when we have to take into account the whole class of teachers· required for a nation. It follows that we are anyhow faced by the question of How to Pay for Education.

When we talk of the cost of education we usually think only of the education of the child, or at any rate of the non-adult. Of course, education ought to continue throughout the whole of life; and, in some sense, it always does so continue. Life, as we say, is itself the great instructor. But we have hitherto made too little account of the desirability of providing formal instruction, and special opportunities for learning, for adults who are willing to take advantage of them. It was a suggestion of William Morris that the community ought to be so glad and thankful that any grown man or woman should desire to be instructed in any subject whatsoever, or to be made wiser, and should be willing to take the trouble to learn, that the community should eagerly provide the tuition and welcome persons of any age, however ignorant, without fee or formality, to its public schools and colleges. Let us, however, postpone for the moment the question of adult education and begin with the sufficiently extensive problem of how to pay for the education of the non-adult.

Now it is worth notice that the old Whig doctrine of " supply and demand," and of the desirability of leaving everybody to buy what he liked, at its price in the market, does not apply to the education of the child. Schooling, like birth and burial, is one of the fundamental human needs that cannot possibly be paid for by the individual concerned, who has simply to suffer, in mind or body, whatever other people choose to inflict upon him. The characteristic Early Victorian notion that schooling was a commodity supplied, not to the child, but to the parent, and that it was accordingly to be provided according to the demand of the parent, and at the parent's expense, went along with the Early Victorian idea of the adult male's " property " in his children, as in his wife, in his church pew, in his vote, in his sinecures, and in anything else that was " his." Needless to say, this idea still lingers. To this day it is almost impossible to make the old-fashioned " man of property " realise, when he professes to desire " equality of opportunity," that it is not " equality of opportunity " *to the children* to condemn them all to whatever education their parents can afford, and may choose, to pay for. And, to take quite a different illustration, it does not seem yet to have occurred to those who, in Parliament or at the Treasury, decide the salary scales of the various grades of public employees, that whilst there may conceivably be reasons for paying some employees thousands a years and some hundreds a year, when the wages of others are reckoned only in dozens or in scores of pounds sterling per annum, yet it is difficult to discover any reason whatsoever for allowing, as we do, to the children of the one grade of Civil Servants any less advantageous opportunities of education than to the children of the other grade.

To come to the financial facts for this country to-day we may estimate that the cost of all the formal education in the United Kingdom, in class or school or college or educational institution of any kind, from the humblest nursery school and kindergarten up to the post-graduate research laboratory of the university—together with the professional private tuition that goes on, but necessarily excluding the incalculable training given by the parents and in the families themselves, does not reach £50,000,000 a year, and is probably much less. We spend, that is to say, on teaching and training the whole of the rising generation, less than 2 per cent. of our aggregate national product or income, rather more than we give for our cigarettes and tobacco, but less than a third of what we devote to alcoholic drink. Thus, our whole expenditure on education is really an astonishingly minute sum. Even including the maintenance of the young people from birth to manhood—the expenses of nursing, minding, feeding, clothing, lodging, teaching, training, and amusing all the boys and girls up to 21, except in so far as a proportion of them have prematurely become producers and are supporting themselves—it is difficult to put the amount that we allot for this purpose in the whole kingdom, including the lavish expenditure on their children of some of the wealthy, at more than £150,000,000 a year. Those under 21 who have not yet entered productive industry number about a third of the whole population. But we do not spend on all their needs, including education, more than a fifteenth of our available income. As a nation we are horribly stingy to our young people. Those who, as parents, sacrifice to their children a large part of their lives and income refuse, as electors, to adopt anything like the same policy for the community as a whole, even when it would involve no additional sacrifice from themselves.

As parents we may be wisely keen on giving our own children the very best equipment for life that we can discover or devise; but as citizens we still habitually ignore the fact that the children, as a whole, are the most profitable asset that the State possesses; that, far more even than our agricultural land, it would pay the community to cultivate them most highly, and that nothing is so wasteful as permitting them to grow up either physically or mentally undernurtured and undeveloped. It used to be predicted before the war that the 20th century would be the century of the child. After the war the world will find it more than ever necessary and profitable to double or to treble the opportunities and advantages that it has hitherto allowed to the young. But shall we be prepared to do so?

Confining ourselves to the one-third of our total expenditure on the non-adult which is devoted to formal education, we see at once that the largest item in the bill is for the salaries of the teachers; the corps numbering, for the United Kingdom, including teachers of all kinds and grades, possibly as many as a quarter of a million men and women, whose salaries and emoluments, shamefully inadequate as they mostly are, must amount to something like 30 millions sterling. It is interesting to note that, so far are we from equality in educational opportunities, that the amount that we spend under this head of teachers' salaries varies from less than 20s. a year for each child in some of the rural elementary schools up to more than £20 or £30 a year for each boy in some of the so-called " public schools " frequented by the sons of the wealthy. The cost per undergraduate of the aggregate teaching staff at a university is, of course, often greater still.

The other large item in the educational budget is the cost of providing and maintaining the buildings in which the instruction is given. This takes the form, in the main, of interest and sinking fund on the loans by means of which the land was bought and the buildings were erected; and it appears to amount, in the United Kingdom, to something like eight or ten millions a year.

Apart from the salaries and emoluments of the teaching staff and the provision and maintenance of the educational buildings, the remaining items are unimportant. But they include the cleaning, lighting, heating, and repairing of the premises, the provision and maintenance of what may be called the educational plant (furniture, equipment, maps, pictures, casts, etc.), and the supply of books, both for use in class and for general reading in libraries.

At present we pay for education in four ways, to the extent of some 20 millions a year out of the rates levied on the householders by the Local Education Authority; to the extent of some 15 millions a year out of the grants-in-aid from the National Exchequer, which are contributed by all the payers of taxes; to the extent, possibly, of two or three millions a year out of the income of endowments bequeathed or given for the purpose; and to an unknown extent, possibly of a couple of millions a year, out of fees paid by the parents. It is difficult to imagine any other way by which the education of young people could be paid for. The three questions that arise seem to be : First, ought anything to be got from fees? Second, ought any old endowments to be permitted to be allocated to particular purposes, or should they be merged in the common educational revenue? And, third, ought the provision made from public revenues to be drawn from local or from national funds?

To take first the question of fees. At present we provide primary education in the public elementary schools without fee; but— mitigated by a more or less extensive supply of free places, exhibitions, and scholarships—we often charge fees in the " higher elementary " and evening continuation schools, we do so almost invariably in the secondary schools, and we do so always in the universities and technical colleges. These fees vary from a merely nominal charge of a shilling or two up to fifty or a hundred pounds a year charged in one or other way for tuition alone at the most expensive colleges. (We must for the moment ignore the additional expenses involved in board and lodging.) It is to be noted that (except in the 500 or 600 " preparatory schools " for the young children of the wealthy; in the still surviving " private venture " secondary schools for girls and in a few cases for boys; and in a few of the so-called " public schools " for boys and more expensive colleges for undergraduates of either sex) the fees charged are insufficient to cover the cost of the education. In the vast majority of cases in which fees are paid the pupil is nevertheless being subsidised—often to an extent far exceeding the subsidy enjoyed by the child in the " free " school—out of the rates and taxes or out of endowments of public character. In fact, it is Eton and Winchester that are, literally and precisely, " charity schools "—not, as one Duchess ignorantly declared, the unendowed public elementary schools. All the universities, not excluding even Oxford and Cambridge, now receive substantial subsidies from the rates or the taxes, just as do all but a few schools, primary or secondary. It would be difficult nowadays to find any family whatsoever, however wealthy or highly placed, in which one or other member has not benefited at some time, often without realising the fact, from the House of Commons Vote for education, or from the rate levied by the Local Education Authority, or from some endowment of public character. Whether the education, to the individual pupil, is or is not " free," it is nowadays, in nearly all cases, subsidised in one or other way by the community. We have lost all such shame as we ever felt, even the most Whiggish among us, at thus benefiting from public money. Why, then, it is naturally asked, should we continue to charge fees to the extent in the aggregate of perhaps a couple of millions a year?

Now the institutions or instructors charging fees in the United Kingdom fall into two categories, according to whether or not they are effectively under the control of the Government or Local Education Authority. By far the most important of them are not under such control. Among these are the 500 or 600 expensive " preparatory schools " at which about 25,000 boys between 9 and 13, coming from rich households, are boarded and lodged and " prepared " for the so-called " public " schools or the Navy; a hundred or two of these " public " schools themselves, existing as self-governing foundations under bodies of trustees, who charge high fees, receive no grants, and have relatively small endowments, or none at all; and the still surviving, entirely unsubsidised " private venture " day and boarding schools for girls and (in a much smaller number of cases) for boys, which charge fees covering the whole cost and even yielding a profit to their proprietors. We cannot very well prohibit these schools from charging the fees that the parents are willing to pay; and so long as we permit persons to have large incomes we cannot prevent their spending part of these incomes in providing extravagantly for their children—even if their object is one no more praiseworthy than to keep them " uncontaminated " by contact with the children of parents with smaller incomes. The same is true of the Universities of Oxford and Cambridge and their constituent colleges, which do not substantially depend on the small grants that they now get from the Government for special departments, and are not, in fact, subject to any effective public control. And with these ᵗ fee-charging institutions we must, for this purpose, class the extensive range of teachers and instructors in music, dancing, drawing, shorthand, bookkeeping, and other " accomplishments," to whom young people voluntarily resort and pay fees in order to acquire something that they, or their parents, desire. With all these fees we cannot practically interfere without an unwarrantable restriction on individual liberty.

The question of the abolition of fees accordingly relates, as a practical issue, to those schools and colleges which are, to any effective extent, under the control of the Government or the Local Education Authority. These comprise the thousand secondary day or boarding schools for boys and girls, which are either maintained by the Local Education Authority or else so extensively aided by its grants or those of the Government as to be practically subject to its decisions; the evening continuation schools and the hundreds of technical and other colleges now almost everywhere maintained by the Local Education Authority with Government aid; and the Scottish, Irish, Welsh, and English universities (other than Oxford and Cambridge) which depend to such an extent on grants from the rates or taxes as to be practically in the hands of the Government.

The arguments in favour of the total abolition of fees in these essentially public educational institutions are strong. It would bring them into line with the public elementary schools. If, as may be hoped, we are now to have universally obligatory training from 14 to 18, at any rate to the extent of eight hours per week, this will certainly have to be provided without fee. The fee, which in this whole class of cases is never anything like adequate to cover the cost, operates as an obstacle to the children of poor parents, and when these struggle to surmount it, constitutes an unfair tax on parental unselfishness and self-sacrifice. And the segregation of children of the parents able to afford the school fee—largely shop-keepers, farmers, and the salariat—maintains, in the public education of the community, an invidious feeling of class " gentility," which is as detrimental to those schools which are despised as being " free," and are resorted to in the main by the children of the wage-earners, as it is to those which snobbishly pride themselves on being " select." Finally, there can be no real Social Democracy without a genuine equality of " common schooling," securing to every citizen, however high he may soar in knowledge or status, a uniform minimum of the elements of civilisation and an identical code of manners in personal relations; and this, it is strongly urged, can be obtained only when all classes use the same schools.

On the other hand, the practical administrator finds great difficulty in abolishing all fees in schools and college. He sees no chance of any universal abolition of such fees; he realises that their abolition in the institutions under municipal or Government control, far from leading to their abolition in those not under such control, would, in the present state of public opinion, certainly fortify the proprietors and governors of these practically independent schools and colleges in their determination to retain their fees, and thus more than ever to mark themselves off from the institutions of the common people. There would accordingly be a worse and more " snobbish " class segregation, certainly a greater diversity of manners, and probably a greater inequality in the elements of civilisation than there is at present. Moreover, though it may seem obvious that the exaction of fees hinders the children of poor parents from taking advantage of secondary schools, technical colleges, and universities, the case becomes less clear upon examination. In many parts of the United States the public secondary schools are as free as the public elementary schools; and in some of the Western States the universities are equally free from fees. But—though this is apparently uncomprehended by any patriotic American—the children of the great mass of the people nevertheless remain as a matter of fact excluded from these institutions. The proportion among the population of free-school Chicago obtaining more than primary schooling is no greater than that among the population of fee-paying London. When Mr. Carnegie threw open the Scottish universities, free of charge, to every Scottish youth or maiden, this virtual abolition of university fees was not found to increase, to any revolutionary extent, the number of their undergraduates; and it has been seriously doubted whether the percentage of children of manual-working wage-earners gaining access to the Scottish universities has been at all increased by practically abolishing the fee-barrier. The fact is that what prevents the children of the manual-working wage-earners from obtaining secondary or university education is not so much the fees that are exacted as the cost of maintenance of the pupil between 14 and 19, and between 19 and 22, together with the family sacrifice involved in forgoing, during these years, any earning of an income in aid of the parental household. To abolish the high school and college fees is not, as might be imagined, to throw open these institutions to wage-earner and employer alike; but almost entirely, whilst leaving the class segregation as before, to confer a financial boon on the middle and upper class. And even when it is only a question of evening continuation schools and technical colleges, the fact cannot be ignored that practical experience of absolutely free admission is not wholly favourable. Where there has been no fee, enrolment has often been multitudinous, but it has been equally light-headed; and it has been followed by an immediate falling away of attendance. It seems as if that which is not paid for, if only by a nominal fee, is too often apt to be valued at the price charged for it. In view of the difficulty of inducing the representatives of the average citizen to devote any public money whatever to higher education, or to the teaching of any but the most flagrantly Philistine subjects, those concerned for the extension of the most valuable of all kinds of education naturally hesitate to sacrifice—almost entirely as a gift to those who do not need public assistance—the income that the fees afford.

Thus, the position is that, with the present distribution of wealth, we cannot, if we would, achieve anything like a universal abolition of educational fees or compel all children and young persons, irrespective of their parents' means or wishes, to sit side by side in the class-room or lecture-hall. We cannot, in fact, make even any considerable progress towards this democratic ideal except step by step with our progress towards equality of income. Here, as elsewhere, political democracy depends on Social Democracy, and Radicalism discovers that, if it is to achieve its own ends, it must evolve into Socialism. In the present intermediate stage the practical administrator, in education as in everything else, has to make what compromise he can.

What we have to assert as the democratic policy in education is, first, that, in the interests of the families concerned, whatever education is made universally obligatory shall also be made entirely gratuitous to the pupil and the parent; and, secondly, in the interests of the community as a whole, that no child or young person, however indigent may be his parents, shall be prevented by poverty from obtaining access to all the education, however prolonged and however costly, that his abilities enable him to take adequate advantage of. Such a policy demands much more than the partial abrogation of educational fees, which is alone within our reach, and is not dependent on their complete and universal abolition.

The first part of the democratic policy in education requires, not merely the removal of fees in the public elementary and continuation schools, but also gratuitous school books and gratuitous access to all the advantages offered by these schools; the ample provision and satisfactory staffing and equipment of such schools in town and country alike, up to the needs of the whole population and of all its separate sections (such as the mentally defective, the blind, the crippled, etc.), and, what is not always remembered, the supply of whatever medical treatment, food, and clothing may be required in the case of the children of indigent parents to enable these, as well as the sons and daughters of parents who are better off, to obtain (as no fewer than one-sixth of all the children in the public elementary schools in this country are now prevented from obtaining) even a reasonable degree of benefit from the educational advantages that are provided. The schools which charge no fee need, in fact, equally with those which charge fees, to be made genuinely accessible to the whole people. In this direction an enormous amount still remains to be done, in the United States and Canada, in New Zealand and Australia, as well as in the United Kingdom, to achieve really " free education " even in the public elementary schools—which may well be deemed a matter of prior importance to the mere abolition of fees in secondary schools and university colleges !

The second part of the democratic policy in education—the effective opening-up to every boy and girl whatever opportunities of education above and beyond the compulsory grades their abilities enable them to take adequate advantage of—involves much more than the abolition of fees. It is only partly satisfied by the provision, from one end of the kingdom to the other, of a sufficient number of " free places " in all schools or colleges receiving any public aid, to be awarded upon proof of aptitude or promise in any direction whatever, to the children of parents able to maintain them at home, but unable to afford the fees for the special instruction they require. Nor would it be any more satisfied if all the school fees were abolished. It demands much more. It insists on the necessity, if the opportunity of the child of wage-earning parents to proceed along the educational highway is to be made a real one, of an adequate supply of maintenance scholarships, covering the full cost of maintenance as well as of schooling, to be awarded at successive ages—say, at 11-12 for the mass; at 14-15 for those who may develop late or have been missed at the first intake; at 18-19 for those whom the community needs to train further in a university, technical, or teachers' training college; and at 22-23 for the specialists destined for post-graduate or research work. These maintenance scholarships will, of course, have to vary in value (especially where they are not made tenable at a residential school or college), beginning, perhaps, with a small sum of £6 or £12 a year, in addition to a free place, and rising to £40, £80, or even £150 a year in the later stages. And in order to ensure equality of opportunity all over the country, to prevent a stingy Local Education Authority from depriving the children within its area of their legitimate opportunities, and to equalise the burden as between rich areas and poor, this great scholarship scheme ought to be national in its organisation and in its financial basis, although as far as possible local in its administration. The experience gained during the last decade with local scholarship schemes indicates that (apart from the definite percentage of free places that all aided secondary schools and university and technical colleges should be required to provide), the national scholarship scheme, in its various grades and different branches of study, ought to extend to the selection, for the whole United Kingdom, of at least 30,000 scholars of either sex and of different ages annually, involving the maintenance, after the scheme had got completely under way, of about 150,000 national scholars at any one time, or about 2 per cent. of the school population. This would involve an addition to the Education Estimates for England and Wales of no more than three or four millions sterling annually; and, unlike the mere abolition of school fees, it would, for the first time, effectively open up to the poor child of any intellectual aptitude or promise a real educational highway.

The question raised by educational endowments has become one of relatively small importance. The democratic purse is now so enormously greater than that of the most munificent testator! The whole mass of such endowments in the United Kingdom, from the " ragged schools " to Eton, from the Oxford and Cambridge Colleges to Mr. Carnegie's libraries, do not amount to as much as the proceeds of a 2d. rate or those of a single penny of the 5s. income tax. This, of course, is no reason why any of the endowments should be allowed to be wasted or misapplied or diverted from any class of beneficiaries for whom they were destined. But it behoves us to keep a proper sense of proportion. We must not allow ourselves to be diverted from securing an adequate appropriation of the national income to education—say, an addition of 30 or 40 millions a year from the rates and taxes—by any idea of improving the application of a few hundreds of thousands a year from educational endowments.

We ought to insist on full and public inquiry into the objects, the past and present administration, the expenses, and the measure of current success of every educational endowment (as, indeed, of every other endowment), not because we allege or suspect that any particular endowment is being wrongly dealt with, but because experience shows that all endowments are, with the lapse of years, apt to go to sleep, to become bound in old routine, to pursue aims and ends that have become obsolete, and—in quite a large proportion of cases—to fritter away money unnecessarily in expenses—in fact, not to put too fine a point upon it, to be misapplied. Moreover, it is the rarest thing in the world for any corporate body to reform itself from within. Every endowment administered by a body of Trustees or Governors ought, whatever its object or purpose, to be systematically overhauled every 20 years—not necessarily to be compulsorily "reformed" (though the liability to such reform should exist), but primarily in order to let in fresh light, to get the proceedings reviewed by outside critics, and to supply the Trustees or Governors themselves with an up-to-date, considered judgment upon their proceedings, which they might be left, in the first instance, to act on or not as they thought fit.

In connection with educational endowments, however, it must be remembered that a great deal of this overhauling has been done, sometimes more than once; and the reports of the Charity Commissioners are full of information as to the educational "charities" that have been in this way very successfully "reformed." Our case should be that, in many cases, and notably in those of the Oxford and Cambridge Colleges, another overhaul is due and overdue; that the needs of the nation in education develop from generation to generation, as well as the principles on which it requires its corporate possessions to be administered; and that, accordingly, each successive generation demands to be assured that all the endowments are being dealt with to the greatest advantage of the community.

But we should be careful not to put our claims on any faulty ground. Thus, it is, broadly speaking, incorrect to assert that the endowments of the Oxford and Cambridge Colleges, or those of Eton and Winchester, were originally given or left for the education of the poor, meaning the manual-working, wage-earning class, whether farm labourer or town citizen. It is safe to say that no such idea entered the head of the mediæval founder of a college or other benefactor. What he wished to endow was the education of priests or philosophers; or, in the most liberal view, the training of men to fill the necessary public offices, and thus serve God in Church and State. He desired, no doubt, that no fit youth should be excluded by mere lack of means, and in mediæval times many of the university students were poor enough; whilst a tiny percentage of them, picked out and aided in some exceptional way, may have come from artisan or peasant homes. But nothing could be more ludicrously at variance with the truth than the impression sometimes indicated in speeches on this subject, that these endowments had been originally devoted to the education of the manual-working or wage-earning class, from which they have been wrongly diverted. The democratic case for an overhaul of the Oxford and Cambridge Colleges, as of all other educational endowments, is that there is ground for the suspicion that the funds are not all being applied in the ways that would now be most conducive to the welfare of the nation as a whole.

Similarly, we should avoid claiming that it would be for the public advantage to use these educational endowments for the maintenance of elementary schools, or for anything else that we can persuade Members of Parliament or of Education Committees to vote out of the taxes or the rates. To apply endowments in order to save expenditure out of the rates and taxes is virtually to confiscate the endowments for the benefit of the owners and occupiers of house property and the payers of income tax, super tax, and estate duties; and to do this in such a way that persons with the largest incomes would find themselves the most benefited. These, at any rate, were not the persons whom the ancient benefactor desired to endow! We do not want, in fact, to "pool" educational endowments for general educational purposes and so reduce either the education rate or the income tax. Hence we should always try to get educational endowments allocated to special purposes which would not otherwise be provided for in our educational budget. Such purposes may most usefully include pioneer work, in subjects or by methods or for sections of pupils, in which educational experiments are required— we are only just beginning to know how to educate! They may usefully include provision for instruction in subjects of which the bulk of the ratepayers or taxpayers do not yet understand the importance, but which far-sighted thinkers believe to be of vital concern. Endowments may usefully be applied in the provision of scholarships, in supplement of the national scholarship scheme, for particular sections (such as adult workmen or the blind or the crippled); or for subjects needing exceptional provision (such as art or music); or for exceptional kinds of help (such as travelling studentships or research fellowships). And in order to secure new initiative and fresh ideas any benefactor should be encouraged to endow any particular subject, any particular section of the population, any particular method of instruction, or any particular institution as to which he has an inspiration or in the importance of which he specially believes.

On the other hand, it is undesirable that any scholarship money should go (as much of what is given out of endowments at Oxford and Cambridge, as at Eton and Winchester, now goes) to pupils whose parents can quite well afford to maintain and educate them without aid from what is essentially public money. Nor can a large part of the expenditure on " idle " fellowships be justified. The most serious indictments against the Oxford and Cambridge Colleges in respect of their endowments are, however, the waste and extravagance of their financial administration, the needless multiplicity of highly paid offices, and the government of the universities essentially in the interests of those who profit by their archaic abuses—offences against the common weal which, in maintaining an atmosphere of hypocrisy, class prejudice, and corruption, do nothing to augment the charm of these ancient seats of learning.

The final question remains of the extent to which the cost of education should fall upon local or upon national funds, on the rates, or on the taxes. The case for making education a national service, entirely provided from the Exchequer, is, at first sight, a strong one. We should get rid at once of the characteristic parsimony of the representatives of the ratepayers; of the inevitable ignorance and narrow-mindedness of the Councillors of Little Pedlington; and of the underpayment of the teachers and the starvation of the schools that are thereby promoted. We should make a full measure of educational opportunities the equal birthright of every child in the kingdom. And what is of very practical importance, we should equalise the burden of education as between those towns and districts, on the one hand, where children are relatively few and the average rateable value is high, and, on the other, those (like West Ham) in which the average rateable value per child is so low that it can be foreseen and calculated that every additional cottage that becomes the home of a family will involve a rise in the education rate. On the other hand, we have to remember that centralised finance inevitably involves central administration, and we stigmatise central administration as bureaucracy. The loss of all local autonomy in education would be grave. And the contrast is instructive between the extraordinary progress during the last half-century of the British educational service, which has been locally administered under central supervision, and the very unsatisfactory condition of the British prison service, which was (in 1878) transferred to central administration with local supervision, and which remains one of the blots upon our civilisation. It is terrible to think how our prisons have lagged behind our schools. We suffer in our schools from the parsimony and the narrow-mindedness of the Local Educational Authorities, but we gain by the initiative of the more enterprising among them, we learn from their experiments, and we are eventually led by emulation to copy their progress. And we at any rate avoid the cramping bureaucratic pedantry which still maintains a prison system which is a disgrace to the 20th century.

What experience has taught us in the United Kingdom is that the most advantageous system is a combination of central and local administration. This combination may, in some cases, take the form of dividing the duties. Thus, there is a great deal to be said for placing whatever public control is exercised over the universities and the teachers' training colleges exclusively in the hands of the Minister for Education. More generally it is found best to share the administration and control between central and local authorities. Here the approved instrument is the grant-in-aid. The local authority is left freedom to administer as it thinks fit (subject to the enforcement of a statutory " national minimum "), but it is encouraged to do more than the minimum by receiving from the Exchequer a grant of part of its expenditure, so adjusted as to increase as the local expenditure rises. The grant may in some cases (as in a national scholarship system) properly amount to the whole, or nearly the whole, of the local outlay. In other cases, where encouragement of a new service is specially needed but a larger measure of local autonomy has to be maintained (as, for instance, in the provision of schools for the mentally defective), the grant may properly amount to 80 per cent. of the local outlay. Usually a grant of 50 per cent. suffices; although a further differentiation between districts of high and low rateable value per child is also required. This system of grants-in-aid of local expenditure has proved, in the United Kingdom of the last three-quarters of a century, to combine the advantages of local autonomy with those of centralised administration, in a manner superior to any other Governmental device. This, at any rate in this country, in our own day and generation, seems how best to pay for education.

OUR OLD EDUCATIONAL ENDOWMENTS.

By J. Arthur Fallows, M.A., Oxon.

After the destruction of the Roman Empire by the barbarian invasions its cultural prestige still remained, and as soon as large States began to reappear, and barbarism lessened, the old classical schools were revived, bishops and princes imitating the Roman Emperors and municipalities in founding both elementary and secondary schools. When a bishop received from a prince an endowment for a cathedral he generally created an elementary school for his choristers and a secondary school, both for fee-paying young gentlemen and for youths to be trained for the priesthood. Such schools were made in England at Canterbury and York. Winchester, the capital of Wessex, contained one of our oldest cathedral grammar schools, to which King Alfred sent his youngest son, Ethelward, who, according to Asser, " became studious in the liberal arts before learning manly arts, namely, hunting and such pursuits as befit gentlemen." Bishops and archdeacons, when they had risen socially and had acquired wealth and power as dignitaries of the Church, endowed schools with free places, so that clever boys of the peasant class and of the poorer urban classes might find opportunities for advancement. In the middle ages most of the parochial clergy were " recruited from the ranks of the peasantry," as they are in France or in Russia to-day. The peasants were eager to place their sons in the ministry of the Church, as it provided one of the few careers where ability counted rather than birth; the tonsure performed on the skulls of those who took even minor orders " freed the son of a serf from servitude " and gave him " benefit of clergy," and the villeins were legally obliged to pay a fee to their lords for permission to " crown " a boy with this pious decoration. William of Wykeham, Chichele, Latimer, and Grosstête were examples of famous clergymen of peasant origin. Latin was studied in the secondary or grammar schools for utilitarian reasons, not only for clergymen but also for bailiffs, architects, musicians, doctors, teachers, travellers, and diplomatists. Not only in cathedral towns, but in almost every market town in England in the middle ages, schools were founded by colleges, chantries, guilds, or hospitals. A college was an endowed body of clergymen, generally meeting in a big parish church, engaged in singing, praying, and teaching, but living in the world, instead of being confined to a monastery, as the monks or regulars were supposed to be confined. " A grammar school was a recognised appendix to a collegiate church." Such colleges existed at Derby, Ripon, Beverley, Warwick, Windsor, Westminster, Christchurch (Hants), Manchester, Rotherham, St. Albans, and other towns. The most famous of them was Winchester College, founded in 1382 by William of Wykeham, mainly for the free education of poor scholars intending to become parish priests. Lady Berkeley founded Wooton-under-Edge School in 1384, " for the maintenance of holy mother Church, and of other liberal arts and sciences, considering that the purpose of many, desiring to be instructed in grammar, is daily frustrated by poverty." Manchester School was founded in 1523, to meet "the great poverty of the common people," and was a public school, as being "open to any man-child of any county or shire." Rotherham College was founded to provide preachers and teachers for the rude highland districts of Yorkshire, and six of the poorest of its pupils were to be fed, clothed, and educated there till the age of 18. At Beverley College some boys paid fees to the master, and others, including all those who came from the song school, paid no fees. St. Albans School was endowed for the maintenance and housing of 16 poor scholars, the master "taking fees from the rest according to ancient custom." Birmingham, Coventry, Louth, and Ludlow had schools connected with guilds. The colleges at Oxford and Cambridge were largely intended for the use of poor students.

A chantry was a small chapel in a church, where a priest was endowed to sing masses for the repose of the soul of the donor, and to teach boys. The Royal Commission of 1548, under the Act of Parliament for the Suppression of Chantries, reported that chantry priests were engaged in teaching at Chelmsford, Great Baddow, Berkhamsted, Lancaster, Newbury, Preston, Middleton, Liverpool, Lincoln, and many other places. Orders were promised for the continuance of the educational work of these suppressed colleges and chantries, but in many cases these orders never appeared upon the scene. In most schools and colleges of the middle ages there were free places for poor scholars, even Queen Mary, in 1554, continuing the old formula— "in order that piety and good learning may flower in the Church, we decree that for ever in the Church of Durham 18 boys, poor and destitute of the help of friends, be nourished on the goods of the Church." In the 15th century endowments were given mainly by clergymen, drapers, and grocers to many places to turn fee schools into free schools. In 1439 God's House was established at Cambridge for the training of teachers for the grammar schools. They were secondary schools of Latin language and grammar, logic and rhetoric, leading on to the universities, and distinguished also from the elementary schools, for the "petties," for reading, writing, and arithmetic, or from song schools for choristers. In Denmark they came to be called Latin Schools, in Germany Gymnasia, in France les lycées, and in those countries they have continued to be cheap and inclusive. Erasmus tried to make them more literary, and the Protestants tried to make them more Biblical.

The monks did little for education, except in the early Cluniac Days. In England many old cathedral and collegiate foundations were handed over by kings and noblemen to bodies of monks, a certain part of the endowments being ear-marked, as before, for educational objects. Their schools were conducted, not by the monks, but by lay teachers in the town. Monasteries in the 15th century had small almonry or choir schools of charity boys, generally to the number of 13 boys in each school, according to A. F. Leach. They also had small schools within their own walls for some of their own youthful novices, often men of noble blood, and were supposed, if Benedictines, to send two students from each abbey to the universities. But, generally speaking, the monks were ill-educated, and did as little as they dared for education. Monks were rich, lazy, and genteel, and were not interested in the grammar schools, which, according to Professor Foster-Watson, "did so much to aid the humbler classes to rise in the social scale." (See his new book on the grammar schools, issued by the Cambridge University Press in 1916.)

In the 16th century the poorer classes lost many of their educational advantages. After the Great Plague had lessened the numbers of the peasantry, and wages had risen and rents fallen, the landlords began to turn the arable strips in the village fields into enclosed pasture fields, and to evict many small holders from their holdings, especially in about one-third part of the country. In some cases this was done by monastic landlords; John Rous of Warwick said, in 1486, "the profit of the enclosures the monks enjoy." More often it was the work of lay landlords. A few schools, such as Eton and Sedbergh, refused admission to the sons of villeins. By the Act of Parliament of 1547, which suppressed chantries, guilds, colleges, and hospitals, hundreds of schools were ruined. In some cases a school survived, the landlord paying a fixed sum to the schoolmaster. Thus all the increment of the estate went to the landlord (including fines and sales of timber), and in course of time, as the value of land increased and that of money decreased, this annual rent charge came to be a wretched pittance. Lever denounced in 1550, in a sermon, the "miserable drowning of youth in ignorance," and said that "many grammar schools founded to bring up poor men's sons in learning now be taken away, by reason of greedy covetousness." In the words of A. F. Leach, the chief authority on the history of English grammar schools, "the chief mischief of the dissolution of these colleges was that it swept into private pockets vast endowments which might perhaps have been appropriated to education." This spoliation was not the wish of the Protestant Reformers. King Henry VIII., in establishing his cathedrals at Peterborough, Westminster, Canterbury, Worcester, Gloucester, Bristol, and Oxford, had decreed that scholars, "poor and destitute of the help of friends and of native talent, as far as may be, should be maintained and instructed at all of them." Cranmer himself was eagerly desirous of helping poor boys to school. He found that "poor men's children are many times endued with more singular gifts of nature, and also commonly more apt to study than gentlemen's sons." He had seen many sons of our best born families "very dull and without all manner of capacity" and unwilling to take the pains to get learning, and he disliked the presence of rich young men at Oxford "qualifying themselves for places in the State by slight and superficial knowledge." (For 300 years this came to be the blight of Oxford.) Cranmer succeeded in preventing the local gentry from extruding all plebeian boys from Canterbury School, but, on the whole, the reforming clergy were too weak to prevent the landlords from impoverishing the people's schools, though Schoolmaster Ascham pleaded that "commonly the meaner men's children came to be the wisest counsellors in the weighty affairs of the realm."

In the century between 1560 and 1660 many new educational endowments were created, largely by evangelical tradesmen, for the benefit of the poorer classes. Schools were founded, e.g., at Tonbridge by a skinner, Daventry by a draper, Rugby by a grocer, Tiverton by a manufacturer, Harrow by a yeoman, and Lancaster by a tallow chandler. Some town councils or guilds, such as Birmingham, Warwick, King's Lynn, and Stratford, bought back their schools. The puritan Archdeacon Johnson founded schools at Oakham and Uppingham. Bishop Jewel and Bernard Gilpin maintained and instructed poor scholars in their homes. Dean Nowell influenced Mrs. Frankland to "help poor toward youths that lack exhibition" at Middleton, Newport (Essex), and at Caius College, Cambridge. Dedham School was endowed to teach freely " 20 of the poorest men's children." John Royse of Abingdon endowed Abingdon School for 63 children of poor widows and other poor men, apt for learning, in the district, without fees, fee-payers being also admitted to the school. William Harper, a tailor, bought chantry lands and endowed Bedford School "for nourishing and educating poor boys of that place." Tailors also endowed Reading and Wolverhampton Schools. Giggleswick scholars were to be "of the poorer sort, although they be not so well learned as other scholars which have rich friends." In 1635 some of these scholars at the university were so poor that the dons were unwilling to be their tutors. At Repton, Manchester, and Worcester, in the 17th century, there were many plebeian students, along with some boys of higher social classes. Christ's Hospital was founded for the use of orphans and foundlings. The sons of "handicraftsmen, mean tradesmen, and painful husbandmen" were educated at Lewisham in 1652, while at Hereford care was to be taken that the "poorer be not sordidly habited to the offence of better quality." The Cromwellians tried to improve the status and salaries of teachers, and even to found a university at Durham, but all these schemes collapsed after the Restoration of 1660, while Dissenters could no longer attend the Universities of Oxford and Cambridge.

Between 1740 and 1840 the condition of the majority of the people in England became worse than at any other period of our history. In most parts of the country, where commons had remained until then, the old grass commons and the arable strips were enclosed by the landlords. This led to the final abolition of the class of yeomen or peasant proprietors, and the reduction of the agricultural labourers to a position of extreme poverty and dependence. In the same period the use of new inventions in big factories lowered the status of handicraftsmen, while wars and the Corn Laws raised rents and the prices of all provisions, especially after the conclusion of the 18th century. Our rural districts now consisted of the three castes of landlords, farmers, and agricultural labourers.

The old grammar schools decayed, partly because of their poor endowments, and partly owing to their narrowly Anglican and Latin character and their refusal to adapt themselves to new conditions; Oxford and Cambridge degenerated for the same reasons.

Only a certain number of these old schools became, for various reasons, prosperous, fashionable, and exclusive. Such were Rugby, Winchester, Eton, Harrow, and Westminster.

The Cathedral Schools in some cases died out, as at Exeter, Salisbury, and Wells; in other cases they lingered on in an impoverished state, "the governing body, the canons, failing to increase the ancient stipend, or provide new buildings, in accordance with the fall in the value of money and modern educational demands." In 1851 the dean and canons at Rochester had increased their own stipends tenfold, while keeping the scholars' grants at the rate of the 16th century. The Rev. Whiston, headmaster of Rochester School, called attention by books and letters to this injustice. Even the new Dictionary of English Church History confesses that "cathedrals have not carried out properly their duties of supporting and teaching poor scholars, with which they were charged." (See page 193 of this book.) Several charity schools had been founded in the 18th century, with humiliating regulations, e.g., in the way of a distinctive dress.

In the latter part of the 19th century many of the old grammar schools were reformed under schemes prepared by the Endowed School Commissioners, schemes which in some cases granted scholarships (often insufficient in amount) to pupils from the elementary Council Schools. But in other cases, as at Bedford, the bulk of the advantages of the old endowments was transferred to the boys of the middle and upper classes. The eight mis-called " public " schools, which had obtained by 1850 the highest social prestige, have become more costly, exclusive, and fashionable than ever before, and have entirely extruded the boys of the plebeian classes for which, with the possible exceptions of Eton and Sedbergh, they were mainly intended. For further details on the subject, the reader should consult the pamphlet by Wilkins and Fallows on English Educational Endowments, published by the Workers' Educational Association in January, 1917.

REFERENCES.—A. F. Leach : " English Schools before the Reforma-tion." Foster-Watson : " English Grammar Schools."

EDUCATION AND THE ORGANISATION OF RESEARCH.*

By Viscount Haldane.

There is a controversy which is doing some harm to the progress of the educational awakening which is taking place in so remarkable a fashion. The question has been sharply raised whether the ideal in education is to be science or the humanities. In a less abstract form the same question has been raised as between the trade continuation school and the secondary school as places for the instruction of the adolescent democracy. Speaking for myself, I look on the disjunction which this question implies as a false one. I believe, on the one hand, that the best forms of scientific teaching are impossible without copious reference to the spirit of the humanities, and, on the other hand, that the teaching of the humanities without steady reference to scientific modes of thought leaves a gap unfilled. Knowledge is one and indivisible, though no single individual can take in the whole which it constitutes. That whole must, just on this account, be ever present as an ideal to the minds of teacher and taught alike, if it be only in the sense that the particular subject which is actually being taught is constantly shown to be merely a fragment of an entirety to which it yet furnishes a guide.

The tables used by the engineer who has to work out the structure of a bridge seem dry and abstract, and they are often left to appear so. And yet they record the outcome of a mighty effort of the spirit. It was when lying in bed and thinking out first principles that on Descartes, a great humanist, there flashed the comprehension that geometry and algebra were intimately related. In his discoveries of co-ordinate geometry and the theories of ordered couples and of vectors he enunciated the principles which are now embodied in the text books of practice which guide the bridge designer in calculating the details of structure he has to plan. These things and many others of the kind may be and ought to be taught with constant reference to the great foundations of abstract thought on which they rest, and if they are so taught they form studies in the spirit of humanism. So in ordinary arithmetic, founded on the discovery of the Arabic numerals and of the value of what to the ancients was not a number at all, o, we have an advance in range of thought which is astounding when it is reflected on. By relieving the brain of unnecessary work such a new notation set it free to concentrate on more advanced problems and to increase the mental power of the race. As has been said, "probably nothing in the modern world would have more astonished a Greek mathematician than to learn that, under the influence of compulsory education, the whole population of Western Europe, from the highest to the lowest, could perform the operation of division for the largest numbers. The fact would have seemed to him a sheer impossibility." Of course, arithmetic, like technical formulas, may be taught in a dry

---

* See " Report of the Committee of the Privy Council for Scientific and Industrial Research for the year 1916-17," published by H.M. Stationery Office; and " Higher Education After the War," by Professor Burnet.

and soulless fashion. But it should not be so, and need not be so. In
this, as in countless other matters, there is a field for a general education of significance which reaches far beyond the subject matter. The
spirit is everything, and if the topics of instruction are used to
stimulate range of outlook the best educational results may follow.
For, as Professor Pringle Pattison tells us in his recently published
Gifford lectures on the " Idea of God," it is true, " as pointed out by
Plato long ago, that ' all nature is akin,' and, therefore, for the
rational mind any actual knowledge is so linked with other truths as
to be capable of carrying us ultimately to the end of the intellectual
world, that is, to the systematic knowledge of the whole."

It is this truth that Kerschensteiner of Munich, who has done so
much to establish the practical possibility of giving general education
in the special trade continuation schools which he introduced, means
when, an idealist in educational aim, he insists on the value of taking
the particular business of life in which a boy or girl is interested by
reason of daily employment in it as a point of application for
significant instruction of a wide nature.

I have said so much in order to try to get rid of the apprehension
that technical education can be no more than instruction in some
business. It may be made so, but it ought not to be made so. All
depends on the teacher and the spirit in which he teaches. This is, of
course, even more certainly true of the higher forms of technical
instruction. No wise person wishes to lose any opportunity of impart-
ing to those under training the meaning and sense of literature and of
art. Education ought to include variety. And it ought also to be
adapted to the needs and aptitudes of the individuals who are being
educated. But a real education in any form may be made to convey
the sense of a larger whole than that with which it is immediately
concerned. Moreover, the process of such education may afford to
the teacher the opportunity of watching his pupils, and of marking out
those in whom he discovers special aptitudes for recommendation to
the authorities for access to further learning. In this fashion a well-
organised system of scholarships will enable the State to get the
advantage of drawing upon a reservoir of special talent which such a
system may render available. There are doubtless countless boys and
girls of humble origin who possess great gifts which their circumstances have rendered it impossible to develop or even discover. But
if continuation schools of a proper kind are made a reality these
nascent minds of quality ought to be selected out of the mass and
given the opportunity of developing talent in the fullest fashion in
still higher institutions.

The scope of such a method of selection is likely to be much
extended by the new demand which has arisen for the application of
high scientific knowledge to industry. It is now being realised that
industry itself dare not stand still as regards method, and that new
discoveries, almost from day to day, are essential in any business for
which it is sought to secure and hold pre-eminence. The State has at
last taken the matter up, and is providing for the development of
research in a way which is bound to extend the field in which special
knowledge finds a market. This must, of course, tell on education,
and must necessitate the provision of new opportunities for study.
The Department of Research which has just been founded has an
organic connection with the Education Department. This connection
is essential. For reseach cannot be extended without the provision of

scientific experts, of whom we train comparatively few at present. Until recently the manufacturers offered but little encouragement to the schools and universities to undertake such training, for the employment of highly trained experts was not a common practice. But now that the industrial world has been awakened to the necessity of applying science to industry there is a better prospect in front of the student who wishes to make such application his profession.

Over the new Department of Research there is a Committee of the Privy Council, containing Ministers and ex-Ministers, and presided over by the Lord President of the Council, who has thus been made the Minister of Research. Under this Committee, which is responsible for it, is the Advisory Council, over which Sir William McCormick presides and of which Dr. Heath is the secretary. This Council, which contains men of the highest scientific and industrial eminence, has been since last autumn a Department of the State, and administers a large grant from the Treasury. It advises the manufacturers as to the researches which ought to be undertaken, and, where the manufacturers cannot do this themselves, it will organise scientific investigation in selected laboratories at the universities and elsewhere. In this way the prospect has arisen of a new employment for students who choose to devote their careers to work of this kind. The education required for preparation is naturally stimulated and provided for. Sir William McCormick has been, it must be borne in mind, for some years the directing spirit of the Committee which is engaged in administering the new funds provided by the Treasury for the development of the university colleges, and he is intimately acquainted with this kind of educational work from a further long experience as secretary of the Carnegie Trust. He is thus qualified as few men could be to direct the operations of the new Research Department, and to stimulate the extension of scientific training of a high order.

It thus appears that within the last few months a substantial advance has been made in the improvement of the educational machinery of the country, and particularly in developing scientific research. How far this advance will be carried depends on whether the general public interest in the subject grows with the growth of the new machinery which is now available. So far the industrial world has shown a keen and satisfactory growth of interest in it, and a disposition to take full advantage of the opportunities offered. But the work to be done, if we are to bring ourselves up to the level of the organisations which some of our foreign competitors in trade possess, is enormous, and the nation cannot afford to rest. For it is true here, as elsewhere, that " to him that hath shall be given."

EDUCATION BY MUSIC.

By Beryl de Zoete.

" There is no method of education so powerful as music, for rhythm and harmony find their way into the inmost soul and implant grace there, so that he who is rightly educated becomes graceful."— Plato.

" He who mingles music with gymnastic in the fairest proportion and best attempers them to the soul, may be rightly called the true musician and harmonist in a far higher sense than the tuner of the strings."—Plato.

" Music, as the Greeks understood it, is the sum of our powers of feeling and thought, an everchanging symphony of spontaneous ideas, shaped by imagination, ordered by rhythm, and harmonised by consciousness. This music is the character of the individual."— Dalcroze.

There has never been a time when in all departments of national life revolutionary counsels had so good a chance of prevailing as at present. The old prejudice against change has been driven to its last trench and there lies quaking. The old goblin of expense is pierced to the heart by the daily cost of war. Labour has felt its power, and under the mask of patriotism has already stooped to play the part of tyrant. What constructive principles shall we bring to the work of education? What rights shall we demand, knowing, as we have now every reason to know, that what we really think worth fighting for we shall obtain. Let us by all means lay at the door of the State the deficiencies in our educational system if we remember that we all live behind the same door. For in a democracy the State is not a sudden miracle, a floating detached splendour, an awful presence, an abstraction. It is a mobile force shaped from within, an active and living image of the people. The nature of that force depends on the conceptions that each citizen has of citizenship; of the rights he may demand and the duties he will perform. There is a right of citizenship which under present conditions is crushed out of existence—the right of every human being to realise his own nature and develop the faculties that are in him. Let us be revolutionary and base our education on the desire to put within the reach of every child such riches of the world as he is capable of enjoying; to make him feel that he may be himself a creator and vitally share in the building up of new worlds. The workers have been so busy fighting for the right to procure by labour a small portion of what many of us have without labour enjoyed as our natural birthright—life under decent physical conditions, a sufficiency of food and leisure—that they have not yet openly taken the field in the cause of education. But, consciously or not, these demands of Labour are not material only. If a line must be drawn between spiritual and material, sound bodies and cultivated minds must be found on one side of it. It is a spiritual claim you make when you demand the minimum possibilities of a decent physical life. Education begins from the first moment of life, and our educational period, if it is to expand at all, must expand backwards as well as forwards.

We are probably all agreed that a national education should not aim at fitting the masses early to become efficient slaves in an industrial state, but at the development of free, vigorous, intelligent individuals. But a large proportion of the children who attend the elementary schools in our big towns are born under unhealthy conditions, live in unhealthy conditions, and are not healthy human beings. Many, judged by a normal physical standard, are deformed; almost all stand in need of corrective gymnastics, as well as of good food, airy homes, large and pleasant spaces for play. These children are often exquisitely gifted and worthy of the best education that can be given them, but they need above all a method of education which should make its appeal to the mind through the body.

Now it is the function of music to inspire movement; movement in the body, and that movement in the spirit which we call emotion. Music supplies the most direct physical and spiritual stimulus known to man. It finds its way, as Plato says, into the inmost places of the soul and there implants itself; it stirs into life the sleeping spirit of man and urges it to expression through the body. Among most primitive peoples rhythm presides over every communal action, to inspire and control. They have no music in which they do not physically participate. Every musical festival is for them a dance and intimate to their life. They all are the composer and orchestra in one.

Yet the organic sensibility to rhythm which is found in almost every human being and which has inspired human labour since history began had been practically neglected as a means of education till it was rediscovered about 20 years ago by a really great teacher, the Swiss musician, Jaques Dalcroze. When teacher of harmony at Geneva he was struck by the lack of relation between the technical ability of his pupils and their actual musical development. Though their time was spent in rendering the works of the great masters they were themselves unrhythmical. Their work was an intellectual exercise, which left their musical being unaffected. Then began for Dalcroze a long series of experiments based on the belief that the rhythms of the body, inspired and controlled by music, might be made the basis of an educational method. With characteristic ardour and invention he used his genius for improvisation to explore the potentialities of the body as a *conductor* of music. He soon found that to understand a rhythm, and to possess a muscular system capable of rendering it physically, were not enough; that there must be set up a rapid communication between brain and muscle. Step by step he was led into a wider circle of educational experience, and so gradually evolved what is now known as the Dalcroze method of rhythmic gymnastics, or Eurhythmics.*

---

* It is difficult, perhaps impossible, to describe the Dalcroze method. It must be seen and experienced to be understood. Below is a rough classification of the exercises:—

1. Division of time and space, which will include all the metrical part of music, the teaching of number, space and figure.

2. Inhibition, i.e., the instant arrest or interchange of movements at a given command, including a clear mental image of the movement which is to be substituted, and of the muscular effect of the arrested movement, and developing both the muscular sense and brain control.

3. Dissociation of movements, a balance and combination of antagonistic movements, as in the balance of contraction in one limb with relaxation in another, or of two rhythms simultaneously realised by clapping and stepping.

4. Dynamic and agogic, i.e., the variation of degrees of emphasis and degrees of speed, involving a systematic study of muscular contraction and relaxation, and an

Artists, psychologists, doctors, teachers, as well as musicians, began to gather round him and to realise, each in his own department, the significance of this discovery of rhythm as a fundamental basis of appeal in each individual. To teach a child to control such of its movements as are naturally automatic, to form fresh motor habits, to produce the maximum effects with the minimum effort, is to give it a clear mental control of its physical powers, to teach it to know itself and to be master of its personality.

Wherever it has been rightly taught—taught that is to say by someone who is alive and eager to appeal to the life-force in others—the value of the method has been placed beyond dispute. It develops self-control, concentration, the power of definite thinking, and of forming clear mental images; above all, it evokes vitality and delight.

Rhythmic gymnastics differs from most systems of gymnastics in several respects. And, first, in the large place it allows to time variation. In ordinary gymnastics the exercises are performed in unvarying periods of time, and the innumerable degrees of contraction of which the muscles are capable are reduced to a few elementary distinctions. Further, in gymnastics the movements are pre-arranged, not spontaneous, and thus give no scope at all to a natural artistic expression. In rhythmic gymnastics there is no such rigid uniformity. The grammar of the movements should certainly be accurately learnt, but accuracy leaves a wide margin for individual temperament when a movement is made in response to a musical impulse. There is no set music in the ordinary teaching of Eurhythmics. The musical rhythm which evokes movement in the body must be improvised if it is to develop and vary with it, and the child is from the first encouraged to improvise and modify rhythms for itself, to create living and rhythmic shapes with the instrument nearest to its hand and directly expressive of its emotions, its own body. With what delight and touching beauty children will thus improvise everyone must know who has seen them freely at play. Here, again, provision is made for the " naughty " child—generally the child whose vitality craves direct expression in movement. Give it but a chance to make patterns with its movement, give it a rhythm to move to, help it to experience varieties of time division, make it devise new shapes, encourage it to experiment in the dynamics of muscular movements (children are always immensely amused and interested to find in what ways they can control, contract, and relax their muscles) and you will not need repressive discipline. No normal being loves disorder for its own sake. Make order interesting, show it in contrast with chaos, and the fascination of helping to produce it will be felt.

The instinct of creation which the teacher is everywhere now beginning to enlist as a self-educative force of immeasured scope

---

education of brain and muscle through the experience of all degrees of motion, force, suppleness, careful preparation, and rapid action.

5. Musical realisations—the phrasing of rhythms, free movement, and plastic expression.

Eurhythmics is taught in over 50 schools and colleges in England and Scotland, throughout three elementary training colleges, and in several elementary schools. Any information as to literature, classes, and demonstrations may be obtained from the London School of Dalcroze Eurhythmics (Principal, Mr. P. B. Ingham), 23, Store Street, London, W.C. 1, or from the Secretary of the Dalcroze Society, Mrs. Eckhard, Broome House, Didsbury, Manchester. The London School would be glad to discuss the formation of a class for members of the W.E.A. in any town where they have a centre.

lies at the heart of the Dalcroze method. His insistence on it as the source of all that makes life worth living for man, and the real basis of a vigorous social state, would alone place Dalcroze among the great teachers of our time. It is the art of life, the creative life, a body and a mind working in harmony, that, rightly understood, his method aims at teaching. Many of the people, of whatever social class, whom we meet daily in the street, have not lived at all in the sense I mean. They have been circumscribed and contracted since their birth; some by riches, some by poverty, but all by the judgments of their class. Devoid of a directing consciousness in themselves they are at the mercy of any bold or imposing judgment. It is splendid to imagine a great nation rising up in strength to demand not the right of conquest, nor the right of possession, but the right of every man born into it to live creatively.

We want some great vitalising influence like this in our educational policy; some big creative impulse. We do not want the children taught a little more of the same thing for a little longer time. You may be quite sure that children whose education up to 10 or 12 years old, had been musical in the sense imagined by Plato in the third book of his " Republic," in the sense actually in process of realisation by Dalcroze, would not be backward. They would be exceedingly forward to acquire rapidly and intelligently and creatively what it is necessary for them to learn in order to play their part in a great Empire. The State will be driven at last to the economy of a more expensive education. Let us enlist all the forces of life on our side, and not be afraid to pitch our demands too high.

NOTE ON THE EDUCATIONAL POSSIBILITIES OF DANCING.

There is an aspect of Eurhythmics which has not yet been championed by educationists, namely, its relation to dancing, yet it is an aspect most fertile in suggestion.

Long before M. Dalcroze gave his first demonstration of Eurhythmics in England, in the winter of 1912-13, he was known to teachers of children by his action songs and musical games. These all have as their basis the development of expression and character and are distinctly dramatic in intention. Carry them further, give them a fuller imaginative content, and we come to the dramatic dance, or the dance as it was understood in antiquity, and is practised even now among the people who still seek in art the expression of their social experiences. We know from many sources that the Greeks danced the great legends of their religion, that their dances were not mere formal patterns in space, but patterns of human fate. Why should not our children also be allowed to dance the stories they learn? Out of these stories they can, with a sufficiently imaginative musical stimulus, improvise dances which will immensely increase their sympathy and their realisation of the imaginative content of the stories. And so literature and history may be taught by movement, too, and pantomime become not an idle pastime, but a means of real education.

M. Dalcroze himself constantly draws suggestions for his plastique from those stories which symbolise the inward conflict of human passion. Recently in a lesson he proposed for a subject " Orestes Striving with the Furies." Four groups, roughly stationed in the four

corners of the room, represented the Furies. Their part was to drive
back Orestes, who baffled by one, then another, sought ever a fresh
outlet for escape. When at last Orestes broke through, the dance
was over.

Of course, the plastic response depends immensely on the musical
improvisation. A whole world of imaginative suggestion moves in
the improvised rhythms of Dalcroze. But the actual harmonic means
he uses are extremely simple. Musical feeling and imagination are
essential to the teaching of Eurhythmics, and teachers who have this,
and can find inspiration in the living world, may, even without great
technical accomplishment, evoke a greater response in their pupils
than some highly diplomaed musicians. For poets need not be
philologists, but they must drink continually at the living source from
which language has sprung.

LIBRARIES.

By B. M. HEADICAR, F.L.A.

(Librarian, London School of Economics and Political Science, University of London).

How many people are there, I wonder, who realise and appreciate the number and nature of the many libraries provided for the edification of the people of the United Kingdom. And among the comparatively few who are familiar with the library service, how many make use of it at all? Again, of those who use the libraries may we not say with absolute truth that, for various reasons, only a minority find their particular needs adequately provided for? How and why is this the case? One reason is that library authorities do not sufficiently advertise the existence of their libraries and the many advantages to be gained by using them. Municipal authorities are fond of advertising their baths and washhouses and other revenue producing establishments, but the libraries which provide, free of cost, mental recreation and stimulus are usually forgotten in this connection. The advantages of libraries should be advertised in such a way that wherever one goes he would be—so to speak—hit in the eye with the facts. Much could be done by articles in the local Press calling attention to new books, special collections, topical literature, and many other features. This is spasmodically done, but rarely systematically. It may be urged that if people want things they will go for them, and that if they will not accept something for nothing they should go without. We know that busy mothers often do not have time to think, let alone read, and the same argument applies in a degree to many workers, and even when they have the time to read the former are unable to leave their homes and go book-hunting. Well, if people will not or cannot come to the libraries—often situated at a distance—the libraries must be brought somehow to them. Is it possible to do this? Certainly, but the old bogey of insufficient income always confronts one. Branch libraries have been established in many large towns to facilitate the loan of books; other places have delivery stations open on one or two nights a week on the outskirts of the district. Blackburn has eight of these stations, and so have Warrington, Halifax, and Sheffield. Travelling libraries also attempt to meet the needs of those who find it difficult to visit the libraries themselves. These travelling libraries are usually in the form of boxes of 50 or more volumes, which are dispatched to police and fire stations, factories, and other institutions, the books being exchanged as the need arises. Bradford has ten travelling libraries working. Much progress has been made in the development of school libraries. These are sometimes distinct branches of, and entirely controlled by, the municipal library, but in some cases—as at Croydon—a grant is made by the Education Committee towards the provision of the necessary books, the library authorities administering the libraries for the schools and providing the staff at the central library for the work of cataloguing, classification, and general organisation. Books are delivered at each school in the borough and interchanged among the schools during vacation. The cost of establishing these libraries in a district containing 60 schools is about £400, and £250 per annum is required afterwards. Blackburn runs 39 school libraries, Warrington 26, Darwen and Wakefield 22 each, and Bury 18, so it will be seen that northern counties have made considerable progress in library extension work. Attempts have been made in America to establish a system of home delivery of books, but very little success seems to have resulted. From the above facts it will be gathered that in many places strenuous efforts have been made to take the libraries to the people, but the efforts are not general, and extension work being dependent largely on the enthusiasm of the library committees frequently suffers from the lack of it. The workers of the country ought to realise what the library can do for them. If they want to improve their knowledge of their trades, to know what things affect the cost of living, why Labour troubles arise, what is happening in the world ; if they want to understand the fundamentals of economics, systems of education, the possibilities of Empire trade, the meaning of Free Trade and Protection, the origin of wars and the blessings of peace ; if they are desirous of knowing how their fellow men live ; if they have a yearning to know more of the beauties of nature, of the wonders of geology, of great men and women ; if they want to find a new job, breed rabbits, grow potatoes, learn the duties of parents, the necessity for clean homes and hands ; if they would understand why thousands of little mites always look pale and careworn, scantily clad and badly fed, and thousands more bright, well-fed and well-clothed ; if they would learn of all that has made and is making life for many miserable and for some full of joy—the library is able to help them without any extra cost to themselves. If they wish to imbibe the writings of great minds, or to procure reading for recreation, to know how to spell Mesopotamia, to find where Salonika is, or to decide where to spend a holiday, the library is the place where all these matters and a multitude of others in some degree are the subjects of discussion in some volume within its walls, all to be had for the mere asking. The more efficient and extensive the library service is, the closer it is brought to the homes of the people, the less possible will it be for any man or woman to remain ignorant of the things that matter. Despite all that the libraries have done and are doing, much remains to be accomplished before our library system can approach the ideal. About 600 districts have established libraries out of the rates, and many of these areas have numerous branch libraries, while in addition there are hundreds of semi-public and institutional libraries providing food for the minds of seekers after knowledge.

One would imagine that, with such a vast collection of libraries as the above, the studious mind should never lack food for thought, and yet not only is the supply of necessary goods as scarce as sugar in 1917, but, just as in the case of the latter commodity, distribution is terribly unequal. This result is largely due to the lack of co-ordination and co-operation among the library authorities of the country, municipal and institutional. Systems of classification and arrangement vary from place to place ; catalogues are differently planned and frequently imperfectly carried out ; bibliographical work is often conspicuous by its absence ; untrained and inexperienced men (and women) are too frequently put in charge of important libraries, and neighbouring authorities do not consult each other with regard to purchases—hence a vast amount of duplication—and there is no system at present whereby it is possible to inquire of some central institution as to the most suitable library for a particular subject, or the whereabouts of particular works. Municipal libraries *do* provide facilities in so far as the central and branch libraries are concerned, but they have usually no knowledge of the contents of non-municipal institutions, and vice versa. Each library is a law unto itself, and generally it does not think outside its own district. What a godsend it would be if there were, say, in Camberwell, Hammersmith, Islington, and Whitechapel, a miniature British Museum reference library, supported and controlled by the local authorities in each area. Is it possible to deny that tremendous advantage to the student and great economy in finance would be brought about if, instead of the usually inadequate municipal reference library, five or six bodies combined to provide north, south, east, and west, a great reference library devoted to that one purpose? You cannot generally discover, except by accident, that a work not available in one library is to be found next door, and the inquirer has to hunt from library to library on the offchance of finding at last the much-sought work. These remarks apply particularly to London. The defect is not so acutely felt in large provincial towns, because in these places the municipal libraries are controlled by one authority, and I see no reason why London should not have its libraries controlled under a similar arrangement. I know a howl will be raised in many directions at the mere suggestion of a single library authority for London, but the inhabitants will never get the best value for money spent on the libraries without some such scheme. I do not for one instant approve of the suggestion of the Workers' Educational Association that libraries should be put under the Local Education Authority. Of the many possible evils which may fall upon the libraries spare us from this one. Libraries are educational, it is true, very much so, but to imagine that to be this simply is the ideal aim and end of public library progress is as inaccurate as a Turkish official communique. Libraries surely are intended to provide mental recreation, to supply information, to inculcate and cultivate a love of reading for reading's sake, to encourage research and to aid the spread of knowledge, if you like, but not to become adult schools, controlled by the mind of a schoolmaster. All this apart from the fact that education authorities will, in the future, have their hands more full than ever of their legitimate work. I should prefer to see a body of experienced librarians and others, outside the immediate control of the municipal authorities, made responsible for the general management of our libraries, endowed with adequate funds and powers, imbued with the minimum of parochialism and having as its ideal the provision of literature of the kind needed in convenient districts, the establishment of a central catalogue and co-operative bibliographies, as well as a central exchange for duplicates and directory of research. In fact, a body which could and would really co-ordinate the activities of the libraries, paying due regard to distinctly local needs. Even an improved Library Association, given these powers, would produce incomparably better results than the present lonely local management, with its committees and sub-committees, handicapped by the delays which are inseparable from such a system. Lending libraries also could be made of immeasurably greater value than they are at present. If you live at the extremity of one district and almost next door to the public library of another you cannot make use of the lending department of the latter, because you are outside its radius, and even if your own library is two miles away that makes no difference. You can either go there or go without your books. You may argue that you help to pay for them, but that does not alter the rule. You must rest content with the fact that you are helping to provide others with literature. Even with co-operative catalogues and unification of service the reader living at a great distance might still feel dissatisfied. It would be cheaper, perhaps, for him to buy a book than pay his fare to London and back in order to see it, but that does not alter the fact that there are many special collections in London which are invaluable to the research student, and a central institution to which application could be made for guidance would be an inestimable boon to many. The new Central Lending Library for students is likely to do great things in future, but it must obviously be handicapped by the fact that it has largely to be its own advertisement. A central board, if it existed, could do a great deal in bringing to the knowledge of the public the facilities provided by that institution. I believe the deficiencies I have mentioned could be quickly remedied if those directly concerned were keen enough to set about the business. One has to confess that many members of library committees, etc., are quite apathetic regarding even their own libraries. Those who object generally to municipalisation or state control of institutions do not want them to be very successful, although they have not always the courage to say so openly. There are, undoubtedly, numbers of them, who think public libraries wrong in principle, but who also believe public tennis courts and bowling greens to be essential to the life of the community. These are the people who can afford to buy the books they want, but who like to get their favourite recreations cheaply.

It is my opinion that there is not sufficient personal contact between our librarians and the readers. If the assistance of the librarian was more often available much greater satisfaction would result to the inquirer. There are libraries in existence where one hardly ever meets the chiefs of the institutions—in fact, many of them think it *infra dig* to be in evidence at the library desk. In many cases, though, the chief librarian is the only member of the staff who has sufficient training and knowledge to be of real help. Of course, there are numbers of assistants who are not only able to help, but ready and anxious so to do, but, unfortunately, there are many who are ready but unable, largely through no fault of their own. How can you expect a man to be a " guide to the literature of any subject " when he has to exist, as is so often the case, on the munificent sum of anything from £1 to £2 a week? Yet many senior library assistants are in this position. Scores of people whom I know personally, who have professional certificates for librarianship and frequently other qualifications as well, have to subsist on a pittance considerably less than that given to a town hall porter. Why is it that the professions which cater for the training of the minds of their fellow men should be considered less worthy of a living wage than others? Teachers and librarians are surely members of honourable callings, and yet they are expected to give of their best for a smaller reward than is given to a full-time bricklayer. I am not suggesting that the latter is too well paid. Far from it. I should like him to get as much as he wants, but I do most emphatically assert that it is a national disgrace that members of library staffs, among others, who can, under proper conditions, become important factors in improving the knowledge of the people, should be so terribly handicapped financially; the argument generally used is that the penny rate limit prevents better remuneration being offered. I agree that the general limiting of the library rate to one penny in the pound, which has been the position more or less since 1850, when the first Public Library Act came into force, should be quickly removed.

It is a startling fact that about half the public libraries in this country have an income of less than £350 per annum, and 200 of these have less than £200. From the income provision has to be made for rents and interest on loans, upkeep of the building, books, and periodicals and salaries, with the result that on the average only one-fourth of the income is available for books and periodicals—the acquisition and use of which is the real purpose—at any rate, the main object—of the institution. A capable librarian and an adequate choice of books cannot be ensured when there is less than £200 a year to share between them and other necessities. As a consequence the "other necessities" have to be supplied, and the balance of the money only is left for the two most essential things.

Library authorities have no right to expect the best results from a staff which is badly underpaid. I know of people who have been members of the staff of a library for ten or twelve years who are at the moment getting the princely wage of 30s. a week! I am confident that if library authorities had any real desire to alter matters, and if they would by their actions show it, the whole position could be changed as easily as a clock could be wound. If the chief librarians of the country had had the opportunity I am sure matters would have been altered for the better years ago, and if the authorities to-day had the courage to cry out unanimously that they were anxious to improve the position, national shame would assuredly effect an alteration. Do not let it be thought that librarians and their assistants generally have no interest in their calling. I believe that the present generation of librarians is, on the whole, a competent and enthusiastic one. The very fact that so many men take up the profession is evidence enough of their interest, for if that were lacking, heaven bless the libraries!—the financial reward offered is not a thing to struggle for. Another proof is the long list of those who have passed the professional examinations of the Library Association, but this has not meant either salvation or security for most of them. A centralised administration could, by the economy resulting therefrom, considerably improve matters even if the rate limit remained. A district reference library could provide twice as many *different* books at half the cost incurred by four different libraries buying almost the *same* books. It would even offer some advantages over the British Museum itself, for the age limit at the latter institution prevents its free use by thousands of people at the most studious age.

Well, then, in the great reconstruction period after the war, what is to be the position of our library system? Almost every other trade and profession in existence will, in all probability, offer greater monetary inducements to employees than before the war, but for the librarian and prospective librarian it looks like being "as you were." There is no Trade Union to take severe measures in cases of low wages and long hours. Almost the first direction in which local authorities turned when the cry of "war economy" was raised was to the library rate. In many places the order was "cut down your demand for books and periodicals." And this at a time when it was more than ever necessary that the poorer sections of the public should

H

read—for only by learning what caused the war, what its consequences will be, and how such a calamity can be avoided in future will the people be able to take a proper part in the work of reconstruction— a thing which is going, I hope, to make a vital difference to the future of every human being. The opportunities for well doing in our libraries will increase exceedingly. In many directions the scope of library work will be considerably extended. The assistance of these institutions will be necessary in many new spheres and in increased ratio in others not so new. We hear of plans for establishing great commercial libraries in many of our large towns, of rural libraries, of co-operation with chambers of commerce and agricultural associations, and many other ideas for extension of labours. Let us hope that the opportunity will be taken at once to systematise the whole field of librarianship, to make the library profession that power for good in the land which it deserves to be. Instead of being " cribbed, cabined, and confined," cold-watered, sometimes ridiculed, often despised, controlled by people with no real sympathy with the work, let the State see to it that in future our libraries are placed in such a position that no single thing essential for their welfare shall be withheld from them. I have thrown out some suggestions. These may not be new to any interested person. They have probably been mentioned and better expressed by scores of other people before me. All the more evidence of their urgency. A well-known Member of Parliament said to me only a few days ago that if it could be shown that there was a real demand from the people for the extension of library work, the removal of the rate limit, and any other necessary legislative action would not be refused by Parliament. At present, he said, it could be urged that such measures were demanded by interested associations, and not by the people at large. Readers may do a lot in this matter. Cannot the workers demand that their libraries shall be at least as well provided for out of the rates as their baths and washhouses—to which, by the way, they have to pay for admission. I believe that it is just as necessary for the community that the libraries and the profession should be soundly re-established as it is for the education profession to be, and no one doubts the needs of the latter. If we can afford £7,000,000 a day for the destruction of men and material, surely to goodness an extra penny in the pound *once a year* will not break the camel's back. And once this has become an accomplished fact half the difficulties will have vanished. Money spent on libraries does not destroy men or material, but it creates and recreates, and the dividend declared in human values makes the institutions gilt-edged securities.

REFERENCES.—J. D. Brown : " Guide to Librarianship." H. G. T. Cannons : " Bibliography of Library Economy." T. Greenwood : " Library Year Book " (fourth edition). " Library Association Year Book."

PART III.

EDUCATION IN OTHER COUNTRIES.

PREFACE.

By Miss T. M. Browne, M.A.

This section makes no attempt at exhaustive treatment. Its aim is to give a short general sketch of the educational systems of other countries, with particular reference to any outstanding features which may be of value for those interested in the future of education in this country. The study of our own problems cannot be complete without some examination of the various ways in which similar problems have been faced elsewhere. The relation of Church and State in matters of education, of State and local authority, the extent of State aid and the effects of State control, the value of private enterprise in education, public interest in education—all such questions may best be considered by studying them in close connection with widely varying systems, which emphasise now one aspect and now another. Nor can the inquiry stop short at education. Other influences—geographical, racial, religious, economic—must be allowed due weight before comparisons or criticisms can justly be made. A general knowledge of this kind is indispensable for all who wish to grapple seriously with the defects of our own system or to judge what place England occupies in the educational development of the civilised world. It will also do much to destroy that insular prejudice against things foreign, which is less excusable in the sphere of education than in any other.

The duty of the State to guarantee to its citizens a minimum amount of free education is now everywhere recognised. Beyond this primary stage the extent of State " interference " varies. Most countries provide facilities to a greater or less degree by the establishment of State secondary schools and by aiding other schools provided they meet certain requirements. As the facilities granted by the State vary, so naturally does the extent of State control, and in this respect the highly centralised French system may be contrasted with our own. Only in Germany as yet does the State insist on a certain amount of continued education after the primary stage. In the United States free State education from the kindergarten to the University is possible.

Such growth of State activity in education usually involves at some time or another a conflict with the voluntary efforts of private persons or associations. On the one hand, a certain amount of State control is necessary to ensure order and stability in any system of education; on the other hand, non-State, " private " schools preserve that freedom of method and initiative which is too often crushed out of a State-controlled institution. As voluntary effort has in the past been directed mainly towards denominational education, the chief problem has been, and often still is, the religious one; and this involves the whole question of the relation of Church and State. The State cannot impose any religious teaching on its citizens against their will, yet it must guarantee efficiency in those schools which claim the right to give religious teaching. Most systems have had to face the problem of adjusting the rival claims. Where sharp denominational differences exist the difficulties are intensified. The policy adopted in many instances, e.g., in our own Colonies, in Holland and Belgium, is to provide secular education only from public funds while giving recognition and financial aid (and therefore to some extent supervision) to the denominational schools. In Holland and Belgium the religious question has always played an important part, and the " private " schools which supply religious teaching occupy a prominent place in the educational system. In Germany denominational teaching is firmly established. Occasionally, as in Norway and Sweden, the controversy has been little felt owing to the uniformity of religious belief and the intimate connection between Church and State.

No very close examination of the financial basis of foreign education is needed to show us how much we have to learn. In this respect we fall far behind America, with its lavish expenditure on public education, and even a small country like Switzerland puts us to shame. To quote the words of the Prime Minister : " Switzerland spends upon education 55 times as much per head of population as this great and wealthy Empire, whose praises we are never tired of singing on our platforms."

There are many other aspects of foreign educational systems which might be examined, and these suggestions only indicate the lines along which more detailed study might work.

The accounts which follow consist of short articles on certain countries which are of particular interest and significance. They bring out general characteristics and indicate the national attitude towards education. The countries so treated include China and Japan, India, France, America, and Denmark. The development of education in the Far East, with its enormous possibilities for the future, is too often entirely neglected, while in the case of India everyone should have some idea of the problems which arise in the educational as in every other sphere from the clash of Eastern and Western ideas. In Denmark the People's High Schools have a particular interest for the W.E.A., and no member should be ignorant of kindred movements abroad which are working for similar ends and are inspired by the same ideals.

Other systems are dealt with in brief summaries giving the main facts, but of necessity omitting much detail. All would repay closer study from such sources as the Special Reports on Educational Subjects issued by the Board of Education and obtainable in any large public library. These are of various dates, and the earlier reports may describe conditions which have since been altered. Vol. 17 contains a full and interesting account of the People's High Schools ; Vol. 3 (1898), of Education in Switzerland; Vol. 8, Norway and Sweden; Vols. 4 and 5, the Colonies. Numerous articles dealing with particular aspects of education may be found in various volumes, e.g., Training of Native Races, Secondary School Education in Germany, etc. Information may also be obtained from Munro's Cyclopædia of Education, which summarises the systems of each country, from the articles in the Encyclopædia Britannica, on " Education " and on the different countries, also from the Year Books of the Colonies and Statesmen's Year Book.

EDUCATION IN AMERICA.

By Professor Gilbert Vivian Seldes.

Good Americans feel about education very much as good drinkers feel about water. In their earlier days they have had some of it and found it inoffensive; they recall the taste vaguely. But as for thinking or talking or writing about it—that is too much.

In some ways that is a dangerous state of mind, but it indicates a thoroughly healthy condition of affairs. (The comparison with drinking must be considered closed.) We give little thought to our education because it is a normal good thing in our lives. It shapes us and transforms us; it deserves, and is beginning to get, more popular thought and more trained experiment; but the best thing and the fundamental thing is that we assume the existence of a good system of education. So much is safe for us.

The difficulty is to tell about this; it is far easier to explain an ice-cream-soda than to tell why one eats bread or breathes air. Education is our air. A child goes to school because that is the normal thing to do, and the time is rapidly coming when young men and young women will go to college because that, too, will be the normal thing. Our colleges will be somewhat different places before that time.

The normal course of education begins with the Kindergarten, but those of the generation before last who happened to be brought up in the country know none of the delights of coloured bits of paper, nor the intricacies of cut-out puzzles. To-day the Kindergarten has spread into rural districts and the cities are plunging heavily on the Montessori method, with variations. We are delaying the beginning of book-learning (there is a distinct prejudice in the words) and are teaching our youngsters to have prehensile fingers and clear observant eyes and good ears. Fifteen years ago the primary school was the beginning of rural education, and it started with slates and pads and pencils. There were four, not three R's : reading, writing, arithmetic, and the teacher's ruler which snapped over awkward hands. The " little red school house," which is the emblem of anti-clericalism in the United States, housed the primary and the grammar grades; it took its pupils through the elementary things, into advanced arithmetic, United States history, and, under energetic teachers, even to the portals of literature. We read " The Idylls of the King " (with notes).

That was up to the age of, say, 17. Thenceforward the country boy had to shift for himself—to travel each day to the nearest " high school " and prepare himself through four years of Latin, mathematics, history, and science, with perhaps a modern language, for college—or to drop his schooling for ever.

To-day the country school, particularly in the east, is equipped with a manual-training department, a domestic science course, lessons in singing, or, sometimes, instrumental music; and it leads directly to the high school. The township, unit in education, and the county, the administrative unit in each State, combine to bring a high school within reach of the smallest town.

The high school is really the centre of gravity in our educational system. Although the college seems to be the storm-centre the appearance is misleading, for everything depends on the style of education which is given to a growing body of boys and girls when they are between 17 and 21 years old. Two high schools at least in the United States are empowered to give the degree of Bachelor of Arts. One of them, the Central High School of Philadelphia, has, beside the ordinary curriculum of Latin, history, science (physics, physiology, botany, zoology, chemistry, and the like), history, English literature, modern languages, and a certain amount of manual training, such things as astronomy, Greek, logic, political science, research courses in modern English literature, ethics, and a host of subjects which are the proper work of college years.

The urban high school is usually two schools by this time; the manual training school will make concessions and teach a bit of Latin; the classical school will teach science, but hardly engineering. Between these two groups the feud is as it should be in accordance with traditions, but it is carried into the Municipal Council chamber and the ancient arguments are periodically heard. Practical training is demanded, and, although the heads of technical schools and of industrial works plead for men with trained minds rather than for technically trained men, the urgency of life pushes the modern school further and further forward. The question which the principal of a large high school has to solve, with his board of education, is whether his school shall prepare for college, shall prepare for work, or shall prepare for living. I should say that the first two receive most attention. The high school in the United States is not yet conscious of its possibilities, for it certainly can develop into the one institution which will give the minimum background against which ordinary American life can be seen in proper colours. The high school still thinks of itself too much as an intermediary stage.

After that, if anything does follow, comes the college or the university. (The only distinction we make is that a university includes a college, which teaches a bit of everything, and has, in addition, professional schools of law, medicine, the sciences, and, to be sure, business.) Here one must write with many reservations, for the college system in America is a rapidly changing one and has many simultaneous phases of development.

The great colleges, in the sense that Oxford and Cambridge are the great colleges of England, will be Harvard, Yale, Princeton (they are all properly universities). Each has its special tone, and each takes pride in that tone—a circumstance which allies them to many smaller colleges and sets them apart from such universities as that of Pennsylvania, which is larger than any of the three, but lacks the tradition of tone almost entirely. Harvard is in Cambridge, a suburb of Boston, and is popularly supposed to maintain the New England tradition; Yale upholds the more vigorous spirit of old New York; Princeton is achieving, partly as the result of President Wilson's reforms, a creditable combination of scholar and gentleman. In all the major colleges of the country some compulsion exists in the matter of choice of studies, the free-elective system (in the good free-will ethic of New England) passed out of existence when Charles William Eliot retired from the presidency of Harvard. The average of required work will be some 16 or 18 subjects in a four-year course, and of these one-third or one-fourth will be related, so that each student will have a concentrated knowledge of at least one subject when he graduates. The system of instruction is largely that of the lecture-room with occasional conferences and outside reading. Princeton has the tutorial system, on the English plan, but nowhere does the system of reading during vacation prevail.

It is hard for a graduate of one of these schools to confess that they are ceasing to be important in American life, but the thing must be said. If they continue to be the finest institutions they will bring leaven into the lump of college men, but they can no longer be the leaven in the lump of our national existence. The same force which prevents us from having a national newspaper seems to make a national university impossible. Its place is taken by the State universities, usually named after the State and usually dependent upon the State's bounty. Many of them prosper because of the lands which the Federal Government set apart for their revenue many years ago; all receive from their States appropriations usually in proportion to the number of students they teach.

The cultivation of " life " in any sense is less intense in the State colleges than it is at the older schools, and even there it falls behind the standards of English colleges. The State colleges tend to be practical. Although the best engineering school is generally supposed to be at Cornell and some of the finest technical schools are at Columbia (both in New York and both belonging to the Harvard-Yale-Princeton group) the schools for agriculture, forestry, mining, and such practical work are generally to be found in the State institutions. Living is cheap there; fees and tuition are reduced to very little by the State, and many scholarships are given. The study of the humanities is not neglected, but the State universities would go on doing their major work if the classical collegiate subjects were dropped altogether. The reason is obvious. Many of the universities were founded in States still pioneer in spirit; as cultivation spreads the colleges will change; in the end they will become the great educative force of the country.

I have not room to discuss the many professional schools and the technical schools. In many of the Eastern colleges a degree is now demanded before a student can enter the law or medical school, but the qualification is not ruinous because many other reputable schools exist, apart from colleges and universities. The standard of scholarship, quite apart from the standard of teaching, at all the professional schools is high. The technical schools hardly need explanation; they are hardly cultural, but they are unquestionably effective.

I have tried to give so far an account of our institutions as they are encountered by the average citizen. That they are encountered may be proved by one of our chief editorial witticisms; we are supposed to spend as much each year on education, or nearly as much, as we spend on chewing-gum. You may take it that our education is faulty because it does not stop us from chewing gum; or you may take it that our system is hopeful because even those who chew gum find place and profit in that system.

The prejudice against men and women of education is almost gone. (I should have mentioned such girls' colleges as Vassar, Wellesley, Bryn Mawr, and Smith before. I should say now that most of the State universities are co-educational.) We demand the right to spend money on education. Those of us who are practical men demand, in addition, that every man who leaves college shall be able to show in dollars and cents that the investment has been good. Others still cling to the perverse idea that the object of college life is to make men not better wage-earners, nor scholars, nor gentlemen, but better citizens. They want the college, and with it the whole educational system, to give discrimination, to make men clear of judgment and generous of mind. In the clash between these two purposes the practical man is winning out, but his victory is his undoing. In spite of his best efforts the school widens out. In spite of him the crux of our system moves gradually upward, so that the grammar school, out of which lads and girls passed at 12 and 13 with their education complete, has become the low standard; in spite of him the high school leads to the college; in spite of him the men and women who go through college are better than efficient.

To describe the effects of our education, even as they are visible over a period of 15 years, would pass beyond the limits of space assigned me. And it would pass beyond the legitimate theme of this article. But perhaps I may say that our democracy is in our education, and it is our education which has made it possible for us to fight for the democracy of the world.

DANISH HIGH SCHOOLS (FOLKEHOJSKOLER).

By Miss A. C. Heath (Tutorial Class Lecturer).

There are certain resemblances between the University Tutorial Class movement and the People's High Schools in Denmark, but there are also certain essential distinctions, and these distinctions seem to lie in the respective qualifications required of the teachers. The Danish movement lays stress upon the teacher's message. He must be a man not necessarily of a specified dogmatic faith, but one with a general optimistic belief in a higher trend of things and a Kingdom of God to come on earth. " His must be the living voice speaking with the accent of conviction in it" (Thornton). He needs "stillness and quiet" (Poulsen). The function of the English Tutorial Class lecturer, on the other hand, is to train minds, not to influence thought, while the following words from Thornton illustrate the Danish point of view: " The Folkehöjskoler teacher, whilst leaving all distinctive religious instruction to the Church, of which he is an attached member, so teaches history both of his own and of other countries as to show that there is a divine purpose running through the ages; that behind all human events there is a higher and spiritual influence making for all that is good and right, in conformity and in union with which he may gladly work for the establishment of a Kingdom of God upon earth."

This important distinction, which, in the present writer's opinion, is the root of the difference between English institutions on Danish lines, such as Fircroft, and the Tutorial Class movement, becomes clear on studying the lives and ideals of the co-fathers of the movement, Bishop Grundtvig and Kristen Kold.

Bishop Grundtvig (1783-1872) passed some years of his early youth in the house of a country clergyman. His leisure hours were spent with the country farmers and their labourers, and it was thus that he acquired his knowledge of and deep love for them.

Denmark, at that time, was passing through a period of stagnation, and Grundtvig, as he grew up, became filled with a desire to awaken his countrymen to new life. Such new life he gradually came to think would come from the formation of schools, " accessible to young people all over the land, where they may readily get leave and opportunity to become better acquainted not only with human nature and human life in general, but with themselves in particular, and where they can receive guidance in all civic relations and become well acquainted with their country's need in all directions, whilst their daily life and love of country are nourished by national speech and historical information, by mutual intercourse with one another, and by the lively songs which are heard through all the period of Denmark's history, and inspire admiration for what is great, warm love for what is beautiful, faithfulness and affection, peace and unity, innocent cheerfulness,

---

Note.—Tenses of the original speech have been transposed.

pleasure and mirth." " Thus," Grundtvig goes on to say in the speech from which we quote, " will be opened a well of healing in the land, which will be sought by crowds from generation to generation," and therein, " past counting, blind people will receive their sight, the deaf their hearing, and the dumb their speech, and there the halt will cast away their crutches and show clearly that the dance trips it lightly through the wood."

The co-father of the movement is Kristen Kold (1816-70), the son of a poor shoemaker. There were three landmarks in Kold's life : the first " when a well-known preacher made me see that our Lord loved mankind, and it was frightful I had not managed to learn that all the years of my life. . . . . I had never seen the like to the life, the zest, the strength and energy that sprang up in me and henceforth made all lessons easy." The second was when, like Grundtvig, he learnt the power of the living voice, and, abandoning obsolete catechetical methods, " talked " the contents of the Catechism to his scholars, and the third when the war over Schleswig-Holstein taught him how the spirit of enthusiasm could be spread.

Kold, by birth and temperament, was able to attract the poorer classes of working men. He shared the sleeping rooms of his pupils and lived with them on a basis of democratic equality.

The spirit of these two men lives in the movement as it is to-day. To-day there are over 70 High Schools whose foundation is due to their inspiration and 14 Agricultural schools founded under the influence of the High Schools. The number of students in the High Schools was 3,273 men and 3,266 women in 1907.* At present the proportion of townsmen among the pupils is small.

The terms are usually of five months' duration for men in the winter and three for women in the summer, though in some of the schools there is co-education during the winter months and a special course for women in the summer as well. Askov has a two years' course.

The cost is less than 8s. 6d. a week in the majority of schools, while a large number of bursaries provided by the State enable the poorest students to enter.

Among these 70 High Schools a little more than half give a purely cultural education—history, literature, mathematics, and natural science—while the remainder add technical subjects. The 14 agricultural schools are in close connection with the High Schools and draw from them their best students.

The High Schools are described as the " hot-bed " of the great Danish co-operative movement, while the fact that 30 per cent. of the 1901 Parliament were ex-High School pupils illustrate the truth of Principal Schröder's claim : " If that which is in a man is set in the right direction it will bear fruit in the whole of his outer activity ; a real enlightenment of spirit in the man of full age will call forth the energy, capacity, and perseverance more necessary than acquirements when it comes to the solution of practical problems."

But the best summary of the work of the schools is contained in these words of Mr. Thornton :—

" Under the influence, continued for months together at the most receptive period of a man's life, in places free from distractions, of

---

* The average age of the students is between 18 and 25.

living word, glad song and genial comradeship, men's natures are expanded; dormant, unsuspected faculties are awakened; the mental horizon is extended; prejudices fall away; desires for new activities arise. These are the purest, most lasting joys. Once gained, they can never be lost. They are independent of time and change. And so it may well be said that the chief result of this 60 years' work is a huge increase in the sum of human happiness."

REFERENCES.—"Cyclopædia of Education" (Sonnenschien). Sadler : " Continuation Schools." Thornton : " Schools (Public and Private) in the North of Europe." Board of Education, Special Reports, Cd. 3537.

EDUCATION IN FRANCE.

By Miss T. M. Browne.

A brief general sketch of education in France, however slight, cannot fail to bring out at many points its contrast with the English system, and the study of these differences is both interesting and valuable. In France may be found in efficient working order a system which does not on the whole appeal to the English attitude of mind with regard to education—a system that is, of complete State control, embracing every department of education and carefully organised under a highly centralised scheme of administration. No doubt those who lay most stress on the value of unhampered initiative and free development will point out the dangers involved in the employment of large numbers of State officials and in the power given to the State to determine the general character and aims of the teaching given in every type of school. On the other hand, those who look rather to the haphazard arrangement and lack of effective supervision in many branches of our educational system will admire the clearness of plan and purpose which avoids wasteful overlapping and makes for order and unity by bringing the smallest country school into direct contact with the Central Authority. There is no room in the French system for the uncontrolled private schools of every grade and every degree of efficiency which are so numerous in England. Private schools of a definitely religious character do exist, and their sharp antagonism to the State schools is due to the conflict between Church and State, which in France has been so bitter. Before the Revolution education in France was developed largely by religious bodies. In particular, through the activity of the Christian Brothers, invaluable work has been done until recent times in the foundation and maintenance of boys' schools. The State reorganisation of education resulted in the withdrawal first of religious instruction (1881) and later of clerical teachers (1886). The Orders then carried on private schools of their own until in 1904 the suppression of religious congregations involved the closing of their schools. In spite of all difficulties lay private schools still exist and are supported entirely by voluntary effort. No one, however, may open such a school without the sanction of the Ministry. The teachers, like those in the public schools, must give a guarantee of efficiency by possessing the State diploma and only the State leaving examinations are recognised.

The Minister of Public Instruction is the supreme head of the whole educational system. He is assisted by a Consultative Committee representing all grades of education. Under him are three Directors for the three departments of primary, secondary, and higher education. Below them come the "rectors," or heads of the 17 "academies" or educational divisions of the country. They are appointed by the President of the Republic and exercise control over all three grades.

Effective supervision is maintained by an important body of inspectors with varying degrees of control. The highest of these are the "inspecteurs généraux." They keep in touch with the general progress of education, and by their agency the Central Authority may exercise its influence and transmit new ideas and suggestions to all parts of a district. " They act as the eyes and ears of the Central Authority and serve also as its mouthpiece."

In addition, each academy or division has its inspector. His close contact with the administrative body, on the one hand, and the schools in their practical working on the other, make him a valuable link between the two. The inspectors for primary schools act under him.

The teachers are all appointed directly or indirectly by the Central Authority. No one may teach without possessing the State certificate, and this maintains a high average of efficiency. Similarly in the secondary schools and Universities only certain diplomas and degrees give the necessary qualifications for teaching.

Primary education is free and compulsory between the ages of 6 and 13. For children under the school age there are numbers of well-equipped kindergarten schools, " écoles maternelles." No religious teaching is given in the primary schools, its place being taken by instruction in " morals " and " civics." Such teaching is expected to be entirely neutral, and nothing must be said which might give offence to any religious beliefs. By endeavouring to instruct the child in his duties towards himself, his neighbour and the State it aims at producing the knowledge and practice of good citizenship.

A distinguishing feature of the French primary system is the extensive provision made for continued education. Primary and secondary education are regarded as distinct from the earliest to the latest stages, and the normal transition is not from the primary to the secondary school, but from the primary to the higher primary school. These schools aim at providing further opportunities for the cleverer children among the working classes. They do not admit all without discrimination, but only those who are fit to profit by continued instruction. All must have the certificate of primary studies (taken from the primary school), and a quarterly examination tests the fitness and progress of the scholar. Instruction is free and numerous scholarships are provided to cover the expense of travelling, clothing, etc. The curriculum of the course, which extends over two or three years, continues and develops that of the primary school. It includes the teaching of literature, political economy, elementary legal ideas, and mathematics. In order to fit the children for their future occupations training is given in agriculture, horticulture, commerce, the work of the shop, and domestic science. Special sections provide training in these branches of work.

The possible danger against which these schools must guard is the diversion of potential workers from industry and agriculture to clerical work and other already overcrowded professions. Here the value of central control is felt. By means of careful returns the general working of the scheme may be judged, and its effects to some extent discovered, by inquiry into the nature of the occupations afterwards taken up by the pupils. Thus, when it was found that the chiefly literary training did not produce the desired results, a more practical character was given to the teaching by the institution of the special courses intended for industrial commercial or agricultural pursuits. Every effort is made to avoid spoiling a child for an occupation for which he would otherwise be well fitted. By giving to every intelligent child the chance of an additional two or three years' training, with little sacrifice on the parents' part, some at least of the great wastage of intelligence, which so often results from the early stoppage of elementary education, may be avoided.

Employers of all kinds are familiar with the type of education given in these schools and recognise its value. They often apply directly to the schools, and special efforts are made to secure suitable occupations for the pupils. In many cases boarding establishments are connected with the schools and have a valuable influence on the children's development.

Secondary education is given in the colleges and lycées. The Baccalauréat, or State leaving examination, which admits to the Universities and to many careers, is taken at the end of the course, which may be either classical or modern in tendency. In the lycées religious instruction may still be given by a chaplain. The Universities number 17 in all, one for each academy. The professors are appointed by the Ministry of Public Instruction and are paid by the State. The University of Paris, in point of numbers, is the largest in the world. In 1910 its students numbered over 17,500. All the Universities are open to women.

Secondary education in France in several ways offers an interesting contrast to our own. There is a tendency to regard it primarily as an intellectual training, and the many different State examinations afford a practical and easily recognised test of the amount of knowledge acquired at the various stages. On the intellectual side alone it undoubtedly stands higher than our own, but it lacks certain valuable elements which foster the all-round development of character. The insistence on physical training and the value of games, the freedom and responsibility of community life, the close relations between master and boys—all these no doubt are sometimes unduly emphasised in English schools at the expense of purely intellectual work, but in their proper place they are important factors in education taken in its widest sense. This spirit is to some extent making its way in France, but it will probably never be allowed to grow to such a degree as to injure the tradition of learning which is such a valued possession of the French schools.

EDUCATION IN THE FAR EAST.

By Professor P. M. Roxby.

In the making of the world's future the Far East is destined to play a part whose importance can scarcely be over-estimated. The gigantic issues involved in the present war and the coming settlement should not blind us to the fact that the world will presently be faced with another set of problems, hardly less momentous and complex than those whose solution Europe and America are now so painfully seeking. These problems are concerned with the future relations of the White and Yellow Races, and they are naturally conditioned, to a very large extent, by the form which economic, social, and political development is taking, or is likely to take, in the Far Eastern countries. There is no need to argue the point that this development is intimately related to the progress of education. We have only to think of Germany to realise that a country's educational system is often not only the lever of its economic and political advance, but is also the index of its aspirations and the key to its social conditions. Anyone who wishes to form some estimate of the Orient in relation to the great drama of world politics must try to gauge the effects which the educational experiments now in progress are likely to have upon its future.

Excluding Indo-China and the Eastern Dependencies of Russia, the Far East now comprises China and Japan, for Korea has become a part of the Japanese Empire, and her educational system is almost entirely controlled by the great Island Power. The educational position in Japan differs fundamentally from that in China, and even in this brief sketch the two countries must be separately treated.

EDUCATION IN JAPAN.

The educational machinery in Japan has been rapidly built up during the last forty years as a part of that wonderful system of State organisation which has transformed a relatively weak and extremely isolated Eastern State into a first-class World Power. Japan indeed was never the comic-opera principality which our grandfathers used to picture, and the pioneers of the new Japan have utilised to the full many forces of strength latent in the old régime. When they realised that if Japan was to hold her own with the great Western Powers she must be drastically reconstituted, they set themselves to the task of transforming, without destroying, the essential fabric of Japanese life, and of adapting Western institutions to the peculiar needs of their own country. The combination of the new with the old is well seen in an educational system which is designed to combine the technical efficiency and training of the West with the inculcation of the special virtues on which they believed the greatness of Japanese national life to depend. Thus we should notice :—

(a) The extreme importance attached to the development of military virtues, the sense of discipline, the habit of unquestioning obedience, the spirit of self-sacrifice, the subordination of personal ambitions to the common good. These aspects of training systematically carried on, form the traditions of " Bushido," the old code of feudal chivalry, tinctured and softened by Buddhist conceptions, which was one of the distinguishing features of Old Japan.

(*b*) The reverence for the person and office of the Emperor as embodying the unity and greatness of Japan. It provides a kind of motive force for the active exercise of the virtues mentioned above. The portraits of the Emperor and Empress, hung in special receptacles in all the higher schools and colleges, have an almost sacred significance, and there are many cases of teachers risking their lives to save them during fires.

(*c*) The maintenance of the Chinese classics, inculcating filial obedience and respect and other typically Eastern virtues, as an essential part of the curriculum.

In these and other similar ways the directors of the educational system of modern Japan have preserved the continuity of Japanese traditions, with unquestionably great results, for there can be no doubt that the wonderful achievements of their armies at Port Arthur and Mukden, and hardly less their great economic progress, have been due quite as much to the maintenance and development of the old typically Japanese virtues as to the extraordinary efficiency of the technical training which they have adopted from the West.

Education in Japan is entirely under Government control, and reproduces in its external aspects many of the features of the Continental, particularly perhaps of the German system. It includes :—

1. A complete system of elementary schools in two grades, ordinary and higher, attendance for a period of six years being compulsory. In the words of the Imperal rescript governing the national system of education : " Elementary schools are designed to give children the rudiments of moral education, and of an education specially adapted to make them good members of the community, together with such general knowledge and skill as are necessary for the practical duties of life, due attention being paid to their bodily development."

An interesting and important point is that as a rule the children of all classes in the locality attend the same school. The staple subjects are morals, the Japanese language, Japanese history, arithmetic, geography, science, drawing, singing, and (for girls) sewing. To these are added in the higher elementary schools manual work and either agriculture or commerce. In some cases there is instruction in English.

2. The system of secondary schools, as originally planned, was based on the French model. The country was divided into eight major school districts, and each of these was to be sub-divided into 32 middle-school districts, with one secondary school in each. The scheme has been considerably modified, but holds good in its main features, and there are now nearly 300 middle schools in Japan, either public schools or private schools directly supervised by the Government. The curriculum includes morals, Japanese language and Chinese classics, foreign languages (English or German), history and geography, arithmetic, natural history, physics and chemistry, drawing, singing, and gymnastics. The course is planned on a five

years' basis (from 12 to 17), and the children who pass through it have already attended the ordinary elementary school course.

3. There is a very complete system for the training of teachers, and special schools are provided for this purpose; generally speaking, the staffing of the schools is good and the size of the classes relatively small.

4. An important feature is the existence of eight high schools, the special object of which is to prepare students either for the Universities or for the Government Services. The great majority of the students who enter these high schools are graduates of the middle schools, and have already reached the age at which the average student enters a University in England. In these schools there is specialised instruction in three categories according to the line of study which the student is going to follow subsequently. One section prepares students specifically for the Colleges of Law and Literature, and the curriculum includes history, logic and mental philosophy, elementary law, and political economy; the second section is preparatory to admission to the Colleges of Science and Engineering or of Agriculture, and the emphasis is given to mathematics, physics, chemistry, geology, etc. The third prepares for the Colleges of Medicine. In all three sections modern language teaching plays a very important part, and includes Japanese, Chinese, English, and either German or French. The European traveller in Japan cannot fail to be impressed by the linguistic attainments of the educated classes. Common also to all three sections is the teaching of ethics and elaborate physical training.

5. The Imperial Universities of Japan gain immensely from the fact that practically all their students have already passed through these high schools. The first year student is usually much better equipped on the linguistic side, and is more ready to profit by the highest instruction which the University can give him, than is the case with his compeer in England. There are already three Imperial Universities in Japan in Tokyo, Kyoto, and Tohoku, respectively, and a fourth is to be founded in the Hokkaido (Yezo), the northernmost and most backward of the central group of islands in the Japanese Archipelago. All of them are heavily subsidised by the State.

Space forbids any detailed account of the organisation of these Universities, but it must be noticed that they consist of " Colleges " where definite courses of instruction are given, and of " Halls " in which, under the guidance of professors, students are prepared for special research. Japan had so much to learn from Europe in the methods and technique of modern science that she has necessarily been mainly occupied in absorbing rather than in adding to the sum of human knowledge, but during recent years she has begun to make important contributions of her own, notably in the science of seismology and in some departments of chemistry.

In addition to the Imperial or State Universities, there are several privately founded special schools or universities, such as the celebrated Keiogijuku, founded by perhaps the most famous of Japanese educationalists, Mr. Fukuzawa. The aims of this institution are thus set forth : " The Keiogijuku is not satisfied with remaining merely a place of cloistered learning. It aspires to be the fountain-head whence flows nobility of character and an intellectual life and moral glory to illumine the path of Japan. Its aim is to make clear those principles which should govern the domestic, social, and national life, not only by preaching, but also by practising them, thus to prove a leading factor in the general welfare of the country."

There is also in Japan a rapidly developing system of higher technical schools and colleges and a growing intimacy of relationship between them and the business classes. The importance of the application of science and research to the different forms of production is thoroughly understood, and in particular it may be noticed that Japanese agriculture, the basis of national life, is being gradually revolutionised by these means.

Finally, a passing reference must be made to the fact that greater provision is being made for the education of women. In the elementary schools boys and girls are frequently taught together, but in the higher grades there are separate higher female schools, and since 1901 there has been a special Women's University. This is probably the most revolutionary feature in the entire educational system, for, as is well known, the status of women in the old Japan was definitely inferior to that of men, and the change promises to produce far-reaching social consequences.

From the slight sketch that has been given it will be seen that the educational system in Japan is singularly complete and in many ways is considerably in advance of ours in England. Perhaps its main feature is its systematic character and its almost complete control and organisation by the State. There are, as has been mentioned, private institutions under the supervision of the State, and there is a good deal of opportunity for individual effort, but the curricula and scope of activity are carefully watched and regulated. There is not as yet anything corresponding to the Workers' Educational Association, and it must be remembered that the industrial association of workers is voluntary, and independent organisation is as yet only in its infancy in Japan. It is only quite recently that trade unions have been recognised and they still work within very restricted limits. Japan in the future will undoubtedly have to face many grave economic and labour problems created by her industrial transformation, but she is likely to face them with all the greater chance of success because, thanks to the wisdom of her statesmen, her people are already relatively highly educated.

EDUCATION IN CHINA.

The problem of education in China is one of great complexity and of immense and far-reaching importance. A slight sketch of the situation which the Chinese reformers have to face will be more useful than a descriptive account of the educational machinery already established.

China is still in the early stages of a transformation which Japan has nearly completed. Systematic attempts to effect reforms on the lines followed in Japan can hardly be said to have begun before the closing years of the 19th century, after the rude awakening which the country received in the Japanese War of 1895. The results are in some ways already remarkable, but in the main they are still weak and fragmentary. For several reasons the problem is far vaster and much more complex than it is in Japan.

1. China is not only a much larger country, it is also far less unified. China is not so much a State as a series of loosely organised societies of the clan type, held together much more by a common written language and by the common heritage of a very ancient and distinctive civilisation than by the organisation of a central government. The sense of nationality, as we understand it in the West and as it is understood in Japan, is only just beginning to animate the masses of the Chinese people. Society is very strong as expressed in the organisation of the family or clan groups and to a large extent also in industrial and trade groups, but is weak as expressed in the activities and control of a public authority. There are also strong provincial feelings and prejudices. The welding of the numerous commercial and provincial groups into one strong, stable nation-state is the chief task of Chinese statesmanship.

2. In Japan this work has been largely carried through by the Elder Statesmen and the Samurai, the old feudal aristocracy of the country, whose willingness to direct its destinies along new lines has been the outstanding feature of the " Meiji " era (age of enlightenment). But in China there is no corresponding governing class. In many ways Chinese society is the most democratic in the world, and there is a striking absence of class distinctions. This fact is a feature of Chinese life which to those who believe in democratic institutions is full of promise, but in this period of rapid transitions it presents many difficulties and dangers. It means that the leaders of the New China must be selected from the masses themselves, trained along new lines, and taught to understand the West without losing touch with their own people. Nobody yet has ever succeeded in dragooning the Chinese into new paths. They are the last people in the world to submit to " Prussianising " methods. All change must come from within by a natural process of growth, following upon the assimilation of new ideas. The student class of China drawn from the people must be one of the principal agents of whatever changes are necessary. Hence immense importance attaches to the training of the student class. It is attended at present by many peculiar difficulties. The old educational régime has been swept away and the establishment of a new system is hampered not only by inexperience and by ignorance of what exactly is required, but also, so far as the central authorities are concerned, by the more immediate need of inaugurating financial, military, and administrative reforms. Colleges for the higher training of students are rapidly coming into existence in most provinces of China, but they all at present labour, to a greater or less degree, under the same disadvantages—an uncertainty of purpose, the lack of a sufficient number of qualified teachers, the absence of suitable books and appliances, and the difficulty of finding the right medium of instruction.

The uncertainty of purpose is very natural. There are many ideals to be harmonised, the ideal of retaining all that is best in the old Chinese culture, the ideal of understanding and utilising the spirit of Western institutions, the ideal of acquiring an adequate knowledge of European science and technology. It is not surprising that in the absence of a centralising authority such as exists in Japan there is at present considerable confusion. The curriculum is generally over-loaded, and the students, notwithstanding their high receptive capacity, usually only acquire a superficial knowledge of any one subject.

China has to rely at present upon a large number of foreign teachers or of native teachers trained in foreign lands. This, again, involves much confusion of methods and ideals. British, French, American, Japanese, and German conceptions of education jostle one another to an extraordinary degree. There are few modern text-books in Chinese on science, history, law, or medicine, and in many of the higher colleges recourse is frequently had to a Japanese version. We have to picture huge classes of Chinese students trying to understand the West by studying a Chinese adaptation of a Japanese interpretation of European books on constitutional government! Then, again, the peculiar structure of the Chinese language presents an enormous difficulty. It enshrines a great literature. It is hallowed by the traditions of four millennia. But it does not lend itself at all readily to the translation of modern technical terms nor to precise scientific statement. Some great Chinese authorities believe that it can never be satisfactorily used as a medium for conveying Western knowledge to the people. What is to take its place? The question is still unsettled, and the unfortunate students often have to receive some of their lectures in Chinese, some in English, some in French, and some in German. European rivalries, too, are naturally reflected in the academic world of China by vigorous efforts to push the claims of particular languages.

These are only a few of many difficulties confronting the educational reformers of China. If their task of reconstructing an ancient civilisation is to be successfully performed, they must not be hurried. The Chinese will not be hustled, but they have a wonderful vitality, and, as their history shows, a great capacity for absorption. It is an old saying that " China is a sea which salts all waters that flow into it." This capacity is now to be put to the severest test, but those who know China best believe that if the Great Powers do not complicate the situation by industrial and political intrigues, she will come through this most critical period of her long history with renewed strength. It is in the interest of the entire world that she should, and it is of the utmost importance to realise that the transformation or reconstruction—call it what you will—of China is only likely to be successful and fruitful of great results if it is carried through gradually without any violent break with the past.

EDUCATION IN INDIA.

By R. M. Joshi, M.A., LL.B. (Bombay).

Pre-British System of Education.—From time immemorial India has been known as a land of schools, of learning, of literature, of philosophy, all inseparably connected with religion. Owing to the difficulty of the Sanskrit language, however, learning was mainly confined to the Brahmans, the priestly class. As teachers of the community they kept schools for the few of a high order and gave oral lessons to the many of a practical character. The Muslims similarly established a few seats of Arabic learning of a high order, and had a school attached to each mosque where the rudiments of knowledge could be acquired by the multitude belonging to that faith. Both the Hindu and Muslim schools emphasised the development of the memory and of the capacity for abstract reasoning rather too much. The number of these schools seems to have been greatly reduced by the political disorders of the 18th century.

Early British Period.—Up to 1813, the East India Company, being mainly a trading firm, did not pay much attention to the education of its Indian subjects. That work was mainly done by the institutions described above, and also by the missionaries who followed in the wake of the traders and combined general instruction with their proselytising propaganda. The indigenous system was broadly taken as the basis and encouraged by men like Warren Hastings. It was in 1813 that a small sum was expressly set apart for expenditure on education. The question whether education should be imparted in Eastern lore through the Indian vernaculars, or in Western science and literature through English as the medium, was decided in favour of the latter, specially by the exertions of Macaulay, whose Minute of 1835 is very important in that connection. In 1837 English was substituted for Persian as the official language. Important posts in Government service were promised for persons knowing English, and that gave an incredible spur to English-teaching schools and colleges for the rest of the century.

The Modern Period, 1854 Onwards.—The foundation of the modern structure of Indian education, however, was laid in 1854 by the Court of Directors' dispatch to the Government of India. That was a very comprehensive document, and forms the basis of the Government policy to-day. It made the State definitely responsible for the education of the subjects. The measures which were prescribed for carrying out this policy were : (1) The constitution of a Department of Public Instruction (in each province); (2) the foundation of Universities at Presidency towns; (3) the establishment of training schools for teachers; (4) the maintenance of the existing Government schools and colleges of a high order, and the increase of their number when necessary; (5) increased attention to all forms of vernacular schools; and, finally (6), the introduction of a system of grants-in-aid which should foster a spirit of reliance upon local exertions. The policy of this dispatch was confirmed by the Crown in 1859 when it took over the administration of India from the Company. In 1857 the Universities of Calcutta, Madras, and Bombay had been incorporated, that of the Punjab followed in 1882, and of Allahabad in 1887. The various Government Departments wanted subordinate public servants; the courts of the Western type wanted lawyers trained in the Western way; there was a good field for doctors of Western medicine; there was room, too, on the lower rungs of the Public Works Departments for surveyors and engineers. All this demand gave an extraordinary spur to higher education, and the Universities turned out numbers of graduates, especially graduates of arts and law, and, to a lesser extent, of medicine and engineering. These were quickly absorbed in public service or private schools for a couple of decades or so, but that very fact put a high premium on the securing of a degree rather than on acquisition of learning. The number of secondary English schools and arts colleges, privately owned and aided by Government, rapidly increased; the number of eager aspirants after Government service increased still more; the habit of cram crept in; the level of higher education was threatened with a decline; primary education receded into the background. In 1882 a Commission, appointed by Lord Ripon, surveyed the situation and made recommendations, but they do not appear to have been acted upon, for Lord Curzon's inquiries in 1901 showed that matters had not improved since 1882, but were, in fact, a little worse so far as primary education was concerned. In the meantime, a revolution was taking place in the economic life of the country. The opening of the Suez Canal in 1869 and its effective use after the seventies, coupled with the rapid development of railway construction in India, was leading to a swift collapse of the indigenous industries of the old-fashioned type and throwing an increasing number of people back on to the land; but there was no definite scheme either of agricultural, or of technical and industrial, or of commercial education, while there were plenty of successful and unsuccessful matriculates and graduates with nothing to do, and the number was each year being substantially added to. Lord Curzon saw this clearly and set to work vigorously, and the substantial progress of education on a comprehensive scale may be dated from 1904. The growing strength of public opinion may also claim a substantial portion of the credit in this matter. Primary, technical, and commercial education are now acknowledged to be matters of special importance, and the Agricultural Departments, instituted in each province by Lord Curzon, have already justified their existence.

Notwithstanding the recent great progress of education, the number of persons who could read and write was, according to the Census of 1911, only 106 males and ten females per 1,000. The persons with a knowledge of English numbered 1.7 millions out of a total population of more than 313 millions.

The educational system comprises : (a) Universities; (b) secondary schools leading up to the matriculation or a school-leaving certificate (these schools are sometimes divided into (i.) high, or English schools, and (ii.) middle, or Anglo-vernacular schools); and (c) primary schools wherein the medium of instruction is always the vernacular of the district. There are also normal schools for training teachers for the primary and secondary schools, technical and commercial schools growing in number since 1907, and some 40,000 schools of the indigenous type still working in their own way and not falling within the system proper. Most of the agricultural schools and colleges are also outside the pale of the Universities or the Educational Departments.

The following table shows the extent of University education in 1915 :—

ARTS COLLEGES.

	Number of institutions.		Number of scholars.
English	120	......	40,067
Oriental	27	......	1,780

COLLEGES FOR PROFESSIONAL TRAINING.

Law	22	......	4,476
Medicine	4	......	1,755
Engineering	4	......	1,268
Teaching	13	......	693
Agriculture	3	......	224
Veterinary	1	......	173
Commercial	1	......	143
Total	195	......	50,579

These are mostly males. The number of females was 406 in arts colleges, one in law, 68 in medicine, and 50 in teaching.

There are five Universities already referred to. A denominational Hindu University is being established at Benares, and there are movements for a Muslim University at Aligarh, and for Universities at Dacca, Patna, Rangoon, Nagpur, and Mysore. In State institutions education is secular. Of the colleges given in the above table those under private management, though aided by Government, are 70 arts, .21 Oriental, one law, three teaching; those unaided by Government are 20 arts, three Oriental, nine law, one teaching; the rest, including most of the professional colleges, are managed by Government. The " teaching " colleges, above referred to, are for training teachers for " secondary " schools.

The figures for secondary and primary education in the same year are as follows :—

	Institutions for Males.		Females.		Scholars. Males.		Females.
Secondary	6,403	...	606	...	1,015,670	...	87,194
Primary	116,077	...	15,709	...	4,521,015	...	930,187
Special : Normal and others	6,589	...	1,218	...	183,375	...	37,035
Private	36,466	...	2,037	...	563,388	...	73,479
Total	165,717	...	19,584	...	6,333,611	...	1,128,420
Grand Total	185,301			......	7,462,031		

The " special " schools include (1915) 663 training schools for masters, with 15,329 scholars; 91 for mistresses, with 2,076 scholars; nine schools of art, with 1,411 scholars; two law schools, with 27 scholars; 24 medical schools, with 3,476 scholars; 18 engineering and surveying schools, with 743 scholars; 198 technical and industrial schools, with 11,176 scholars; and 61 commercial schools, with 2,628 scholars.

Of the " secondary " schools 438 are managed by Government, 1,292 by local funds and Municipal Boards, 3,988 are " aided," and 1,262 " unaided." The Government only intend to keep " model " secondary schools, about one in each district, and leave the rest to local initiative aided by public funds.

Of the " primary " schools 1,173 are managed by Government, 36,304 by local funds and Municipal Boards, 78,978 are " aided," and 15,251 " unaided." The Government do not desire to keep any " primary " school themselves, but merely to aid private enterprise.

Of the " special " schools 500 are managed by Government, 350 by local funds and Municipal Boards, 5,193 are " aided," and 1,757 are " unaided."

The total expenditure on public instruction in 1914-15 was about 1,092 lakhs of rupees. (A lakh equals 100,000 Rs. 15 equals £1.)

The following table gives the sources and objects of that expenditure :—

SOURCES.

Provincial revenues	(about)	423 lakhs.
Local funds	,,	167 ,,
Municipal Boards	,,	44 ,,
Fees	,,	286 ,,
All other sources :—		
Private	,,	163 ,,
Public	,,	10 ,,
Total	,,	1,093 ,,

OBJECTS.

Arts colleges	(about)	63 lakhs.
Professional colleges	,,	28 ,,
Secondary schools	,,	278 ,,
Primary schools	,,	267 ,,
Special schools :—		
Training	,,	27 ,,
Others	,,	39 ,,
Buildings	,,	178 ,,
Furniture and apparatus	,,	21* ,,
University	,,	24 ,,
Direction	,,	9 ,,
Inspection	,,	47 ,,
Scholarships held in—		
Arts colleges	,,	$4\frac{1}{2}$,,
Professional colleges	,,	$1\frac{1}{2}$,,
Secondary schools	,,	7 ,,
Primary schools	,,	$1\frac{1}{2}$,,
Special schools	,,	2 ,,
Miscellaneous	,,	$94\frac{1}{2}$† ,,
Total	,,	1,092 ,,

* Special grants only.   † Evidently including foreign.

The expenditure on education has been rapidly increasing during the last decade, and especially during the last quinquennium.

PRESENT PROBLEMS IN EDUCATION IN INDIA.—The following are some of the pressing problems : (1) *Universities.* To provide facilities for post-graduate training and research; to increase hostel accommodation in affiliated colleges; to provide higher technological and commercial education. (2) *Secondary Schools.* To advance corporate life by increasing the number of hostels and encouraging outdoor games; to relieve the rush towards external examinations like the matriculation (i.) by instituting suitable school-leaving certificate examinations of the " internal " type, and (ii.) by providing technical, commercial, and agricultural divisions in each " model " secondary school, so as to encourage the choice of a practical career by youths; to find a satisfactory solution of the conflict between English and the vernaculars as the medium of instruction in secondary schools; to increase the number of trained teachers; to improve the prospects of teachers in " aided " schools. (3) *Primary Schools.* To expand the sphere of literacy as quickly as possible; to make the acquisition of at least a smattering of English possible in the upper forms of a primary school, knowledge of English having now become valuable in all walks of life. (4) *Education of girls.* To take advantage of awakened public opinion in this matter to further the cause of women by providing institutions of all grades for them. (5) To help *the Muslims* to make up lost ground in education. (6) To provide special facilities for the " *depressed* " and " *backward* " classes to enlighten themselves. (7) To consider the wisdom of the policy of perpetuating class distinctions by instituting special schools and colleges for landholders' sons in imitation of the *Chiefs' colleges* already started.

SWITZERLAND.

The educational system of Switzerland is marked by the complete-ness with which every grade is organised, though the type of organisation varies from canton to canton, as might be expected where differences of race and language exist. The cantons, though for certain purposes united as a Federation, yet remain in reality small separate " States," controlling their own affairs and showing a strong feeling of independence and local patriotism. The Federation lays down certain general principles with regard to education—it must be sufficient, compulsory, gratuitous, and free to members of all religious bodies without offence to their beliefs. (This does not rule out denominational teaching, provided that attendance is not compulsory.) No person may open a private school without the permission of the Central Authority. Subject to this general oversight, the cantons frame their own laws and carry on their own administration, and so for practical purposes are the supreme educational authorities. The result is a great variety of detail according as the conditions in each canton vary. In some, e.g., Zurich, there is much greater decentralisation than in others.

Both primary and secondary schools are public in the sense that they are used by all classes and are supported by public funds. No grant is dependent on attendance or results. Only a small proportion of the funds is paid directly by the Federation. The canton is largely responsible for the finances of higher education where the schools provide for large areas, while the local authority, the commune, supplies the greater part of the funds needed for primary schools, for which it forms the unit of administration. Local interest in educational work is thereby stimulated.

The school age is from 7 to 14 (6 or 6½ in some cantons).

A child may leave a primary school at 10 and attend for two or four years a " secondary " (i.e., higher grade) school, provided for the district by several communes combined. Above these come the " middle " (i.e., secondary) schools of every type.

The State examination, which every recruit must take at the age of 20, exerts an indirect influence by encouraging the continuation of study, and also by testing the permanent value of the education received at the primary schools.

There are seven Universities under the control of the cantons. The only educational institution directly managed by the Federal body is the great Polytechnic of Zurich.

BELGIUM.

The question of religious instruction has influenced the character of the primary schools in Belgium. The laws concerning this have varied with the political party in power. A law of 1879 removed obligatory religious teaching from the communal (i.e., public) schools, and the opposition of the Catholic majority resulted in the foundation of private denominational schools whose pupils soon outnumbered those of the communal schools. In 1884 liberty was given to the commune to provide religious instruction and also to " adopt " and maintain the denominational schools, though leaving them freedom in method, appointment of teachers, etc. In 1907 there were 4,598 communal and 2,693 " adopted " schools.

There is Government inspection with regard to the conditions required for gaining the grant, but the communes (i.e., the local authority) have a large measure of independence and are responsible for primary education.

The school age is 6—14. A small fee is charged, but instruction is free for those who cannot afford it. About one-third of the teachers in primary schools are members of religious orders.

For children under school age (from 3 to 6), extensive provision is made in the " *school gardens*," which, like the primary schools, are communal, " adopted," or private. They receive grants from the State and are under State inspection, but are to a large extent managed by the commune. There are over 2,700 of these schools, of which about two-thirds were " adopted." The schools aim at the development of the child's physical, mental and moral faculties by stimulating its activities in the right direction. Froebel methods are used. Special stress is laid on hygiene, and cleanliness is a condition of admission. By these means the health and happiness of the children is fostered and the effects of a bad environment counteracted. The teachers are specially trained, and the success of the system is impossible without their sympathy and enthusiasm.

There are two types of State secondary school. The Athenées Royaux, or higher secondary schools, numbering 35, are for boys only. The classical and modern courses run parallel with each other and the leaving examination admits to the University. In the lower secondary schools, (88 for boys, 40 for girls), more emphasis is laid on studies of immediate utility. The diploma, normally taken at 15 after a three years' course, is of value in business life. The tuition fees are low and there are a number of scholarships.

Ample provision is made for technical, commercial and industrial education, through the co-operation of the State, the commune and private bodies.

In addition to the independent University of Brussels and the Catholic University of Louvain, there are two Universities under State control.

HOLLAND.

In Holland, as in Belgium, denominational teaching has been the cause of much dispute. By a law of 1857 secular teaching alone was to be provided at the public cost. In 1889 private denominational schools were allowed a Government grant and they now occupy an important place in the educational system. Primary education is compulsory between the ages of 6 and 13, but is not entirely free. By a law of 1900 each commune must organise a continuation school for those who wish to profit by it. The necessary age is from 12 to 16 and pupils must first have passed through the primary course. This compulsory provision of facilities for continued education beyond the primary school marks a great advance.

Above the primary schools come the Burgher (Intermediate) Schools, which must be provided by every commune with a population of 10,000. They are intended for future artisans and labourers, and are now represented chiefly by evening schools. The age of admission is 12 or 13 years and the course covers three or four years. As there is no State subsidy the entire expense falls on the local authority. In many cases there are no fees, and where they are charged, poor children may obtain free places. The records of attendance and results are very satisfactory. In 1910 there were 81 of these schools.

Secondary Schools are of two types. The Higher Burgher Schools, 77 in number, supply a three or five years' course in which scientific subjects occupy a prominent place. There are no scholarships or bursaries, but a remission of fees may be obtained by special application. The diploma taken at the end of the course is of value in commercial and civil life and admits to the Polytechnic at Delft or to the medical and science courses at the Universities.

There is no Government grant for the Higher Burgher Schools for girls (of which there are 15), but the communes give liberal support.

The second type of higher secondary school is the *gymnasium* provided in all towns of 20,000 inhabitants. These have replaced the Latin schools which prepared for the Universities, and their leaving examination admits to the Universities, whereas a pupil from the Higher Burgher School must take a course of Latin and Greek after his diploma if he wishes to enter other than the scientific faculties. In 1910 there were 31 public and as many private gymnasia.

Specialised trade schools exist for various branches of work—navigation, fishing, and in particular for agriculture, for which there are several State establishments.

Provision for higher education includes three State Universities, the Communal University of Amsterdam, the Polytechnic of Delft which gives advanced technical training, and a number of denominational institutions.

SWEDEN.

In Sweden (and also in Norway) there is close connection between the State and the Established (Lutheran) Church, due to the prevailing uniformity of religious belief. Ecclesiatical and educational matters are controlled by the same department of State and the clergy take a prominent part in education. Primary education is free and the school age is from 7 to 14. At 9 a pupil may pass to the lower and at 14 to the higher secondary school. The majority of these State secondary schools are for boys. They are highly developed and the fees are low, so that private schools are not numerous. On the other hand, the majority of girls' secondary schools are private. Private schools may obtain State recognition, and thereby gain the right to hold the State leaving examination. They then receive grants, but this does not hamper their freedom or make for too great a uniformity.

In the State leaving examination, taken at 18, and necessary for entrance to the University, an interesting feature is the viva-voce examination, which is of wider range than the written section, and embraces all subjects taught in the later years of the school course.

It is conducted by the teachers of the school and by Censors (who are usually University Professors) appointed for the purpose.

In Swedish methods of instruction extensive use is made of *sloyd*— a system of handwork for the educational development of boys and girls. Large numbers of foreign teachers visit the Government seminary, at which a free course of instruction is given during the summer. Sweden also occupies the foremost place as regards physical training, Ling's organised system of gymnastics being everywhere in use. All instructors are trained at the Central Gymnastic Institute.

As the result of private enterprise the People's High Schools spread from Denmark to Sweden, which now has 28 of these schools. They provide mainly for the rural population and the average age is 20 to 22. The course covers the winter months of two successive years. The first year's course follows the original Danish model in being purely educational, the second gives a technical training, chiefly in agriculture. The movement also spread to Norway, which has 15 People's High Schools. In addition to these schools there are many workmen's institutes which organise lectures and discussions.

Sweden has two Universities, both under State control.

ITALY.

Public schools of every grade are maintained by the State, which requires other public schools to conform to the rules of the State schools. No private person may open a school without State authorisation.

Free and compulsory primary education dates from 1877. The schools are maintained by the communes, sometimes with State aid. Boys and girls are educated separately. There are two grades, the lower, with school age from 6 to 9 years, the higher from 6 to 12 years. There must be at least a lower grade school in every commune, and where there is no other, compulsory attendance at a day school ceases at 9 years. Good kindergarten schools are very numerous. Institutions for children from $2\frac{1}{2}$ to 6 years number over 3,000.

A proportion of 7 in 1,000 of the population receives secondary education. In over a thousand secondary schools the education given is classical, in about 400 it is technical.

The number of illiterates is large, being approximately 50 per cent., but each year shows a decrease.

There are 21 Universities, together with other institutions for higher education.

CANADA.

In 1867 the legislative bodies of each province were given the exclusive right to pass laws on matters concerning education, provided that the rights and privileges possessed before this by the denominational and separate schools were maintained. In general, education in the Protestant communities is not under the control of religious bodies. In the French and Irish Catholic communities religious instruction forms part of the education given. In some provinces Catholics have the right to form " separate schools " for elementary education, the local rates for these schools being separately levied and applied. In the French-speaking province of Quebec, the system of education differs from that of the other provinces. Two separate committees exist for Catholic and Protestant education, and each has final control over its own schools. There is no compulsion, and subject to certain safeguards small fees are payable. In all other provinces education is free and compulsory under conditions which vary from province to province. In all provinces the cost of education is defrayed from public funds, provincial and local. The present total expenditure is more than four times that of 1901. Secondary schools, colleges and Universities exist under Government control in all the provinces.

___

SOUTH AFRICA.

At the Union, which came into force in 1910, the Central Authority took over the administration of University education, while other branches were left to the control of the separate provinces. Primary education is compulsory throughout the Union except in a few districts in Cape Colony, and is free, except in Natal and a few special cases in other provinces.

Except in about 15 per cent. of the schools in Cape Colony, there is strict separation of white and coloured children. The education of the natives is largely carried on by State-aided missionary schools. There are also a number of State schools for coloured children.

The educational system of South Africa is influenced by the prevalence of two distinct languages, English and Dutch. In Cape Colony English is the medium of instruction in 90 per cent. of the schools. As Natal is almost entirely British, the question scarcely arises. In the Transvaal the early stages of instruction are in the child's native tongue. After this, English is gradually introduced. There has been most friction in the Orange Free State. At present a child is taught up to the age of 4 in the language he best understands, after this in both languages, though the parent may obtain exemption from one or the other.

The Cape University is an examining body only. Numerous University Colleges prepare for its degrees. At Johannesburg there is a flourishing school of mines and technology.

___

AUSTRALIA.

The educational systems of the different States are quite independent of one another and of the Federal Government, but there are no marked differences between them. Public education tends to become centralised and systematic, since it is controlled and supported by the State without interference on the part of the locality in which the school may be. Primary education is free, compulsory, and in the main, secular, though periods may be set apart for instruction by clergymen of different denominations.

Every effort is made to extend facilities for education to the thinly peopled districts. Where there are about twelve children small provisional schools are formed, where less than this, they are visited on alternate days, and sometimes an itinerant teacher travels from house to house.

In several districts small scattered schools have been replaced by a well-equiped central institution, to which the children are conveyed without charge.

Secondary and continuation schools need developing. In New South Wales there are two types of the latter—-artisan schools for boys learning trades and commercial schools for boys entering business. Special attention has been given to agricultural training in ordinary schools and in training institutions.

NEW ZEALAND.

Apart from the private schools (which in 1915 numbered 321), education is in the hands of the State. It is compulsory between the ages of 7 and 14, free, and entirely secular. The proportion of illiterate persons is low, being only 17 per cent.

The *primary schools* in 1914 numbered over 2,000, with a high average attendance and an average number of 37 pupils to a class. The Education Department issues monthly the " School Journal," an illustrated paper containing articles on subjects of educational interest—nature knowledge, the history and geography of New Zealand, current topics, etc. This is circulated free among the pupils of the primary schools, and may be bought by the private schools.

The approximate cost of primary education per head (19s. 3d.) is higher than in Great Britain, and the total amount spent on education is one and a-half millions.

In *secondary education* the free place system is used to the full advantage. In the 33 secondary schools and 60 district high schools (in which there are both primary and secondary departments), junior and senior free places are tenable. Only 16 per cent. of the pupils receiving secondary education in these schools pay fees.

There are also day technical schools which provide for children who would not otherwise receive a secondary education; 91 per cent. of these pupils hold free places from the primary schools. In addition to purely technical subjects, a certain amount of time must be given to other subjects, such as English and arithmetic.

There are also a number of primary and secondary schools for the natives. The University is an examining body with three constituent colleges, to which scholarships given from private endowments or from public funds may be obtained.

W.E.A. classes were started in 1915. The expense is borne by the University. As yet there is no State subsidy, but local bodies have contributed funds.

PART IV.

THE UNIVERSITIES AND THE WORKERS.

THE UNIVERSITIES AND PUBLIC OPINION.

By A. E. Zimmern

(Hon. Treasurer of the W.E.A., late Fellow and Tutor of New College, Oxford).

What is the place and function of Universities in a modern democratic community? What can a democracy reasonably expect from its great seats of learning, which, whatever their mode of government, are in effect, and are rightly regarded by the public, as national institutions? How can Universities best make their own special contribution " to the life " of a democratic Commonwealth?

The approaching extension of the franchise lends point to such inquiries, for it confronts British Universities with new problems and opportunities which will at once test the wisdom and public spirit of their rulers and inmates and determine the nature and extent of their influence in the post-war generation.

Fifty years ago, when the franchise was first extended to the working class, Robert Lowe, in a memorable sentence, declared that " we must educate our masters." The words were spoken half in jest, but they bear a deeper meaning than their author realised. When he spoke of " our masters " he was thinking of the newly enfranchised working class. But the real masters of Britain, as of every community, are those who control the sources of knowledge. It was at least as important in 1867, if Robert Lowe had only known it, to educate the Universities in their civic and national responsibilities as to set up schools in every parish, for if the great storehouses of the nation's knowledge are divorced from the general life of the community the very foundations of popular government are undermined. Power, whether political or of any other kind, is simply applied knowledge. It can only be wielded effectively by men and women who *know*, instead of merely " thinking " or " believing " or " understanding " or " guessing " or taking on trust because they have heard it on a platform or " seen it in print." If the opinions in accordance with which the country is governed are based on ignorance and prejudice, and the knowledge upon which they should be based is stored up and jealously withheld in exclusive corporations, the last state of democracy will be worse than the first.

The power of the people must be based, in a word, not on opinion, but on knowledge, and on a recognition of the large and important mass of " hard facts " which it is beyond the power of organised opinion to alter. The tendency to forget this, the temptation to believe that Parliamentary majorities and conference resolutions are trumpet-blasts at which the walls of Jericho will fall down, is the besetting sin of modern popular movements, and its wide prevalence is perhaps the main reason why, in spite of several generations of skilful and sustained agitation, Democracy in Europe and overseas is not yet master in its own house. It must win the keys of knowledge before it can wield the sceptre of power.

Happily, in England at any rate, some of the " masters " took the hint in a way unintended by Robert Lowe. The last two generations bear witness to a gradual awakening of a sense of national responsibility on the part of the British Universities, and to their increasing desire to emerge from academic seclusion, and to extend the range of their activities and influence. The success of the W.E.A. in recent years has, perhaps, tended to throw somewhat unduly into the shadow the achievements of the pioneers of the various forms of " University Extension "—a work which was due, unlike the W.E.A., to the initiative of University men, and has done, and is doing, much to sow seed which has borne fruit in numerous ways throughout the community.

Relatively small in bulk as such work has been, we may, nevertheless, regard it as having established the broad principle that the University in a modern community cannot remain a self-centred and exclusive corporation living for itself alone. Its knowledge, its opportunities, its equipment, its " atmosphere " are national possessions, held in trust by each passing generation of students and teachers for the benefit of the community as a whole. But the wider possibilities inherent in this recognition are still imperfectly realised. It is worth while trying to see whither it leads us.

The work of a modern University is, in the broadest sense, of two kinds—teaching and thinking. It is at once a school and an intelligence department; or, to put it in Army language, it is both an officers' training corps and the General Staff of the community. It exists both to prepare young people in body, mind, and character for the active work of life, and to help people of all ages to gain an understanding of the meaning of life in all its different phases. It is faced with a two-fold task of *training* and of *interpretation*.

Of the work of the University as a training school little need be said here. Mr. Sidney Webb, with his love for enshrining romantic themes in committee room phraseology, has described this side of University work as that of a "technical school for the brain-working classes." However much such a definition may grate upon all to whom College life calls up indelible memories of friendship and happiness in grey quadrangles and spacious gardens, it stresses the undeniable fact that for entry into certain kinds of employment a University education, that is, an education prolonged for three or four or even more years beyond the secondary school stage, will always remain, if not indispensable (as in Germany) at any rate extremely useful. Happily, it is becoming increasingly recognised both by psychologists and by practical men, that a prolonged general education is the best preparation for most occupations which require a high level of brain power and concentration, so that British Universities are not likely to fall into the German error of turning what should be a seat of education and of the liberal arts, and of training for service, into a battleground of competing and

J

unrelated specialisms. The danger, however, does exist, and no one who has watched the reaction of British academic opinion to the war can be quite easy in his mind as to the future of the broader traditions of the British University course. Yet the response of the Universities to the call of the war should be sufficient to show that, with all their undeniable intellectual shortcomings, the Universities have not failed to give their inmates a sense of the paramount duty of national and social service, which is, or should be, the first element in a technical or professional equipment.

On this side of University work, apart from the maintenance of the liberal tradition, and its perpetual enrichment by contact with life and experience, the main problem is that of securing access for all those young people who are capable and desirous of receiving such a training. This is an immense task, but the main burden of it, in England at any rate, must fall for the next few years on the secondary schools. There is, unhappily, little ground for thinking that the University provision of the country, meagre though it is compared with what it might be, is not adequate to meet the needs of the young people who are capable of profiting by it. A University is not a glorified high school. It is not meant for boys and girls who are still in the text book stage and unable to study without spoon feeding and direction. It is intended for students who, however scanty their knowledge, however vague and chaotic their ideas as to their future occupation, have some independent intellectual life of their own, who value ideas and the contact of mind with mind, and who come to a seat of learning, not simply to scramble through some bread-winning test, but, whether consciously or not, to satisfy the needs of their growing spirit. It is not easy to devise tests which shall attract all those, however "wild," for whom the University has something to offer, and exclude all those, however bookish, for whom, at this stage, direct contact with life would be a better education ; existing scholarship and matriculation arrangements, still more, existing scales of fees, are plainly not contrived for this end ; but to suggest their amendment in detail goes beyond the scope of this paper. It is sufficient to say that, in exercising their function of selecting students for admission to their ordinary courses, Universities are performing a national service, and that if they do not, or cannot, exercise it in the best interests of the nation it is the duty of the nation to interfere.

The other side of University work, what has been called the work of thinking or of interpretation, it is too broad and various to be described in detail, but perhaps it can be summarised under three heads :—

First, it is the duty of a University to maintain a high standard in all studies and subjects which come within its range. Perhaps it would be simpler to say that its duty is to foster a love of truth ; but truth in the ordinary sense of the word is too narrow and intellectual a term. A University should be a centre of taste, of the love of beauty, as well as of truth ; its concern is with all the large and enduring interests of life, and those who are following the quest of the spirit in any field of endeavour, whether the world calls them artists or architects or musicians, philosophers or historians, biologists or chemists, social workers or statesmen in politics or industry, should feel equally at home within its walls. Modern life with its sick hurry and divided aims, its ruthless and mechanical "drive," is in ceaseless conflict with the healthy creative instincts of the artist, and with the scholar's sensitive love of accuracy and balance and intellectual justice. It is the function of the University to maintain and diffuse respect for all sincere and fundamental achievement, to proclaim the cause of quality against quantity, of simplicity against showiness, of honesty against flattery, of precision against phrase-making; to cause men to feel shame at the hasty production and shallow judgment which pass muster in the crowded metropolis; to be a haven of refuge where men acquire or renew kinship with the spirit of truth ' which must preside over every fruitful undertaking or activity of mankind. If the Universities do no more for us in the next generation than reform the headlines of our newspapers and banish shop-window methods from our public life, they will have served democracy well.

Secondly, it is the duty of a University to undertake what is called "research," that is, to increase human knowledge, or, by interpreting existing knowledge, to increase our understanding of it. That is a task which has always been associated with Universities, but in recent times, when the teaching function of Universities has come more to the front, it has been apt to be neglected or relegated to the interstices of a busy teacher's time. It is often forgotten that teaching and research are different kinds of work, and often best undertaken by different persons. The "researcher" is primarily interested in his subject; the teacher is primarily interested in his students; the two interests, happily, are often combined; but all modern Universities should find room for a certain number of those rare and difficult minds who find their highest satisfaction in simply adding to the accumulated store of human knowledge.

Thirdly, the University exists to perform what can be called a function of *mediation*; to bring its knowledge and outlook to bear, as a helpful and reconciling influence, on the problems of the day. The true University spirit is not dry, thin, vacuous, pedantic, superior, or, as the phrase goes, academic; it is understanding, and sympathetic, health giving, and vitalising. A democracy in which the University played its proper part in public life would be equally free from pedantry in its professors, and from vulgarity and rant in its politicians. There would be constant action and inter-action between theory and practice, between book-learning and experience, between students of all ages and occupations. Political science would no longer be reserved for University lectures and remain conspicuous by its absence on party platforms or in election literature; and our elder statesmen, men who had acquired ripe wisdom in the service of the State, would be chosen naturally, and as of right, to positions of influence and authority over young minds, too often reserved at present for teachers who have long since ceased learning. Elections would still preserve the old-time fighting flavour so dear to the heart of the pugnacious Briton, but the issues to be decided in them would be thrashed out in fair-tempered, if vivacious, discussion between speakers and voters who had acquired intellectual seriousness and a due sense of their responsibility. Candidates would learn to revise their methods and would find it impossible to remain ignorant of some of the very elements of the work which they are asking authority to undertake. Men would learn to look to the Universities for guidance and inspiration. Constitutional problems would be discussed at leisure, as in Ireland at this moment, within the four walls of a University, with a library within call. Nor would experiments be made upon the long suffering body politic by practitioners imperfectly acquainted with social anatomy.

It is one of the ironies of the modern age that Democracy has become the dominant political creed at a time when the problems of society and government are more difficult and complex, less easy of understanding by the plain man, than ever before in human history. Simple solutions are preached on every hand, but every fresh attempt to apply them breeds fresh disillusionment, till the " revolutionary tradition " has been worn threadbare, and men are tempted to relapse into a cynical and contemptuous despair. For the problems of the modern time defy simple solutions, as Russia is learning to her cost; and it is Plato's philosopher-king rather than a many-headed multitude of tired toilers who is really required to solve them. If Democracy is to survive as an effective force, if government by the people is not to perish from the earth, the people itself must strive to acquire the spirit and temper of the philosopher; it must learn to recognise wisdom and sincerity when it sees them; it must fortify itself against the attempted tyranny of the expert and the assaults of reaction by making the University aware of its needs, and securing that its knowledge and equipment are made freely and constantly available for the service of Democracy.

What does such a policy involve in practice? Nothing less than a new system of education for adult citizens superimposed upon the system already provided for young people. Perhaps " system " is the wrong word for something that must of necessity be voluntary, elastic, spontaneous, and largely self-governing, as the experiments made by the W.E.A. in that direction have shown. But our statesmen and Universities have still to realise, in full measure, that it is farcical to call a community " democratic " unless its citizens have adequate leisure for attention to public affairs, and unless those who hold the keys of knowledge provide the opportunities for the wise and profitable use of such leisure. Democracy has still to win its spurs. It is living to-day upon the failures of alternative systems of government. Only through the fruits of adult education can it secure an intrinsic and lasting justification. When every town and village in Britain is a home of University study, in the widest sense of the word, then we can say with assurance that our country is made " safe for Democracy."

Have the British Universities realised the work that lies ready to their hands in this task of interpretation and mediation? Can they do so until their personnel has been largely humanised and enriched, and their range of interest and study extended and broadened? Is it likely that the necessary changes in University policy and government will be effected in time to meet the urgent needs of the enlarged democracy? Will war, the greatest of educators for a nation like ours, which has always learnt best in the school of experience, send a freshening breeze through the cloisters and council rooms of our academies? The optimist will not offer a direct answer to these questions. He will prefer to leave them with a question mark.

THE PROBLEMS OF UNIVERSITY GOVERNMENT.

By H. A. Grimshaw.

No one claims that the Universities, old or new, of this country serve the interests of the nation to the fullest degree of their capacity. For many reasons the older foundations have tended to lag behind, socially and educationally : to be utra-conservative in their educational effect, and to stress certain aspects of social life, which, though perhaps valuable in themselves, may be gained at too great a cost, and, if overstressed, may become positively detrimental. On the other hand, the newer Universities have not as yet secured positions in the world of thought at all comparable, in the estimation of society generally, with those of Oxford and Cambridge. They have been none too receptive of new ideas and ideals : they have been governed by men imbued with the traditions of the Cam and the Isis, and though it must be admitted that they have here and there adapted themselves most admirably to the needs of the populations and the industries of their areas, the initiative in such breaches of formalism and educational conservatism has come, for the most part, from outside. Rich men have endowed chairs in more modern subjects of study; Chambers of Commerce or other associations of business men have pressed for and assisted financially the inception of courses of study suited to the needs of the district in which the University is situated; even, at times, the organised workers have made successful demands for changes in or extensions of University facilities. But it is seldom indeed that a University has deliberately set itself to fill that position in the national life which educationists think it should occupy.

This failure is to be attributed in part to the unsatisfactory financial arrangements of the Universities as a whole. Whilst, because of the large ancient endowments of the older Universities, the study of certain subjects is richly rewarded by fellowships, chairs, and so on of great pecuniary value, other subjects of much larger importance to the modern world are left to struggle as best they may on the proceeds of tuition fees, a few fellowships, and recently endowed chairs, and are able to offer little inducement, as a rule, to the best minds. The difficulty of reforming this evil result of the " dead-hand " is, of course, great, but society ought not to allow itself to be thus permanently injured. It has allowed the endowments of hundreds of " knitting " and " grammar " schools to be converted to the uses of the modern secondary schools, and it should not hesitate similarly to modernise the endowments of the ancient University curriculum. With the newer Universities, of course, this difficulty does not arise, or at any rate not to the same extent. Their income is derived from grants from the Central and Local Government Authorities, from fees, and from voluntary contributions and bequests. Whilst the grants and fees are fairly stable and dependable, the other sources are extremely variable and unreliable. Yet it is on these last that the Universities must rely most largely for the power to extend their curricula and capacities.

And even when a generous donor has been discovered, he has at times enforced conditions incompatible with the best interests of education, or has perpetuated mistakes and misunderstandings which the lapse of a few years has brought to the light. Though it would be untrue to say that the British Universities have suffered or have been controlled to anything like the same extent as some of the American Universities, which have been founded or have received endowments at the hands of the multi-millionaires, yet there is a possibility of similar dangers. Some few years ago a lecturer in the States was dismissed because he had advised his students to read Bernard Shaw on some point or other, and there have been bad cases in America during the present war of the expulsion of lecturers and professors who disagreed, on war questions, with the financial supporters of their Universities.

There is perhaps less objection to the method of using the Universities which is said to have become common in America of late. When a business magnate or a firm wishes to pursue some line of research it makes use of the University organisation by the simple method of financing, for a shorter or longer period, a special piece of research work. It may, of course, do this by providing a research-studentship for a limited period, and in this way attain its end with less expense than would be the case if the work had to be done by the firm itself. This method, under careful supervision, might be useful to the furtherance of the University function of the pursuit of scientific knowledge, and it does not appear to expose the University to the danger of control by the financial interests.

But clearly Universities should not be dependent upon their chances of discovering rich donors—the " Form of Bequest " printed by almost every college in a prominent position in its Calendar is a perpetual annoyance to the present writer—nor subject to their whims, opinions, or convictions in regard to what should be studied and taught. Finance controls the curricula of all the Universities to a much larger extent than is safe for the interests of society. The remedies lie in the direction, first, of largely increased expenditure from the public funds, and, second, in the conversion of ancient endowments to modern uses. But finance is not the whole matter, and increased grants will not of themselves bring about the close relations between University education and education generally, or between the Universities and society at large in its social, political, and economic aspects, which the ratepayers and taxpayers ought to expect, and which democracy must demand. There remain certain problems of University government.

A University is, on the one hand, an organisation for teaching, and on the other an organisation for the pursuit of scientific truth. Its professors and lecturers have, therefore, two functions: they are teachers and they are scientists. As scientists their interest lies entirely in the furtherance of the sum of human knowledge, and they should endeavour, and do for the most part so endeavour, to approach their task without bias or prejudice of any kind in the true spirit of sceptical inquiry, whether their object be the testing (rather than the supporting or attacking) of the theories and the conclusions which existing science puts forward or accepts, or the exploring of new, hitherto untouched fields of knowledge. The essential thing is that they should be independent. For the scientist outside the University one may say that this independence has now been gained. Since the middle of the 19th century the attitude of the unscientific world has changed; particularly is that the case with the religious world, which instead of attacking the discoveries of science as false because not easily " squared " with the doctrines of theology, now has expanded its theological " scheme of things entire " in order to admit what appeared to be incompatible. But the University scientist is still subject to certain influences which tend to restrain him. He is at the same time a servant and a savant, and the conditions of his service may lessen the value of his science. In this country we have contrived to combine independence with efficient public service in the office of judge. (It may even be urged that we have succeeded in giving to judges too great an independence, though this view might not be pressed were the judges appointed by methods more likely to secure the ablest men.) The professor or lecturer, as scientist, is in a position entirely analogous with that of the judge as interpreter of the law. The judge does not make the law (in the ordinary sense) any more than the scientist makes the truth. Without pursuing the analogy between " the law " and the laws of natural science, it can be asserted that it is the business of both judges and scientists to find out the law or the truth and to express it.

But the University scientist is also a teacher, and here the case for independence is not quite so clear. Waiving for the moment the question as to who decides what is to be taught, it is easily seen that there is a certain mass of knowledge which, in all lands and under all circumstances, is passed on by each generation to the next and forms the basis upon which communal life is made possible. That mass of knowledge increases as civilisation increases, and, as Professor John Dewey shows, necessitates formal (as distinct from casual or incidental) educative method even in very early stages of social life. In the highly civilised countries of the West the amount of such fundamental knowledge is formidable, and is ever increasing as the concept of progress in society widens. Yet its passing on from each generation to the next is the first condition of progress, and there can be no hesitation as to whether it shall be taught or not. For those teachers, therefore, whose important function it is to pass on what might be called the fundamental social knowledge which makes the existence of society possible there can in the nature of things be little independence as to the matter which is to be taught. Society as a whole must decide, and in that decision the teacher has no more part and no more importance than any other man. It is possible indeed that he should have less influence than the political scientist or the sociologist. It is true that he has expert knowledge as to what *can* be taught to the coming generation, and *when*, and *how*. But on the subject of *what* should be taught society must overrule him.

This is supported further by a consideration of the necessities of the position. A whole new population is to be educated, in the sense that it is to be trained to take its part in the society to which it has been added, and when it is considered that part of that population is constantly shifting from place to place it is obvious that, unless such shiftings are to be disastrous to the education of the individuals concerned, there must be a certain degree of uniformity as to the matter taught.

All education, however, is not of equal importance in transmitting social values. It may seem paradoxical to say that the higher the stage of education the less important does it become from this point of view, but it is undoubtedly so. The fundamental social knowledge to which I have referred consists not only of knowledge in the ordinary sense, but of acquired habit and custom—the habit, for example, of obedience to certain social laws, not always expressed in Statute Books or enforced by police, as well as a general habit of obedience to those which are so expressed and enforced. But science is not confined to these fundamentals. It reaches out and up, winning from ignorance new facts and new laws, which in the process of time are welded in with the fundamental social knowledge, perhaps displacing some portion of it, but ever laying wider foundations for the erection of a nobler society. There is no well-marked dividing line between that which is part of the foundation and that which science is testing and trying, and so there can be no well-marked line between that knowledge which must be passed on to the next generation and that which may perhaps be rejected, and is at any rate not as yet so fully accepted as to be built easily into the social basis. So also no line can be fixed beyond which it can be said that the teacher must be independent. What can be said, however, is simple and adequate for the case here dealt with. It is that the higher the type of education becomes the less necessary is it for society to insist on uniformity in what is taught, and the more necessary is it that the teacher should exercise a wide independence. Obviously society must retain some control. How that is to be done, and to what extent, are perhaps the two most vital problems of University government.

A suggestion is obtained from the discussion now going on with regard to the control of industry. The Syndicalist doctrine would place the organisation and control of all matters *within* an industry in the hands of the persons directly concerned—those engaged in it. But Syndicalism admits that this is not and cannot be all that is required, for a particular syndicate is not an isolated entity, but touches at all points and is dependent upon other syndicates. Therefore some function must be allotted to the combined mass of these external entities. As to what exactly that function shall be there may be different opinions; as to what in general terms it must inevitably be there can be no ambiguity. It must be, since the external bodies taken together are the consumers of the product of the syndicate, the ultimate decision as to what the syndicate should produce. The control system would thus be one of syndicate plus consumer.

University government is at present of this type, but with two very important defects. The first lies in the composition of the syndicate itself. Possibly in mediæval times the control of curricula could hardly be entrusted to society in general, and there might be much to say for retaining it in the hands of the teachers and of those who had benefited by their teaching. Practically the same position obtains to-day in the older Universities. *No proposal for change can be made except by the associated teachers, nor adopted without the consent of the associated ex-students.* But teachers as a body are almost invariably behind the times with regard to curricula. They are usually at least a half-century behind, and they may be several centuries. They are experts, and like other experts they incline to conservatism. The cause lies in the nature of their occupation, and is common to all those who act or expound " with authority." That there are brilliant exceptions goes without saying, but that these remain exceptional is only too obvious from the history of attempted reform in recent years. The initiative in change under these circumstances is confined to a class little prone to initiative movements, which by the nature and conditions of its service becomes temperamentally opposed to change and powerful in resisting it. The struggles anent the admission of women to degrees, and the bitter controversy about compulsory Greek, are sufficient witness to this. Reform must, therefore, take the line of providing methods by which changes can be introduced more readily, and the Universities brought into more and more direct relation to society and its needs.

In other words, the consumers must have a greater influence in the decision as to what shall be taught. And this brings out the second defect of the existing system. The position of the organised consumers in a Syndicalist state is represented in University government by the associations of the ex-students, called Convocation usually, and consisting of all those who have graduated at the University and have taken the trouble to pay a small registration fee. They retain *for life* the power of giving their " placets " or " non-placets " upon all questions of change. The vast majority of them, as is inevitable, get completely out of touch with the progress of learning, and, engrossed in other interests, are only too prone to regard departure from the methods they themselves followed as dangerous, if not positively injurious. The country parsonages, for instance, are the great obstacle to women's education at Oxford and Cambridge. One remedy suggests itself : it is that this power should be limited to a few years after graduation in the case of all except those who remain in close touch with University life and education. Even then the graduates may be regarded rather as an association of ex-consumers, with less direct interest than those who are actually students. It is arguable that to hand over the control of the curricula to students themselves, unchecked, would lead to more satisfactory results, from a social point of view, than the present system. Their demands (expressing, of course, those of their parents also) would certainly bear a more direct relation to the needs of society than is reflected in the " non-placets " of the country parsonages or in the inertia of the teachers. In this connection it is interesting to note that in the American Universities the system of " Options " under which students have a much greater range of choice of subjects of study than is usually the case here, has resulted in the almost complete disappearance of Latin and Greek.

It remains true, of course, that the interests of the outside consumers are not represented only by Convocations. The outside world can and does, as has been pointed out, exercise some control. But in the past, and very largely also in the present, that control has been exercised by one class of society only, the wealthy, and has been subject to the enormous influence of the conservative governing bodies of the Universities themselves, effectually checking most tendencies towards progress. In the modern Universities the inclusion of representatives of outside interests upon the controlling authorities— the Senates, Courts of Governors, and so on—is a step in the right direction, but much too timid a step. More should be done in the way of securing for the general public a stronger direct influence.

The ideal solution for all these difficult problems is one which will secure, on the one hand, the fullest possible independence to the teaching staff, and, on the other hand, a complete control by society over what part the University shall play in the satisfaction of the needs of the community.

The actual government of a northern (English) University is vested in a Court, representative of outside interests, and a Vice-Chancellor, who represents the Court in, and presides over, the Senate, which is a body of teachers. This arrangement probably contains the germ of the ideal system of University government. The function of the Senate must, however, be carefully defined. Its members are scientists as well as teachers, and, as such, are entitled to the highest independence possible over the subject matter of their teaching. But that independence and its accompanying authority should be confined to science, and should not be admitted in matters of administration. They are not, for example, likely to be very successful in deciding what exact educational function the University should perform for the best advantage of the community it serves. But when that decision has been made, when it has been decided, for example, that Greek, or Chinese, or dyeing, or metallurgy, is to be taught in a particular University, the scientist-teachers to whom the subject is entrusted must be given a free hand.

It is clearly the function of the Court of Governors to decide how best the University can serve the community in its choice of subjects to be taught. But it must be made more fully representative of the consumers of the University product than is the case at present. Particularly the State's views should be more adequately expressed on the Court, not because the State pays in the form of grants part of the direct cost—the kind of bargaining spirit which admits the State or its representatives into a share in management commensurate with the direct assistance given by the State is an anachronism, and belongs to the individualist thought of the early 19th century—but because the State is the largest and the most effective organisation of consumers. The local authorities also are organisations of consumers with a more special interest, who are possessed also of a more special knowledge of local needs. These central and local authorities should, in the interest of the general body of consumers as a whole, have a powerful representation on the Court of Governors. At the present moment the London County Council—a local authority controlling to a large extent the lives and fortunes of a population larger than that of Canada—is represented in the government of London University by two members of the Senate out of 59; the Board of Education, standing for the whole population of the British Isles, has four.

But the power which it is suggested should be given to the representatives of the central and local authorities should be distinguished from *direct control* either by the Board of Education or by that " body " and the local authorities acting together. The objections to direct control are insuperable in the present writer's view. It would make the securing of the independence of the teacher still more difficult, in the first place, and, in the second place, it would establish bureaucracy in exactly the position in which it is capable of most harm. The University government, once constituted, must be possessed of a very large measure of independence of action. Its constitution should ensure that it is kept in touch with the extra-University world, but should at the same time remove the dangers which would arise from direct State control. The representation of the *general body of consumers* being thus provided for, there can be only advantage obtained from the representation on the Court of *specially interested consumers.* These may be Chambers of Commerce and other organisations of the business world; Employers' Federations, Trade Unions, and Co-operative Societies in the industrial world; learned societies; organisations of teachers; societies which have the furtherance of education as their aim; societies which devote themselves to the study or improvement of social conditions—all the wealth of voluntary organisation which a highly civilised country offers should be made of use in this vital function of deciding what the University shall do for the community. And last, but almost of the first importance, the students themselves who are at the moment at work, and perhaps also the students who have within a reasonable period completed their studies and passed into the working world, should be in a position to be heard through their delegates on the Court of Governors.

These suggested changes would be comparatively easy to make in the cases of the modern Universities. The older ones, however, do not require modification, but revolution. Under their present constitutions it is impossible to secure reforms at all adequate to the need the nation has of their services. The necessary revolution might be carried out by a statutory Commission with power to shape a new constitution on the lines suggested above. Not rigidly on those lines, however, for it is only in a very limited sense that either Oxford or Cambridge is important educationally to its particular locality, and, therefore, the part played by the local authorities in government may be less than where a University models itself largely on the needs of local industry, and the greater importance of the old Universities to national life warrants society in general, rather than the people of a locality, in taking a larger share in control than in other cases. The Commission should also be empowered to withdraw those endowments attached to subjects no longer of the first importance in an altered world, and to employ them for the furtherance of other studies, not necessarily in the colleges to which the endowments were originally directed; in short, to mobilise these educational funds and re-assign them in accordance with modern needs. We must be prepared to sacrifice some of the patina of these ancient institutions in order to fit their metal with less friction into the modern machine.

In the third place, the Commission should have full powers to regulate the relationship between the University and its constituent colleges. At present these latter are wealthy and proportionately independent, and their relation to the University is the greatest obstacle to reform. (Similarly the most difficult problem in the government of London University is its relation to the Imperial College of Science.) Such institutions must be content to forego a large measure of their independence, and must subordinate themselves to the interest of the University of which they form a part.

These rearrangements being made, the Commission should take steps to assure to the University a large measure of independence for the future, under a constitution similar to that suggested above as approaching the ideal, with full independence for the teaching staff, combined with control by consumers so far as the direction of output is concerned.

In conclusion, it is hoped that a case for a revision of University government has here been made out. It is impossible within the limits of the space allotted to indicate all the problems which have arisen, and which need the careful attention of society if the Universities are to take their rightful place as the leaders of education in a democratic state. The position of the University as head and guide of the lower educational institutions of the nation has not been here touched upon, yet it is obviously of enormous importance, and the recent Education Bill foreshadows an extension of its function in this respect. But only a reformed University can carry out this function satisfactorily. Again, there is the problem of inter-University collaboration. We speak of a student of " a University " : why not of a student of " the Universities "? For clearly, to provide thorough courses of study in all the Universities, or in many of them, in the same subjects involves a considerable amount of waste, which might be to a large extent avoided if the students were permitted to attend more than one centre of learning. Or, possibly, the interchange of professors and lecturers might conduce to the same end. The peculiar advantages obtained by the system of residential Universities suggest a further question. The more modern institutions cannot offer these advantages : their students are for the most part drawn from the localities and reside in their own homes. Without arguing on the advantages and disadvantages of this in comparison with the other system, one may suggest the possibility of there being a distinct and useful part to be played by a residential University in a system of non-residential ones.

And, finally, the recent development of the modern Universities has brought with it certain problems of internal organisation which are becoming increasingly difficult and important. The status of the " Professor " is one of these. It is rapidly becoming more and more difficult to say with any accuracy what the title means, either from the point of view of position in the world of learning, or from those of emoluments and duties. In some Universities the Professor is of relatively small importance : he may do little lecturing, leaving the burden of the actual teaching to an overworked and often seriously underpaid lecturer. There are certain instances well known in University circles of abominable slave-driving of this type. Again, a lecturer or reader in one University (e.g., at Oxford) may be actually of much superior standing than a Professor elsewhere from all points of view. Efforts are now being made to correct some of these evils and anomalies by the formation of an Association of University Lecturers, and it may be hoped that some good will result.

But these and many similar defects of the existing organisation will be righted the more easily if the Universities individually are reformed in the directions here indicated, and if they can be brought to regard themselves as parts of the national system of education, working rather in collaboration than in competition with one another, subordinating their individual interest to the general educational welfare, and making this last their one great aim.

THE TUTORIAL CLASS MOVEMENT.

BY WINIFRED BEATON

(Assistant Secretary, Central Joint Advisory Committee on Tutorial Classes).

History.

The W.E.A. and the Tutorial Class movement are the natural outcome of forces which have for the last 25 years been gradually finding expression among an increasing number of working men and women. The co-operative movement, the Working Men's College and University Extension, have in different ways aimed at satisfying the same desire for education. But there has always been a large body of working people who desired not merely short series of lectures, but intense and continued study, and who sought education in order to get to the heart of many problems that had for long beset them and which insistently demanded solution.

It was given to Albert Mansbridge to see that the time had come when working men and women must refuse to have education bestowed upon them from above, but must themselves know what they desired and so organise that desire that they might by their own efforts obtain it.

In 1903, at a conference at Oxford, the Workers' Educational Association was initiated by a small group, of whom Mr. and Mrs. Mansbridge were the leading spirits. In 1907, as the result of a conference of Universities and workpeople held in Oxford, a committee was formed to go into the question of the establishing of Tutorial Classes, and in the autumn of that year two Tutorial Classes were undertaken under the auspices of the University of Oxford at Rochdale and Longton and the beginning of a class met at Battersea under London. Six more classes started in 1908 and in 1909 six Universities were at work. The Report on Oxford and Working-Class Education was produced early in 1909, and in it the lines on which Tutorial Classes should work were laid down. In August, 1909, again at a conference, this time of Universities, held at Oxford, the Central Joint Advisory Committee on Tutorial Classes was initiated, with Mr. Mansbridge as honorary secretary. This committee by its constitution is enabled to count among its members representatives of every University and University College in England and Wales (a unique achievement) and also representatives of Labour. It exists to help Universities to work along the lines of the Oxford report with the institution of Tutorial Classes as its ideal, and is ready when desired to advise any University or University College, and so assist in securing a reasonable amount of uniformity in the conduct of the classes, and also to act at the request of Universities as a common channel of approach to such bodies as the Board of Education, Local Education Authorities, the Gilchrist and other educational trusts to appeal for aid, financial and otherwise.

Growth.

During its ten years of life the movement has grown with great rapidity. From two classes in 1907-8 it had increased to 152 in 1914-15—a steady increase, as will be shown from the following :—

	1907-8	1908-9	1909-10	1910-11	1911-12	1912-13	1913-14	1914-15	1915-16	1916-17
Classes ..	2	8	32	72	102	117	145	152	121	99
Students..	83	237	1117	1829	2485	3176	3234	3110	2414	1927

Since then, owing to the war, the number has decreased somewhat, but this was to be expected, and when the number of students in the forces or employed, with continuous overtime, on Government work is considered it is indeed surprising that in the current session 1917-18 there are 121 classes in Great Britain alone successfully carrying on three-year courses. In the first winter of war the loss to the classes caused by the going of students was so great that the Board of Education made special concessions for that winter, so that they should not be submerged financially through the patriotism of their members. It is interesting to note that such was the enthusiasm for the movement that in some cases fathers and mothers took the places of their sons to help to carry on the work, and one class held near a big munition factory has been maintained entirely by the women who were left, the discussion being full of keenness and enthusiasm. There seems little doubt that as soon as opportunity affords the number of classes will again increase.

Summer Schools.

In 1910 the first summer school of the movement was held in Oxford, and a school has been held under that University each summer since that date, while other Universities who have taken up this feature of the work are Bangor, Cambridge, Durham, Leeds, and London. Some of these schools are residential, some (e.g., London) are arranged for four consecutive Saturdays during the summer. The residential schools, such as Bangor and Oxford, are an invaluable means of giving the students a taste of university life, as they take place in the long vacation, and students are thus able to live in college and get some sense of the University environment. The level of the work is high, and to one not accustomed to hear discussions amongst working people an evening in the common room at a summer school when University and Labour men of all sorts and conditions are probing the ideas of a lecturer is a revelation. Since the war the summer schools have turned eagerly first to the study of modern European history, and, secondly, to the problems of reconstruction after the war.*

Overseas.

The movement overseas originated in 1913 with a visit of Mr. and Mrs. Mansbridge to Australia. There are now 40 classes in New South Wales alone, with a total Government grant of £5,150. All the Governments give grants with the exception of West Australia, where owing to drought and the war the Government have not felt able to aid financially, though they sympathise with the ideals of the movement. In New Zealand there are 25 classes, all of which were started in time of war; in itself a notable achievement. The total number of students in Australia, Tasmania, and New Zealand is well

---

* The summer school held in 1917 at Oxford was considerably helped and stimulated by the presence of three Australian tutors: F. A. Bland, M.A., and Duncan Hall, M.A., of Sydney, and B. H. Molesworth, M.A., of Brisbane. The fresh and living interest in Colonial and International questions which they introduced makes it greatly to be hoped that the interchange between Overseas and Home tutors and students may become a great feature of the movement as soon as circumstances permit.

over 2,000 and thousands attend the lectures and educational conferences arranged by the W.E.A.*

In Canada W.E.A. groups have been started, and Tutorial Classes are being carried on in Montreal and Toronto. The Canadian tutors are convinced that if once the movement were thoroughly organised in Canada, and steps are being taken to that end, it would not be behind Australasia in enthusiasm.

In South Africa there are W.E.A. branches and Tutorial Classes in Durban and Johannesburg. It is recorded that two years ago during the time of riot in Johannesburg the class which was then meeting continued a vigorous discussion of an economic subject to all appearance oblivious of the disturbance outside.

Management.

The classes are under the management of Joint Committees of the Universities and University Colleges, composed of an equal number of representatives of Labour organisations nominated by the W.E.A. and of representatives nominated by the University. There are now Joint Committees under the Universities of Birmingham, Bristol, Durham and Newcastle, Leeds, Liverpool, London, Manchester, Oxford, and Sheffield, and the University Colleges of Nottingham, Reading, Wales (Aberystwyth), and South Wales (Cardiff), and classes have been conducted under the University College of North Wales, Bangor. Joint Committees on slightly different lines are now in operation in Scotland, at Aberdeen and Edinburgh, and the movement is spreading to Glasgow and Dundee. In Ireland classes have been running for seven years in Belfast and a Joint Committee has recently been formed at University College, Cork. Thus the movement is now firmly rooted over the whole of Great Britain.

Each Joint Committee is responsible for the conduct and management of its classes.

Finance.

As regards finance, the classes, if recognised by the Board of Education, which is the case for every good class, can claim under certain conditions a block grant of £30. At the outset the two classes at Rochdale and Longton were paid under the Technical School Regulations at the rate of 5s. per student fulfilling an attendance of 20 hours or over. A year later this grant was raised to 8s. 6d. per student under the regulations for literary and commercial subjects, a special clause being inserted to provide for them. In 1913, as the result of representations made on behalf of the Universities by the Central Joint Advisory Committee, special regulations for University Tutorial Classes were drawn up by the Board of Education, giving a block grant of £30 to each class, and in consequence of further negotiations on the part of the Committee this grant was increased to £45 a class in 1917. The regulations also allow special conditions for the shift system and for advanced classes for students who have been through a three years' class and wish to do advanced

---

* Two tutors have gone from Great Britain to the aid of the sister movement. Meredith Atkinson, who was the first to go from England, has been for three years Director of Tutorial Classes at the University of Sydney, and now holds a similar post at the University of Melbourne. Herbert Heaton, who went first to Tasmania, has now gone from the University of Hobart, where he was Director of Tutorial Classes, to take up a similar post at the University of Adelaide.

work in the same subject. Grants are received in many cases from Local Education Authorities, and from bodies such as the Gilchrist Educational Trust. All these grants are counted as part of the contribution of the local W.E.A., which aims at sharing half the expense of the class. The movement has always received sympathy, co-operation, and invaluable help from all these bodies, but even these grants naturally do not by any means cover the cost of a class, and the remainder is provided by the Joint Committee. Several Joint Committees have fixed grants from the University, and in one or two cases a University agrees to make up any deficit there may be on the year. In the case of Oxford and Cambridge, contributions are in addition received from individual colleges, but it is clear that when all these sources of revenue are taken into consideration the incomes of Joint Committees are fluctuating and uncertain, and there can be no doubt that this financial uncertainty prevents them from increasing the number of classes at the rate they would like to do, and also prevents the W.E.A. from organising these to the extent which would otherwise be possible.

Class=Work.

From the outset the students of Tutorial Classes set a high ideal before them. They were not isolated cases of men and women who wished to leave their fellow workers and follow ambitious careers; they were pioneers in a movement which they hoped would lead to a national system of education in which all should have the opportunity to cultivate a humane and broadminded attitude, and none should be denied the knowledge for which he hungered. It followed, naturally, that the spirit of the movement was pure, and that no material advantage was sought. The goal before it was an educated democracy, a community in which not only the so-called governing classes, not even only the working classes, but every section should be represented with fairness and governed with justice. No examination or diploma marks the end of the course, and it is worthy of notice that, though early in the movement it was thought by some to be advisable to give testamurs to students at the end of a three years' class, these were never given because the students did not wish for them.

The classes are held for three consecutive years in one subject and " must aim at reaching, within the limits of the subject covered, the standard of University work in Honours." It is recorded that when the movement was still in its infancy a sceptical professor of history was confronted with a pile of unselected essays, and so far forgot scepticism as to pronounce the judgment that a large proportion of them were worthy of Honours students of the University. Indeed, he afterwards became the tutor of a successful class.

Choice of subject has tended as a result of the war to become more restricted than before. The normal thing is for a class to choose Economics, this being the subject with which the students have had most to deal and then to proceed to some other study, such as philosophy, psychology, history, or literature. A year or two before the war the number of literature and philosophy classes was steadily increasing, and the Board of Education had approved music as a tutorial class subject, but with the war the choice of subject has swung back almost exclusively to Economics and History. It is hoped that this tradition will not be too closely followed in the future. Already Australia has been more enterprising in the choice of subject, such experiments as classes in electricity, musical æsthetics, and chairmanship being carried on successfully.

It must not be forgotten that the students who undertake to join a Tutorial Class know that it is a somewhat arduous piece of work that they are entering upon. They undertake definite pledges of attendance and essay work, promising to attend regularly, unless prevented by an unavoidable cause, and to do such written work as may be required. Although in the written work a satisfactory standard must be reached, the tutor is wisely left to use his own discretion regarding each individual student, for it must be remembered that at the beginning of a class a student may never have attempted to write an essay of any sort, and he may even be gradually led to find his first method of expression by giving his opinions in letter form.

When one considers the enormous obstacles of overtime, poor homes, want of rest and quiet, against which working men and women have to fight in their desire for deeper knowledge, it brings some realisation of the strength of the compelling force which enables them triumphantly to overcome such difficulties.

Class Method.

It is an essential principle of the Tutorial Class that the students should govern the class. No tutor can be foisted upon a group if the students are unwilling, and the students also have the right of choice as regards the subject. The classes meet 24 times in the six months, October to April, each meeting consisting of two hours, the first given up to the lecture by the tutor and the second to discussion of it. It is this discussion which marks the movement out from the educational efforts which gave it birth. A vital and frank discussion of such a subject as Economics is greatly hindered if the class takes the form of an audience such as those attending University Extension lectures, but in a gathering of not more than 30 the atmosphere is immediately more conducive to free expression of opinion, and no one who has attended a Tutorial Class could fail to be struck by the tolerant and, at the same time, candid discussion of problems which the students feel to be of burning interest.

Tutors.

The tutor is not a person set apart, as more than one newly fledged graduate has found to his cost; he is one of the students and must discuss on the same basis as they. In such a subject as Economics, though the tutor may know the theoretical side better than his students, they in their turn know vastly more than he of the over-burdening practical problems involved. Immediately this is recognised it is possible to see to some extent the unlimited potentialities of a movement which so connects, on University lines, members of a University and of Labour.

The choice of a tutor is all important, but this appointment involves a difficulty. It is not desirable that tutors should consider tutorial class work as a stepping-stone to careers in other spheres, but with their present status and remuneration to make such teaching a life work involves a greater sacrifice in many ways than the movement has a right to demand. Until Tutorial Class work is put on a sounder financial basis it seems impossible that Joint Committees can see their way to improve the general conditions under which tutors work or to persuade Universities to give more general facilities to tutors for keeping in close touch with University work, a very important thing for the health of the classes.

Libraries.

Another great difficulty which has always confronted the Tutorial Class movement is that of the supply of books. The majority of Joint Committees have travelling libraries, but they are not nearly adequate to the demand. The W.E.A. started a small library in co-operation with Toynbee Hall in 1912, and by this means was able to give considerable help to classes, but the urgency of the problem became so obvious that in 1915, through its honorary secretary, the Central Joint Advisory Committee made representations to the Carnegie United Kingdom Trustees for a grant to initiate a central library for students. A grant to allow of an experiment for five years was given by the Trustees, and the Central Library for Students was then launched as an entirely new and separate body. Its aim is to ensure that *bonâ-fide* students coming under its notice shall be helped in their studies if they are unable to obtain the use of the necessary books elsewhere, and also " to stimulate and develop higher study on the part of those, for the most part isolated students, who owing to the lack of facilities and of guidance in reading have been content with a lower level of knowledge than they are capable of acquiring." The library, therefore, confines itself as much as possible to the purchase of the dearer books of reference which cannot easily be obtained through any other channel. Although the library has only recently issued its first annual report, the demand for books and the support it has received show that its conception as a library to meet the needs of every kind of student is the right one, and that it fills a long-felt want. If it continues to grow as it has done during its few months of existence the book problem will in a short time be approaching a solution.

Ideals and the Future.

Before passing to any indication of the future, it may be well to consider whether the movement has followed the lines laid down and whether it is fulfilling the purpose for which it was created.

In the main the essential ideals behind the movement are unspoilt, and it is true to say that the W.E.A. and Tutorial Class movement is a great university of working people. If one ventured a criticism one would say that its whole future depends upon the upholding of the ideals which created it. As the movement grows danger grows, and it would be no slight catastrophe if the tutorial classes produced a cult of freakishness or, worse still, of priggishness. For this reason the care needed in the choice of tutors should be urgently emphasised. The tutor and students have a wonderful opportunity, simply by unconscious example, of influencing each other in the direction of tolerance, *esprit de corps*, a broadminded attitude towards those who differ in opinion, and that true education which leads to a realisation of the comradeship which should exist in and link up all sections of the community. Through their effects on the tutor the students may exert a great influence on University thought. It is only when the best points of each are assimilated by the other that the ideal of a Tutorial Class is attained. The Tutorial Class movement must lead to no pseudo-culture, neither must it prove a stepping-stone for ambition, nor be the unconscious tool of any organisation. The pioneers of the movement knew well that book-learning was not education, and if the students and tutors once forget that the whole spirit behind the work is lost. That " W.E.A. spirit," intangible, but none the less real, which gripped many who " came to scoff and remained to bless," has marked this movement out as not only an educational, but as a spiritual force. And if it is to continue to be more than merely an educational organisation which arranges classes this spirit must be in it. It has in the past owed much to its fine tutors and to its devoted class secretaries, who have at considerable sacrifice to themselves done all in their power to spread the ideals of the movement; it was built up on sacrifice and without it would be no longer vital.

Of the problems ahead post-Tutorial Class work is one of the most pressing. In the Oxford Report on Working-Class Education it is recommended that students from the Tutorial Classes should be enabled " regularly and easily to pass into residence at Oxford and to continue their studies there." But it was felt that this was an experiment which should not be hastened, and scholarships which might have been used for one student at a University were instead divided to enable several to attend a Summer School. Two tutorial class students have become tutors, and successful tutors, of tutorial classes, and it is hoped that this will become more and more possible. Already, principally through the enthusiasm of the Longton Tutorial Class, a sister movement has come into being, and students from tutorial classes go weary miles after their day's work to lead study groups in the many isolated mining villages of Staffordshire, so that now a great federation of study groups has grown up.

Advanced, fourth year, or seminar classes are other methods by which students continue to work after finishing a three years' course, and many enter another class in a different subject.

Chiefly out of the need for a common meeting-place there have arisen here and there in recent years W.E.A. Houses, such as Chorley College, Manchester College, and Sheffield W.E.A. House, where students and W.E.A. members may have a home, where meetings may easily be arranged, and where all the W.E.A. work of the district may centre. There is every possibility that these W.E.A. Houses will grow in number as time goes on.

Yet despite these and other difficulties, if one looks at the future before the movement, should it continue to develop along spiritual lines, its possibilities seem unlimited. It has drawn the Universities and Labour together; why should it not unite other, until now, equally divergent sections of the community? There is a Tutorial Class for Members of Parliament in Australia. Would the same be altogether undesirable in Great Britain? There is no trade or profession in which a Tutorial Class would be useless or futile. Again, is there any limit but the boundaries of the world to the movement's possibilities for expansion? Already it has found a sure place in four Continents. It has friends in Europe; it has friends in America; why should it fail to be international? To achieve even the beginnings of this, those who believe in it in Great Britain and in the Dominions Overseas must make it their peculiar care to see that the work is not retarded in its development by hindering conditions of finance and administration. If these are removed a crucial step would be taken, and the way would be left clear for the fulfilment of that ideal of an educated world which is the goal of all reformers.

STATISTICS OF CLASSES.

Arranged according to subject.

Subject.	Number of classes.			Number of students enrolled.					
				Men.			Women.		
	1914-15.	1915-16.	1916-17.	1914-15.	1915-16.	1916-17.	1914-15.	1915-16.	1916-17.
Economics and Industrial History	77	57	50	1287	765	661	294	254	292
Local Government	3	1	—	52	7	—	3	5	—
Psychology and Philosophy	9	14	14	133	168	141	98	143	130
Plato's Republic	—	1	10	—	12	—	—	2	—
English Literature	15	17	10	183	149	80	144	206	148
Modern European History and History of Political Freedom	32	10	10	426	166	106	182	51	81
Biology	4	4	5	59	55	47	13	25	58
Music	—	1	1	—	4	4	—	19	17
Unemployment	1	—	—	14	10	—	1	—	—
Growth of English People	—	1	1	—	10	11	—	5	—
History of Western Civilisation	—	1	4	—	70	39	—	7	16
Political Science	6	5	—	102	27	—	20	10	36
Studies in Social Science	2	2	1	30	49	14	13	15	—
Sociology	3	5	—	35	14	13	31	32	11
Evolution of Government	1	2	1	9	—	6	10	12	—
Ethics	1	—	1	17	—	—	2	—	—
British Constitutional Development	—	—	1	—	—	—	—	—	5
European Art and Culture	—	—	1	—	not known	—	—	not known	10
	154	121	99	2347	1506	1122	811	786	804

Estimated number of students since beginning .. .. .. 8,000 (approximate).

Estimated number of students who have done more than three years' work .. 500 (approximate).

STATISTICS OF CLASSES.

University.	Number of classes.			Number of students enrolled.					
				Men.			Women.		
	1914-15.	1915-16.	1916-17.	1914-15.	1915-16.	1916-17.	1914-15.	1915-16.	1916-17.
Birmingham	6	6	5	81	56	73	45	27	44
Bristol	5	4	—	83	36	—	35	25	?
Cambridge	5	2	2	68	29	36	27	8	8
Durham	9	7	4	187	84	47	36	36	17
Leeds	13	14	14	173	203	185	66	90	81
Liverpool	19	14	11	229	146	63	111	122	99
London	26	21	22	383	248	226	149	122	235
Manchester	17	13	8	219	135	88	98	96	58
Nottingham University College	6	6	2	110	80	25	29	32	12
Oxford	16	11	10	271	168	127	75	63	81
Queen's College, Belfast	1	1	2	10	10	11	13	7	16
Reading University College	2	2	2	35	21	11	21	19	18
Sheffield	10	11	13	151	145	172	37	49	69
Aberdeen	—	1	1	—	14	15	—	5	5
Edinburgh	—	4	3	—	59	43	—	77	61
Univ. College of Wales, Aberystwyth	10	—	—	190	—	—	55	—	—
Univ. College of N. Wales, Bangor	4	4	—	50	72	—	—	8	—
Univ. College of S. Wales, Cardiff	5	—	—	107	—	—	14	—	—
	154	121	99	2347	1506	1122	811	786	804

THE UNIVERSITY TUTORIAL CLASS:
FROM A STUDENT'S POINT OF VIEW.

BY MISS N. SCRUTON.

Several years' membership of a tutorial class has convinced me that this kind of educational opportunity is peculiarly fitted to meet the needs of workingmen and won en. I am attempting to describe a tutorial class in the hope that some fellow workman or woman will say, " This looks like what I want," and will take steps to find out whether it is or not.

A tutorial class meets for two hours. Usually the tutor lectures for the first hour, and the other half of the time is given up to discussion. The lectures are as far removed as possible from what are known as " popular lectures " which ought to have nothing in them "which 500 people cannot all take in at a flash just as it is uttered." As I think of the lectures which I have heard in tutorial classes (dealing for the most part with some branch of social science) their chief characteristics seem to have been : Getting back to beginnings; patient tracing of developments; revelation of the infinite complexity in human affairs.

Occasionally, in the discussion hour, when some traditional position is fiercely attacked and desperately defended, the talkers may momentarily strive for victory, but normally, the main business of the discussion—to get nearer the truth of the matter—is kept well in sight. Sometimes a timid student will very hesitatingly put a query or express an opinion, and the tutor (if he is possessed of the gift of sympathetic understanding) will say, " Yes, your point is so and so," showing to the rest of the listeners the sense which really lay was at the bottom of an almost unintelligible utterance. Frequently the remark of a classmate, whose industrial experience had been hard like my own, would throw what I had learnt from the lecture into quite a new perspective. It was during a tutorial class discussion that I caught my first glimpse of the potentiality of organised Labour.

Then there are essays to write, and these present a considerable amount of difficulty to people of 30 or 40 years of age, who have attempted nothing in the shape of " composition " since they were twelve or thirteen. The material out of which the essay has to be made frequently defies manipulation, and the essayist is neither surprised nor pained at the tutor's comment, " You do not see the wood for the trees." Some of us will never write what can be truthfully called a creditable essay, but all who really try soon learn the folly of using shibboleths, of making assertions without giving reasons, and understating the case with which they do not agree.

Given earnest minded students and tutors of the right kind, there seem to me tremendous possibilities in the tutorial class method, not only for the development of the exceptional student, but for (what is often regarded too lightly) the widening and deepening of life for the so-called " ordinary " man or woman.

BANGOR SUMMER SCHOOL.

By A. N. Shimmin.

The Bangor Summer School is conducted by a Committee of representatives from the University Tutorial Classes Joint Committees of Belfast, Bristol, Leeds, Liverpool, Manchester, Nottingham, Sheffield, and Wales. The lectures and tuition at the school are given in the buildings of the University College of North Wales, and, in the main, the students aie housed during their stay in the hostels connected with the college.

The first meeting of the school was held in 1913, so that the larger part of its history is identical with the war period. This has meant some diminution in the number of men students, but so far from there having been a decreasing vitality the whole educational work of the school has made great progress, and has achieved a high standard in all directions.

The figures relating to the attendance of students are as follow :—

	Men.	Women.	Total.
1913	98	26	124
1914	87	36	123
1915	73	41	114
1916	41	40	81
1917	34	31	65
Totals	333	174	507

The students are mostly tutorial class students or ex-members of such classes, and the records indicate, as might be expected, that the greater portion of them come from classes which are supervised by the four Northern Universities. The ages of the students range mainly from 25 to 40 years, though quite 10 per cent. of each year's membership have been between 40 and 50 years of age.

The following table shows at a glance the constitution of the school membership. Every effort has been made annually to induce artisans to attend in larger numbers, but it must be recognised that the sacrificing of the only holiday of the year is too big a claim on many who would otherwise be only too glad to attend. The vital fact at once emerges, on the other hand, that many students *do* devote their annual week or fortnight to a stay at the school, and the success of the school has been determined in a large measure by the work of these people.

	1913.	1914.	1915.	1916.	1917.
Artizans	87	82	59	37	35
Clerks	14	19	22	11	10
Teachers	15	10	18	19	14
Domestics	8	12	15	14	6

In the first year economics and industrial history claimed the attention of the vast majority of the students, but literature and psychology have attracted more students as the school has developed, and there is now no danger of limitation of subjects, as may be seen from the admirable yearly prospectus.

Since the inauguration of the school the average period of weekly tuition (in lectures, study groups, or in private) has been from 23 to 26 hours—to say the least, a highly creditable standard.

The teaching work is, normally, in the hands of university lecturers and tutors, whose stay varies from two to four weeks in most cases. Two general lectures are given during each week, at which the attendance of all students is compulsory. But the essential feature of the educational work is the " seminar " or " study-group," in which three or four students meet daily to discuss with their tutor their special subject of study.

For two years now this method has been in operation, and in view of the greater continuity and thoroughness of study it has been voted both by students and tutors a real success. The cases of weak students or of specially advanced students are met by periods of personal tuition.

Every year the students' reports have gone to show how deeply summer school study is appreciated, largely because of the freedom of the method employed and, on the other hand, the exchange of view which membership of a miscellaneous study group affords.

The social side, though second to the distinctly educational work, is by no means neglected. It has proved, in fact, a powerful force in the educational life of the school. Three or four days a week excursions take place, and almost every evening a sing-song, concert, or impromptu debate. Everywhere the spontaneity of the students' efforts is most noticeable. The Sunday night addresses and debates have become institutions, and every week have revealed the catholicity of taste among the students.

The school is inspected by the Board of Education, and a substantial grant is paid each year by the Board on the work done at the school. The other part of the financial liabilities has been met each year by contributions from the University Committees and the W.E.A. and by students' fees. The Gilchrist trustees have contributed to the Scholarship Fund, by means of which grants-in-aid are made to assist students whose attendance would otherwise be rendered impossible.

Events have justified the optimism of the School Committee in carrying on throughout the war, and the claim of the 1917 report that " Bangor Summer School must become a permanent institution " is well supported by the history of the first five years.

It is, however, only one of the summer schools held in the country. There remains the great work of co-ordinating existing efforts, and of increasing the number of places at which such thoroughly useful meetings can be held.

UNIVERSITY TUTORIAL CLASSES :
TUTORS' CONFERENCE.

The first Conference of Tutors of University Tutorial Classes was convened by the Workers' Educational Association in the Victoria University, Manchester, in January, 1910. Since then there has been a Conference every year to discuss the special problems connected with the teaching and organisation of Tutorial Classes. Until 1915 Conferences were convened by the Central Joint Advisory Committee, in 1911 at Cambridge, in 1912 at Oxford, in 1913 at Leeds, in 1914 at Cambridge, in 1915 at Liverpool. At Liverpool the Conference decided to constitute itself a permanent body, and appointed a Committee to make arrangements for the next meeting and to draft a constitution for submission to it. The next meeting, in January, 1916, was held in University College, London, when the following constitution was adopted :—

CONSTITUTION.

1. The organisation shall take the form of an Annual Conference and a Standing Committee.

2. Membership of the Conference shall, on payment of an annual membership subscription of half-a-guinea, be open to all persons who have taken Tutorial Classes in the winter 1912-13 or since, and to all persons who shall take Tutorial Classes in the future.

3. The Standing Committee shall have power to invite to the Conference such visitors as they think fit; such visitors shall have the right to speak, but not to vote.

4. The Conference shall hold at least two sessions, one of which shall be confined to members.

5. The Standing Committee shall consist of a Chairman and Secretary elected at the Conference, and of five representatives elected by postal ballot, no two of whom shall represent the same University or University College.

At the same meeting the following statement was adopted :—

REPORT ON STATUS AND REMUNERATION OF TUTORS.

The status and remuneration of tutors and the relation of tutors to the junior staffs of the Universities which they serve are interconnected problems, and might be made the subject of a single set of recommendations. Present arrangements are unsystematic, a state of things largely due to the rapidity with which the Tutorial Class movement has grown and the difficulty of finding tutors. Last winter two tutors took five classes each, 14 four each, five three each, 16 two each, and 39 one each. Six tutors took classes for more than one University. The " part-time " tutors included barristers, schoolmasters, University professors and lecturers, and students engaged in research. The normal method of remuneration is the payment of £60 to £80 per class, the tutor's salary depending on the number of classes his Joint Committee could give him and he could take. Some Universities have appointed " staff tutors " at fixed salaries. No University has made arrangements for all its tutors to lecture inside the University, and many have no official status as members of the staff; but a number of the tutors (in addition to part-time tutors, whose chief work is intra-mural teaching) do, as a matter of fact, give courses inside their University without having the status of lecturers, and a number have that status.

The system that obtains in most other branches of teaching—of relying almost exclusively on full-time teachers—would seem to be neither possible nor desirable in the Tutorial Class movement. The number of classes and the subjects chosen for study vary too much from year to year to keep up a staff of full-time tutors regularly and fully occupied. And the movement gains from the variety of teachers working in it, and from the association with its work of members of the professorial staffs of the Universities and of teachers whose experience and ordinary work are not academic. Uniformity of status is difficult to secure, because there may be great variations in the qualifications of a number of tutors, all well qualified to take classes; tutors whose main occupation is the conduct of Tutorial .Classes may, however, reasonably expect some increase in remuneration with increased experience.

On the other hand, the present lack of system has dangers for the movement.

. 1. It may lead to the appointment of teachers who have neither the qualifications which would be required of an intra-mural teacher in that subject nor other qualifications which fit them for the work. The tendency of such appointments in the long run would be to reduce Tutorial Classes from the rank of University classes to that of continuation school classes (which are a good thing, but are a different thing), and to hinder the full recognition of extra-mural teaching as an integral and honourable part of University work.

2. The normal position of a full-time tutor—an intellectual casual—may deter good men from taking up the work and lead present tutors to seek other positions which give them security of tenure, even when they would prefer their present work.

3. There is the danger that the tutorial system may be used to keep down the small salaries paid to some intra-mural teachers for their real work.

The conditions of the problem are different in the older and the newer Universities. In the older Universities the payment per class has been comparatively high ($£80$ and $£72$), the Joint Committees have endeavoured to give tutors full employment when they wanted it, and the college system makes the whole organisation of the University different. The great bulk of Tutorial Class work, however, is done by the newer Universities, and the following suggestions have reference primarily to them :—

1. The existing arrangement for selecting tutors—the Joint Committee—was devised to meet Oxford conditions. Its continuance is, however, essential in all Universities (a) to secure the confidence of Labour in the teaching; (b) to give the classes and the W.E.A. a check on the appointment of tutors who are not suited to the special conditions of Tutorial Class teaching. The tutors are University teachers, and the privileges and dignities which University status carries with it should be extended to them.

2. The demand for classes in Economics, Economic History, and cognate subjects is large enough and steady enough in most areas to make possible the appointment of staff tutors, with security of tenure and at a salary fixed irrespective of the number of classes arranged. Such tutors should be lecturers (or professors) in the Department of Economics or History. As the movement develops the appointment of staff tutors in other subjects should become possible.

3. No tutor should be paid less than £60 a class. Staff tutors, whose main occupation is the taking of Tutorial Classes, ought to have a commencing salary of £300 a year, and all tutors who regularly take more than one class ought to be on a scale.

The present officers of the Conference are :—

Chairman, Arthur Greenwood, 9, Erskine Hill, Golder's Green, N.W. 4.

Secretary, Henry Clay, Cedar House, Epping, Essex.

The following memorandum, adopted at the Conference of 1917 in Manchester, may also be quoted :—

MEMORANDUM ON THE UNIVERSITY TUTORIAL CLASS MOVEMENT
SUBMITTED TO THE RECONSTRUCTION COMMITTEE.

1. Growth of the Movement.

University Tutorial Classes were established at Longton and Rochdale in January, 1907. The growth of the movement was as follows :—

	1908-9.	1909-10.	1910-11.	1911-12.	1912-13.	1913-14.
Classes	8	32	72	102	117	145
Students	237	1,117	1,829	2,485	3,176	3,234

The early classes were given to Economic History and Economics. As the number of classes has increased the range of studies has widened. There were before the war classes in Political History (English and European), Political Science, Sociology, English Literature, Psychology, Ethics, Geography, Music, and Natural Science.

2. Composition of the Classes.

The following is an analysis of the occupations of 3,035 students in 1913-14 :—

Clerks and Telegraphists.*	Teachers.	Textile.	Domestic.	Engineers.	Shop Assistants.
623	308	235	193	177	160

Miners, etc.	Printing.	Metal.	Building.	Carpenters and Joiners.	Other Factory.
148	144	95	83	82	65

Railway.	Tailors and Dressmakers.	Insurance.	Postmen, Trams, Police.	Potters.	Boot, Shoe, and Leather.
63	61	59	58	57	52

Warehousemen.	Labourers.	Foremen and Managers.	Food.	Bookbinders.	Miscellaneous.
47	31	26	25	9	234

* Of the clerks and telegraphists 210 were in London classes.

More significant than the paid occupations of the student is their voluntary work. No complete record of this has ever been made. The following particulars relating to four classes, which happen to be available, are not unrepresentative : Class A served two industrial villages with a joint population of 18,000; Class B was recruited mainly from an Adult School Sub-Union in London; Classes C and D were organised by W.E.A. branches in county boroughs.

	A	B	C	D
Trade Union officials	3	1	7	5
Trades Council officials	3	—	1	1
Officials of political associations	2	2	1	2
Voluntary educational work	5	2	5	3
Friendly society officials	1	1	1	3
Directors of co-operative societies	2	1	2	1
Teachers or officials in Adult Schools or Sunday Schools	7	5	5	3
Local preachers	1	1	1	—

In illustration of the same point, it may be mentioned that the tutor of the above classes had among his present and past students twelve City and Borough Councillors. The sacrifices made by Tutorial Class students to attend the classes, to do the necessary reading and essay work, are another illustration of their quality. Long hours and exhausting work, overtime and unemployment, the pressure of voluntary public work, and even the shift system do not prevent the great mass of members from fulfilling the onerous conditions of membership; the proportion of attendances made to attendances possible is usually 75 per cent. or over. The classes have acquired a new social importance from the missionary or " extension " work undertaken by them. One student has given as many as 77 lectures in one winter, taking complete responsibility for four classes, and submitting his notes beforehand to his tutor for correction. The four classes in the Potteries have established an organisation which is this winter maintaining 36 daughter classes, all taken by voluntary teachers. Similar work is being done elsewhere, either by the direct method of establishing daughter classes or by permeating existing organisations—literary societies, co-operative educational activities, Adult Schools, Trades Councils, etc.—and raising the standard of voluntary education generally. It is worth noting that the officials and Executive Committee of the W.E.A. District which organises most Tutorial Classes (more than one-third of the whole) are almost all of them either tutors or students of Tutorial Classes.

3. Standard of Work.

The academic quality of the work of Tutorial Classes varies and generalisation is difficult. It varies with the quality of the tutor and the time he can give to each class, with the care with which the class was organised, with the number of books accessible to the students.

One tutor finds that his students in social history will read Stubbs, Maitland, and Vinogradoff; others are satisfied if their students read Townsend Warner's popular text-book. Another tutor finds that from a quarter to a half of a class taking 19th century industrial history will read at least Dicey's " Law and Opinion " and Webb's " History of Trade Unionism." While most of the essays done are of value only as exercises, some Tutorial Class essays have been published in the

" Economic Journal " and other periodicals. Comparisons with the work of undergraduate University students are not helpful. The range of studies is not the same, social studies occupying a much larger place in Tutorial Classes than in other University work. The Tutorial Class student has had no secondary education; the undergraduate has had no experience of industry and politics. The Tutorial Class student comes to the lecture with questions and ideas that he wants to discuss; the undergraduate more usually comes with a notebook which she proposes to fill. The Tutorial Class student wants knowledge; the undergraduate may want knowledge, but his immediate object is a degree. It is, however, safe to say that in the field of history, economics, and moral and political philosophy the work of Tutorial Classes is on the average not below " pass " standard and under favourable circumstances is of " honours " standard.

4. Organisation and Staffing.

While Universities regard Tutorial Classes as University work and receive Board of Education grants on that condition, the treatment that in some cases they have accorded to Tutorial Classes varies much more than their treatment of intra-mural work. This may be illustrated by reference to the financing of classes and the position of the tutors. Financial arrangements vary with the circumstances of different Universities. The chief expenses, however, everywhere are tutors' salaries, travelling expenses, and cost of organisation; the chief sources of income are Board of Education grant (a maximum of £30 per class), contributions from Local Education Authorities, and the University contribution. The Oxford Committee estimates that the University must expend £70 per class over and above Board of Education grants and local sources of income without allowing anything for cost of organisation; its expenditure for all purposes from University sources on 19 classes and a Summer School in the year 1913-14 was over £1,400. The total University grant for all purposes in the case of the 16 Manchester classes in 1913-14 was £450, in the case of the ten Leeds classes in the same year was £150; in other cases the expenditure was much lower. Similar variations occur in expenditure on organisation. Two Universities have appointed Organising Secretaries specially, who work in co-operation with our Workers' Educational Association as far as possible. Two Universities subscribe £50 and one £25 to the funds of W.E.A. district organisations and leave the organisation in the main to them. The other Universities and University Colleges leave the organisation to the W.E.A. without making any such contribution to the expense. Tutorial Classes are only a part of the W.E.A.'s work, and the W.E.A.'s resources are far from adequate to its work; hence the organisation of Tutorial Classes is seldom perfect.

It follows that the position of the staff is also unsatisfactory. Intra-mural teachers are appointed for a term of years at a definite salary, which they receive irrespective of the attendance and work of their classes. Some Tutorial Class teachers have been given similar conditions of appointment, but the great majority are appointed for a session and for one or more classes. Some Universities, without guaranteeing full-time employment, make it their policy to plan out their work ahead in such a way as to ensure full-time employment for those tutors who desire it; other University authorities have sometimes not made up their minds how many classes they intend to run a month after the session has begun, so that the chief risk and uncertainty of the work is thrown on the tutors. Some Universities give their Tutorial Class teachers the status of lecturers in the department of the University devoted to the teacher's subject, or make arrangements for them to lecture in the University in the summer term; others treat them as outsiders, employed for a particular piece of work which carries with it no status in the University.

The reason usually given for not improving the conditions of Tutorial Class teaching is lack of resources, which means simply that other kinds of University work are considered more important. The reason is sometimes given that Tutorial Class teachers have not the academic qualifications possessed by intra-mural teachers. In that case a breach of faith with the students and the Board of Education was committed in appointing them, the Board's grant being paid only on the condition that the instruction given is of University standard and students invited to join on the same condition.

5. The Claims and Possibilities of the Tutorial Class Movement.

The Tutorial Class movement is capable of almost indefinite extension. The conditions and expense of an intra-mural University education make it very difficult for more than a small minority of the population to avail themselves of its advantages. The Tutorial Class, on the other hand, does not take its students away from their work, claiming as it does only a portion of their leisure. It does not take them out of their social class. Its cost per student is relatively slight. It extends, therefore, the possibility of University education from the small minority to the great majority of the population.

The experiment of offering University teaching to students who have had no secondary education has been successful, because the students were men and women of adult age and some social experience, who brought active questioning minds to the study of problems in which their class was vitally interested. Zeal for knowledge, as shown by the sacrifices made to obtain it, and social importance, as shown by the amount of public work undertaken by ex-students, are much greater in the case of Tutorial Classes than of most intra-mural University classes. The number of officials of working-class movements in Tutorial Classes at the moment gives them a special claim to consideration, but it must be remembered that they meet also the need of the natural scholar who has missed the ladder of education. And it is an error to suppose that only the man of exceptional ability can profit by membership of a Tutorial Class; owing to defective organisation many existing classes are not " selected " at all, and it has been well established that the Tutorial Class system is of benefit to people of the same intellectual type as the undergraduates who spend three years in a University and fail to take a pass degree. Any improvement of elementary education or extension of facilities for secondary education will widen the scope of the Tutorial Class without making it unnecessary, since the need which the Tutorial Class meets, the need of the adult, who wishes to supplement his own experience, reading and reflection by organised study, is a permanent and a growing need. On the other hand, it is doubtful whether the demand for improvement in the earlier stages of public education will ever attract the popular support necessary for effective reform if the level of education among adult voters is not raised by some such direct method as the Tutorial Class. In this connection the indirect influence of Tutorial Classes in training leaders for less formal educational groups is important.

A great development of Tutorial Class work could not but react favourably on other University work. If the differentia of University teaching is the combination of research with teaching, Tutorial Class work, involving as it does constant contact and discussion with men and women who are actively interested in and possess some experience of the problems studied, provides an atmosphere at least as favourable to research in the field of history, economics, literature, and the mental and moral sciences as that of intra-mural teaching. The development of the Tutorial Class system would provide the newer Universities with such a staff of teachers as would make possible the adoption of a tutorial system inside the University—a different thing from using Tutorial Classes to eke out the inadequate salaries of lecturers whose real work is inside the University. At the same time, .it would remove the reproach that Universities are institutions designed for the benefit of the middle and upper classes with such members only of the working class as are endeavouring to leave that class.

The development of the Tutorial Class movement to the present date, however, has done little more than show its possibilities. With additional resources it would be possible to reduce the number of classes that a single tutor takes and makes possible individual tuition; facilities could be given for research; smaller classes of more carefully selected students could be held on similar lines; resident tutors could assist tutorial students in the preparation of lectures for subordinate classes. Such developments, and others that experiment might lead to, would be applications of the principle that the extra-mural University student is as worthy of consideration as the intra-mural student.

Additional resources must come from the Government, since the education of the working classes is not an object that appeals strongly to the kind of people who endow Universities.

The claim of the movement on the Government is a double claim; the claim of all University education, the extension of which to all who desire it is made possible by this system, and the special claim of the workers whose educational needs were neglected in adolescence and youth. For the ideal of the Tutorial Class movement is not the mere extension of the continuation school system to adults, but, in a phrase of Dr. Sadler's, decentralised University work of the highest quality.

Additional resources are needed in two directions. Extension is obstructed by the expense of classes to the Local Education Authorities or other local authorities undertaking the classes; development by the inability and in some cases unwillingness of University authorities to treat Tutorial Classes as being of the same importance as intra-mural work. The former obstruction would be removed by increasing the present Board of Education grant per class; the latter calls for a grant-in-aid based on a different principle. The original establishment and the subsequent development of the Tutorial

Class system was due to the willingness of some University authority to apply their own resources to the work.

Other authorities, as the figures of expenditure, etc., given above indicate, although not refusing to take the work up, have not attached the same importance to it. Experiment is necessary to discover improved methods of organising and conducting classes, and in the interests of the classes quite as much as of the tutors, some means must be devised of giving Tutorial Class teaching the same advantages and attractions as other kinds of University teaching. Such attempts to devise new methods and to remove the unsatisfactory elements in the position of tutors will be made if the Universities that have done most for the movement in the past are given the means for further development of their work.

We suggest, therefore, that, in addition to the grant paid on the class, the Government should make to Universities and University Colleges a block grant-in-aid for Tutorial Class work equal to, or proportionate to, their expenditure on the work from their own resources. Thus the Government assistance will be applied at the point where it is likely to have most effect, and will stimulate the Tutorial Class movement without carrying with it any extension of State control.

ASSOCIATION OF TUTORIAL CLASS TUTORS OF THE UNIVERSITY OF LONDON.

The Association of Tutorial Class Tutors of the University of London was formed at the beginning of the 1916-17 session. All the London tutors who conducted classes during the session are members of the Association.

Owing to the abnormal conditions it has not been possible for the Association to hold many meetings, nor has it been thought advisable at present to frame a definite constitution for the Association. The objects of the Association are, briefly, to promote the interests of the tutors, and to enable the tutors to take a more active and collective part in the development of the Tutorial Class movement in the London area.

The conditions and the difficulties caused by the war have shown more clearly than ever that the present standard of remuneration, the security of tenure, and the status of tutors leave much to be desired. It is unsatisfactory that tutors should not only be unable to depend upon the guarantee of a minimum annual salary, but should also be unable to forecast between the close of one session and the beginning of the next whether they will have one, two, or more classes, or no classes at all. Tutors are thus placed in a difficult situation, and are thereby often prevented from giving their best thought and work both to their own classes and to the development of the Tutorial Class movement as a whole. The Association fully realises the difficulties which confront the Board of Education and the University in regard to these matters at the present time, and it also fully realises that these difficulties will remain in the transition period which will follow the war. But the Association is of opinion that the tutors and the movement as a whole will gain if the discussion of these problems and the framing of concrete proposals for their solution are made one of its main objects.

The more strictly educational activities of the Association will aim at providing opportunities for the discussion of such questions as—

(1) The position and the development of elementary and continuation education in their relation to the higher education of working people;

(2) raising the standard reached by the average Tutorial Class student;

(3) the organisation of seminary work;

(4) the training of students for civic and educational work;

(5) means of bridging over the second and third years and the third and fourth years of Tutorial Classes with regard to the retaining of original students, the recruiting of new students, and maintaining continuity of studies;

K

(6) co-operation with the Joint Committee and the Workers' Educational Association towards increasing the demand for Tutorial Classes;

(7) co-operation with the National Association of Tutors;

(8) the relations, actual and possible, competitive and co-operative between University Extension Classes and Tutorial Classes.

The Association will also aim at holding periodical meetings for the discussion of general or particular difficulties which arise in Tutorial Class work; for the comparison of personal experiences, methods, and experiments, etc.

The Secretary (pro tem.) of the Association is Edward McGegan, 11, Carlyle Square, Chelsea, S.W. 3.

UNIVERSITY EDUCATION FOR WOMEN.

By Miss A. M. A. H. Rogers.

Facilities for study are given to women at all the Universities of the United Kingdom. The eight modern Universities of England (Birmingham, Bristol, Durham, Leeds, Liverpool, London, Manchester, Sheffield), the four Universities of Scotland (Aberdeen, Edinburgh, Glasgow, St. Andrews), the two Universities of Ireland (Trinity College, Dublin, the National University), and the University of Wales admit them to membership and to graduation in Arts, Science, Literature, Medicine, Law, and Music, and, except at Durham, in Theology. In most cases, if not in all, women are eligible for appointments. Speaking generally, some knowledge of two modern languages, ancient or modern, and of mathematics is required for matriculation, and a University education is secured by the requirement of attendance at a certain number of lectures. London stands almost alone in not requiring any guarantee of such an education in the case of the external students, towards whom it stands in the relation of an examining and not of a teaching body. These Universities, with the exception of Trinity College, Dublin, and Durham, are not residential, but have halls or hostels for women students, which differ from colleges in their method of government and absence of provision for education within their walls. Holloway College and Westfield College are residential colleges, which prepare students for the London examinations, but are not, like Bedford College for Women, colleges of the University. King's College for Women is at present in a period of transition, which has been prolonged by the war. Information as to these Universities should be addressed to the Registrar, and in the case of the residential colleges to the Principals. Oxford and Cambridge hold a position unique among Universities as regards their women students. Women are admitted at Oxford to all the examinations qualifying for degrees in Arts,* at Cambridge to the Tripos (i.e., Honour) Examinations in these subjects, and at both to Examinations in Music and to the Preliminary and Intermediate Examinations in Medicine, but not to the Final Examination. They can also obtain recognition for research work. They are not, however, members of the University, and have no right to share its education, to compete for its scholarships and prizes, or to hold its appointments. They do not wear its academical dress, they are not subject to its discipline, and they do not obtain degrees. In spite of these disabilities they have the full advantage of a University education, as they are by courtesy (and on payment of fees when required) admitted to nearly all the lectures and laboratories. The University examiners cannot refuse to examine them. The scholarships open to them are small in amount and few in number. The students have a certain recognised status, but the tutors and lecturers of their colleges, though personally treated with great courtesy by the men tutors, are not formally recognised as University teachers. The prestige of Oxford and Cambridge is, however, so great that the disadvantage to their

---

* This includes Degrees in Science, as at the Scottish Universities.

women students of a state of things which cannot be considered permanent is less than might have been anticipated. Attempts made towards the end of the last century to obtain the admission of women to degrees were unsuccessful. The question will be raised again at Oxford after the war, and will no doubt lead to sin.:lar action at Cambridge. The main difficulty lies in the democratic method of government enjoyed by Oxford and Cambridge, and well-established democracies have neither in ancient nor in modern times shown any particular readiness to give women a share in power or money. An apparent concession is made to women at both these Universities by allowing them to enter for examinations under special conditions. Latin and Greek are still obligatory in what is practically the entrance examination at both Universities, but at Cambridge women may substitute modern languages for both, and at Oxford a modern language for Greek. Women are also allowed at Oxford, unless they read Science, to omit the Intermediate Examination, and are not restricted, as men are, to a limited period of study for Honours. Unfortunately, these modifications of the course have been utilised as an argument against the degree, and should be used as rarely as possible. Girton College requires all its students to take the men's course. Pass students are not admitted at Cambridge, and only rarely at Oxford. A University degree is practically necessary for a good post in a secondary school, but the Oxford Pass Course is very ill adapted to the requirements of girls' schools. The full degree course covers three years. The three terms are each of eight weeks' duration, but Honour work is arranged to cover a considerable part of the vacations, and at Cambridge many students reside for a short vacation term. Women can also take one of several University Diplomas. The requirements for admission are less rigid than for the degree course, and the course need not cover more than two years. The Diplomas in Geography and in Economics and Political Science (Oxford only) are the most useful to ordinary students. Neither Oxford nor Cambridge can supply hospital facilities for the full Medical Course, which must be completed in a large city, but can be begun at the University, where Chemistry, Physiology, and Anatomy can be studied.

At Cambridge there are two residential colleges for women, each having its own staff of teachers and lecturers. Girton is at a little distance from Cambridge, but its students can easily attend lectures in the University. At Oxford there are four residential colleges— Lady Margaret Hall, Somerville College, St. Hugh's College, St. Hilda's Hall. There is also a body of students called the Society of Oxford Home-Students, organised under a principal and governing body of its own and quite independent of the colleges. These five bodies are styled in the University Statutes " Recognised Societies of women students " and their students are entered on a University register. The University has constituted a Delegacy for women students, consisting of both men and women, through which it deals with the students, but the Societies make their own arrangements for tutorial instruction and each has its own educational staff.

The lectures attended are for the most part those given by and for men in the University, but a certain number are given by the women teachers. The Association for the Education of Women in Oxford acts as a link between the past and present students and the five Recognised Societies. It provides an office which serves as a bureau of information, a library, and lecture-rooms in a central University building, and makes the formal arrangements for admission of students to University lectures and for the payment of fees to lecturers. General inquiries as to education in Oxford should be addressed to the Secretary, A.E.W. Office, Clarendon Building, Oxford; detailed inquiries as to colleges and home-students to the respective Principals. (Address of Principal of Oxford Home Students: Mrs. Johnson, 5, South Parks Road, Oxford.) The expenses of a University education at a residential college are from about £85 to about £100 a year. This includes board, residence, and tuition, but not personal expenses, travelling, or books. The expenses of a home-student may be considerably less. These students live in their own homes or with relations in Oxford, or in private families, or sometimes in lodgings, and pay for such tuition as they require. They can, therefore, more easily adapt their expenses to their means. An older student has more liberty as a home-student than if she lived in a cottage, where the rules are necessarily made for young students. St. Frideswide's is a Roman Catholic hostel for home-students.

Members of the W.E.A. who contemplate study at one of the older Universities may feel sure that they, like other genuine students, will be cordially welcomed and can obtain a very excellent education if they will bear a few facts in mind. Both Universities are ancient and somewhat prejudiced institutions, which, until the middle of the last century, took account only of men students. They have their own rules as to the examinations qualifying for admission to University courses, and these are apt to prove a difficulty to students whose education has been on very different lines from that of boys' public schools. Care should be taken that a woman student has had such a preliminary preparation, especially in languages, as will enable her to profit by University teaching. The Universities are situated in towns of very moderate size, and the rules of discipline and etiquette are adapted to places where students attract more attention than they do in a large city. Women students must be prepared to adapt themselves both in educational and social matters to conditions with which they may not entirely sympathise and which they find irksome, and must take the rough with the smooth, or they will not get the full benefit of University life. The collegiate system of Oxford and Cambridge makes the intercourse between men and women students less unconstrained than it is at modern co-educational Universities, but, on the other hand, the relations of the teachers, whether men or women, with the individual pupils is more intimate, owing to the tutorial method of teaching created by that system.

SETTLEMENTS.

By Hilda Cashmore
(Warden, University Settlement, Bristol).

" The settler of a University Settlement . . . looks not to a church buttressed by party spirit nor to a community founded on self-helped respectability. He looks rather to a community where the best is most common, where there is no more hunger and misery, because there is no more ignorance and sin, a community in which the poor have all that gives value to wealth, in which beauty, knowledge, and righteousness are nationalised. The equal capacity of all to enjoy the best, the superiority of quiet ways over those of striving and crying, character as the one thing needful, are the truths with which we have become familiar, and on these truths we take our stand."

These words are the charter of the Settlement Movement. They were first spoken in St. John's College, Oxford, in 1885, when Canon Barnett put into words the idea which was in the minds of the young men of that generation when they sought fitly to commemorate the eager spirit of Arnold Toynbee, by the foundation of the first English Settlement. It is quite true that the old Settlement movement was an upper class movement, an effort of those students who as members of the older Universities, and as the heirs of all the ages were anxious to share the gifts so freely bestowed on them, to make an act of restitution to those from whom they had been withheld. It is true that their free offer of friendship was the holding out of hands to less fortunate members of the community whose desire for friendship had to be aroused and won; that their determination to work at social study and scientific research found them engaged in study of methods which seem strangely old-fashioned and out of date to-day; that the leadership they offered was the leadership of a class. This was inevitable, and all honour is due to their humanity that they could brook no delay in returning to the community what the community had given so generously. But free sharing of the common heritage of the past, simple friendship based on common human interests, hard study of our social diseases, and a constructive imagination turned to the problem of the community of the future, these simple and fundamental conceptions which lie at the heart of the Settlement movement are as vital to-day as ever.

The hard things said of the Settlement movement really only show that the balance has happily shifted, that education is no longer the property of a class. The ideal of a community " where the best is most common, in which beauty, knowledge, and righteousness are nationalised," is already shared by working men and women, artisans and casual labourers, as well as university graduates, and men of leisured upbringing.

The Settlements of the future must be voluntary associations of men and women of all classes who have seen the vision of a community spiritually awake, in which human beings shall be ends in themselves, and not merely means to material ends, who have learnt that class consciousness is a weakness, not a strength, and class segregation impossible to men inspired with a common ideal. The members of the community shall be the pioneer and the voluntary element in a conscious attempt to work out a new democratic state, a state measuring values and apportioning them by the measure of their spiritual quality, and testing material prosperity not by the market value of goods only but by their potential power to develop full personality. They shall be the explorers; those who go in front at their own risk and make out new paths in the trackless land ahead. They shall be the brethren of the common pity reverently waiting behind to succour those who have been trampled down, worn out and cast aside by the thoughtless progress of the crowds moving forward. They shall be a fellowship of men and women who are not seeking place or authority or riches, but are consumed with the desire to serve their generation. They shall study life for life's sake, putting aside preconceived theories. They shall see in the living present as it is played out before their eyes the eternal issues. They shall have the courage to look good and evil in the face. They believe that the issues of life have no final answer here, and are content to share daily in the experience of common life, and patiently to brood over its meaning. They will prize the gifts of the mind; they will welcome ideas as men welcome the spring. They will demand for themselves and for others leisure to think, and above all, and persistently, leisure to live. They will ask nothing for themselves, and have nothing for themselves but what they will ceaselessly demand for each member of the community.

So much for the spirit of the Settlements; the spirit of human companionship, patient study, dauntless experiment.

The next point is their characteristic mission to-day. They should be the solvents of antiquated prejudices just because they touch life at so many points. They should be the training ground for the new social students of the future. They must not be laboratories in which the superior "brain" fashions theories from the cold observation of the sufferings of men, an effort in which heart and hand are separated. But they must be workshops in which brain and hand work faithfully together, to refashion tools for the service of men in the future, and to discover the faults in the mechanism of society.

An ideal Settlement is a group of people tacitly pledged to share what they have got to the full, if it is music, or art, or intellectual ability, or business, or domestic skill, or the gift of healing. They are tacitly pledged to keep the door open, to create an atmosphere so alive, and yet so patient of difference, that a meeting ground is made for men and women of various classes and of conflicting views, a place for free discussion and for the birth of new ideas.

Such an ideal allows the widest possible divergence of method. Settlements of many kinds have sprung up. The following attempts a rough classification :—

1. THE UNIVERSITY SETTLEMENTS OF GREAT BRITAIN AND THE COLLEGE SETTLEMENTS OF AMERICA.*

These have broadened their methods but their underlying aims remain the same. They have never been officially attached to the

---

* The following are University Settlements: Birmingham Women's Settlement; Bristol University Settlement; Cardiff University Settlement; Edinburgh University Settlement; Glasgow, Queen Margaret Settlement; Glasgow, University Students Settlement; Liverpool University Settlement; Cambridge House; London, Mansfield House; Oxford House; London, Toynbee Hall; Women's University Settlement ; Manchester University Settlement.

Universities, but have always been voluntary associations of members of various Universities. They now exist in almost every University town of England and Scotland, and abound in the great American cities. Hull House, Chicago, stands to the American College Settlement movement as Toynbee Hall to the English. Oxford and Cambridge have in all cases chosen London for the field of their enterprise.

2. SETTLEMENTS FOUNDED BY THE GREAT PUBLIC SCHOOLS.

e.g., St. Hilda's East, Rugby House, Wellington College Mission, United Girls' Schools Settlement.

3. SETTLEMENTS EMPHASISING RATHER THE CIVIC ASPECT OF THEIR WORK.

e.g., The Browning Settlement, Passmore Edwards Settlement.

4. SETTLEMENTS WHICH HAD THEIR ORIGIN PARTLY IN THE HOME MISSION WORK OF THE CHURCHES, PARTLY IN THE INSPIRATION OF THE UNIVERSITY SETTLEMENT MOVEMENT.

e.g., Women's Presbyterian Settlement, Talbot House, Lady Margaret Hall Settlement, The Red House, Leeds, Canning Town Settlement, Woodbrooke Settlement, Settlement of the Holy Child, Bishop Creighton House Settlement.

TABLE OF SOME CHARACTERISTIC DEVELOPMENTS OF THEIR WORK.

1. The organisation of various forms of philanthropic work.

2. Civic work of all kinds.

3. All kinds of experimental social work in connection with the needs of children and young persons.

4. Educational work.

5. Music, art, recreation of all kinds.

6. Health work.

7. Higher education of adult men and women and of adolescents.

8. Social research.

9. Definite training of " social workers."

One or two illustrations of work which is characteristic of all the Settlements may be given :—

1. The educational programme of Toynbee Hall for this session, 1916-1917, illustrates the educational work, both on the side of formal teaching and that of education by fellowship—

(*a*) Classes are advertised in—

Literature, drama, languages, history, economics and social science, hygiene and first aid, art, music, and gymnastics.

(*b*) Educational clubs, such as—

Toynbee Natural History Society.
,,   Art Club.
Toynbee Hall Ambulance Division.
,,   ,,   Guild of Compassion.
,,   ,,   Choral Class.
,,   ,,   Folk and Morris Dancing.
,,   Shakespeare Society.
,,   Travelling Club.
,,   Antiquarian Club.
,,   Chess Club.

2. CIVIC WORK.—A glance at the annual reports of the University Settlements shows the following :—

(*a*) WORK in connection with the Board of Education and Educational Authorities on Care Committees in Infant Welfare Associations, Invalid Schools, Play Centres (now just emerging from the experimental stage and receiving grants from the State).

(*b*) BOARD OF TRADE.—After-Care Committees, apprenticeship schemes.

(*c*) Insurance Committees.

(*d*) Boards of Guardians.

(*e*) Work in connection with the activities of the Local Government Board.

(*f*) Pensions Committees.

(*g*) War Savings Commitees.

An interesting experiment has lately been made in the foundation of Barnett House, Oxford. It is an institution which has for its principal objects the promotion of the systematic study of social and economic problems, of university settlements, and of the higher education of wage earners.

If sympathetically developed it should be able to exercise a powerful influence in emphasising the underlying unity of aim of many widely scattered groups of workers, who, through the very nature of their absorbing work in their particular districts, tend to lose touch with one another, and with some of the wider issues.

3. Again, the foundation of the English provincial Universities has emphasised a very important development of the Settlement idea. All the great cities which have recently obtained their University charter have spontaneously produced their Settlements. From their insistence on the folly of letting ignorant and unsympathetic hands deal with the intricacies of social administration there has grown up the new development of the Social Study Courses at the provincial Universities, themselves in touch with the experimental work carried on in the Settlements. The courses are so arranged that theoretical study and experimental contact with the machinery of society are pursued side by side. There remains a tacit understanding that education in social problems is dead unless it is carried on in the common room and the club through immediate action of mind on mind, irrespective of class.

The following Settlements train students in connection with the University Social Study Courses :—

Birmingham Women's Settlement.
Birmingham Woodbrooke Settlement.
Bristol.—University Settlement.
Leeds.—The Red House.
Liverpool University Settlement.
Liverpool.—Victoria Women's Settlement.
Belfast.—Women Workers' Settlement.
London.—Canning Town Women's Settlement.
Creighton House.
Lady Margaret Hall Settlement.
Passmore Edwards' Settlement.
Presbyterian Women's Settlement.
Ratcliff Settlement.
St. Helen's House, Stratford.
St. Hilda's East.
Talbot House.
Toynbee Hall.
United Girls' Schools Settlement.
Women's University Settlement.

The movement is full of promise, but it brings with it dangers. The " professional social worker " has come to stay, and the demand on University Settlements to equip themselves to seize upon and quicken the spirit of this new development is urgent.

If Settlements seize the opportunity and demand a higher standard of training the worst dangers of a bureaucracy out of touch with the heart of the people may be stayed, but they must take care that the magnitude of the task does not stifle their spirit and turn them into mere professional training colleges. They must insist on small numbers, on remaining social clubs linking together those of all classes who are looking out into the future and launching the experiments which can still only be undertaken by those who can take risks.

The future of Settlements is quite uncertain. The promise is very fair, but it is a promise to the spirit rather than to the work of the founders. If those who call to the younger generation for support still make their appeal to the generous-minded of all schools of thought, and can show them the kind of comradeship that is needed, they will inevitably bring to themselves fitting members for their societies. If in their plea for more efficient social service, more reasoned and balanced thinking, they can still keep the spirit of the movement the future of social training is largely in their hands. If the Settlements make their claim on all citizens; if class distinctions within them are unthinkable; if they really give a clear lead, and create joy and beauty and reverence in their neighbourhoods, there is no doubt of the co-operation of their fellow-workers in every city, and their opportunities for mutual education are unlimited.

REFERENCES.—Jane Addams : " Twenty Years at Hull House " (Macmillan). Barnett : " Worship and Work " (Garden City Press, Letchworth); " Vision and Service " (Hazell, Watson, and Viney). Werner Ticht : " Toynbee Hall and the Settlement Movement " (Bell and Sons). Branford : " Interpretations and Forecasts " (Duckworth).

UNIVERSITY REPRESENTATION IN PARLIAMENT.

The right of returning Members to Parliament, for long held by Oxford and Cambridge Universities, was extended to London and the Scottish Universities by the Reform Acts of 1867 and 1868. Parliament refused at the time to grant a similar privilege to ecclesiastical Durham, even though grouped with the then Radical London. Thenceforward the position was that Oxford and Cambridge returned two Members each, London one, Edinburgh and St. Andrews together one, Glasgow and Aberdeen together one, Dublin one. The Representation of the People Act of 1917 (8 Geo. V. C. 64) has changed the position, bringing into representation the Welsh and the newer English Universities, and giving an additional Member to Scotland. Oxford, Cambridge, and London remain as before. Durham, Manchester, Liverpool, Leeds, Sheffield, Birmingham, and Bristol Universities together retain two Members. The four Scottish Universities, forming one constituency, will in future return three Members, and the University of Wales will send one. The total (including Dublin) will thus be twelve.

The qualification of a University voter is determined by Section 2 of the new Act, which runs :—

" A man shall be entitled to be registered as a Parliamentary elector for a University constituency if he is of full age and not subject to any legal incapacity, and has received a degree (other than an honorary degree) at any University forming, or forming part of, the constituency; or, in the case of the Scottish Universities, is qualified under Section 27 of the Representation of the People (Scotland) Act, 1868 (31 and 32 Vict. C. 48); or, in the case of the University of Dublin, has either received a degree (other than an honorary degree) at the University, or has obtained a Scholarship or Fellowship in the University whether before or after the passing of this Act."

Women are admitted to the University franchise under the same Act, Section 4 (2) :—

" A woman shall be entitled to be registered as a Parliamentary elector for a University constituency if she has attained the age of 30 years and either would be entitled to be so registered if she were a man, or has been admitted to and passed the final examination, and kept under the conditions required of women by the University the period of residence necessary for a man to obtain a degree at any University forming, or forming part of, a University constituency which did not at the time the examination was passed admit women to degrees."

The wording of this clause is likely to lead to considerable trouble ; probably several cases will have to be decided by the Courts before the Oxford or Cambridge woman student will know precisely whether she will be entitled to the vote or not.

The passing of a final examination for a degree is not, as the above clauses alone would seem to imply, the sole qualification necessary. Clause 19 runs : " . . . . the governing body of every University forming, or forming part of, a University constituency shall cause a register to be kept in such form and made up, if desired, to such dates as they may direct, of persons entitled to vote in respect of a qualification at their University, and shall make the register available for the purpose of University elections for the constituency, and shall on the application of any person allow that person at all reasonable times to inspect and take extracts from the said register :

" Provided that the governing body may direct that a person who before the passing of this Act has received a degree, but was not entitled to vote in respect thereof, shall have no right to be registered unless he makes a claim for the purpose.

" The governing body of any such University may charge such fee as they think fit, not exceeding £1, in respect of registration to any person who receives a degree at their University after the passing of this Act, or who has received a degree before the passing of this Act, but was not entitled to vote in respect thereof." There is thus no difference in the nature of the present and past qualifications, except as regards the admission of women.

Clause 20 (1) provides that " at a contested election for a University constituency where there are two or more Members to be elected any election of the full number of Members shall be according to the principle of proportional representation, each elector having one transferable vote as defined by this Act." This will apply to all the University constituencies, except London and Wales.

Schedule V. of the Act provides for the method of conducting elections. The Returning Officer is the Vice-Chancellor in the cases of Oxford, Cambridge, London, and Wales; for Dublin he is the Master of Trinity ; for the combined University constituency an officer (" Vice-Chancellor, Principal, or Corresponding Officer of one of the combined Universities ") is to be appointed by the Board of Education. The poll is to be open five days, and voting is not by ballot, but by voting paper in a prescribed form. Votes may be forwarded by post.

The University voter will be in most cases a plural voter, but he (or she) is limited by Clause 8 (1) to the exercise of two votes only, one on the residence qualification, and not more than one " by virtue of other qualifications of whatever kind."

The University Franchise is not regarded with any high degree of favour by the general public, and with positive disfavour by the Labour Party. Yet it has never, probably because of the small number of Members returned, been made in any sense a " burning question." It is an anomalous " fancy franchise " in a democratic system, however, and the value of its retention is very questionable.

The present Parliamentary representation of the Universities is given below. The figures in brackets give the electorate at the last election (December, 1910, except where otherwise stated) :—

OXFORD (7,135).

Lord Hugh Cecil (U.) .... Unop.

Bye-election, June 30th, 1914.

Right Hon. R. E. Prothero (U.)..................... Unop.

CAMBRIDGE (7,228).

J. F. P. Rawlinson, K.C. (U.) .... Unop.

Bye-election, February 16th, 1911.

Sir J. Larmor, D.Sc., F.R.S. (U.) 2,308

Not Elected.

H. Cox (Ind. U.) 1,954
T. Page (Ind. U.) 354

LONDON (6,960).

Sir P. Magnus, Bart. (U.) 2,579
Sir V. Horsley, F.R.C.S. (L.) 1,857

EDINBURGH AND ST. ANDREWS (12,756).

Bye-election, August 10th, 1917.

Sir W. W. Cheyne, Bart., K.C.M.G. (U.) ...... Unop.

GLASGOW AND ABERDEEN (13,254).

Sir H. Craik, K.C.B. (U.) .... Unop.

DUBLIN.

Right Hon. Sir E. H. Carson, K.C. (U.) ...... Unop.

Bye-election, February 5th, 1917.

A. W. Samuels, K.C. (U.) 1,481

Not Elected.

Sir R. Woods 670

THE UNIVERSITIES.

ENGLAND.

BIRMINGHAM.

The Scientific College, founded by the public spirit and munificence of Sir Josiah Mason, was incorporated as the Mason University College in 1897. In 1900 this institution absorbed the Medical and Dental Departments of Queen's College in 1892 and became the Birmingham University in 1900.

It is governed by a Court of the usual composite character, and a small Council, which wields the effective power, and the Senate, which includes the Principal, the Vice-Principal, the Deans of all the Faculties, and all the Professors of the University for the time being.

The Mason Scientific College was founded " for the promotion of thorough systematic education and instruction specially adapted to the practical mechanical and artistic requirements of the manufactures and industrial pursuits of the Midland District of England," and the University has specialised in, without, of course, confining itself to, engineering, mining, metallurgy, brewing, and commercial studies. A Day Training College for elementary teachers is conducted in connection with the University. The Faculties are arts, science, medicine, and commerce. A degree in dentistry is a feature of the medical side.

About 1,000 students are taught annually, among whom the arts and science courses appear to be most popular.

BIRMINGHAM AND THE W.E.A.

HISTORICAL.

From 1905 to 1908 the Birmingham Workers' Educational Association was aided by a group of members of the University staff, who organised courses of lectures at the University in the evening. The University was not concerned officially in the promotion of the lectures, but it granted the free use of a lecture theatre.

In 1908 the Senate sanctioned the establishment of a Social Study Diploma and the formation of a Social Study Committee. The Committee consisted of members of the University staff, together with other persons, who were co-opted on account of their interest and experience in social work in the city. The functions of the Committee were twofold : first, to provide a course of systematic instruction, combined with practical training, for those who wished to engage in public and social service, and, second, to organise classes and lectures in the evening for working men and women in conjunction with the Workers' Educational Association. The first-named course of instruction was given in the daytime and led up to a Diploma, but the evening classes were of a slighter character and consisted of courses of from five to ten lectures each. They did not receive a grant from the Board of Education.

In 1910 the Senate sanctioned the formation of a Joint Committee similar to those at work in connection with other Universities, and the Social Study Committee handed over to the new Committee the work of conducting the evening lectures. The Joint Committee abandoned the evening lectures in their old form and proceeded to establish in their place University Tutorial Classes, and also extended operations to other towns.

GRANTS FROM THE UNIVERSITY.

From 1906 to 1909 the Social Study Committee made an annual grant of £25 to the Midland Workers' Educational Association. In 1910 the University Council gave a grant of £25 to the Birmingham Workers' Educational Association. In 1911 the University Council made a grant of £100 to the Joint Committee, and this was increased immediately afterwards to £310 a year, which is the annual grant at the present time. The Joint Committee gives £50 a year to the Midland Workers' Educational Association for secretarial work in connection with the Committee.

THE PRESENT POSITION.

The present relations are based upon the following recommendations, passed by the City Council in February, 1912, and attached to the grant made to the University from the city rates :—

" It is desirable that the University should :—

(a) maintain such Tutorial Classes as may be considered desirable by the Joint Committee of the University and working-class representatives ;

(b) appoint junior lecturers in such subjects as Economics, History, and Literature (or such others for which there may be a demand in working-class circles), who should be appointed with the definite object of devoting part of their time to giving evening lectures to adult workers at the University itself or in other parts of Birmingham."

The recommendations were accepted by the University Council, and at the request of the Joint Committee the Council decided to make an annual grant of £310 to the Committee, and to sanction the appointment of two assistant lecturers, one on Economics and the other on Literature, who should devote half their time to work under the Joint Committee. In addition to his ordinary University work, each of these lecturers is required to take one Preparatory Class, to give four courses of six lectures each session, and to give not more than three single lectures each session. It is the practice for the Joint Committee to appoint a member of the Labour side of the Committee (usually the Secretary) to act with the head of the faculty concerned in selecting the candidates for these lectureships.

OTHER AID GIVEN BY THE UNIVERSITY.

The University grants the free use of rooms for all Workers' Educational Association classes, lectures and meetings, and a porter has been specially engaged to enable the University to be open in the evening.

Since 1909 a library and reading-room has been at the disposal of Workers' Educational Association members and students each week evening, and since 1911 this room has been used in the daytime for secretarial work in connection with the Workers' Educational Association and the Joint Committee.

July, 1917.   T. W. PRICE.

BRISTOL.

The University of Bristol was founded under a Charter granted in 1909 at the petition of University College, Bristol, and of the Society of Merchant Venturers of the City of Bristol. The latter society has assisted vitally in the foundation of the University, has placed its buildings at the University's disposal, and has undertaken to provide and maintain the Faculty of Engineering. University College, Bristol (incorporated in 1876), was dissolved on the formation of the University. There are four associated institutions, the Royal Agricultural College (Cirencester), the Bristol Baptist College, the Western College, Bristol (Theological), the Theological College (Salisbury), and the National Fruit and Cider Institute (Long Ashton). There is a University Hall of Residence for Women at Clifton, and Training Departments for teachers in elementary schools have been set up.

Government is on the lines of the modern Universities (see Manchester). Some members of the Court are appointed by bodies representative of the working classes, including the Workers' Educational Association, the Bristol Trades Council, etc.

The Faculties are in arts, science, medicine, and engineering. Some 1,600 or 1,700 students (including 700 or 800 evening students) attend the courses.

BRISTOL AND THE W.E.A.

The University received its Charter in 1909. Before the University began its career the older University College came into sympathetic touch with the Workers' Educational Association, and some members of the staff, notably the Principal, Dr. C. Lloyd Morgan, Mr. J. H. Priestly (now Professor of Botany at Leeds), and Professor G. H. Leonard (who has been President of the Bristol University since its inception) took an active part in starting the Workers' Educational Association in Bristol.

A Joint Committee for Tutorial Classes was established in 1912 and the first class was started in Bath. In the following year three classes were started in Bristol. The four classes ran for the normal period of three years. Application to the University for a class to continue for the fourth year was declined, and it was further resolved by the University that no further classes should be sanctioned during the period of the war, the view being held that, contrary to the practice in other Universities, the expense could not be justified, and since the practice of the University is to appoint its Committees annually the Joint Committee was not re-appointed, so that at the present time the University is out of touch with the general movement.

Soon after the granting of the Charter the Workers' Educational Association organised a deputation to the present Vice-Chancellor to make representations respecting the charges for evening classes in the University. As a result the evening classes and short courses were, with few exceptions, thrown open to the workers free of charge upon presentation of a recommendation from the Workers' Educational Association, National Union of Teachers, Trade Unions, Adult School Union, and the Bristol Education Committee. This has since been modified, and students are now asked to pay a fee of 1s. for registration as students. In the interest of students to whom even this small charge might be a deterrent this may be remitted upon the Vice-Chancellor's recommendation.

Extra-mural lectures have been a feature of the work of the University. Courses of lectures on Economics, History, etc., have been arranged and held in schools and other buildings lent to the University in a central position in the city. These lectures have always been appreciated, especially as the University is somewhat inaccessible to large numbers of workers.

The University subscribes £5 a year to the funds of the Bristol Branch and the Tutorial Class Joint Committee voted £5 a year to the Western District Workers' Educational Association as a contribution towards the cost of organising Tutorial Classes. It also grants free use of rooms for Workers' Educational Association Council meetings, lectures, demonstrations, etc. Members of the staff help very generously in giving lectures, demonstrations, etc.

The Merchant Venturers' Technical College (which is the Faculty of Engineering in the University) also grant the free use of rooms for meetings, lectures, and social gatherings. Members of the staff also generously give their services as lecturers.

The question of the future financing of Tutorial Classes is one that must receive careful consideration, especially in the case of Bristol, where the Local Education Authority unfortunately decided not to give financial support to these classes on the ground that a penny rate is already levied for the University. About £3,000 is earmarked for Bristol scholarships and bursaries, and the contention is that Tutorial Classes should be provided for out of this rate, as is done in the case of Birmingham. The basis on which Tutorial Classes have been organised by the University is that a class costs £70 annually. This includes the provision of books. Of this amount the local branch of the Workers' Educational Association is charged £40. Of this sum £30 can be earned in grant from the Board of Education. A small variable grant is received annually from the Gilchrist Trustees for one class. This is based on the attendance and essay work. The Workers' Educational Association is, therefore, responsible for £10 per class and any loss in grant caused by insufficiency of essays or attendance.

The future of Tutorial Classes in the Bristol district will depend upon the attitude of the University towards the question of finance. It would seem that one of two things must happen : either the University must take greater financial responsibility or the Board of Education must make larger grants.

One of the most pressing needs of the western district is the appointment of junior lecturers at the University (following the precedent set at Birmingham) who could give their time in the evenings to lecturing for Workers' Educational Association branches, especially on Economics, History, and Literature. The lack of suitable lecturers and the expense of travelling prevents the development of the Workers' Educational Association in towns where there is a good opening for educational work amongst the adult population.

UNIVERSITY SETTLEMENT.—This institution, though not officially connected with the University, is linked to it by strong personal ties with certain members of the staff and through the interest of many of the students. It is the centre of numerous Workers' Educational Association activities, and a room is given over to the Workers' Educational Association at a nominal rental. This is used as a reading-room and contains an excellent library which is strong on the Economic side. This is managed by a Joint Committee of the Settlement and the Workers' Educational Association. The residents render good service by lecturing, and one year classes for the Settlement Girls' Clubs are organised under the auspices of the Workers' Educational Association. The Settlement affords an excellent medium by which University men and women can come into contact with members of the Workers' Educational Association and kindred organisations.

W. R. STRAKER.

CAMBRIDGE.

" The Chancellors, masters, and scholars of the University of Cambridge " were incorporated by the 13th Eliz. c. 29. Seventeen colleges—Peterhouse (founded A.D. 1284), Clare (1326), Pembroke (1347), Gonville and Caius (1348), Trinity Hall (1350), Corpus Christi (1352), King's (1441), Queen's (1448), St. Catharine's (1473), Jesus (1496), Christ's (1505), St. John's (1511), Magdalene (1519), Trinity (1546), Emmanuel (1584), Sidney Sussex (1596), Downing (1800)—and one Public Hostel—Selwyn College (1882)—form this " literary republic." " All these societies . . . . are maintained by the endowments of their several founders and benefactors. Each (the Public Hostel included) is a body corporate, bound by its own statutes, but it is likewise controlled by the paramount laws of the University."

Government is by a Senate and the Council of the Senate, and is of the worst possible type. Nothing can be offered to the Senate (a body of ex-students) for confirmation without the sanction of the Council (a body of teachers and ex-students). A proposal offered to the Senate or confirmed by it is known as a Grace. Heads of colleges, except the Provost of King's and the President of Queen's, are called Masters.

The income of the University, as distinct from the colleges, is derived from certain property, the fees of students at examinations, the trading profit of the University Press, a quarterly " tax " on members of the University, and from contributions of the various colleges.

Admission to membership of the University is possible, under certain conditions, for students who are not members of any college or hostel. (See Cambridge University Calendar.)

CAMBRIDGE UNIVERSITY AND THE WORKING CLASSES.

Until modern times the work of a University was, almost of necessity, limited to what was done within its own walls. Men were trained for many walks of life, and they influenced their fellows in all parts of the country. It was never supposed, however, that University teaching and examinations could be carried out except in the immediate surroundings of the University itself. Modern facilities of travel made a new departure possible, but a change would not have taken place except for the greatly increased feeling of responsibility to the nation which was so marked among the best University men about the middle of the Victorian period. Both Oxford and Cambridge instituted their local examinations in 1858, but these are mainly, though not entirely, confined to candidates of school age. Various schemes for the teaching of adults were in the air about the same time, but the first official recognition was given by the University of Cambridge in 1873, when the " local lectures " were established. James Stuart, Fellow of Trinity College, and afterwards Professor of Mechanism, was the real founder, and continued his interest in the scheme till his death in 1913. " University Extension," as it came to be called, and the title has been officially adopted at Oxford, was closely connected in Professor Stuart's experience with two bodies : the North of England Council for Promoting the Higher Education of Women and the workmen employed in the railway works at Crewe. From that day to this both types of student have been catered for. In some centres the audience is largely composed of women ; in others workingmen greatly predominate—the University always tries to get all classes to join. It cannot be maintained that the number of working-class people who have been influenced is as great as was hoped in the early days of the movement, but a great measure of success has been attained, especially in some districts. In the eighties and nineties there was great activity in the mining villages of Northumberland, and in more recent times successful courses have been held at Seaton Delaval. In 1909, in that centre, 180 students attended a twelve-lecture course, 35 staying to the class afterwards, 23 wrote the weekly papers, and 15 passed to final examination. In the neighbouring county of Durham the work has been carried on at New Herrington almost continuously since 1900, generally, however, by six-lecture courses. A very promising start was made at Hetton-le-Hole in 1915 In the Michaelmas Term of that year there was an average attendance of 720 at a course on " Scientific Progress in Recent Times," notwithstanding the fact that a thousand men from the place had joined the Army. The audience consisted almost entirely of miners and their families. Courses have also been given on " The Map of Europe " and " Some Makers of Modern History." Working-class students attend the lectures in considerable numbers at Leicester, Northampton, Norwich, York, and other centres. Barnstaple might not seem a promising place for such a purpose, but ever since the war began, the average attendance at a twelve-lecture course has been 269, a large number being artisans. Real determination on the part of a few leaders has often produced a wonderful result, but many a promising experiment has failed for lack of funds. Since 1902, Local Education Authorities have been able to give assistance in subjects other than technical, and the Board of Education has come to the rescue in many centres. It is increasingly felt that the liberal education of adults is a vital matter for the country. Cambridge has not done as much as she would have liked, but it is something for her to report that from 1873 to 1916 her local lectures were attended by an aggregate average of 414,635, mostly at twelve-lecture courses; 155,830 attended the class; 55,488 wrote the papers; 38,016 certificates were granted on the joint result of paper-work and examination after regular attendance at lectures and classes of a full course.

Oxford had the honour of starting the Tutorial Classes in 1908 in connection with the Workers' Educational Association. Cambridge followed suit in 1909, and four years later formed a Joint Committee of Management, consisting of five representatives nominated by the Association, with five resident members of the Senate. The Tutorial

Class system is now well known as an admirable means of intensive study extending over at least three years. Lack of funds has so far hampered the extension of the work, but there is great hope of development after the war. Higher education cannot be expected to pay for itself, whether in connection with the local lectures or the Tutorial Classes. The future of the movement depends on the cordial co-operation of the Board of Education, Local Education Authorities, the Universities, and Labour organisations.

The effort of the University for the working classes must, by the necessities of the case, be mainly extra-mural, and Cambridge has shown her belief in it by the devotion of many of her best sons during the last half-century. She is, however, always anxious to keep the door open for working-class students to enter the University itself. The number of such students who have won her scholarships and bursaries in mediæval and modern times is very large. By means of them the State and the professions have been greatly strengthened. Up to the present, however, no system has been devised which will bring to Cambridge for a period of study workingmen who will go back to their old occupations. In 1913, partly by the aid of the Leicester Town Council, a Tutorial Class student came to Trinity College and for two years did admirable work, mainly in economic subjects. No further step has been taken in this direction, and the matter is encompassed by obvious difficulties. It is a great problem of the future, but many Cambridge men will not be satisfied till it has been solved on lines which are satisfactory from both the democratic and educational standpoints.

D. H. S. CRANAGE.

DURHAM.

Durham University is unique among British Universities in that, whilst being of comparatively modern creation, its charter having been granted in 1837 by William IV., it has connections leading back to the 13th century. A Hall for Durham students was founded at Oxford about the end of that century, and was refounded, still at Oxford, a century later as Durham College by Bishop Hatfield. The Reformation deprived the Abbey of Durham of its revenues, however, and Durham College became Trinity College in 1555 on a new foundation. Both Henry VIII. and Cromwell are said to have intended founding a college in Durham itself, but nothing was done until 1831, when the Dean and Chapter of Durham promulgated the scheme which led to the charter of 1837. The University was ecclesiastical in its inception, the Dean and Chapter of Durham Cathedral being Governors, but the actual administration is in the hands of the Warden, a Senate, and Convocation. As at Oxford, disciplinary matters are confided to two Proctors, nominated annually by the Warden. The needs of the district are those connected with mining and engineering, and instruction in these subjects was commenced as early as 1837, but subsequently relinquished. In 1871 the University co-operated with the North of England Institute of Mining and Mechanical Engineers in the foundation of a College of Science—the Armstrong College—at Newcastle-on-Tyne. This college forms the scientific side of the University, and was incorporated in it in 1874. Other institutions forming part of the University are Bishop Hatfield's Hall (1846), St. Chad's Hall (1904), St. John's Hall (1909), and the Women's Hostel

(1899) at Durham, and the Durham College of Medicine (1851) at Newcastle.

In 1895 degrees were established for women, who may now take any courses except those in theology.

EARLY EXTENSION WORK.

(COMMUNICATED BY DR. JEVONS.)

In 1886 the University of Durham undertook to give outside Durham evening lectures and such instruction as was given to students in Durham. After attending such lectures for two years, and passing the necessary examinations, such students were admissible to the final year's course of study in the University, and after a residence of not less than three terms were eligible for the final examination for the degree of B.A. Evening lectures under this scheme were given in Sunderland by the University classical tutor, Mr. F. B. Jevons, and some students eventually proceeded to the B.A. It proved, however, impossible to keep the scheme in operation long, partly because a knowledge of both Latin and Greek was required of the students, and partly because a year's residence in Durham was demanded. But the scheme included some provisions which since then the Board of Education has required of University Tutorial Classes as conditions of earning the grants offered by the Board. Thus the University required that : (a) " Before or after each lecture a class shall be held by the lecturer for catechetical or informal teaching, in which each student shall receive individual teaching." (b) " In the subject-matter of each lecture questions shall be set. The student shall submit his or her answers to the lecturer for correction or comment." The scheme, therefore, though it failed to survive, has its importance as one of the early stages in the process outside of the development of University Tutorial Classes.

THE UNIVERSITY OF DURHAM JOINT COMMITTEE, 1911—1916.

BY MISS STEVENSON (ARMSTRONG COLLEGE).

Until 1916, when new Joint Committees were formed for the Durham and Newcastle divisions separately, the Tutorial Classes in connection with the University of Durham were all managed by one Joint Committee, which held its meetings in turn in one of the colleges of the University or in a building belonging to one of the bodies represented on the Committee. The bodies were, in 1911, the Durham Miners' Association, the Northumberland Miners' Association, the National Amalgamated Union of Labourers, the Durham County Club and Institute Union, the Boilermakers' Society, the Co-operative Union, the Adult School Union, and the Workers' Educational Association. Beside the members directly connected with the University the Secretaries of the Northumberland and the Newcastle Education Authorities and the Durham County Higher Education Secretary were members of the Committee. The Joint Secretaries were Mr. J. W. Lee (succeeded in 1915 by Mr. J. G. Trevena) and Professor Hallsworth.

This Joint Committee did not entirely restrict its activities to Tutorial Classes. In November, 1911, it accepted responsibility for preliminary courses of lectures, which were being arranged in different centres, on the understanding that the local expenses should be borne by the local body through whom the courses were arranged. In January, 1912, it sanctioned special short courses of lectures at Blyth, Jarrow, and Hebburn.

But the record of this Joint Committee is mainly a record of increasing activity in starting and maintaining Tutorial Classes and of increasing need of funds. The principle on which it worked was that no new class should be started without financial responsibility being undertaken for it by the local organisation. The sum to be raised locally was fixed first at £40, and later at £55 per class per year for three years. The local organisation was also to be responsible for the provision of a class-room and all other local arrangements. It was expected that the greater part of the cost might be defrayed by grants from the Board of Education, grants from Local Education Authorities, and contributions from co-operative societies, Trade Unions, etc. The Joint Committee was to provide the tutor and the class library. The need of books is now largely met by the Central Library for Students; but in these earlier times we find the Joint Committee making special grants for books and raising a fund to buy books by an appeal to private individuals.

Grants were received from the following sources : The Gilchrist Trustees, Armstrong College, the Durham Colleges, the Central Office of the W.E.A., the Local Education Authorities of Wallsend, Middlesbrough, West, and from Durham County Council for classes held within its administrative area. The Northumberland County Council showed no interest in Tutorial Classes, and the Newcastle Education Committee took the view that such classes should not be directly recognised by it, and could be helped by Armstrong College out of the grant given to the college by the city.

The subjects in which classes were held were : Modern History, Industrial History, Economics, Social Problems, and Literature. The tutors were : Mr. Meredith Atkinson (who left in 1914 to become Director of Tutorial Classes in the University of Sydney), Mr. P. A. Brown, Professor Hallsworth, Professor Vickers, Dr. Lilias Macgregor, Mr. J. W. Ramsbottom, Mr. R. Wilson, Mr. Dainton, and Mr. Moles. The number of classes held in 1911-1912 was nine, and in 1912-1913 was nine, and in 1913-1914 was twelve. This progress was checked by the war. Mr. Brown at once joined the Army, never to return. Mr. Ramsbottom also enlisted. New classes which had been planned could not be started. Mr. Wilson was, however, appointed as a whole-time tutor to take four classes. In 1913-1914 there were eight classes, and in 1915-1916 there were four.

Successful Summer Schools were held under the Joint Committee in 1913 and 1914. After the war began it was not found possible to arrange for them.

The last meeting of this Committee was held in May, 1916. Its last piece of work was to co-operate with the north-eastern district of the W.E.A. in arranging for the citizen lectures given in connection with the meeting of the British Association in Newcastle in September, 1916.

LEEDS.

The University of Leeds grew out of the Yorkshire College, with which was incorporated the Leeds School of Medicine. In 1887 the Yorkshire College was admitted as a constituent part of the Victoria University. In 1904 it received its charter as a separate University. No provision was made in the charter for the representation of the working class upon the University Court or Council, though in practice Labour has had some indirect representation through the medium of the provision for the representation of local authorities. On the other hand, ancient companies and modern industrial concerns found a place. In addition to this, all donors of £1,000 become life members of the Court, and any " company, society, or partnership firm " giving a donation of a similar amount has the right to nominate a member of the Court. The University Council, which is the important administrative body, is more strictly representative. There are a considerable number of " Advisory Committees," but of these the Committee for Tutorial Classes and Extension lectures is the only one on which workpeople are directly represented.

The University has developed on lines very similar to those of other Northern Universities. It may, roughly, be stated to be an institution of science, medicine, and technology, to which has been added an arts side. This affects considerably the kind of source from which students are drawn. Certainly the conception which is often voiced in Labour circles of the University being the preserve of the nobility and the very rich does not apply to the University of Leeds. Although exact statistics are not available, it is quite clear that the great bulk of the students are drawn from the homes of the professional, trading, and better paid wage-earning classes. In the year 1913-14 (the session immediately preceding the war) the number of full-time students in the University was 663. Of these 49 held Fellowships, Scholarships, and Studentships awarded by the University itself, and 131 were there by virtue of holding Scholarships awarded by local authorities. There were also about 150 King's Scholars, but some of these probably held other Scholarships, and are, therefore, included in the preceding figures. In addition, there were some Training College Studentships given by the local authorities to holders of King's Scholarships, and a large number of evening studentships and exhibitions given in aid of attendance at short courses.

The evening courses in science and technology appear to be attended almost entirely by the industrial class. The fee per session for whole or part group course is 10s. 6d., and in many cases even this is not paid. The number of evening students in 1913-14 was 217.

The Agricultural Department has, both within the University buildings and in its extra-mural work throughout the country, done a considerable amount of work specially designed to meet the needs of working people. The lectures and other work on gardening, stock rearing, etc., reach many hundreds of people each year.

In common with the other modern Universities, the University of Leeds, as yet, can scarcely claim to be a competitor of the ancient Universities in its influence upon the arts and in providing the personnel of a political governing class. Whether it is possible to have a free growth of ideas on political, economic, and philosophic subjects in an institution which is predominantly technological may be a matter for debate, but it is true that compared with the provision of aids to material production the arts side appears to be somewhat starved and ill-developed. Probably this side has not had sufficient intimate touch with the outside world to exert the full measure of its influence, but in the University Tutorial Class movement has been opened one channel which will have a beneficial effect in this connection.

LEEDS UNIVERSITY AND THE TUTORIAL CLASS MOVEMENT.

The Tutorial Class movement and the work of the Workers' Educational Association generally has, from the outset, had the strong support of some individual members of the University staff, who have given very valuable assistance. The attitude of the University as an official body is more difficult to define. It agreed quite readily to set up a Tutorial Classes Committee, and the chief officers of the University have been active workers on that Committee. At the same time the financial assistance has been meagre. The grant by the University Council towards the cost of Tutorial Classes was, in the early years, £50 per annum. More recently it has been £150 per annum, with an additional £20 towards the upkeep of the travelling library. How this compares with the general expenditure of the University may be gathered from the following items taken from the accounts for the year 1913-14.

Salaries of staff, £43,356 (this does not include the salaries of Tutorial Class tutors, which are paid by the Committee); stamps, £307; telephones, £115.

As a Tutorial Class under the Leeds Committee costs between £65 and £70 per annum, of which £30 comes from the Board of Education, heavy contributions have had to be obtained from Local Education Authorities and local centres of the movement. There are hopes, however, that the University contributions will, in the future, be considerably increased. Very recently a special grant of £200 has been given to meet a deficit in the accounts of the Committee and to assist in the establishment of new classes.

In spite of financial stringency, the Tutorial Class movement has progressed and is ever widening its influence. Even the rupture between the Workers' Educational Association and the University during the Leeds municipal strike did not stop an increase of classes. The quality of the work cannot be denied. In the session 1916-17 there were 14 classes at work with an average attendance percentage on *all* students varying from 96.8 to 73.9. The average for the whole of the classes under the Committee was 81.2.

The University has always readily granted the free use of rooms for class and general Workers' Educational Association purposes.

University Extension lectures, as distinct from Tutorial Classes, do not excite much demand. As the cost of these lectures is wholly borne by the local centres this is not surprising. It would probably be possible to increase the demand from working-class societies for Extension lectures very considerably if the Board of Education and the Universities were prepared to spend money on them.

Quite recently the University has held special courses for the training of welfare workers. This work is intended to be for the benefit of working people, but as among working people themselves there is a divided opinion as to the value to them of some of the manifestations of the welfare movement, it would be premature to discuss the value of the University contribution to this work.

G. H. T.

LIVERPOOL.

University College, Liverpool, was founded by Royal Charter in 1881, and three years later became a constituent college of the Victoria University. By the Liverpool University Act of 1903, however, the University College was separated from the Victoria University, and it received an independent charter in the same year. That charter establishes a system of government on the lines usually followed in the modern Universities (see Manchester).· Affiliated or partly affiliated institutions are St. Aidan's College, Birkenhead, Edge Hill and Mount Pleasant Training Colleges, and the Harris Institute, Preston.

Degrees are granted in arts (including architecture and commercial science), science, medicine (including hygiene and diplomas in public health, tropical medicine, etc.), dental surgery, veterinary science, law, and engineering. There is an important School of Tropical Medicine.

The students number over 1,000, of whom some 800 prepare for degrees or diplomas of the University. The degree in engineering is of increasing popularity.

LIVERPOOL AND THE W.E.A.

By G. W. Coupland, M.A., B.Sc., Litt.D.

The aims and objects of that portion of the W.E.A. movement which is closely connected with the University of Liverpool are those of the movement in the country at large, and its recent activities have been, like those of other sections, influenced and shaped by the peculiar circumstances of the time. Thus a large number of lectures and special classes have been held, beyond the ordinary courses, on problems of import for the present and future. With regard to the more normal work of the W.E.A., it may be briefly said here that in a geographical region stretching from Barrow to Crewe there has ,been no slackening of effort during the war. Further, and this is essential, there is at the present time a clear recognition on the part of those concerned, both in the University and outside it, of the enormous importance of the work, of the possibilities of its almost boundless extension in the future in this area, of the need for directing an increasingly large measure of University activity to this great task. There are many obstacles in the path of advance. All can and will be passed. One only will have a considerable retarding effect—the lack of tutors. It is to be hoped that the W.E.A. will speedily apply itself to the consideration of this cardinal difficulty, for most of our hopes and schemes are vain until it be removed.

[Two Tutorial Classes were started in Liverpool in 1909 and progress was rapid. In 1911-12 there were eight, in 1913-14 twice as many, and a maximum of 19 was reached in 1914-15. Since then the war has, of course, interfered here as in so many other useful things. Economic subjects have been the chief, but not the exclusive studies of the Lancashire and Cheshire students.]

LONDON.

London University dates from the period when, debarred from entry to the existing Universities, or dubious of the value of the education these provided, certain elements of the population founded schools on the joint stock principle. Jews and Unitarians were shut out from Oxford, Cambridge, and Durham, or were under certain disabilities there; the followers of Bentham did not find there the kind of education they required. University College School was a " joint stock " school founded by such men in 1822, which was opened as " The University of London " in 1828, but did not receive official sanction until 1836, when it was incorporated as " University College, London." At the same time, the University of London was instituted as a body for granting degrees by examination. The " cits' " University was heavily satirised. " What is the good of the mathematics, classics, or political economy taught to a youth weighing tea and sugar? " asked the author of a pamphlet " On the Probable Failure " of the new University. Barham (" Ingoldsby ") wrote " The London University; or Stinkomalee Triumphans : An Ode to be Performed on the Opening of New College of Grafton Street East " :—

" Whene'er with pitying eye I view
Each operative sot in town,
I smile to think how wondrous few
Get drunk, who study at the U-
niversity we-ve got in town."

. . . .

" There's Jerry Bentham and his crew,
Names ne'er to be forgot in town !
In swarms like Banquo's long is-sue,
Turk, Papist, Infidel, and Jew
Come trooping on to join the U-
niversity we've got in town."

In spite, however, of furious opposition from the products of the older Universities, due largely to the religious quarrel—for the latter were strongly Anglican—but perhaps most largely to a typically English form of snobbery, the University went ahead under a State-created Senate, the constitution of which was intended to safeguard the nation from all probable or possible evil consequences. From 1836 to 1858 its functions were limited to the examination of the students of certain affiliated colleges, but in the latter year it was allowed to examine anybody in almost anything. Consequently there have developed external and internal sides of the University, with external and internal examinations, the former being open to anyone, anywhere, whether a prescribed course of study has been undertaken or not.

In 1878 the whole University system of examination, degrees, honours, and prizes was thrown open to women. London has thus the credit of being the first University in Great Britain thoroughly to recognise the importance of the higher education of women.

Practically the only tie between the University and the affiliated institutions, down to 1900, was the loose yet galling one of examination, and in that year a reconstitution took place, by which a number of these institutions have been recognised as " schools of the

University." Since then three institutions—University College, Gower Street, W.C. (1907), King's College, and King's College for Women, Strand, W.C. (1910)—have been incorporated in the University. The recognised "schools of the University " are :—

The Imperial College of Science and Technology, Imperial Institute Road, S.W., including the Royal College of Science and the Royal School of Mines, Exhibition Road, S.W., and the City and Guilds (Engineering) College, Exhibition Road, S.W.

Royal Holloway College for Women, Englefield Green, Surrey.

Bedford College for Women, Regent's Park.

East London College, Mile End Road, E.

London School of Economics, Clare Market, Kingsway, W.C. 2.

The S.E. Agricultural College, Wye, Kent.

Westfield College, Kiddespere Avenue, Finchley Road, Hampstead.

London Day Training College, Southampton Row, W.C.

New College, Finchley Road, Hampstead, N.W. (Congregational).

Hackney College, Hampstead (Congregational).

Regent's Park College (Baptist).

King's College, Theological Department, Strand, W.C. (Church of England).

Wesleyan College, Richmond.

St. John's Hall, Highbury (Church of England).

St. Bartholomew's Hospital Medical School, W. Smithfield, E.C.

St. Thomas's Hospital Medical School, Albert Embankment, S.E.

Westminster Hospital Medical School, Caxton Street, S.W.

Guy's Hospital Medical School, Borough, S.E.

St. George's Hospital Medical School, Hyde Park Corner, S.W.

London Hospital Medical School, Turner Street, Mile End, E.

Middlesex Hospital Medical School, Union Street, W.

Charing Cross Hospital Medical School, Charing Cross, W.C.

London School of Medicine for Women (Royal Free Hospital), 8, Hunter Street, W.C.

University College Hospital Medical School, University Street, W.C.

King's College Hospital Medical School, Denmark Hill, S.E.

St. Mary's Hospital Medical School, Praed Street, Paddington, W.

London School of Tropical Medicine, Albert Docks, E.

Lister Institute of Preventive Medicine, Chelsea Bridge Road, S.W.

Royal Army Medical College, Grosvenor Road, S.W.

Royal Dental Hospital and London School of Dental Surgery, 32, Leicester Square, W.C.

Naval Medical School, Greenwich.

National Dental Hospital and College, 187-191, Great Portland Street, W.

There are also about 30 institutions which have recognised teachers of the University, among which Goldsmiths' College, New Cross, S.E., was presented to the University by the Goldsmiths' Company in 1904, and is now an important training college for teachers, with science, engineering, and building departments in addition.

The University itself is inadequately housed in the pretentious Imperial Institute, South Kensington, and the problem of securing a more suitable building, or a site for a new erection excited some controversy before the war. The chief suggestions were that Somerset House be taken over, that an entirely new building be erected on a site facing the Embankment, and that the new headquarters be erected outside London.

The government is on lines established by the London University Act of 1898 and the statutes adopted under it.

The " supreme governing body and executive " of the University is the Senate of some 54 members, presided over by the Chancellor. Four members are appointed by the King with the advice of the Privy Council, 16 elected by Convocation, and 16 by the Faculties. The Royal Colleges of Physicians and of Surgeons nominate two each, as do also University College, King's College, and the Incorporated Law Society. Each of the four Inns of Court sends one member; the Corporation of London appoints one, two represent the London County Council, and one is sent by the Council of the City and Guilds of London Institute.

There are three standing Committees of the Senate, the Academic Council, the Council for External Students, and a standing Board to promote the extension of University teaching. Their names indicate their functions.

At the head of the University is the Chancellor, who is elected by Convocation for life. The Vice-Chancellor, appointed by the Senate from its own body, acts in case of the absence of the Chancellor or during a vacancy. His term of office is one year.

Convocation comprises all registered graduates, plus the Chancellor and other officers. It elects its own Chairman and Deputy-Chairman.

The Faculties are in arts, science, theology, laws, medicine, music, engineering, economics, and political economy (including commerce and industry). Except in medicine, mining, and architecture, external students are admitted to all degree examinations without regard to the courses of study they have pursued. This feature of the University has been the subject of much criticism in recent years. On the one hand, it is claimed that the external student, missing the very real advantages of the corporate and social life of the University, cannot usually attain the intellectual standard which a London degree should represent, and that the external degree is obtainable by mere " cramming." On the other hand, it is retorted that if by " cramming " it is possible to obtain a degree, the examiners are to be blamed. It is certain that the external degrees of London incite very large numbers of students to pursue intense courses of study, privately or with such help as their neighbourhood affords, who would otherwise perhaps waste their energy in diffusion, and the abolition of these degrees would be felt to be a national loss.

LONDON UNIVERSITY AND TUTORIAL CLASSES.

The beginnings of the Tutorial Class movement in London may be traced to a small body of students who gathered round Professor Geddes at Battersea in 1907. But it was in July, 1909, that the Joint Committee for the Promotion of the Higher Education of Working People was formed on the usual basis, and immediately the Committee began its work of ascertaining what demand existed in London for Tutorial Classes. The result was prompt and decisive; and consequently, instead of the two or three classes contemplated, five classes were arranged, four of them to study Industrial History and Economics. From that time there was steady growth up till the outbreak of war. In 1913-14 there were 30 Tutorial Classes under the

London Joint Committee, the first residential Summer School had been held, and various experiments in the development of the work had been made. When the war came, London had to bear the full brunt of it, and the utmost efforts were needed to keep classes going. At present (April, 1918) 19 classes and two preparatory classes are finishing their session's work on the whole with credit and success. The proportion of women students is much larger (some classes have been specially started for them), and the average age of the men students is higher than was formerly the case. The area of subject has been widened—this year three classes have been studying Psychology on experimental lines, several classes have seriously tackled the Problems of Social, Political, and Economic Reconstruction; and there have been classes in History (including Modern European History), Sociology, Biology, Economics, and Literature. A Literature Class has produced a magazine.

Among the important questions engaging the attention of the Committee before the war was that of advanced study. There is nothing better being done for evening students than Tutorial Classes, but the system is never affirmed to be ideal. It is the first fruits; the promise of greater achievements to come. Several London classes in their fourth year (and even in their third year) have undertaken seminar work which gave students the opportunity of concentrating on some one specific subject. Several students went to courses at the London School of Economics and some received private tuition from distinguished scholars, such as G. M. Trevelyan, G. P. Gooch, and R. H. Tawney. The question of post-Tutorial work will require to be worked out in the future.

When the war broke out 20 or 30 London students and tutors were in the middle of an unforgettable fortnight at Eton; it was the first residential London Summer School. It has been impossible to repeat that wonderful experience, but year after year the Saturday Summer School has been held, and for four Saturdays in the summer various University buildings in London have opened their doors to the frankly democratic life of the Tutorial Classes and the W.E.A. The greatest lecturers in the country have come to the school.

With all its amazing complexities and baffling difficulties London will present after the war a tremendous opportunity for Tutorial Classes, and for work at both ends of that scale—for more frankly elementary work and for more specialised and advanced work. If the standard can be kept high and even raised, if the corporate side of the work can be emphasised, and if the education can be related both to the finest sort of individual culture and to the elevation of social life, the movement in London may enter on a larger era of usefulness in the near future.

MANCHESTER.

In 1846, John Owens, of Manchester, bequeathed a sum of almost a hundred thousand pounds for the foundation of a college to give instruction in " such branches of learning as are usually taught in the English Universities." To the Owens College, thus founded, was amalgamated in 1872 the Manchester Royal School of Medicine, and in the following year building was begun on the present site. Since then the story is of continued extension. In 1880 the Victoria

University was founded by Royal Charter, and Owens became a constituent college. A clause in the Charter permitted the admission of other similar institutions, and in 1884 University College, Liverpool, in 1887 Yorkshire College, Leeds, were so admitted.

The development of these northern towns, and the need for specialisation with regard to the industries of their respective areas, however, brought about a desire for change, and in 1903 University College, Liverpool, applied for the foundation of a separate University in that town. In the result, three Universities were created from the constituent parts of the one. Manchester retained the title (the Victoria University of Manchester), but in 1903 and 1904 respectively the Liverpool and Leeds Universities were established.

The authorities of the University are the Chancellor, Vice-Chancellor, and Pro-Vice-Chancellors, the Court of Governors, the Council (23 members), the Senate (46 members), the Boards of Faculties (arts, science, law, music, medicine, commerce, theology, and technology), and Convocation. The executive body is the Council, which consists of the Chancellor, Vice-Chancellor, at least four of the members of the Senate who are members of the Court, and of other members of the Court chosen by the Court to secure the representation of Convocation and of the Manchester City Corporation. The University Court is a much larger body, constituted on lines adopted in most of the more modern English Universities. Besides the officers of the University and representatives of the Senate, of the Boards of Faculties and of Convocation, there are five members appointed by the Lord President of the Council, representing the central government, and others appointed by various local authorities, the intention being clearly to keep the University and its studies in constant contact with the general life of the community.

The total number of students reaches close upon 2,000, and includes about 500 women. Medicine attracts the largest number, but it is closely followed, as would be expected, by science. About 150 of the women are students of the University Training College attached to the University.

MANCHESTER AND THE W.E.A.

By G. W. Daniels.

In common with the majority of English Universities, the most important way in which the University of Manchester offers facilities for adult education is by the provision of Tutorial Classes, organised in connection with the Workers' Educational Association. The scheme was inaugurated in April, 1909, by a Joint Committee, consisting of representatives of the University, the Co-operative Union, the National Conference of Friendly Societies, the Northern Counties Amalgamated Association of Weavers, the Miners' Federation of Lancashire and Cheshire, the Lancashire and Cheshire Federation of Trades and Labour Councils, and the Workers' Educational Association. Since its formation the Joint Committee has been constituted of an equal number of representatives of workers' organisations and of the University, with the Vice-Chancellor as chairman and a representative of Labour as vice-chairman.

In the first session (1909-10) nine classes were carried on in various Lancashire towns, and the number gradually increased until the session 1914-15. In the two following sessions, owing to the crisis through which the country is passing, a reduction took place, but in the present session (1917-18) ten new classes have been organised, bringing the total number near to the pre-war figure.

During the nine sessions in which the Joint Committee has been in existence 45 Tutorial Classes, taking a three years' course of study, have been established in 24 centres. Of these classes 27 have successfully completed their three years' course, while two proceeded to a fourth year; five disbanded after two years' study, and the remainder (14 in number) are now in existence. In addition, six advanced classes (composed of students who have completed a three years' course and who are considered to have reached a stage when they can profitably undertake advanced study) have been conducted, also 14 special " one-year " classes. The following figures show the number of classes and students (not including the one-year classes) in each session since the Joint Committee was formed :—

		Classes.	Students.
Session	1909-10	9	299
,,	1910-11	13	380
,,	1911-12	14	348
,,	1912-13	15	402
,,	1913-14	16	366
,,	1914-15	17	317
,,	1915-16	13	231
,,	1916-17	8	146
,,	1917-18	14	360

The subjects of study, chosen by the students, in the 51 classes comprehended in the above table show the following selection :—

Industrial History and Economics	29	classes.
Political History	5	,,
Psychology	8	,,
Literature	5	,,
Philosophy	3	,,
Natural Science	1	,,

In addition to the work undertaken by the Joint Committee in the establishment of Tutorial Classes, the consistent support which has been given to the Bangor Summer School, since its inception in 1913, ought to be mentioned. Each year a substantial sum has been granted towards the expenses of organisation out of the funds placed at the disposal of the Joint Committee by the Council of the University, and several members of the Joint Committee have taken an active part in the work of the Committee which is responsible for the Summer School. In view of the circumstances which have obtained since 1914, there is much ground for encouragement in what has been, and is being, done by the Manchester University Joint Committee, but those who are acquainted with the vast population working and living in the area of which Manchester is the University centre know that, as yet, only a tentative approach has been made to the large problem of providing facilities for the study of those subjects in which adults have shown themselves to be interested. Sufficient experience has been gained, however, to warrant the belief that solution of the problem of adult education in such an area lies largely with the extension of the range of subjects studied in the classes and an increase in the number of classes formed. It is evident that there is a latent demand for such classes ready to express itself wherever opportunity is presented. In the formation of the Joint Committee, in its composition, and in the interest which has been taken in its work, the University of Manchester has shown that it is alive to its responsibilities as regards adult education, and there is every reason to believe that any future demands made upon it will meet with a ready response.

OXFORD.

The beginnings of Oxford University are to be found in corporations or guilds of teachers and scholars, traceable as early as the end of the 12th century, and perhaps even earlier, for Theobaldus Stampensis and Robert Pullein are recorded to have taught in 1120 and 1133 respectively. By the 13th century the University had become of sufficient importance to warrant the attention of Kings and Popes— the former because the feuds between " town " and " gown " became at times serious enough to be of national importance. It is said that the number of scholars was to be reckoned in thousands, and there was as yet little in the way of a disciplinary code. During the 13th century the four great orders of mendicant friars were attracted to Oxford, and their schools and lectures seem to have been exceptionally popular. With them two of the most well-known names in mediæval learning, Roger Bacon and Friar Bungay, are associated. Other orders founded schools at Oxford also; the Benedictines quite early, the Cistercians in 1437. But the Friars' Preachers were important enough in the 14th century to make a bold bid for control of the University, only countered after a hard struggle.

The Reformation brought changes; many of the colleges were dissolved, some even dismantled, and the reaction under Mary was not long-lived enough entirely to restore them to their former position. After that the Protestant colleges—first of which was Jesus in 1571— were established, but only slowly. Though the early Stuart times saw Wadham and Pembroke founded, the Civil Wars put an end to the encouragement of learning for almost a century. From the Stuart time is to be dated the peculiarly English development of a University of *colleges*, rather than of teachers and students. The new system, by restricting students to the lectures provided by their own college, had very ill effects, and has now long been abandoned in practice at Oxford, though, of course, the lecturers at each college regard the student members as their particular charge.

The colleges are, in the order of their foundation, University College (founded 872(?) and endowed in 1249), Balliol (founded 1263-8), Merton (1264), Exeter (1314), Oriel (1326), Queen's (1340), New (1379), Lincoln (1427), All Souls (1437), Magdalen (1458), Brasenose (1509), Corpus Christi (1516), Christ Church (1546), Trinity (1554-5), St. John's (1555), Jesus (1571), Wadham (1612), Pembroke (1624), Worcester (1714), Hertford (1740), Keble (1870). There is also a Public Hall, St. Edmund Hall (1269), and three private halls (Marcon's, Pope's, and Parker's) under licensed masters.

Since 1910 certain societies for women students are " recognised " : Lady Margaret Hall (1878), Somerville College (1879), St. Hugh's College (1886), St. Hilda's Halls (1893), and the Society of Oxford

Home-Students. Women are not eligible either for membership of the University or for admission to degrees, but they have, since 1884, been gradually admitted to all examinations in arts and music. The University diplomas (except the one in military science) and some of the certificates are open to women.

The colleges are corporate bodies themselves, and are not directly governed by the laws and regulations of the University. All members of the colleges are also members of the University.

The government of the University (under the Oxford University Act of 1854 and the Universities of Oxford and Cambridge Act of 1877, and in part under the Statutes of Archbishop Laud) is vested in the Chancellor, the High-Steward, the Vice-Chancellor, the two Proctors, and in certain bodies. Of these, the *Hebdomadal Council* (the Chancellor, Vice-Chancellor and the ex-Vice-Chancellor, the Proctors, and 18 other members elected by Congregation) is the most important, since it has the initiative in most matters concerning the University. Its suggested legislation is submitted to the *Congregation* (consisting for the most part of the teaching staff and administrative officials of the colleges and the University), which has the power of adopting, amending, or rejecting the proposals. Statutes which are adopted by Congregation are generally submitted to *Convocation*, a much larger body, comprising all the Masters of Art and the Doctors of the various Faculties who are registered in the books of the University.

There is also a General Board of Faculties, which may initiate proposals with regard to studies and examinations.

The chief executive officers are the Vice-Chancellor, who is nominated annually by the Chancellor from among the Heads of colleges, and the Proctors, who are elected annually by the colleges and halls in turn. The Chancellor is elected for life by Convocation.

The Faculties are Arts (including music and education), natural science (including rural economy and forestry), theology, law, and medicine. The number of undergraduates in 1913-14 was 3,838, to which must be added 391 women students in the various recognised societies.

The University conducts local examinations and grant certificates in four grades, and, in conjunction with Cambridge, will undertake the examination of such schools of the highest grades as wish it. In this connection also certificates are granted.

OXFORD UNIVERSITY TUTORIAL CLASSES COMMITTEE.

It was to the University of Oxford that the Workers' Educational Association in 1907 made their memorable demand which marked a new phase in English education and led to the establishment of the Tutorial Class movement. The demand was met, a Joint Committee of Labour and University representatives set up, and two experimental classes—one at Rochdale and the other at Longton—established in January, 1908, under the tutorship of Mr. R. H. Tawney. It was soon evident that the desire of working people for continuous intensive study was a real one, and until the work was taken up by the other Universities the resources of the Oxford Committee were strained to the utmost, and, as will be seen by the particulars set out below, they rapidly extended their operations. The number of Oxford classes conducted each session since the beginning is shown in the following table :—

Year.	No. of Classes.	
1908 (January-April)	2	
1908-9	8	
1909-10	12	
1910-11	14	
1911-12	16	and 3 provisional classes.
1912-13	17	
1913-14	18	
1914-15	14	and 2 provisional classes.
1915-16	11	and 2 provisional classes.
1916-17	10	and 2 provisional classes
1917-18	11	

The reduction in the number of classes since 1914 has been due to the war, and arises out of causes which scarcely need explanatior., the chief of which was financial, one of the results of the war being to reduce the Committee's income and obliging them to cut their garment according to their cloth. The Committee, however, being thoroughly convinced of the educational value of their work, its importance in the national scheme of education and the possibilities of its future development, determined to keep as much continuity as possible. They have, for instance, in co-operation with the W.E.A., encouraged groups of students, for whom a Tutorial Class cannot for the time being be provided, to keep together as voluntary study classes, and have given what help they could by lending books, providing syllabuses, and arranging for occasional visits of tutors whenever opportunity offered. In 1910 the Committee initiated an important development in the shape of a residential Summer School at Oxford for students from the classes. The idea was that students should be brought into actual contact with the University, should have opportunities for individual teaching by scholars and specialists in their particular subjects, and to meet and exchange ideas with students from other centres. The school was necessarily experimental in the beginning, but the appreciation of the students and the educational results convinced the Committee that it would form in the future one of its most important activities. This conviction has been fully borne out, and the school has since continued to be an annual feature of the Committee's work. Several of the colleges have from year to year given facilities for the school : Balliol College from the first has placed accommodation at its disposal both for lectures and tuition and residential purposes. New College has also provided accommodation for each of these purposes, and Christ Church for residence. Up to date about 350 students have resided in college during their summer course. For the first few years until Summer Schools were established by other Joint Committees the strain on the Oxford School was very great. As the other Summer Schools came into being and the strain became reduced, the Oxford Committee began to consider on what line their school could most usefully develop. This seemed to be in the provision of intensive study for students who could stay at the school for a month or longer, as well as provision for short-period students to a slightly more limited extent than in the early years. The war interrupted this development, but it will probably be continued when normal times return. A great part of the work of tuition and lectures at the school has been done voluntarily by resident Professors and tutors in the University, who have rendered invaluable service. The following table shows the number of students attending the school since 1910 :—

Year.	No. of Students.
1910	89
1911	173
1912	215
1913	138
1914	140
1915	49
1916	74
1917	70 (estimated).

Thus nearly 1,000 students, mostly Trade Unionists, have passed through the school, and of these about 70 have stayed for a month or longer, and been enabled to follow a co-ordinated course of study suitable to their individual needs. The school had endeavoured to meet the particular educational requirement of each individual student, and the bulk of the work has been done by individual tuition.

There is one particular in which it is recognised that the work of the Oxford classes needs greatly strengthening, and that is in the systematised provision of a greater amount of individual tuition throughout the three years' course. This obviously is a most difficult problem to solve in view of the fact that the students' time is restricted to the scanty leisure remaining after the working day and that tutors' opportunities are limited by the exigencies of travelling. Efforts have been made not only to provide more individual tuition, but to prevent the classes becoming stereotyped into one hour's lecture and one hour's discussion, and new experiments in class methods have always been encouraged. In a few years before the war a nearer, but by no means complete approach was made towards attaining a satisfactory system of individual tuition. Consultation with tutors and classes has shown the nature of the difficulties and made clear that no one method can be applied to every class. During the war the solution is postponed, but this is a problem to which the Committee will give serious attention afterwards.

A feature of the Oxford work is the constant endeavour of the Joint Committee to keep in close touch with their classes—a desirable policy, as the centres are " far flung," ranging from Chatham and Bournemouth in the south, to Leeds and Lincoln in the north. For some time past it has been the custom of the Committee to invite delegates from their classes to meet them once a year at Oxford for the purpose of free discussion and exchange of opinion on the progress of the work. These meetings have proved of the greatest value and interest. It is also the practice of one or more members of the Committee to visit each class in its third year to form an opinion as to the general results of the course and elicit the views of students on matters of mutual concern. By these and other means the democratic nature of the classes is preserved, and the work shaped to the needs of the students. As regards the students themselves, they feel that the movement is their own, to make or to mar, and thus their sense of responsibility is deepened.

During 1916-17 Oxford was responsible for ten full Tutorial Classes and two provisional classes; and, in addition, provision was made in co-operation with the local W.E.A. branches for continued study in the cases of a few groups of old students who had passed through a Tutorial Class course, but for whom a class was not available for the time being. The total number of students enrolled was 306 (202 men and 104 women), of whom the great majority were manual workers, the following figures being illustrative of the occupations :—

Textile trades (spinners, weavers, carders, etc.), 28; engineers (fitters, iron turners, blacksmiths, etc.), 30; potting industry (pressers, casters, mouldmakers, gilders, decorators, etc.), 37; miners, etc., 11; railway servants, 5; bricklayers and plasterers, 5; carpenters and joiners, 5; tailors and tailoresses, 20; shop assistants, 11; shoe and leather workers, 5; printing trades, 5; house painters, 3; Trade Union organisers, 2; women (chiefly artisans' wives engaged in domestic duties), 21. The following, among other occupations, were also represented, viz., cardboard maker, baker, gas meter inspector, tramway pointsman, postman, milliner, basket maker, gardener, pedlar, carter, school attendance officer, butcher, and small cultivator. In addition, there were on an average three or four students in each class engaged, some in clerical work, and others in elementary school teaching.

There are signs of a growing educational demand on the part of women, and it is notable that one of the most successful of the Oxford classes last session was one composed almost entirely of working women.

The Joint Committee have stated their belief that there will be after the war a greatly increased demand upon the Universities by the workers for the provision of a " liberal education," and have expressed their hope to be able to take their full share in this extension. To make this possible Tutorial Class finance must be placed on a firmer footing, and it is hoped that this period of educational reconstruction will not be allowed to pass without that desirable object being effected. It is true that as regards Oxford, there will be great difficulties in increasing the contributions from the colleges and University. All the colleges are now practically empty of students and thus are faced with financial problems of their own, and it must be some time before the University can return to normal conditions. It is impossible to conclude this short review of the Oxford work without recording how greatly it has been indebted, especially in its formative period to the resource, the untiring energy and inspiration of Mr. A. Mansbridge, whose recent retirement from the Committee and from the position as Joint Hon. Secretary, which he had held since the beginning, is much regretted.

June, 1917.

OXFORD UNIVERSITY EXTENSION.

The University Extension movement for the provision of higher adult education began at Cambridge in 1873 and at Oxford in 1878. A special Delegacy for its control was set up at Oxford in 1892. The choice of lecturers and the control of finance is in the hands of Local Committees; in the year before the war (1913-14) Oxford had 114 of these in actual work. The lecturers are appointed by the Central

Authority, which also conducts the examination at the end of each course; every course consists of at least six lectures.

The method of instruction is as follows : When a course has been chosen a syllabus of it (60 copies) is sent down to guide the reading of students, and a library of books bearing on the subject. Every lecture is followed by a class, at which questions are asked and difficulties answered; the lecturer also sets and corrects essays for those who choose to do them. In 1913-14 Oxford had 41 lecturers engaged, 131 courses were given, and the number of students attending was about 12,500. The war has naturally caused some falling off in the number of students and lectures, but on the whole the work has been maintained.

The payment to lecturers varies with their position and experience; experience shows that the cost per lecture, including besides the lecturer's fee and expenses, room rent, advertising, etc., varies from £5 to £6 at most.

Meetings of students and lecturers are held at Oxford in August every other year, when courses of lectures are given on the various aspects of some special subject or subjects. Certificates of work done under certain conditions are recognised by the University as exempting from some of its own degree requirements.

The Secretary is Mr. J. A. R. Marriott, M.P., Fellow of Worcester College, Oxford, and the full title of the Delegacy is " for the extension of teaching beyond the limits of the University."

SHEFFIELD.

The University of Sheffield serves an area which has many peculiar features. In the industrial life of the city itself it might almost be said that there are two Sheffields.

While the armament and heavy steel industries show examples of the most advanced forms of large scale production and modern capitalism, the cutlery trade clings tenaciously to the system of small masters and to a type of industrial organisation having many features in common with that of the 18th Century. The city has two influential Co-operative Societies and there are two Trades Councils, i.e., the older " Federated Trades Council " and the newer " Trades and Labour Council."

Being situated at the extreme south-west of Yorkshire, the University includes in its area of influence South Yorkshire and parts of Derbyshire, Nottinghamshire, and Lincolnshire. Thus it serves an area predominantly occupied in mining, iron and steel, and agriculture.

It received its Charter in 1905 and was the successor to the University College of Sheffield. Like the other Yorkshire University, its technological side looms very large.

The constitution of the University Court is very wide and includes representatives of some purely Sheffield organisations, among which the Federated Trades Council finds a place. Donors of £1,000 in one sum or in instalments become life members of the Court, and even " every such donor making the requisite donation by Testament shall be entitled by Testament to appoint or to authorise his personal representatives on one occasion to appoint one person to be a member for life."

Five hundred pounds secures a place for ten years and every Corporate body of Association giving £1,000 may also nominate a member for a term of ten years. The University Council, which is the really important body, is more strictly representative.

The number of evening students attending the University is very large, particularly on the technological side. The following figures will emphasise this fact. In the year 1913-14 there were 317 full-time students attending courses for degrees or diplomas of University standard, and 117 students attending post-graduate courses. For the evening courses 1,290 students attended the Applied Science Department alone, while 250 took courses in Arts, Pure Science, and Law.

The fact that, apart from the Applied Science Department of the University, there is no good technical school in the city, accounts to a great degree for these large numbers, but even with an allowance on this score they still indicate that a substantial number of members of the working class must come into direct contact with some side of the University. The University has also been very ready to provide free popular lectures.

There are no statistics available as to the number of full-time students who formerly attended a public elementary school, but what evidence there is tends to show that it must be large. The amount received in fees in the year 1913-14 was £8,922, while on the other side of the account £2,077 was expended by the University itself in scholarships and prizes. In addition, scholarships were awarded by Local Authorities.

The amount of support which a modern University receives from public sources is often under-estimated. In 1913-14 the total income of the University of Sheffield was £50,434. Of this £14,595 came from the State and £17,726 from Local Authorities (£13,006 being from the city of Sheffield). Endowments provided £4,671, fees £8,922, and miscellaneous donations about £1,000. The rest mainly comprises payments for work done, bank balance brought forward, etc.

SHEFFIELD AND THE W.E.A.

The University has, particularly in more recent years, done its utmost to meet the demands for University Tutorial Classes. This side of its work has, however, peculiar difficulties to face. A large proportion of working people in the area are engaged in employment of a very arduous and exhausting kind. Further, the shift system is very common, and, although recent regulations of the Board of Education have made it possible to hold a class in duplicate, this merely mitigates the evil a little. An extensive application of the shift system in any district is a source of social disintegration. Women have their menfolk coming in to meals and sleep at all times of the day and night, and the same people can never be sure of meeting together twice consecutively. In spite of this the number of Tutorial Classes has steadily risen, even during the war, and in 1916-17 there were 14 classes at work.

The finances of the Tutorial Classes are merged in the ordinary accounts of the University and no limit has been set on the amount available for this purpose. Each item has, however, to be sanctioned by the University Council.

The Tutorial Classes Committee has not experienced any difficulty on this account. The Council has in recent years sanctioned each year the expenditure of £5 per class on the class library. A further £5 per class per year has been granted for summer school scholarships. For the year 1916-17 the total on these two items alone, if fully expended, will be £140. Contributions towards the cost of Tutorial Classes are received from the West Riding County Council. In other cases the University has borne the whole cost above the Board of Education grant, and no request is refused because a local contribution is not forthcoming.

The University has given further assistance to the work of the Tutorial Classes and the W.E.A. generally by the free loan of two houses near the University to be used as a W.E.A. House. The management of the House is under the control of the local branch of the W.E.A. As membership of the House is only 1s. per annum, and for this there is the use of a reference library, writing and conversation rooms, and admittance to weekly lectures, etc., it will be realised that this contribution by the University might be made of great value to working people. The free use of rooms in the University also is always readily granted.

THE UNIVERSITY COLLEGES.

EXETER.

The Royal Albert Memorial College was founded in 1865, and became a University College in 1901. Its most important feature is its work as a training college for teachers in elementary schools, but it also provides courses in preparation for the degrees of London University and the diplomas (in education) of London and Cambridge Universities and of the College of Perceptors. It conducts also a School of Art, Junior Engineering and Technical School, and it organises evening classes. Seven or eight hundred students are thus provided for.

NOTTINGHAM.

The University College of Nottingham was incorporated by Royal Charter in 1903. Courses of study are provided for the degrees of London University, for the diplomas of the college itself and of other institutions, and for the elementary teacher's certificate of the Board of Education. Among the diplomas granted by the college itself those in mining, engineering, and commerce have been established with an eye to the needs of the district.

The total number of students for the session 1917-18 was 1,838, of whom 514 were day and 1,324 evening students. During the war a Military Science Department has been organised.

The college takes part in the organisation of Tutorial Classes " anywhere in the East Midlands." Such classes are held at present in Leicester and Nottingham.

READING.

The history of Reading University College begins in 1860, when classes in science and art were begun under the late Science and Art Department of South Kensington. In 1885 Oxford University Extension lectures were begun, and the Reading University Extension

Centre-developed into considerable importance. In 1892 these two institutions were amalgamated. The Aylesbury Dairy Institute of the British Dairy Farmers' Association was moved to Reading and connected with the " University Extension College," as it was then called, in 1895. Incorporation (as a company limited by guarantee and with no power of taking profits) followed in 1896. In 1899 Oxford University admitted " Reading College " to affiliation, and the name was changed to University College, Reading, in 1902. A movement is now on foot to establish an independent University.

Preparation is given for London University degree examinations, the Cambridge teacher's certificate, and a number of diplomas (letters, science, agriculture, dairying, commerce, music, horticulture, and the fine arts). For agricultural studies the college has a farm at Shenfield. The college is also recognised as a training college for teachers.

Abour 1,000 students attend the various day or evening lectures.

Tutorial Classes are organised by a Joint Committee representing University College and the Reading Branch of the W.F.A.

SOUTHAMPTON.

The history of the Hartley University College, Southampton, is similar in some respects to that of University College, Reading. The Hartley Institute was founded in 1862, and incorporated as a University College in 1902. It is affiliated to Cambridge University.

The degrees for which preparation is given are those of London University. There is an important Department of Engineering, and the college is a recognised institution for the training of teachers in elementary schools. Some 600 students attend the evening classes, about 50 take the full courses in preparation for degrees, and as many more for the various diplomas and certificates of the college itself and of other institutions.

SCOTLAND.

ST. ANDREWS.

The University of St. Andrews is the oldest in Scotland, having been founded in 1411 by Kerry Wardlaw, Bishop of St. Andrews. It formerly included three colleges—St. Salvator (founded in 1450), St. Leonard (1512), and St. Mary (1537)—but the two first were united in 1747. The University College of Dundee was founded in 1880 and affiliated to the University in 1897.

Government is in the hands of the Chancellor, Rector, and the University Court—a composite body presided over by the Rector, and comprising the Principals of the colleges, the Lord Provosts of St. Andrews and of Dundee, and a number of Assessors nominated by the Chancellor and the Rector, or elected by the General Council or the Senatus Academicus. The Court's decisions require the assent of the Chancellor. The Senatus Academicus consists of the Principals and Professors of the University, and its function is to regulate and superintend the teaching and discipline. Its President is the Principal of the United Colleges of St. Salvator and St. Leonard, who is ex-officio

Principal of the University. There is a right of appeal in most cases from the Senatus Academicus to the Court. The General Council dates from the Universities (Scotland) Act of 1858, but its constitution has been several times changed since then. It comprises the Chancellor, the members of the Court, the Principals, and all graduates of the University, as well as matriculated students, who have fulfilled certain conditions. Its function is " to take into consideration all questions affecting the well-being and prosperity of the University, and to make representations from time to time on such questions to the University Court." It also elects the Chancellor of the University, who holds office for life. The Rector is elected by the matriculated students for a term of three years, and no Principal or Professor of any Scottish University is eligible. The Vice-Chancellor is nominated by the Chancellor.

In normal times the number of students received is about 500, of whom some 30 to 40 per cent. are women. The Faculties are arts, science (including agriculture and engineering), divinity, and medicine (including public health). Studies have a less " modern " bias than the new English Universities; the arts course is most commonly taken, though science and medicine attract fair numbers. St. Mary's College has been restricted to the teaching of theology since 1579. The University acts only as an examining body in the case of the well-known L.L.A. diploma for women.

GLASGOW.

Glasgow University dates from 1450, when it was created under a Bull by the Pope Nicholas V. From James VI., in 1577, it received a charter and a considerable addition to its funds, and since that time its history is of extension in every possible direction. In 1870 the University was transferred to new and more commodious premises, erected to the designs of Sir G. Gilbert Scott at Gilmorehill, at a cost of over half-a-million, but subsequently considerable extensions have been found necessary.

Since 1893 women students have matriculated and graduated from Queen Margaret College, which was amalgamated with the University in that year, and is now devoted exclusively to women's education and forms the Women's Department. The Royal Technical College, Glasgow, was affiliated in 1912.

Government is of the same type as that of St. Andrews (q.v.). The Rector is elected by the matriculated students divided into four " nations "—a curious feature.

The courses of study provided are of great variety, the University having, as have the younger English Universities, made provision for graduation in subjects intimately connected with the industry of the neighbourhood, the courses in marine engineering being especially important. Of the 3,000 students in attendance, however, rather more than a third take the arts courses, about one-fourth take the well-known Glasgow medicine course, and one-sixth follow lectures in science. Law, theology, and mixed courses account for the rest. In normal times rather more than half the students are women. Some well-known names are associated with Glasgow, the most famous perhaps being that of Adam Smith.

314

ABERDEEN.

Aberdeen University was founded in 1494-5 by William Elphinstone, Bishop of Aberdeen, under the authority of a Papal Bull obtained at the instance of 'James IV. In 1505 the College of St. Mary, afterwards called King's College, was founded within the University, and in 1868, after a long independent existence, the Marischal College (founded in 1593) was added.

Government is on the lines laid down by Universities (Scotland) Act of 1889, and does not differ essentially from that of the other Scottish Universities.

About 1,000 students are provided for annually in the Faculties of arts, science (including agriculture), divinity, law, and medicine, including public health). From a quarter to a third of the students are women. The courses in arts and in medicine are followed by the great majority of the alumni.

EDINBURGH.

The " College of Edinburgh," or " The Town's College," was founded in 1583 by the Town Council of Edinburgh. There is no charter of foundation extant, but the college had from the first the privilege of granting degrees. Though the college came to be styled the " University of Edinburgh," it remained under the control of the Town Council until 1858, when the Universities (Scotland) Act conferred upon it, in common with the other Universities of Scotland, a new and autonomous constitution.

The University is housed at present in the " Old Building," on the site of " Kirk o' Field," the scene of the murder of Darnley, and in four other institutions; the New Buildings (School of Medicine) and the M'Ewan Hall, Teviot Place; the Music Class-Room, Park Place; the John Usher Institute of Public Health, Warrender Park Road; and the Engineering and Natural Philosophy Departments in Infirmary Street. The " Old Building " is of considerable architectural interest, having been designed by Robert Adam, and begun under his superintendence in 1789. His death, coupled with lack of funds, marred the design, however, and weaker hands completed it in 1828 at a total cost of £160,000.

The government of the University is organised on the lines of that of St. Andrew's (q.v.). The total revenue is about £120,000, of which some £35,000 is received from the Central or Local Government Authorities. From 3,000 to 4,000 students matriculate annually, the Arts and Medicine Faculties being by far the most popular. The Faculty of Music attracts a few students.

THE SCOTTISH UNIVERSITIES AND THE W.E.A.

The W.E.A. north of the Tweed works under rather different conditions from those prevailing in England and Wales. In Scotland the School Board still remains the local authority in education, and the Scotch Education Department can only support Tutorial Classes if they are under the control of the local School Board. Consequently financial responsibility has to be accepted by the School Board, and the classes are regarded as part of its continuation classes scheme. The following details will illustrate the circumstances in which the existing Scottish branches developed and the relations between the Association and the Scottish Universities.

ABERDEEN.—A number of persons interested in the W.E.A. began visiting local meetings of Trade Unions in 1913. They also approached members of the University staff and of the local School Board. A preliminary meeting was held in April, 1913, presided over by the Principal of the University, and it was agreed to form a branch. A small Provisional Committee secured the affiliation of 25 bodies, and it also attracted individual members by arranging a course of lectures for the winter 1913-14 on " Some Problems of Citizenship." The lectures were given in the University building, and twelve of them were delivered by members of the staff. The class-room, with heating and lighting, was provided free of charge. In due course a constitution was drawn up and the Association fully established. During the summer of 1914 the Executive Committee of the Association sent a deputation to meet representatives of the University Court and Senatus to discuss the question of starting Tutorial Classes. The University representatives were sympathetic and promised to put the matter before the Court and the Senatus. A deputation then waited on the Continuation Classes Committee of the School Board. The Committee agreed to bring the question before the School Board itself. As a result of these interviews, the University and the School Board appointed representatives to meet representatives of the W.E.A. to discuss the whole position at a joint meeting, the object being to form a Joint Committee which would have control of the classes if they were formed. The joint meeting, with the Principal in the chair, adopted this course, each body electing its own representatives. The School Board undertook financial responsibility for the classes; the University agreed to provide the class-room, heating, and lighting, and also to give a donation of £5 a year to each class to form a reference library. The fee for each class was fixed at 5s. for a course of 24 lectures. The fees were to be paid to the School Board and were not returnable. The Joint Committee exercised control over the classes. The procedure agreed upon was that the Association was to express its wishes to the Joint Committee and the University was to recommend the tutor for any class it was decided to hold, while the School Board had to approve of the nomination and make the appointment. The tutor's fee was fixed at £40 for 24 meetings of the class. During 1914-15 two classes thus constituted enrolled more than 15 students, the minimum required by the School Board. The war, however, seriously damaged the prospects for 1915-16. Only one class could be arranged, and this continued to meet in 1916-17. Each year the University has made the grant of £5 to the classes for books and the arrangements about the meeting-place have been continued. The authorities of the University of Aberdeen have from the outset shown a keen interest in and sympathy with the local work of the W.E.A.

EDINBURGH.—A public meeting to consider the proposal to form an Edinburgh Branch of the W.E.A. was held on the 26th October, 1912. Professor Richard Lodge presided, and an address was delivered by Mr. Albert Mansbridge. As a result a Provisional Committee was appointed, which set itself to secure individual members and affiliated societies. The University of Edinburgh was asked for its sympathy and co-operation, and the Scotch Education Department was approached to ascertain on what terms it could make grants to W.E.A. classes. The Department intimated that it was unable to assist unless the Association had the concurrence of the local School Boards. In January, 1913, it was agreed to invite the School Boards of Edinburgh and Leith to receive deputations, Professors Lodge and Darroch consenting to act on the deputations. Meanwhile, four Tutorial Classes were held as an experiment, and they met with moderate success. In reply to the deputation, the School Boards promised to consider the question of joint control of the classes. It was finally arranged that the Edinburgh School Board should assume financial responsibility for the Edinburgh classes, the local branch appointing an Advisory .Committee to make recommendations and reports to the Board. Professor Darroch was elected convener of this Advisory Committee and he still retains that office. The Leith School Board vested the supervision of its classes in a Joint Board of Managers. In each case the University of Edinburgh nominated two representatives to act on these administrative bodies. The Clerk of the Board requests the Advisory Committee (in the case of Edinburgh) classes) to visit the classes each session and to report to the Board on their progress. From the outset there was a feeling that the classes would gain many advantages from meeting within the University. In September, 1914, the Edinburgh School Board received an intimation from the University Court that it was prepared to provide accommodation for the classes on very reasonable terms. Classes were, therefore, held in a University class-room until the session 1916-17, when the School Board could not see its way to continue paying the sum charged by the University and the classes were removed to their new school at Boroughmuir. The School Board had also given the use of the Royal High School for two series of public lectures arranged by the branch in the spring of 1915 and 1916. A deputation waited on the new Principal (Sir J. A. Ewing) in the course of this summer and was most sympathetically received. They were advised to apply to the University Court for assistance in the form of a grant of the free use of a lecture-room on three evenings a week for the classes. The Court resolved to grant this request at its meeting on 16th July. The three classes running this winter, therefore, meet in the University. Since the formation of the branch the Association has had the active support of Professors Sir Richard Lodge (president of the branch), Darroch (convener of the Advisory Committee), and Seth (vice-president). Several lecturers have taken classes.

The experiment of holding classes at Leith never met with any considerable support, and it has been abandoned since the outbreak of the war.

The financial arrangements in Edinburgh differ from those in Aberdeen. The class fee is 3s. for a course of 24 lectures, and the School Board has agreed to hand back 6d. from each student's fee to the branch. The tutors are paid £16 for 24 class meetings. The Association itself makes grants annually, usually of £1, to assist students in forming class libraries.

GLASGOW.—In Glasgow the position is not yet so clearly defined as in Aberdeen and Edinburgh. The School Board, which pays the lecturer and provides the room, agreed to run certain lecture-courses in Economics and History under the auspices of the W.E.A. This is the second session of this arrangement, and the results have been, so far, gratifying. In addition, a public lecture-course at intervals of one month on educational subjects has been arranged for this winter. Professor Darroch, of Edinburgh University, and Dr. Boyd, of Glasgow University, have delivered the first two lectures of the series. Progress is being made in increasing membership of the Association and in enlisting the co-operation of Trade Unions.

IRELAND.

THE NATIONAL UNIVERSITY OF IRELAND.

The Irish Universities Act of 1908, and the charter granted under the provisions of that Act, provides for the incorporation of Queen's College, Cork, Queen's College, Galway (to be known henceforward as the University Colleges of Cork and Galway respectively), and " a new college to have its seat in Dublin," into the National University of Ireland. The " new college " is University College, Dublin. St. Patrick's College, Maynooth, is a recognised college of the University.

The governing authorities are the Chancellor (elected by Convocation), the Vice-Chancellor (elected by the Senate), and Pro-Vice-Chancellors (also elected by the Senate) ; the Senate, presided over by the Chancellor, and comprising the Presidents of the constituent colleges, six representatives of the governing body of University College, Dublin, and four from each of the other two constituent colleges, eight representatives elected by Convocation, four co-opted members, and the Registrar. Convocation consists of all the aforementioned officers of the University, together with all registered graduates of the University who have fulfilled the conditions of enrolment in Convocation. There is also a Board of Studies and the Faculties, presided over by the Vice-Chancellor, and including the Professors, lecturers, and other teachers in the University. The Vice-Chancellor is the chief executive officer, and the real governing power resides in him and in the Senate. Convocation has no powers beyond those of electing representatives to the Senate and " discussing and pronouncing an opinion on any matter whatsoever relating to the University."

The Faculties are arts, philosophy and sociology, Celtic studies, science, law, medicine, engineering and architecture, and commerce.

The National University, thus reconstructed, took the place of the former Royal University of Ireland, dissolved by the same Act (Irish Universities Act, 1908). The change put an end to the system of granting degrees to external students on the result of examination only, a system now obtaining only in London University and (so far as the B.A. is concerned) in Dublin.

QUEEN'S UNIVERSITY IN IRELAND.

University (formerly Queen's) College, Cork, was founded in 1845, along with the Queen's Colleges of Galway and Belfast, under the Act of that year, entitled " An Act to enable her Majesty to endow new Colleges for the Advancement of Learning in Ireland." The University was incorporated in 1850, under the name of the Queen's University in Ireland, and comprising the three above-mentioned colleges.

A further change took place in 1882, when the Queen's University
was dissolved, and a new charter was granted constituting the Royal
University of Ireland from the same three constituent colleges.

BELFAST.

The Queen's University of Belfast was constituted by a charter of
1908 on the dissolution of Queen's College, Belfast, which had been
incorporated in 1849. There are two recognised colleges of the
University, in addition to the former Queen's College. Part of the
degree courses in engineering and textile may be taken at the
Municipal Technical Institute, Belfast, and part of the training in
agriculture is given at the Royal College of Science, Dublin.

Government is by the Chancellor and Pro-Chancellors, the Vice-
Chancellor (the executive head), the Senate, Convocation, and the
Academic Council.

The Faculties are of arts, commerce, law, medicine, and science.
Medicine absorbs the largest number of students, but the arts and
science degrees are also favoured. The annual number of students is
between 500 and 600.

DUBLIN.

" Dublin University " and Trinity College, Dublin, are in practice
interchangeable terms. Trinity College was founded by charter of
Elizabeth in 1591 as " unum Collegium noster Universitatis."

Government is in the hands of a Board, composed of the Provost
and Senior Fellows, with representatives of the Junior Fellows and
the Professors; the Visitors (the Chancellor of the University and the
Lord Chief Justice of Ireland); the Senate, comprising the Chancellor
and all such Doctors or Masters of the University as comply with
the conditions of enrolment; and the Council, consisting of the
Provost, the Senior Lecturer, the Registrar, and 16 Senators
representative of various sections or Faculties. The effective governing
body is the Board.

The University sends a representative to Parliament.

About 1,000 student undergraduates attend annually (some for
examination only) in the arts courses. A peculiar feature of Dublin
is that students takng professional degrees are compelled to take an
arts degree also. The most important " school," from a numerical
point of view, is that of medicine, which has usually some 250 students
at work.

THE IRISH UNIVERSITIES AND THE W.E.A.

By M. W. ROBIESON.

There are three Universities in Ireland, with six colleges, or seven
if we include Maynooth. Conditions of University life and teaching,
and still more the environment of the college, vary very much from
one to another; so that it would be unreasonable to expect any great
uniformity in the endeavour to make higher education available for
workers. Only in two of these colleges up to the present has any
sustained attempt been made to solve the problem.*

* I desire to acknowledge indebtedness to Mr. Conrad Gill, M.A., Belfast and
Professor A. J. Rahilly, M.A., Cork, for much of the detailed information contained
in this article.

In connection with the **Queen's University of Belfast** there has been a branch of the W.E.A. in existence since 1910, and Tutorial Classes have been conducted since the same date. The difficulties it has had to meet have arisen from the peculiar conditions of the Labour movement in Belfast, the resemblance of which to similar movements in Great Britain is more apparent than real. Most of the usual organisations have at least a nominal existence, but their significance and influence are generally rather different. At present it is still true that the traditional division of political parties is little affected by economic conflict, and that the workers exhibit, on the whole, an unusually low degree of interest in social questions. Those who have been attracted to the W.E.A. are for the most part drawn from amongst those who have broken away from party politics. The I.L.P., for example, which is apparently growing in Belfast, though it is largely an offshoot from the same movement on the Clyde, has supplied a number of members. So also have the Trade Unions, though there is much room for development in this direction. Between the Co-operative Society and the W.E.A. there has been throughout a close connection. Certain of the meetings and classes have been held in the Co-operative Hall and lectures have been arranged jointly by the W.E.A. and the Co-operative Society. During the past 18 months two courses have also been carried through in association with the Central Presbyterian Association.

The Tutorial Classes, which are organised by the University, have been principally in the hands of one of the lecturers of the University, with occasional assistance from other members of the staff and other persons interested in this type of work. The classes averaged about 20, and have covered a considerable range of subjects— Social Economics, Economic History, General History, Geography, Child Study, etc. It is usual also to arrange one or two public lectures each winter and to conduct a series of Saturday evening meetings for members at which papers are read on very various subjects and followed by a discussion. The attendance is comparatively small but regular.

The prospects of further development of the movement appear to be very encouraging provided that the finance problem can be solved. At present the Tutorial Classes are provided by the University, and the tutors are not specially paid for this work. The roots of the difficulty are that no public body in Ireland can normally give grants for higher education—except, of course, for technical education under the direction of the Department of Agriculture and Technical Instruction—and that there is no Local Education Authority at all. Were it possible for the Treasury to give a grant additional to the general grant to the University, or for the Commissioners of Education to move in the matter, very considerable developments might be possible. The Belfast Branch of the W.E.A. is preparing a statement, to be sent to the Chief Secretary, showing the need for working-class education in Ireland, and it hopes to arrange for a conference on the same subject.

During the sessions 1915-16 and 1916-17 very successful " economic conferences " were held at **University College, Cork.** These lectures and discussions were due to the initiative and self-sacrificing labour of two Professors, the college merely supplying a room. The audience, which in the end numbered over 400, consisted chiefly of workingmen and women and students. At the close of each lecture a vigorous discussion ensued, and the workers soon became accustomed to put their point of view and to argue. The subjects discussed included Poverty, Housing, Insurance, Casual Labour, Town Allotments, Women Workers, and Socialism. A few lectures were also delivered in Limerick and Waterford. The two Professors to whom the enterprise is due have also started a " University and Labour Series " of pamphlets, two of which have already been published, a third being in the press.

As a result of this voluntary campaign and of the response of the local Trades Council, the Corporation was induced to make a grant of £150 per year for the purpose of University Extension in virtue of a hitherto unused power under the Irish Universities Act (1908). Hence in the coming session the National University will for the first time attempt in a small way the education of adult workers.

Nothing permanent or definite has yet been done in **Trinity College, Dublin, University College, Dublin, University College, Galway, or McCrea=Magee College, Derry.**

It is very difficult to estimate the prospects of the whole movement in Ireland. It does seem clear that the conditions, except to a slight extent in Belfast, differ altogether from those in England; so that the analogy of English experience is not particularly helpful. Even in Belfast, which is in some respects similar to the North of England towns and in others to Glasgow, public opinion on social questions in general is in much the same state as it was in England 40 or 50 years ago. In the ordinary English sense there is hardly any Labour movement in Ireland. There is a certain amount of Trade Union activity and a revolutionary Labour section more or less closely connected with the Sinn Fein body. Even there, however, strongly political or national sentiments play as vigorous a part as those more distinctive of working-class movements. On the other hand, the spread of this sort of education to the rural districts may prove easier in the future in Ireland than in England, because of the Irish Agricultural Organisation Society, which might very possibly be linked up with the Universities. The solution of the problem as a whole will probably be reached along rather different lines from England and a new type of organisation developed with some distinctive national features. It is impossible that the present situation in Ireland can leave this problem unaffected, and it is common knowledge that the younger generation of University men and women is profoundly affected by political and social ideas very different from those of previous academic generations. My impression is that there may result a closer relation between the Universities and the workers than is to be found anywhere in Great Britain; but this is not· yet certain because the economic divisions involved are very far from having worked themselves clear.

WALES.

UNIVERSITY OF WALES.

The University of Wales was founded by charter in 1893. It has no teaching staff, and the three constituent colleges (University Colleges of Wales, Aberystwyth; of North Wales, Bangor; of South Wales and Monmouthshire, Cardiff) have separate charters and independent government. The functions which the University has so far carried out are those of organising and co-ordinating examinations and the granting of degrees. Some half-dozen Theological Colleges are associated with the University.

The Faculties are of arts or letters, science, theology or divinity, law, medicine, and music.

The most important post, that of Vice-Chancellor, is held in turn by the Principals of the three colleges for a two years' term.

UNIVERSITY COLLEGE OF WALES.

This college at Aberystwyth was founded in 1872, and was for ten years maintained by the voluntary contributions of the Welsh people. It received a charter of incorporation in 1889. Government is on the same lines as that of the other Welsh University Colleges (see University College of South Wales).

The departments of study undertaken at Aberystwyth include arts, science, law, agricultural and technical instruction, and instrumental music. There is also a Training College for teachers of elementary and secondary schools. The most highly developed feature of the curriculum is probably instruction in agriculture. From 400 to 500 students are registered annually.

UNIVERSITY COLLEGE OF SOUTH WALES AND MONMOUTHSHIRE.

This college was founded at Cardiff as the result of public meetings and subscriptions, and was opened in 1883. The Cardiff Corporation provided £10,000 of the original funds and the late Marquis of Bute a similar sum. Subsequent developments have added a School of Science and Technology, a Commercial School, and other departments to the original equipment, and in 1890 a Day Training College for elementary teachers was opened.

The authorities of the college are the President, Vice-President, the Court of Governors, the Council, and the Senate. The Court of Governors is constituted somewhat similarly to that of Manchester (q.v.), with, however, a provision for the inclusion of persons who have " contributed £500 and upwards to the funds of the college." The Council is the executive body.

The college educates students, of course, for the degrees of the University of Wales, but it also grants certain diplomas, notably in agriculture. There are usually some 500 students, of whom about one-third are women.

THE UNIVERSITY COLLEGE OF NORTH WALES.

The University College at Bangor was established in 1884 as the result of the Report of a Departmental Committee appointed in 1880 to inquire into the conditions of intermediate and higher education in

Wales and Monmouthshire. It became a constituent college of the the University of Wales in 1893. The studies pursued there are, of course, largely in preparation for the degrees of the University, and the courses are also recognised by the University of Oxford.

The college is recognised by the Board of Education as a training college for teachers in elementary schools, and a course is provided for teachers in secondary schools. Courses in agriculture are an important feature.

Normally from 300 to 400 pupils study at Bangor.

THE UNIVERSITY COLLEGE OF WALES AND THE WORKERS.

There has been a tradition in Wales that the Welsh University, through its constituent colleges at Aberystwyth, Bangor, and Cardiff, has been a people's University from its inception. If we judge from the large number of sons and daughters from the ranks of the working class population that have successfully entered and graduated at the University, it is true. This traditional educational equality of opportunity does not do away with the tremendous inequality of sacrifice involved in the maintenance of such workers' children at any one of the above institutions. Suffice it to say that the totally inadequate scholarship system, rooted in the county school system of Wales, is a very unsatisfactory solution of the economic aspect of college education in Wales. This is the real justification of the demand now made before the Royal Commission on Welsh University Education, that the scholarship system be abolished and a system of free education with maintenance grants, if necessary, be given to all who aspire to a University education.

It is not in the above sense of how the University of Wales has provided for professional training for the sons and daughters of the workers of Wales that I want to dwell on, but the aspect of University education that touches the adult workers themselves. This aspect of University education rises above the bread and butter plane, where the workers seek no reward for seeking and obtaining knowledge, above the intrinsic joy and zest which they gain from such a course. This organised demand by workers for the facilities to study, under the best possible authorities, subjects touching their daily lives as units· of society, is only part of the movement now labelled as "The University Tutorial Class Movement," inaugurated some years ago by Mr. Albert Mansbridge, of W.E.A. fame.

The Tutorial Class movement has taken root at the three colleges, where very successful classes have been held for several years. In Aberystwyth and Cardiff University Colleges there are joint committees of the usual type consisting of Labour and academic representatives responsible for the classes. At Bangor the classes were looked on as one of the normal activities of the college. Ultimately, it is hoped to get a properly constituted joint committee at Bangor.

The subjects most in demand by students in North, South, and West Wales were those fascinating subjects of an economic or historical character that dealt with some aspect of social life.

Few though the number of classes (dependent often on the number of tutors available) appear to be,* one must not think that the

---

* See Appendix Summary.

workers of Wales are satisfied with this number. Were it not for the totally inadequate supply of tutors (due mainly to a totally inadequate supply of money at the disposal of the three colleges to support and develop this aspect of University education) the district secretary of the W.E.A. for Wales could have started tutorial classes in 50 different centres in rural and in thickly populated industrial districts in Wales.

Unfortunately, the War with its toll on the small band of tutors and the disorganisation of University finance, wrecked (for the time at any rate) the promising beginnings of the Tutorial Class movement in Wales, so that for the session 1916-1917 we can record no single University Tutorial Class as existing under any of the three University colleges.

All lovers of the W.E.A. and the Tutorial Class movement are setting their hopes on a revival of learning that will take place in Wales when the War is over. They are looking forward to the practical application of some of the recommendations of the Royal Commission on Welsh University Education, which will more than make up for the set-back we have had since the outbreak of the European Armageddon.

No account of the Tutorial Class movement in Wales would be complete without reference to two institutions closely related to it—one outside the movement, as it were, and the other born of it. These institutions are the National Library of Wales, and the Bangor Summer School respectively.

Under the guidance of Mr. John Ballinger, M.A., the National Library of Wales has helped the Tutorial Classes most materially through its excellent supply of book-boxes, containing a suitable selection of text books recommended by tutors for reading in connection with their courses.

Since 1913 regularly every year Tutorial Class students from Wales have had the inestimable joy and privilege of meeting fellow students at the Bangor Summer School, where tuition was given during certain weeks in July and August under ideal college conditions. The need and justification of this institution is shown by the fact that, despite the abnormal condition experienced through the War, the school has been successfully held in 1914-1915-1916 and 1917.

What little we have accomplished in Wales in the past we hope to multiply a hundredfold in the future.

" Nid da lle gellir gwell."*

John Thomas, Hon. Secretary, W.E.A., for Wales.

———

References.—Albert Mansbridge : " University Tutorial Classes." Report of Royal Commission on University of Wales. Reports of W.E.A. for Wales, 1907-1917. Thomas D. Lleufer : " University Tutorial Classes for the Workers."

---

* Translated : " Not good where there can be better."

PART V.

THE WORKERS' EDUCATIONAL ASSOCIATION.

LEADING FACTS IN THE HISTORY OF THE WORKERS' EDUCATIONAL ASSOCIATION.

By the Rev. W. Temple, President.

It was in the summer of 1903 that a conference was called in Oxford, representative of the various Labour and educational organisations in the country, to consider the formation of such a society as the Workers' Educational Association. This conference was convened by a group of workingmen who felt that the linking up of universities and Labour, for which the University Extension Movement had stood, was urgently necessary, but, so long as the bridge was built from one side only, unattainable. No doubt the ideals with which University Extension started included the fashioning of such a link, and in the case of certain lecturers the gulf had been successfully bridged; but this was rare. There was need for a movement from the other side. The point of view predominant in the social circles from which members of the University were drawn, and the point of view predominant in the Labour world, were too diverse to permit of real unity unless there was some means by which Labour could become articulate and express its educational ideals to the University.

The conference of 1903 voted into existence what is now known as the Workers' Educational Association, though at first it was known by a more cumbrous name. Two years later a similar conference was held, and another in 1907, the last of the series, at which an invitation was made from the representatives of Labour to the Vice-Chancellor of the University that he should appoint seven members of the University to meet with seven representatives of Labour that they might confer together and report upon " Oxford and Working-Class Education." The report, which was issued with that phrase as its title, remains one of the standard documents in the history of the movement. Its chief recommendation was the formation in Oxford of a committee similar to that which had drawn it up for the purpose of establishing and supervising University Tutorial Classes in working-class areas. Such a committee was formed at once, a small modification of one of the University statutes being made in order to facilitate this; and the example has been followed, though the exact model has not always been adopted, in all other universities in England and Wales. Moreover, there is now a Central Joint Advisory

Committee, consisting of representatives of the universities, of the Joint Committees, and of the W.E.A., for the co-ordination of this work. For the history of the Tutorial Class Movement we must refer to the book, " University Tutorial Classes," by Albert Mansbridge, who has from the beginning been the inspirer, as he was the founder, of the whole W.E.A. movement and what has sprung from it.

It was in the autumn of 1908 that I had the honour to be elected President, and this step was taken by way of completing the earlier constitution of the W.E.A.

One of the most hopeful signs of the days in which we are living is the revived interest in education shown by nearly all Labour gatherings. The reason for this is not simple; it is rather the result of many converging forces. Perhaps chief among them are these. It becomes more and more plain that education is the way to power, and that, as the Bishop of Oxford once told an annual meeting of the Workers' Educational Association, " even though the workingmen become strong and clamorous and carry out a revolution, they will be trodden down again under the heel of knowledge unless they get it for themselves, for ignorance will always be trodden under foot of knowledge." Education thus becomes more and more necessary to the realisation of anything like true democracy. But there is also another reason. The more thoughtful minds in the Labour movement have become increasingly convinced that the real root of social problems is spiritual. It is not merely the inequitable distribution of the proceeds of industry against which they protest and rebel; it is still more the low estimate of the worker's personality which goes along with this. Our present system constitutes a standing insult to the personality of the poor man; he is dependent upon the goodwill of others to an extent which those others would never tolerate if they held a view of his personality such as either religion or any wholesome ethics would require them to hold. To give or to receive charity is excellent when equality is first assured; but to be dependent upon anything in the nature of charity for the reasonable necessities of civilised life is an outrage. And it is by education that the working classes can most effectively assert their true personality. If a man is a little inarticulate, rather halting and clumsy in expression, he is easily set down, if not defeated, by someone whose faculty may in itself be less but has been more highly trained. Education is, in fact, essential to the realisation of real liberty.

But it is not only in this way that education and liberty are linked together; not only must there be education if there is to be liberty in the State, but also there must be liberty in the school if there is to be education. Intellectual effort may indeed be made in partnership, but it cannot be undertaken by one person simply on behalf of another, nor can intellectual culture be in any way imposed on one person by another. It is essential to the life of the mind that each person should truly live it for himself. No doubt our minds grow through intercourse with other minds, but they must themselves be active in this intercourse, and that not only by way of pure reception. What we learn by heart, unless it comes as the summary of what we have already learnt to understand and to believe, is very rapidly forgotten, or, even if the words are remembered, exercises little influence on the rest of thought or on conduct. If by knowledge we mean merely the acquisition of information then education is concerned with something much more than knowledge, for it is always mainly interested in the reasons for things, and above all in the process whereby the reasons for things are found. We shall only obtain the kind of education which gives the fullest human development if we abandon all effort to impose upon the mind of the learner any beliefs—religious, political, economic, historical, or of whatever kind they may be—and desire first and foremost that the learner shall make up his own mind on as complete a presentation of the facts as can be produced. Thus in the sphere of religion it is far better that a man should hold a heresy which he genuinely believes than that he should tamely acquiesce in the acceptance of an orthodoxy, even on the supposition that the orthodoxy is indeed the truth. The same is true in every other department. This does not mean that every student should have to begin each subject at the very start as if no others had started before. It is reasonable to teach the multiplication table instead of leaving the child to discover it for himself, because in that way an immense amount of time is saved. But all who teach should be carefully on their guard against imposing a particular interpretation of facts. The aim must be to assist the student to make discoveries, and above all to develop the faculty whereby such discoveries are made. The wise student will, of course, get·the help of minds more mature than his own to guide his in his study. If an interpreter of his subject is available he will seek out the interpreter and use his interpretation as a clue. But he will always distinguish between what he believes provisionally because he has been told it, and what he believes with real assurance because after full examination he has tested it.

Plainly these principles must be applied with increasing care as the age of the student advances and his capacity for criticism becomes greater. In adult education they should reign completely. Here there should be no attempt either to impose or even to suggest one interpretation as that which it is desirable that the student should hold. The tutor or leader of a class will indeed give his own interpretation, but he will give it as something submitted to the criticism of those whose thought he is helping to guide. For he is not teacher only, while they are learners only, but all are learners together, one of them having the advantage of having begun study some years earlier than the rest. This is the spirit which in the Workers' Educational Association we desire to promote, for we believe that just as education is essential to freedom so is freedom essential to true education. There should be no aim beyond the building up into its fulness of the real personality of the student; that personality is both individual and social, and only if both his individuality and his membership of the community are simultaneously fostered by his education is that education worthy of its name.

When the war broke out it became necessary to determine what was the Association's attitude. But this was really easy. It must call upon men and women everywhere to study the occasions of the great catastrophe and form their own judgments about it. Naturally the war has diminished some of the activities in which the Association was engaged or to which it had given rise, but there can be no doubt that after the war the opportunities of work will be far greater than before. Our principle throughout has been that the Association should be a federation of Labour and educational organisations. Gradually, as the work has become strengthened in various parts of the country, districts were formed with a large amount of local autonomy, and the general development of the work necessitated a revision of the constitution, which took effect in 1916.

The W.E.A. may justifiably believe that it has exercised some influence on the development of the whole educational system, even apart from the work that it has set on foot itself. The Board of Education has taken a strong interest in it from the outset, and representations made by it have always received full attention. It has been careful to maintain complete freedom from all sectarian or party political interest; it unites upon its platform all who desire to spread true education in the spirit of that freedom which is essential to education among the working people. It has no doctrine to teach except that people who desire to study should have the opportunity of studying, and that in their study they should make up their own minds.

In the stimulation of interest in reconstruction the Association has taken its full part, and its chief activity during the past 18 months has been concerned with forming a series of recommendations which may give both the goal at which we are to aim and the steps which we are to take to reach it. These recommendations are given in full on pages 341-9. Having furnished its own policy the Association called a general conference of Labour and educational bodies, which met in the Central Hall, Westminster, on May 3rd, and passed a series of resolutions, which embodied in general outline the principles elaborated with more detail in the series of recommendations given below.

REFERENCES.—A. Mansbridge : " University Tutorial Classes." J M. Mactavish : " What Labour Wants from Education."

THE W.E.A.: ITS PROPAGANDA, ORGANI-
SATION, AND METHOD.

By J. M. Mactavish, General Secretary, W.E.A.

PROPAGANDA.

The propagandist is anathema to the conventionalist, for the latter lives by authority, regulates his life by rule, immerses himself in technique and machinery, and worships forms and traditions.

The propagandist, generally a layman, is a rebel against accepted authority. He is an idealist and lives by faith. Unhampered by the traditions, conventions, formulas, or technique; ignorant, it may be, of practical difficulties, he none the less visualises possibilities, inspires faith, and paves the way for the experts who later on realise the dreams of the dreamers Of such stuff have been made the men and women who have fertilised the soil out of which there have grown new social hopes, who have driven the intellectualists to their studies, and made the " dismal science " the most living science of our times.

Can the propagandists do for education what they have so often accomplished for religion and in more recent years for the social sciences? Can they lift it out of the deadening grip of codes, curricula, time-tables, reports, returns, inspections, and other machinery which has made so many of our schools institutions for " the diffusion of useful knowledge," whereby interest is destroyed and pedantic pedagogy reigns supreme? Can they give to the people a new faith and hope in education? " 'Tis a consummation devoutly to be wished."

But the small measure of success that has attended the efforts of those who have hitherto attempted it does not inspire great hope. Half a century of public education which has produced little more than a small percentage of experts, a large percentage of illiterates, and a great mass of apathy and indifference is a deadweight not easily removed.

Yet, despite past failures and present difficulties, there are many indications that we are on the eve of a great awakening. The war has destroyed many well-worn paths along which in pre-war days the human mind was content to amble. Authorities, opinions, notions, and prejudices have gone down like nine-pins before the vibration of the far-flung battle line of a world in arms, and men and women are seeking new anchorage for storm-tossed minds. With the removal of the old authorities who used to pilot their lives they have discovered how ill-equipped they are to find new ones. From this discovery of " the fullness of our ignorance and the emptiness of our knowledge " there has sprung a demand for education which, if stimulated and wisely guided, gives new hope for the future. " We are too hungry to wait " was the reply of a group of workingmen whose leisure time was already fully occupied with Trade Union, co-operative, and other work when it was suggested that the formation of a W.E.A. class should be postponed till the autumn. All over the country W.E.A.

conferences on education have aroused an enthusiasm which a few years ago expressed itself only on social and economic questions. The National Conference, convened by the W.E.A. on May 3rd, 1917, was a further indication of how widespread the interest has become, while the Co-operative Congress at Cardiff, epoch-making both in spirit and decisions, gave more time to the consideration of education than to any other subject. But if this wave of enthusiasm is not to recede, leaving behind it no permanent results, it must be inspired with a deeper purpose than has hitherto been given to education.

The instruction, so oft miscalled education, received by the great mass of the working-class, has been so scanty, disciplinarian, uninteresting, and painful that it is only by giving to them new conceptions of the purpose of education and associating these with the ideals agitating the working-class mind that we can hope to maintain the new interest that has been awakened and prevent its exploitation in the interest of mere technical efficiency.

The gigantic sacrifice of life, limb, treasure, and civil rights made in the name of national liberty has given to the cause of freedom a new and powerful impulse. It is no longer a mere abstraction. It has taken on a new and deep significance. It has been paid for in such an outpouring of the world's best blood as is without parallel in history, and the public mind will seethe, surge, and insist until that which has been so dearly bought has in a large measure been attained. This gives to the teacher and educationist a new atmosphere to work in and to the propagandist a new soil in which good seed well sown will bring forth a rich harvest; for, for many days to come the public mind will be susceptible and receptive of all that promises to make for freedom.

The establishment of international law for the maintenance of peace and order, even if supported by international armed force, can do no more than hold in check untrained human passions which may at any time again o'erwhelm us. Economic betterment may prove no more than a gilded cage against the bars of which the human spirit may beat its wings in vain. True freedom springs from within; it cannot be imposed from without. It is the product of an education that gives the possession and use of one's full powers, coupled with a knowledge of the truth. It is this conception of education that gives to the propagandist his great opportunity.

Man is not made, he grows. All that a child may become it potentially already is. The child is the parent of the adult as truly as the man and woman are the parents of the child. It is the business of education to aid the child, adolescent and adult to become, to grow, and so realise those latent powers for good with which every normal child has been endowed even before it enters the world. In a primitive community where the social environment is accepted as permanent all that is needed is that its members should adapt themselves to it. But in a highly organised, industrial community, whose members have become conscious of its injustices and their power to change it, it is only by the development of their capacity to feel, think, and will aright that we can hope to equip them for the great task of so moulding their social and industrial environment as to provide the maximum stimulus to human freedom and growth.

This conception of education as stimuli to the growth of those human powers which make us " masters of our own destiny " may seem commonplace to the educationist. But it is not so with the people, for the atmosphere in which their children are taught has been poisoned by commercialism. To purify the atmosphere, awaken faith, and arouse interest and enthusiasm is the work of the propagandist. This he can do only by idealising education, by helping the people to conceive of it as the process by which we develop those great natural gifts, emotional, intellectual, and volitional, which in turn fit us to put into the human environment what we want to get out of ourselves.

ORGANISATION AND METHOD.

But missionary zeal, no matter how well informed, is not of itself enough. Divine madness is a noble passion, but if its victims only shoot at the moon they accomplish nothing. We may " hitch our wagon to a star," but the law of gravitation is still too strong for poor mortals. Successful propaganda necessitates careful and thorough organisation.

In this the W.E.A. has proved so successful that until a better method is devised it certainly holds the field. It constitutes an alliance of Labour and learning, which foreshadows greater social and industrial changes than have yet been accomplished, for it promises to equip the working class for gaining such control over its economic conditions as will secure a measure of social and industrial freedom hitherto unachieved.

The units of the association are its branches, which are constituted on lines somewhat similar to Trades Councils. They are local federations of Trade Union branches, Trades Councils, co-operative societies, Adult Schools, Teachers' Associations, and other bodies operating within the branch area; in addition to which individuals interested in education are accepted as members.

Hitherto the activities of the branches have for the most part been confined to organising classes, study circles and lectures, safeguarding the freedom of its classes from any interference with the right of students to select their subject and their tutor, to consult all authorities on the course of study that is being pursued, and the free and frank exchange of opinions between tutors and students. This safeguarding of the freedom of the class is the more necessary, inasmuch as the interests of the great majority of students naturally turn to those subjects which are directly related to those social and industrial problems which constitute the issues raised by political parties in their appeals for public support. To prevent anything in the nature of proselytizing it is necessary that tutors should be as familiar with the writings of Marx as of Marshall, with the teachings of Socialism and Syndicalism as with Liberalism and Conservatism. Nor is the converse less necessary. Only by being able to introduce his students to the best authorities in all schools can the tutor hope to stimulate independent thought on the part of his students.

But past experience and new needs are rapidly increasing the activities of the branches. While in the more placid areas literature, languages, and the more or less academic study of the social sciences may suffice, in the more strenuous industrial centres there is a rapidly increasing demand for opportunities for the study of more immediate and pressing problems. This is all to the good. Previous to the war, the rank and file of the Labour movement were for the most part content to accept the opinions put forward by accepted leaders. There was little independent discussion, and less independent thought, for, although the meetings of the organised Labour movement always invite discussion, they are none the less partisan gatherings, and as such tend to stifle that free exchange of opinion which is so valuable in stimulating new ideas, and which is only found at its best in gatherings of an inclusive character.

During the period of reconstruction, however, old problems will reassert themselves with increased intensity, and will require to be considered in the light of new conditions, while many new problems will emerge. The difficulties and dangers arising from demobilisation and dislocation of industry are already receiving considerable attention by conferences, summer schools, and Government Committees, and a more or less constructive policy appears to be in process of formulation. But much still remains to be done before the new ideas, to which these efforts have been given birth, can be translated into action.

Within the Trade Union and co-operative movements new opportunities, responsibilities, and needs will call for very careful consideration, while serious problems of organisation and policy are still awaiting solution.

The insistent demand for working-class control within the workshop has already received a great deal of approval, but very little thought has yet been given to the practical difficulties that must inevitably arise when the time comes to give effect to the recommendations of the Whitley Committee.

Each city and town will be faced with problems peculiarly their own, calling for sound judgment on the part of its public representatives and enlightened intelligence on the part of its citizens.

Public opinion and political differences will, as a result of their temporary suppression, break out with increased intensity and bitterness, and in the midst of this electric atmosphere vital national and international questions will have to be fought out and settled.

It is impossible to say in what attitude of mind our soldiers and sailors will return to us, but we may be assured that they will come back with a greatly increased sense of ownership in the country they have fought for. Faced with such a multiplicity of problems, in the solution of which they will be expected to play a part, to whom are they to look for enlightenment and guidance? For it must be remembered that, through the great majority of working people leaving school at an early age, they have been deprived of the mental training that would enable them to readily adapt their minds to new conditions and problems.

Obviously, many will return to their old allegiances and accept the dictates of Press and party leaders, whose minds have become so fagged and overstrained by the prolonged stress of the war that they are incapable of fresh and vigorous thought. Others will turn to those to whom public passion and heat will for some time give undue prominence. But always there will be a considerable percentage who will seek for opportunities for careful investigation, independent thought, associated study, and discussion with kindred spirits.

These are the hope of the future, and in the national interest as well as in the working-class interest the opportunities they seek for ought to be provided. For this work W.E.A. branches are peculiarly fitted. Conferences, representative of all bodies within the branch areas, should be convened on all problems affecting the well-being of the community. The more highly controversial the problem the greater the need for free and dispassionate discussion. From such conferences classes or study groups should be formed to consider and, if necessary, report to a later conference. Only in small associated groups is intensive study possible. The more numerous the groups the more valuable will be the final report and the finer the training received by those who take part. Much of this work, however, will call for the services of trained leaders or teachers, and will probably involve a greater financial outlay than can be borne by a large number of branches.

University Tutorial Class Joint Committees, which consist of an equal number of Labour and university representatives, provide tutors for Tutorial Classes. These committees constitute an important link between the universities and the working-class movement, while the experience which the tutors derive from their classes corrects the academic outlook of university graduates by bringing them in direct touch with the realities of industrial and social life. This, in turn, is having its effect on the outlook of our universities, which have for too long nourished their undergraduates on histories that are seriously misleading because of their incompleteness and on social and economic theories, many of which the most intelligent workers regard as woeful misinterpretations of facts.

In one year classes, where courses of study similar to that undertaken by Tutorial Classes are pursued for one year only, tuition is given for the most part by university graduates and teachers. Grants paid partly by the Board of Education and partly by Local Education Authorities enable branches to pay small tuition fees to many of such tutors. A considerable number, however, render voluntary service, both in teaching and lecturing, in preference to accepting payments that have no relationship to the services rendered. As a result the demand for one year classes is already very much in excess of the available number of teachers. If, however, branches increase their activities on the lines suggested above the shortage of teachers will be greatly increased. For this reason Tutorial Classes must aim more and more at inspiring and equipping their students to become teachers and leaders of classes and study groups. Ruskin College, the Working Men's College, and the Central Labour College must each contribute its quota. The policy of class-conscious isolation pursued by the Plebs League must not be allowed to deter students from the Central Labour College sharing in work that is so vitally important to the future of the working-class movement. No matter whether the teacher be a follower of Marx or Marshall so long as he does not seek to proselytize his students, aids them to select, arrange, and sift the facts of the problems, and tests the value of what he has achieved by the amount of independent thought existing in the class, his services ought to be enlisted.

It may be thought, however, that such educational work should not be aided by grants from public funds. The prevailing opinion that the study of controversial questions is not a fit object for grant-aid is in no small measure due to the public opinion existing on the problem of denominational teaching. Yet there is perhaps no question on which there is greater need for serious associated study and frank dispassionate discussion as there is on religion. Dogmatic instruction in theology is often as detrimental to true spiritual growth as dogmatic instruction in economic theories is to an intelligent understanding and treatment of social and industrial problems. Serious study of conflicting theological views, coupled with a frank exchange of opinions, would do much to sift the chaff from the wheat, stimulate thought, and make for a greater tolerance.

What applies to theology applies to all controversial questions affecting the well-being of the community. Since members of the community will give their adherence to one or other of the many conflicting schools of thought, if healthy development of intellectual and religious life is to be assured by avoidance of blind adherence to obsolete authorities, provision must be made for the study and discussion of all such questions, and grants should be available for the remuneration of all teachers or tutors, *irrespective of the subject studied*, provided the inspector is satisfied that the teacher is qualified to teach, that his treatment of the subject is educationally sound and non-partisan in character.* To encourage the study of professional, commercial, and technical subjects, by the payment of grants while refusing to assist the study of other subjects that are equally vital to the mental and spiritual well-being of the community on the ground that they are controversial, is enthroning Philistinism and damning back the finest qualities of our people. Meantime, it is well that those who fear the revolutionary influence of trained mental power and knowledge should recognise that if adequate public facilities are not provided for the serious study of working-class problems in an educational atmosphere, with the assistance of qualified teachers and tutors, that which the public purse will not do for them they will do for themselves, and " they who pay the piper will call the tune." Adult working-class interests centre round social and industrial problems. They are seeking a way out. Assisted in the right way they will find it, and untimately effect social and industrial changes by bloodless and peaceable methods. But if denied such assistance they will approach the study of these problems embittered by the injustices of their industrial experiences, and the old gospel of " an eye for an eye and a tooth for a tooth " will find a new application.

But the activities of W.E.A. branches must go beyond the convening of conferences and the organisation of classes and study circles. The next Education Act will not accomplish all that the W.E.A. has asked for. Nor has the W.E.A. asked for all it would like to secure.

But it will give greatly increased powers to Local Education Authorities. It will be the business of W.E.A. branches to induce Education Authorities to use these powers to the full with the minimum of delay, while at the same time stimulating public opinion to make such fresh demands as will assure further legislation in the direction of a broad highway of free education from elementary school to the university.

By such methods each branch can gradually build up a working-class college for its own area, of which it will be the executive, for the

---

* This does not mean that the tutor is to have no views of his own, but that he must not seek to impose them on his students. However strong his personal opinions, he must do his best to state the case from every point of view.

essentials of a college are neither land nor buldings, but groups of associated students having a corporate life and taught by efficient teachers. Such colleges will gradually become the intellectual centres from which all new thought affecting the life of its area will radiate.

But local branches can only attain maximum strength and influence through a national association. Hence the need for a Central Council, representative of all branches, and of other national bodies affiliated to it. The functions of the central authority are to co-ordinate and express the common will of the movement, formulate national policy, organise and use national influence for national purposes, convene national conferences, launch fresh efforts, assist weak centres and build up a national alliance of labour and learning by awakening the interest and securing the affiliation of national Trade Unions, co-operative societies, teachers' associations, and universities. But no central authority can adequately co-ordinate and express the common will of innumerable branches, classes, and study circles scattered all over the kingdom, or carry the propaganda of the W.E.A. into centres in which no branch or classes have yet come into existence. This difficulty has called into existence district organisations with a constitution similar to that of their branches. Within clearly defined limits districts, like branches, are autonomous bodies. Their powers of autonomy are limited by the decision of their branches and affiliated bodies and also by the decisions of the Central Council. But inasmuch as they operate over a larger area and attract to themselves the most active members in their districts there is always a possibility of district activities overshadowing branch activities. But as the future success of the movement depends on thorough branch organisation and work this danger must be averted, and it can only be averted by each branch taking the liveliest interest in the work of its own district and by insisting on its right to contribute its full quota to the national movement, deriving in return inspiration from the knowledge that it is sharing in work that has become national and international in its scope.

With such organisation and methods as has been here briefly and inadequately sketched, constituting a network of local, district, and national agencies, inspired by the spirit of social service, we may hope gradually to build up a truly educated democracy, fitted for the task of harnessing all that man has achieved over the blind forces of nature to the emancipation of the people and the true service of mankind.

THE W.E.A. IN AUSTRALASIA.

By F. A. Bland, Lecturer, Sydney University.

Called into being in 1913 as a result of the visit undertaken by Mr. Albert Mansbridge, at the invitation of Australian Universities, the W.E.A. has proved another instance of the facility with which British institutions can be adapted to the varying needs of a new environment overseas. The invitation itself was additional evidence of the deep concern in education which in recent years has been manifesting itself. Over 100 years ago one of the Governors of New South Wales asserted that there was no place in the world where the education of the people was a more sacred duty, but he was indicating a policy which was in advance of current thought, both in England, and in what subsequently came to be called Australia. The recognition by the authorities of that " sacred duty " was tardy. Almost a century was to pass ere the democratic communities under the Southern Cross realised that they could neither develop the material resources of their continent, nor make any lasting contribution to the higher ideals of life and civilisation unless a radical change were made in their attitude towards education. The need once recognised, action promptly followed. Obsolete systems were remodelled in the light of the ripest experience of other countries. From primary school to University a royal road was constructed along which might travel the sons and daughters of the poorest citizens unhindered by the cramping chains of lack of means. In such an atmosphere the W.E.A. obtained a ready hearing, a hearing all the more sympathetically given since it represented a response to an already articulate demand on the part of many adults to be provided with means to participate in that which was now to be the right of their children. The progress to the goal of an enlightened industrial democracy was not to be deferred for a generation till the new policy had borne fruit, but was to be commenced immediately by the co-operation of Governments, education authorities, universities, and workers.

After a visit of 17 weeks, characterised by ceaseless activity, Mr. Mansbridge was able to report to the parent body in London that " in every State, university and trades hall are now making common cause in the development of education." In New South Wales and Tasmania financial assistance was forthcoming, enabling work to be commenced at once. Mr. Meredith Atkinson, M.A., tutorial class lecturer of the University of Durham, was appointed director of tutorial classes in Sydney University, and was charged also with supervising the movement generally in Australia, and in Tasmania Hobart University appointed Mr. H. Heaton, M.A., as lecturer, with the condition that he was also to be tutor and organiser for the W.E.A. Mr. Atkinson at once found his hands full; enthusiasm was high, and possibilities limitless. But then the war came, and Australia found herself whirled immediately into the vortex of the collossal struggle. Confronted with this turn of events, the W.E.A. momentarily staggered, but in new South Wales, Tasmania, and Victoria, where Government grants and financial assistance has already been given, events proved that there was no cause for alarm. In all the other States, authorities, like their colleagues in England, were unwilling to hazard additional expenditure upon education, although one day this will doubtless provide one of the greatest safeguards against a recurrence of the events of July-August, 1914.

Repeated representations and negotiations and a calmer review of the situation subsequently resulted in Queensland putting £1,500 in the estimates for additional university lectureships, out of which tutorial classes will be provided; in South Australia promising £1,300 for like work, and increased grants being made in the three neighbouring States of New South Wales, Victoria, and Tasmania.

New Zealand, visited by Messrs. Atkinson and D. Stewart in February-March, 1915, made a response magnificent beyond expectation. Undeterred by the ever-increasing demand the war was making upon its manhood and its resources, tutorial classes sprang into existence at many centres in New Zealand, their path smoothed by generous financial assistance from the universities and Municipal Councils. In New Zealand the movement has, if possible, been even more successful than in Australia. The university colleges have given substantial assistance, and the Municipal Councils of Auckland, Wellington, and Christchurch have also contributed. Only the war has delayed the Government grant which had been promised.

The advent of the W.E.A. has provided an increased stimulus to educational thought in Trade Union circles. Standing for an alliance between labour and learning, the W.E.A. has been closely connected with the Trades Halls in each city, and finds in trade organisations the bulk of its affiliated bodies. This connection was at first misunderstood in circles outside the Labour world owing to the special significance attaching in Australia to the terms "labour" and "worker." It also gave rise to misconceptions in the mind of some Trade Unionists, who, overlooking the real nature of the W.E.A., saw in it an excellent channel for propounding their own particular political beliefs. Thus one of the largest federations or employees seriously offered to subsidise tutors for the W.E.A., provided they had the choice of tutors and text-books.

In the process of enlightenment the Trade Unionist has been led to examine the foundations of his beliefs and the reactions of his policy, and this cannot but be beneficial to all parties. Tutorial classes and study circles; regular meetings at Trades Halls, where delegates have rubbed shoulders with non-unionists and academics; conferences such as that organised at the Sydney Trades Hall and at Sydney University upon "Trade Unionism in Australia," when delegates assembled from the whole State to discuss the history and tendencies of Trade Unionism; or public lectures—all have contributed to destroying complacency and self-satisfaction and to awakening a spirit of inquiry. Tasmania can boast that the W.E.A. has been responsible for reaching one-tenth of the total population. Could this but be followed up how rapid might be the advance towards an enlightened democracy!

There are two features worth noting in reviewing the work of the W.E.A. The first is that almost all the classes are at present working in the capital cities, where it would be anticipated there would be ample facilities for obtaining from other sources the education the W.E.A. seeks to give. In that respect, however, conditions are different from England. The number of voluntary organisations, such as adult schools, working men's colleges, and the like, is very small. Evening lectures, too, at the universities, until recently have been limited both in scope and quantity. The W.E.A. is, therefore, indeed cultivating new ground, but it is not unmindful of the necessity of extending its activities to the country towns. This has already been commenced, and it is thought that this will be the most fruitful field, for here there will not be the same intensive industrial life, nor the continuous distractions which crowd upon the city dweller and prevent his becoming a serious student.

The other feature is that the far greater proportion of classes have chosen industrial history and economics as their subject of study. This is mainly a reaction against the previously existing condition. At the close of the 19th century there were still some States which had no university, and, incredible as it may seem in a community which has been making bold social and industrial experiments, in no university was there any systematic study of economics. The Chairs of Sociology and History also were insufficiently endowed, and the main energies of the universities were concentrated upon the professional schools of medicine, engineering, and law. Public administration and commercial subjects found no place in the curricula. The university was quite out of touch with the great bulk of the citizens, and the academic was an object of suspicion in the industrial and commercial world. The position is improving daily; almost all Governments have proved willing to provide an increasing endowment for Chairs of Economics, Education, History, as well as Applied Science.

These schools are now thronged with students, and the number of W.E.A. classes is a measure of the need felt by the country for some guidance in those problems which confront them at every turn. Already students of the W.E.A. have in New South Wales been returned to the State Legislature, and the university from being a thing apart is coming more and more to be a vital force in the life of the community.

SUMMARY.

Figures convey no adequate idea of the growth or vitality of the W.E.A., but the following summarises its progress in Australia :—

NEW SOUTH WALES.—Government grant of £3,000 to tutorial classes and a direct grant of £150 to the W.E.A. for expenses. Director of tutorial classes appointed. Twenty-one tutorial classes, many study circles, 73 affiliated organisations, and 115 individual members.

Conferences organised upon (1) Trade Unionism in Australia (a result of which is an authoritative publication, " Trade Unionism in Australia," dealing with the history, tendencies, and reaction of Trade Unionism in Australia); (2) sex hygiene. Two summer schools held at Blackheath, Blue Mountains.

TASMANIA.—A special lecturer and W.E.A. organiser appointed. Government grant £675. Four tutorial classes and two study circles in Hobart and Launceston. Lectures and classes in 1915 reached 2,000 people (one-tenth of population). At the end of 1916 Mr. Heaton was appointed to a professorship at Adelaide University; Mr. D. B. Copland has been appointed as his successor.

M

VICTORIA.—Government grant £300 with prospects of substantial increase. Tutorial classes four, and study circles; 30 affiliated organisations, four branches.

NEW ZEALAND.—Government grant suspended. University grant £1,200. Municipal Councils of Auckland, Wellington, and Christchurch £100 each. Fifteen tutorial classes, many study circles, and public lectures.

QUEENSLAND AND SOUTH AUSTRALIA.—Have received promise of grants of £1,500 and £1,200 respectively. Here and in West Australia tutorial classes and study circles have been working for the past three years and many bodies have affiliated with the association.

The war has made recurring levies upon the officials of the W.E.A., and the conscription issue made the existence of even an organisation claiming to be non-party political difficult, but, inspired by the past and confident of the future, new members of the W.E.A. are continually stepping up to take vacant places. The ideal set before members is the building up of an organisation truly representative of working-class opinion on educational questions, which should participate actively in moulding an educational system in accordance with democratic ideas and aspirations, and should provide a common meeting-ground for all, who, though differing on other questions of vital importance, are united in their desire to raise the intellectual standard of Australian democracy.

A JUNIOR FELLOWSHIP OF THE W.E.A.

By W. E. Simnett.

To friends of the W.E.A. perhaps one of the most inspiring and significant developments of the movement of late is the crusade which it has undertaken on behalf of youth. After the war the problem of youth, of the education and training of the new generation, will indeed be of the first importance.

While other articles in these pages deal with the continued education and industrial training of adolescents, it is proposed here to consider briefly some aspects of social environment.

Under normal conditions the great majority of boys and girls finish schooling about the age of 14 and " go to work." Of these, a certain number subsequently attend more or less regularly at evening classes, or devote a portion of their scanty leisure to some form or another of self-improvement; but it may be safely assumed that the average boy or girl in all large towns makes somewhat the same use of leisure time as that graphically described for us by one of the Editors of this Year Book in his study of boy life and labour in Birmingham.

This matter of the use of leisure is permanent. Even when the day continuation school is established the question of the social and cultural use of leisure in adolescence will remain, although our working youth will then be, as we hope, not only freer, but better fitted to make use of their own time than they now are. Under present conditions, however, from 14 onwards, working girls and boys, after spending a long, tiring, and probably monotonous day in factory, shop, or office, have only a brief hour or two, apart from Saturday afternoons and Sundays, in which to satisfy all their cravings for pleasure, romance, adventure, and excitement. Long before our schemes for compulsory further education mature there will be ample scope for voluntary effort in helping our working youth to make the most pleasurable and fruitful use of the time that is their own in the critical and formative years between 14 and 18 or 20.

Here, we suggest, is an opportunity for the W.E.A. In this fatal hiatus between schooldays and the period when an all too small fragment of the great army of youth normally comes under the influence of movements concerned with higher education, the great leakage occurs of which bodies like the W.E.A. are striving to recover the best elements a long way down the stream. We must move up to the sources.

Our starting point should be fixed at the schoolgates. The minimum age for membership of the W.E.A. is 16, but in point of fact, its influence reaches probably very few under the age of, say, 18. Why not have a Junior W.E.A., or rather a Junior Fellowship, for young people between 14 and 18?

Let us see what this would mean. It means that the Fellowship must become a movement as ardent and fine as that which the W.E.A. itself inaugurated, and that the keynote of this movement must be the same principle of democratic self-government out of which grew the Tutorial Class and all the activities for which the W.E.A. stands to-day. Many agencies are now beneficently concerned with the welfare of working boys and girls, both at home and at work (see, for instance, " The Boy in Industry " pamphlet), but it is no depreciation of their efforts to say that the true salvation of the boy or girl must lie at last in his and her own hands.

In dealing with incipient democracy we must adopt democratic methods. The self-governing group, with which we are familiar in W.E.A. circles, arbiter of its own educational destiny, must reproduce itself, although in more elastic form, in the Junior Fellowship. How may this be done?

In " Progress " for January, 1916, the present writer has suggested a plan based upon the Old Scholars' Association of the Elementary Schools, and to this article* he would refer those who may be interested for a fuller account of the problem and of the proposed " Fellowship " than can be attempted in the limited space available in this Year Book. Briefly, it is proposed that the formation of Old Scholars' Associations should be encouraged in every elementary school, and that from these should be formed self-governing groups of boys and of girls who should seek, with the assistance of a leader, but by their own initiative and conscious effort, some definitely cultural aim. This may be either intensive or general, according to the tastes of those composing the group, which should not be too large for each individual to feel that he or she is taking an active and necessary part in its affairs. Some examples of possible group activities are given in the article referred to, together with suggestions for joint functions and for co-operation with other organisations.

To every W.E.A. member and to every class and group of students it should be a duty and a privilege, in the new days that are drawing near, to interest themselves actively in the schools of their neighbourhood. In the past Tutorial Class students have themselves formed and led introductory classes, so that others might in turn tread the paths of higher education. So we may hope that leaders and helpers will be forthcoming for the junior groups formed on the " Tutorial " model from the " old scholars " of the elementary school.

That what we suggest is neither extravagant nor impracticable is attested by the excellent work which is being done, or was done before the war, by several Old Scholars' Associations in London, which were capably organised and managed (to a large extent by the old scholars themselves), and which led a full and varied life of social and educational activity.

With the assistance of the Education Department of the L.C.C. the writer had proposed to undertake an investigation of the possibilities of such associations, which he hopes to carry out as soon as military duties and the resumption of normal conditions will permit. For the present he desires to urge upon the Workers' Educational Association the claims and fitness of working youth to benefit by the same methods and organisation which has brought higher education and culture to adult working democracy, and to suggest that this field of labour is peculiarly *our* heritage. He has proposed a plan whereby the schools may be naturally utilised and each centre linked up in the Fellowship, and he hopes to see this plan, with such modifications as experience and criticism may suggest, put into operation immediately after the war. In the meantime, he invites suggestions and help from all readers of this Year Book who are interested in the problem of " After School."

---

* " After-School." " Progress," January, 1916. (P. S. King and Son, 6d. net).

EDUCATIONAL RECONSTRUCTION.*

The Recommendations of the Workers' Educational Association to the Reconstruction Committee.

14, Red Lion Square, Holborn, W.C.,†
November 24th, 1916.

To the Secretary of the Reconstruction Committee.

SIR,—On behalf of the Workers' Educational Association, I beg to enclose herewith copies of a number of resolutions, together with explanatory matter, drawn up by that body with request that you will communicate them to the Sub-Committee which has been appointed to review the whole field of national education.

The resolutions embody the conclusions of the Association, after as careful inquiry and discussion as time permitted, into those aspects of the problem of education on which it felt entitled, and indeed impelled, in virtue of its professed objects and the experience of its members and affiliated societies, to offer a considered opinion.

It may be well to state briefly how the resolutions came into being and what body of opinion they represent.

The Workers' Educational Association‡ is a federation of 2,150 working class and educational bodies in England and Wales, including 737 Trade Unions, Trades Councils and Branches, 381 Co-operative Committees, 302 Adult Schools, Brotherhoods, etc., 12 University bodies, 9 Local Education Authorities, 170 Working Men's Clubs, Institutes, etc., 138 Teachers' Associations, 91 Educational and Literary Societies, 46 Classes and Study Circles, and 264 various societies, mainly of workpeople.

Affiliated bodies which are national in their scope are represented on the central governing body of the Association. Those which are local are represented on the governing bodies of the branches and districts by which the work of the Association is carried on, in close contact with Universities and Local Education Authorities, in different parts of the country.

Before making any effort to formulate a policy on the problem of Educational Reconstruction, we decided to consult, as far as possible, the working class as a whole. With this object in view, we issued last August a pamphlet, " What Labour Wants from Education," to all Trades Councils, Trade Union Branches, Co-operative Societies, Adult Schools, etc., in England and Wales. The pamphlet contained a series of questions which these bodies were requested to discuss and answer. Apart from a free distribution of 25,000 copies, 45,000 copies have been sold since last August. This indicates the widespread interest taken in the question and the extent of the field covered by our inquiries before formulating any proposals for the consideration of your Committee.

The resolutions which we now submit to you originated in the central body of the Association. They were submitted in draft to

---

* All the references in the footnotes are to Education Bill No. 2.
† The W E.A. has now moved to 16, Harpur Street, W.C. 1.
‡ On 1st June, 1917, the W.E.A. had 2,336 affiliated bodies. (See page 350.)

the nine local districts of the Association, and by them to their local branches, 160 in number, and to their affiliated societies. After being considered at branch meetings they were discussed at representative Council meetings of the districts to which amendments from the branches and local affiliated societies were submitted. Finally they were submitted to a meeting of the Central Council of the Association on November 18th, 1916, at which 133 amendments sent in by districts and national affiliated bodies (practically all of them embodying points of substance) were discussed and in a large number of cases embodied. In their present form they therefore represent the result of the deliberations of the Association as a whole, arrived at both in its local centres and through its affiliated bodies, and testify to the keen and widespread interest which the news of the appointment of your Committee has aroused in working-class circles.

A few words should be added in explanation of the character of the proposals submitted.

We are fully aware that the proposals taken by themselves may appear to be somewhat cut-and-dried and to lay undue stress on questions of organisation and machinery. We were, however, expressly authorised by the Central Council of the Association to affirm to your Committee with all possible emphasis that such an interpretation of the motive embodied in the proposals would be directly contrary to the spirit and purpose of those whose views they represent.

In the opinion of the Association, the ideal underlying educational reform, in whatever direction it is undertaken, must be essentially humane and, in the broadest sense of the word, spiritual, and no improvements in legislation or administrative machinery can hope to achieve success unless those who are responsible for their working bear this fact constantly in mind. The object of the proposals submitted is not simply to improve the educational machinery of the country; they have been conceived in the hope and desire that they may serve to set free the spiritual forces which the war has so strikingly brought to light in every section of the people, nowhere more than among the working class, and that they may thus contribute to the promotion of the work of reconstruction which must of necessity fall in so large a part upon the shoulders of the coming generation.

Yours faithfully,

J. M. MACTAVISH, General Secretary.

THE HIGHWAY OF EDUCATION.

RESOLUTION 1.—THE IDEAL.

That the broad principle of free education through all its stages, including that of the University, be accepted.

PRACTICAL PROPOSALS.

RESOLUTION 2.—YOUNG CHILDREN.*

(a) That the age for compulsory attendance at schools should be raised to six years, and it should be compulsory for the Local Education Authority to establish and control a sufficient number of Nursery Schools for the children within their areas between the ages of two and six;

(*b*) that attendance at these schools should be free; and *that they be open to all whose parents desire them to attend ;*†

(*c*) that the Nursery Schools should be under the special supervision of the School Medical Officer, and attention in them should be mainly directed to the cultivation in the children of good physical habits, and healthy bodily development, play and rest whenever possible in the open air forming an important part in the curriculum;

(*d*) that the Nursery Schools should accommodate small groups of children and should be so distributed as to be near the homes of the children;

(*e*) that the Head of the Nursery School should be a teacher who has special qualifications for the training of young children.

> * The provisions of the Bill on this subject are contained in Clause 19, and are to the effect that Education Authorities shall be empowered to apply, or aid the supply, of Nursery Schools for children over two and under five years of age, " whose attendance at such a school is desirable for their healthy, physical and mental development."

RESOLUTION 3.—UNIVERSAL FULL-TIME EDUCATION.*

We are of opinion that the age for exemption from compulsory full-time attendance at school should be 16, and to this end we recommend :—

(*a*) That universal full-time education continue to the age of 14, no exemptions being granted under that age, and that no child should leave school until the end of the terms, Christmas, Easter, or Midsummer, in which he attains the age of 14;

(*b*) that it be compulsory for all Local Education Authorities to raise the leaving age to 15 (without exemptions) within a period of five years, and that Local Education Authorities be granted powers forthwith to make bye-laws to raise it to 16;

(*c*) that when the school leaving age is raised above 14, Local Education Authorities should be required to grant maintenance allowances to children above that age where necessary;

(*d*) that education during the compulsory full-time period, more especially in the upper standards, should be organised with a view to its continuance during adolescence;

(*e*) that the employment of children for profit or wages outside school hours during the compulsory full-time school period be prohibited.

> * The age of full-time attendance is dealt with in Clause 8 of the Bill. That Clause provides —(*a*) that no exemption from school attendance below the age of 14 shall, in future, be permitted, (*b*) That education authorities shall be empowered to make bye-laws requiring the full-time attendance at school of children up to the age of 15.
>
> The employment of school children is dealt with in Clauses 13, 14, and 15. They may be summarised as follows :—
>
> (*a*) A child under 12 may not be employed at all.
>
> (*b*) A child over 12 may not be employed on a school day before the close of school hours, or on any day before 6 a.m. and after 8 p.m.
>
> (*c*) A child may not be employed in any factory or workshop under the Factory or Workshops Act, or in any mine or quarry.
>
> (*d*) A Local Authority may prohibit or regulate the employment of any child if it is satisfied that such employment is injurious to the child's health or education.

---

† The words in italics were added to the resolution after the introduction of Education Bill No. 1.

RESOLUTION 4.—HIGHER EDUCATION.

I. SECONDARY EDUCATION.

A.—Part=time education between the age of exemption from com= pulsory full=time attendance and 18.*

(*a*) That compulsory part-time education of not less than 20 hours per week (including time spent in organised games and school meals) be provided free for all such young persons as are not receiving full-time education ;

(*b*) that the hours of labour for all young persons under the age of 18 be limited to a maximum of 25 per week ;

(*c*) that the distribution of hours throughout the year upon the above basis should be arranged, where necessary, to meet the needs of seasonal industries and other circumstances ;

(*d*) that the education in such schools should be directed solely towards the full development of the bodies, minds, and characters of the pupils ; that it should therefore be intimately related to the environment and interests of the pupils, and should contain ample provision for physical well-being, including organised games and school meals ;

(*e*) that the teachers in such schools should enjoy status and emoluments similar to those of teachers in other secondary schools.

†(*f*) that no exemptions be granted to young persons under the age of 18 years.

†(*g*) that uncompromising opposition be offered to any attempt to secure the recognition of works schools as places of education within the meaning of the Act.

> * The principal provisions of the Bill on this subject are contained in Clauses 3, 10, 11, and 12, and may be summarised as follows: (*a*) Attendance at continuation schools shall be obligatory for all young persons between 14 and 18 (unless they are receiving, or have received, efficient instruction in some other manner) as they reach the age of 14. Young persons who have passed any examination equivalent to University Matriculation or who have been under full-time instruction in an efficient school until the age of 16 are exempt. (*b*) Such attendance shall take place for 320 hours in each year (*i.e.*, an average of 8 hours per week for 40 weeks). (*c*) After the lapse of 5 years from the appointed day, the Board of Education may, if it thinks fit, make an order increasing the hours of compulsory attendance required by the Act.

B.—Full Secondary Education.*

(*a*) That all children admitted to a Secondary School should have reached an approved standard of education, the ground of transfer being the fitness of the scholar for the broader curriculum ;

(*b*) that free provision should be made for all who are eligible and desirous to enter such schools, such provision to include a satisfactory maintenance allowance where necessary ;

(*c*) that the number of Secondary Schools of varying types should be largely increased, and that the curriculum be made more variable to meet the interests of individual scholars ;

(*d*) that facilities should be provided for the transfer from part-time to full-time secondary education ;

(*e*) that the requirements of a liberal education should be regarded as paramount in the organisation of every type of secondary school ;

---

† These clauses were added on 25th September, 1917.

(*f*) that the distribution and organisation of secondary schools should be such as to promote equality of access to University education of the highest type for students in every local area.

* There is no proposal in the Bill on Secondary Education. The W.E.A. regards this as a grave blot on the measure, especially in regard to the abolition of fees and the establishment of an adequate system of maintenance allowance.

II. UNIVERSITY EDUCATION.

(*a*) That no student should be accepted as an undergraduate of a University or University College who has not previously attained an adequate educational standard satisfactory to the University Authorities;

(*b*) that free provision should be made for all who reach this standard, adequate maintenance grants being given where financial circumstances require them, and, further, that until such time as free University education is provided, the number of scholarships, the value of each scholarship and the method of selection should be such that no student should be debarred by financial circumstances from becoming an undergraduate;

(*c*) that greater facilities should be provided whereby men and women able to profit by a special period of study at a University should be enabled to do so without an entrance examination;

(*d*) that all Universities and University Colleges conforming to Board of Education requirements should receive from the State such grants in aid as will enable them to be efficiently staffed and equipped;

(*e*) that it should be a condition of payment of State grants in aid to Universities and University Colleges that they make adequate provision for University Tutorial Classes;

(*f*) that since an essential part of the work of a University lies in affording facilities for the advancement of knowledge, more adequate provision should be made for scientific and literary research conducted with this object;

(*g*) that workpeople, together with other sections of the community, should be directly represented on the governing bodies of all Universities and University Colleges.

III. TECHNICAL EDUCATION.

(*a*) That in the interests alike of education and of economic efficiency, a sound general education in childhood and adolescence is the necessary foundation for any specialised course of technical or professional training, both in town and country, and that, therefore, technical education should be regarded as supplementary to secondary education;

(*b*) that, owing to the immense variety of occupations in a modern community, and the wide differences between them, both in the amount of special training necessary to efficiency and the prospects of permanent employment for young workers, it would be impracticable, as well as undesirable, for the State to attempt to enforce any compulsory system of technical education;

(*c*) that since the trades and industries and professions of the country exist in order to serve the needs of the community, technical education should, as far as possible, be divorced from the prevalent atmosphere of commercialism, and be regarded as a training in public service; and that this aspect of the subject should be kept in view in the organisation of the courses of instruction;

(*d*) that Technical Schools should be administered by a body on which employers and workpeople chosen by their respective trade organisations should be equally represented, together with members of the Education Authority, and that there should be special advisory committees of employers and workpeople for special trades;

(*e*) that close contact should be maintained between Universities and technical institutes, and between technical institutes and schools and workshop practice, and that workpeople should also be represented on the University Committees concerned;

(*f*) that, subject to the preceding conditions, an extension of technical and professional education is highly desirable in the national interest;

(*g*) that such education should be free, and that until this is provided there should be a generous provision of scholarships with adequate maintenance grants, so that duly qualified students from the full-time and part-time Secondary Schools and from evening classes in technical schools, whose special bent lies in the direction of scientific and technical work, may pass forward to full-time day courses of instruction (followed by research) in Universities, Technical Colleges, and the larger Technical Schools.

RESOLUTION 5.—CORPORATE LIFE.

Since experience has shown the great educational value of corporate life in schools it is necessary—

(*a*) that adequate playgrounds and playing fields, with the necessary equipment and free transit to them when necessary, should be provided for all schools;

(*b*) that greater freedom of access for children to playgrounds should be allowed out of school hours;

(*c*) that children should be encouraged to arrange their own games and other activities, and that facilities should be given for the development of special aptitudes;

(*d*) that as far as possible the help of the children should be enlisted in the management of school life.

Further, it is desirable, with a view to the development of corporate life in our schools—

(*e*) that the greatest possible freedom be given to both teachers and pupils, and that teachers be not required to adhere rigidly to a prescribed time-table or a fixed syllabus;

(*f*) that the growing practice of a common school meal be encouraged;

(*g*) that because of the importance of the development of a sense of beauty in early years the school buildings and interiors should be designed with this end in view.

RESOLUTION 6.—PHYSICAL EDUCATION.*

That, in view of the general obligation of the State to safeguard the physical well-being of the children of the nation and of the serious defects of their health revealed by the School Medical Service, ampler provision for ⸫ ⸱ physical well-being is indispensable to the proper working of our educational system.

With this in view it is necessary—

(*a*) that it be compulsory for all Local Education Authorities to set up and maintain such a Medical and Dental Service as will secure adequate inspection and treatment to all scholars attending the schools within the area of the respective authorities ;

(*b*) that the system of school meals be so extended and improved as to overcome the evils of under-feeding and malnutrition ;

(*c*) that greater facilities for physical training should be provided, including the organisation of games and the use of simple equipment, and also bathing ad swimming where possible ;

(*d*) that the policy of establishing schools on the outskirts of towns, where facilities for open-air teaching and playing fields can be more easily provided, should be encouraged, with the necessary arrangements for conveyance and common meals ;

(*e*) that ample provision be made for the fullest possible education of all children who are physically or mentally deficient.

> * Theproposals of the Bill with regard to this subject are contained in Clauses 17 and 18. They may be briefly summarised as follows : (*a*) A Local Education Authority may maintain holiday or school camps, centres and equipment for physical training, playing fields, school baths, and other facilities for social and physical training. (*b*) A Local Education Authority shall have, in relation to children in secondary schools and continuation schools, the same powers and duties with regard to medical inspection and treatment as it has with regard to children in elementary schools—*i.e*, it *must* inspect them and it *may* provide treatment for them.

RESOLUTION 7.—SIZE OF CLASSES.*

We are of opinion that no class in any school ought to contain more than 30 pupils, and to this end we recommend :—

(*a*) That the necessary steps be taken immediately to increase the supply of qualified teachers and school accommodation so as to reduce classes to 40, with a view to a further reduction to 30 ;

(*b*) that a standard of not more than 30 be adopted for all new and remodelled schools, that a separate class-room be provided for each class, and that the present minimum basis of floor space per child be largely increased.

> * There is no proposal in the Bill on this subject.

RESOLUTION 8.---THE SUPPLY OF GOOD TEACHERS.*

To provide an adequate supply of good teachers it is necessary—

(*a*) that there be free access to training facilities for the teaching profession, accompanied by adequate maintenance grants where required ;

(*b*) that the salaries paid and pensions provided should be such as will induce the best men and women available to enter and remain in the profession, with equal pay for equal service ;

(*c*) that intending teachers should be enabled to pass through a period of study at a University of at least a year's duration before entering the profession, and that the colleges where professional training is provided should be closely connected with a University ;

(*d*) that every possible facility should be provided for present unqualified teachers to qualify, and that the appointment of unqualified teachers be discontinued ;

(*c*) that the highest positions in the educational service should be open to teachers who are fitted to fill them.

* There is no proposal with regard to the supply of teachers in the Bill.

RESOLUTION 9.—PUBLIC LIBRARIES.*

That, in view of the importance of extending and developing the work of the public libraries in town and country, it is desirable that they should be brought into closer connection with the general educational system of the country :

With this end in view the separate library rate should be abolished, and the provision and upkeep of public libraries should be entrusted to the Local Education Authority as an integral part of the scheme for its area.

* No proposal in regard to Public Libraries is made in the Bill.

RESOLUTION 10.—DISTRIBUTION OF COST.*

(*a*) That each Local Education Authority be required to submit to the Board of Education a complete scheme of education for its area, together with estimates of the cost ;

(*b*) that 75 per cent. of the total cost of any approved scheme be met by the National Exchequer, but that

(*c*) the Board of Education be empowered to reduce the grant where—

(1) the teaching staff is insufficient in quality or numbers or the salaries paid are inadequate ;

(2) the number of scholars in any class exceeds 40 ;

(3) the number and variety of educational institutions are not adequate ;

(4) the medical inspection and treatment and supply of school meals are not adequate ;

(5) the Local Education Authority fails to administer its bye-laws ;

(6) where any other part of the scheme is not carried out to the satisfaction of the Board of Education ;

(*d*) That the Board of Education be required to give a special grant to meet the needs of areas where—

(1) the school population is high ;

(2) the rateable value is low as compared with the cost of education.

* Clause 38 (2) of the Education Bill provides that the grants paid to a local authority shall be "not less than one-half of the net expenditure of the authority."

RESOLUTION 11.—EDUCATIONAL ENDOWMENTS.*

That since the proper use of educational endowments is important to the development of a national system of education, it is desirable :—

(*a*) that a public and intelligible statement should be made periodically as to the amount of such endowments, the sources from which they are received, and the way in which they are controlled and expended ;

(*b*) that there should be an inquiry into their origin and history ;

(*c*) that action should be taken for their better distribution where this would appear after inquiry to be desirable in the interests of the educational development of the country.

> * Clauses 39—41 provide for the administration of Educational Endowments by official trustees.

RESOLUTION 12.—WORK OF THE W.E.A.*

That, since the character of British democracy ultimately depends on the collective wisdom of its adult members, no system of education can be complete that does not promote serious thought and discussion on the fundamental interests and problems of life and society, such as is promoted by the W.E.A.; that while we are of opinion that it is against the best interests and free development of the Association to accept a grant from the State for general purposes, we regard it as necessary, in order that the voluntary contributions to the Association should be free for educational propaganda work, that grants should be made towards the cost of organisation of definite and recognised pieces of work, such as University Tutorial Classes and one-year classes. We regard this need as being of national importance, more especially in the difficult period after the war. We, therefore, recommend :—

(*a*) That the Board of Education grant to University Tutorial Classes be equal to 75 per cent. of the tutor's salary and 75 per cent. of the proved cost of organisation and administration ;

(*b*) that the Board of Education grant to one-year classes be 75 per cent. of the total cost of organisation, tuition, and administration.

> * The Educational Bill does not deal with the work of the W.E.A.

(a) MILITARY TRAINING.*

That Clauses 3 and 17 of the Bill should be amended by the insertion of the words to the following effect : " Provided, however, that the physical training in question shall not be of a military bias or intention."

> * There is no provision to this effect in the Bill.

(a) CHILDREN EXEMPTED UNDER 14.*

That provision be made in the Bill for the continued education of children under 14 on the appointed day, who have left school before the Act comes into force.

> * There is no proposal with regard to such children in the Bill.

(a) CHILDREN ABNORMALLY EMPLOYED DURING THE WAR.*

That provision be made, either in this or in a separate Bill, for the education of juveniles prematurely exempted from school attendance during the war.

> * There is no proposal with regard to such children in the Bill.

(a) CONSTITUTION OF EDUCATION COMMITTEES.

That provision be made to secure that the co-opted members of Education Committees include representatives of all branches of the teaching profession and of the organised workers.

> * There is no provision to this effect in the Bill.

(a) These clauses were added to the W.E.A. programme on 25th September, 1917. That is, after the introduction of Education Bill No. 2.

THE W.E.A. : ITS CONSTITUTION AND ACTIVITIES.

At the close of the year 1916-17 the Association registered 10,750 members and 2,336 affiliated organisations, mainly Labour. These were organised in 191 branches, 10 districts, and the Central Association. The branches and districts are for most purposes autonomous bodies, governed by their own members and affiliated bodies.

The Central Association acts as a co-ordinating body and is alone responsible in questions of national policy. It is governed by a Council composed of six representatives from each district and one representative from each affiliated society. The Central Council meets at least twice in each year. The Executive Committee is elected by the Council at its annual meeting in July and is composed of one representative of each District Council and six representatives of national affiliated societies. The Central Association is financed by contributions from the districts, the amount of which is determined by the Central Council from time to time, by contributions from national bodies (the minimum affiliation fee to the Central Council is £2 2s.), and by donations from individuals.

WORK.

The main work of the Association has been, and will continue to be, to arouse and satisfy the desire for education among adult men and women. Its special function has hitherto been, and must remain, the creation, in harmony with Labour and educational agencies, of a system of adult education which is in essence a Workers' University.

CLASSES AND LECTURES.

The Association is largely responsible for organising Tutorial Classes in addition to organising and running one-year classes, study circles and lectures.

During the year 1916-17, 99 Tutorial Classes were carried on, as compared with 121 the previous year, the number of students being approximately 1,926, as compared with 2,414; 121 Tutorial Classes have been running throughout the winter 1917-18, but the number of students is not yet known. History and economics continue to be the favourite subjects in the Tutorial Classes, the growing interest in the problems of national reconstruction having greatly encouraged this.

In the year 1916-17 there were 154 one-year classes and 70 study circles, as well as 526 public lectures. Of these, 25 one-year classes, 24 study circles, and 146 lectures were on subjects connected with the war. In addition 131 lectures, conferences, and discussions on " Educational Reconstruction " and nine dealing specially with " Child Labour and Education " were organised; 118 informal talks to W.E.A. members were also arranged.

Besides the above, strictly organised by the Association, very many lecturers have been supplied to other bodies, one branch alone having arranged as many as 327 addresses for other societies.

SUMMER SCHOOLS.

Summer Schools have become an increasingly important part of the work of the Association. Experience at these has shown the wisdom of giving the fullest opportunities for personal and informal intercourse between tutor and students, and, if necessary, of reducing the number of lectures in order to facilitate this. In 1917 much attention was naturally devoted to the problems of reconstruction which will arise after the war. At Cambridge, eleven Tutorial Class students attended a course of study upon " The Economics of Land." At Oxford, while special provision was made, when possible, for students who desired assistance on some special subject, the plan of study was grouped under the three headings of domestic, foreign, and imperial reconstruction. On an average, each student in the Oxford School spent 22 hours a week in class and tuition. At all the schools there was a happy combination of serious study with a spirit of comradeship.

In addition, the London Joint Committee organised meetings on four successive Saturdays, general lectures being given in the afternoons, and three concurrent Tutorial Classes being held in the evenings. The number of students attending the meetings each Saturday varied from 250 to 300.

In 1917, Summer Schools were held at :—

Bangor.—July 7th to August 25th.

Cambridge,

London (Saturday School).—June 2nd, 9th, 16th, and 23rd.

Oxford.—June 30th to August 18th.

For 1918, Summer Schools are being arranged at :—

Bangor.—July 6th to August 24th.

Cambridge.—August 1st to 13th.

London (Saturday School).—May 25th, June 1st, 8th, and 15th.

Oxford.—July 6th to August 17th.

ONE=YEAR CLASSES.

One of the most serious problems of the immediate future is the finance of the one-year classes of the Association. At present the Association is largely dependent on the voluntary or semi-voluntary services of tutors. Most of these classes have been splendidly served, but, if they are to maintain the great place to which their work entitles them, they must be placed on a financially firm basis.

W.E.A. COLLEGES.

An interesting development of the work of the Association is the establishment of W.E.A. Colleges in different parts of the country.

BOOKS.

The problem of the supply of books has from the first been a serious difficulty in all W.E.A. classes. The Universities have done much to assist the students in this matter, but were unable to meet the great need of the Tutorial Classes and still more of the one-year classes. Various methods have been tried to solve the problem. In addition to the libraries lent by the Universities, there appear now to be two principal roads to a solution.

By arrangement with publishers and authors the Association has secured special editions of standard books needed by our students. The scheme at present is hardly past the experimental stage, but already cheap editions have been arranged of the following books : " History of Trade Unionism," " Industrial Democracy," and " Prevention of Destitution," by S. and B. Webb; " The World of Labour," " Labour in War Time," " Self-Government in Industry," " Trade Unionism on the Railways," by G. D. H. Cole; " Women in the Engineering Trades," by B. Drake; " Trade Unionism," by C. M. Lloyd; " The Industrial Outlook," by various writers; "The War of Steel and Gold" and " A League of Nations," by H. N. Brailsford; " The War and Democracy," by various writers; " The Tutorial Class Movement," by A. Mansbridge; " Essay Writing," by Arnold Freeman and B. L. K. Henderson; " Great Britain After the War," by Arnold Freeman and Sidney Webb; " Nationality and Government," by A. E. Zimmern. Special terms have been arranged for the following periodicals : " The Athenæum," " The Political Quarterly " and " The Round Table." The W.E.A. has also co-operated with other organisations, such as the Athenæum Literature Department and the Fabian Research Department, in order to secure special cheap editions for its members and students.

THE CENTRAL LIBRARY FOR STUDENTS.

The Central Library for Students, founded on the initiative of the W.E.A., has provided the second avenue by which a solution of this problem is being approached. It is willing to supply books, usually the more expensive kind, to any classes in connection with the W.E.A., or to any members of the W.E.A. ; 5,299 volumes were issued during the year 1917-18. Anyone desiring to borrow books should write to 20, Tavistock Square, London, W.C. 1. The only charge made is that of carriage. The Committee would like to feel that their educational work is being strengthened by a full use of the library.

WOMEN'S CLASSES.

The Women's Classes have had a struggle to maintain their membership, owing to war work, irregular hours, etc., and they have in most cases struggled successfully, though in one or two centres classes have had to cease for a time. It is interesting to note that where there are no special Women's Classes there is an increasing proportion of women students in the mixed classes.

In the special Women's Classes first aid, home nursing, and hygiene are among the most popular subjects; the rest of the classes are divided among history, literature, nature study, French, singing, embroidery, dressmaking and millinery, and elementary biology.

A large number of lectures are regularly arranged for women's organisations, such as Women's Co-operative Guilds, Mothers' Clubs, Women's Labour Leagues, Y.W.C.A.

RURAL WORK.

The rural work of the Association has suffered more than any other activity through the difficulties caused by the war. In the several districts, where the movement was taking root in small villages, the obstacles caused by increased railway fares and disorganisation of trains have made it almost impossible to continue the work. Everywhere financial stress is hampering growth, but there is good ground for the belief that when the opportunity arrives the work in villages will grow rapidly; this appears to be especially so in the Eastern, South-Eastern, and Western Districts. A special committee of the Central Council is at present inquiring into the whole subject.

EDUCATIONAL RECONSTRUCTION.

While the first task of the Association is to stimulate and provide for the demand for adult education, it is concerned with the education not only of men and women, but of the children who will be the men and women of the future. Education is continuous, because life is continuous. If the adult is to win the opportunities for freedom of thought and self-expression which should be the birthright of every human being, the personality of the child must not be stunted by premature wage-earning.

In order to unite opinion upon the subject of Educational Reconstruction after the war, the Association in September, 1916, appointed a committee to draft recommendations which might be put before the public and the Government. The committee submitted its report to the Council on 18th November, 1916. The proposals contained in it have been widely discussed in the press and on the platform. A very large number of conferences upon them have been organised by the districts in different parts of the country. They were adopted, with certain small amendments, at a National Conference of Working-Class and Educational Organisations held at the Central Hall, Westminster, on May 3rd, 1917.

THE " HIGHWAY " AND LITERATURE.

The " Highway," the official organ of the W.E.A., is published monthly. In addition, pamphlets and leaflets are issued from time to time on educational questions and the work of the W.E.A.

THE W.E.A. OVERSEAS.

The movement in Australia and New Zealand, where remarkable progress has been made, is described in the article by Mr. F. A. Bland.*

In South Africa, where there are two branches, at Johannesburg and Durban, classes and lectures are held each winter and considerable headway is being made.

In Canada the foundations of a strong W.E.A. are being laid; the great need of the moment is an organiser. A class in Economics and Educational Problems, under the leadership of an old friend of the Association, Professor J. A. Dale, has been meeting for the past three

* See pages 335-338.

years in Montreal. Latest reports indicate that in the near future big developments are to be looked for in Toronto and other cities.

It is most satisfactory to see that wherever experiments on the lines of the Association's work are made, they meet with the same enthusiastic reception as they have won in Great Britain.

EASTERN DISTRICT.

Founded in 1913. This is one of the newest districts of the Association, and until the end of last year was entirely dependent on voluntary effort for organising and secretarial work. The district has now, however, secured the services of a full-time secretary and solid progress is being made. Last year (1917) the district reported that, despite the difficulties arising from the war, remarkable progress had been made during the year. Three new branches were formed at Bedford, Halstead, and Hitchin, and one was in process of formation at Chelmsford. At Norwich active work was resumed after being temporarily suspended in 1916. Activities at Colchester and Letchworth were still suspended. A considerable difficulty was found in the maintenance of classes, but in this work success was achieved by six branches and a class was also maintained at St. Albans, where there is as yet no branch. Kettering and Ipswich made study circles a prominent feature of their work. Twenty-seven lectures were organised in the district, of which four at Brentwood were arranged as a course. The district was active in the campaign on Educational Reconstruction. Two representative conferences were called by the Ipswich Branch, four other branches organised meetings, and a meeting was also arranged at Boxmoor. During the past year the work has grown rapidly. The life of the branches has been intensified, a new branch has been formed at Braintree and the work is being carried into new districts.

LONDON DISTRICT.

The vastness of London, its cosmopolitan population, its lack of local life and feeling, presents a difficult problem to the W.E.A. Remarkable success was achieved in the year ending July, 1917, the last for which complete statistics are available.

The work was more diversified and extensive than in previous years. There were 22 University Tutorial Classes, taking economics, history, literature, political science, and natural science; nearly 70 one-year classes and study circles (many of which were women's classes), taking a very wide range of subjects, history, literature, economics, singing, gardening, domestic science, etc.; lectures in hospitals; visits to places of historic interest, including several arranged specially for wounded soldiers to St. Paul's, Westminster Abbey, the Houses of Parliament; 440 lectures in W.E.A. branches and local organisations; three series of lectures in Central London; 25 educational conferences and addresses. In the latter half of 1917 a number of large representative conferences were held on Educational Reconstruction at which the programme of the W.E.A. was strongly supported.

Three new affiliations were secured during the year, and the number of individual members of the district was nearly doubled, being 224.

The outstanding feature of the work during the past year has been the rapid development of the outlying districts. Tutorial Classes have been started at Finchley, Wood Green, Tottenham, Harrow, and Wealdstone, and one-year classes at Kew and Crayford. Branches have now been formed at Crayford, Kew, and Wealdstone. The work of the other branches has continued to develop except in one or two places where war service has made too heavy a call on our workers.

MIDLAND DISTRICT.

The Midland district is one of the oldest. Much good work has been accomplished, although the district has suffered considerably through the difficulties arising out of war conditions. Activities have been temporarily suspended in five centres, but active work has been carried on by 20 branches, including two new ones at Colwich and Hereford. During the past two winters, particular attention has been given in classes, lectures, and conferences to social and economic reconstruction. In January, 1917, an eight days' school, which was attended by 58 students, was held in the University of Birmingham, for the study of Labour Problems and the War. The district has been active in prosecuting a campaign on Educational Reconstruction. All Labour and educational organisations in the district were invited to co-operate, and four very successful conferences were organised.

NORTH=EASTERN DISTRICT.

The North-Eastern district of the W.E.A. was formed in the autumn of 1910, with Mr. J. W. Lee as secretary, and the late Dean Kitchen, of Durham, as the first chairman. As the work in the district developed and the tutorial class movement began to be known, the formation of a University Joint Commitee was essential, and the Durham University Joint Committee was formed in the spring of 1911. Mr. P. A. Brown was appointed tutor, and classes were organised for the autumn of 1912 at Ashington, Gateshead, Sunderland, Hartlepool, and West Stanley (2). On the death of Dean Kitchin, in 1912, Dr. F. B. Jevons, M.A., became chairman of the District Association, which office he still holds. The growth of the W.E.A. in the North-East was steady, and at the end of the first complete year, 48 organisations had affiliated to the district and ten branches of the W.E.A. had been formed. Under the guidance of Mr. Lee activity increased, and when he resigned from office in the autumn of 1914, he had laid securely the foundations of a strong organisation in the North of England. His successor—Mr. J. G. Trevena—took up the work in the first shock of the European War. It was doubtful for some time what effect the war would have on the movement, but after nearly four years of hostilities, the W.E.A. in the N.E. district emerges with its activities widened and its position consolidated. Labour has learned the importance of education, and 107 organisations have now rallied to the support of the W.E.A. The individual members in the district number 100. Nineteen branches are in existence and doing what educational work is possible. During the past session four University tutorial classes have been held and 24 preparatory classes. Three large representative conferences have been called during the past year to discuss the various problems in connection with the campaign on Educational Reconstruction, and in this way much valuable propaganda has been done.

In furtherance of this campaign on Educational Reconstruction, two district conferences, attended by about 450 delegates each, have been held—October, 1916, and February, 1917. Branch conferences have been held in the following centres : Bishop Auckland, Carlisle, Darlington, Stockton and district, including Hartlepool and Middlesbrough. The pamphlet on " Educational Reconstruction " has been sent from the district office to working-class organisations in the North of England to the number of about 2,200. A vigorous circulation of the pamphlet has also been carried on in each of the branches. Draft resolutions have been circulated similarly, and have in many cases been forwarded to official circles. The pamphlet has been brought well to the notice of the press, which has given space to W.E.A. proposals.

NORTH=WESTERN DISTRICT.

Originally covering a much wider area than at present, this district was founded in 1906. The growth of the work necessitated the division into the present North-Western and Yorkshire Districts in 1914. War conditions have seriously affected the work of some branches, and the activities of several others are suspended.

But during the year 1916-17 activity in Stockport was resumed, new branches were formed at Wigan and Pendlebury, 21 additional societies affiliated, and the individual membership increased by 15. In connection with the campaign on Educational Reconstruction, 20 conferences and meetings were held, and numerous deputations were received by Trade Unions, Working Men's Clubs, etc., with good results. Nineteen Tutorial Classes were held during the year, as compared with 27 during the previous year. In addition to these, seven special one-year classes were organised by Manchester University. The Summer School at Bangor was very successful, 81 students taking part.

Since the introduction of the Education Bill, special efforts have been made to overcome the opposition of certain sections of the cotton operatives to the abolition of the half-time system, special pamphlets and leaflets have been issued, conferences have been held, and a large number of meetings addressed.

In the latter half of 1917 and during 1918 new ground has been cultivated in North Lancashire, Westmorland, and Cumberland. Several branches have been formed and a special Committee constituted to organise the work in the district. The early results in this region are full of promise.

SOUTH=EASTERN DISTRICT.

This district originally comprised the whole of the present district, the London district, and the Eastern. The growth and spread of the work soon made division necessary. Up till now it has been found impossible to engage the services of a full-time secretary, but the district has been well served by the part-time secretaries who have carried on the work. In the year 1917, the outstanding feature was the work of the twelve study groups that were organised. Several branches arranged courses of lectures and single lectures. The district was very active in the campaign on Educational Reconstruction. Many of the branches organised well-attended conferences at which the proposals of the W.E.A. were strongly supported. Work was opened in several new districts, and developments were hoped for at Staines and Hythe. The individual membership of the district increased to 36, and there were 21 affiliated bodies. New branches were formed, and have already done good work, at Ashford, Horsham, Eastleigh, and one in connection with the Holiday House at Burghfield Common. This made a total of 27 branches in the district; of these, seven have suspended activities during the war. As an earnest of the future, few developments could be more welcome than the rise of groups of branches such as have recently come into being in Kent and around Southampton. The movement in this district is full of vigour.

WELSH DISTRICT.

During the first years of the war, the work in Wales suffered considerable interruption, but, despite difficulties, the organisation was kept intact, and several of the branches throughout the period did considerable work. In cases where Tutorial and other classes found it impossible to continue their regular course, the members met as study groups. The two most active branches were undoubtedly Cardiff, where a successful course of lectures was held, and an energetic campaign on Educational Reconstruction conducted, culminating in a thoroughly representative conference; and Penarth, where a successful class on " European Politics of the 19th Century " was held, and various other activities continued. Lectures and classes were also held by the branches at Barry, Bridgend, Cardiff, and Llantwit Major. The interest aroused by the W.E.A. campaign and the Government inquiry into University education has rapidly created an atmosphere which entitles us to look to the future with confidence. The full results of this will not be achieved for some time, but already considerable developments are taking place. During the winter 1917-18, two full-time tutors were at work in the district. The classes were keen and the work good. At the close of the session the members of several of the classes arranged a programme of work for the summer, so that next winter the demand for Tutorial Class facilities may grow more rapidly.

WESTERN DISTRICT.

Notwithstanding the many difficulties created by the war, the work of the district has been well maintained. Attention has been mainly directed to sustaining existing branches rather than attempting to start new ones. A new branch was formed during the year 1916-17, at Stroud. An excellent start has been made and there is great promise of rapid development.

The district at one time consisted of 21 branches, a number of which were rural, but the war and other causes have been responsible for ten of these closing down. It is hoped that the majority will resume their useful work as soon as possible. The remaining eleven have done good work; eight have successfully run grant-earning classes throughout the winter, two have done well in other ways, and one made a plucky attempt under difficult circumstances.

The outstanding feature of the district is the magnificent record of work accomplished by the Bristol Branch. Heavy demands for lecturers and leaders have been made, but with few exceptions these have been all met, thanks to the generous way in which those appealed to placed their services at the disposal of the W.E.A.

With a strong centre like Bristol as a base, it only needs adequate financial support for large developments in the Western district, especially in Somerset, where the work of the W.E.A. has been very successful.

The question of Educational Reconstruction has received a considerable share of attention. Very successful conferences have been held at Bath and Bristol, and good discussions have taken place in other branches. Travelling expenses, especially with the abnormal rail fares, have prevented conferences being arranged in scattered areas. Two thousand copies of the W.E.A. Recommendations have been circulated to Trade Union branches and other working-class organisations. Resolutions approving these proposals have been passed by numerous bodies and forwarded to Members of Parliament and also to public bodies.

Quite one of the most cheering developments during recent months has been the rise of the W.E.A. in Devon and Cornwall. Till now this district has been somewhat isolated from W.E.A. influences. Mr. Straker, the Western district secretary of the W.E.A., spent two months in the district last year (1917); the response was magnificent. Three branches have already been formed and one is in the course of formation. With the services of a full-time organiser, great progress is anticipated in the south-western counties.

YORKSHIRE DISTRICT.

Originally included in the North-Western district, the growth of the work in Yorkshire necessitated the establishment of a new district in 1914. Although its history has thus been cast almost entirely in the period of the war, it is a record of continuous growth. By the solidity of its work, the district has obtained a very large degree of support from the Labour Movement. In the year 1916-17, owing to the pressure of war conditions, three branches (with the exception of holding a class) had to suspend their activities. On the other hand, three new branches were formed. The total branch membership of the district increased from 1,448 individual members to 1,600, and 357 affiliated societies to 389. The corresponding figures for the district are 289 to 323 individual members, and 31 to 36 affiliated societies. The district was very active in the campaign on Educational Reconstruction, and four representative conferences were held in the county. In addition there was held a considerable number of local conferences of working people. A strong effort has since been made to secure the strengthening of the Education Bill. The Holiday School at Ingleton met twice during the year, and on each occasion with success. The number of one-year classes and study circles has decreased during the year, but the number of Tutorial Classes has increased—31 having been held.

SCOTLAND.

During the past two years the position of the W.E.A. in Scotland has been consolidated and preparations made for a considerable advance at an early date. New branches have been formed in Ayrshire and Dundee. In each of the other three branches the number of individual members and affiliated societies has increased. In July, 1916, the Provisional Council for Scotland was formed to co-ordinate the activities of the branches and generally to develop the work of the W.E.A. in Scotland. A number of organisations have affiliated to the new Council. Lecture courses were conducted in Edinburgh and Aberdeen during the winter months. In 1916-17 classes were organised by each of the three branches—Edinburgh, three classes : economics, literature, and philosophy; Aberdeen, a third year Tutorial Class in applied economics; Glasgow, three classes, two of which dealt with Scottish history and literature in the 19th Century, and the third dealing with economics. In Aberdeen and Edinburgh the classes were organised by Joint Committees composed of representatives of the University, the School Board, and the W.E.A. Branch. In Glasgow a Joint Committee has not yet been formed. The work has been greatly hampered by the prevailing conditions due to the war. The measure of success, however, is sufficient to justify the belief that the movement has taken a firm root in Scotland.

IRELAND.

The Belfast Branch has made progress in spite of many difficulties. A Tutorial Class has been studying the History of Western Civilisation, while another class has taken as its subject " Fifty Years of Social and Economic Idealism." Informal talks have been given on Saturday evenings and Sunday rambles have been organised. The branch have given special attention to the problem of Educational Reconstruction, and have produced their own proposals for Ireland. These have been widely discussed and supported.

For the two sessions 1915-17, " Economic Conferences," attended by an audience of workers and students which increased from 60 to 400, were held at University College, Cork. These were practically University Extension Lectures, followed by animated discussions, but they were directed and managed entirely by the initiative and enterprise of Professor Rahilly and Professor Smiddy. In connection with the Conferences a " University and Labour " series of pamphlets has been started. Owing to this successful effort, the Corporation of Cork was induced to use its hitherto neglected power under the Irish Universities Act (1908), and to make a grant of £150 for next session's Extension Lectures and Tutorial Classes. This is the first grant ever made in Ireland for the purpose. A Joint Committee has been formed and will, it is hoped, link its activities and affiliate with the W.E.A. During the past year Tutorial Classes have been started under the leadership of Dr. Burke.

W.E.A. PUBLICATIONS.

	Post Free. Per copy. s. d.	Per doz. s. d.	Per 100, s. d.
The " Highway " (monthly)	o 1½	o 10*	—
" The Choice Before the Nation "	o 2	1 9	—
" How to Amend the Education Bill " ..		Free.	
" Democracy or Defeat," by R. H. Tawney ..	o 1½	o 9	6 o
" Educational Reconstruction," being the Recommendations of the W.E.A. to the Reconstruction Committee..	o 1½	o 9	6 o
" What Labour Wants from Education," by J. M. Mactavish	o 1½	o 9	6 o
" English Educational Endowments," by H. T. Wilkins and J. A. Fallows, M.A... Cloth	1 o	9 o	—
Paper	o 6	4 6	—
" Bibliography of Reconstruction "	In course of preparation		
" An Introduction to the Study of Social Problems," by Arnold Freeman	Reprinting		
" War and the Workers "	o 1½	o 9	
" Trade Unionism in Australia," by Meredith Atkinson, M.A.	1 6	15 o	—
" First Aid to Essay Writing," by Meredith Atkinson, M.A.	o 3½	2 6	18 o
" Some Thoughts on Education and the War," by R. H. Tawney	o 1½	o 9	6 o

* For quantities not less than two dozen.

W.E.A. CHEAP EDITIONS.*

	Usual net price s. d.	Cheap Editions. Per copy. s d.
" The Industrial Outlook," Edited by H. Sanderson Furniss	3 6	1 6
" Great Britain After the War," by Sidney Webb and Arnold Freeman	1 o	o 6
" Memorandum on the Industrial Situation After the War." The Garton Foundation	1 o	o 9
" Labour in War Time," by G. D. H. Cole .. ..Out of print		2 6
" The World of Labour," by G. D. H. Cole	4 6	2 6
" Self-Government in Industry," by G. D. H. Cole ..	4 6	2 6
" Restoration of Trade Union Conditions," by Sidney Webb	—	1 o
" Trade Unionism," by C. M. Lloyd	2 6	1 6
" Women in the Engineering Trades," by B. Drake..	2 6	1 6
" Prevention of Destitution," by Mr. and Mrs. Sidney Webb	6 o Cloth	2 4
	Paper	1 10
" A League of Nations," by H. N. Brailsford	5 o	2 o
" The War of Steel and Gold," by H. N. Brailsford..	3 6	2 o
" The War and Democracy," by several writers ..	2 6	2 o
" University Tutorial Classes," by A. Mansbridge ..	2 6	1 4
" Essay Writing," by B. L. K. Henderson and Arnold Freeman	1 6	1 4

* No bookseller can be supplied with copies of these cheap editions for sale,

SOME OTHER PAMPHLETS AND CHEAP EDITIONS.

POST FREE.

	Per copy. s. d.	Per doz. s. d.	Per 100. s. d.
" Christmas Eve," by Browning	0 1½	—	—
" Address to the Swindon Branch, W.E.A.," by Robert Bridges, Poet Laureate ..	0 2½	—	—
" Old Worlds for New," by A. J. Penty ..	3 10	—	—

	Usual net prices.	Cheap Editions. Post free. Per copy.	Per doz. plus half carriage.
" An Introduction to the Study of International Relations," by A. Greenwood and others.	2 0	1 4	12 0
" International Finance," by Hartley Withers	3 6	1 4	13 0
" Nationalism and Internationalism," by Ramsay Muir	4 6	1 6	13 6
" Mutual Aid," by P. Kropotkin	6 0	1 8	—
" Conflicting Ideals of Woman's Work," by B. L. Hutchins	—	1 0	10 0
" Reorganisation of Industry"..	—	1 0	10 0
" Urban and Rural Industry "	—	1 0	10 0
" Some Economic Aspects of International Relations "	—	1 0	10 0
" The People's Year Book"	—	1 4	10 6
" The Labour Year Book, 1918 "	Ready shortly.		

In addition to these, the following Magazines can be obtained at special rates :—

	Usual Annual Subscriptions.	Subscriptions through W.E.A.	Carriage free. Per doz. copies.
" Round Table " (quarterly)	10 0	6 0	14 0
" Athenæum "	14 0	6 0	4 6

Owing to increasing costs none of the prices given above can be guaranteed.

W.E.A. DIRECTORY.

CENTRAL ASSOCIATON.

General Secretary : J. M. MACTAVISH, 16, Harpur Street, W.C. 1.

EASTERN DISTRICT.

District Secretary : G. H. PATEMAN, 276, Cherryhinton Rd., Cambridge.

Bedford.—Secretaries : H. WASH, 3, Palmerston Street, Bedford; Miss COOK, 158, Hurst Grove, Bedford.

Braintree.—Secretary : STEPHEN WOOD, Mount Road, Braintree.

Chelmsford.—Secretary : Mrs. AUSTIN, Louisa Villa, Great Baddon, Chelmsford.

Colchester.—Secretary : H. P. WILSON, Technical College, Colchester.

Halstead.—Secretary, W. KNOWLES, 52, Tidings Hill, Halstead, Essex.

Hitchin.—Secretaries : T. G. WILLIAMS, 11, Bancroft, Hitchin; Mrs. IMPEY, 2, Whinbush Road, Hitchin.

Ipswich.—Secretary : S. J. HUTLEY, " Osterley," Stradbroke Road, Ipswich.

Kettering.—Secretaries : Miss S. GREEN, 29, Cobden Street, Kettering; G. CHESTER, 88, Nelson Street, Kettering.

Letchworth.—Secretary : Mrs. POOLE, 78, Pix Road, Letchworth.

Lincoln.—Secretary : H. YEX, 12, Pennell Street, Lincoln.

Luton.—Secretary : H. EDWARDS, 5, Avondale Road, Luton.

Norwich.—Secretary : Miss A. L. LONG, 5, Sewell Road, Norwich.

Wellingborough.—Secretary : C. W. PAGE, 33, Ferrestone Road, Wellingborough.

LONDON DISTRICT.

District Secretary : H. GOODMAN, 16, Harpur Street, W.C. 1.

Battersea.—Secretary : L. KNOTTLEY, 55, Parma Gardens, Battersea, S.W.

Camberwell and Southwark.—Secretary : Mr. HIGGINS, 157, Lynton Road, S.E. 1.

Crayford.—Secretary : W. CARR, 97, Green Walk, Crayford.

Croydon.—Secretary : H. H. SIDEY, 155, Windmill Road, Croydon.

Deptford.—Secretary : T. W. HOWARD, 176, Malpas Road, Brockley, S.E. 4.

Hampstead and Kilburn.—Secretary : S. G. KIRBY, 19, Gascony Avenue, W. Hampstead, N.W. 6.

Ilford and District.—Secretary : J. HUTTON, 12, Brisbane Road, Ilford, Essex.

Kew and Richmond.—Secretary : Miss A. JACOBS, 10b, Waterlow Place, Kew Green.

Lambeth.—Secretaries : A. H. JENN, Durning Library, Kennington Cross, S.E. 11; J. HOPKINS, 21, Rita Road, South Lambeth Road, S.W. 8.

Leytonstone, Leyton, and Walthamstow.—Secretary : Mrs. JENNER, 174, Twickenham Road, Leytonstone.

Marylebone and North=West London.—Secretary (Acting) : Miss L. PRENTICE, 53, Waverley Avenue, Wembley.

Metropolitan.—Secretary : H. GOODMAN, 16, Harpur Street, Holborn, W.C. 1.

St. Mary Cray and Orpington.—Secretary : E. A. EDMED, Cambria, Moorfield Road, Orpington.

Southall.—Secretaries : A. E. HALL, 15, Waltham Road, Southall; Mr. WHILSMITH, 91, Townsend Road, Southall.

Uxbridge.—Secretary : H. T. HAMSON, Thornby, Walford Road, Uxbridge.

Waltham Cross and Cheshunt.—Secretary : Miss WELSFORD, High School, Waltham Cross, Herts.

Wealdstone and Harrow.—Secretary : G. A. JORDAN, 5, Roxboro' Road, Harrow.

Wood Green and District.—Secretary : Miss G. A. HUTTON, 79, Duckett Road, Harringay, N. 4.

MIDLAND DISTRICT.

District Secretary : T. W. PRICE, The University, Edmund Street, Birmingham.

Birmingham.—Secretaries : T. W. PRICE, The University, Edmund Street, Birmingham; Lieutenant W. J. WOOLDRIDGE (on active service); Lieutenant F. W. GADSBY (on active service); Mrs. J. BURLEY, The Spinney, Yardley Wood Road, Moseley, Birmingham.

Colwich and District.—Secretary : LANCE G. E. JONES, School House, Colwich, Staffs.

Coventry.—Secretary : J. K. HARRISON, 84, Highland Road, Earlsdon, Coventry.

Derby.—Secretary : T. W. TOWNSEND, 90, Almond Street, Derby.

Dudley and District.—Secretaries : E. GRUBHAM, 4, Walford Street, Tividale, Tipton, Staffs; G. E. LUCAS, 11, Compton Road, Cradley Heath, Staffs.

Hereford.—Secretaries : J. S. PRICE, 8, Scudamore Street, White Cross, Hereford; E. J. WILSON, St. Omer, White Horse Street, Ryelands, Hereford.

King's Norton.—Secretaries : A. J. BROUGHALL, 86, Watford Road, King's Norton; W. HARDY (on active service); Miss M. A. GRIFFITHS, 21a, Sycamore Road, Bournville.

Leicester.—Secretary : F. SALTER, 43, Conway Road, Leicester.

Nottingham and District.—Secretary : R. G. RADFORD, 113, Stanley Road, Nottingham.

Nuneaton and District.—Secretaries : F. JOHNS, Germoe, Earls Road, Nuneaton.

Rugby.—Secretary : F. J. GIBSON, 64, Stephen Street, Rugby.

Shrewsbury and District.—Secretary : A. HALLETT, Restholme, Meole Brace, Shrewsbury.

Sutton=in=Ashfield.—Secretary : A. ROBINSON, Church View, Alfreton Road, Sutton-in-Ashfield.

Tamworth.—Secretary : H. F. WALKER, 26, Cruft Street, Tamworth.

Tysoe.—Secretary : Miss E. PARGETER, Upper Tysoe.

Wellesbourne.—Secretary : E. H. FROST, School House, Wellesbourne.

NORTH=EASTERN DISTRICT.

District Secretary: Mrs. J. G. TREVENA, 84, Westmorland Road, Newcastle-on-Tyne.

Annfield Plain.—Secretary: C. SMITH, 13, Tower Road, Greencroft, Annfield Plain, Co. Durham.

Bishop Auckland and District.—Secretary: R. THOMPSON, Ravensworth, Cockton Hall, Bishop Auckland.

Blyth and District.—Secretaries: Miss I. EADINGTON, 5, Hedley Avenue, Blyth; L. S. J. COTTRELL, Rowley Street, Blyth.

Carlisle.—Secretary: J. T. COULTHARD, 30, Leatham Street, Carlisle.

Darlington.—Secretary: F. SMITHSON, 24, Milton Street, Darlington.

Easington and District.—Secretary: G. S. PHELP (absent on war service); Secretary (acting): E. J. JONES, 19, Easington Street, Easington Colliery, Co. Durham.

Gateshead.—Secretary: E. OATES, 3, Queen's Terrace, Gateshead.

Hartlepool.—Secretary: Miss MARY WARD, 16, Thornton Street, West Hartlepool.

Jarrow and Hebburn.—Secretary: T. A. HUDSON, 8, Gray St., Jarrow.

Middlesbrough.—Secretaries: W. STEPHENSON, 129, Victoria Road, Middlesbrough; E. HOLMES, 1, Southfield Road, Middlesbrough.

Newcastle=on=Tyne.—Secretaries: A. G. EVERY, 39, Lavender Gardens, West Jesmond, Newcastle-on-Tyne; A. B. DODD, 10, Mather Street, Newcastle-on-Tyne.

Shildon and Eldon.—Secretary: J. CALLAGHAN, 6, Halls Row, Eldon, Bishop Auckland.

South Shields and District.—Secretary (acting): J. J. GIVENS, 225, Mile End Road, South Shields.

Spennymoor.—Secretary: Miss N. STEWART, 14, King Street, Spennymoor, Co. Durham.

Stockton, Thornaby, and District.—Secretary: G. H. HEPPLESTON, 23, Newtown Avenue, Stockton-on-Tees.

Sunderland.—Secretary: H. BAINBRIDGE, 34, Mount Rd., Sunderland.

West Stanley.—Secretary: FRANK BLACKWELL, Wylam Terrace, Shield Row, West Stanley.

NORTH=WESTERN DISTRICT.

District Secretary: E. J. HOOKWAY, College House, Brunswick Street, Manchester.

Accrington.—Secretary: S. POTTS, 42, Elmfield Street, Church, Lancs.

Altrincham.—Secretary: S. ANDREW, 75, Stamford Park Road, Hale, Cheshire.

Aspatria.—Secretary: ISAAC ALLEN, 6, Brayton Road, Aspatria.

Bacup and District.—Secretary (*pro tem.*): J. M. AYLMER, Dale Street, Bacup.

Barrow=in=Furness.—Secretary: A. BOND, 43, Hill Road, Barrow-in-F.

Birkenhead.—Secretary: W. GREEN, 150, Peel Street, Tranmere, Birkenhead.

Blackburn.—Secretary: F. GARSTANG, 11, Manor Road, Blackburn.

Blackpool.—Secretary: E. STEVENSON, 10, William Street, Little Layton, Blackpool.

Bolton.—Secretary: JOHN DARBYSHIRE, Corporation Chambers, Corporation Street, Bolton.

Chorley and District.—Secretary: E. BIBBY, W.E.A. College, Chorley.

Cleator.—Secretary : W. G. MURRAY, 27, Trumpet Terrace, Cleator, Cumberland.

Colne.—Secretary : W. HIGSON, Public Library, Colne.

Congleton.—Secretary : E. NADIN, Mill Lane, Dane-in-Shaw, Congleton.

Crewe.—Secretaries : W. H. PRICE, 3, Clifton Avenue, Crewe; Miss M. RILEY, 26, Cemetery Road, Crewe.

Darwen.—Secretary : L. S. NOBLE, 30, Limes Avenue, Darwen.

Farnworth and District.—Secretary : JOHN E. HALL, 3, Barnes Terrace, Bank Top, Kearsley, Farnworth.

Glossop.—Secretary : G. E. COLCLOUGH, 18, Church Street, Glossop.

Haslington.—Secretary : J. GREENWOOD, 28, New Street, Haslington, Crewe.

Heywood.—Secretary : O. GRIFFITHS, 113, Bamford Road, Heywood, Lancs.

Kendal.—Rev. C. E. MERCER, Kendal.

Lancaster.—Secretary : T. PARKER, 118, Conkton Road, Lancaster.

Leigh.—Secretary : J. STOTT, 38, Railway Road, Leigh, Lancs.

Littleborough.—Secretary : J. DEARDEN, 7, Central Ave., Littleborough.

Liverpool.—Secretary : G. H. LEAROYD, 16, Rowson St., New Brighton.

Macclesfield.—Secretary : CHARLES YATES, Moorlands, Hollins Road, Macclesfield.

Manchester, Salford, and District.—Secretaries : E. REAY, 13, Norton Street, Brook's Bar, Manchester; E. FISHER, 4, Piercy Street, Ancoats, Manchester.

Middleton and District.—Secretary : J. H. ROBERTS, 12, Clark Brow, Middleton.

Nelson.—Secretary : J. PROCTOR, 62, Clayton Street, Nelson.

Oldham.—Secretary : FRED MAIEY, 19, Coppice Street, Oldham.

Penrith.—Secretary (*pro tem.*) : W. JOHNSTON, 4, King Street, Penrith.

Pendlebury.—Secretary : W. WATKISS, 6, Ethel Avenue, Pendlebury.

Preston and District.—Secretary : R. A. HOLDEN, Greenbank, Lostock Hall, Preston.

Rochdale.—Secretary (acting) : Miss E. M. FOUNTAIN, Harelands, Rochdale.

St. Helens.—Secretary : Rev. H. SHORT, Laurel Dene, Hard Lane, St. Helens.

Shavington.—Secretary : J. W. PLATT, Shavington Villa, Shavington, near Crewe.

Southport.—Secretaries : Miss M. HULL, 2, Beecham Road, Southport; J. H. NEWTON, 162, Kew Road, Birkdale, Southport.

Stockport.—Secretary : HARRY SHELDON, 121, Petersburg Road, Edgeley Park, Stockport.

Wigan.—Secretary : J. RUCK, 67, Hodges Street, Wigan.

Workington and District.—Secretary : W. H. BAILEY, 50, Pow Street, Workington.

SOUTH-EASTERN DISTRICT.

District Secretary : E. W. WIMBLE (absent on war service); District Secretary (*pro tem.*) : Mrs. WHITAKER, York Cottage, Bracknell, Berks.

Aldershot and District.—Secretary : A. GREGORY, Merridale, Cranmore Lane, Aldershot.

Ascott=under=Wychwood (Rural).—Secretary : Miss SMITH (absent on war service); Secretary (*pro tem.*) : A. W. H. BRYAN, The Grange Cottage, Ascott-under-Wychwood.

Ashford.—Secretary : E. TONG, 44, Christchurch Road, Ashford, Kent.

Bournemouth.—Secretary : J. S. RAINER, 6, King's Park Road, Bournemouth.

Bracknell (Rural).—Secretary (acting) : Miss ALDER, High Street, Bracknell, Berks.

Canterbury.—Secretary : A. GLANVILLE, Plas Issa, Cromwell Road, Canterbury.

Chatham.—Secretary : T. HARMER, 23, New Street, Chatham.

Chipping Norton (Rural).—Secretary : H. SANDLES (absent on war service).

Coln, Hatherop, and Quenington.—Secretary : A. V. LEWIS, Woodside, Quenington, Fairford, Glos.

Cowes.—Secretary : A. FIELDING, 36, Pelham Road, Cowes.

Eastleigh.—Secretary : F. SMITH, Crescent House, Ramsey, Eastleigh.

Epwell (Rural).—Secretary : Mrs. A. M. CLEYDON, Yarn Hill Farm, Epwell, Banbury.

Folkestone.—Secretary : W. MONCRIEFF, 21, Guildhall St., Folkestone.

Froxfield (Rural).—Secretary : Miss V. CUMMINS, Froxfield, Petersfield.

High Wycombe.—Secretary : Mrs. H. N. REID, Glasnevin, West Wycombe Road, High Wycombe.

Horsham.—Secretary : Miss L. J. CHURCHMAN, 5, Middle St., Horsham.

Maidstone.—Secretary (*pro tem.*) : S. E. STEELE, 63, St. Philip's Avenue, Maidstone.

Midhurst.—Secretary : Miss L. ATKINSON, Heathlands, Bepton Road, Midhurst.

Oxford.—Secretary (*pro tem.*) : *GEORGE CARTER, 5, Leckford Place, Oxford.

Peppard (Rural).—Secretary : J. HARRIS, Highway Cottage, Shiplake Dale, Peppard, Oxon.

Petersfield.—Secretary : Miss J. CUMMINS, Froxfield, Petersfield.

Portsmouth.—Secretary : T. E. HICKEY, 30, Claremont Road, Fratton, Portsmouth.

Reading.—Secretaries : T. W. E. SPIR, 6, Beresford Road, Reading; F. W. PADLEY, 2, Eldon Place, Reading.

Redhill.—Secretary : T. W. REED, 41a, Grove Hill Road, Redhill.

Sibford (Rural).—Secretary : H. H. LONG, Sibford Ferris, Banbury.

Smeeth.—Secretary : A. WEATHERELL, School House, Smeeth.

Southampton.—Secretary : Miss M. CAMPBELL, 9, Forest View, Southampton.

Stoke Row (Rural).—Secretary : Miss E. C. TURNER, Well Cottage, Stoke Row, Henley-on-Thames.

Wittersham.—Secretary : J. UDALL, School House, Wittersham.

Woking.—Secretary : Mrs. AUBREY, 20, Eve Road, Woking.

Yarnton (Rural).—Secretary : Mrs. DRINKWATER, Station House, Yarnton, Oxon.

WELSH DISTRICT.

District Secretary : Dr. S. H. WATKINS, 34, Station Rd., Penarth, Glam.

Barry.—Secretary : J. F. MEDHURST, 18, Westward Ride, Garden Suburb, Barry, Glam.

Bridgend.—Secretary : W. J. EATON, 97, Grove Road, Bridgend, Glam.

Caerau.—Secretary : F. PEARSE, 9, Treharne Rd., Caerau, nr. Bridgend.

Cardiff.—Secretary : J. C. ASHE, 16, Lon Isa, Rhiwbina, near Cardiff.

Cymmer.—Secretary : Miss M. A. POPHAM, Laurel House, Boyton Road, Cymmer, Port Talbot, Glam.

Fforest Fach.—Secretary : J. HARDING GEORGE, Pant-y-Meillon, Fforest Fach, Glam.

Llanelly.—Secretary : F. BROWN, 8, Stafford Street, Llanelly.

Llantwit Major.—Secretary : Miss J. TRIGG, East Street, Llantwit Major, Glam.

Llefeni.—Secretary : J. T. JONES, Foalfruog Farm, Aberldejend, Merionethshire.

Neath.—Secretary : W. J. DAVIES, 18, Eastland Road, Neath, Glam.

Newport.—Secretary : R. E. DAVIES, Marlow House, Christchurch Road, Newport, Mon.

Penrhiwceiber and Mountain Ash.—Secretary : P. THOMAS, T. Harris Terrace, Penrhiwceiber.

Penarth.—Secretary : R. JAMES, Alexandra Park, Penarth.

Port Talbot.—Secretary : E. P. REES, 35, Castle Street, Aberavon, Glam.

Swansea.—Secretary : S. REES, 7, Phillips Parade, Swansea.

Tredegar.—Secretary : G. DAVIES, B.A., 25, West Hill, Tredegar, Mon.

WESTERN DISTRICT.

District Secretary : W. R. STRAKER, 27, Morgan St., St. Paul's, Bristol.

Bath and District.—Secretaries : E. H. BENCE, Ivy Lea, Bloomfield Park, Bath ; W. H. ROBINSON, 3, Great Stanhope Street, Bath ; Mrs. MITCHELL, 26, Queenwood Avenue, Fairfield Park, Bath.

Bridgwater.—Secretary : W. H. COUSINS, 23, Wimbledon Road, Bridgwater.

Bristol and District.—Secretaries : Miss L. B. JAQUES, 106, Richmond Road, Montpelier, Bristol ; W. R. STRAKER, 27, Morgan Street, St. Paul's, Bristol.

Chisledon (Rural).—Secretary : W. J. HART, Webb's Farm, Chisledon, Wilts.

Frome.—Secretaries : Miss M. A. BARKER, 12, Nunney Road, Frome ; Miss A. C. CROCKFORD, The Ferns, The Butts, Frome.

Marlborough.—Secretary : A. J. STEELE, 13, St. John's Close, Marlborough.

Nursteed (Rural).—Secretary : Mrs. THORNELEY, The Elms, Nursteed, Devizes.

Paulton.—Secretary : J. MATTHEWS, Farrington Gurney, near Bristol.

Radstock.—Secretary : W. J. BIRD, Garfield Cottage, Wells Road, Radstock.

Rodbourne Cheney (Rural).—Secretary : E. G. LEWIS, South View, Rodbourne Cheney.

Salisbury.—Secretary : Mrs. CONMEADOW, 70, St. Ann's St., Salisbury.

Shipham.—Secretary : J. GATEHOUSE, School House, Shipham, Winscombe, Somerset.

South Gloucester.—Secretary : S. A. UNDERDOWN, Wick, near Bristol.

Street and District.—Secretary : H. J. SHARMAN, 112, High Street, Street, Somerset.

Stroud (Glos.).—Secretaries : R. R. DOBSON, Marling School, Stroud; Miss C. F. SMITH, The Acre, Stroud; T. HANDFORD, 3, Brightside, Horns Road, Stroud.

Swindon.—Secretary : H. WHITING, 16, Durham Street, Swindon.

Taunton.—Secretary : W. S. DENTON, Dunelin, South Road, Taunton.

Wells and District.—Secretary : Miss R. A. KELLAND, 13, St. Cuthbert Street, Wells, Somerset.

Winscombe and District (Rural).—Secretaries : Miss M. ELDRIDGE, Glanville, Winscombe; Miss M. R. GOWING, Mayfield, Winscombe; —. RANSFORD, Mendip Library, Winscombe.

Winterbourne Valley (Rural).—Secretary : Miss SHEARER, Whye Farm, Winterbourne Bassett, Wilts.

Woodborough (Rural).—Secretary (*pro tem.*) : Mrs. RADCLIFFE, Woodborough, Wilts.

Wroughton (Rural).—Secretary : J. J. CANT, 35, Swindon Road, Wroughton, Swindon.

Yeovil.—Secretary : C. J. LONGMAN, 32, The Avenue, Yeovil.

SOUTH=WESTERN DISTRICT
(At present attached to Western District).

Exeter.—Secretary : T. H. COYSH, 35, Monkswell Road, Exeter.

Newton Abbot.—Secretary : J. MERCER, 37, Chelston Road, Newton Abbot.

Plymouth.—Convener of Provisional Council : J. SMALL, J.P., 54, Laira Bridge Road, Plymouth.

Torquay.—Secretary (*pro tem.*) : Miss PEARSON, Ballybrock, Westhill Road, St. Mary Church, Torquay.

YORKSHIRE DISTRICT.
District Secretary : G. H. THOMPSON, 21, Brudenell Road, Hyde Park, Leeds.

Batley.—Secretary : B. INESON, 7, Transvaal Ter., Carlinhow, Batley.

Bingley.—Secretary (*pro tem.*) : Miss E. A. PERFECT, 5, Beck Houses, Park Road, Bingley

Bradford.—Secretary : Miss A. R. WHITAKER, 102, Jesmond Avenue, Bradford.

Brighouse.—Secretary : N. B. GRAVES, 24, Gathorne Street, Brighouse.

Chesterfield.—Secretary : S. H. HARRISON, 40, Compton Street, Chesterfield.

Cudworth.—Secretary : G. BELL, 139, Barnsley Road, Cudworth.

Denaby Main.—Secretary : Miss M. HORSFALL, 52, Ravensfield Street, Denaby Main.

Doncaster.—Secretary : Miss L. M. STOCK, 41, Christchurch Road, Doncaster.

Ecclesfield.—Secretaries : Miss S. M. R. HAYES, M.A., Cross Hill, Ecclesfield, near Sheffield; J. E. LOWE, 25, Cross Hill, Ecclesfield, near Sheffield.

Halifax.—Secretaries : DRYDEN BROOK, 108, Dudwell Drive, Skircoat Green, Halifax; JAMES FLETCHER, 23, Union Street South, Halifax.

Hebden Bridge.—Secretaries : S. CRAVEN, Rydal Dene, Hebden Bridge.

Huddersfield.—Secretaries : J. M. EVANS, Beech House, Netherton, Huddersfield ; Miss A. SMITH, 128, New Hey Road, Huddersfield.

Hull.—Secretary : F. HOLMES, 130, Worthing Street, Newlands, Hull.

Ilkley.—Secretaries : G. H. PLOWS (on active service), 2, Grosvenor Terrace, Ilkley; Miss E. G. BIRKIN, Trafalgar Road, Ilkley.

Keighley.—Secretaries : J. COLEY, 24a, Mornington Street, Keighley ; H. THOMAS, 63, Hebden Road, Haworth, Keighley.

Leeds.—Secretary : H. WHEWELL, 31, Burley Lodge Terrace, Hyde Park, Leeds.

Maltby.—Secretary : Miss E. M. HENERY, 3, Cliff Villas, Rotherham Road, Maltby.

Mexborough.—Secretary : J. H. CROWTHER, 1, Foundry Lane, Mexborough.

Rotherham and District.—Secretary : JOSEPH SMITH, 79, Netherfield Lane, Parkgate, near Rotherham.

Scarborough.—Secretary : C. HURD, 147, Prospect Road, Scarborough.

Sheffield.—Secretaries : E. SIMPSON, W.E.A. House, 278, Weston Bank, Sheffield ; T. FISHER, 27, Richards Road, Heeley, Sheffield.

Shipley and District.—Secretary : T. B. KNOX, 27, Westcliffe Road, Shipley.

Silsden.—Secretary : S. TEAL, Dale View, Silsden, *via* Keighley.

Sowerby Bridge.—Secretary : T. JOHNSON, School House, Sowerby, Sowerby Bridge.

Spendborough (late Cleckheaton).—Secretary : H. SUTCLIFFE, St. Luke's Terrace, Cleckheaton.

Stockbridge.—Secretary : M. SWALLOW, Rundell Road, Stocksbridge, near Sheffield.

Todmorden.—Secretaries : Miss EMILY S. ASHWORTH, 6, Byrom Street, Todmorden ; F. ROGERS, 4, Beaumont Street, Todmorden.

Wakefield.—Secretary : B. JOHNSON, 10, Earl Street, Wakefield.

Wensleydale.—Secretary : Miss NAN CROSBY, Bainbridge, Askrigg, Yorks.

York.—Secretary : F. NORTH, 48, Fairfax Street, York.

IRELAND.

Belfast and District.—Secretary : SAMUEL KYLE, 42, Bray Street, Belfast.

Cork.—Secretary : Professor H. RAHILLY, The University, Cork.

SCOTLAND.

District Secretary : Mrs. STEWART, 7, Mantone Terrace, Edinburgh.

Aberdeen and District.—Secretary : Miss R. M. GLEN, 40, Beaconsfield Place, Aberdeen.

Ayrshire.—Secretary : Mrs. CLIMIE, 25, Armour Street, Kilmarnock.

Dundee.—Secretary : Miss E. BATTING, Grey Lodge Settlement, Wellington Street, Dundee.

Edinburgh.—Secretary : Miss A. L. MACDONALD, 23, Dublin Street, Edinburgh.

Glasgow and District.—Secretary : HUGH B. GUTHRIE, 4, James Gray Street, Langside, Glasgow.

N

PART VI.

EDUCATIONAL MOVEMENTS.

TRADE UNIONISM AND EDUCATION.

By G. D. H. Cole.

It is a charge very often brought against the working classes that they are apathetic about education. There is certainly a sense in which this is true, but no less certainly untrue are some of the conclusions most often drawn from its truth. The workers are apathetic about education, but so is every other class in the community, and I think it can be said that the workers' record compares favourably with that of other classes. Especially true is this when the circumstances of the normal working-class family are taken into account. It is difficult for parents who have not been educated themselves to believe in the value of education for their children; often, too, it is difficult for them to forego the earnings which the children can make when they leave school or out of. school hours. Nor is the actual character of the education provided always encouraging to the worker; for it seems to them far too much directed to the manufacture of clerks and teachers, and far too little to the real broadening of life.

Yet, in face of all these obstacles, Labour, so far as it has been articulate, has always stood for better education. Year after year the Trades Union Congress and the Labour Party have pressed for educational reform, and even in Lancashire and Yorkshire, the homes of the half-time system, the active Trade Unionists have been almost unanimous in seeking the advancement of education and the abolition of child labour.

So far as concerns the passing of resolutions and the framing of policies Labour's record is certainly better than that of any other class. But the complaint is often made by members of other classes that there the matter ends. For instance, when the universities, local authorities, or the State are asked to make fuller provision of Tutorial Classes for adult workers the opposition almost always takes the line that the Trade Unions ought to pay for such forms of education, and that their unwillingness to do so proves that there is no real working-class demand, and, therefore, no need to provide facilities.

This is a most astonishing argument. Who ever argued that, because the upper classes are not willing to provide the money for upper class education—which is only solvent because of its heavy endowments and subsidies—therefore upper class education has no claim to exist? Whoever argued that because the British Medical Association will not pay for the training of the doctors they are to be accused of gross dereliction of duty? Education is a national burden, the cost of which ought to fall upon the nation; and this applies with just as much force to the education of adults as to that of children. The universities are recognised as an integral part of our national system of education, and we cannot justly or logically take any other view of the various kinds of classes and summer schools which form the foundations of the workers' university.

The education of children forms too great a burden to be borne by private enterprise except for the richer classes. The actual provision of educational facilities by the workers is therefore almost confined to classes for adults. We must now try to see what Trade Unionism has done to provide this kind of education and what have been the ideals which have inspired it.

The stimulus to action, and the first practical steps towards action, have in almost all cases been unofficial. Ruskin College, founded by the efforts of private educationists of Labour sympathies, only subsequently enlisted the support, and passed under the government, of its affiliated Trade Unions and Labour bodies. The Workers' Educational Association, originally the product of the conversations of certain workingmen with certain scholars, only subsequently secured the affiliation of many of the great Trade Unions and of their branches throughout the country. The Central Labour College, founded by the seceders from Ruskin College in the strike which preceded its definite passage under Labour control, has only recently passed under the complete guardianship of the South Wales Miners' Federation and the National Union of Railwaymen.

These three organised institutions form the main channels by which the Trade Union movement plays a definite part in the provision of adult working-class education.* Two of them are actual residential colleges, to which students are sent for a year or more with maintenance scholarships from their Labour organisations. Ruskin College also organises a large system of tuition by correspondence, and undertakes various other pieces of educational work, while the Central Labour College, in addition to correspondence courses, itself organises classes in many working-class districts.

The W.E.A. differs in character both from Ruskin College and the Central Labour College. It is an association of labour and educational bodies as well as individuals, and its aims include general educational propaganda, as well as the actual provision of certain types of education. It agitates for educational reform, it provides classes, and it co-operates with the universities in organising tutorial classes and summer schools.

If this is the machinery by which Trade Unionism plays a part in education what are the ideals behind it? The Plebs League, which is the propagandist body associated with the C.L.C., directs a continual stream of criticism against the W.E.A. The W.E.A. sets out to be " non-party political "; the C.L.C., or at least the Plebs League, is aggressively Marxian in outlook and teaching. The W.E.A. claims to teach " impartially "; the organ of the Plebs

---

* For the part played by the Co-operative Movement see the special article on pp. 374-76.

League takes as its motto the words " I can promise to be candid, but not impartial."

Both these organisations base their appeals for support to the Trade Unions on the principles for which they stand. The C.L.C. and the Plebs League stand openly for the class struggle, and the education which they seek to impart is a revolutionary education, intended to minister to the overthrow of the existing order. The W.E.A. speaks of education as an end in itself, of the need to allow the student to make up his own mind, of the danger of binding down tutor and student to a narrow orthodoxy which restricts not only their outlook, but also their mental development.

Fundamentally we all know the difference between education and propaganda. Propaganda is an attempt to bring others to one's own point of view; education is an attempt to equip others with the means of making up their own minds. Both are legitimate forms of activity; the point is that they are *different*.

The difference between the W.E.A. and the C.L.C. is not the difference between education and propaganda, but the difference between an educational institution and a school for propagandists. In short, both have their place, but their places are different.

When, therefore, the W.E.A. and the C.L.C. make their claims for Trade Union support those who treat their claims as fundamentally irreconcilable are wrong. If all the C.L.C. says about the W.E.A. is true, then the working class ought to take the whole educational system out of the hands of the State and run it for themselves on Socialist Sunday School lines. If all some W.E.A extremists say in defence of the W.E.A. is true, then there is no place for propaganda at all, and all propagandist societies (including the W.E.A. itself in its other activities) ought to shut down. But if neither of their views is right, what are the respective spheres of education and propagandist training?

When we want to train a teacher or a doctor or a minister of religion we generally try to give him first a good general education and then a good specialised training. This is what should be done with the Labour propagandist also. First educate and then train for propaganda; or, if the two must go on at the same time, make education in all cases the basis of propaganda. Let a man try to understand all points of view before he begins trying to refute any of them. It must be allowed that, under present-day conditions, this ideal is often difficult of realisation. The well-qualified teacher has too often a governing-class outlook, and the good text-book suffers from the same defect. Bit by bit this is being remedied as a supply of teachers and text-books with democratic outlook is created; but there is still bias enough to account fully for counter-bias on the other side. Against the bias of the so-called " impartial " education the C.L.C. designedly sets another bias. It is right if it clearly recognises this bias as a corrective and the work based upon it as training for propaganda rather than education properly so called; but it puts itself in the wrong as soon as it claims to be the only true working-class education.

The opposition of the C.L.C. to the W.E.A. has seemed to many a dangerous hindrance to the awakening of the Trade Union movement to a full appreciation of the importance both of educating the workers and of training Labour leaders and propagandists for their work.

Perhaps, however, in the long run it will rather tend to stimulate interest in both problems. At the beginning of this article I defended Labour against the charge of educational apathy by a comparison of its attitude with that of other classes. The defence was strictly comparative. Labour is apathetic, even if it is not so apathetic as others.

What, then, ought Trade Unionism to do for education? It ought, of course, to throw itself with far greater vigour into the national campaign for educational reform. But also it ought in its own interest and not because the upper classes tell it so, to be far more active in the provision of educational facilities for its members. It ought to capture the active control and direction of the W.E.A. and of the C.L.C., as it could quite easily do if it liked; it ought to make every Trade Union, Trades Council, district, and branch a centre of educational activity by running classes of its own, and by co-operating and subscribing where other bodies set up classes. It ought to set about framing for itself an educational policy both for children and for adults, and it ought to face and answer for itself the problems raised in this article and elsewhere in this book. If it will do that it will find that a great mass of democratic opinion among teachers and educationists will rally to its aid, and it will be well on the way to equipping itself with that educated rank and file through which alone the emancipation of Labour can be accomplished.

THE CO-OPERATIVE MOVEMENT AND EDUCATION.

By George Stanton

(Vice-President of Midland Co-operative Educational Association; Associate Editor of " Co-operators' Year Book ").

Education has been the great dynamic force behind the progress of the co-operative movement from the days of Robert Owen to those of our own time. The founders of the modern movement—the Rochdale Pioneers—men of truly heroic commonsense—made their first rule, " That a definite percentage of profits should be allotted to education." Through all its developments the co-operative movement has remained faithful to the example of its founders, and the model rules of the Co-operative Union recommend to every society the putting aside of 2½ per cent. of its " surplus " as a purely educational fund and the election of a special committee for its administration. While it cannot be said that this excellent advice is strictly followed, co-operators do spend each year something like £100,000 in varied educational and propagandist activities, ranging from the granting of scholarships to Oriel College, and classes upon social and economic subjects, to musical festivals. As long ago as 1885 a Central Educational Committee of the Co-operative Union was established for the purpose of directing and co-ordinating educational policy and work; and the purpose of co-operative education was defined at that date as " primarily the formation of co-operative character and opinion; and, secondarily, though not necessarily of less import, the training of men and women to take part in industrial and social reforms and municipal life generally." To-day a vast network of educational machinery links up the movement to a yet broader and more idealistic programme of social and humanistic education, and there is a project now being considered by the movement—as the outcome of a recent survey—to revise the whole educational constitution, from the Central Committee of the Co-operative Union to the Sectional Educational Associations and the local Educational Committees, with a view to accomplishing still more intensive work. Mr. Fred Hall, M.A., the adviser in studies to the Union, laid before the delegates at the Swansea Co-operative Congress this year, a considerably extended programme of subjects and methods of work, which it is hoped to have fully organised and at work as war circumstances allow, in order that co-operators may take their responsible share in the opportunity of educational reconstruction now facing the nation.

While co-operators have always recognised that they had their own peculiar educational needs, and have directed a continuous effort to the promoting of co-operative efficiency both in the business and social senses, upon the broad platform of educational reconstruction, they may be said to share the W.E.A. outlook and ideals. At the Swansea Congress, for example, the following comprehensive resolution was enthusiastically adopted after a splendid debate expressive of " the W.E.A. spirit " :—

" That this Congress, convinced of the important contribution which a satisfactory system of education can make to the welfare of the nation, and dissatisfied with the present scope and organisation of education in the United Kingdom, demands a reorganisation of education on lines that will facilitate the fuller development of the childhood, manhood, and womanhood of the nation; and, in particular, insists: (1) That the present half-time system be abolished, all exemptions below the age of 14 discontinued, the leaving age at the close of the war being raised to 15; (2) that continued education be compulsory up to the age of 18, free from specialised craft education; (3) that maintenance grants for students be provided where necessary; (4) that the Government take such steps as are necessary to enable qualified candidates to pass to the universities unhindered by considerations of expense; (5) that recognition be given to the importance of the teacher's personality in education by raising the status and increasing the salaries of teachers, to provide them with adequate reward for their services and as a means of attracting and retaining in the service of education the men and women best fitted for the teaching profession."

Mr. W. R. Rae, in moving this, said that "the working classes would receive just as much education as they asked for "; they had to pass from the stage of urging and asking to that of insisting and demanding. Co-operators wanted the road from the elementary school to the university to be easy for their children to tread.

It is of interest to note that many co-operative societies, in common with Trade Unions, are claiming direct representation upon local Education Authorities.

To briefly classify the varied aspects of educational work carried on by co-operators is impossible in a short article. An annual programme, however, is drawn up by the Central Educational Committee which forms the basis of most of the effective work done nationally and locally. There is a comprehensive scheme of class work, including courses upon such subjects as Co-operation, Industrial History, Economics, and Citizenship; to these have been added specialised courses of study like co-operative finance, statistical research, Trade Unionism, economics of industry, welfare of the group, constitutional history, sociology, political science, the art of teaching, and after-war problems. Students unable to attend classes are provided with tuition by correspondence.

Less direct, but not less effective educational work, is done through the agencies of children's and young people's circles and women's and men's guilds. There is a constant distribution of social literature within the movement, and most of the societies' records and " Wheatsheafs " devote some part of their pages to educational matters. The propagandist meeting and lecture is also another ever-present feature of co-operative activity.

Most Educational Committees provide scholarships in connection with local secondary and higher grade schools for their members' children, and for the older people in connection with university lecture schemes. Usually the most helpful relations exist between these committees and local branches of the W.E.A.

A special feature of co-operative educational work is that of the training of co-operative employees in technical and general subjects. Tuition is offered in salesmanship, business organisation, and management, with special courses in bookkeeping and clerical subjects. Courses of study for secretaries and managers of societies upon subjects like commercial and co-operative law, auditing, advertising, money, banking, and prices, etc., are now under consideration.

There is also a liberal provision of recreative efforts like concerts, tea meetings, choirs, flower shows, and excursions, which, although of only limited educational value, do a great deal to stimulate the social life of co-operative societies.

Since 1913 there has also grown up within the movement a remarkable enthusiasm for summer schools. In 1916 three of these gatherings were organised in different parts of the country and attended by large numbers of students. Week-end lecture schools are also a successful feature of co-operative educational work. It is hoped as the outcome of these to establish a purely co-operative college in the near future.

A recent innovation is the issuing of an admirable quarterly magazine, the " Co-operative Educator," which aims at supplying a journalistic platform for co-operative educationalists; it is proposed to make it a monthly after the war. Apart from this, the educationalists of the movement have lately been actively endeavouring to raise the general standard of co-operative journalism.

The establishment of a Co-operators' Educational League has also been decided upon, which will endeavour to organise in its ranks all who are connected or interested in co-operative education; a development which, as the Central Educational Committee's report to Congress puts it, " can hardly fail to produce good results."

Under all these circumstances it is well-nigh impossible, as it would be imprudent, at present, to suggest other things which co-operative educationalists might do. They are making progress quite as rapidly as the complex developments and circumstances they have to face will allow. It is certain that their influence upon the movement was never greater than at present; the war seems to have given impetus to their zeal. They have definitely linked up the commercial and intellectual phases of the movement in a close, vital relationship. Practically, the whole of the decisions of the Swansea Congress were evidence of how they have quickened the mind of the movement and made it alert to the new responsibilities and opportunities the war has brought. They are gradually displacing the huckstering spirit of " divi-hunting " with a broader vision of the fundamental idealism upon which the application of co-operative principles to human affairs is based. After the changes in the general constitution of the movement, to be decided upon at Manchester Congress in 1918, there is a prospect of education taking a still more important place in co-operative activity. Co-operation stands for the necessity of knowledge to combat social evils and economic injustice; it realises that knowledge is the basis of progress and freedom, and that a democracy that wishes to make social and industrial progress and establish liberty must be educated.

REFERENCES.—C. R. Fay : " Co-operation at Home and Abroad " (King). C. Webb : " Industrial Co-operation " (Co-operative Union). " Report of Swansea Co-operative Congress, 1917 " (Co-operative Union). " General Co-operative Survey : Second Interim Report " (Co-operative Union). " Report on Co-operative Production " (Fabian Research Department). " Report on the Co-operative Movement " (Fabian Research Department).

Examinations.—Examinations, founded in 1854, are held annually by the society, through the agency of local committees, at various centres in the country. They are open to any person. The subjects include the principal elements of commercial education and music. This year the number of entries was 26,185, including 279 prisoners of war or interned men at Ruhleben, Groningen, Chateau d'Oex, and Mürren. The number of centres was 379.

Library and Reading-room.—The library and reading-room are open to Fellows, who are also entitled to borrow books.

Election of Fellows.—Candidates are proposed by three Fellows, one of whom, at least, must sign on personal knowledge; or are nominated by the Council.

The annual subscription is two guineas, payable in advance, and dates from the quarter-day preceding election; or a life subscription of 20 guineas may be paid. There is no entrance fee.

Secretary, G. K. Menzies, M.A., John Street, Adelphi, London, W.C. 2.

LONDON SCHOOL ATTENDANCE OFFICERS' ASSOCIATION.

Mr. J. H. Patterson, 8, Granville Road, Wandsworth, London, S.W. 18.

SCHOOL ATTENDANCE OFFICERS' NATIONAL ASSOCIATION.

Q.M.-Sergt. H. R. Armstrong, " C " Company, 87th .T.R.B., Hornsea, East Yorks.

ROYAL SOCIETY FOR THE PROTECTION OF BIRDS.

The Secretary, 23, Queen Anne's Gate, S.W. 1.

THE BOY SCOUT MOVEMENT.

The Boy Scout Movement was founded by Sir Robert Baden-Powell in 1908, and now has a membership of about 250,000.

The aim of the movement is to develop good citizenship among boys by forming their character—training them in habits of observation, obedience, and self-reliance, inculcating loyalty and thoughtfulness for others, teaching them services useful to the public and handicrafts useful to themselves, promoting their physical development and hygiene.

The system of instruction is contained in "Scouting for Boys" (1s. 6d.) and "The Wolf Cub Handbook" (1s. 6d.), both by the Chief Scout.

Boys are divided into (a) Wolf Cubs, aged 8-12 ; (b) Scouts, aged 11-18. Wolf cubs are graded as follows: A tenderpad must know the cub law, signs, and salute. The law is : " The cub gives in to the old wolf; the cub does not give in to himself." After three months' service he may become a one star cub by showing knowledge of the Union Jack, four knots, certain physical exercises, and why to keep nails and teeth clean. After six months, he may become a two star cub if he knows the alphabet in Morse or semaphore, eight points of the compass, two verses of " God Save the King," how to clean a cut finger, and why dirt in a scratch is dangerous, and other tests. A two star cub is eligible for badges, *e.g.*, collector, woodworker, house orderly, athlete.

Scouts are graded as follows: A tenderfoot must know the scout law, signs, and salute. There are ten Scout laws. The first is "A Scout's honour is to be trusted," and the rest lay down, similarly, loyalty, usefulness, brotherhood, courtesy, kindness to animals, obedience, cheerfulness, thrift, and purity. A second-class scout has passed tests in first aid, signalling, tracking, fire-lighting, cooking, compass, and thrift. A first-class scout has passed tests in swimming, signalling, dealing with accidents, reporting a journey, cooking, map-drawing, woodwork, judging distances and weights, and training a tenderfoot. A second-class scout is eligible for proficiency badges, of which there are 55, covering such groups as public service, *e.g.*, fireman, ambulance man; trades, *e.g.*, plumber, miner; hobbies, *e.g.*, naturalist, photographer.

It is laid down as essential that the troop work shall be done in patrols, *i.e.*, groups of about eight boys under the leadership of one of themselves, a system which trains them in self-government.

Considerable stress is laid on outdoor work, which culminates in the annual camp, and physical exercises and gymnastics form an important item in the training.

The uniform and the ceremonial inculcate smartness, and appeal to the craving for romance.

Wolf cub work is not merely elementary scout work, but includes story telling, play acting, and organised games and dances.

The headquarters office is at 25, Buckingham Palace Road, S.W. 1.

BRITISH AND FOREIGN SCHOOL SOCIETY.

Mr. W. Prydderch Williams, 114, Temple Chambers, London, E.C.

THE EDUCATIONAL SECTION OF THE BRITISH ASSOCIATION.

The Educational Section of the British Association, which held its first meeting in 1901, differs from other educational societies in having wider aims and in being unable by its constitution to keep or publish any list of members. Anyone may become a member of the British Association by paying an entrance fee of £1 and an additional £1 as subscription for the first year (no technical qualifications being required), and any member of the Association may attend the meetings and take part in the discussions of the educational section, the aim of which is to advance the study of the science of education by bringing together for discussion all who are interested in the subject either as teachers in elementary or secondary schools, as lecturers in universities, as administrators of the Education Acts, or as psychologists.

The work of all sections of the British Association is carried on during the intervals between the annual meetings by organising committees consisting of the officers of the section, past presidents, and certain other members elected by the committee of the section. Probably, however, the most useful work of the sections is done by the various committees elected each year by the Committee of Recommendations upon the nomination of the sectional committees. During the past few years the more important of these educational committees have been those which have investigated (*a*) the influence of school books on eyesight, (*b*) the mental and physical factors involved in education, and (*c*) science teaching in secondary schools, all of which have published reports which have received a wide circulation. At the present time committees are engaged in considering (*a*) the educational value of museums, (*b*) the influence of the free place system upon elementary and secondary education, and (*c*) the best means of giving effect to suggestions for educational reform.

The office of the British Association is at Burlington House, S.W., the President of the educational section is Sir Napier Shaw, and the Recorder is Mr. Douglas Berridge, 1, College Grounds, Malvern.

THE NATIONAL BROTHERHOOD COUNCIL.

The Secretary, 37, Norfolk Street, Strand, W.C. 2.

CONFERENCE OF CATHOLIC COLLEGES.

The Conference of Catholic Colleges was established in January, 1896, and at the present time about 90 schools are represented on it. The qualification for membership is that the school is subject to Roman Catholic Bishops or to one of the religious orders (Jesuits, Benedictines, etc.); this is equivalent to saying that the school is a public and not a private school.

The object of the Association is to facilitate the interchange of ideas and information on all school matters, *e.g.*, teaching, examinations, scholarships, internal management, and organisation generally, with special reference to the conditions in force at Catholic colleges and convent schools; also to watch over Catholic interests in case of any proposed legislation as to secondary schools, and to take such steps as may be considered advisable to procure due consideration for such interests.

The President is elected annually, but the Secretary retains his position from year to year. The Conference meets every year and generally at one of the Catholic colleges.

The Conference is represented on the Federal Council of Secondary School Associations.

Secretary, the Rev. Canon Driscoll, M.A., Cardinal Vaughan School, Addison Road, London, W.C. 14.

THE CHILD STUDY SOCIETY, LONDON.

The society was founded in 1894; reconstituted in 1907. It numbers among its members representatives of educational science teachers, medical experts, and others interested in child study.

The object of the society is the scientific study of the mental and physical condition of children and also of educational methods, with a view to gaining greater insight into child-nature and securing more sympathetic and scientific methods of training the young.

Lectures and discussions on educational questions bearing upon child study are arranged in the spring and autumn. Reading circles are held and visits arranged to institutions where child study methods are practised.

The society has recently drawn up and issued a memorandum on the educational principles upon which should be based all future school reform.

The Association, of which London forms part, issues a quarterly journal, " Child Study," maintains a library, and arranges a conference.

Hon. Secretary, W. J. Durrie Mulford. Offices : 90, Buckingham Palace Road, London, S.W. 1.

THE STUDENT CHRISTIAN UNION OF GREAT BRITAIN AND IRELAND.

The aim of the movement is to lead students in British Universities and Colleges into full acceptance of the Christian Faith in God— Father, Son, and Holy Spirit; to promote among them regular habits of prayer and Bible study; to keep before them the importance and urgency of the evangelisation of the world, the Christian solution of social problems, and the permeation of public life with Christian ideals; and to lead them into the fellowship and service of the Christian Church.

Founded 1892.

Secretary : Rev. Tissington Tatlow, 32, Russell Square, W.C. 1.

CHURCH EDUCATION CORPORATION.

This Educational Trust was formed in 1900 with the object of founding secondary schools for girls and a training college for women secondary teachers. It established and maintains Sandecotes School, Parkstone, Dorset; Uplands School, St. Leonards-on-Sea ; and Milham Ford School, Oxford. Its training college for women secondary teachers, Cherwell Hall, Oxford, is recognised by the Board of Education, by the Oxford University Delegacy, and by the Cambridge University Syndicate. In 1917 the Council became the trustees for carrying out an educational endowment for the benefit of daughters of the clergy of the Church of England who have lost one or both parents. In addition to liberal assistance to such children during school life the Trust provides for university or other special training.

Secretary : Charles C. Osborne. Offices : 34, Denison House, Westminster, London, S.W. 1.

THE GENERAL ASSOCIATION OF CHURCH SCHOOL MANAGERS AND TEACHERS.

The objects of the Association are :—

1. To bring school managers and teachers who are members of the Church of England into closer union, for the purpose of enabling them to give expression to their opinions on any public question affecting national education.

2. To promote definite religious teaching in elementary schools, and to enable managers and teachers to lend their combined influence to secure its efficiency.

3. To enable managers and teachers to exert their due influence in the protection of the many important interests common to both, which are seriously affected from time to time by the regulations of the Board of Education, by Local Education Authorities, and by other causes.

Organising Secretary: Miss E. M. Parham, 132, Argyle Road, Ealing, W. 13.

THE CHURCH SCHOOLMASTERS AND SCHOOLMISTRESSES' BENEVOLENT INSTITUTION.

The Church Schoolmasters and Schoolmistresses' Benevolent Institution provides annuities to aged and infirm teachers or widows of teachers, home allowances to necessitous orphans of teachers, financial assistance during illness or other temporary difficulty, assists the thrifty to purchase annuities at a reduced rate, etc. It is not " a teachers' association, but many teachers are subscribers.

Founded 1857. Membership, about 12,000.

General Secretary: John West, the National Society's House, 21, Great Peter Street, Westminster, S.W. 1.

CITY AND GUILDS OF LONDON INSTITUTE.

A. L. Soper, Gresham College, Basinghall Street, E.C. 2.

THE CIVIC AND MORAL EDUCATION LEAGUE.

The object of the League is to promote systematic civic and moral education and to make the formation of character the chief aim in school life. It is essentially an educational body, and uses the following among other propaganda methods :—

1. Holiday meetings for teachers and social workers have been held at Ludlow, Newbury, Aberystwyth, and London.

The object of these meetings has been to foster a friendly spirit between various groups of workers, and to arouse and stimulate feelings of active goodwill between citizens by a close study of what a citizen's life has been, is, and might be.

Discussions have been organised on school-work in relation to civic and moral problems, e.g. : (a) Ethical Problems, (b) Civics Teaching in Schools, (c) The Relations between Religions and Moral Education, (d) Sex-Knowledge and Sex-Ethics, (e) Social Eugenics, etc.

2. Lectures and discussions are organised on such topics as those mentioned above.

3. Syllabuses are drawn up and published for use in schools, clubs, and other centres of social and educational work.

Pamphlets and books are published by the League, and it is hoped also to continue the issue of a magazine after the war.

4. A training scheme is in process of being organised at the Lecture Centre at 11, Tavistock Square.

5. A library exists for the use of members, and books may be borrowed or read in the office. Standard and modern books on

questions relating to civic and moral education are to be found on the shelves, and after the war it is hoped to enlarge this side of our work.

6. The League has formed, and is finding, opportunities of influencing educational legislation and administration in accordance with its object.

Further particulars as to membership and requests for help or suggestions for the work of the League will be welcomed by the Secretary, 11, Tavistock Square, London, W.C. 1.

CLASSICAL ASSOCIATION.

Hon. Secretaries : M. O. B. Caspani, M.A., University College, London; W. H. Duke, M.A., Jesus College, Cambridge.

CLUB AND INSTITUTE UNION.

Secretary : B. T. Hall, Club Union Buildings, Clerkenwell Road, E.C. 1. (See pages 383-85.)

THE CO-OPERATIVE UNION EDUCATION COMMITTEE.

C. E. Wood, Holyoake, Hanover Street, Manchester. (See pages 374-76.)

COUNTY COUNCILS ASSOCIATION.

The Association consists of representatives of every County Council in England and Wales, with the exception of Cardiganshire and Merionethshire. The President for the current year is the Earl of Northbrook, the Chairman of the Executive Council is the Right Hon. Henry Hobhouse, and the Vice-Chairman is Sir W. Ryland D. Adkins, M.P.

The Education Committee consists of one representative of the Education Committee of every Council belonging to the Association, and the secretaries or directors of education are also entitled to attend. The Chairman is Sir Henry Hibbert, M.P. (Lancashire), and the Vice-Chairman is Mr. H. Mellish (Notts.).

The object of the Committee is to watch over and protect the interests, rights, and privileges of the County Councils as Local Education Authorities, as they may be affected by legislation, public or private, of general application to counties, or by the action of Government Departments ; to obtain and disseminate information on educational matters of importance to County Councils generally, and in other respects to take such action as may be desirable in circumstances in which county education authorities generally may be interested.

Secretary of the Committee as well as of the Association, G. Montagu Harris, 82, Victoria Street, Westminster, S.W. 1.

THE DALCROZE SOCIETY OF GREAT BRITAIN AND IRELAND.

Objects.—To encourage the study of Dalcroze Eurhythmics, to make and print a register of members, and to encourage and help musicians to train as teachers with M. Jaques-Dalcroze. Annual subscription, 2s.

Founded July, 1915. Membership (1916), 300.

Hon. Secretary: Mrs. M. L. Eckhard, Broome House, Didsbury, Manchester.

THE IMPERIAL SOCIETY OF DANCE TEACHERS.

The Imperial Society of Dance Teachers seeks to promote " a uniform system of instruction, based upon universally recognised technicalities of art and a faithful adherence to its orthodox principles."

Founded 1904. Organ : " The Dance Journal " (monthly).

THE DECIMAL ASSOCIATION.

E. Merry, Finsbury Court, Finsbury Pavement, London, E.C.

SCHOOL DENTISTS' SOCIETY.

Hon. Secretary : William Fisk, Street Lodge, Watford, Herts.

DESIGN AND INDUSTRIES ASSOCIATION.

The aim of the Association is to stimulate and encourage excellence of design and workmanship in British industry through the co-operation of manufacturers, distributors, designers, educationists, and the general public. It accepts the position of machinery in manufacture, but seeks so to extend the influence of design that all things, even those of common use, may be made with that fitness and economy which render workmanship beautiful. It pursues its aim by holding exhibitions of the best current examples of commercial products; by publishing literature, by propaganda in the Press, and by lectures; by forming trade groups of manufacturers, designers, and distributors, and by providing means of co-operation between individuals; by endeavouring to bring education throughout the country into closer relationship with industry.

Hon. Secretaries : Cecil C. Brewer and Hamilton T. Smith, 6, Queen Square, London, W.C. 1. (Telephone No. : Museum 2521.)

ASSOCIATION OF DIRECTORS AND SECRETARIES FOR EDUCATION.

Austin Keen, M.A., County Education Offices, Cambridge.

THE ROYAL DRAWING SOCIETY.

Founded 1888. Incorporated 1902.

The Royal Drawing Society was founded and exists for the development of the child's natural love of picture-making. In order to make drawing an integral part of general education, it encourages this natural development of drawing, untrammelled by any convention, as a means of expressing character, intelligence, and initiative.

This object is promoted in schools by the society's examinations and by the exhibition of drawings held annually in London. About 1,500 schools and 70,000 pupils are now connected with the society.

Drawings done at home are sent to the society for helpful criticism and advice in the " red books " three times yearly.

The society also trains teachers in its studios and holds examinations for the teacher-artist certificates, in which candidates must qualify in teaching and theory of teaching, as well as in actual drawing. Some results of the 30 years' work of the society may be seen in its books of reproductions.

Art Director and Honorary Secretary, T. R. Ablett, F.R.C.S. Gallery and offices : 50, Queen Anne's Gate, Westminster, S.W. 1.

DUTY AND DISCIPLINE MOVEMENT.

The Secretary, 117, Victoria Street, S.W. 1.

"EDUCATION AS NATIONAL SERVICE."

TRAINING SCHEME AND LECTURE CENTRE FOR TEACHERS AND SOCIAL WORKERS.

This lecture centre has been opened this year for educational propaganda. The new methods in education are based on reverence for the individuality of the pupil or student and a belief that development and progress take place best in an atmosphere of freedom.

The application of these principles to every form of social and educational effort is a matter of great importance, and is necessary to ensure success to movements which are intended to be progressive and educative. These principles are making teaching itself a more attractive and congenial profession.

The object of the Committee is to find men and women willing to prepare themselves for such work, and schemes of training have been arranged for that purpose. It is hoped that after the war many men and women (e.g., the V.A.D. workers) may be set free to take part in social and educational work.

There is urgent need for young men and women to prepare themselves :—

1. To undertake civic and other forms of public work, including committee work and public speaking.

2. To serve on local Councils, Education Committees, Care Committees, etc.

3. To work in settlement schools for mothers, etc.

4. To take classes in play centres, boys' clubs, girls' clubs, or in the Workers' Educational Association, etc.

5. To undertake research in education, regional survey, and social work.

Many who begin some form of such work with enthusiasm give it up after a time, though with adequate preparation they might have been encouraged to continue and even extend their efforts.

Each student will undertake a course of study planned for the particular work chosen and in accordance with previous experience and education. Use will be made of lecture courses given at different colleges in London as well as those at the lecture centre. Visits of observation will be made to special institutions.

Hon. Dean : Mrs. Mackenzie, M.A., 11, Tavistock Square, London, W.C. 1.; Tutor, Miss Margaret Frodsham, B.Sc., assisted by other lecturers.

THE ASSOCIATION OF EDUCATION COMMITTEES.

The Association of Education Committees consists of practically the whole of the Education Committees of County and non-County Boroughs and Urban Districts in England and Wales. Its objects are to watch over and ·protect the general interests of education, and particularly those affected by legislation, or departmental administration.

Each Education Committee nominates delegates, who meet in conference once a year in London, to the number of some hundreds. From these an Executive Committee of 36 members is chosen annually. They meet in London five or six times in the course of the year, to adopt a united policy on current educational questions, and make representations, as they may deem necessary, to Parliament, the Board of Education, or other authorities.

During the past year the Executive Committee, on the instructions of the annual conference in 1916, put to the Education Committees a series of questions relating to educational reform, and in April last they issued an exhaustive report, largely based on the replies they received. In this they advocated a large number of the reforms embodied in the Education Bill brought before the House of Commons by the President of the Board of Education in August, 1917.

Hon. Secretary, Frank J. Leslie, 21, Harrington Street, Liverpool.

THE NATIONAL ASSOCIATION OF EDUCATION OFFICERS.

The National Association of Education Officers consists mainly of the chief education officers of local bodies.

Founded 1909. Membership, 130.

Organ : " School Government Chronicle."

Hon. Secretary : A. R. Pickles, Education Offices, Town Hall, Burnley.

EDUCATION REFORM COUNCIL.

The Education Reform Council was formed in April, 1916, by a conference held by invitation of the Teachers' Guild and presided over by Sir Henry Miers. Its declared object is ; " To consider the

O

condition of education in England, and to promote such reform and developments as may appear desirable." Nine investigating committees were appointed, and their conclusions are embodied in the volume, " Education Reform," which was published in July, 1917.* This volume contains full information as to the resolutions passed by the Council and all official information ; it also includes a valuable " Foreword " by the chairman, Dr. William Garnett.

The Education Reform Council state that the reforms proposed have as their aim to widen educational opportunity ; to train all for work and leisure ; to utilise more effectively national resources, human and material ; to fit the growing generation for the service of home, society, and the State ; to admit all to the quest for goodness, truth, and beauty ; to make better citizens. Such are the ideals ; they are not likely to be the subject of controversy. The practical recommendations for making an approach to those ideals naturally range from suggestions for large administrative change to small (but not unimportant) details about class instruction or school baths. As it is obviously impossible to refer, even briefly, to the work of each committee, we select, as typical for the present article, the first-mentioned aim, viz., " to widen educational opportunity." To achieve this purpose the Education Reform Council advises that organised education should continue for every boy and girl until at least the age of 17. Statutory distinctions between higher and elementary education should not be allowed to hinder progressive organisation, e.g., the development of the type of school known in London as Central Schools. Local authorities should be required (not merely permitted) to aid higher education, and the limit of 2d. to the higher education rate in the county areas should be removed. Varying types of continuation schools should be encouraged, and the Education Reform Committee are in hearty agreement with the Workers' Educational Association in urging that in no school should the work be restricted to vocational subjects, but should (a) prepare for citizenship, (b) develop personality, (c) meet physical needs. Each continuation school should have a corporate life of its own. The number of efficient secondary schools should be increased, and pupils at any recognised school should be eligible for State scholarships for prolonging secondary education after 16 or tenable at the universities.

The importance of securing as teachers men and women with the necessary spirit and ability is strongly emphasised, as is also the need to reduce the size of classes in elementary schools. A special feature of the " Medical and Health " Committee's report is the proposal for more thorough grading of children, with increased attention to those who are a little below average in book-learning. Among the duties assigned by the Education Reform Council to the provincial associations is the co-ordination within their areas of scholarship provision, " whether such scholarships be derived from Local Education Authorities, endowments, or other sources, and to award State scholarships." Is it too much to hope that this suggestion may lead to a treatment of endowments on truly democratic principles, in proper co-ordination with State and rate grants, while respecting the desire of the pious founder to benefit the locality?

---

* Published by P. S. King and Son, or may be obtained direct from the Teachers' Guild, 9, Brunswick Square, W.C. 1. price 5s.

We will conclude with a resolution relating to the Workers' Educational Association, which was adopted and published by the Education Reform Council in 1916: "The classes carried on under Joint Committees of the Universities and the Workers' Educational Association are doing work which is of national importance and deserves increased State support. If the existing grants to the Three-Year and One-Year Classes were augmented the admirable work now done could be extended."

Hon. Secretary: G. F. Daniel, Education Reform Council, 9, Brunswick Square, W.C. 1.

EDUCATIONAL COLONIES AND SELF-SUPPORTING SCHOOLS ASSOCIATION.

The objects of the Association are to advocate a reform of our educational system under which children would receive a thorough training—manual, physical, and scholastic—and maintenance when necessary, paying for it at the completion of their training by a short period of employment that would be profitable both economically and educationally. To advocate this educational reform as a means of simplifying the solution of our greatest social, imperial, and military problems.

Hon. Secretary: J. B. Pennington, I.C.S. (ret.), 3, Victoria Street, Westminster, S.W. 1.

THE UNION OF EDUCATIONAL INSTITUTONS.

This union was founded 22 years ago as the Midland Counties Union of Educational Institutions; but seven years ago several of the Western Counties applied for affiliation, and it was then decided to alter the title.

The aims of the union have always been to help in the extension of education in technical and evening schools and classes. To secure this end a very broad and comprehensive set of syllabuses of instruction is issued annually, and these syllabuses are constantly under revision to keep them up-to-date and to meet the varying requirements of different industrial conditions and the growing knowledge in the various subjects.

These revisions are always based upon suggestions and proposals made by acting teachers throughout the area of the union's work, and conferences of teachers and inspectors are held from time to time upon sections of the syllabuses.

The single subjects for which syllabuses are issued number 80, and in addition there are complete syllabuses for three, four, and five year courses in agriculture, the building trades, mechanical engineering, and mining, while the needs of the younger students are met by preliminary groups divided into technical, commercial, general, domestic and rural series.

Examinations are held annually at very low fees, and the number of exercises worked this year is over 15,000. Founded 1895.

Secretary: W. J. Harris, F.C.I.S , Arden Road, Dorridge, Birmingham.

EMPIRE EDUCATIONAL LEAGUE.

F. E. Tillemont-Thomason, Parliament Chambers, Westminster, S.W. 1.

LEAGUE OF THE EMPIRE.

Mrs. Ord Marshall, 28, Buckingham Gate, Westminster, S.W. 1.

THE ENGLISH ASSOCIATION.

This Association was instituted in 1907 for the purpose of affording opportunities for intercourse and co-operation amongst all those interested in English language and literature, of helping to maintain the correct use of English spoken and written, of promoting the due recognition of English as an essential element in the national education, and of discussing methods of teaching English and the correlation of school and University work, and of encouraging and facilitating advanced study in English language and literature. Meetings are held to further these objects, and reports of papers read or discussions held at such meetings, as well as other leaflets, are printed by the Association. The central body has nearly 1,000 members, and there are branches of the Association in Birmingham, Bristol, Cumberland, Westmorland, Durham, Liverpool, Manchester, Newcastle, Sheffield, Yorkshire, Aberdeen, Dundee, Edinburgh, Glasgow, Kelso, St. Andrews, Stirling, South India, and Toronto. The annual subscription is 5s. and life membership entails a payment of £3 3s.

Secretary: A. V. Houghton, Imperial College Union, South Kensington.

ESPERANTO ASSOCIATION, BRITISH.

Mr. M. C. Butler, 17, Hart Street, Bloomsbury, W.C. 1.

FABIAN RESEARCH DEPARTMENT.

The Department originated in the Fabian Society, but membership is open to all Socialists, Co-operators, and Trade Unionists. The most important of its activities is now " The Trade Union Survey," which is under a special Committee, in which Trade Unionists and other research workers sit together. On this side of the Department the Parliamentary Committee of the Trades Union Congress and the Parliamentary Committee of the Scottish Trades Union Congress are affiliated to the Department, together with 33 national Trade Unions, 59 Trades Councils, and 17 Local Labour Parties.

It is proposed to open a Co-operative Section. There are 19 associations affiliated to the Department, making a total of 128.

Secretary: G. D. H. Cole. Acting Secretary: Miss Margaret I. Postgate, 25, Tothill Street, Westminster, S.W. 1. (Telephone: Victoria 1915.)

FEDERATION OF EDUCATION COMMITTEES.
(WALES AND MONMOUTHSHIRE.)

The objects of the Federation are :—

1. To watch over and protect the general interests of education in Wales and Monmouthshire, as they may be affected : (a) By legislation of general application to education districts, ·either by public or private Bills ; (b) by the administration of the various Departments of the Government which may exercise jurisdiction over or in relation to the work of education ; and

2. To take action in relation to any other subject in which Education Committees generally may be interested.

Twenty of the 29 Education Committees in Wales and Monmouthshire belong to the Federation, including all the education authorities of the two most populous counties—Glamorganshire and Monmouthshire.

Messrs. J. J. Jackson, B.A., Director of Education, Cardiff, and T. Botting, B.A., B.Sc., Director of Education, Aberdare, Joint Honorary Secretaries.

THE FROEBEL EDUCATIONAL INSTITUTE.

The Froebel Educational Institute was founded in 1892 for the training of teachers of young children and the education of children up to the age of 14. For these purposes it maintains three departments : –

1. A training college for the teachers of young children with accommodation for 100 women students.

2. A school adjoining for 200 boys and girls between the ages of 3 and 14.

3. A school at 1, Challoner Street, West Kensington, for 100 boys and girls between the ages of 3 and 12.

All three departments have their full complement of students or children.

The supporters of the Froebel Institute believe that infinite harm is done by faulty education in the earlier years of a child's life, and that permanent good can most surely be attained if the education is sound from the outset. The Institute, therefore, makes a special study of young children, and of the conditions and activities which are found to promote their development most effectively.

The training given in the college enables its students to be useful in many directions, and helps them to adjust themselves to the various and varying conditions of life or to modify these when possible and advisable. It proves helpful not only to those who adopt teaching as a profession, but also to others who care for the welfare of the young.

Secretary : Arthur G. Symonds, M.A., the Incorporated Froebel Educational Institute, Colet Gardens, West Kensington, W. 14.

THE FROEBEL SOCIETY.

The Froebel Society was founded in 1874, and has taken an active part throughout the 43 years of its existence in helping to widen educational opportunity and to promote developments in education, more especially with regard to young children. It is largely owing to the work of this society that many teachers have received a special but broad training, and have been recognised in their professional capacity by the creation of the certificates of the National Froebel Union. In consequence the children attending many elementary infant schools, as well as kindergartens, are being educated on the lines of their own natural development, and the principles of education which have been advocated and put into practice in schools for young children are now permeating the upper departments of schools and are influencing parents, inspectors, Education Committees, and others who are interested in education.

The Froebel Society's headquarters are in London, but it has many active branches throughout the country. Its objects are carried out through meetings, conferences, lectures, and demonstrations; through the publications of the journal, " Child Life," and by the issue of other publications dealing with the proper education of young children. The society has an excellent library dealing with the care and education of children, and a reading-room, where members can see all the leading educational magazines and papers of England and America.

The society sends a representative to the Teachers' Registration Council, and has often approached the Board of Education with regard to matters relating to preparatory and nursing schools and the training of teachers, etc.

The society generally seeks to keep abreast of, and take part in, reforms which are being made in educational matters throughout the country. It has a large representation upon the board of the National Frobel Union.

Secretary : Miss Courtenay, the Froebel Society and Junior Schools Association, 4, Bloomsbury Square, London, W.C. 1.

THE NATIONAL FROEBEL UNION.

The National Froebel Union holds examinations and grants diplomas to teachers and those training teachers for kindergarten work.

Founded 1887.

Secretary : Miss E. H. Maclean, Norwich House, Southampton Street, Bloomsbury, W.C. 1.

GEOGRAPHICAL ASSOCIATION.

The Hon. Secretary, 40, Broad Street, Oxford.

ROYAL GEOGRAPHICAL SOCIETY.

Arthur R. Hinks, F.R.S., Secretary, Kensington Gore, S.W. 7.

GILCHRIST EDUCATIONAL TRUST.

The Trustees have the duty of administering a fund left by Dr. John Borthwick Gilchrist, who died in 1841, and under the terms of whose will they may devote either the interest or the principal of the fund to the encouragement of education and learning in any part of the world. With such unfettered powers it has been necessary to proceed along lines of a strictly limited policy, and the present Trustees have followed the practice of their predecessors in making it their chief aim to give financial assistance to educational schemes of a pioneer character that appear to promise such success as shall ensure of their becoming self-supporting in the near future or make such an appeal to the educational authorities of the country that they may be adopted as a part of the national system of education. The considerable success that has attended these efforts has been summarised in an address given by the Chairman in 1910, printed copies of which may be obtained from the Office of the Trust.

A special effort has been made continuously since 1865 to encourage a love of study among the masses throughout the country by the institution of series of popular lectures. These have mainly been on science, but others have been introduced dealing with history, art, and subjects of social interest, and the Trustees are prepared to consider the inclusion of other subjects. Series of five lectures each have generally been arranged in the winter at 20 selected towns.

Copies of the conditions under which grants of these lectures are made may be obtained from the Office of the Trust, the chief condition being that the Trustees shall be satisfied of the promise of the lectures leading either to the establishment of some new form of educational work in the town or to the further development of some form already existing.

Secretary : A. H. Fison, D.Sc.   Office : 1, Plowden Buildings, Temple, E.C. 4.

LIVERPOOL UNION OF GIRLS' CLUBS.

Hon. Secretary : Miss D. M. Crosfield, 3, Fulwood Park, Liverpool.

NATIONAL ORGANISATION OF GIRLS' CLUBS.

Secretary : Mrs. A. Glover, 118, Great Titchfield Street, W. 1.

GUILD OF THE EPIPHANY.

The Guild of the Epiphany is a society for women teachers in secondary schools and other women who are actively promoting or who desire to promote the highest interests of education. Candidates for admission must be members of the Church of England or of other churches in full communion with her.

Secretary : Mrs. R. Vaughan Johnson, Wimseyes, Banstead, Surrey.

EDUCATIONAL HANDWORK ASSOCIATION.

This Association represents the oldest organisation in this country having for its object the promotion of handwork as a means of education. In the early eighties the " Sloyd Association of Great Britain and Ireland " was formed, the northern members of which very soon resolved themselves into a separate body called the " Educational Handwork Union." The fusion of these two bodies in 1904 brought into existence the " Educational Handwork Association." The main objects of the Association are :—

1. To serve as a means of intercourse between members and others interested in educational handwork.

2. To make educational handwork better known, and to show its importance as an essential factor in education by means of lectures, demonstrations, and discussions.

3. To promote the introduction of educational handwork into *all* primary and secondary schools, so as to provide for the harmonious development of the pupils.

4. To encourage and assist wherever possible in the provision of special training of teachers.

The Association has made rapid progress since the amalgamation. Over 60 branches have been formed in various parts of the country, at whose meetings hundreds of lectures are given annually.

The journal of the Association—" Educational Handwork "—is now in its tenth year of issue and has attained a circulation of over 8,000 copies.

Summer schools for the training of teachers in handwork have been held for many years under the auspices of the Association, and thousands of teachers have attended thereat.

The lending library contains most of the up-to-date books bearing on the pedagogies and activities of handwork in education.

The Board of Examinations for Educational Handwork was formed by the two Associations in 1898 for the purpose of providing students of handwork with credentials of their ability to teach this subject.

All persons interested in education are eligible for membership, and may join at any time on payment of a minimum subscription of 2s. 6d. per annum.

Full particulars and specimen copies of the journal may be obtained from the Hon. Treasurer and Secretary, J. Spittle, F.E.I.S., 16, Cambridge Road, Huddersfield.

THE HISTORICAL ASSOCIATION.

The objects of the Association, which number some 1,250 members, are to collect and distribute information on all matters relating to the study and teaching of history, to encourage local centres for the discussion of such questions, to represent to education authorities and the general public the needs and interests of historical study and teaching, and to co-operate with other associations in the furtherance of kindred objects.

Branches of the Association have been formed at Birmingham, Bradford, Bristol, Derby, Exeter, Leeds, Liverpool, London, Manchester, Nottingham, Sheffield, Southampton, and York.

The Association has published a series of leaflets dealing with bibliographies and other subjects, a series of five leaflets on English history in contemporary poetry, and a set of six constitutional documents, such as the Magna Carta (translated) and the Petition of Right. An Annual Bulletin of historical literature is published in July, and the Association also issues a quarterly journal, "History."

The annual subscription to the Association is 5s., and the annual subscription to "History" is 3s. for members and 4s. 6d. to non-members.

Secretary : Miss M. B. Curran, 22, Russell Square, London, W.C. 1.

ROYAL HISTORICAL SOCIETY.

Hon. Secretary : H. E. Malden, M.A., 22, Russell Square, W.C. 1.

NATIONAL HOME-READING UNION.

The National Home-Reading Union exists to guide readers in the choice and use of books and provide a means of continuous education. In return for a very small fee it offers : (1) Courses of reading with select lists of books in poetry, drama, fiction, language, history, biography, travel, philosophy, economics, nature-study, science, art, and general literature; (2) a magazine published monthly during the session (October to May); (3) companionship in systematic reading and study in circles. There are three sections of membership : the special course dealing in an advanced manner with a variety of subjects; the general course suitable for those who prefer to read more widely without entering into the detailed study of the special course, and the young people's course, intended primarily for children of school age, but also useful to those who, having left school, desire help in continuing their own education and in cultivating the habit of profitable reading. The annual fee for each section entitles members to receive the monthly magazine and the book list of the section to which they belong. All information may be obtained from the Secretary.

General Secretary : Miss Jeanie I. Swanson, 12, York Buildings, Adelphi, W.C. 2.

EDUCATIONAL KINEMATOGRAPH INTERNATIONAL COUNCIL.

Morley Dainow, 22-24, Great Portland Street, W. 1.

LABOUR COLLEGE
(Until recently the Central Labour College).

Secretary : T. Lowth, Unity House, Euston Road, N.W. 1.

SCOTTISH LABOUR COLLEGE (PROVISIONAL COMMITTEE).

The proposal to found a Labour College for Scotland was first made at a representative Conference held in Glasgow in February, 1916. Various causes connected with the war delayed action being taken for some time. During the winter 1917-18 the Provisional Committee started 17 Sunday and evening classes in economic and political subjects. The average attendance was over 75 per cent. of the 1,500 students enrolled. The classes were held in various towns in Lanarkshire, Dumbartonshire, Renfrewshire, and Fifeshire. The Glasgow Plebs League, which works in close co-operation with the College Committee, organised 19 classes, with a total of about 1,000 students. The greatest difficulty of this movement has been to secure the services of the requisite number of qualified tutors.

At a Conference held in Glasgow on March 16th, 1918, the constitution of the Committee was adopted.

Secretary : J. F. Armour, Scottish Labour College Committee, 65, West Regent Street, Glasgow.

THE UNION OF LANCASHIRE AND CHESHIRE INSTITUTES.

The Union of Lancashire and Cheshire Institutes has for its objects the advancement of literature, science, and the fine arts, including their application to industry, commerce, and domestic life, and for this purpose it shall have power (*a*) to act as an examining board, or to appoint examining boards and examiners, and to issue awards to successful candidates; (*b*) to collect and receive contributions, subscriptions, gifts or legacies, and hold funds and property for the objects of the Union or any of them, as the donors may direct; (*c*) by means of voluntary contributions, subscriptions, legacies, or the funds of the union, to offer to students of evening classes in union prizes, exhibitions, and scholarships; (*d*) to maintain a reference library for the use of members, teachers, and officials of the institutes; (*e*) to maintain a circulating village library; (*f*) to co-operate with the County Councils in the geographical counties of Lancashire, Cheshire, and Westmorland, the High Peak Parliamentary Division of Derbyshire, and the Higher Education Board of any district of the Isle of Man, and also with any institutions or societies in these said counties and in the Isle of Man for the purposes of the above objects of the Union.

Founded 1839.

Secretary : John T. Coles, F.C.I.S., 33, Blackfriars Street, Manchester.

THE LING ASSOCIATION.

The Ling Association (*a*) grants diplomas in the Swedish system of gymnastics; (*b*) aims at improving the conditions of employment of its diploma or certificated members; (*c*) serves as a propagandist agency for extending and perfecting the Ling system of physical culture.

Founded 1899.

Organ (in conjunction with the two following societies) : " The Journal of Scientific Physical Training " (four-monthly).

Secretary : Miss Hankinson, 19, Briston Grove, Crouch End, N. 8.

LONDON SCHOOLS DINNER ASSOCIATION.

Arthur H. Ward, 32, John Street, Theobald's Road, London, W.C. 1.

MANCHESTER AND SALFORD DISTRICT EDUCATION ASSOCIATION.

F. Willett, 49, Spring Gardens, Manchester.

MATHEMATICAL ASSOCIATION.

Hon. Secretaries : C. Pendlebury, M.A., 39, Brandenburgh Road, Chiswick, W. 4, and Miss Punnett, London Day Training College, Southampton Row, W.C. 1.

ASSOCIATION OF MEDICAL OFFICERS OF SCHOOLS.

Drs. W. Attlee, R. C. Elmslie, and G. Chaikin, 11, Chandos Street, W. 2.

MODERN LANGUAGE ASSOCIATION.

The Modern Language Association was founded in 1892, with the object of raising the standard of efficiency in linguistic teaching, promoting the study of modern languages, and obtaining for them in educational curricula the position to which their importance entitles them. The present number of members is about 1,100, all but a small number of whom are teachers in universities and schools. The Association's magazine, " Modern Language Teaching," appears eight times a year and is supplied gratis and post free to all members. The Association also supports the " Modern Language Review," a quarterly journal of philology and research in modern and medieval literature. It possesses a Travelling Exhibition of books for use in teaching modern languages and a collection of lantern slides. Recently the Association has been instrumental in obtaining the institution by the Universities of Oxford, Cambridge, and London of special examinations in French and German for teachers. It has also influenced school examinations usefully. Before the war it co-operated with foreign societies in promoting the exchange of children between English and Continental families, and it is hoped to resume this work after the re-establishment of peace.

Modern Language Association : Steeple, Kingsway, Gerrards Cross. Hon. Secretary : G. F. Bridge, M.A. (Telephone : Gerrards Cross 139.)

MONTESSORI SOCIETY, LONDON.

This society exists for the promotion of the study of the educational ideas of its distinguished president, the Italian lady doctor, Dr. Maria Montessori, and for the encouragement of the foundation of schools and classes conducted on the system of auto-education, which she advocates as the result of her experiments in the field of education. The work of the society comprises propaganda lectures, which are usually open to non-members on payment of a fee of 6d. It has a panel of lecturers whose names and approximate fees it can give particulars of to any societies or private individuals desirous of arranging lectures on this method of teaching. More intensive work is carried on by means of study circles confined to those who either belong to the society already or join it on purpose to take a study circle course. Such a course consists of at least ten lectures, and visits to schools are usually arranged. The tuition fee is half-a-guinea, in addition to the half-crown to the society. During the year 1916-17 six study circles were at work. The number of students in each is limited to 30, so that real teaching may be done. In August, 1916, a very successful summer school was held, at which there was a continuous course of lectures and observation in a school for three weeks. This was in the Berkshire village of Wootton.

Since September, 1915, the society has been responsible for an observation school, in which 20 children are educated on this method by a teacher holding the international Montessori diploma. This school does not claim to be a demonstration school or to materialise fully Dr. Montessori's ideal, but it affords interesting matter for study. It is supported by means of a special donation fund, and visiting is confined to donors.

Activities already carried on to some extent, but which will be vigorously developed in the near future, are a registry for Montessori teachers, a library for students, and a correspondence bureau for giving information about the method.

The Secretary is Mr. Hutchinson, 49, Gordon Mansions, W.C. 1.

UNION OF GRADUATES IN MUSIC (INCORPORATED).

Dr. E. F. Horner, F.R.C.O., etc., 19, Beverley Road, Anerley, S.E. 20.

GIRLS' SCHOOL MUSIC UNION.

Miss Cecilia Hill, Wentworth Hall, Mill Hill, N.W.

THE INCORPORATED SOCIETY OF MUSICIANS.

The Incorporated Society of Musicians conducts examinations and grants certificates to teachers, but it is concerned with executants rather than teachers. It was founded with the object of promoting whatever may tend to the elevation of the status and the improvement of the qualifications of all members of the musical profession, or advance musical education.

Founded 1892.

General Secretary : Hugo Chadfield, 19, Berners Street, W. I.

NATIONAL EDUCATION ASSOCIATION.

The National Education Association consists of persons approving of its objects and subscribing annually to its funds, local branch associations formed in different parts of the country, and affiliated organisations formed for other objects but embracing those of the National Education Association.

The constitution and policy of the Association are controlled by a Council of 300 members, representing all parts of England and Wales, which is elected annually by the subscribers, branches, and affiliated bodies.

The Association, which was formed at the beginning of 1889, has for its objects :—

1. To promote a system of national education which shall be in all its grades efficient, progressive, and unsectarian, and shall be under popular control; and also to oppose all legislative and administrative proposals having a contrary tendency.

2. To secure the universal establishment of representative authorities in districts of suitable area, and having under their control unsectarian schools within reasonable reach of the population requiring them.

3. To secure the abolition of fees in all elementary schools, and the opportunity of free or aided education for deserving pupils in higher schools and colleges.

4. To obtain facilities for the better training of teachers in unsectarian institutions under public management.

The Association is not a party organisation, the Association, and especially some of the local branches, forming a common platform for men and women of all parties and creeds to meet in support of educational progress.

Secretary, A. J. Mundella, Caxton House, Westminster, S.W. 1.

THE NATIONAL SOCIETY.

Objects : The promotion of the education of the poor in the principles of the Church of England.

Founded in 1811; incorporated in 1817.

Full membership is secured under its constitution to persons subscribing a guinea a year, or contributing ten guineas at one time. The number of members is about 3,700. There are also a large number of subscribers of smaller sums, and a recent development, especially in Leeds, has been the enrolment of subscribers of 1s. a year among members of the working-classes, who recognise the great benefit which they or their children have derived from attendance at Church schools, and who desire to help the society in its endeavours to maintain the position of those schools. Of such schools there are about 10,500. The methods of the Society's action in pursuance of its objects include the making of grants-in-aid of the building, extension, improvement, and repair of Church schools, and in aid of the maintenance of Church Training Colleges at which elementary school teachers are prepared for the work of their profession by a two years', and sometimes a three years', course. The Training Colleges of St. Mark's, Chelsea, and St. John's, Battersea, for men and Whitelands College, Chelsea, for women are under the control of the National Society, receiving substantial annual grants (£1,219 in 1916); and in the same year £2,289 was granted in aid of the maintenance of residential Diocesan Training Colleges in various parts of the country. Grants towards the building enlargement, improvement and repair, of Church day schools were paid to the amount of £4,050 in 1916. The Society also actively promotes, by training courses for teachers and demonstrations, the improvement of methods of religious education both in Day and Sunday schools. In this connection there have been published in recent years from its depository more than 20 volumes of carefully graded Sunday School lessons, together with papers giving guidance as to the use of these courses of lessons in Day schools.

Organ of the Society.—The " School Guardian," an Educational Review issued monthly at 1d., which contains notes of the month covering all matters of general educational interest whether elementary or secondary, and is in the forefront of the advocacy of educational reform, with special reference to the interests of the working classes. It also contains from month to month articles by eminent educationists and helpful reviews of educational books.

Secretary : Talbot Baines, 19, Great Peter Street, Westminster, S.W. 1.

___

YOUNG NATURALISTS' LEAGUE.

President : W. Percival Westell, 8-11, Southampton Street, Strand, London, W.C. 2.

___

NATURE STUDY SOCIETY.

Wilfred Mark Webb, F.L.S., F.R.M.S., The Hermitage, Hanwell, W. 7.

___

THE SCHOOL NATURE STUDY UNION.

The School Nature Study Union aims at bringing together, for mutual help and advice, those interested in Nature Study in general, and its place in education in particular. This it seeks to do by the following means:—

1. Meetings in winter, at which papers are read by specialists on various aspects of Nature Study.

2. Excursions throughout the year for purposes of practical Nature Study.

3. The quarterly publication of an official organ, entitled " School Nature Study," containing general reports of the work of the union, résumes of the papers read at the meetings, practical articles which are reprinted in leaflet form, reviews of books, and other matters of interest.

4. Annual conferences and exhibitions.

5. Co-operation with other societies whose work may touch that of the union.

The union has organised sections for the more detailed and definite treatment of certain aspects of nature study, thus:—

1. The Photographic Section applies itself to Nature photography and ecological record.

2. The Gardening Section deals with horticultural principles and operations mainly as applied to school gardens.

3. The Microscopic Sections provides opportunity for the study of such facts of nature as a microscope reveals, and practice in the use of a microscope.

Hon. Secretary: H. E. Turner, 1, Grosvenor Park, Camberwell, S.E. 5.

NEW IDEALS IN EDUCATION.

New Ideals in Education began as an informal association of friends of education sharing the same views and sympathies.

OBJECTS OF CONFERENCE.

Having begun as an informal association of friends of education, sharing the same views and sympathies, the Conference Committee has now assumed the character of a permanent Council governed by a definite constitution. It does not exist to voice the opinions of any particular pedagogical school or to give exclusive assistance to any sectional propaganda. Its members work together upon the basis of a common conviction that a new spirit, full of hope for the world, is stirring in education; and the purpose of their activities is to aid that spirit wherever and in whatever form it is striving to express itself. An attempt to characterise a vital movement in a single sentence is apt to be misleading as well as ineffective, but it may be said that the essentials of the new spirit, as the Committee conceives it, are reverence for the pupil's individuality and a belief that true individuality—surest antidote to the poison of egoism—grows best in an atmosphere of freedom. The object of the conference is to draw together in fellowship, under pleasant holiday conditions, all who are seeking to embody this spirit in their work, to offer them a platform for the discussion of difficulties and the communication of the results of experience or reflection, to bring isolated experimenters into touch with one another, and to give to pioneering work the encouragement of criticism and recognition.

The first conference was held at Runton, 1914. A full report of the proceedings was published, which can be obtained for 1s. 6d. from the Conference Secretary, 24, Royal Avenue, Chelsea, S.W. 3.

The second conference, under a new name, "New Ideals in Education," was held at Stratford-on-Avon, 1915. A full report of proceedings was likewise published.

The third conference was held at Oxford in 1916, the report costing 2s.

The fourth conference is being held at Bedford College, 1917. The report will be published shortly at 1s. 9d.

Conference Committee: Chairman, the Earl of Lytton ; vice-chairman, Dr. Macan, Litt.D. Master of University College, Oxford; Sir Frank Benson, LL.D. ; W. Laurence Bradbury, proprietor of "Punch"; *Lady Betty Balfour ; Miss Cross, Principal of King's Langley School, Herts; Miss Crouch, headmistress, Deansfield Road L.C.C. School, Eltham; E. P. Culverwell, Professor of Education, Dublin University ; Rev. A. A. David, D.D., Headmaster of Rugby School ; *Bertram Hawker ; Miss Caroline Herford, Manchester University; *Edmond Holmes, late Chief Inspector of Schools, Board of Education ; Miss Hawtrey, Principal of Training College, Darlington ; Mrs. Meyrick Jones ; *Dr. C. W. Kimmins, Chief Inspector of Schools, London County Council ; Homer Lane, Superintendent of the Little Commonwealth ; Mrs. Robert Martin Holland ; *Albert Mansbridge, late secretary Workers' Educational Association ; Miss Mercier, late Principal of Training College, Leeds ; Mrs. Mackenzie, late Professor of Education at Cardiff University ; Lady Isabel Margesson ; W. Lee Mathews ; Beresford Melville, late Chairman Montessori Society; Right Hon. Sir William Mather, LL.D., Chairman of the Froebel Institute ; *T. P. Nunn, M.A., D.Sc., Prof. of Education, London University ; Miss De Norman, late H.M. Inspector of Schools ; *Miss Rennie, Hon. Secretary of the Montessori Society ; Miss Leila Rendel, Director of the Caldecott Community; *The Countess of Sandwich ;

H. Bompas Smith, Prof. of Education, Manchester University; *E. Sharwood Smith, Headmaster of Newbury Grammar School; Miss Mildred Swannell, Froebel Lecturer; Miss Melian Stawell; Capt. St. John, Treasurer of the Montessori Society; Dr. Michael Sadler, Vice-Chancellor of Leeds University; H Tunaley, late H.M. Inspector of Drawing, Board of Education; Christopher Turnor; Dr. Yorke Trotter, London Academy of Music; W. B. Griffiths Vaughan (Grenadier Guards); Dr. Jane Walker, Nayland Sanatorium; *Miss Alice Woods, late Maria Grey Training College.

The Secretary, Miss N. B. Synge, 24, Royal Avenue, Chelsea, S.W. 1.

Those marked with an asterisk are on the Executive Committee.

NORTH STAFFORDSHIRE MINERS' HIGHER EDUCATION MOVEMENT.

Secretary : E. S. Cartwright, Barnett House, Broad Street, Oxford. (See pages 386-87.)

THE NORTHERN COUNTIES EDUCATION LEAGUE.

The objects of the League are :—

1. To defend the principles of popular control and religious liberty in national education.

2. To demand that all schools and colleges receiving Government grants or local rates shall be brought under popular control.

3. To obtain through England and Wales the establishment of directly elected authorities in areas of suitable size for educational purposes only.

4. To secure that training colleges and the offices of teacher and pupil teacher, now maintained at the public cost, shall be thrown open to all, without test of creed or denomination, and that teachers shall be engaged solely for the work of education and shall not be required to undertake or perform extraneous duties.

5. To advocate the omission of sectarian and theological teaching from State-paid education, and the substitution of moral and citizen training.

They lay stress on the lengthening of the school life, the provision of better school buildings, and better opportunities for physical development, and inveighs against the junior technical school. The Secretary is Mr. Charles Peach, and the offices of the League are at 5, Cross Street, Manchester.

BIRMINGHAM NURSERY SCHOOLS' ASSOCIATION

(originally known as the Birmingham People's Kindergarten Association).

The above Association has been in existence 14 years. Its aim is to give the children of the people between the ages of 2 and 6 years the best in education, viz. : to set free the individuality of the child. For this reason the number of children in the Nursery Schools are limited to 30 ; for then the teacher and her helpers can give individual care and attention to each child.

The aims of the work are :—

1. To build up character through mutual service for one another and through activities in connection with the care of plants and pet animals.

2. To develop self-control and independence through freedom and liberty, yet not at the expense of the community life.

3. To lay a foundation for life in the acquisition of habits of order and cleanliness, thus helping the child to appreciate and to desire beauty in its surroundings.

4. To train the senses and hand-power at a time when the sense-organs and muscles are in process of development.

5. To give the child new and varied experiences of the social life of man, thus forming a basis for its self-expression work.

6. To endeavour through stories, game and song, to deepen the impressions received, and to stimulate the imagination.

Co-operation with the Home :—

Every effort is made by the teachers to keep in close touch with the parents so that they may continually consult together as to the best way of dealing with each individual child.

The mothers are invited to be present at the medical inspections, and they and the teachers endeavour together to carry out the advice of the doctors so as to improve the health of the children.

The Hon. Organising Secretary is Miss Julia Lloyd, Farm, Sparksbrook, Birmingham.

MANCHESTER AND SALFORD ASSOCIATION FOR DAY NURSERIES AND NURSERY SCHOOLS.

The Manchester and Salford Association for Day Nurseries and Nursery Schools was founded in April, 1916, as a result of a conference convened by the National Union of Teachers, Schools for Mothers, Women's Citizens' Association, and the Manchester Society for Women's Suffrage. It was established for the purpose of founding day nurseries and nursery schools, and to promote State and municipal action for the benefit of children under school age. It has established three nurseries, two of which are co-operating with other institutions, the third being mainly for the children of munition workers. Each nursery is managed by a House Committee, and each has an honorary medical officer. It is hoped that several new nurseries will be opened before long in districts where the need is urgent. The three nursery schools, and six day nurseries, which were established before this Association was started, are now affiliated to it.

Hon. Secretary : Miss M. S. Beard, Grosvenor Chambers, 16, Deansgate, Manchester.

THE NATIONAL ASSOCIATION FOR THE ORAL INSTRUCTION OF THE DEAF.

This Association has a training college for teachers and a school for children at 11, Fitzroy Square, London, W. 1. It endeavours to provide an adequate supply of trained teachers for the schools of the country. The students take the Joint Examination Board for Teachers of the Deaf for their professional diploma and their academic attainments are tested by the Board of Education. The aims of the

Association are : (*a*) to promote the pure oral system of teaching deaf and so-called dumb children by lip-reading and articulate speech, to the rigid exclusion of the finger alphabet and all artificial signs; and (*b*) to train teachers of this system for public and private work. The Hon. Secretary is Dr. D. A. H. Moses, 11, Fitzroy Square, W. 1.

THE OXFORD AND CAMBRIDGE SCHOOLS EXAMINATION BOARD.

The Board was established in 1873 to inspect and examine schools preparing boys for those Universities and to grant certificates on the results of the examination. Its work was early extended to girls' schools. The Board has also from time to time conducted examinations for various Education Authorities. The certificates granted by the Board are recognised by many other Universities and professional bodies.

The examinations of the Board are mainly of two kinds—school examinations and examinations for certificates.

Annual conferences with representatives of the Head Masters' Conference, the Head Masters' Association, and the Head Mistresses' Association, for the discussion of the regulations and of any questions which may arise on the conduct of the examinations are held. The Board also holds conferences, as occasion arises, with other bodies representing those interested in the teaching of particular subjects. It is also prepared to receive representations from individual teachers.

Membership consists of the Vice-Chancellors of the Universities of Oxford and Cambridge and a number of heads and fellows of colleges in those Universities.

Secretaries : P. E. Matheson, M.A., New College, Oxford; A. W. Pickard, Cambridge M.A., Balliol College, Oxford; T. G. Bedford, M.A., Sidney Sussex College, Cambridge.

Address : Schools Examination Office, Balliol College, Oxford.

OXFORD UNIVERSITY EXTENSION.

The University Extension Movement for the provision of higher adult education began at Cambridge in 1873 and at Oxford in 1878. A special delegacy for its control was set up at Oxford in 1892. The choice of lecturers and the control of finance is in the hands of local committees; in the year before the war (1913-14) Oxford had 114 of these in actual work. The lecturers are appointed by the Central Authority, which also conducts the examination at the end of each course. Every course consists of at least six lectures.

The method of instruction is as follows : When a course has been chosen, a syllabus of it (60 copies) is sent down, to guide the reading of students, and a library of books bearing on the subject. Every lecture is followed by a class, at which questions are asked and difficulties answered; the lecturer also sets and corrects essays for those who choose to do them. In 1913-14 Oxford had 41 lecturers engaged, 131 courses were given, and the number of students attending was about 12,500. The war has naturally caused some falling off in the number of students and lectures, but on the whole the work has been maintained.

The payment to lecturers varies with their position, and experience shows that the cost per lecture, including, besides the lecturer's fee and expenses, room rent, advertising, etc., varies from £5 to £6 at most. Meetings of students and lecturers are held at Oxford in August every other year, when courses of lectures are given on the various aspects of some special subject or subjects. Certificates of work done under certain conditions are recognised by the University as exempting from some of its own degree requirements.

The Secretary is J. A. R. Marriott, M.P., Fellow of Worcester College, Oxford, and the full title of the Delegacy is "For the extension of teaching beyond the limits of the University."

PARENTS' NATIONAL EDUCATIONAL UNION.

The Parents' National Educational Union was founded in 1887 in response to a demand from thoughtful parents.

The Union aims at giving opportunities for the study of Educational problems, and a meeting ground for intercourse between parents, teachers, and all who are interested in education.

The central principles are: (1) That a religious basis of work be maintained. (2) That the series of addresses and other means employed by the Union shall be so arranged as to deal with education under the following heads: (a) Physical; (b) Mental; (c) Moral; and (d) Religious. (3) That arrangements concerning lectures, etc., be made with a view to the convenience of fathers as well as of mothers. (4) That the work of the Union be arranged to help parents of all classes.

The objects are: (a) To assist parents of all classes to understand the best principles and methods of education in all its aspects, those which concern the formation of character, as well as actual methods of teaching. (b) To create a better public opinion on the subject of the training of children, and with this object in view to collect and make known the best information and experience on the subject. (c) To afford to parents opportunities for co-operation and consultation, so that the wisdom and experience of each may be profitable to all. (d) To stimulate their enthusiasm, through the sympathy of numbers acting together. (e) To secure greater unity and continuity of education by harmonising home and school training.

Central Office: 26, Victoria Street, S.W.; Hon. Organising Secretary, The Hon. Mrs. Franklin; General and Organising Secretary, Miss Parish.

THE INCORPORATED BRITISH COLLEGE OF PHYSICAL EDUCATION.

This College was founded in 1891 and was incorporated in 1897. Its objects are the provision of a high-class instruction in the principles and practice of physical education, the development of a national system suitable to the national temperament and tastes, the holding of examinations and the granting of certificates to successful candidates, and to promote physical education generally in the true sense of the word. Although its aims are chiefly concerned with the educational side of the subject, it also encourages recreative schemes of a useful character. Copies of the syllabus of examinations may be obtained on receipt of two penny stamps from Frank H. Gelling, Hon. Secretary, 5 and 7, Johnson Street, Notting Hill Gate, London, W. 8.

NATIONAL LEAGUE FOR PHYSICAL EDUCATION AND IMPROVEMENT (INCORPORATED).

OBJECTS.

1. To stimulate public interest in the physical condition of the people throughout the kingdom.

2. To establish close association and centralisation of all Societies and individuals trying to combat such influences as tend to produce national physical deterioration.

3. To aid existing organisations.

4. To start organisations for physical health and well-being wherever none exist.

This movement is on strictly non-political and undenominational lines.

Founded in 1905.

Secretary : Miss Halford, 4, Tavistock Square, London, W.C. 1.

EVENING PLAY CENTRES COMMITTEE.

In June, 1917, there were 25 Play Centres under the London Evening Play Centres Committee, held in Council Schools lent by the L.C.C. to the Committee, free of all charges for cleaning, heating, and lighting. Each centre is under the direction of a paid superintendent, who is assisted by a paid staff, supplemented by voluntary workers wherever such help is available. The centres are open five nights in the week, from 5-15 p.m. to 7 p.m. or 7-15 p.m., and for an hour and a-half on Saturday mornings, for 40 weeks in the year. From Easter onwards the centres are in the playgrounds, and the staff at each centre is then reduced to a games master, a games mistress, and a working woman, in addition, of course, to the superintendent.

Hon. Secretary : Mrs. Humphrey Ward, Passmore Edwards' Settlement, Tavistock Place, W.C. 1.

PLEBS LEAGUE.

Mrs. W. Horrabin, 176, Springvale Road, Sheffield. (See pages 390-91.)

ASSOCIATION OF PREPARATORY SCHOOLS.

F. Ritchie, 156, Sutherland Avenue, London, W. 9.

PRIVATE SCHOOLS ASSOCIATION (INCORPORATED).

Chairman of Council : Mr. S. Maxwell, M.A., LL.B., Manor House School, Clapham Common, S.W.

LONDON PROGRESSIVE EDUCATION COUNCIL.

Miss Constance Williams, Caxton House, Westminster, London, S.W. 1.

REPRESENTATIVE MANAGERS OF LONDON COUNTY COUNCIL ELEMENTARY SCHOOLS.

Henry W. Pyddoke, Oxhill, Loughton, Essex.

ROYAL SANITARY INSTITUTE.

1. Founded in 1876 to promote the advancement of sanitary science in all or any of its branches and to diffuse knowledge relating thereto.

2. Holds congresses and meetings in London and throughout the country for the discussion of public health questions.

3. Maintains in London a permanent Museum of Sanitation and Hygiene and a large library.

4. A journal of proceedings is published.

5. Holds training courses for public health officials twice a year, commencing in February and September.

6. Carries out standard examinations in various centres for sanitary officers, meat and food inspectors, women health visitors, maternity and child welfare workers, and in sanitary science as applied to buildings and public works, and in school hygiene, including elementary physiology, in the United Kingdom, and in the Dominions beyond the seas.

Secretary and director, E. White Wallis, F.S.S., 90, Buckingham Palace Road, S.W. 1.

RUSKIN COLLEGE.

Sam Smith, Ruskin College, Oxford. (See pages 388-89.)

JOINT SCHOLARSHIPS BOARD.

H. Bendall, M.A., 37, Norfolk Street, W.C. 2.

THE SOCIETY OF SCHOOLMASTERS.

The Society of Schoolmasters was founded for the relief of necessitous schoolmasters and similar charitable purposes.

Founded 1798.

Secretary : A. Llewelyn Roberts, B.A., 40, Denison House, 296, Vauxhall Bridge Road, London, S.W. 1.

BURGH AND PAROCHIAL SCHOOLMASTERS' WIDOWS' FUND.

The Burgh and Parochial Schoolmasters' Widows' Fund has for its object the relief of widows and orphan children under 17 years of age of contributors, who were Scottish burgh and parochial schoolmasters appointed prior to the coming into force of the Education (Scotland) Act, 1872. The fund is now administered under a Provisional Order confirmed by Parliament in 1913.

Founded 1806. Membership 58. (No new members were admissible after 1873.)

Clerk : John Ewart, W.S., 58, Frederick Street, Edinburgh.

ASSOCIATION OF SCHOOL BOARD CLERKS AND TREASURERS IN SCOTLAND.

W. Higgins, 21, West Nile Street, Glasgow.

SCHOOLS MUTUAL AID SOCIETY.

Object.—The promotion of correspondence and exchange of objects of local interest between city and country schools. The country schools send letters and nature specimens to their city friends, and the town schools return letters, pictures, postcards, magazines, drawings, and other objects. Careful instructions are given to avoid the uprooting of rare plants, taking of birds' nests, etc.

Expenses.—Nine City and County Councils (including the L.C.C.) grant 10s. per year per school for postage expenses. Many schools pay their own postage. Over 380 schools are in correspondence at the present time. The expenses of the Hon. Secretaries and of those schools which cannot pay their own postage are met by subscriptions.

Full Title.—" Schools Mutual Aid Society " (S.M.A.).

Hon. Secretary, Miss O. L. Cobb, 40, Redlands Road, Reading.

BRITISH SCIENCE GUILD.

Miss A. D. L. Lacey, 199, Piccadilly, W.

SCOTTISH SCHOOL BOARDS ASSOCIATION.

James Cuthbert, Mar Street, Alloa.

SECONDARY EDUCATION ASSOCIATION OF SCOTLAND.

George C. Pringle, M.A., High School, Peebles.

SECONDARY SCHOOLS ASSOCIATION.

R. S. Hyams, 25, Victoria Street, Westminster, S.W. 1.

THE SECONDARY SCHOOLS' SCRIPTURE TEACHING CONFERENCE.

The Secondary Schools' Scripture Teaching Conference aims at improving the Bible teaching in public and secondary schools.

A Report was published of each annual conference (1912, 1913), but the work has been suspended during the war.

Founded 1912. No regular membership.

Hon. Secretary : N. P. Wood, Bishop Stortford College (at present serving in the Army). Chairman of Committee (acting as Hon. Secretary) : H. Cradock-Watson, Merchant Taylors' School, Crosby, Liverpool.

THE SESAME HOUSE ASSOCIATION.

The Sesame House Association was formed in 1916 of former students of Sesame House for Home-Life Training, St. John's Wood, London, and of others interested in the educational ideas for which it stood.

Sesame House aimed at the practical establishment of ideal home-life. The needs of children from babyhood to school age and the needs of the community were studied practically and theoretically. Every member of the household shared responsibility for the order and beauty of the surroundings. The various branches of domestic work were brought into a harmonious whole by the unifying principle running throughout. It is hoped that in the immediate future centres of a similar kind will be started, and that members of the Association will be able to assist in a practical way those who undertake such work.

Apply for further information to Miss Last, late Principal of Sesame House for Home-Life Training from 1907-1916, at Dew Green Cottage, Felden, Boxmoor, Herts.

SHAFTESBURY SOCIETY AND RAGGED SCHOOL UNION, 1844.

For the physical, moral, and religious welfare of the poorest children and young persons, chiefly in London and district. It operates chiefly through 140 Branches and affiliated Missions, and 4,000 voluntary teachers and workers. It maintains Holiday Homes at Bognor, Southend, Windsor, a Residential School for crippled children at Bournemouth, a Camp House for School Journeys at Loughton, and administers the "Fresh Aid Fund" for London area. The Cripple Mission has under visitation, or in Cripple Parlours, 7,700 children, to whom help is given in the supply of spinal carriages, surgical appliances, holidays, etc. Other agencies include the Barefoot Mission, the Poor Children's Boot Fund, the London School Dinners' Association, and the Yule Tide Association. Infant welfare work is represented by several Day Nurseries and Schools for Mothers. The total income 1916-17 amounted to £30,000, mainly derived from voluntary contributions.

Hon. Secretary, Arthur Black; Director: Sir John Kirk, J.P., 32, John Street, Theobald's Road, W.C. 1. (Telephone: Holborn, 1,951.)

THE SIMPLIFIED SPELLING SOCIETY.

The aim of the Simplified Spelling Society (of which Professor Gilbert Murray is President) is to remedy the grave disadvantages resulting from the innumerable inconsistencies and irrationalities of English spelling. A fairly consistent representation of the sounds of the language will greatly lighten the work of the learner and make the teaching of spelling an easy and rational process instead of a laborious drilling in unreason.

This reform will mean a practical prolongation of every child's school life, since the time now wasted on spelling can be devoted to other subjects of real—as opposed to conventional—importance. When it is considered that this benefit will be reaped, not by any limited class, but by all coming generations of English speakers, the importance of the work undertaken by the society cannot fail to be recognised.

The Secretary will send free literature on application to the Simplified Spelling Society, 44, Great Russell Street, London, W.C. 1.

THE SMITH TRAINING COLLEGE OF THE ROYAL NORMAL COLLEGE FOR THE BLIND.

This college is recognised by the Board of Education as a training college for school teachers, and Government grants are made as in training colleges for the sighted.

Founded 1895.

Address : 108, Church Road, Upper Norwood, S.E. 19.

JOINT SOCIAL STUDIES COMMITTEE.

This Committee was formed in July, 1916, as the outcome of an inquiry instituted by the Personal Service Association into the provision of training for voluntary social workers, and consists of representatives of the constituent colleges of the University of London and other bodies offering social training. Its function is to ensure the provision of adequate and systematic courses of instruction and practical experience for social workers. As far as possible schemes of study already in existence will be utilised, including, when practicable, evening classes on social and economic subjects provided by the Workers' Educational Association. It is proposed to form a union of voluntary workers as soon as a sufficient number qualify by undergoing the requisite training, and a Provisional Committee has been appointed to act as a temporary executive. Full particulars may be had from the Secretary, Miss Low, at the office, 11, Marble Arch, W. 1. (Telephone number : Paddington 3687.)

SOWERBY DIVISION CONFERENCE OF YOUTH.

This Association of Bible Classes, Mutual Improvement Societies, and other educational bodies in the Sowerby Parliamentary Division of Yorkshire was formed in 1894.

Its primary object was to provide a common platform where youth of all sections might meet to discuss the questions of the day.

At the annual meetings in January each year two sessions are held, afternoon and evening, at each of which an address is given, followed by a discussion. A meeting is also held in the summer, taking the form of a ramble and open-air meeting, at which natural science and local history receive special attention.

A list of lecturers is published for the use of affiliated societies during the winter session.

The Conference, which is affiliated to the Yorkshire District of the W.E.A., has a membership of 45 societies.

J. H. Greenwood, 172, Horton Grange Road, Bradford.

THE STATE CHILDREN'S ASSOCIATION.

The State Children's Association stands for the principle that the home is the foundation of the State and that the home-reared child, whose personality has developed under family influence and affection, makes the best and most valuable citizen. Recognising that economic conditions press more heavily on widowed or deserted mothers and their children than on any other class, the Association have conducted an active campaign for mothers' pensions in each case.

Secretary : F. Penrose Philp, 53, Victoria Street, S.W. 1.

THE TEACHERS' CHRISTIAN UNION.

The Teachers' Christian Union is an inter-denominational guild of men and women teachers of all grades, the aim of which is to emphasise the spiritual side of educational work and to unite teachers in seeking through Christian education a solution of social problems.
Organ : " Quarterly Papers for Teachers."
Secretary : Miss W. M. Mowll, 26, George Street, Hanover Square, W.

THE TEACHERS' LEAGUE OF THE SOUTH LONDON HOSPITAL FOR WOMEN.

The Teachers' League of the South London Hospital for Women exists " to support a bed or beds in the private wards of the South London Hospital for Women (Incorporated) for the use of members during sickness, who are unable to pay for medical treatment and whose cases the medical staff of the hospital consider suitable for in-patient treatment."
Founded 1912. Membership, 200 to 250.
Hon. Secretary : Miss J. Harsett, 17, Grey Coat Gardens, S.W. 1.

UNIVERSITY OF CAMBRIDGE: TEACHERS' TRAINING SYNDICATE.

The college of this Syndicate, which is entirely for men, is suspended for the period of the war. The examinations for secondary school teachers is still continued.
Secretary : W. G. Bell, M.A., 1, St. Mary's Passage, Cambridge.

ASSOCIATION OF TECHNICAL INSTITUTIONS.

The Association of Technical Institutions was formed in 1894, and consists of 104 leading institutions distributed throughout the British Isles. The objects of the Association are to promote the efficient organisation and management of technical institutions, facilitate concordant action among governing bodies, and aid the development of technical education. The Association from its inception has been in close touch with local, central, and governmental institutions dealing with the development of technical instruction.
The affairs of the Association are managed by a Council, consisting of a president, chairman of the Council, vice-chairman of the Council, hon. treasurer, hon. secretary, and twelve members, half of whom are governors and half principals of technical schools and colleges.
Founded 1894.
Hon. Secretary : F. Wilkinson, F.G.S., Director of the Technical School, Bolton.

THE THEOSOPHICAL EDUCATIONAL TRUST
(In Great Britain and Ireland) Limited.

The Theosophical Educational Trust was established with the object of bringing into full realisation the ideals advocated by the Theosophical Fraternity in Education. By running various types of experimental schools, and by rendering both financial and other assistance to the pioneer schools affiliated to it, the Trust provides proof of the possibility of its aims, and at the same time supplies actual working material through which its own ideas can be continually checked, sifted, and readjusted to actual fact. The Trust answers the doubters and hesitants in the only convincing way, namely, by showing them its theories in successful practice, and demonstrating that the ideals, though far reaching, are yet closely in touch with the limits of actuality.

SCHOOLS FOUNDED BY THE TRUST.

The Garden City Theosophical School (founded 1915), Letchworth, Herts.

The Brackenhill Theosophical Home School (founded 1917), Bromley, Kent. (Free school supported by voluntary contributions)

SCHOOLS AFFILIATED TO THE TRUST.

The Essendon School, Skegness, Lincolnshire.
Penrith New School, Church End, Finchley, N.W. 4.
The Leinster House School, Hyde Park, W. 2.
The London Garden School, St John's Wood, N.W. 3.

Secretary : Mrs. Ensor. Registered Offices : 11, Tavistock Square, London, W.C. 1.

THE THEOSOPHICAL FRATERNITY IN EDUCATION.

Motto : " Education as Service."

Aims.— 1. To further the ideals in all branches of education. 2. To secure conditions which will give freedom for its expression.

Organ of Fraternity.—An international magazine devoted to the spreading of the new ideals in education will be started as soon as the paper restrictions permit.

During the present critical period of our nation's history and the consequent survey of our resources, education has been, and is, passing under very close scrutiny.

Most thinking people have come to regard the war as the birth-throes of a new era, and have realised that education is the most potent instrument of preparation for it. Without a fundamental change in the attitude towards life of the citizens of to-morrow, the ideals of the pioneers of this new era can never be realised. Education can effect that change, but it must be a type of education different from that which has hitherto been prevalent.

There has been a widespread consideration of educational reconstruction, and many schemes have been promulgated, among which that of the W.E.A. stands out prominently as voicing the demands of the workers. Most of the schemes hitherto published deal, however, with organisation, administration, salaries, size of classes, the school-leaving age, and so forth. This side, which may be termed reconstruction from without, is very necessary, since new wine cannot be put into old bottles, but it cannot be too emphatically asserted that changes in the outer or form side are not going to suffice. There must also be reconstruction from within. The school discipline, the curricula and methods of teaching must be so reformed as to give the children a more spiritual conception of life, to train their creative intellect and to make individuality and character pre-eminently important. Harmful competition must be eliminated and replaced by co-operation. For autocratic discipline must be substituted democratic self-government. In a word, we must provide the education which will produce fit citizens of a real democracy, a democracy of individuals able to think and decide questions for themselves, determined that strength and power shall be used for service and not for self-aggrandisement.

The Theosophical Fraternity in Education was founded to stand for both the outer and the inner spheres of educational work, to synthesise the many different notes sounded by the various educational reconstructive movements and to draw together in a world-wide fellowship, free from class or professional grade distinctions, all who are seeking to embody the new ideals in their teaching work. It offers a wide platform for the discussion of the practical application of the new ideals in the schools of to-day. It brings isolated experimenters together and offers them the strength of union, and the consequent encouragement so much needed by pioneers.

This fraternity is unique in the breadth of its appeal, its world-wide membership, and its policy of inclusiveness.

Membership is open to all teachers. Associateship is offered to all people who are interested, however remotely, in the work for which the fraternity stands.

The subscription is 2s. per annum in both cases (exclusive of the monthly magazine).

Offices.—11, Tavistock Square, London, W.C. 1.

THE UNIVERSITY OF MANCHESTER.

UNIVERSITY EXTENSION COMMITTEE.

The general object of University Extension is to enable wider audiences to share the results of human culture, whether ancient or modern, by bringing them into close contact with the best thought of present and past times, and by developing their interest in history, literature, art and science by means both of lectures and of class and study work. Not the least of the objects of the movement is to meet the growing demand for sound knowledge in the field of economics.

Apart from this general aim, the Manchester University Extension also fulfils the more special end of providing a link between university teaching and the other parts of the educational system. This it does by organising courses in connection with education authorities, by bringing the University into closer relations with educational institutions, and by the special facilities it offers to teachers who wish to acquaint themselves with the results of recent inquiry and observation on the subject of education.

Secretary: H. P. Turner, M.A., LL.B., University of Manchester.

UNIVERSITY EXTENSION GUILD.

Messrs. A. P. Griffiths and E. H. Short, 449, Birkbeck Bank Chambers, High Holborn, W.C. 1.

UNIVERSITY OF LONDON: BOARD TO PROMOTE THE EXTENSION OF UNIVERSITY TEACHING.

The purpose of the university extension lectures and classes carried on by the university through the Board to Promote the Extension of University Teaching, is to provide means of higher education for persons of all classes engaged in the regular occupations of life. The majority of the courses are carried on in the evening.

It has been found that university extension serves two distinct purposes; one is to awaken and stimulate an interest in the study of history, economics, literature, art, natural science, and other subjects; the other is to supply systematic and continuous teaching in these subjects by means of sessional and terminal university extension courses, and more especially by the connected courses extending over a period of several years, which are arranged under the scheme for the diploma in the humanities, and by means of the university tutorial classes for working people, organised by the Joint Committee for the Promotion of the Higher Education of the Working People appointed by the Senate to co-operate with the University Extension Board in this branch of their activities.

Courses and classes are carried on every year with the help of local committees at a large number of centres throughout London and the surrounding district.

Some particulars of special developments and recent activities of the movement will be found elsewhere in this volume in the account of the work carried on by the Univerity of London during the war.

Further information with regard to university extension work and the establishment of local centres may be obtained from the Registrar, John Lea, M.A., University of London, South Kensington, S.W. 7.

UNIVERSITY OF LONDON GRADUATES' ASSOCIATION.

A. S. E. Ackerman, B.Sc. (Engineering), 25, Victoria Street, S.W. 1.

UNIVERSITY OF WALES.

The Guild of Graduates of the University of Wales, existing mainly for educational purposes, has instituted different committees or sections to undertake work or research in different departments of study. The results are published in " Transactions of the Guild," in other journals, or in separate volumes. The most successful sections have been the Literature Section, the Dialect Section, and the Anthropological Section. It is composed of all graduates of the University of Wales of two years' standing as such, all members of the teaching staffs of the constituent colleges, and all students of the constituent colleges who graduated in any University of the United Kingdom prior to, or within two years after the date of the Charter of the University.

Founded 1893. Membership, 3,600.

Clerk : Professor William Jenkyn Jones, Aberystwyth.

UNIVERSITIES' SETTLEMENT ASSOCIATION IN EAST LONDON.

Toynbee Hall, Whitechapel.—Evening classes for adults in economics, history, literature, and languages, especially Russian; also in elocution and drama, folk and Morris dancing, and physical exercises. In addition to the above, classes are held in first aid to the injured, home nursing, hygiene, etc., and there is a Toynbee Hall Branch of the St. John Ambulance Brigade.

Educational Societies.—The Toynbee Shakespeare Society and the Toynbee Art Club meet weekly; the Toynbee Natural History Society monthly.

The Toynbee Hall rooms are used for educational purposes by various societies, such as the Mile End Literary and Social Union, the "New Era Circle," the B'noth Zion Association, and the Sinai League.

Several companies of Girl Guides and two companies of Scouts, including the Toynbee Company, hold meetings and classes at Toynbee Hall; the Tower Hamlets Cadets use one of the buildings—Balliol House.

The Students' Union aims at encouraging a spirit of fellowship among the students, and a room with a piano is set apart for their use as a common room and place of social meeting. They are allowed the free use of the library, with its valuable collection of books on economic subjects.

Secretary : F. F. Hitchcock, The Warden's Lodge, Toynbee Hall, 28, Commercial Street, E. 1.

THE UPLANDS ASSOCIATION.

The aims of the Association are :—

1. To provide means of active study and co-operation for persons (and especially for parents and teachers) interested in educational reform, that is, in the reform of school life and teaching.

2. To associate such persons by means (*a*) of a summer meeting, and opportunities for study or conference at other periods of the year; (*b*) of a circular as the organ of the Association.

3. To publish, as occasion seems to require, principles of reform in education.

4. To take active steps towards the practical working out of principles of reformed education, (*a*) by reporting in the circular any efforts in schools and other institutions where such principles are being adopted or tried, and (*b*) by endeavouring to set on foot at least one school in close connection with this Association.

The Committee undertook last year to draft a series of statements, and have been engaged during this year's meeting in adding to these some considerations on physical education. They are, of course, subject to revision, and we intend to go forward, as time permits, treating of all topics within our sphere that seem to be of real importance.

Principles of reform in school life and teaching :—

1. All types of schooling to be pursued so far as climatic conditions will permit in the open air.

2. The school should form a centre for communal activity in which the scholars realise their domestic, industrial, and civic dependence upon their fellows.

3. Individual differences in child nature, and the study of stages in development, should be recognised in any reform of school practice.

4. Balance should be maintained between intellectual, æsthetic, and practical experience, in contrast to the traditional curriculum of schools which exalts unduly the sphere of knowledge as a factor in human development.

5. It is incumbent on places of education to promote mutual understanding and respect between the two sexes; especially at the present epoch when public opinion is recognising the partnership of men and women in public affairs.

This duty can be discharged (1) by extending the association of men and women teachers on the staffs of schools and colleges. (2) By investigations as to the limits within which co-education can be approved. Experience indicates the benefit of co-education up to the age of 11 or 12 years and again after the age of 18. During the intervening years separation may be advisable, not only in the pursuits followed by scholars, but in school attendance; unless a new type of school community could be devised which would recognise the instinctive desire for separation, as well as the benefit gained by social experience. Inquiry along such lines is therefore advocated. (3) By associating fathers and mothers more closely with the aims and methods of the school to which their children belong.

6. Under normal circumstances, a scholar should be educated at home, or in a school near his home at least until the age of 11 or 12 years.

Secretaries : Miss M. M. Mills and Miss A. F. Purvis, 25, Andover Road, Southsea, Hants.

URBAN DISTRICT COUNCILS ASSOCIATION.

A. J. Lees, Palace Chambers, Bridge Street, Westminster, S.W. 1.

VICTORIA LEAGUE.

The Victoria League is a non-party Association of British men and women, founded in 1901 for the purpose of promoting closer union between British subjects living in different parts of the world.

The League organises personal intercourse by means of introductions, maintains clubs for overseas soldiers in London and Edinburgh, and secures a welcome for British subjects throughout the Empire.

Through its educational organisation the League circulates books and newspapers, promotes correspondence between schools and individual children in different parts of the world, and organises lectures. These lectures are given both to adult and juvenile audiences. Wherever desired, they are illustrated by lantern slides. Lectures to soldiers in camp have been a special feature since the outbreak of war, while a scheme for supplying lectures to soldiers in hospital has been successfully inaugurated in the summer of 1917.

It is intended to give such lectures as may be useful to soldiers in supplying information likely to help them on their return to civil life.

Secretary : Miss Drayton, 2, Millbank House, Westminster, S.W. 1.

COMMITTEE ON WAGE-EARNING CHILDREN.

" Formed in 1900 to increase the efficiency and promote the reform of existing legislation for the protection of children in employment."

Hon. Secretaries : Miss N. Adler, 121a, Sinclair Road, Addison Gardens, W. 14 ; Miss Alice C. Franklin, 35, Porchester Terrace, W. 2.

IRISH ASSOCIATION OF WOMEN GRADUATES AND CANDIDATE GRADUATES.

Founded March 14th, 1902. The objects of the Association are to be an organisation of University women connected with Ireland and a means of communication and united action in matters affecting their interests, and to secure that all the advantages of University education in Ireland should be open equally to women with men.

Secretary : Miss C. Ryan, B.A., Tracy College for Girls, Corysfort, Blackrock, Dublin.

THE ASSOCIATION FOR THE EDUCATION OF WOMEN IN OXFORD.

The Association for the Education of Women in Oxford (founded 1878) unites in one society the men and women who admit women students to their lectures or give them private instruction, and the students who have passed the final degree examination of the University. Its office acts as a bureau for general information as to the facilities for study offered to women at Oxford, and through its report it keeps its members informed of the general progress of women's education in that University. It has in many ways promoted the interests of Oxford women students, particularly in the matter of obtaining admission to university lectures and the opening of examinations. It has a library and a loan fund, and awards annually a studentship granted by the Gilchrist Trustees. The names of women who desire to attend university lectures are entered, and the fees are paid through its office, and are not sent direct to the lecturers.

Secretary : Miss A. M. A. Rogers, 39, Museum Street, Oxford.

NATIONAL UNION OF WOMEN WORKERS OF GREAT BRITAIN AND IRELAND.

The objects of the Education Sectional Committee of the National Union of Women Workers are to bring together women representing every phase of education for common consultation on matters of vital interest and to form a link between them and the public.

The whole Committee, which consists of about 120 members resident in all parts of the British Isles, meets quarterly. There is a small sub-committee, which meets when necessary.

During the last year the Committee has considered the Interim Report of the Consultative Committee on Scholarships for Higher Education, and the Final Report of the Departmental Committee on Juvenile Education in relation to Employment after the War. It has also taken an active interest in the question of the regulation of cinematograph shows, and arranged an important deputation to the Home Office asking for better conditions in the buildings, and for the proper censoring of films.

The Committee has spent much time and given careful consideration to the question of educational reform, and is glad to see that many of its proposals are embodied in Mr. Fisher's Education Bill now before Parliament.

Hon. Secretary : Miss Elsie M. Zimmern, Parliament Mansions, Victoria Street, S.W. 1.

WOMEN'S GARDENING ASSOCIATION.

T. Chamberlain, F.R.H.S., 62, Lower Sloane Street, S.W. 1.

WOMEN'S INDUSTRIAL COUNCIL (INCORPORATED).

Secretary : Miss F. V. M. Taylor, 7, John Street, Adelphi, Strand, W.C. 2.

WORKERS' EDUCATIONAL ASSOCIATION.

J. M. Mactavish, 16, Harpur Street, Theobald's Road, Holborn, W.C. 1. Holborn 3033. (See Part V.)

Y.M.C.A. EDUCATION COMMITTEE.

Secretary : The Rev. B. A. Yeaxlee, Tottenham Court Road. (See pages 380-82.)

Y.W.C.A. EDUCATION COMMITTEE.

Miss Walters, 25, George Street, W. 1.

PART VII.

THE ORGANISATION OF THE TEACHING PROFESSION.

INTRODUCTION.

BY MRS. SIDNEY WEBB

The teacher—that is to say, the person who earns his livelihood by instructing others—is one of the oldest of professionals. Yet in the considerable research which I undertook when preparing my monograph on " English Teachers and Their Professional Organisation," I was unable to discover any organised association of teachers in this country until the establishment of the College of Preceptors in 1846. During the Middle Ages, the classic period of vocational organisation, when the priests, the lawyers, the merchants, the craftsmen—even if we include the manor, the agriculturists—had, all of them, their respective corporate entities, and enjoyed within these corporations considerable rights of self-government and common regulation, extending sometimes to non-members, there seems never to have arisen any " craft," " mystery," " company," or " guild " of teachers. It may be that the immemorial connection between the occupation of teaching and the vocation of the priests, or of the " religious," prevented in the past any separate organisation. Certainly in our own country, and within our own experience, this close connection has militated against the rise of professional organisation among teachers. For the first half of the 19th century we see both the headmasters of the endowed and public schools and the professors and tutors at the two great Universities usually in holy orders, looking in ecclesiastical dignity to a good living, a deanery, or a bishopric. It was not until there existed a large body of lay teachers, dependent for their livelihood or status on the practice of teaching, that we see arising professional organisations of teachers for the advance of science and art of teaching, and for the protection of the personal dignity and the standard of life of the teacher. What is the size and character of the world of teachers, and how far is it organised? According to the Census of 1911* there are more than 300,000 persons in the United Kingdom who claim to gain their livelihood by teaching—that is to say, about a quarter of a million in England and Wales. But teaching is an elusive expression and

---

* In the absence of authoritative up-to-date information, I have deemed it best to utilise pre-war statistics for the existing educational interregnum. What will be the number of teachers available after the war is beyond the knowledge even of the President of the Board of Education himself.

may mean anything from the work of a Regius Professor to the occupation of an alphabet-teaching nursery maid, from the responsible administrative position of a headmaster to the drudgery of the supplementary teacher—what used to be called an " Article 68 "— whose only obligatory qualification,- it has been scoffingly said, consisted in being over 18 years of age and vaccinated! The amount and the method of remuneration of this undefined class are extraordinarily varied. Within the world of teachers there are men and women at salaries ranging from as little as £30 to as much as £3,000 a year, innumerable types of pieceworkers, fee-takers, and independent home-workers, and quite a number who are still unabashed profit-makers. The subjects dealt with by the teacher are bewildering to their range and in their value; I need cite only " the three R's," history, literature, science, foreign languages, religion, the arts and crafts, scientific industries, the physical faculties of man, whether normal or defective, domestic economy, and practically all forms of games and recreation. The teacher may, indeed, be said to have taken the whole world for his province! As for the " methods " used, they vary from the immemorial birch to the best equipped laboratory; they alter from year to year, from place to place, and are the special hunting ground of the inventor and the crank. There is, in fact, no vocation which is at once so undefined and so variegated as that of the instructor. In spite of this extreme heterogeneity, we discover certain distinctive features marking out teaching from other professions. In the first place, it is predominantly feminine; out of the quarter of a million persons in England and Wales claiming to be teachers, at least 175,000 are women; and we find this femininity repeated in the largest separate sections of the world of teachers. Moreover, though teachers include the most diverse types of men and women, there are certain solid blocks which stand out as being composed of persons with uniform antecedents, a like training, and similar pecuniary circumstances, with a sufficiently defined common interest and a sufficiently developed common technique for a real professional solidarity. Out of the 250,000 teachers in England and Wales at least 150,000 are known to be at work all day in the public elementary schools, and of these about 100,000 are organised.

In the public secondary schools there are about 15,000, with probably as many more in the still existing private secondary schools, and of these secondary school teachers about 8,000 belong to professional associations. Another 10,000 may be allocated to Universities and technical institutes and to the specialist institutions of different kinds and grades, of whom perhaps one-third will be members of one or other of the many specialist professional organisations. That leaves some 60,000 or 70,000 out of the quarter of a million about whom nothing positive is known. These are assumed to be " private teachers," such as music, dance or drawing teachers, and all grades of private tutors and governesses, paid by individual customers, and at work in their own or other people's homes. Among these there is practically no organisation.

Elementary School Teachers.

By far the largest and best organised class is that of the teachers in the compact world of the public elementary school. By means of their powerful organisations the elementary school teachers have protected and improved the standard of life for their class alike in salaries and in pensions; they have gained a much valued freedom from " compulsory extraneous tasks "; they have been saved from petty tyranny and unjustifiable dismissal; they have been greatly relieved from the pressure of mechanical codes and exacting inspectors; and they have seen the professional prospects of their own class widen by the opening to them of the inspectorate and of the secondary and technical schools. But they have done more than improve the material conditions of the teaching class. They have settled in their own favour the question of whether or not the employees of the public authority have the full rights of citizens. The N.U.T. and the L.T.A. have successfully asserted the right of their members to take the fullest possible part, both as voters and canvassers and as elected representatives in local government, including even the controversies of educational administration. They have compelled each successive Ministry to appoint teachers' representatives on Royal Commissions and Departmental Committees, and they have secured their co-option on Local Education Committees. In all these ways the elementary teachers, through the power of their organisation, have enhanced the social and professional status of their class. Fifty years ago the University don or the Eton master would have regarded as a revolutionary absurdity the suggestion that the elementary school teacher—the purveyor of the three R's to the proletariat—was a fellow professional whom he had to meet on terms of equality. To-day a professor or a public schoolmaster finds himself sitting side by side with the elementary school teacher on professional organisations, such as the Consultative Committee of the Board of Education or the Teachers' Registration Council, and he sees that the elementary teacher has as good a chance as himself of a knighthood, and a far better chance of a seat in Parliament or even in the Cabinet. Against this success the organisations of elementary school teachers have to admit one big failure—a failure which has prevented any remarkable, or, as I should say, any adequate rise in the remuneration of the ordinary class teacher. They have failed to control, or even to regulate, the entry into their profession; and, unlike the medical practitioners, they have failed to standardise the qualifications required for public employment. There are still 40,000 uncertificated and 12,000 supplementary teachers, many of whom, owing to their lack of any recognised professional qualifications, are earning less than the wage of an unskilled labourer.

But, altogether apart from activities in which teachers have seen material and spiritual advantage to themselves, I think no competent investigator can doubt that the work of the N.U.T. and the L.T.A., taken as a whole, has had a beneficial effect on the great community of working-class children. Smaller classes, really compulsory attendance, the better enforcement of the Education Act, the abolition of half-time, the prevention of the painful employment of children after school hours, the raising of the age at which the child may leave school, the prevention of street trading by children, the enforcement of attendance at continuation schools, with the consequent reduction in the hours of labour of the adolescent, have all formed part of the permanent policy of the N.U.T. The adoption of medical inspection and treatment, the feeding of necessitous children, the general improvement of the conditions of working-class life—all these reforms have received the warm support of the representatives of teachers in Parliament and on local authorities. In more ways than one the N.U.T. has identified itself with the needs of the wage-earning class family, and with the educational aspirations of the most enlightened of the manual workers. The very rise of the elementary school teacher in social status and self-respect—the very promotion of the instructor of the workman's child from a servile menial to a highly trained professional—implies an addition to the dignity and self-respect of the wage-earning class itself.

Secondary School Teachers.

It is not too much to say that the past half-century has revolutionised upper and middle-class education from top to bottom. The tutor or governess, visiting or residential, has been largely superseded by the school, the school has been subjected to an ever-increasing amount of outside inspection and standardisation, whether voluntary or compulsory; and the " private venture " schools have been increasingly overshadowed by the publicly controlled institutions. But in spite of this steady trend towards increasing organisation and collective control, secondary education, as compared with elementary education, remains to this day haphazard in its diversity. Out of the 30,000 persons claiming to be teachers in secondary schools, perhaps one-half are still at work in definitely private schools, carried on for profit by individual proprietors, whilst the other 15,000 are in the service of a miscellaneous array of Governing Committees of all sorts—Trustees of educational endowments, the Courts of Livery Companies descended from the Guilds, directors of joint stock companies formed for public objects, County Councils and Borough Councils and other Local Government Authorities and mixed Boards of Governors made up of all these elements. These varieties among employing authorities are paralleled by differences among the employed. In contrast with the relatively simple world of elementary school teachers, the world of secondary school teachers, even to-day, shows a great variety in status, in the method of remuneration, in the other conditions of employment, and in the amount, kind, and quality of the work demanded. Hence we find no one professional organisation, such as the N.U.T., representing all grades of secondary school teachers. Two organisations— the College of Preceptors and the Teachers' Guild of Great Britain and Ireland—have attempted to do so, but they have not succeeded. We see, on the contrary, at least a dozen organisations, arising at different dates, having members of different grades or kinds, with different interests, different methods, and concerned with different educational ideals and different forms of technique.

Teachers of Special Subjects.

Besides the head and class teachers in elementary and secondary schools engaged in teaching the ordinary subjects, there is in England an ever-shifting *personnel* of teachers of special subjects, or teachers using methods adapted to particular kinds of pupils, whether these are taken individually or in schools of various grades, or in university, technical, or normal colleges. I find it difficult to estimate, even roughly, how many specialist teachers there are or how they are distributed. Of music and drawing there are, we know, instructors of every kind and grade; there are thousands of teachers of manual training, gymnastic, dancing, and domestic subjects; the teachers in technical institutes and those in training colleges, together with the teachers of the deaf, the dumb, the blind, and the mentally or physically defective, have each their specialities; there is the specialist of the kindergarten, whilst the teachers of shorthand, bookkeeping, and commercial subjects feel themselves to be a class apart from the elementary or secondary school teachers. Professional organisation of some kind has arisen among each of these groups of teachers. But these associations are of a curiously mixed character. Sometimes (as is most common in music) the body admitted to the Teachers' Registration Council as representing a particular section of the teachers of special subjects is merely a school or college, or a group of such institutions, such as the Guildhall School of Music or the Association of Technical Institutions. Sometimes the body thus admitted, though partly composed of teachers, includes in its membership a large element of non-teaching philanthropists or amateurs of the subject. Of such we may instance the National Society of Physical Education, the Educational Handwork Association, or the Royal Drawing Society. Or the body may be composed partly of executants of the art, who are only part-time teachers and some of whom have never been teachers, as in the Royal College of Organists and the Incorporated Union of Graduates in Music. In the aggregate, possibly as many as 10,000 specialist teachers are members of one or other of the score of associations of this nature that I have so far been able to discover. It is difficult to make any common statement with regard to the strength and effectiveness or the professional policy of so heterogeneous a collection of societies. They vary, in fact, almost indefinitely, from what I suspect to be little more than societies for giving their members high-sounding certificates to old-established colleges with charters, from newly formed propagandist organisations of missionary fervour, up to bonâ-fide professional associations of teachers concerned in a particular method or subject-matter of instruction. The contempt of the Englishman for science, art, and technology has left the realms of these distinctively " modern " subjects the happy hunting ground of the private adventurer. The trail of profit-maker in schools, in plant, in text-books, and, above all, in certificates for teachers and pupils may be discerned, though it can hardly be described, in many organisations which claim to be professional associations of teachers. Moreover, in no other section of the teaching world is the busy amateur or the " society " patron so in evidence.

THE NEED FOR THE ORGANISATION OF THE TEACHING PROFESSION.

By William J. Pincombe

(General Secretary of the London Teachers' Association).

The teaching profession is organised to an extent probably unknown in any other profession in this country. It is not an uncommon thing for a teacher to belong to three or four different organisations drawing their membership from among teachers and officered and controlled by teachers, but, in spite of this fact, the teaching profession might be much better organised. There are nearly a dozen national organisations, that is, associations of teachers professing to cover the whole of the country, either from one centre with individual membership, or by local branches or associations. There are the National Union of Teachers, the Head Teachers' Association, and the National Federation of Class Teachers (all composed largely of elementary school teachers), four or five distinct organisations. of secondary school teachers (masters and mistresses, head teachers and assistant teachers) and several others. Mrs. Sidney Webb, in her painstaking investigation of the subject of organisation among teachers, noted the extraordinary number and variety of teachers' associations. Wherever 20 or 30 teachers are gathered together to do the same work, or even if scattered through a wide area, there is fertile soil for a new association, and it will not be long before one of the more energetic members of the group has organised a new society, with its president, treasurer, secretary, and committee. Investigators are sometimes surprised at the vast number of small Trade Unions connected with particular industries. Their number is not greater, nor their character more diversified, than the multitudinous organisations among teachers. But there is one notable difference. The industrial worker almost invariably joins one organisation only, and, indeed, may not join more than one. The teacher has a choice of half-a-dozen and often uses all his opportunities. In London, for instance, it is possible to find many teachers who are members of (1) the National Union of Teachers, (2) my own organisation (the London Teachers' Association), (3) the Head Teachers' Association, and, say (4) the Association of Head Teachers of Central Schools, and, possibly, several other bodies, such as the Child Study Society or the Historical Association. There are secondary school teachers who belong to the N.U.T., to one of the secondary school organisations (such as the A.M.A.), the L.T.A., and two or three " subject " associations. Constantly one hears the remark : " It is so difficult to belong to everything, there are so many meetings to attend." Ridiculous though it may appear to say so, in view of this state of affairs, it can easily be demonstrated that the teaching profession is still sadly lacking in organisation along vital lines.

In the forefront of most programmes of educational reform drawn up by teachers' organisations (whether they be predominantly elementary or secondary or University) is the demand for a national system of education. But teachers who contend so strenuously for a national system of education have failed hitherto to secure even the semblance of national unity among themselves. They have not even secured territorial unity. In many towns it is possible to find half-a-dozen branches of different national organisations, each meeting separately, knowing little of one another or one another's members, and working in the dark so far as the interests and activities of all the others are concerned. In a capital city such as London this multiplication of territorial branches of national organisations is intensified. A really practical step towards a national system of education could be taken by teachers themselves securing unity within the sphere of their own organisations.

A remarkable thing has just taken place in Scotland, the country with the best educational system in the world. The Scottish teachers have made up their minds that what has been good hitherto shall be better still in the future. Their first step towards educational reform has been the abolition of sectionalism in their own profession, and, accordingly, they have accomplished the fusion of the Educational Institute of Scotland, the Scottish Class Teachers' Association, and the Secondary Education Association. But even before the union of the three bodies had taken place, they had formed between them a Scottish Education Reform Committee, which drew up a report entitled " Reform in Scottish Education." Of all the reports upon educational reform (dozens of them have been published in England and Wales) there is not one so comprehensive, so complete, so authoritative, and so businesslike as that published by the Scottish Education Reform Committee. The programmes of English teachers' associations by comparison with it are meagre and insignificant.

No one would be so foolish in these days as to suggest an immediate coalescence of all the English teachers' organisations. In spite of its remarkable progress, the National Union of Teachers has failed to " steam roller " other teachers' organisations out of existence—they have become stronger on the whole. But English teachers can make some effort, at least, to follow the excellent example of their Scottish colleagues.

One will not presume to define methods. This, however, is certain. Teachers who demand so vehemently a national system of education stultify themselves by their own divisions, and it is notorious that the Board of Education and the Local Education Authorities are well aware of and probably take advantage of this lack of unity. Small groups of teachers, such as those working in the Universities and the secondary school teachers and the growing groups of technical teachers, somewhat naturally, fear that their representations and counsels may be swamped in such an organisation as the National Union of Teachers, composed largely of teachers working in elementary schools. The continued existence of separate and sectional organisations must be accepted as inevitable, at any rate for a long time to come, but there is no excuse whatever for disunion and separation in regard to many matters of common policy. Whether it be by federation or by a National Council with local Councils or by Joint Committees, it is sincerely to be hoped that English teachers will attempt immediately to secure some measure of that greater unity which their Scottish colleagues have already achieved.

While on the subject of organisation, it is to be regretted that there is little or no communication between the teachers' associations of this and other countries. It is true that there is an interchange of a few courtesy greetings at certain annual conferences, but that is about all. There is no interchange of ideas. There is no attempt, for instance, on the part of the Irish or the Scottish teachers to inform their English colleagues of the state of education in those countries. The Scottish educational system is held up as a model, but no attempt is made by English teachers to obtain information of educational developments in the North. Again, there is practically no communication between the teachers' organisations of Great Britain and those of Canada, Australia, New Zealand, and South Africa. The fact is that the educational system of this country is insular and provincial. It is absolutely free—only too free—from that better kind of Imperialism which connotes mutual aid within the Empire. The teachers of Western Europe have been well organised for years, but there have been hardly any points of contact between them and the teachers of our own country. It is not too much to believe that fraternisation between teachers' organisations might have done something to avert war, or, if war indeed were inevitable, the existence of friendly relations between the teachers' organisations of the Entente countries would certainly have been of the greatest value in educating public opinion and the development of closer sympathies between the Allied peoples. There have been minor and isolated attempts to bring together teachers within the Empire and from different countries, but up to the present there has been nothing even distantly approaching deliberate and sustained effort in this direction.

Organisation is good if it promotes comradeship, associated effort, and combined action. But organisation—mere machinery—as an end in itself is a poor thing to work for. The real value of better organisation and greater unity within the teaching profession of this country will be tested by their direct effect upon the welfare of education. The nation has the right to demand from its teachers both a critical and a creative policy in regard to education. The attitude of teachers in the past has been, however, too often of a passive character. Movements, reforms, and sometimes thoroughly vicious tendencies have been imposed from above or thrust in from without. The teachers' attitude has been critically receptive or merely acquiescent according to circumstances and conditions. The time has arrived for something better than that. There must be a great Council of the teaching profession. The nucleus exists already in the Teachers' Registration Council. To this Great Council of the teaching profession teachers themselves must look for a lead in regard to all matters affecting the welfare of the profession, and possibly for a great deal of distributed information with regard to the technique of their work. The Board of Education must be made to realise that in the Great Council of the teaching profession there has emerged at last an authoritative body from which the opinions of teachers may be obtained and to which should be referred all questions affecting teachers and relating to educational practice. If the Teachers' Registration Council is to become merely the custodian of a register of names or a guinea-collecting agency, it will be an excrescence and a useless and wasteful consumer of energy which might be much better employed.

Discussion has taken place recently as to whether teachers' organisations should enter into closer relations with the Labour Party. There is a great deal to be said on both sides of the subject. Cautious observers contend that teachers are the trusted servants of the nation—entrusted indeed with the nation's most important service—and that, in their corporate capacity, therefore, teachers would be well advised to keep entirely free from the entanglements of party politics. It would be profoundly regrettable, urge those who argue thus, if all the advice and wisdom of the teaching profession in regard to educational matters were placed at the service of one political party only, and that the Liberal Party, and the Conservative Party, and the new Labour and Socialist Parties that may be started (and there will probably be several) were regarded merely as political opponents. There is room, however, for a great deal more active co-operation between teachers and all those working for the uplifting of the masses of the people. The active association of teachers' organisations with the Workers' Educational Association is an excellent illustration of what is possible. There is room for a great extension. Teachers should be entering into agreements for co-operative activity with Trade Unions, doctors, nurses, and workers in every department of social activity. Every public authority in the country should consult the teachers or should be approached by teachers' organisations with regard to the utilisation of public property and amenities in the best interests of the children. Every public library should have upon its committee a representative from the teachers of the district, and the librarian should be in communication with every school—elementary, secondary, and technical—in the area served by his library. Every committee controlling public baths and every superintendent of a swimming bath should be in contact with the teachers to see how best the baths can be used in the interests of the children. Those responsible for the management of parks, open spaces, and recreation grounds should be eager to consult teachers, and teachers should be equally anxious to offer advice and assistance in making the best use of these preserves of health, education, and pleasure. In the administration of education itself there should be consultation between teachers of all grades of schools. It is intolerable, but unfortunately it is too often true, that the headmaster of a great public school or of a grammar school or of one of the newer secondary schools, does not even know the names of the head teachers of the elementary schools outside his gates. This must be altered.

Another result of better organisation and closer co-operation among teachers will be the pooling of the best ideas in educational practice. At present, if a teacher or a group of teachers discovers a new or improved method in technique nobody benefits except a limited circle. An enterprising publisher may give greater publicity to an experiment as a commercial speculation, or an inspector may be interested and pass on the idea to others. Sometimes a masterful inspector or director of education will put pressure on teachers to adopt the new method, which is one of the worst things that can happen. Greater unity among teachers should increase greatly the amount of inter-communication and facilitate the creation of a body of common opinion upon matters of professional practice and technique which should be of value to all. There are certainly 150,000, and possibly 200,000, full-time teachers in this country. The number of educational newspapers and journals is ridiculously small, and their circulation notoriously falls greatly below the number of teachers. It is not creditable to the teaching profession that so many teachers never see a professional journal. There should be twice as many educational newspapers in this country as there are at present, with vastly larger circulations than anything now conceived possible. There should be at least one educational quarterly, at least one educational monthly, and half-a-dozen first-class journals devoted to the technique of teaching, and a large number of organs of information, of opinion, and of discussion. Unfortunately teachers have been so poorly paid in the past that the newspaper bill almost came under the heading of " luxuries." The salaries of teachers are to be substantially improved, it is hoped, and with that improvement there should be a margin for books, for subscriptions to learned societies, and for the purchase of educational reviews, journals, and pamphlets.

In conclusion, the teaching profession is handicapped by parochialism and sectionalism. The teachers' horizon too often is bounded by the school wall, and the outlook of the corporate body extends too seldom beyond the city or county boundary. Provincialism and insularity are too markedly the characteristic of teachers' organisations. Closer union, associated effort, solidarity, community of spirit, if not identity of machinery, must replace the present confusion. An Imperial Union and international communications must be ·set up as soon as possible. The enormous dynamic forces of the teaching profession must be pooled for the benefit of all. Linked up with those who are working to promote the health and welfare of the people and the children of the people, the teachers must be regarded no longer as a cloistered class living and labouring apart from the main streams of life and reality. The teachers themselves must create a great literature of education. They must be also the custodians and generators of a body of authoritative opinion upon all matters relating to education, preserving always the opportunity for the free play of thought and activity, so that there may be life and not death for the insurgent forces which make for progress.

THE TEACHERS' REGISTRATION COUNCIL.

By Dr. F. B. Jevons.

The Teachers' Registration Council is authorised by the Education Act of 1907, and was established by a Privy Council Order on the 29th February, 1912. This Order provides that the Council shall consist entirely of teachers, except that the Chairman, who must be selected from outside the Council, need not be a teacher. The members of the Council number 44, of whom eleven represent the teaching staffs of Universities, eleven the Associations of Teachers in Public Elementary Schools, eleven the Associations of Teachers in Secondary Schools, and eleven the various Associations of Specialist Teachers. It will be seen that the Council represents every type of teaching work, and, although its first duty is to frame and keep a register of teachers, it is obvious that many other duties spring from this. Thus Mr. J. A. Pease (now Lord Gainford), addressing the first meeting of the Council, said :—

" All he had to do was to welcome the Council and congratulate them on having come together. Their object would be not only the formation of a register of teachers. There were many other spheres and fields of usefulness for a Council representative of the teaching profession. He hoped that they would be able to speak with one voice as representing the teaching profession, and that the Board would be able to consult with them. So long as he was head of the Board they would always be most anxious to co-operate with the Council, and would attach due weight to their views. He hoped that they on their side would realise some of the Board's difficulties, and that the atmosphere of friendly relationship which he trusted had already been established would continue."

In pursuance of this idea the Council has been freely consulted by the Board of Education on many matters relating to educational administration. For example, the Board submitted to the Council the draft of its introductory chapter to the new edition of " Suggestions for Teachers," and in the complete document just issued many of the Council's suggestions have been incorporated. Similarly, the Council was able to influence very greatly the constitution of the new Secondary School Examinations Council, and at the present time it is occupied in considering the Education Bill with a view to suggesting amendments in order that the measure may find an early place on the Statute Book.

Most important of all the Council recognises the essential unity of the teaching profession, and is anxious to prescribe in every branch a standard of attainment and of training for the work which shall place all teachers on a true professional level. It is evident that this cannot be accomplished unless and until the Council is seen to have the support of the great majority of intelligent and qualified teachers. When this has been gained the Council will be in a position to press the demands of registered teachers for better salaries and adequate pensions, for reasonable freedom in their work, and for the right to be consulted freely by the administration when new regulations are being framed. In all professions a register of qualified persons is the starting point for the development of a professional status, and the small and single payment of one guinea, with no annual subscription, seems a small sacrifice in view of the possibilities which lie before a united body of teachers working through a representative Council and resolved to place their calling on that level of public regard to which it is entitled.

THE NATIONAL UNION OF TEACHERS.

The National Union of Teachers, consisting of over 94,000 members, is, whether estimated in numbers or in political influence, the foremost professional association of the kind in this country, and probably it would be true to say that it is the premier professional union in the world. The Union was inaugurated for purposes of protection and defence as well as for mutual assistance, in 1870, and since that date its history has been a history of continued success; as its membership has increased so have its activities increased and its operations extended. Every aspect and form of education is dealt with, most of the improvements in Acts, Codes, and other regulations on education being due to the Union's suggestions. Nearly all the present improved conditions of school life are due to its efforts—the establishment of healthier school surroundings, the adoption of satisfactory schemes of medical inspection, extension of school life, reduction in the half-time system, modification of Factory Acts, the abolition of the principle of payment for teachers according to mechanical results, being all the outcome of Union activity. With it also rests much responsibility for clauses in the Children Act relating to juvenile smoking, the supply of alcoholic liquors to children, and the Street Betting Act of 1907.

The Union is the recognised medium for teachers' communication with the Press, with Ministers of Education and Parliament, being represented in the House of Commons by two of its leading officials. Every phase of the teachers' professional life and duty is dealt with, legal help is afforded when necessary, and sustenance to those who suffer financial loss in defence of professional rights or position. Many of the benefits which the Union has effected for the teacher can hardly be over-estimated; amendments in the organisation and selection of the inspectorate, improvements in teachers' qualifications, extension of facilities for training, etc., are but few of the great essentials which have been secured. Again, the right of certificated teachers to have their names enrolled in a comprehensive register was obtained after years of strenuous effort, and the establishment of the Registration Council became an accomplished fact in 1913, with seven members of the Executive as Councillors. By repeated claims the Union has also secured the establishment of a general scheme of superannuation and local service systems of pensions under some of the local authorities for secondary, technical, and elementary school teachers. And here let it be urged that the majority of the benefits secured are enjoyed by all—members of the Union and non-members alike.

The Teachers' Provident Society forms an important branch of the work, and was inaugurated in 1878 for the purpose of enabling members to secure such benefits as sick pay, life assurance, pensions, endowments, etc., at low rates of contribution. The society has a State insurance section, and is approved for the purpose of administering the National Insurance Act of 1911. There is, in addition, a benevolent and orphan fund attached to the Union, which maintains two orphanages, grants temporary relief to infirm teachers and widows of teachers, and renders other beneficent help.

Nearly 13,000 members of the National Union of Teachers are serving with his Majesty's forces, about 900 have been killed or have died as the result of war conditions, while many have been honoured for gallant services. Between 200 and 300 Belgian refugee teachers have been housed and cared for, some of them being still maintained by their fellow teachers in this country. In connection with war matters less particularly affecting teachers the Union has been instrumental in obtaining improved pensions and allowances for widows and dependents of soldiers and sailors, and has taken an active part in the national war savings campaign, as well as in many other matters of great public moment.

THE SHEFFIELD TEACHERS' EDUCATION CAMPAIGN OF 1917.

By W. H. Robinson.

In 1913 the Sheffield Teachers' Association formed an Education Campaign Committee, to which all the other educational associations in the city sent representatives, to visit various organisations and address them on the subject of education. The committee suspended its activities when war broke out, but in the summer of 1917 the association decided to resume the campaign, and a new committee was formed. In the election of this committee the association was guided by one principle only—the selection of representative teachers of all grades who would take an active part in the campaign. So much general agreement was shown by the members that, after the first meeting of the committee, the campaign was in full swing. The Campaign Committee prepared a statement of principles which it hoped to see embodied in an Education Bill, but before it had begun to lay its scheme before the public Mr. Fisher's Bill was introduced. This necessitated a hasty change of plan. The attitude of the committee to the new Bill was promptly defined, and it was decided that the first phase of the campaign should be directed to persuading the public to give the Bill its heartiest support as an earnest endeavour to lay the foundations of a sound system of national education.

Over 700 organisations—social, religious, political, and industrial—were approached, and when the committee next met it was faced by invitations from 50 organisations, representing all shades of public opinion. Every member of the committee was a busy person. Most of them were engaged in evening as well as day school work and in other activities, but all felt that this campaign must be carried through at any cost, and their enthusiasm was increased by an address from Mr. Fisher himself to the Sheffield Teachers' Association. The first body to receive a deputation happened to be the local branch of the National Association of Insurance Agents. An assistant master in an elementary school gave a brief outline of the idea of the Education Bill, and a secondary school assistant master gave an address on the meaning and possibilities of a sound system of national education. A keen discussion took place, and then a member of the audience asked : " What can we do immediately to support this campaign? " He thereupon proposed a resolution, which was carried unanimously, welcoming the Education Bill, and pledging those present to support it in every possible way. The secretary of the branch was instructed to send a copy of the resolution to the President of the Board of Education, the local M.P., the Chairman of the Education Committee, the Press, etc. The Chairman referred with pride to the fact that as a youth he had done his first public speaking in favour of the 1870 Bill. The deputation left the meeting feeling that the campaign had opened well. The next day a deputation was received by a meeting of delegates of the Toolmakers' Society, at which there were present the secretaries of all the local branches. The audience listened with great interest to the deputation, and took part in an animated discussion of the subject from many points of view. After the deputation had left a resolution was passed unanimously, heartily supporting the Bill, and recommending their branches to do the same and to receive deputations at once.

The beginning of the campaign was typical of its progress. Without exception, every society which was visited welcomed the deputation most cordially, listened attentively, discussed the problem intelligently, sought for information, and was not only willing, but anxious, to receive suggestions as to how the members could best further the campaign. Every aspect of the problem—economic, social and educational, primary and secondary—has been discussed, and no one type of audience has been more cordial than another in its earnest support of the campaign. For instance, the Chemical and Pharmaceutical Society was as keen as the most advanced branch of the National Union of Railwaymen. The National Union of Clerks and the Amalgamated Union of Operative Bakers and Confectioners were both anxious to demand more than the Fisher Bill proposes. During a single week, a political club, with 100 members present, a literary and debating society, with a full attendance of 50 or 60, a branch of the Blacksmiths' Union, a branch of the Amalgamated Society of Engineers, several branches of the National Union of Railwaymen, the Adult School Union, and a special meeting of the Iron, Steel, and Metal Dressers' Union, at which 250 men were present, were addressed by members of the Campaign Committee, and all enthusiastically passed resolutions giving their heartiest support. An Adult School in one of the outlying villages celebrated its eleventh anniversary by having an education campaign itself and inviting speakers from the Campaign Committee to address meetings in the morning, afternoon, and evening on education. During the month of October nearly 40 deputations were received by various societies. On one Sunday alone eleven members of the Campaign Committee addressed eight different meetings. The Sheffield Evangelical Free Church Council called a special meeting to receive a deputation and subsequently took an active part. The Assurance Managers' Association and the Executive Committee of the Guild of Help, the Independent Labour Party, and the Theosophical Society, the Sheffield Trades and Labour Council, and the Esperanto Society, the Ethical Society and the Federated Trades Council, the Friendly Societies' Council, and men's, women's, and Neighbour Guilds stood side by side with Trade Union branches in the Campaign Committee's programme of deputations for November. Every organisation needed an address to suit its own individuality, but all were equally interested in the broad national question.

The temporary withdrawal of the Bill in December practically marked the end of the first phase of the campaign, though the committee continued to keep in touch with all the forces making for progress in public opinion on education.

The first piece of spade work has been done. There is now a great instructed mass of public opinion, found mainly in organised bodies, which has some ideal of education, and a desire to do what is possible towards realising that ideal locally. The task of the Campaign Committee in its next phase, therefore, is to decide what reforms are practicable and show how best a great organised effort can be made to secure them.

DIRECTORY OF TEACHERS' ORGANISATIONS.

[NOTE.—In editing this Directory of Teachers' Organisations, we have tried to include only those educational bodies which are exclusively or predominantly associations of teachers and which exist for professional or " Trade Union " objects. This is not easy, because many societies are of a mixed character and many declare their aims vaguely. " Subject Associations " (like the Royal Historical Society), philanthropic agencies (like the Society of Schoolmasters), and all other educational bodies which did not seem to demand inclusion here have been placed in the Directory in Section VI. Compilation has been greatly facilitated by Mrs. Sidney Webb's generous permission to use her monograph on " English Teachers and Their Professional Organisation " (published as two supplements to the " New Statesman " of September 25th and October 2nd, 1915); and also by the assistance of Mr. Frank Roscoe, secretary of the Teachers' Registration Council, and Mr. W. J. Pincombe, secretary of the London Teachers' Association. We desire also to thank the many individuals who have forwarded us statements for insertion. Will secretaries during the current year kindly forward full and up-to-date particulars concerning their societies in order that next year the Directory may be made complete and accurate? Further information regarding Teachers' Associations may be found in the Directory of Educational Associations, published each March by the " Journal of Education," in the " Schoolmasters' Year Book and Directory," in the Directory of Women Teachers, etc. Inverted commas are employed in the statements to indicate quotation from a society's own declaration of its aims.]

The Aberdeen County Schoolmasters' Association was intended originally for the promotion of brotherly feeling among the schoolmasters and the furtherance of education in the three counties. Its present object is the promotion of secondary education in the country schools and the interests of teachers participating in the Dick Bequest, from which grants are paid for secondary education.

Founded 1862. Membership, 60.
Hon. Secretary : M. G. Gerrard, M.A., Bucksburn.

The Accountant=Lecturers' Association exists " to provide an organisation for accountants engaged in teaching, lecturing, or otherwise connected with commercial education, and generally to do all such things as may be necessary to elevate the status and procure the advancement of such accountants." Membership is restricted to members of the Institute of Chartered Accountants and the Society of Incorporated Accountants and Auditors, or persons who have passed the final examination of either of those bodies, but the Committee has limited power to admit other persons as hon. members.

Founded 1914.
Hon. Secretary : M. Moustardier, G.S.A.A., A.C.I.S., 29, Kenninghall Road, Clapton, E. 5.

The Art Teachers' Guild shares with the National Association of Art Masters and the Royal Drawing Society the privilege of electing one member of the Teachers' Registration Council. It was established " to bind together those interested in the teaching of art in schools, to study and discuss methods of such teaching, and to aid in the development of the same." The bulk of its members are art mistresses.

Founded 1900. Membership, about 260.

Organ : " The Art Teachers' Guild Record " (four-monthly).

Secretary : Miss Ethel M. Spiller, 11, Highbury Crescent, N. 5.

The Association of Assistants in Central Schools, London, endeavours to promote the interests of teachers and scholars in Central Schools.

Founded 1912. Membership, 346.

Hon. Secretary : Miss A. C. M. Drinkwater, B.A., 52, Amerland Road, West Hill, Wandsworth, S.W. 18.

The Association of Assistant Mistresses in Public Secondary Schools is a parallel organisation to the Association of Headmistresses, with which it has worked in harmonious and efficient co-operation, to raise the dignity and improve the quality of the profession of women teachers.

Founded 1889. Membership, about 1,700.

Secretary : Miss K. Andrews, 30, Clanricarde Gardens, Notting Hill Gate, W. 2.

The Association of Book=keeping Teachers aims at providing an organisation " for the purpose of doing all such things as may be necessary to elevate the status of its members and of the profession generally," etc. It gives diplomas in the teaching of book-keeping.

Founded 1904. Membership, 350.

Organ : " The Book-Keepers' Magazine " (monthly).

General Secretary : G. T. Barton, " Daneside," 13, St. George's Avenue, Ealing, W. 5.

The Association of the Headmasters of the Endowed Schools in the Midland Counties.

Founded 1871. Membership, about 80.

Hon. Secretary : Rupert Deakin, 34, Bunbury Road, King's Norton, Birmingham.

The Association of Headmistresses unites the heads of girls' public secondary schools. It was founded largely through the efforts of Miss Beale and Miss Buss.

Founded 1890. Membership, over 400.

Secretary : Miss Ruth Young, 92, Victoria Street, London, S.W. 1.

The Association of Preparatory Schools is composed of headmasters of privately owned boarding schools for boys up to 15, which have the special business of preparing the sons of well-to-do parents for public schools of the type represented in the Headmasters' Conference.
Founded 1892. Membership, 500 odd.
Organ : " The Preparatory Schools Review."
Hon. Secretary : F. Ritchie, 156, Sutherland Avenue, W. 9.

The Association of Public School Science Masters has for its objects : " (a) To promote the teaching of natural science in public schools; (b) to afford a means of communication between natural science teachers in public schools themselves and between them and others engaged in teaching natural science elsewhere; (c) to afford a means of communication between natural science teachers in public schools and examining bodies."
Founded 1900.
Secretaries : C. L. Bryant, Harrow School; F. G. Beesley, St. Olave's School, Tooley Street, S.E. 1.

The Association of Secondary Teachers in Ireland has for its objects the improvement of secondary education generally and particularly of the status of assistant teachers.
Founded 1890. Membership, about 500.
Hon. Secretary : T. J. Burke, Blennerville, Tralee, Co. Kerry.

The Association of Teachers of Domestic Subjects was first organised in 1896 as a Sectional Committee of the National Union of Women Workers. It became a distinct organisation in 1902. The exclusively feminine membership consists of " persons holding teachers' diplomas from a recognised training school " and " other persons who are teaching or supervising in direct connection with domestic subjects." It is, in fact, a " Subject Association " concerned with the technique of its science and craft, and in part a professional organisation aiming at an elevation of the status of its members.
Founded 1896. Membership (in 1916), 1,671.
Secretary : Miss K. M. Buck, Hastings House, 10, Norfolk Street, Strand, W.C. 2.

The Association of Teachers in Technical Institutions represents a part of the teaching profession which bids fair to become the most important of all its specialised sections. It admits " all teachers in technical institutions," both men and women, " other than those engaged solely in secondary school work." It counts among its members principals as well as assistants, and aims especially at securing adequate professional control over the curriculum its members have to teach.
Founded 1904.
Organ : " The Technical Journal " (monthly).
Hon. Secretary : P. Abbott, B.A., 5, West View, Highgate Hill, N. 19.

The Association of Tutorial Class Tutors under the University of London exists to serve the interests of the tutors and to develop and extend Tutorial Class work in the London area. (See Part IV.) Founded 1917. Membership in 1917 consisted of every London tutor engaged in Tutorial Class work in 1916-17.

Secretary : E. McGegan, University Hall of Residence, 10 and 11, Carlyle Square, Chelsea, S.W. 3.

The Association of University Women Teachers includes not only head and assistant secondary school mistresses, but also principals, professors, and tutors in Universities. A main object is " to protect and improve the status and to further the legitimate interests of women teachers." It runs an Appointments Bureau for its members. (See Part IV.)

Founded 1883. Membership, over 2,800.

Secretary : Mrs. B. Brough, 59, Cambridge Street, Hyde Park, W. 2.

The Association of University Lecturers. (Being organised.)

The Birmingham Council and Voluntary School Head Teachers' Association " formulates the opinions of head teachers employed in the area of the Education Authority and lays such opinions before the Education Committee when desirable."

Founded 1896. Membership, 350 to 400.

Hon. Secretary : J. G. Forrester, Tindal Street, Birmingham.

The Catholic Headmasters' Association aims at protecting the interests of the Catholic Secondary Schools under the Intermediate Board and at making suggestions to the Board on educational matters.

Founded 1888. Membership, 35 headmasters and 15 heads of convent schools.

Hon. Secretary : Very Rev. P. J. Canon Marshall, St. Brendan's Seminary, Killarney.

The Central Association of Irish Schoolmistresses aims at " promoting the higher education of women in Ireland; affording means of communication and co-operation between schoolmistresses and other ladies interested in education ; watching over the interests of girls, especially with regard to secondary and university education."

Founded 1880. Membership, about 70.

Hon. Secretary : Miss L. O. Rowletts, B.A., Kilronan, Clanskeagh, Dublin.

The College of Preceptors is the oldest professional organisation of teachers of any kind. In spite of a liberal constitution, the college has remained essentially the organisation of the schoolmaster who is himself the *entrepreneur*, contracting personally with each parent ; and it has always refused to take on any of the functions common to the Trade Union or professional association of salaried persons, which claim to arrange by their own representatives, in discussion with their employers, for a share in the control of the service. It offers diplomas for Associate, Licentiate, and Fellow. Membership is open to all ranks of teachers.

Founded 1886. Membership, about 1,000.

Secretary : G. Chalmers, Bloomsbury Square, W.C. 1.

The College of Teachers of the Blind exists, *inter alia*, " to raise the status of teachers of the blind by forming them into a college with a recognised position as specialists in the work of education." It holds examinations and grants certificates and diplomas.

Founded 1907. Membership, about 240.

Hon. Registrar : Henry Stainsby, c/o National Institute for the Blind, 224-228, Great Portland Street, London, W. 1.

The Conference of Headmistresses of Public Secondary Schools in the Administrative County of London is one of the local Associations which are affiliated to the Association of Headmistresses.

Founded 1908. Membership, 54.

Secretary : Miss Hanbidge, M.A., Central Foundation School, Spital Square, E. 1.

The Conference of University Tutorial Class Tutors meets annually to discuss the problems connected with the teaching and organisation of Tutorial Classes. (See Part IV.)

First Conference 1910.

Hon. Secretary : Henry Clay, Cedar House, Epping, Essex.

The Council of Principals of Schools and Institutions for the Deaf was created and continues to exist for the consideration of problems—educational, physical, and financial—affecting special schools for the deaf as viewed more particularly by committees and principals. It is now an integral part of the National Association of Teachers of the Deaf with which it amalgamated ten years ago, but has its own body of officials.

Founded 1860.

Organ : " The Teacher of the Deaf."

Hon. Secretary : Mr. G. H. Greenslade, Doncaster.

The Council of Principals of Training Colleges under Government Inspection (open to the Principals of all such Training Colleges and the Principals or responsible heads of such training departments attached to Universities or University Colleges) has for its objects " to consider and discuss matters affecting the interests of such Training Colleges, mainly with reference to administration and finance, and to take such action thereon as may be desirable."

Founded 1913. Membership, about 75.

Hon. Secretary : The Rev. Canon Stuart Blofeld, Saltley College, Birmingham.

The Educational Institute of Scotland.—" . . . . as there is no organised body in Scotland whose duty it is to ascertain and certify the qualifications of those intending to enter upon this office, and whose attestation shall be sufficient recommendation to the individual and guarantee to his employers, it is expedient that the teachers of Scotland, agreeably to the practice of other liberal professions, should unite for the purpose of supplying this defect in the educational arrangements of the country, and thereby of increasing their efficiency, improving their condition, and raising the standard of education in general."

Founded 1847. Membership, about 14,000.

Organ : " Educational News " (weekly).

Secretary : Hugh Cameron, M.A., F.E.I.S., 34, North Bridge, Edinburgh.

The Faculty of Teachers in Commerce " is the largest and most influential organisation of commercial teachers in the United Kingdom, and is devoted exclusively to the interests of commercial teachers and commercial teaching." It includes the Incorporated Societies of Shorthand Teachers, Book-keeping Teachers, Typewriting Teachers, and Specialist Teachers.

Incorporated 1916.

General Secretary : W. H. Jones, 8, Birch Grove, Rusholme, Manchester.

The Federal Council of Secondary School Associations was founded to enable secondary teachers to act unitedly upon particular questions without jeopardising the independence of the various sections. The constitution provides for the representation of each body affiliated by three representatives (though the Headmasters' Conference decides to send one only). It has played a considerable part in forming the Teachers' Registration Council, in raising the status and salary of the secondary school teachers, etc.

Founded 1906.

Secretary : R. F. Cholmeley, M.A., Owens School, Islington, N. 1.

The Friends' Guild of Teachers has been established " to form a body which will represent all teachers connected with the Society of Friends and which will be able to speak with professional weight on educational subjects," etc.

Founded 1896. Membership, 276.

Hon. Secretary : Jane H. Williamson, Ackworth School, Pontefract.

The Headmasters' Conference is an annual meeting of headmasters belonging to the hundred or so " public schools " that are in close connection with the two older Universities.

Founded 1869. Membership, about 120.

Hon. Secretary : W. A. Boulkeley Evans, 12, King's Bench Walk, Temple, E.C. 4.

The Imperial Union of Teachers was inaugurated by the League of the Empire. In July, 1912, under the auspices of the League, a first Imperial Conference of Teachers' Associations was held and a second is to be held at Toronto by invitation of the Government of Ontario.

Founded 1913.

Organ (of the League) : " The Federal Magazine."

Hon. Secretary (of the League) : Mrs. Ord Marshall, 28, Buckingham Gate, S.W. 1.

The Incorporated Association of Assistant Masters in Secondary Schools includes the assistant masters not only of endowed or publicly maintained schools, but also of private venture schools. It has developed an important " Legal Department " for the defence of the professional rights of its members.

Founded 1891. Membership, about 5,200.

Hon. Secretary : A. Blades, B.A., Sloane School, Chelsea, S.W. 1.

The Incorporated Association of Assistant Mistresses in Public Secondary Schools exists " (1) to promote the cause of education generally; (2) to protect and improve the status and to further the legitimate professional interests of teachers."

Founded 1884. Membership, over 2,000.

Secretary : Miss K. Andrews, 30, Clanricarde Gardens, W. 2.

The Incorporated Association of Headmasters includes the headmasters of schools of every type in which secondary education is provided; " it sends representatives to the Teachers' Registration Council, the Federal Council of Secondary Schools' Associations, and to every other body upon which secondary education is represented; through its officers it is in constant touch with the representative bodies of the other sections of the teaching profession, with the Universities, and with the Board of Education; it has provided witnesses before every Royal Commission that has dealt with educational matters, including the Royal Commission on the University of London, and the Royal Commission on the Civil Service; it has both on its own initiative and through the Federal Council made persistent and not unsuccessful efforts to improve the status of teachers, to promote a general scheme for pensions, and to bring about the much desired organisation of a system of public examinations.

" The officials of the Association are always at the service of members, for the giving of information, and, so far as they may be able, of advice upon doubtful or difficult positions; and where legal questions of general interest arise, the Honorary Legal Adviser is available for consultation through the Legal Committee of the Council."

Founded 1890. Membership, 615.

Organ : " Review " (terminally).

Hon. Secretaries : R. F. Cholmeley, Owen's School, Islington, N. 1; W. Jenkyn Thomas, Hackney Downs School, Clapton, E. 5.

The **Incorporated Gymnastic Teachers' Institute** has for its objects the better definition and protection of the profession by a system of examinations, the issue of certificates, and the registration of teachers of gymnastics, fencing, and other subjects relating to gymnastics and physical education. The Institute consists of Fellows, Members, and Associates. No teacher is admitted to membership without passing the required examinations. The certificates granted are for the British System of Physical Training and the Swedish System of Physical Training, also for the Elementary School Teachers' Drill Certificate.

Founded 1897.

Hon. Secretary : Mr. T. Williams, 25, Chalcroft Road, Lee, S.E. 13.

The **Incorporated Society of Commercial Teachers** insists upon not only a secondary school standard of general culture, but also upon proof of competency to teach at least three separate commercial subjects before granting its dignities of Fellow and Associate. It includes a large number of the principals of the Commercial Departments of the Municipal Technical Institutes in the North of England.

Founded 1909.

Secretary : T. B. Brown, F.S.A.A., 49, Victoria Buildings, Manchester.

The **Irish Protestant National Teachers' Union** exists to obtain security of tenure for Protestant teachers in Ireland.

Organ : " The Irish Protestant National Teachers' Annual."

Hon. Secretary : I. M'Loughlin, B.A., Clandelrye, Belfast.

The **Institute of Commercial and Specialist Teachers** is open to all teachers specialising in one or more subjects.

Founded 1910.

Assistant Secretary : A. E. Hazell, 57, Frobisher Road, Hornsey, N. 8.

The **London Dalcroze Teachers' Union** exists to " further the development of Eurhythmics in England and to maintain the standard of work."

Founded 1916. Membership, 25.

Hon. Secretary : Winifred E. Houghton, c/o London Dalcroze School, 23, Store Street, W.C. 1.

The **London Head Teachers' Association** has objects identical with those of the National Association of Head Teachers, to which it is affiliated.

Founded 1899. Membership, about 1,400.

General Secretary : D. H. Cassels, 38, Parkview Crescent, New Southgate, N. 11.

The London Married Women Teachers' Association exists " (1) to safeguard the interests of married women teachers; (2) to gain security of tenure and compensation for unjust dismissals; (3) to secure compensation for loss of pensions and breakdown allowances; (4) to afford opportunities for married women teachers to interchange opinions and take action where necessary on subjects of educational importance."

Founded 1909. Membership, about 250.

Hon. Secretaries : Mrs. Kate M. Dice, 23, West Hill, Sydenham, S.E. 26; Mrs. Muir Stanbury, L.C.C. Central Boys' School, Haverstock Hill, N.W. 3.

The London Teachers' Association includes teachers of all grades employed in schools aided or maintained by the L.C.C. Within the L.C.C. area it is sovereign in all matters concerning the relation of the teacher to the local authority, apart from questions of " legal benefit." These, and issues arising out of the relation of London teachers to the Board of Education, are within the competence of the N.U.T. (Over 12,000 members of the L.T.A. are also members of the N.U.T.) The L.T.A. is conspicuous for its success as an " Association of Consumers," organising foreign travel, country holidays, etc., as well as for its success as a professional organisation. Attempts have been made, but hitherto without success, to secure amalgamation between the N.U.T. and the L.T.A.

" The primary object of the Association is to ascertain, represent, and support the collective opinions of teachers working under the administration of the London Education Authority upon all matters affecting education and the interests of teachers. From the point of view of educational administration, the Association concerns itself more with the proceedings of the L.C.C. as the Education Authority than with the proceedings of Parliament or the administrative Acts of the Board of Education."

Founded 1872. Membership, 20,500.

Organ : " The London Teacher." Weekly circulation, 19,500.

General Secretary : William J. Pincombe, 9, Fleet Street, London, E.C. 4.

The London Union of Commercial Institutes consists of the members of the staffs of the Senior Evening Commercial Institutes under the London County Council. Membership is limited to the actual members of the staffs of the above-mentioned institutes, together with those qualified instructors who are in the approved panels; 95 per cent. of the principals and instructors are members of the Union. The objects of the Union are :—

1. To hold conferences and meetings for the discussion of professional affairs, interests, and duties; the reading of papers and the delivery of lectures; to collect, collate, and publish information of service or interest to members of the profession and the public at large.

2. To secure for the members of the Union such definite professional standing as may assist them in the discharge of their duties.

Founded 1913. Membership, 500, plus 200 on active service.

Organ : " Commercial Institutes Staff Gazette."

Secretary : H. Hemmings, 59, The Avenue, N. 10.

The London University Extension Lecturers' Association promotes fellowship among extension lecturers in the London area, protects and advances their material interests, " besides serving as a most useful channel of communication between the University Extension Board and the lecturers as a body." All lecturers under the Board are eligible for membership. Usually meets once a year.

Founded 1906. Membership, 30 to 40.

Acting Secretary : P. Gaskell, 35, Acacia Road, St. John's Wood, N.W. 8.

The Metropolitan Evening Institutes' Association (formerly the Metropolitan Evening Teachers' Association) exists to protect the interests of its members.

Founded 1895.

Hon. Secretary : W. J. Kenyon, 33, Queen's Road, Finsbury Park, N. 4.

The Music Teachers' Association tries to " promote progressive ideas upon the teaching of music, especially with a view to the recognition of heads of schools and others of the value of music study as an integral part of the child's general education." Membership is open to teachers of music and also to those studying to become teachers and others interested.

Founded 1908. Membership, 900.

Organ : " The Music Student."

Hon. Secretary : Arthur J. Hadrill, 24, Westmount Road, Eltham, S.E. 9.

The National Association of Head Teachers has for its main objects : (1) To further the cause of education generally ; (2) to further the physical, mental, and moral welfare of the children of the nation ; (3) to provide a ready means of communication between the head teachers of the country, and of ascertaining and giving expression to their opinions ; (4) to provide a means of taking united action whenever necessary ; (5) to safeguard the authority and interests of head teachers, to render sympathy and help to members in circumstances of difficulty, and to raise teaching to the dignity of a profession.

Founded 1897. Membership, over 6,000.

Organ : " The Head Teachers' Review."

Secretary : J. E. Dogherty, 25, Queen's Road, Newcastle-on-Tyne.

The National Association of Manual Training Teachers exists for the " dissemination of educational views on the question of manual training " and " to take united action in any matter affecting the interest of the profession."
Founded 1891. Membership, over 1,000.
Organ : " Manual Training " (monthly).
Assistant Hon. Secretary : C. H. Lineham, 262, Laburnum Grove, Portsmouth.

The National Association of Non=Collegiate Certificated Teachers, without publishing statistics of membership, claims to represent the 40,500 teachers who have received the Board of Education certificate but have not had a college training. In its own words :, " The Association exists primarily to protect the interests of certificated teachers who have obtained their ' diploma ' without the aid of a college course. While recognising the benefits which should accrue from a properly organised college course, which should be made obligatory with regard to all *future* teachers, it works for the removal of any disability that may be imposed by the Board of Education, Registration Council, or Local Education Authorities upon *existing* non-collegiate certificated teachers." It aims at the " unity of the profession " by the recognition of "the Government Certificate" as the " qualifying diploma," and stands for : " One diploma for those thoroughly qualified, and no petty distinctions."
Founded 1899.
General Secretary : Mr. J. Langton, F.R.G.S. (Past President), 2, Comberton Road, Upper Clapton, London, E. 5.

The National Association of Teachers of the Deaf exists " to further the cause of the education of the deaf ; to afford opportunities for the discussion of professional and educational topics ; to promote the professional interests of the teachers ; to arrange for holding biennial conferences ; to render advice and assistance to members in connection with their work ; to form a register of teachers and of the vacancies occurring. It has now been decided to amalgamate the National Association of Teachers of the Deaf with the " College of Teachers of the Deaf," so that the whole professional interests and the granting of diplomas will be linked up in the new " National College of Teachers of the Deaf." This comes into force January, 1918.
Founded 1895. Membership, 387.
Organ : " The Teacher " (bi-monthly).
Hon. Secretary : F. G. Barnes, Homerton College, E. 9.

The National Federation of Catholic Teachers' Associations desires " (*a*) to promote the welfare of Catholic education ; (*b*) to facilitate interchange of thought and co-operation amongst those engaged or interested in Catholic education ; (*c*) to give advice and help to members in times of difficulty ; (*d*) to secure the direct representation of Catholic teachers on the Executive of the N.U.T."
Founded 1907. Membership, 3,369 (exclusive of members with the Forces).
Hon. Secretary : W. Merrick, 18, Elleray Road, Pendleton, Manchester.

The National Federation of Class Teachers was founded to attend to the interests of class teachers as distinct from those of head teachers (whose influence in the N.U.T. has always been dominant). It holds its own local meetings and national conferences. It has a large representation on the N.U.T. Executive and insists upon putting its own point of view in deputations and memorials to the Board of Education and Local Education Authorities.

Founded 1894. Membership, 19,500, plus 10,000 on active service.

Organ : " The Class-Teacher " (bi-monthly).

Secretary : Harry Pearson, " Broxton," Grove Road, Hoylake, Cheshire.

The National Federation of Women Teachers is the most powerful of the teaching organisations which cater expressly for women. It is a Federation formed out of the local associations which sprang up during the " woman's rights " agitation of 1900 to 1910. Its object is to improve the position of the woman teacher, and especially to secure " equal pay and equal increments " for men and women teachers of the same professional status. It aims also at securing " more women on the N.U.T. Executive," " representation of women on all Educational Authorities," and the Parliamentary franchise for women teachers.

Founded 1911. Membership, not precisely known. During 1917 70 branches have been formed, some with a membership of 200 or 300.

Organ : " The Schoolmistress."

General Secretary (pro tem.) : Miss A. S. Byett, L.L.A., 93, Grantham Road, Birmingham.

The National Society of Art Masters was established as the " Society of Art Masters " and until 1902-3 it was composed exclusively of the heads of the 200 or so " Schools of Art " in the Metropolis and other large centres, which received the grants of the Science and Art Departments. From 1902-3 the society has broadened its basis in order to include also those who were teaching art in elementary schools, etc. Like many other organisations of specialist teachers, it aims at conducting its own examinations and at granting its own certificates, with regard not only to each successive crop of art teachers, but also to the pupils in all the schools staffed by its members.

Founded 1888. Membership, 700.

Secretary : Alfred Shuttleworth, A.R.C.A., 45, Bedford Row, London, W.C. 1.

The National Union of Uncertificated Teachers seeks to promote the interests of the 40,000 elementary school teachers (nine-tenths of them women) who are excluded from membership of the N.U.T. because they do not possess a Board of Education certificate. Supplementary teachers (who have no organisations of their own) may become members. Statistics of membership are not published.

Founded 1913.

Hon. Secretary : Miss E. Walsh, 30, Hylton Crescent, Prestwich, Manchester.

The Private Schools Association exists to protect the interests of efficient private schools.

Incorporated 1884.

Organ : " Secondary Education," published twice a term.

Chairman of Council (to whom all communications should be addressed) : S. Maxwell, M.A., LL.B., F.R.A.S., Manor House School, Clapham Common, S.W. 4.

The Schoolmasters' Association has for its objects (i.) " to advance the interests of secondary education in Ireland," and (ii.) " to afford its members the advantages of mutual counsel and support." Consists of members (Headmasters of Irish secondary schools) and associates (Headmistresses of Irish secondary schools).

Founded 1869. Membership (including Associates), 100.

Hon. Secretary : J. Thompson, M.A. (Cantab), M.R.I.A., The High School, Dublin.

The Secondary Education Association of Scotland exists to promote " the interests of teachers in the intermediate and secondary schools, and generally to further the cause of higher education in Scotland."

Founded 1909. Membership, about 1,600.

Organ : " The Secondary School Journal."

Secretary : George C. Pringle, M.A., F.R.S.E., High School, Peebles.

The Secondary School Teachers' War Relief Fund exists to " supplement, where necessary, any State or other provision made for secondary school teachers who have been disabled through the war or for the dependants of those who have been so disabled or who have fallen in their country's service. Allowances are made such as will enable the recipients to live with the same degree of comfort as they have been accustomed to."

Founded 1916.

Hon. Secretary : G. D. Dunkerley, B.Sc., The Grammar School, Watford.

The Secondary, Technical, and University Teachers' Insurance Society seeks " to provide for the relief or maintenance of members during sickness or other infirmity " ; " to be an approved society within the meaning of the National Insurance Act." Membership is restricted to secondary, technical, and university teachers, including teachers in private employ.

Founded 1912. Membership, about 11,000.

Secretary : C. J. Mills, A.F.I., 10, Mecklenburgh Square, W.C. 1.

The Sheffield Commercial Teachers' Union consists of teachers of commercial subjects in the service of the Sheffield Town Council. Its object is " to render mutual assistance in working the syllabuses of the Sheffield Education Committee, to provide substitutes for members, and assist in appointments."

Founded 1915. Membership, 40 to 50.

Hon. Secretary : F. Franks, 26, Hardwick Crescent, Sheffield.

Le Société des Professeurs de Français en Angleterre. a pour but : " Intellectuel—de fournir des Professeurs de Français dévoués instruits, et dont les aptitudes soient reconnues officiellement ; Matériel—de grouper les Professeurs dans une Société amicale, et de les aider dans leurs difficultés présentes ou dans celles de leur vieillesse, autant que les moyens de la Société le permettent. La solidarité doit être un des plus chers devoirs des Professeurs entre eux ; Patriotique—de faire connaître et aimer la France. Aujourd'hui plus que jamais, tout Professeur de Français doit avoir à cœur de montrer les trésors d'idéal de liberté, de justice, de vie intellectuelle qui se trouvent dans une âme française. Pour appartenir à la Société, il faut : offrir des garanties de savoir et de compétence pédagogique constatées par les diplômes français (Brevet de l'enseignement primaire, Baccalauréats de l'enseignement secondaire, Licences ou Diplômes d'études supérieures de l'enseignement supérieur, Agrégations, Doctorats) ou anglais. Présenter des qualités morales reconnues et attestées. Etre en règle avec la loi militaire. Payer sa cotisation : 10s. 6d. par an."

Etabli, 1881. Les Membres, 250.

Les Sécretaires : Mm. B. Minssen et A. Fortin, Sackville House, 7, Red Lion Square, W.C. 1.

The Society of Pitman's Certified Teachers of Shorthand is made up exclusively of holders of Pitman's Teacher's Certificate.

Founded 1905.

Organs : " Pitman's Yearbook and Diary " and " The Shorthand Teacher's Magazine."

Acting Secretary : F. G. W. Lester, 13, Solon New Road, Clapham, S.W. 4.

The Teachers' Guild has aimed from its establishment at the inclusion in its membership of teachers of every kind—an ideal achieved largely through the efforts of the Guild by the establishment of the Teachers' Registration Council.

Founded 1884. Membership, about 2,000.

Organ : " The Teachers' Guild " (quarterly).

General Secretary : F. Fairman, M.A., 9 and 10, Brunswick Square, W.C. 1.

The Teachers' Training Association consists of persons engaged in the " professional training of students preparing to take a University Diploma or Certificate in Education," i.e., the staffs of the training departments attached to Universities.

Founded 1907. Membership, over 90.

Hon. Secretary : Miss S. Melhuish, M.A., Bedford College, London.

The Training College Association exists " to furnish opportunity for the discussion of educational questions, especially those relating to the training of teachers, and for the expression of a collective opinion thereon." Membership is confined to (1) the principals and all members of the teaching staffs of training colleges and training departments recognised by the Board of Education, and (2) other persons, approved by the Association, who are, or have been, engaged in the work of training teachers.

Founded 1892. Membership, about 450.

Organ : " The Journal of Experimental Pedagogy and Training College Record."

Hon. Secretary : Major H. E. Griffiths, St. John's College, Battersea, S.W. 11.

The Union of Directors of Music in Secondary Schools is a male society confined to the principal teachers in large schools who have under their direction several other teachers of music. It aims at the increase of the quantity and the improvement of the quality of the instruction of music in large schools, principally the well-known " public schools " for boys.

Membership, about 100.

Secretary : Rev. Dr. Rowton, Folkestone.

The Union of Teachers of the Deaf on the Pure Oral System believes that the " oral system of teaching deaf mutes is well established in the United Kingdom, and that it has become a duty to protect the work and show its superiority."

Founded 1894. Membership, 70.

Hon. Secretary : J. W. Fisher, 27, Arvin Road, Highbury, N. 5.

The Welsh County Schools Association " holds periodical meetings for the discussion of educational problems; provides its members with opportunities for interchanging opinions on all matters affecting the control and internal organisation of the county schools of Wales; seeks to influence public opinion on educational questions, to watch all legislation dealing with secondary education, and generally to protect the interests of its members." Headmasters and headmistresses of secondary schools are alone eligible for membership.

Founded 1895. Membership includes almost all those eligible.

Organ : " County Schools Review " (terminally).

Hon. Secretary : D. E. Williams, M.A., Gowerton, South Wales.

The West Riding Association of Organising Masters and Secretaries for Technical Education " associates and unites the organising masters and secretaries in technical and other forms of higher education in the West Riding of Yorkshire."

Founded 1904. Membership, about 4,000.

Secretary : G. C. Hewitt, Ripponden, Halifax.

The Yorkshire Headmistresses' Association was formed for the purpose of discussing matters of educational importance specially relating to Yorkshire schools.

Founded 1910. Membership, about 50.

Hon. Secretary : Miss Nodes, Municipal High School, Doncaster.

DIRECTORY OF EDUCATION AUTHORITIES.

ENGLAND.

County Boroughs, Boroughs, and Urban Districts are distinguished by the letter (C.B.), (B.), and (U.D.) respectively.

All correspondence should be addressed to the Borough or District Education Offices.

An asterisk denotes those Local Education Authorities having only concurrent powers under Section 3 of the Education Act, 1902.

BOARD OF EDUCATION.

President: The Right Hon. H. A. L. Fisher, M.P., Whitehall, S.W. 1.

Parliamentary Secretary: The Right Hon. J. Herbert Lewis, M.P., Whitehall, S.W. 1.

Permanent Secretary: Sir L. Amherst Selby-Bigge, K.C.B., Whitehall, S.W. 1.

LOCAL EDUCATION AUTHORITIES.

ACCRINGTON (B.), Lancs.—A. H. Aitkin, Solicitor, Clerk, Education Offices, Town Hall, A.

ACTON (U.D.), Middlesex.—F. A. Everitt, Secretary, Education Department, Council Offices, A., W. 3.

ALDERSHOT (U.D.), Hants.—Norman Clinton, Clerk, 4, Station Road, A.

ASHTON-IN-MAKERFIELD* (U.D.), Lancs.—Albert Sykes, Secretary, Council Offices, Bryn Street, A.-in-M.

ASHTON-UNDER-LYNE (B.), Lancs.—Lieut.-Colonel D. H. Wade, Secretary, Education Office, A.-under.-L.

AUDLEY* (U.D.), Staffs.—J. J. Nelson, Solicitor, Secretary, Education Offices, A.

BACUP (B), Lancs.—W. Unwin, Secretary, Education Offices, B.

BANBURY (B), Oxfordshire.—A. Stockton, Clerk, Town Hall, B.

BARKING TOWN (U.D.), Essex.—J. T. Edwards, Secretary, Public Offices, B.

BARNSLEY (B.), W. Riding.—D. Paul, Secretary, Education Office, B.

BARNSTAPLE (B.), Devonshire.—G. W. F. Brown, Secretary, on military service.—E. J. Buckingham, Acting Secretary, The Strand, B.

BARROW-IN-FURNESS.—A. Hawcridge, Director of Education, Town Hall, B.-in-F.

BATH (C.B).—The Town Clerk, Guildhall, B.

BATLEY (B.), W. Riding.—G. R. H. Danby, M.A. (Oxon.), Director of Education, Education Offices, B.

BECKENHAM (U.D.), Kent.—F. Stevens, Clerk, Council Offices, B.

BEDFORD (B), Beds.—S. C. George, F.C.I.S., Secretary, Bromham Road, B.

BEDFORDSHIRE.—H. E. Baines, Director of Education, Shire Hall, Bedford.

BERKSHIRE.—W. C. F. Anderson, M.A., Secretary, Shire Hall, Reading.

BERWICK-UPON-TWEED (B.), Northumberland.—James Gibson, Acting Clerk, Town Clerk's Office, B.-upon-T.

BEVERLEY (B.), E. Riding.—J. W. Mills, Clerk, 31, Lairgate, B.

BEXHILL-ON-SEA (B.), E. Sussex.—A. B. Lawson, Secretary, Town Hall, B.-on.-S.

BILSTON (U.D.), Staffs.—F. O. Beech, Secretary, Town Hall, B.

BIRKENHEAD (C.B.)—R. T. Jones, Secretary, Town Hall, B.

BIRMINGHAM (C.B.).—J. A. Palmer, Secretary, Margaret Street, B.

BISHOP'S CASTLE* (B.), Salop.—E. Griffiths, Secretary, Castle Street, B.C.

BLACKBURN (C.B.).—A. H. Whipple, M.A. (Cantab), B.Sc. (London), Director of Education, Library Street, B.

BLACKPOOL (C.B.).—J. 11. Greenwood, Acting Director, Town Hall Street, B.

BLYTH (B.), Northumberland.—H. T. Rutherford, Secretary, 1, Stanley Street, B.

BOLTON (C.B.).—F. Wilkinson, F.G.S., Director of Education, Nelson Square, B.

BOOTLE (C.B.).—F. K. Wilson, Secretary, Town Hall, B.

BOSTON (B.), Lincs. (Holland).—G. Harless, Secretary, Municipal Buildings, B.

BOURNEMOUTH (C.B.).—F. W. Ibbett, M.A., Director of Education, Education Offices, Municipal Buildings, B.

BRADFORD (C.B.).—A. C. Coffin, B.A., Town Hall, B.

BRIDGNORTH* (B.), Salop.—F. R. Cooksey, Secretary, 60, High Street, B.

BRIDGWATER (B.), Somerset.—A. King, Town Clerk, Clerk's Office, B.

BRIDLINGTON (B.), E. Riding.—G. G. O. Sutcliffe, J.P., Solicitor, Clerk, Quay Road, B.

BRIERLEY HILL* (U.D.), Staffs.—W. Waldron, Secretary, High Street, B.H.

BRIGHOUSE (B.), W. Riding.—T. Walling, M.A. (Cantab), Secretary, Manor House, B.

BRIGHTON (C.B.).—F. H. Toyne, B.A., Secretary, 54, Old Steine, B.

BRISTOL (C.B.).—W. A. Adams, Secretary, Guildhall, Bristol.

BROMLEY (B.), Kent.—F. H. Norman, Secretary, Municipal Buildings, Bromley.

BUCKINGHAMSHIRE.—E. G. Watkins, Secretary, County Hall, Aylesbury.

BURNLEY (C.B.).—A. R. Pickles, M.A., Director of Education, Town Hall, B.

BURTON-ON-TRENT (C.B.).—L. E. Burgess, M.A., Secretary and Director of Education, Guild Street, B.-on.-T.

BURY (C.B.).—J. Haslam, Town Clerk, 8, Bank Street, B.

BURY ST. EDMUNDS (B.), Suffolk.—J. H. Wakefield, Secretary, Town Hall, B. St. E.

CAMBRIDGE (B.), Cambs.—E. Jenkins, Secretary, Guildhall, C.

CAMBRIDGESHIRE.—A. Keen, M.A., Education Secretary, Education Office, County Hall, Cambridge.

CANNOCK (U.D.), Staffs.—W. E. Swift, Council Offices, C.

CANTERBURY (C.B.).—H. Fielding, Town Clerk, 15, Burgate Street, C.

CARLISLE (C.B.).—A. H. Collingwood, 15, Fisher Street, C.

CHADDERTON (U.D.), Lancs.—A. Crompton, Secretary, Town Hall, C.

Q

CHATHAM (B), Kent.—A. J. Harris, Clerk, Town Hall, C.

CHELMSFORD (B.), Essex.—G. Melvin, Town Clerk, 16, London, Road, C.

CHELTENHAM (B.), Gloucester.—W. T. Long, Secretary, Municipal Offices, Promenade, C.

CHEPPING WYCOMBE (B.), Bucks.—A. J. Clarke, Clerk, Town Clerk's Office, High Wycombe.

CHESHIRE.—R. P. Ward, Director of Education; W. R. Hall, Secretary for Higher Education, County Education Office, City Road, Chester.

CHESTER (C.B.).—A. E. Lovell, M.A., Secretary and Director of Education, Town Hall, C.

CHESTERFIELD (B.), Derbyshire.—W. Jacques, Secretary, Foljambe Road, C.

CHICHESTER (B.), W. Sussex.—J. W. Loader Cooper, Town Clerk, C.

CHISWICK (U.D.), Middlesex.—W. H. Lane, Education Clerk, Education Office, Town Hall, Chiswick, W.

CHORLEY (B.), Lancs.—R. L. Roby, Secretary, Town Hall, C.

CLITHEROE (B.), Lancs.—W. S. Weeks, Town Clerk, Town Clerk's Office, C.

COLCHESTER (B.), Essex.—E. H. Bultitude, Trinity Street, C.

COLNE (B.), Lancs.—H. Hartley, Secretary, Town Hall, C.

CONGLETON (B.), Cheshire.—H. Latham, Secretary, Chapel Street, C.

CORNWALL.—F. R. Pascoe, B.A., J.P., Secretary, County Hall, Truro.

COSELEY (U.D.), Staffs.—F. J. C. Poole, F.R.G.S., Secretary, Council House, C., near Bilston.

COVENTRY (C.B.).—F. Horner, B.A., LL.B., Secretary, Council House, C.

CREWE (B.), Cheshire.—H. D. Struthers, Director of Education, Municipal Buildings, C.

CROYDON (C.B.).—J. Smyth, Clerk, Education Office, Katharine Street, C.

CUMBERLAND.—C. Courtenay Hodgson, M.A., Secretary, The Courts, Carlisle.

DARLINGTON (C.B.).—A. C. Boyde, M.A., LL.B., Secretary, Education Office, North Lodge, D.

DARWEN (B.), Lancs.—W. Bretherick, Secretary, Technical School Buildings, D.

DEAL (B.), Kent.—A. C. Brown, Solicitor, Town Clerk, 127, High Street, D.

DERBY (C.B.).—W. Cooper, J.P., Secretary, Education Office, Becket Street, D.

DERBYSHIRE.—A. J. Jenkyn Brown, Director of Education, County Offices, Derby.

DEVIZES* (B.), Wilts.—W. H. Titcombe, Secretary, 31, St. John Street, D.

DEVONSHIRE.—J. F. Young, Secretary, County Education Office, The Castle, Exeter.

DEWSBURY (C.B.).—S. G. Bibby, Secretary, Town Hall, D.

DONCASTER (B.), W. Riding.—R. D. Simpson, Secretary, Wood Street, D.

DORSETSHIRE.—C. G. Bone, Secretary, County Offices, Dorchester.

DOVER (B.), Kent.—R. E. Knocker, Town Clerk, 69, Castle Street, D.

DUDLEY (C.B.), Worcester.—J. M. Wynne, Director of Education, St. James's Road, D.

DUKINFIELD (B.), Cheshire.—W. Weild, Secretary, Town Hall, D.

DURHAM (B), Durham.—W. R. Wilson, Secretary, 68½, Saddler Street, D.

DURHAM (County).—A. J. Dawson, Clerk, Shire Hall, Durham.

EALING (B.), Middlesex.—J. B. Johnson, Barrister-at-Law, Secretary, Town Hall, Ealing, W. 5.

EASTBOURNE (C.B.).—H. W. Fovargue, Town Clerk, the Town Hall, E.

EAST HAM (C.B.).—F. R. Thompson, Secretary, Education Office, East Ham, E. 6.

EAST RETFORD (B.), Notts.—W. P. Jones, E. R.

EAST RIDING.—(See Yorkshire.)

EAST SUFFOLK.—(See Suffolk.)

EAST SUSSEX.—(See Sussex.)

ECCLES (B.), Lancs.—S. H. Neave, Secretary, Town Hall, E.

EDMONTON (U.D.), Middlesex.—A. Heap, LL.B., B.A., Secretary, Brettenham Road, Upper Edmonton, N. 18.

ELY (ISLE OF).—(See Isle of Ely.)

ENFIELD (U.D.), Middlesex.—N. Hepworth, Secretary, Public Offices, E.

ERITH (U.D.), Kent.—A. T. Flux, Director of Education, Picardy, Belvedere.

ESSEX.—J. H. Nicholas, M.A., Secretary, County Offices, Chelmsford.

EXETER (C.B.).—H. Armitage, Clerk, 39, Southernhay West, E.

FALMOUTH (B.), Cornwall.—E. E. Armitage, Secretary, Municipal Buildings, F.

FARNWORTH (U.D.), Lancs.—H. Rostron, B.Sc., Secretary, Town Hall, F.

FAVERSHAM (B.), Kent.—G. Tassell, Clerk, 20, West Street, F.

FELLING (U.D.), Durham.—W. P. Parkin, Clerk, Council Buildings, F.

FINCHLEY (U.D.), Middlesex.—J. Cogdale, Secretary, Church End, Finchley, N.

FOLKESTONE (B.), Kent.—T. Wilkinson, Clerk, The Old Harvey Grammar School, F.

GATESHEAD (C.B.).—R. T. Edington, Secretary, Prince Consort Road, S., G.

GILLINGHAM (B.), Kent.—W. Taylor, Acting Secretary, Gardiner Street, G.

GLOSSOP (B.), Derbyshire.—J. Walkden, C.C., Secretary, Howard Chambers, G.

GLOUCESTER (C.B.).—P. Barrett Cooke, Secretary, 9, Berkeley Street, G.

GLOUCESTERSHIRE.—H. W. Household, M.A. (Oxon)., Secretary, Shire Hall, Gloucester.

GOSPORT AND ALVERSTOKE (U.D.), Hants.—G. R. Walker, High Street, Gosport.

GRANTHAM (B.), Lincs. (Kesteven).—G. E. Sandy, Secretary, Guildhall, G.

GRAVESEND (B.), Kent.—H. Hampton Brown, Town Clerk's Office, G.

GREAT YARMOUTH.—(See Yarmouth.)

GRIMSBY (C.B.).—D. Chandler, Clerk, Eleanor Street, G.

GUILDFORD (B.), Surrey.—F. G. Shirley, Acting Secretary, Technical Institute, Park Street, G.

HALIFAX (C.B.).—W. H. Ostler, Secretary, West House, King's Cross Street, H.

HAMPSHIRE.—D. T. Cowan, M.A., Director of Education, The Castle, Winchester.

HAMPTON* (U.D.), Middlesex.—E. Cozens, Secretary, Public Offices, H.

HARROGATE (B.), W. Riding.—J. Turner Taylor, Town Clerk, 5, Haywra Crescent, H.

HARTLEPOOL (B.), Durham.—H. W. Bell, Town Clerk, Borough Buildings, H.

HARWICH (B.), Essex.—G. D. Hugh-Jones, Secretary, 42, Church Street, H.

HASLINGDEN (B.), Lancs.—H. A. Collinge, Secretary, Municipal Offices, H.

HASTINGS (C.B.).—P. O. Buswell, Secretary, 18, Wellington Square, H.

HEANOR* (U.D.), Derbyshire.—H. C. Preston, Secretary, Mansfield Road, H.

HEBBURN (U.D.), Durham.—T. Stuart, Clerk, 2, Coquet Street, H.

HEMEL HEMPSTED (B.), Herts.—L. Smeathman, Secretary, Town Hall, H. H.

HENDON (U.D.), Middlesex.—J. Anderson, Secretary, Council Offices, Hendon, N.W. 4.

HENLEY-ON-THAMES,* Oxfordshire.—A. Caldecott, Town Clerk, Town Clerk's Office, H.-on-T.

HEREFORD (B.), Herefordshire.—R. Battersby, Town Clerk, Town Hall, H.

HEREFORDSHIRE.—J. Wiltshire, Secretary, Shire Hall, Hereford.

HERTFORDSHIRE.—Sir C. E. Longmore, Clerk of the County Council; A. R. S. Hallidie, Chief Education Officer, Hertford.

HESTON AND ISLEWORTH (U.D.), Middlesex.—M. Armstrong, Secretary, Council House, Hounslow.

HEYWOOD (B), Lancs.—A. Lewis, B.A., Barrister-at-Law, Director of Education, Municipal Buildings, H.

HINDLEY (U.D.), Lancs.—I. C. Pharoah, Secretary, Council Offices, H.

HOLLAND.—(See Lincolnshire.)

HORNSEY (B.), Middlesex.—A. W. Allen, M.A., Secretary, 206, Stapleton Hall Road, Stroud Green, N. 4.

HOVE (B.), E. Sussex.—S. G. Dancy, Secretary, Third Avenue, H.

HUDDERSFIELD (C.B.).—O. Balmforth, J.P., Secretary, Peel Street, H.

HULL (C.B.).—J. T. Riley, D.Sc., Director of Education, Albion Street, H.

HUNTINGDONSHIRE.—F. L. Turk, Acting Clerk, 36, High Street, Huntingdon.

HYDE (B.), Cheshire.—S. Ashworth, Secretary, Technical School, H.

ILFORD (U.D.), Essex.—W. S. Torbitt, M.A., LL.M., Secretary, Cleveland Road, I.

ILKESTON (B.), Derbyshire.—S. F. James, Town Clerk, Town Hall, I.

INCE-IN-MAKERFIELD (U.D.), Lancs.—W. Smith, Secretary, Council Offices, Ince, near Wigan.

IPSWICH (C.B.).—G. Billam, Secretary, Tower House, Tower Street, I.

ISLE OF ELY (County).—J. H. Haigh, B.Sc., Secretary, County Hall, March.

ISLE OF WIGHT (County).—J. Dufton, County Clerk, 20, Holyrood Street, Newport, I.W.

JARROW (B.), Durham.—T. H. Spencer, Secretary, Town Hall, J.-on-T.

KEIGHLEY (B.), W. Riding.—H. Midgley, Secretary, Town Hall Square, K.

KENDAL (B.), Westmorland.—J. E. Bolton, Town Clerk, 14, Kent Street, K.

KENT.—F. W. Crook, Secretary, Sessions House, Maidstone.

KESTEVEN.—(See Lincolnshire.)

KETTERING (U.D.), Northants.—J. Bond, Clerk, Council Offices, K.

KIDDERMINSTER (B.), Worcestershire.—W. M. Roden, Secretary, Town Hall, K.

KING'S LYNN (B.), Norfolk.—H. M. Howard, B.A., Secretary, London Road, K. L.

KINGSTON-UPON-THAMES (B.), Surrey.—H. T. Roberts, Secretary, Technical Institute, Kingston Hall Road, K.-on-T.

LANCASHIRE.—H. Lloyd Snape, D.Sc., Ph.D., Director of Education, County Offices, Preston.

LANCASTER (B.), Lancs.—G. H. Mitchell, Secretary, Town Hall, L.

LEAMINGTON SPA.—S. Mellows, B.Sc., Director of Education, Town Hall, L. S.

LEEDS (C.B.).—J. Graham, Secretary, Calverley Street, L.

LEEK* (U.D.), Staffs.—A. Vinen, Secretary, Nicholson Institute, L.

LEICESTER (C.B.).—R. T. B. Edge, Secretary, Town Hall, L.

LEICESTERSHIRE.—W. Allport Brockington, M.A., Director, 33, Bowling Green Street, Leicester.

LEIGH (B.), Lancs.—J. Ward, J.P., Director of Education, Town Hall, L.

LEWES (B.), E. Sussex.—C. H. Morris, Secretary, Eastgate Street, L.

LEYTON (U.D.), Essex.—R. Vincent, Clerk, Town Hall, Leyton, E. 10.

LINCOLN (C.B.).—R. C. Minton, Secretary and Inspector, Corporation Offices, Saltergate, L.

LINCOLN (Holland).—A. A. Crabtree, Secretary, Sessions House, Spalding.

LINCOLNSHIRE (Kesteven).—H. Donaldson, Secretary, 64, London Road, Grantham.

LINCOLNSHIRE (Parts of Lindsey).—S. M. Grant, Secretary, 286, High Street, Lincoln.

LIVERPOOL (C.B.).—J. G. Legge, Director of Education, 14, Sir Thomas Street, L.

LONDON.—Sir R. Blair LL.D., Education Officer, Education Offices, Victoria Embankment, W.C. 2.

LOUGHBOROUGH (B.), Leicestershire.—E. A. Jarratt, Secretary, Ashby Road, L.

LOWESTOFT (B.), E. Suffolk.—R. B. Nicholson, Town Clerk, Town Hall, L.

LUDLOW* (B.), Salop.—J. H. Williams, Secretary, L.

LUTON (B.), Beds.—P. J. Carter, Secretary, Town Hall, L.

LYNN.—(See King's Lynn.)

MACCLESFIELD (B.), Cheshire.—W. Grieves, Secretary, Town Hall, M.

MAIDENHEAD (B.), Berks.—H. E. Davies, Clerk, Guildhall, M.

MAIDSTONE (B.), Kent.—E. W. B. Abbott, Barrister-at-Law, Secretary, Faith Street, M.

MANCHESTER (C.B.).—S. Iley, B.A., Director of Education, Deansgate, M.

MANSFIELD (B.), Notts.—J. Harrop White, Clerk, Bank Chambers, M.

MARGATE (B.), Kent.—E. Brooke, Town Clerk, 13, Grosvenor Place, M.

MIDDLESBROUGH (C.B.).—E. Beckwith, B.Sc. (London), Director and Secretary, Municipal Buildings, M.

MIDDLESEX.—B. S. Gott, M.A., Secretary, Guildhall, Westminster, S.W. 1.

MIDDLETON (B.), Lancs.—R. Parkes, Secretary, Post Office Buildings, M., near Manchester.

MORECAMBE (B.), Lancs.—T. Barrow, Secretary, Technical School, M.

MORLEY (B.), W. Riding.—R. Brown, Secretary, Peel Street, M.

MOSSLEY (B.), Lancs.—W. A. Mayall, Secretary, Town Hall, M., near Manchester.

NELSON (B.), Lancs.—J. Skinner, Secretary, Market Street, N.

NEWARK (B.), Notts.—H. H. Osborn, Secretary, Old Magnus Buildings, N.

NEWBURY (B.), Berks.—R. H. Jeeves, Secretary, Municipal Offices, Mansion House Street, N.

NEWCASTLE-UNDER-LYME (B.), Staffs.—G. C. Till, Secretary, Education Offices, Lad Lane, N.-under-L.

NEWCASTLE-UPON-TYNE (C.B.).—P. Sharp, B.Sc., Director of Education, Northumberland Road, N.-upon-T.

NEWPORT (B.), Isle of Wight.—F. D. Shields, 37, Quay Street, N., I. of W.

NEW WINDSOR (B.), Berks.—W. Baxter, J.P., Secretary, Town Hall, W.

NORFOLK.—T. A. Cox, Secretary, Shire Hall, Norwich.

NORTHAMPTON (C.B.).—S. Beattie, Secretary, 4, St. Giles Street, N.

NORTHAMPTONSHIRE.—J. L. Holland, B.A., Secretary, County Education Offices, Northampton.

NORTH RIDING.—(See Yorkshire.)

NORTHUMBERLAND.—C. Williams, Secretary, The Moothall, Newcastle-on-Tyne.

NORWICH (C.B.).—A. H. Miller, Town Clerk, Town Clerk's Office, N.

NOTTINGHAM (C.B.).—W. J. Abel, B.A., Barrister-at-Law, Clerk, South Parade, N.

NOTTINGHAMSHIRE.—B. W. L. Bulkeley, Director of Education (on service).—J. Bramley, Acting Director of Education, Shire Hall, Nottingham.

NUNEATON, Warwickshire.—F. S. Clay, Clerk, Bridge House, N.

OLDBURY (U.D.), Worcestershire.—S. Vernon, LL.B., Secretary, O., near Birmingham.

OLDHAM (C.B.).—J. Rennie, Secretary, Union Street West, O.

OSSETT (B.), W. Riding.—E. Lucas, Secretary, Town Hall, O., Yorks.

OSWESTRY* (B.), Salop.—G. W. Ferrington, Secretary, 18, Arthur Street, O.

OXFORD (C.B.)—R. Bacon, Town Clerk, Town Hall, O.

OXFORDSHIRE.—P. Elford, M.A., Secretary, County Offices, Oxford.

PENGE (U.D.), Kent.—C. G. Liddle, Secretary, Town Hall, Anerley, S.E.

PENZANCE (B.), Cornwall.—T. H. Cornish, Clerk, 8, Parade Street, P.

PETERBOROUGH (B.), Northants.—H. Wilson, Solicitor, Clerk, Queen Street, P.

PETERBOROUGH, SOKE OF.—(See Soke of Peterborough.)

PLYMOUTH (C.B.).—E. C. Cook, Secretary, Cobourg Street, P.

PONTEFRACT (B.), W. Riding.—W. Haddock, Secretary, Municipal Offices. P.

POOLE (B.), Dorset.—C. Lisby, Secretary, P.
PORTSMOUTH (C.B.).—G. W. Allen, Secretary for Elementary Education, Education Committee's Offices, Town Hall, P.—H. E. Curtis, Secretary for Higher Education, Municipal College, P.
PRESTON (C.B.).—A. J. Berry, M.A., Director of Education, Roebuck Chambers, Lancaster Road, P.
PUDSEY (B.), W. Riding.—W. B. Burnell, Secretary, P., Yorks.
RADCLIFFE (U.D.) Lancs.—S. Mills, Secretary, Council Offices, R.
RAMSGATE (B.), Kent.—A. B. Clarke, Clerk, Albion House, R.
RAWTENSTALL (B.), Lancs.—J. E. Kirk, Secretary, Peel Street, Cloughfold, R.
READING (C.B.).—H. T. Pugh, Clerk, Blagrave Street, R.
REIGATE (B.), Surrey.—E. H. Bourne, Secretary, Municipal Buildings, Reigate.
RICHMOND (B.), Surrey.—H. Sagar, Town Hall, R.
ROCHDALE (C.B.).—J. E. Holden, Secretary, Baillie Street, R.
ROCHESTER (B.), Kent.—A. Kennette, Town Clerk, Guildhall, R.
ROTHERHAM (C.B.).—J. A. Muir, Secretary, Imperial Buildings, R.
ROWLEY REGIS (U.D.).—D. Wright, Secretary, Old Hill, Staffs.
RUTLAND.—J. C. Kernick, Secretary, Oakham, R.
RYDE (B.), Isle of Wight.—E. Hunt, Clerk, Town Hall, R.
ST. HELENS (C.B.).—J. A. Hartley, Secretary, 17, Cotham Street, St. H.
SALFORD (C.B.).—R. Martin, Secretary, Chapel Street, S.
SALISBURY (B.), Wilts.—G. Harris, 3, Castle Street, S.
SCARBOROUGH (B.), N. Riding.—R. Underwood, Secretary, Town Hall, S.
SCILLY ISLES (County).—E. N. V. Moyle, Secretary, Council Offices, St. Mary's, I. of S.
SHEFFIELD.—G. S. Baxter, Secretary, Leopold Street, S.
SHIPLEY (U.D.).—W. Popplestone, Secretary and Director of Education, Saltaire Road, S.
SHREWSBURY (B.), Salop.—R. F. Prideaux, Clerk, on military service.—A. Evans, Acting Clerk, the Guildhall, S.
SHROPSHIRE.—E. Crowte, Clerk, County Buildings, Shrewsbury.
SMETHWICK (C.B.).—A. H. Sears, Secretary, Council House, S.
SOKE OF PETERBOROUGH.—W. J. Deacon, Clerk, Cross Street, Peterborough.
SOMERSET.—C. H. Bothamley, M.Sc., F.I.C., County Education Office, Weston-super-Mare.
SOUTHAMPTON (C.B.).—T. Williams, Secretary, St. Mary Road, S.
SOUTHEND-ON-SEA (C.B.).—J. W. Barrow, Secretary, 11, Nelson Street, S.-on-S.
SOUTHPORT (C.B.).—F. W. Teague, Secretary, 2, Church Street, S.
SOUTH SHIELDS (C.B.).—V. C. Carter, Secretary, Municipal Buildings, S. S.
STAFFORDSHIRE.—G. Balfour, Director of Education, Stafford.
STALYBRIDGE (B.), Cheshire.—J. W. Simister, Secretary, Portland Chambers, S.
STOCKPORT (C.B.).—A. Lawton, M.A., Secretary, Town Hall, S.
STOCKTON-ON-TEES (B.), Durham.—J. Tweedy, Secretary, 32, Dovecot Street, S.-on-T.
STOKE-ON-TRENT (C.B.).—Dr. W. L. Freeman, Director of Education, Town Hall, Hanley.

STONE* (U.D.), Staffs.—C. H. Matthews, Secretary, Westbridge House, S.

STRETFORD (U.D.), Lancs.—G. H. Abrahams, Solicitor, Clerk, Council Offices, Talbot Road, Old Trafford.

SUFFOLK, EAST.—W. E. Watkins, Secretary, County Hall, Ipswich.

SUFFOLK, WEST.—F. R. Hughes, Secretary, Shire Hall, Bury St. Edmunds.

SUNDERLAND (C.B.).—H. Reed, Secretary, 15, John Street, S.

SURREY.—W. W. Finny, M.A., Secretary, County Education Offices, Kingston-on-Thames.

SUSSEX, EAST.—E. Young, Secretary, County Hall, Fisher Street, Lewes.

SUSSEX, WEST.—L. Thompson, Secretary, Thurloe House, Worthing.

SUTTON COLDFIELD (B.), Warwickshire.—R. A. R. Nadin, Secretary, Council House, Sutton Coldfield.

SWINDON (B), Wilts.—W. Seaton, Secretary, Town Hall, S.

SWINTON AND PENDLEBURY (U.D.), Lancs.—W. T. Postlethwaite, LL.B., O.B.E., Secretary, Council Offices, Swinton, Manchester.

TAUNTON (B.), Somerset.—W. H. Bailey, Town Clerk, Municipal Buildings, T.

TIPTON (U.D.), Staffs.—H. B. Potts, Secretary, Owen Street, T.

TIVERTON (B.), Devonshire.—E. F. C. Clarke, Clerk, 24, Gold Street, T., Devon.

TODMORDEN (B.), W. Riding.—J. Whitehead, Clerk, Roomfield, T.

TORQUAY (B.), W. Riding.—S. H. N. Lane, Secretary, Town Hall, T.

TOTTENHAM (U.D.), Middlesex.—W. Mallinson, Clerk, Philip Lane, S. Tottenham, N. 15.

TRAWDEN* (U.D.), Lancs.—J. Aston, Secretary, Council Offices, T.

TROWBRIDGE* (U.D.), Wilts.—H. Ledbury, F.A.A., Secretary, 51, Fore Street, T.

TUNBRIDGE WELLS (B.), Kent.—W. C. Cripps, Town Clerk, Town Hall, T. W.

TURTON* (U.D.), Lancs.—J. B. Goulburn, Secretary, Council Offices, Bromley Cross, near Bolton.

TWICKENHAM (U.D.), Middlesex.—H. J. Saunders, F.C.I.S., Clerk, Town Hall, T.

TYNEMOUTH (C.B.), Northumberland.—S. Oldroyd, Secretary, 26, Northumberland Square, North Shields.

UTTOXETER* (U.D.), Staffs.—F. F. Hawthorn, Secretary, U.

WAKEFIELD (C.B.), W. Riding.—P. Glover, Secretary, Town Hall, W.

WALLASEY (C.B.), Cheshire.—T. Samuel, Director of Education, Central Park, Liscard, W.

WALLSEND (B.), Northumberland.—M. W. Graham, Secretary, Town Hall, W.-on-T.

WALSALL (C.B.).—W. Scarlett, Acting Secretary, Council House, W.

WALTHAMSTOW (U.D.), Essex.—T. W. Liddiard, Secretary, High Street, W., E 17.

WARRINGTON (C.B.).—J. M. Murray, M.Sc., Secretary and Director, Sankey Street, W.

WARWICKSHIRE.—B. King, M.A., Director of Education, 22, Northgate Street, Warwick.

WATERLOO WITH SEAFORTH (U.D.), Lancs.—T. Baleson, M.A., Director of Education, Town Hall, W.

WEDNESBURY (B.), Staffs.—E. F. Knowles, Secretary, Walsall Street, W.

WEST BROMWICH (C.B.).—J. E. Pickles, M.A., B.Sc., Director of Education, High Street, W. B.

WEST HAM (C.B.).—G. E. Hilliary, Town Clerk, The Grove, Stratford, E. 15.

WEST HARTLEPOOL (C.B.).—J. G. Taylor, Secretary, Park Road, W. H.

WESTMORLAND.—C. J. R. Tipper, B.Sc., Director, Lowther House, Kendal.

WEST RIDING.—(See Yorkshire.)

WEST SUFFOLK.—(See Suffolk.)

WEST SUSSEX.—(See Sussex.)

WEYMOUTH (B.), Dorset.—G. P. Symes, M.V.O., B.C.L. (Oxon), Secretary, 9 and 10, East Street, W.

WHITEHAVEN (B.), Cumberland.—W. D. P. Field, A.C.I.S., Secretary, Town Hall, W.

WIDNES (B.), Lancs.—H. S. Oppenheim, J.P., Town Clerk, Town Hall, W.

WIGAN (C.B.).—G. H. Mockler, Director of Education, Borough Court and Offices, King Street, W.

WIGHT (ISLE OF).—(See Isle of Wight.)

WILLENHALL* (U.D.), Staffs.—L. Meek, Solicitor, Secretary, 33, Market Place, W.

WILLESDEN (U.D.), Middlesex.—F. Jobbins, Secretary, Municipal Offices, Dyne Road, Kilburn, N.W.

WILTSHIRE.—W. Pullinger, M.A. (Oxon), Director of Education, County Offices, Trowbridge.

WIMBLEDON (B.), Surrey.—A. S. Sheidon, Clerk, 58, Pelham Road, W., S.W. 19.

WINCHESTER (B.), Hants.—T. Holt, Clerk, Guildhall, W.

WINDSOR.—(See New Windsor.)

WOLSTANTON UNITED (U.D.) Staffs.—E. Hollinshead, Secretary, Town Hall, Chambers, W. U.

WOLVERHAMPTON (C.B.).—B. H. Preston, Secretary, Town Hall, W.

WOOD GREEN (U.D.), Middlesex.—J. Rushforth, Secretary, Town Hall, W. G., N. 22.

WORCESTER (C.B.).—The Town Clerk, Clerk to Education Committee.— T. Duckworth, Clerk to Higher Education Sub-Committee, Victoria Institute, W.—F. T. Spackman, Clerk to Elementary Education Sub-Committee, Hound's Lane, W.

WORCESTERSHIRE.—A. W. Priestley, M.A., B.C.L., Director of Education, 37, Foregate Street, Worcester.

WORKINGTON (B.), Cumberland.—E. J. Hepworth, Secretary, W.

WORTHING (B.), W. Sussex.—J. K. Allerton, Town Clerk, Municipal Offices, W.

YARMOUTH (C.B.).—F. W. Wroughton, Clerk, 28, South Quay, G. Y.

YEOVIL (B.), Somerset.—H. C. C. Batten, Secretary (on active service). —R. L. Hiscott, Acting Secretary, Town Clerk's Office, Y.

YORK (C.B.).—J. H. Mason, Secretary, Clifford Street, Y.

YORKSHIRE, E. Riding.—J. Bickersteth, Clerk, County Hall, Beverley.

YORKSHIRE, N. Riding.—J. C. Wrigley, Secretary, County Hall, Northallerton.

YORKSHIRE, W. Riding.—W. V. Dixon, Clerk, County Hall, Wakefield.

WALES.

ABERDARE (U.D.), Glam.—T. Botting, B.A., B.Sc., Director of Education, 42, High Street, A.

ABERTILLERY (U.D.), Mon.—A. Llewellyn, Secretary, 1, King Street, A.

ANGLESEY.—R. H. Williams, Secretary, Llangefni, A.

BARRY (U.D.), Glam.—T. B. Tordoff, Clerk, Council Offices, Holton Road, B., Glam.

BRECKNOCKSHIRE.—A. Leonard, Secretary, County Hall, Brecon.

CARDIFF (C.B.).—J. J. Jackson, B.A., Director of Education, Education Offices, City Hall, C.

CARDIGANSHIRE.—J. James, M.A., Director of Education, Cambrian Chambers, Aberystwyth.

CARMARTHEN (B.), Carmarthenshire.—T. Walters, 31, Quay Street, C.

CARMARTHENSHIRE.—J. W. Nicholas, Secretary, Carmarthen.

CARNARVONSHIRE.—E. R. Davies, Secretary, Old Bank, Carnarvon.

DENBIGHSHIRE.—J. C. Davies, M.A., Director, Market Street, Ruthin.

EBBW VALE (U.D.), Mon.—T. Hughes, Secretary, District Council Offices, E.V.

FLINTSHIRE.—J. B. Evans, M.A., Director of Education, County Offices, Mold.

GLAMORGANSHIRE.—J. James, Ph.D., Education Official, County Hall, Cardiff.

LLANELLY (B.), Carmarthenshire.—I. W. Watkins, Coleshill Terrace, L.

MERIONETHSHIRE.—R. Barnett, Secretary, Towyn.

MERTHYR TYDFIL (C.B.).—R. Elias, M.A. (Cantab), Director of Education.

MONMOUTHSHIRE.—C. Dauncey, Secretary, County Council Offices, Newport, Mon.

MONTGOMERYSHIRE.—L. Phillips, Clerk, County Offices, Plasyndre, Newtown, North Wales.

MOUNTAIN ASH (U.D.), Glam.—A. Morgan, Director of Education, Town Hall, M.A.

NEATH (B.), Glam.—A. J. Evans, 38, Queen Street, N.

NEWPORT (C.B.).—T. A. Eaves, Secretary for Elementary Education, Charles Street, N.—G. W. Moores, Secretary for Secondary Education, Technical Institute, Clarence Place, N.

PEMBROKE (B.).—R. D. Lowless, Secretary, P.

PEMBROKESHIRE.— H. E. H. James, Director of Education, 8, Victoria Place, Haverfordwest.

PONTYPRIDD (U.D.), Glam.—D. M. Jones, Secretary, P.

RADNORSHIRE.—H. V. Vaughan, Clerk, County Offices, Llandrindod Wells.

RHONDDA (U.D.), Glam.—T. W. Berry, Director of Education, Pentre, R.

SWANSEA (C.B.).—T. J. Rees, B.A., Director of Education, Grove Place, S.

WREXHAM (B.), Denbigh.—L. Taylor, Clerk, Guildhall, W.

SCOTLAND.

SCOTCH EDUCATION DEPARTMENT.

SECRETARY.—Sir John Struthers, K.C.B., LL.D. London : Dover Street, Whitehall, S.W. Edinburgh : 14, Queen Street.

THE SCHOOL BOARDS.

THE CLERK AND THE SCHOOL BOARD OFFICES.

ABBEY ST. BATHANS, Berwick.—L. A. W. Tulloch, Abbey St. Bathans, Grantshouse.

ABDIE, Fife.—J. M. Kinlay, Parish Council Office, Newburgh.

ABERCORN, Linlithgow.—R. Amos, Galascrook, Philpstoun, West Lothian.

ABERDALGIE, Perth.—Condi, Mackenzie, and Co., W.S., Perth.

ABERDEEN BURGH.—T. Hector, 22, Union Terrace, A.

ABERDOUR, Aberdeen.—J. P. Smith, New Aberdour, A.

ABERDOUR, Fife.—J. Russell, S.S.C., 95, Hanover Street, Edinburgh.

ABERFOYLE, Perth.—J. Dunlop, LL.B., 109, Bath Street, Glasgow.

ABERLADY, Haddington.—Interim Clerk, Rev. I. M. Murray, U.F. Manse.

ABERLEMNO, Forfar.—J. S. Gordon, The Cross, Forfar.

ABERLOUR, Banff.—Messrs. Kemp and Auchinachie, A.

ABERNETHY, Perth.—J. M'Kinlay, Parish Council Office, Newburgh, Fife.

ABERNETHY AND KINCARDINE, Inverness.—J. Grant, Royal Bank, Grantoun-on-Spey.

ABERNYTE, Perth.—Rev. W. L. Milroy, Abernyte Manse, Inchture.

ABOYNE AND GLENTANAR, Aberdeen.—C. C. Smith, A.

ACHARACLE, Argyll.—A. D. Gillies, Ranachan, Strontian, Argyll.

AIRDRIE BURGH, Lanark.—B. Motherwell and W. R. Mitchell, B.A., B.L., Royal Bank Buildings, No. 10, Bank Street, A.

AIRLIE, Forfar.—J. Davidson, Kirriemuir.

AIRTH, Stirling.—W. Simpson, Solicitor and U.P. Office, Charing Cross, Grangemouth.

ALFORD, Aberdeen.—C. P. Moir, Fernbank, A., N.B.

ALLOA BURGH, Clackmannan.—A. L. Roxburgh, British Linen Bank Buildings, A.

ALLOA (Landward), Clackmannan.—J. W. Moir, 18, Bank Street, A.

ALLOWAY, Ayr.—A. J. Gray, 29, Northpark Avenue, Ayr.

ALNESS, Ross.—F. W. Macdonald, A.

ALVA, Clackmannan.—J. Reed, A.

ALVAH, Banff.—J. MacWilliam, Blythstane, A., Banff.

ALVES, Elgin.—C. G. Mackenzie, National Bank Buildings, Forres.

ALVIE, Inverness.—J. MacBean, Alvie Parish Office, Kincraig.

ALYTH, Perth.—D. S. Kidd, Solicitor and Notary, A.

AMULREE, Perth.—J. Fergusson, Bank of Scotland, Pitlochrie.

ANCRUM, Roxburgh.—T. Kennedy, A.

ANNAN, Dumfries.—J. Roddick, Commercial Bank Buildings, A.

ANSTRUTHER, EAST AND WEST, Fife.—A. C. Mackintosh, National Bank Buildings, A.

APPLECROSS, Ross.—D. Mackenzie, Torridon, Ross-shire.

APPLEGARTH AND SIBBALDBIE, Dumfries.—D. Cormach, W.S., Royal Bank Buildings, Lockerbie.

ARBIRLOT, Forfar.—W. K. Macdonald, Town Clerk, Arbroath.

ARBROATH BURGH, Forfar.—W. H. Alexander, 62, High Street, A.

ARBROATH AND ST. VIGEANS (Landward), Forfar.—N. McBain, 15, Hill Street, A.

ARBUTHNOT, Kincardine.—J. Andrew, Bervie, Kincardineshire.

ARDALLIE, Aberdeen.—F. Gellie, Ellon.

ARDCHATTAN AND MUCKAIRN, Argyll.—Rev. C. D. MacIntosh, M.A., Connell, Argyll.

ARDCLACH, Nairn.—W. Murdoch, 39, High Street, Nairn.

ARDERSIER, Inverness.—H. T. Donaldson, British Linen Bank Buildings, Nairn.

ARDGOUR, Argyle.—J. G. Ewen-Watson, Estate Office, Fort William, Inverness-shire.

ARDNAMURCHAN, Argyll.—A. D. McKenzie, Swordle, A.

ARDOCH, Perth.—W. M. Jeffray, Auchterarder.

ARDROSSAN, Ayr.—K. Wood, jun., Burgh Chambers, A.

ARISAIG AND MOIDART, Inverness.—A. Gibson, A., Inverness-shire.

ARNGASK, Perth.—A. A. Hutton, St. Ronans, Glenfarg.

ARROCHAR, Dumbarton.—-C. Henderson, Leighness, A.

ASHKIRK, Selkirk.—M. McCall, British Linen Bank, Hawick.

ASSYNT, Sutherland.—J. Gordon, Lochinver, Lairg.

ATHELSTANEFORD, Haddington.—A. Hendrie, Court Street, Haddington.

AUCHINDOIR, Aberdeen.—J. Paterson, Brawland-by-Rhynie.

AUCHINLEEK, Ayr.—J. Thomson, Main Street, A.

AUCHTERARDER, Perth.—T. E. Young, W.S., Union Bank Buildings, A.

AUCHTERDERRAN, Fife.—R. Small, Town House, Lochgelly.

AUCHTERGAVEN, Perth.—T. Young, Bankfoot.

AUCHTERHOUSE, Forfar.—A. Jamieson, Pitnappie, Newtyle.

AUCHTERLESS, Aberdeen.—-J. Stephen, Templand Cottage, A., Aberdeenshire.

AUCHTERMUCHTY, Fife.—W. Oliphant, Bank of Scotland, A.

AUCHTERTOOL, Fife.—M. Nicol, Kirk Wynd, Kirkcaldy.

AULDEARN, Nairn.—A. Blackhall, Royal Bank, Nairn.

AVOCH, Ross.—G. M. Cameron, A.

AVONDALE, Lanark.—J. Barrie, Kirk Street, Strathavon.

AYR BURGH.—J. H. Goudie, 70, Wellington Chambers, A.

AYR (Landward).—-A. J. Gray, 29, Northpark Avenue, A.

AYTON, Berwick.—G. M. Geddes, A., Berwickshire.

BALDERNOCK, Stirling.—W. Galloway, Rosslyn, Balmore-Torrance, Glasgow.

BALFRON, Stirling.—J. Henry, Clachan House, B.

BALLANTRAE, Ayr.—J. R. G. Phillips, School Board Offices, B.

BALLINGRY, Fife.—W. Wilson, Crosshill, Glencraig, Fife.

BALMACLELLAN, Kirkcudbright.—-P. Gifford, 188, King Street, Castle Douglas.

BALMAGHNE, Kirkcudbright.—J. Dunn, 63, King Street, Castle Douglas.

BALMERINO, Fife.—W. Scott, Gauldry, Wormit.

BALQUHIDDER, Perth.—D. McLaren, 55, Main Street, Callander.

BANCHORY-DEVENICK, Kincardine.—W. Littlejohn, 222, Union Street, Aberdeen.

BANCHORY TERNAN, Kincardine.—J. Merson, High Street, B.

BANFF.—J. A. Badenoch, F.S.A.A., 27, High Street, Banff.

BARGRENNAN, Kirkcudbrightshire.—D. W. Nicholson, 64, Victoria Street, Newton Stewart.

BARR, Ayr.—J. Laing, Bridgend, B., Girvan.

BARRA, Inverness.—A. McElfish, Procurator Fiscal's Office, Lochmaddy.

BARRY, Forfar.—D. Kidd, Rowan Cottage, Carnoustie.

BARVAS, Ross.—W. J. Clarke, County Buildings, Stornoway, N.B.

BATHGATE BURGH, Linlithgow.—W. Cæsar, Bloomfield House, B.

BATHGATE (Landward), Linlithgow.—W. Cæsar, Bloomfield House, B.

BEATH, Fife.—P. M. Connell, Guildhall Chambers, Dunfermline.

BEDRULE, Roxburgh.—Rev. J. Stevenson, M.A., Bedrule Manse, Jedburgh.

BEITH, Ayr.—A. Smith, B.

BELHELVIE, Aberdeen.—R. Rae, Balmedie, Aberdeen.

BELLIE, Fochabers, Morayshire.—C. and T. C. Gray, Bank House, Fochabers.

BENDOCHY, Perth.—J. B. Miller, Blairgowrie.

BENHOLM, Kincardine.—W. Low, Seaview Terrace, Johnshaven, Montrose.

BERVIE, Kincardine.—J. Andrew, King Street, B.

BIGGAR, Lanark.—J. Herriot, National Bank, B.

BIRNIE, Elgin.—A. F. Macdonald, 54, High Street, Elgin.

BIRSAY AND HARRAY, Orkney.—D. Marwick, Wideford, Kirkwall.

BIRSE, Aberdeen.—W. Wright, Birse, Aboyne, Aberdeenshire.

BLACKFORD, Perth.—J. Lawson, B.

BLAIR ATHOLL.—G. Forrest, School Board Office, B. A.

BLAIRGOWRIE AND RATTRAY, Perth.—R. R. Black, Bank Street, B.

BLAIRINGONE, Kinross.—J. Bleloch, Wellhall, Dollar, Clackmannan.

BLANTYRE, Lanark.—J. Brown, Parish Council Chambers, High Blantyre.

BOHARM, Banff.—Messrs. Thurburn and Fleming, 163, Mid Street, Keith.

BOLESKINE AND ABERTARFF, Inverness.—W. W. Jack, Bank of Scotland, Fort Augustus.

BOLTON, Haddington.—Rev. J. Barr, Service, Bolton Manse, Haddington.

BONHILL, Dumbarton.—J. Brown, Alexandria.

BORGUE, Kirkcudbright.—W. W. Morrison, County Buildings, Kirkcudbright.

BORROWSTOUNNESS, Linlithgow.—J. C. Liddle, Bank of Scotland Buildings, Bo'ness, West Lothian.

BORTHWICK, Edinburgh.—W. Y. Johnstone, Gorebridge.

BOTHWELL, Lanark.—R. Kerr, 50, Cadzow Street, Hamilton.

BOTRIPHNIE, Banff.—Messrs. Thurburn and Fleming, 163, Mid Street, Keith.

BOURTIE, Aberdeen.—W. Moir, Shadowside, Inverurie.

BOWDEN, Roxburgh.—J. A. Porteous, British Linen Bank, Newtown, St. Boswells.

BOWER, Caithness.—J. G. Baikie, Gillock of Bower.

BOYNDIE, Banff.—A. Still, Birchwood Cottage, Boyndie.

BRACADALE, Inverness.—J. Mackenzie, Dunvegan, Isle of Skye.

BRECHIN BURGH, Forfar.—J. S. Kinghorn, LL.B., 16, St. David Street, B.

BRECHIN (Landward), Forfar.—A. Philip, 5, Swan Street, B.

BRESSAY, Shetland.—R. D. Ganson, Brentham Place, Lerwick.

BROUGHTY FERRY, Forfar.—E. Cowan, Royal Bank Buildings, High Street, Dundee.

BRYDEKIRK, Dumfries.—W. Cruickshank, Royal Bank Chambers, Annan.

BUCHANAN, Stirling.—W. Macpherson, Blairnurich, Drymen, Glasgow.

BUITTLE, Kirkcudbright.—J. E. Milligan, Clydesdale Bank, Dalbeattie.

BUNKLE AND PRESTON.—N. J. Leitch, B.

BURNTISLAND, Fife.—R. Brown, 41, High Street, Burntisland.

CABRACH, Banff.—J. L. Craig, 27, Fife Street, Dufftown.

CADDER, Lanark.—J. Hurll, B.L., 75, St. George's Place, Glasgow.

CADDONFOOT, Selkirk.—D. G. Stalker, British Linen Bank, Galashiels.

CAERLAVEROCK, Dumfries.—Rev. T. D. McIlvean, The Manse, Caerlaverock, Dumfriesshire.

CAIRNIE, Aberdeen.—J. Stuart, Huntly.

CALDERHEAD, Lanark.—J. Sneddon, C.A., Herald Buildings, Brandon Street, Hamilton.

CALLANDER, Perth.—D. McLaren, 55, Main Street, C.

CAMBUSLANG, Lanark.—R. Duncan, 116, Main Street, C.

CAMBUSNETHAN, Lanark.—T. Smith and R. Ingram, Commercial Bank, Wishaw.

CAMERON, Fife.—W. Morton, Bonnytown, Strayithie, R.S.O.

CAMPELTOWN, Argyll.—M. Dick, C.

CAMPSIE, Stirling.—J. H. Wyllie, 105, West George Street, Glasgow.

CANISBAY, Caithness.—D. Keith-Murray, B.L., Thurso.

CANONBIE, Dumfries.—G. Irving Bell, Linen Bank Buildings, Langholm.

CAPUTH, Perth.—R. Hunter, Tay Farm, Meikleour.

CARDROSS, Dumbarton.—D. Shaw, Station Place, Renton, Dumbartonshire.

CARESTON, Forfar.—Messrs. J. and D. G. Shiell, 16, St. David Street, Brechin.

CARGILL, Perth.—W. Duncan, Post Office, Burrelton, Perthshire.

CARLUKE, Lanark.—J. Barr, British Linen Bank, C.

CARMICHAEL, Lanark.—G. H. Harrison, Carstairs, Lanark.

CARMUNNOCK, Lanark.—W. Fleming, Windlaw, C.

CARMYLLIE, Forfar.—J. Mackintosh, 107, High Street, Arbroath.

CARNBEE, Fife.—C. H. Maxwell, Town Clerk's Office, Anstruther.

CARNOCH, Ross.—W. Mackenzie, County Buildings, Dingwall.

CARNOCK, Fife.—W. Bald, 126, Dewar Street, Dunfermline.

CARNWATH, Lanark.—T. Smith, C.

CARRINGTON, Edinburgh.—Rev. W. E. Grimwood, C., Gorebridge.

CARSPHAIRN, Kirkcudbright.—C. E. Stewart, Carsphairn, Dalry, Kirkcudbrightshire.

CARSTAIRS, Lanark.—G. H. Harrison, C., Lanark.

CASTLETON, Roxburgh.—J. Barrie, 3, Oliver Place, Hawick.

CATHCART, Renfrew.—G. J. Cameron, 104, West Regent Street, Glasgow.

CAVERS, Roxburgh.—J. Conn, Royal Bank Buildings, Hawick.

CAWDOR, Nairn.—R. M. Lockie, Nairn.

CERES, Fife.—J. Pearson, C.

CHANNELKIRK, Berwick.—H. M. Liddell, Avon House, Oxton, Berwickshire.

CHAPEL OF GARIOCH, Aberdeen.—J. Diack, jun., East Balholgardy, Inverurie.

CHIRNSIDE, Berwick.—D. Denholm, C.
CLACKMANNAN, Clackmannan.—A. P. Moir, 22, Bank Street, Alloa.
CLARKSTON, Lanark.—G. B. Motherwell, jun., 4, East High Street, Airdrie.
CLATT, Aberdeen.—G. Spence, Kirkton, C.
CLEISH, Kinross.—R. Shorthouse, Kelty Bridge, Blairadam, Kinross.
CLOSEBURN, Dumfries.—D. Paterson, Solicitor, Thornhill, Dumfriesshire.
CLUNIE, Perth.—R. R. Black, Bank Street, Blairgowrie.
CLUNY, Aberdeen.—J. Smith, Bristow, Sanchen, Aberdeen.
CLYNE, Sutherland.—Rev. J. Spark, M.A., Clyne School Board, Brora, N.B.
COCKBURNSPATH, Berwick.—J. Wight, Ecclaw, C.
COCKPEN, Edinburgh.—D. D. Tod, Bonnyrigg, Midlothian.
COLDINGHAM, Berwick.—T. P. Doughty, Ayton, Berwickshire.
COLDSTREAM, Berwick.—A. M. Porteous, 5, Tweed Terrace, C.
COLINTON, Edinburgh.—M. W. Scott, C., Midlothian.
COLL, Argyll.—D. S. Fotheringham, Arinagour, C., Oban.
COLLACE, Perth.—J. Campbell, 5, St. John Street, Perth.
COLLESSIE, Fife.—J. L. Anderson, Town Clerk, Gupar.
COLOMONELL, Ayr.—G. Rowan, Barrhill, Ayrshire.
COLONSAY AND ORONSAY, Argyll.—A. McNeill, Colonsay-by-Greenock.
COLVEND, Kirkcudbright.—J. M. Austin, High Street, Dalbeattie.
COMRIE, Perth.—J. P. Mitchell, B.L., Dunira Street, C.
CONTIN, Ross.—D. Cameron, Strathpeffer, Ross.
CORSOCK, Kirkcudbright.—J. Murdock, Drumwhim, C.
CORSTORPHINE, Edinburgh.—J. E. Cowan, J.P., Bank of Scotland, C., Midlothian.
CORTACHY AND CLOVA, Forfar.—J. Edwards, Bearfauld, C., Kirriemuir.
COUPAR ANGUS, Perth.—R. K. Macintyre, Town Hall, Coupar Angus.
COULL, Aberdeen.—W. Kennedy, Springbank, C., by Aboyne.
COVINGTON AND THANKERTON, Lanark.—J. F. Shirley, Charleston, Lanark.
COYLTON, Ayr.—J. Hay, 2, Barns Street, Ayr.
CRAIG, Forfar.—G. M. Wills, Town Clerk's Offices, Montrose.
CRAIGIE, Ayr.—Miss J. L. R. Campbell, The Manse, Craigie, Kilmarnock.
CRAIGNISH, Argyll.—T. Koy, J.P., F.E.I.S., Ardfern, Argyll.
CRAIL, Fife.—J. Guthrie, Anstruther.
CRAILING, Roxburgh.—C. W. Anderson, 38, High Street, Jedburgh.
CRAMOND, Edinburgh.—C. Waldie, S.S.C., 1, Dean Terrace, Edinburgh.
CRANSHAWS, Berwick.—A. Purdie, C.
CRANSTON, Edinburgh.—T. Hanton, Tyne Ford, Midlothian.
CRATHIE AND BRAEMAR, Aberdeen.—A. M. Shirran, Union Bank, Braemar.
CRAWFORD, Lanark.—E. Kerr, Hawthorn Cottage, Abington, Lanarkshire.
CRAWFORDJOHN, Lanark.—J. A. Renton, C.
CREICH, Fife.—D. C. Clark, Luthrie, Cupar, Fife.
CREICH, Sutherlandshire.—D. Shaw, Bonar Bridge, Ardgay.
CRICHTON, Edinburgh.—A. D. Wallace, Pathhead Ford, Midlothian.
CRIEFF, Perth.—M. Finlayson, C,
CRIMOND, Aberdeen.—D, Morgan, Greenbank, Lonmay.

CROMARTY, Ross.—J. Ross, Commercial Bank Buildings, C.

CROMDALE, Elgin.—D. D. Cameron, 39, The Square, Grantown-on-Spey.

CROSS, BURNESS, AND NORTH RONALDSHAY, Orkney.—J. Baillie, Central School-house, Sanday, Orkney.

CROSSHILL, Ayr.—T. Johnstone, Post Office, C., Ayrshire.

CROSSMICHAEL, Kirkcudbright.—W. Gillespie, Castle Douglas.

CROY AND DALCROSS, Inverness and Nairn.—H. T. Donaldson, British Linen Bank Buildings, Nairn.

CRUDEN, Aberdeen.—C. Middleton, Bank House, Cruden Bay, Port Erroll.

CULLEN, Banff.—W. C. Paterson, 22, The Square, C.

CULROSS, Fife.—A. J. Ross, High Street, Kincardine.

CULSALMOND, Aberdeen.—J. Duguid, St. Sairs, C.

CULTER, Lanark.—J. Walker, The Schoolhouse, Culter, Biggar.

CULTS, Fife.—J. Thoms, Canada Cottage, Ceres, Fife.

CUMBERNAULD, Dumbarton.—R. Short, Bank House, C., Glasgow.

CUMBRAE, Bute.—W. Crawford, 42, Stuart Street, Millport.

CUMLODDEN, Argyll.—J. Lindsay, County Buildings, Inverary.

CUMMERTREES, Dumfries.—Rev. A. Sinclair Nicol, Manse of C., Annan.

CUPAR ANGUS, Perth.—R. K. Macintyre, Town Hall, C. A.

CUPAR DISTRICT, Fife.—J. L. Anderson, Town Clerk's Office, C.

CURRIE, Edinburgh.—W. A. Morrison, Currie, Midlothian.

DAILLY, Ayr.—Miss G. Wilson, D., Ayrshire.

DAIRSIE, Fife.—D. H. Murray, M.A., North Union Street, Cupar, Fife.

DALGETY, Fife.—W. Burt, 30, Queen Anne Street, Dunfermline.

DALKEITH, Edinburgh.—J. C. Sturrock, Municipal Buildings, D.

DALLAS, Elgin.—C. G. Mackenzie, High Street, Forres.

DALMELLINGTON, Ayr.—A. S. Glass, D.

DALMENY, Linlithgow.—G. Sanderson, Mid Terrace House, South Queensferry.

DALRY, Ayr.—P. Comrie, 44, New Street, D.

DALRY, Kirkcudbright.—W. Morrine, Union Bank, D., Galloway.

DALRYMPLE, Ayr.—W. B. Addison, 75, Dalblair Road, Ayr.

DALSERF, Lanark.—J. Anderson, "Dunarle," Netherburn, Lanarkshire.

DALTON, Dumfriesshire.—D. McJerrow, Town Hall, Lockerbie.

DALZIEL, Lanark.—T. M. Young, School Board Office, Motherwell.

DAVIOT, Aberdeen.—W. Baxter, Old Meldrum.

DAVIOT AND DUNLICHTY, Inverness.—J. S. Fraser, Queensgate Chambers, Inverness.

DELTING, Shetland.—C. R. Hughson, Firth, Mossbank, Lerwick.

DENNY, Stirling.—A. Hendry, D.

DESKFORD, Banff.—Miss J. Cruickshank, Berryhillock, D., Cullen.

DINGWALL, Ross.—A. Ross, D.

DIRLETON, Haddington.—A. D. Wallace, 10, East Road, North Berwick.

DOLLAR, Clackmannan.—A. M. J. Graham, 18, Mar Street, Alloa.

DOLPHINTON, Lanark.——. Ash, 14, Young Street, Edinburgh.

DORES, Inverness.—A. Urquhart, Errogie, Stratherrick.

DORNOCH, Sutherland.—A. Innes, D.

DORNOCK, Dumfries.—M. Little, British Linen Bank Buildings, Annan.

DOUGLAS, Lanark.—A. Hutchison, Main Street, D.

DOUGLAS WATER, Lanark.—G. Welsh, Anstruther Place, D. W.

DRAINIE, Elgin.—J. H. Glennie, 56, High Street, Lossiemouth.

DREGHORN, Ayr.—N. Auld, Springside, Kilmarnock.

DRON, Perth.—Messrs. Condie, Mackenzie, and Co., 75, George Street, Perth.

DRUMBLADE, Aberdeen.—G. H. Horn, School Cottage, D., Huntly.

DRUMELZIER, Peebles.— J. McLean, Broughton.

DRUMOAK, Aberdeen.—J. Merson, High Street, Banchory, Kincardine.

DRYFESDALE, Dumfriesshire.—D. McJerrow, Town Hall, Lockerbie.

DRYMEN, Stirling.—T. Peden, D.

DUFFUS, Elgin.—J. S. George, Hopeman, Morayshire.

DUIRINISH, Inverness.—J. Mackenzie, Dunvegan, Isle of Skye.

DULL, Perth.—D. Macdiarmid, F.S.A.A., Bank of Scotland House, Aberfeldy.

DUMBARTON BURGH.—A. Roberts, Municipal Buildings, D.

DUMBARTON (Landward).—G. Boyd, County Buildings, D.

DUMFRIES BURGH.—A. D. Robson, 98, Irish Street, D.

DUMFRIES (Landward).—B. McGowan, 135, Irish Street, D.

DUN, Forfar.—A. Middleton, 93, High Street, Montrose.

DUNBAR BURGH, Haddington.—C. C. Patterson, 105, High Street, D.

DUNBAR (Landward), Haddington.—J. D. Brooke, D.

DUNBARNEY, Perth.—J. Paul, Murray Place, Bridge of Earn, Perth.

DUNBLANE AND LECROPT, Perth.—A. B. Barty, High Street, D.

DUNBOG, Fife.—J. Anderson, Schoolhouse, D., Newburgh.

DUNDEE BURGH, Forfar.—J. E. Williams, D.

DUNDEE (Landward), Forfar.—J. G. Shiell, 5, Bank Street, D.

DUNDONALD, Ayr.—R. Young, Troon.

DUNFERMLINE, Fife.—D. Gorrie, 104, High Street, D.

DUNINO, Fife.—J. Clement, Balkailthey, Stravithie.

DUNIPACE, Stirling.—W. Hendry, 194, Stirling Street, D., Denny.

DUNKELD AND DOWALLY, Perth.—R. McGillewie, Union Bank of Scotland Limited, D.

DUNLOP, Ayr.—J. G. Wyllie, Dunlop.

DUNNETT, Caithness.—W. M. Brims, Royal Bank Buildings, Thurso.

DUNNICHEN, Forfar.—J. Young, Letham, Forfar.

DUNNING, Perth.—W. Henderson, Muirhead, D.

DUNOON AND KILMUN, Argyll.—M. D. Macpherson, 160, Argyll Street, D.

DUNOTTAR, Kincardine.—J. Mitchell, 8, Margaret Street, Stonehaven.

DUNROSSNESS, Shetland.—J. J. Goudie, Braefield, D.

DUNSCORE, Dumfries.—J. E. Laurie, D., Dumfriesshire.

DUNS, Berwick.—T. More, 12, Newtown Street, D.

DUNSYRE, Lanark.—J. Haddow, Dunsyre, Carstairs Junction.

DURISDEER, Dumfries.—R. Wilson, 47, High Street, Sanquhar.

DURNESS, Sutherland.—C. Mackenzie, D., Lairg.

DURRIS, Kincardine.—J. J. Mackenzie, 11, King Street, Aberdeen.

DUTHIL AND ROTHIRMURCHUS, Inverness.—J. Grant, Royal Bank, Grantown-on-Spey.

DYCE, Aberdeen.—H. W. J. Paton, Oakhurst, D.

DYKE, Elgin.—C. G. Mackenzie, High Street, Forres.

EAGLESHAM, Renfrew.—W. Browning, Gilmour Street, E.

EARLSTON, Berwick.—R. A. Dodds, Bank House, E.

EASSIE AND NEVAY, Forfar.—J. Butter, Kirkhill, Meigle.

EAST KILBRIDE, Lanark.—R. Gibson, 104, West Regent Street, Glasgow.

EASTWOOD, Renfrew.—J. C. Brown, 6, Carmen Drive, Shawlands.

ECCLES, Berwick.—A. P. Stevenson, 2, Bridge Street, Kelso.

ECCLESMACHAN, Linlithgow.—J. J. Cochrane, County Buildings, Alloa.

ECHT, Aberdeen.—J. Coutts, The Square, Kintore.
ECKFORD, Roxburgh.—R. Shanks, The Square, Kelso.
EDAY, Orkney.—W. Paterson, Beggshouse, E., Kirkwall.
EDDERTON, Ross.—D. Ross, Oriel Cottage, Edderton.
EDDLESTON, Peebles.—C. Gillespie, Eddlestone Schoolhouse.
EDDRACHILLIS, Sutherland.—Cuthbert Cowie, Scourie.
EDGERSTON, Roxburgh.—S. Hilson, County Buildings, Jedburgh.
EDINBURGH.—J. Stewart, S.S.C., Castle Terrace.
EDINKILLIE, Elgin.—Messrs. C. G. Mackenzie, High Street, Forres.
EDNAM, Roxburgh.—A. Lillie, 66, Woodmarket, Kelso.
EDROM, Berwick.—J. Cameron, E.
EDZELL, Forfar.—T. Adam, Anglis Memorial Hall, E.
ELGIN BURGH.—E. D. Jameson, Bank House, 90, High Street, E.
ELGIN (Landward).—A. F. Macdonald, 54, High Street, E.
ELIE, Fife.—A. M. Cook, Clydesdale Bank Buildings, E.
ELLON, Aberdeen.—A. J. Raeburn, LL.B., 44, Market Street, E.
ENZIL, Banff.—J. Dawson, Gollochymill, Port Gordon.
ERROLL, Perth.—W. Goodall, Union Bank, E.
ERSKINE, Renfrew.—R. and T. Russell, 7, High Street, Paisley.
ESKDALEMUIR, Dumfries.—J. Malcolm, Schoolhouse, E., Langholm.
ETTRICK, Selkirk.—W. Hunter, County Clerk's Office, Selkirk.
EVIE AND RENDALL, Orkney.—D. Marwick, Wideford, Kirkwall, Orkney.
EWES, Dumfries.—R. McGeorge, National Bank Buildings, Langholm.
EYEMOUTH, Berwick.—R. Muir Lang, E.
FALA AND SOUTRA, Edinburgh.—J. Duncan, Magazine House, Ford, Midlothian.
FALKIRK, BURGH.- G. Blane, Garrison Chambers, Vicar Street, F.
FALKIRK (Landward), Stirling.—D. Kennedy, 10, Newmarket Street, F.
FALKLAND, Fife.—A. Anderson, Bank Buildings, F., Fife.
FARNELL, Forfar.—C. M. Denholm, Forebank House, Brechin.
FARR, Sutherland.—A. Argo, Golspie
FEARN, Ross.—S. J. D. Fraser, Ballindram, F.
FENWICK, Ayr.—J. Currie, Post Office, F.
FERN, Forfar.—W. Anderson, 10, St. Mary Street, Brechin.
FERRY-PORT-ON-CRAIG, Fife.—H. T. Baxter, 87, Commercial Street, Dundee.
FETLAR, Shetland.—J. Hughson, Hubie, F.
FETTERCAIRN, Kincardine.—J. Davidson, North of Scotland Bank, Fettercairn.
FETTERESSO AND RICKARTON, Kincardine.—J. B. Cunningham, 28, Cameron Street, Stonehaven.
FINDO GASK, Perth.—W. Henderson, Muirhead, Dunning, Perth.
FINTRAY, Aberdeen.—J. S. Shewan, 143, Union Street, Aberdeen.
FINTRY, Stirling.—G. May, 39, Randolph Road, Stirling.
FIRTH AND STENNESS, Orkney.—W. Sinclair, Finstown, Kirkwall.
FLISK, Fife.—D. M. Dingwall, F., Newburgh, Fife.
FODDERTY, Ross.—C. Fraser, Westpark Cottage, Strathpeffer.
FOGO, Berwick.—J. Duns, Duns.
FORDOUN, Kincardine.—R. L. Crabb, North Bank House, Stonehaven.
FORDYCE, Banff.—W. Ingram, Portsoy, Banff.
FORFAR BURGH.—A. Hay, 16, East High Street, F.
FORFAR (Landward).—T. C. Lowson, 34, Castle Street, F.
FORGAN, Fife.—J. Allison, M.A., LL.B., 61, Reform Street, Dundee.
FORGANDENNY, Perth.—A. C. Campbell, 38, Tay Street, Perth.

FORGLEN, Banff.—A. Kindness, Grange Villa, Turriff.
FORGUE, Aberdeen.—G. Winton, F., Huntly, N.B.
FORRES, Elgin.—C. G. Mackenzie, High Street, F.
FORTEVIOT, Perth.—J. P. Kennaway, Solicitor, Union Bank Buildings, Auchterarder.
FORTINGALL, Perth.—A. Clow, Aberfeldy.
FOSSOWAY AND TULLIBOLE, Kinross.—J. Wilson, Kirkland Place, Kinross.
FOULDEN, Berwick.—J. Shed, Springbank Villa, Ayton, Berwickshire.
FOVERAN, Aberdeen.—G. Lindsay, Newburgh, Aberdeen.
FOWLIS EASTER, Forfar.—G. Colston, Schoolhouse, Fowlis, Invergowrie, Dundee.
FOWLIS WESTER, Perth.—M. Finlayson, Crieff.
FRASERBURG, Aberdeen.—A. Henderson, F.S.A.A., 62, Cross Street, F.
FRIOCKHEIM, Forfar.—A. Oliver, Brothock Bank House, Arbroath.
FYVIE, Aberdeen.—W. Thomson, F.
GAIRLOCH, Ross.—W. B. McRae, Poolewe, Ross.
GALASHIELS BURGH, Selkirk.—D. Craighead, Ladhope Vale, G.
GALASHIELS (Landward), Selkirk.—W. Little, National Bank of Scotland Limited, G.
GALSTON, Ayr.—R. Blair, British Linen Bank, G.
GAMRIE, Banff.—G. S. Riddell, Macduff.
GARGUNNOCK, Stirling.—R. Whyte, 4, King Street, Stirling.
GARTLY, Aberdeen.—W. Grant, Faich Hill, G., N.B.
GARTMORE, Perth.—H. D. McLellan, 48, Barnton Street, Stirling.
GARVALD, Haddington.—J. Boucher, Garvald, Prestonkirk, East Lothian.
GARVOCK, Kincardine.—W. J. C. Reed, Laurencekirk.
GIGHA AND CARA, Argyll.—W. W. Philip, Estates Office, Isle of Gigha.
GIRTHON AND ANWOTH, Kirkcudbright.—R. S. Glover, Bank of Scotland, Gatehouse.
GIRVAN, Ayr.—T. G. Tait, Church Square, G.
GLADSMUIR, Haddington.—W. H. Ferme, Haddington.
GLAMIS, Forfar.—J. A. Fisher, Royal Bank House, G.
GLASGOW, Lanark.—J. Clark, M.A., 129, Bath Street, G.
GLASS, Aberdeen.—J. Dickson, 9, The Square, Huntly.
GLASSARY, Argyll.—A. Dewar, W.S., Lochgilphead.
GLASSERTON, Wigtown.—J. J. Colquhoun, 23, George Street, Whithorn.
GLASSFORD, Lanark.—J. Hunter, 45, Millar Street, G.
GLENARAY, Argyll.—J. Lindsay, Solicitor, Inverary.
GLENBERVIE, Kincardine.—J. B. Connon, Stonehaven.
GLENBUCKAT, Aberdeen.—J. Thomson, The Mains, G.
GLENCAIRN, Dumfries.—D. Corson, Moniaive, Thornhill.
GLENCORSE, Edinburgh.—C. H. Jones, 1, The Square, Penicuik.
GLENDEVON, Perth.—W. N. Russell, Schoolhouse, G., Dollar.
GLENELG, Inverness.—J. Macrae, Knoydart Mallaig.
GLENGAIRN, Aberdeen.—James Low, Station Square, Ballater.
GLENGARRY, Inverness.—D. Macaulay, Bank Buildings, Invergarry.
GLENISLA, Forfar.—D. Graham, Dalvaine, G.
GLENMUICK AND TULLICH, Aberdeen.—J. Simpson, Union Bank, Ballater.
GLENORCHY AND INISHAIL, Argyll.—A. McLaine, Municipal Buildings, Oban.
GLENRINNES, Banff.—J. Innes, The Square, Dufftown.

GLENSHIEL, Ross.—J. Mackintosh, Fernfield, Nostie, Kyle.

GOLSPIE, Sutherland.—D. George, G., Sutherland.

GORDON, Berwick.—R. A. Dodds, Commercial Bank, Earlston.

GOUROCK, Renfrew.—G. Dunlop, B.L., 9, Kempock Street, G.

GOVAN, Lanark.—M. MacLeod, 151, Bath Street, Glasgow.

GRANGE, Banff.—J. Clarke, Croftgibb Grange, Keith.

GRANGEMOUTH, Stirling.—J. Burnett White, B.L. Bank Buildings, G.

GREENLAW, Berwick.—D. Leitch, Greenlaw, Berwickshire.

GREENOCK, Renfrew.—A. F. Niven, Municipal Buildings, Wallace Place, G.

GRETNA, Dumfries.—R. P. McDougall, Town Hall, Annan.

GUTHRIE, Forfar.—G. F. Sellar, Bank Buildings, Friockheim.

HADDINGTON BURGH AND PARISH.—T. W. Todrick, Court Street, H.

HALF MORTON, Dumfries.—D. MacGregor, Estate Office, Springkell, Ecclefechan.

HALKIRK, Caithness.—H. J. Mackay, H.

HAMILTON, Lanark.—R. Kerr, 50, Cadzow Street, H.

HARRIS, Inverness.—J. MacKenzie, Tarbert, H.

HAWICK BURGH, Roxburgh.—W. Hume, Commercial Bank Buildings, H.

HAWICK (Landward), Roxburgh.—J. Barrie, 3, Oliver Place, H.

HERIOT, Edinburgh.—D. M. Ironside, H., Stow.

HOBKIRK, Roxburgh.—T. Cuthbertson, F.E.I.S., H., Hawick.

HODDAM, Dumfries.—J. R. Byers, Solicitor, Royal Bank Buildings, Lockerbie.

HOLM, Orkney.—J. Sinclair, Upper Breckquoy, H.

HOLYWOOD, Dumfries.—A. Dobie, 1, Galloway Street, Maxwelltown, Dumfries.

HOWNAM, Roxburgh.—A. O. Riddell, 40, Bridge Street, Kelso.

HOY AND GRAEMSAY, Orkney.—W. L. Ritch, Windywalls, Graemsay, Stromness, Orkney.

HUMBIE, Haddington.—W. Guthrie, Humbie, East Lothian.

HUME AND STICHILL, Berwick.—J. Cairns, 27, Woodmarket, Kelso.

HUNTLY, Aberdeen.—J. Dickson, 9, The Square, H.

HUTTON, Berwick.—A. P. Hope, Sunwick, Berwick-on-Tweed.

HUTTON AND CORRIE, Dumfries.—J. McClure, The Clydesdale Bank Limited, Lockerbie.

INCH, Wigtown.—A. McC. Parker, 23, Charlotte Street, Stranraer.

INCHINNAN, Renfrew.—A. R. Harper, Town Clerk's Office, Renfrew.

INCHTURE, Perth.—L. Melville, 61, Reform Street, Dundee.

INNERLEITHEN, Peebles.—W. W. Thomson, Bank of Scotland, I.

INNERWICK, Haddington.—P. Purdie, The Schoolhouse, I.

INNERWICK (Glenlyon), Perth.—D. P. Webster, Schoolhouse, I., G., Aberfeldy.

INSCH, Aberdeen.—Rev. J. Irvine, The Rectory, I.

INSH, Inverness.—J. Cameron, I.

INVERARITY, Forfar.—J. S. Gordon, The Cross, Forfar.

INVERARY AND GLENARAY, Argyll.—J. Lindsay, County Buildings, I.

INVERAVON, Banff.—C. J. Macpherson, Solicitor, Dufftown.

INVERCHAOLAIN, Argyll.—T. McNab, Toward Point, Argyllshire.

INVERESK, Edinburgh.—J. Richardson, 183, High Street, Musselburgh.

INVERKEILOR, Forfar.—A. Inglis, I.

INVERKEITHING, Fife.—R. Baxter, 16, High Street, I.

INVERKEITHNY, Banff.—R. Alexander, Ladybank, I., Turriff.

INVERKIP, Renfrew.—G. Dunlop, B.L., 2, Church Place, Greenock.
INVERNESS BURGH.—H. M. Graham, 51, Church Street, I.
INVERNESS (Landward).—J. S. Fraser, Queensgate Chambers, I.
INVERURIE, Aberdeen.—W. M. Cowie, 39, West High Street, I.
IRONGRAY, Kirkcudbright.—R. Adamson, 98, Irish Street, Dumfries.
IRVINE BURGH, Ayr.—W. C. Wilson, 148, High Street, I.
IRVINE (Landward), Ayr.—A. F. McJannet, British Linen Bank, I.
JEDBURGH BURGH, Roxburgh.—D. M. Sturrock, Solicitor, J.
JOHNSTONE, Dumfries.—D. McJerrow, Town Hall, Lockerbie.
JURA, Argyll.—F. W. McGillivray, Craighouse, J., Argyll.
KEIG, Aberdeen.—W. Anderson, West Cividly, K.
KEIR, Dumfries.—J. Young, jun., Waterside Mains, K., Thornhill,
   Dumfries.
KEISS, Caithness.—A. Bruce, County Buildings, Wick.
KEITH, Banff.—Messrs. Thurburn and Fleming, 163, Mid Street, K.
KEITHALL AND KINKELL, Aberdeen.—W. Craig, East Hillhead, Keithall,
   Inverurie.
KELLS, Kirkcudbright.—R. Johnstone, New Galloway.
KELSO, Roxburgh.—T. D. C. Smith, 66, Woodmarket, K.
KELTON, Kircudbright.—R. N. Ramsay, 63, King Street, Castle
   Douglas.
KEMBACK, Fife.—W. S. Birrell, National Bank House, Cupar, Fife.
KEMNAY.—A. Whyte, K.
KENMORE, Perth.—C. J. D. Munro, Union Bank Buildings, Aberfeldy.
KENNETHMONT, Aberdeen.—J. Reid, Beaview, Aberdeen.
KENNOWAY, Fife.—E. G. Greig, Commercial Street, Methil.
KETTINS, Forfar.—R. Watson, Cupar, Angus.
KETTLE, Fife.—A. Angus, King's Kettle, Fife.
KILARROW AND KILMENY, Argyll.—M. Mactaggart, Royal Bank Build-
   ings, Browmore, Islay.
KILBARCHAN AND HOUSTON, Renfrew.—J. M. Porteous, Bank
   Buildings, K.
KILBIRNIE, Ayr.—J. Lusk, National Bank Chambers, New Street, Dalry.
KILBRANDON AND KILCHATTAN, Argyll.—N. Macdougall, School Board
   Office, by Balvicar, Oban.
KILBRIDE, Bute.—J. B. Sweet, Bank of Scotland, Lamlash, Arran.
KILBUCHO, BROUGHTON, AND GLENHOLM, Peebles.—D. Tudhope, 34, St.
   Andrew Square, Edinburgh.
KILCALMONELL, Argyll.—D. Macfarlane, Union Bank, Tarbert,
   Lochfyne.
KILCHOMAN, Argyll.—M. Mactaggart, Royal Bank Buildings, Bowmore,
   Islay.
KILCHRENAN AND DALAVICH, Argyll.—D. Macintyre, K.
KILCONQUHAR, Fife.—J. B. Cowan, Solicitor, Colinsburgh.
KILDALTON, Argyll.—J. Robertson, Royal Bank Buildings, Port-Ellen.
KILDONAN, Sutherland.—A. Argo, Golspie.
KILDRUMMY, Aberdeen.—W. Beattie, Corbanchory, Cushnie, Alford.
KILFINAN, Argyll.—W. Stirling, Royal Bank House, Tigh-na-bruaich.
KILFINICHEN AND KILVICKEON, Argyll.—A. M. McGregor, Bunessan,
   Oban.
KILLEAN AND KILCHENZIE, Argyll.—A. Stewart, 11, Argyll Street,
   Campbeltown.
KILLEARN, Stirling.—J. W. Thomson, Post Office, K., Glasgow.
KILLEARNAN, Ross.—G. Lang, Strathcannon, Muir of Ord.

KILLIN, Perth.—P. Stewart, Fernbank, K.
KILMACOLM, Renfrew.—J. C. Huie, Royal Bank, K.
KILMADOCH, Perth.—J. A. McLean, Doune.
KILMILLIE, Inverness.—J. Watson, Parade House, Fort William.
KILMANY, Fife.—D. M. Rollo, 67, Crossgate, Cupar.
KILMARNOCK BURGH.—J. P. Stevenson, County Buildings, K.
KILMARNOCK (Landward), Ayr.—J. P. Stevenson, County Buildings, K.
KILMARNOCK, Dumbarton.—J. Dunlop, LL.B., 109, Bath Street, Glasgow.
KILMARTIN, Argyll.—A. Dewar, W.S., Lochgilphead.
KILMAURS, Ayr.—D. Carruthers, 13, Duke Street, Kilmarnock.
KILMODAN, Argyll.—M. Clark, Glendaruel, Colintraive.
KILMONAVAIG, Inverness.—G. J. Ewen-Watson, Estate Office, Fort William.
KILMORACK, Inverness.—J. McKenzie, Bank of Scotland, Beauly.
KILMORE AND KILBRIDE, Argyll.—D. MacGregor, Clydesdale Bank Buildings, Oban.
KILMORY, ARRAN, Buteshire.—C. Sym, Machrie Bay, Arran.
KILMUIR, Inverness.—J. Macnab, F.E.I.S., K., Portree, Skye.
KILMUIR EASTER, Ross.—W. J. Caroline, Portleich, Delny.
KILNINIAN AND KILMORE, Argyll.—A. Allan, of Aros, Aros House, Tobermory.
KILNINVER AND KILMELFORD, Argyll.—J. Campbell, Clachan, Seil.
KILRENNY, Fife.—C. H. Maxwell, Town Clerk's Office, Anstruther.
KILSPINDIE, Perth.—Messrs. Condie, Mackenzie, and Co., 75, George Street, Perth.
KILSYTH, Stirling.—J. B. Frew, Burngreen, K.
KILTARLITY, Inverness.—A. C. MacLeod, Beauly, K.
KILTEARN, Ross.—G. S. M. Mackintosh, Castle Street, Dingwall.
KILWINNING, Ayr.—R. C. King and F. W. Paterson, 20, Howgate, K., N.B.
KINCARDINE, Perth.—A. Paterson, 62, Port Street, Stirling.
KINCARDINE, Ross.—M. M. Macleod, Ardgay.
KINCARDINE O'NEIL, Aberdeen.—J. McLaggan, Torphins.
KINCLAVEN, Perth.—J. Cree, Airntully, Stanley.
KINELLAR, Aberdeen.—N. Smith, K., Aberdeen.
KINFAUNS, Perth.—Messrs. Condie, Mackenzie, and Co., 75, George Street, Perth.
KINGARTH, Bute.—J. Mackinnon, 11, Albert Place, Rothesay.
KING EDWARD, Aberdeen.—P. Duncan, Balchers, K. E., by Banff.
KINGHORN, Fife.—J. Drummond, 54, High Street, K.
KINGLASSIE, Fife.—R. Small, Town House, Lochgelly.
KINGOLDRUM, Forfar.—Rev. J. C. Jack, The Manse, K., by Kirriemuir.
KINGSBARNS, Fife.—C. H. Maxwell, Town Clerk's Office, Anstruther.
KINGUSSIE, Inverness.—G. Masson, Bank of Scotland, K.
KININMONTH, Aberdeen.—W. Gall, Middleton Hythie, Mintlaw, N.B.
KINLOCHLUICHART, Ross.—D. Mackenzie, Garve, Ross.
KINLOCH RANNOCH, Perth.—D. Macdiarmid, F.S.A.A., Bank of Scotland, Aberfeldy.
KINLOSS, Elgin.—C. G. Mackenzie, High Street, Forres.
KINNAIRD, Perth.—Messrs. Condie, Mackenzie, and Co., 75, George Street, Perth.
KINNEFF AND CATTERLINE, Kincardine.—A. Watt, Hilton, Stonehaven.
KINNELL, Forfar.—A. Oliver, Brothock Bank House, Arbroath.

KINNETTLES, Forfar.—J. A. Fisher, Royal Bank House, Glamis.
KINNOULL, Perth.—M. Bates, Royal Bank Buildings, Kinnoull Street, Perth.
KINROSS.—W. K. Falconer, K.
KINTAIL, Ross.—J. T. MacRae, Inverinate, Kyle.
KINTORE, Aberdeen.—J. C. Innes, Dyce Villa, Inverurie.
KIPPEN, Stirling.—P. Hay, Claymires, Buchlyvie.
KIRKBEAN, Kirkcudbright.—R. Hunter, K., Dumfries.
KIRKCALDY AND DYSART, Fife.—J. L. Innes, 220, High Street, K.
KIRKCALDY AND DYSART (Landward), Fife.—W. M. Dow and J. Inglis, British Linen Bank Buildings, K.
KIRKCOLM, Wigtown.—J. Reid, K., Stranraer.
KIRKCONNELL, Dumfries.—R. Wilson, 47, High Street, Sanquhar.
KIRKCOWAN, Wigtown.—J. Millar, K.
KIRKCUDBRIGHT.—A. Cavan, K.
KIRKDEN, Forfar.—G. F. Sellar, Bank Buildings, Friockheim.
KIRKGUNZEON, Kirkcudbright.—J. Little, Commercial Bank, Dalbeattie.
KIRKHILL, Inverness.—T. G. Gillespie, Commercial Bank of Scotland Limited, Beauly.
KIRKHOPE, Selkirk.—W. Hunter, 4, Market Place, Selkirk.
KIRKINNER, Wigtown.—J. Christison, Barglass, K.
KIRKINTILLOCH BURGH, Dumbarton.—D. Patrick, Council Chambers, K.
KIRKINTILLOCH (Landward), Dumbarton.—C. R. Motherwell, 76, Cowgate Street, K.
KIRKLISTON, Linlithgow.—T. Hood, Gowanbank, K., West Lothian.
KIRKMABRECK, Kirkcudbrightshire.—D. W. Nicholson, 60, Victoria Street, Newton Stewart.
KIRKMAHOE, Dumfries.—W. Dickson, Meadow Bank, K., Dumfries.
KIRKMAIDEN, Wigtownshire.—P. M. Rodie, Windmill, Logan, Stranraer.
KIRKMICHAEL, Ayr.—J. Andrew, Parish Council Office, K.
KIRKMICHAEL, Banff.—C. M. Ross, Argyle House, Tomintoul.
KIRKMICHAEL, Dumfries.—I. Edgar, 19, Bank Street, Dumfries.
KIRKMICHAEL, Perth.—J. Mackenzie, K.
KIRKNEWTON AND EAST CALDER, Edinburgh.—D. Finlay, Council Chambers, East Calder, Midlothian.
KIRKOSWALD, Ayr.—D. Robertson, Parish Council Office, K., by Maybole.
KIRKPATRICK DURHAM, Kirkcudbright.—F. J. Connolly, 63, King Street, Castle Douglas.
KIRKPATRICK FLEMING, Dumfries.—J. B. Leslie, East Lodge, Mossknow, Ecclefechan.
KIRKPATRICK JUXTA, Dumfries.—W. Tait, Church Place, Moffat.
KIRKURD, Peebles.—J. Runciman, 27, Hope Street, Lanark.
KIRKWALL COMBINED, Orkney.—J. Begg, County Buildings, K.
KIRKWALL (Landward), Orkneys.—J. L. Low, 5, Broad Street, K.
KIRRIEMUIR, Forfarshire.—J. Wilkie, 42, Bank Street, K.
KNOCKANDO, Elgin.—J. W. Mackie, Royal Bank Buildings, Elgin.
KNOCKBAIN, Ross.—D. Stuart, Ord, Muir of Ord.
LADY, Orkney.—W. Muir, Inkerman, Sanday.
LADYKIRK, Berwick.—A. M. Porteous, 5, Tweed Terrace, Coldstream.
LAGGAN, Inverness.—F. McIntosh, L., Kingussie.
LAIRG, Sutherland.—A. Gray, Culmaily, L.
LANARK.—J. F. Shirley, Charteston, L.
LANGHOLM, Dumfries.—R. McGeorge, National Bank Buildings, L.

LANGTON, Berwick.—T. More, 12, Newtown Street, Duns.
LARBERT, Stirling.—J. M. Yellowlees, L.
LARGO, Fife.—H. Percival, St. Hildas, Crescent Road, Lundin Links, L.
LARGOWARD, Fife.—J. B. Cowan, Solicitor, Colinsburgh.
LARGS, Ayr.—R. Wood, 8, Bath Street, L.
LARKHALL, Lanark.—W. Cunningham, Union Bank, L.
LASSWADE, Midlothian.—C. K. Brown, J.P., Eliza Bank, Loanhead, Midlothian.
LATHERON, Caithness.—C. F. and C. Reid, Skail, Lybster, N.B.
LAUDER, Berwick.—G. L. Broomfield, L.
LAURENCEKIRK, Kincardine.—J. G. Devlin, High Street, L.
LEADHILLS, Lanark.—G. Menzies, Townfoot, L.
LEDGERWOOD, Berwick.—R. Martin, L., Earlston.
LEITH BURGH, Edinburgh.—F. J. Trotter, 7, Links Place, L.
LEOCHEL-CUSHNIE, Aberdeen.—J. Dunn, Eninteer, Alford.
LERWICK, Shetland.—R. D. Garson, Brentham, L.
LESLIE, Aberdeen.—J. Anderson, Bogs of Leslie, Insch.
LESLIE, Fife.—W. Taylor, Parish Council Office, L.
LESMAHAGOW, Lanark.—J. N. Gilmore, L.
LESWALT, Wigtown.—T. M. Hunter, Union Bank Buildings, Stranraer.
LETHENDY AND KINLOCH, Perth.—J. Stewart, Union Bank Buildings, Blairgowrie.
LEUCHARS, Fife.—W. S. Birrell, National Bank House, Cupar.
LEVERN, Renfrew.—R. S. Stewart, Barrhead, Glasgow.
LIBBERTON, Lanark.—W. B. Smellie, Schoolhouse, L., by Thankerton.
LIBERTON.—T. J. Cochrane, 2, Abercromby Place, Edinburgh.
LIFF, BENVIE, AND INVERGOWRIE, Forfar.—R. C. Thomson, 11, Reform Street, Dundee.
LILLIESLEAF, Roxburgh.—W. Hume, Royal Bank Buildings, Hawick.
LINLITHGOW.—J. Russell, J.P., 49, High Street, L.
LINTON, Roxburgh.—A. O. Riddell, 40, Bridge Street, Kelso.
LINTRATHEN, Forfar.—G. Milne, Middle Coul, Kirriemuir.
LISMORE AND APPIN, Argyll.—D. Macintyre, Port Appin.
LITTLE DUNKELD.—A. Harris, Gowrie Cottage, L. D.
LIVINGSTONE, Linlithgow.—W. M. Miller, Parish Council Office, Blackburn, Bathgate.
LOCHALSH, Ross.—C. Macrae, 14, Bank Street, Plockton.
LOCHBROOM, Ross.—D. S. Ross, Ullapool.
LOCHCARRON, Ross.—R. T. M. Sinclair, L.
LOCHGELLY, Fife.—R. Small, Town House, L.
LOCHGILPHEAD, Argyll.—A. MacEwan, Union Bank Buildings, L.
LOCHGOILHEAD AND KILMORICH, Argyll.—R. Brown, 174, West George Street, Glasgow.
LOCHLEE, Forfar.—J. Crowe, Parish Council Chambers, Tarfside, Brechin.
LOCHMABEN, Dumfries.—J. B. McNish, Town Clerk, Town Hall, L.
LOCHRUTTON, Kirkcudbright.—Messrs. Craig and Geddes, 8, English Street, Dumfries.
LOCHS, Ross.—W. J. Clarke, County Buildings, Stornoway, N.B.
LOCHWINNOCH, Renfrew.—P. McKinlay, 21, High Street, East L.
LOGIE, Fife.—D. M. Rollo, 67, Crossgate, Cupar.
LOGIE, Stirling.—R. A. Hill, Bridge of Allan.
LOGIEALMOND, Perth.—W. Murray, Chapelhill, by Methven, Perthshire.

LOGIE BUCHAN, Aberdeen.—J. Mark, The Square, Ellon.
LOGIE COLDSTONE, Aberdeen.—A. Farquharson, Loanhead, Dinnet.
LOGIE EASTER, Ross.—M. Macrae, Kildary.
LOGIE PERT, Forfar.—A. Middleton, 93, High Street, Montrose.
LOGIERAIT, Perth.—W. A. MacIntosh, Logierait, Ballinluig.
LONGFORGAN, Perth.—D. M. Boyd, Parish Council Office, L.
LONGFORMACUS.—T. More, 12, Newton Street, Duns.
LONGSIDE, Aberdeen.—G. Davidson, Longside.
LONMAY, Aberdeen.—J. Gregory, Crimonmogate Estates Office, L.
LOTH, Sutherland.—A. McEwen, L., Sutherland.
LOUDOUN, Ayr.—J. Mair, Clydesdale Bank, Newmilns.
LUMPHANAN, Aberdeen.—G. Spark, Faburn, L.
LUNAN, Forfar.—J. A. Lindsay, 186, High Street, Montrose.
LUNDIE, Forfar.—J. Macdonald, Dryburgh, Lochee.
LUSS, Dumbarton.—G. R. Murray, Municipal Buildings, Helensburgh.
LYNE, Peebles.—T. Russell, Board of Trade Buildings, High Street,
  Peebles.
MADERTY, Perth.—M. Finlayson, Crieff.
MAINS AND STRATHMARTINE, Forfar.—W. L. Moncur, 9, Ward Road,
  Dundee.
MAKERSTOUN, Roxburgh.—A. M. Porteous, 5, Tweed Terrace,
  Coldstream.
MANOR, Peebles.—W. Lyon, Bank of Scotland Buildings, Peebles.
MARKINCH, Fife.—G. G. N. Douglas, School Board Office, M.
MARNOCH, Banff.—W. Grant, 33½ Main Street, Abercherder.
MARYCULTER, Kincardine.—J. Gray, 31, Adelphi, Aberdeen.
MARYKIRK, Kincardine.—F. Duncan, Luthermuir, Laurencekirk.
MARYTON, Forfar.—C. M. Denholm, Forebank House, Brechin.
MAUCHLINE, Ayr.—J. D. Macmillan, M.
MAXTON, Roxburgh.—J. A. Porteous, Bank House, Newtown St.
  Boswells.
MAYBOLE, Ayr.—P. Paterson, B.L., 92, High Street, M.
MEARNS, Renfrew.—J. Wright, Newton Mearns, Glasgow.
MEIGLE, Perth.—W. Leslie, jun., The Square, Meigle.
MELDRUM, Aberdeen.—W. Baxter, Old Meldrum.
MELROSE, Roxburgh.—J. A. Smart, Royal Bank Buildings, M.
MENMUIR, Forfar.—A. Philip, 5, Swan Street, Brechin.
MERTOWN, Berwick.—T. Boyd, Bourtree Cottage, Maxton, Newtown
  St. Boswell's, Roxburgh.
METHLICK, Aberdeen.—J. Allan, The Village, M.
METHVEN, Perth.—T. Robertson, M., Perth.
MID-CALDER, Edinburgh.—H. O. I. Curle, M.-C.
MIDDLEBIE, Dumfries.—W. Jardine, Eaglesfield, Ecclefechan.
MIDMAR, Aberdeen.—J. Strachan, Birley, M.
MILLBREX, Aberdeen.—W. Thomson, Fyvie.
MINNIGAFF, Kirkcudbright.—D. W. Nicholson, 64, Victoria Street,
  Newton Stewart.
MINTO, Roxburgh.—A. Haddon, 7, Tower Knowe, Hawick.
MOCHRUM, Wigtown.—J. J. Dunlop, Portwilliam.
MOFFAT, Dumfries.—W. Tait, Church Place, M.
MONEYDIE, Perth.—A. L. Smith, Stanley, Perth.
MONIFIETH, Forfar.—D. Gowans, 25, Ferry Road, M.
MONIKIE, Forfar.—R. Stevens, J.P., 62, Seagate, Dundee.
MONIMAL, Fife.—J. L. Anderson, Town Clerk's Office, Cupar.

MONKTON AND PRESTWICK, Ayr.—H. Boyd, 57, Main Street, Prestwick.
MONQUHITTER, Aberdeen.—P. Cowie, Netherton, Turriff.
MONTROSE BURGH, Forfar.—D. S. Campbell, 93, High Street, M.
MONTROSE (Landward), Forfar.—W. C. Walls, High Street, M.
MONYMUSK, Aberdeen.—R. Grant, Pitfichie Cottage, M.
MONZIEVAIRD AND STROWAN, Perth.—J. Sharpe, M., Crieff.
MOONZIE, Fife.—J. Bethune, Schoolhouse, M., Cupar, Fife.
MORDINGTON, Berwick.—Rev. H. Fleming, M., Berwick-on-Tweed.
MOREBATTLE, Roxburgh.—W. Muir, Broomlands, Kelso.
MORHAM, Haddington.—W. Graham, Schoolhouse, M., nr. Haddington.
MORTLACH, Banff.—C. J Macpherson, Fife Street, Dufftown.
MORTON, Dumfries.—D. Paterson, 1, West Morton Street, Thornhill.
MORVERN, Argyll.—A. McLaine, Municipal Buildings, Oban.
MOULIN, Perth.—H. Mitchell, Pitlochry.
MOUSWALD, Dumfries.—Rev. A. Angus, M., Ruthwell.
MOY AND DALAROSSIE, Inverness.—J. Mackintosh, 17, Queensgate, Inverness.
MUCKART, Perth.—J. Wilson, Kinross.
MUIRAVONSIDE, Stirling.—A. Hunter,'Royal Bank Buildings, Falkirk.
MUIRKIRK, Ayr.—J. Caldwell, Wellwood Street. M.
MURROES, Forfar.—H. A. Forsyth, Murroes Schoolhouse, Dundee.
MUTHILL, Perth.—M. Finlayson, Crieff.
NAIRN BURGH.—H. T. Donaldson, British Linen Bank Buildings, N.
NAIRN (Landward).—A. Robertson, County Buildings, N.
NAVAR AND LETHNOT, Forfar.—W. Paterson, Schoolhouse, Lethnot, Brechin.
NEILSTON, Renfrew.—W. Fife, 56, Main Street, Barrhead.
NENTHORN, Berwick.—W. C. Bradford, The Schoolhouse, N., Kelso.
NESTING, LUNNASTING, WHALSAY, AND SKERRIES, Shetland.—G. G. Irvine, Symbister, Whalsay, Shetland.
NEW ABBEY, Kirkcudbright.—J. Henderson, 123, Irish Street, Dumfries.
NEWBATTLE, Edinburgh.—A. Spark, Crawlee's Cottage, N., Dalkeith.
NEWBURGH, Fife.—G. Lindsay, N.
NEWBURN, Fife.—D. Brown, Largo Place, Largo.
NEW BLYTH, Aberdeen.—G. W. Cowie, Easterbo, Turriff.
NEW CUMNOCK, Ayr.—J. Moodie, N. C.
NEW DEER, Aberdeen.—P. Crighton, Main Street, N. D.
NEWHILLS, Aberdeen.—The Very Rev. Dean Wiseman, Bucksburn, Aberdeen.
NEWLANDS, Peebles.—W. Gordon, 45, High Street, Peebles.
NEW LUCE, Wigtown.—C. Kenmuir, Kenmuir's Hotel, N. L.
NEW MACHAR, Aberdeen.—H. W. J. Paton, 74, Union Street, Aberdeen.
NEW MONKLAND, Lanark.—G. B. Motherwell and W. R. Mitchell, B.A., B.L., 10, Bank Street, Airdrie.
NEW OR EAST KILPATRICK, Dumbarton.—W. Higgins, 21, West Nile Street, Glasgow.
NEW PITSLIGO, Aberdeen.—G. Robertson, 81, High Street, N. P.
NEW SPYNIE, Elgin.—R. B. Gordon, County Buildings, Elgin.
NEWTON.—J. Brownlee, Alpha Cottage, Millerhill, Midlothian.
NEWTYLE, Forfar.—A. E. Gray, Belmont Street, N.
NIGG, Kincardine.—D. M. Walker, 5, Walker Road, Aberdeen.
NIGG, Ross.—S. J. D. Fraser, Ballindrum, Fearn.
NORTH BERWICK, Haddington.—A. D. Wallace, 10, East Road, N.B.
NORTH BUTE, Bute.—J. M. Lamont, 12, Castle Street, Rothesay.

NORTH KNAPDALE, Argyll.—H. McDiarmid, 48, Argyll Street, Lochgilphead.
NORTHMAVINE, Shetland.—C. A. A. Harrison, Swarthoull, N., Shetland.
NORTH UIST, Inverness.—R. F. Matheson, Dunvegan, Isle of Skye.
OATHLAW, Forfar.—A. Hay, 16, East High Street, Forfar.
OBAN BURGH, Argyll.—C. R. Jolly, 26, Alexandra Place, O.
OCHILTREE, Ayr.—R. Hay, School Board Office, O., by Cumnock.
OLD CUMNOCK, Ayr.—A. Brakenridge, Glaisnock Street, C.
OLD DEER, Aberdeen.—A. Clark, Old Deer, Mintlaw Station.
OLDHAMSTOCKS, Haddington.—D. Brown, O., Cockburnspath, Berwick.
OLD LUCE, Wigtown.—J. Cullen, jun., Glenluce.
OLD MACHAR, Aberdeen.—G. T. Duncan, 139, King Street, Aberdeen.
OLD MONKLAND, Lanark.—R. Gray, Municipal Buildings, Coatbridge.
OLD OR WEST KILPATRICK, Dumbarton.—D. Walker, 57, Kilbowie Road, Clydebank.
OLRIG, Caithness.—J. Gunn, Castletown, Thurso.
ORDIQUHILL, Banff.—W. Gray, Mill of Park, Cornhill.
ORMISTON, Haddington.—A. Turnbull, O.
ORPHIR, Orkney.—J. Wishart, Westquoy, O., Kirkwall.
ORWELL, Kinross.—B. Murphie, Minathort.
OXNAM, Roxburgh.—J. D. Little, O., Jedburgh.
OYNE, Aberdeen.—J. Diack, jun., East Balholgardy, Inverurie.
PAISLEY BURGH, Renfrew.—J. Hamilton Pullar, 92, High Street, P.
PAISLEY (Landward), Renfrew.—J. B. Stirling, 28, High Street, Johnstone.
PANBRIDE, Forfar.—D. O. Young, Newington, 7, Philip Street, Carnoustie.
PARTON, Kirkcudbright.—W. Gillespie, Castle Douglas.
PEEBLES.—W. Lyon, Bank of Scotland, P.
PENCAITLAND, Haddington.—P. Cossar, P., Edinburgh.
PENICUIK, Edinburgh.—C. H. Jones, 1, The Square, P.
PENNINGHAME, Wigtown.—D. W. Nicholson, 64, Victoria Street, Newton Stewart.
PENPONT, Dumfries.—J. Alexander, 3, West Morton Street, Thornhill.
PERSIE, Perth.—J. B. Miller, Blairgowrie.
PERTH BURGH.—R. Martin-Bates, 1, Rose Terrace, P.
PETERCULTUR, Aberdeen.—A. Sands, 8, Golden Square, Aberdeen.
PETERHEAD BURGH, Aberdeen.—T. Mackie, Court House Buildings, P.
PETERHEAD (Landward), Aberdeen.—T. Mackie, J.P., F.S.A.A., Court House, P.
PETTINAIN, Lanark.—L. A. Morrison, Murrayfield, Biggar.
PETTY, Inverness.—J. S. Fraser, Queensgate Chambers, Inverness.
PITSLIGO, Aberdeen.—F. C. Grant, Rosehearty, Fraserburgh.
PITTENWEEM, Fife.—A. C. Mackintosh, Town Clerk's Office, P.
POLWARTH, Berwick.—J. Duns, Duns.
PORT GLASGOW BURGH, Renfrew.—J. Hood, Clydesdale Bank Buildings, P.G.
PORTMOAK, Kinross.—W. Curtis, Scotlandwell, Leslie, Fife.
PORT OF MONTEITH, Perth.—P. Hay, Claymires, Bucklyvie, Stirling.
PORTPATRICK, Wigtown.—R. M. McClew, Craigview, P.
PORTREE, Inverness.—G. M. Fraser, National Bank, P.
PREMNAY, Aberdeen.—A. J. M. Troup, Ythan Grove, Insch.
PRESTONKIRK, Haddington.—A. E. Wright, National Bank, P.
PRESTONPANS, Haddington.—R. H. Hunter, P.

RAFFORD, Elgin.—G. C. Mackenzie, High Street, Forres.
RATHEN, Aberdeen.—G. Dawson, Mill Farm, Lonmay.
RATHO, Edinburgh.—J. Anderson, 63, George Street, Edinburgh.
RATHVEN, Banff.—J. Archibald, Bank of Scotland Buildings, Buckie.
RAYNE, Aberdeen.—J. Wight, Durno, Pitcaple.
REAY, Caithness.—Miss A. H. MacLeod, R.
REDGORTON, Perth.—A. L. Smith, Cambridge House, Stanley, Perth.
RENFREW.—A. Wright, Brown Institute, R.
RERRICK, Kirkcudbright.—J. Williamson, M.A., LL.B. County Build-
    ings, Kirkcudbright.
RESCOBIE, Forfar.—J. S. Gordon, The Cross, Forfar.
RESOLIS, Ross.—E. Scott, Newmills Cottage, R.
RHYND, Perth.—Messrs. Condie, Mackenzie, and Co., Perth.
RHYNIE, Aberdeen.—J. Murray, R.
RICCARTON, Ayr.—J. D. Mackintosh, 42, Bank Street, Kilmarnock.
ROBERTON, Roxburgh.—J. Wilson, R., Hawick
ROGART, Sutherland.—A. N. Macaulay, Golspie.
ROSEMARKIE, Ross.—J. Henderson, Town Clerk, Fortrose.
ROSNEATH, Dumbarton.—A. McNeilage, Burnside, Kilcreggan.
ROSSKEEN, Ross.—W. George, High Street, Invergordon.
ROTHES, Elgin.—R. D. Stuart, Seafield Square, R.
ROTHESAY BURGH, Bute.—W. Grant, 20, Castlehill Street, R.
ROTHIEMAY, Banff.—Messrs. Thurburn and Fleming, 163 Mid Street,
    Keith.
ROUSAY AND EGILSHAY, Orkney.—J. G. Craigie, Wasbister, Kirkwall.
ROW, Dumbarton.—A. Kyle, Municipal Buildings, Helensburgh.
ROXBURGH.—R. Shanks, The Square, Kelso.
RUTHERGLEN, Lanark.—Messrs. A. and A. Macallan, 90, Main Street,
    Rutherglen.
RUTHVEN, Forfar.—H. V. Cuthbert, c/o A. M. Ferguson, Alyth, Perth.
RUTHWELL, Dumfries.—J. S. Kerss, Hope Cottage, R.
SADDELL AND SKIPNESS, Argyll.—J. MacKinven,Carradale, Argyll.
ST. ANDREWS AND DEERNESS, Orkney.—W. P. Drever, Albert Street,
    Kirkwall.
ST. ANDREWS BURGH, Fife.—H. Thomson, Town Clerk, 115, South
    Street, St. Andrews.
ST. ANDREWS (Landward), Fife.—C. S. Grace, Royal Bank Buildings,
    St. A.
ST. ANDREWS LHANBRYD, Elgin.—J. W. Mackie, Royal Bank Buildings,
    Elgin.
ST. BOSWELLS, Roxburgh.—J. A. Porteous, British Linen Bank,
    Newtown, St. Boswells.
ST. CYRUS, Kincardine.—J. R. Findlay, Royal Bank Buildings,
    Montrose.
ST. FERGUS, Aberdeen.—W. Nicolson, 1, Jamaica Street, Peterhead.
ST. MADOES, Perth.—W. Goodall, Union Bank, Errol, Perth.
ST. MARTIN'S, Perth.—J. Campbell, 5, St. John Street, Perth.
ST. MONANCE, Fife.—D. Cook, Anstruther.
ST. MUNGO, Dumfries.— J. McClure, Clydesdale Bank, Lockerbie.
ST. NINIANS, Stirling.—J. Dobbie, 3, Port Street, Stirling.
ST. QUIVOX AND NEWTON-ON-AYR (Landward), Ayr.—J. Fergie, Gibbs-
    yard, St. Q., near Ayr.
SALEN, Argyll.—A. Macfarlane, 53, Main Street, Tobermory.
SALINE, Fife.—P. M. Connell, Guildhall Chambers, Dunfermline.

SALTOUN, Haddington.—G. P. Smyth, East Salton, Pencaitland, East Lothian.
SANDSTING AND AITHSTING, Shetland.—W. Slatter, Reawick, Lerwick.
SANDWICK, Orkney.—W. Smith, Newark, S., by Stromness.
SANQUHAR, Dumfries.—R. Wilson, 47, High Street, S.
SAVOCH, Aberdeen.—A. Coburn, Annochie Auchnagatt.
SCONE, Perth.—W. G. McFarlane, Parish Council Office, S.
SCOONIE, Fife.—G. McIntosh, Royal Bank Buildings, Leven, Fife.
SELKIRK BURGH.—W. Hunter, 13, West Port, S.
SELKIRK PARISH.—J. Macaulay, 4, Market Place, S.
SHAPANSEY, Orkney.—W. Robertson, Balfour, Kirkwall.
SHETTLESTON, Lanark.—J. Watson, 24, St. Vincent Place, Glasgow.
SHOTTS, Lanark.—J. Hutton, Commercial Bank, Whitburn, West Lothian.
SKELMORLIE, Ayr.—R. H. Hamilton, Clydesdale Bank, S.
SKENE, Aberdeen.—J. Johnstone, Advocate, 80, Union Street, Aberdeen.
SKIRLING, Peebles.—D. S. Moncrieff, S., Biggar.
SLAINS, Aberdeen.—J. Sangster, Schoolhill Cottage, S., Ellon.
SLAMANNAN, Stirling.—A. J. Christie, 175, St. Vincent Street, Glasgow.
SLEAT, Inverness.—R. Macdonald, National Bank, Portree.
SMAILHOLM, Roxburgh.—J. Brown, S., Kelso.
SMALL ISLES, Inverness.—Miss Campbell, Canna, by Oban, Kildonan, Eigg, Oban.
SNIZORT, Inverness.—G. M. Fraser, National Bank, Portree.
SORBIE, Wigtown.—E. Copland, The Crescent, Garlieston.
SORN, Ayr.—J. Allan, St. Germain Street, Catrine, Ayr.
SOUTHDEAN, Roxburgh.—A. C. Milne, The Orchard, Lanton, Jedburgh.
SOUTHEND, Argyll.—J. Lothian, Argyll Street, Campbeltown.
SOUTH KNAPDALE, Argyll.—J. Lindsay, Solicitor, Ardrishaig, Argyll.
SOUTH RONALDSHAY AND BURRAY, Orkney.—J. Drever, Uppertown, Hoxa, S.R., Orkney.
SOUTH UIST, Inverness.—A. McElfrish, Procurator Fiscal's Office, Lochmaddy.
SPEYMOUTH, Elgin.—W. S. Murdoch, Garmouth, Moray.
SPOTT, Haddington.—R. Waddell, S., Dunbar.
SPRINGFIELD, Fife.—J. Beveridge, Brighton Cottage, Cupar.
SPROUSTON, Roxburgh.—A. O. Riddell, 40, Bridge Street, Kelso.
STAIR, Ayr.—R. Sloan, Keyshill, S.
STENSCHOLL, Inverness.—Rev. C. Mackay, The Manse, S., Skye.
STENTON, Haddington.—W. Buchan, Bielgrange, Prestonkirk.
STEVENSTON, Ayr.—A. Wilson, 55, New Street,-S.
STEWARTON, Ayr.—W. Macrae, Royal Bank, S.
STIRLING BURGH.—J. C. Muirhead, 2, Dumbarton Road, S.
STOBHILL, Edinburgh.—W. Y. Johnstone, Gorebridge.
STOBO, Peebles.—T. S. Glover, The Schoolhouse, S.
STONEHOUSE.—A. Anderson, S.
STONEYKIRK, Wigtown.—J. McCaig, School Board Office, S.
STORNOWAY, Ross.—W. J. Clarke, County Buildings, S.
STOW, Edinburgh.—W. Adam, S.
STRACATHRO, Forfar.—C. Ferrier, Clydesdale Bank Buildings, Brechin.
STRACHAN, Kincardine.—J. Rust, The Belts, S.
STRAITON, Ayr.—J. McFadzean, S., Maybole.
STRALACHLAN AND STRACHUR, Argyll.—M. Morrison, S., Greenock.
STRANRAER, Wigtown.—A. S. Carnochan, Wellington House, Princes Street, S.

STRATH, Inverness.—G. M. Fraser, National Bank, Portree.
STRATHBLANE, Stirling.—J. Henry, Chachan House, Balfron.
STRATHDON, Aberdeen.—G. Todd, Bellabeg, S.
STRATHMIGLO, Fife.—W. Oliphant, Edenside, S.
STRICHEN, Aberdeen.—H. E. Penwill, 30, Bridge Street, S.
STROMNESS, Orkney.—W. McKay, St. Abbs Villa, S.
STRONSAY, Orkney.—R. Mitchell, Whitehall Village, S.
STRONTIAN, Argyll.—G. J. Ewen-Watson, Estate Office, Fort William, Inverness-shire.
SWINTON, Berwick.—A. M. Porteous, 5, Tweed Terrace, Coldstream.
SYMINGTON, Ayr.—D. Carruthers, 13, Duke Street, Kilmarnock.
SYMINGTON, Lanark.—J. L. Spence, S.
TAIN, Ross.—J. Munro, 6, King Street, T.
TANNADICE, Forfar.—A. MacHardy, Town Chamberlain's Office, Forfar.
TARBAT, Ross.—H. Thomson, Portmahomack.
TARBERT, Argyll.—D. Macfarlane, T.
TARBOLTON, Ayr.—A. Guthrie, T.
TARLAND, Aberdeen.—J. Hopkins, T.
TARVES, Aberdeen.—J. Marr, Bracklay, T.
TEALING, Forfar.—W. Bell, Balmirth, T.
TEMPLE, Edinburgh.—J. Low, T., Gorebridge.
TENANDRY, Killiecrankie, Perth.—J. Marshall, T., Killiecrankie.
TERREGLES, Kirkcudbright.—J. Johnstone, Waterside, T., Dumfries.
TEVIOTHEAD, Roxburgh.—R. Purdom, Hawick.
THURSO, Caithness.—J. W. Galloway, jun., T.
TIBBERMORE, Perth.—R. Jack, T., Perth.
TILLICOULTRY, Clackmannan.—T. J. Young, F.C.I.S., Forrester House, T.
TINGWALL, WHITENESS, AND WEISDALE, Shetland.—R. Inkster, Scalloway, Shetland.
TINWALD, Dumfries.—Messrs. Craig and Geddes, 8, English Street, Dumfries.
TIREE, Argyll.—M. McLean, Kirkapol, T.
TONGLAND, Kirkcudbright.—W. Nicholson, jun., Justice of Peace Clerk's Office, Kirkcudbright.
TONGUE, Sutherland.—Rev. D. Lundie, T., Lairg.
TOROSAY, Argyll.—A. McLaine, Municipal Buildings, Oban.
TORPHICHEN, Linlithgow.—L. Lawson, T., Bathgate.
TORRYBURN, Fife.—W. Burt, 30, Queen Anne Street, Dunfermline.
TORTHORWALD, Dumfries.—J. Henderson, Sheriff Clerk's Office, 123, Irish Street, Dumfries.
TOUGH, Aberdeen.— J. Davidson, Whitehouse, Aberdeen.
TOWIE, Aberdeen.—J. Thomson, The Mains, Glenbuchat, Aberdeen.
TRANENT, Haddington.—J. Richardson, Musselburgh.
TRAQUAIR, Peebles.—D. Nicholson, M.A., LL.B., 5, Leithen Crescent, Inverleithen.
TRINITY GASK, Perth.—M. Finlayson, Crieff.
TROQUEER, Kirkcudbright.—A. Dobie, 1, Galloway Street, Maxwelltown, Dumfries.
TROSSACHS, Perth.—P. Buchanan, Commercial Bank, Callander.
TULLIALLAN, Fife.—J. Simpson, Forth View, Kilbagis Street, Kincardine-on-Forth.
TULLYNESSLE AND FORBES, Aberdeen.— J. Lawson, Scotsmill, Alford, N.B.

TUNDERGARTH, Dumfries.—J. McClure, Clydesdale Bank, Lockerbie.
TURRIFF, Aberdeen.—W. F. Stewart, 46, High Street, T.
TWEEDSMUIR, Peebles.—Rev. W. S. Crockett, The Manse, T., Peebles-shire.
TWYNHOLM, Kirkcudbright.—P. Gifford, 188, King Street, Castle Douglas.
TYNRON, Dumfries.—D. Corson, Moniaive, Thornhill.
TYRIE, Aberdeen.—R. Pittendrigh, jun., Newseat, Fraserburgh.
UDNY, Aberdeen.—W. Will, Mains of Pitmedden, U.
UIG, Ross.—W. J. Clarke, County Buildings, Stornoway, N.B.
UNST, Shetland.—H. W. L. Hunter, Ernsdale, Balta Sound, U.
UPHALL, Linlithgow.—R. C. Wilson, Cerinia Place, Broxburn.
URQUHART, Elgin.—J. McIsaac, Royal Bank Buildings, Elgin.
URQUHART AND GLENMORISTON, Inverness.—W. Mackintosh, Drum-nadrochit.
URQUHART AND LOGIE WESTER, Ross.—W. Campbell, Conon Bridge, Ross.
URR, Kirkcudbright.—J. Little, Commercial Bank, Dalbeattie.
URRAY, Ross.—A. Logan, Logie House, Muir of Ord.
WALLS AND FLOTTA, Orkney.—J. M. F. Groat, Northrow, Longhope, Orkney.
WALLS, SANDNESS, PAPA, AND FOULA, Shetland.—J. Georgson, School Board Office, W., Shetland.
WALSTON BY BIGGAR, Lanarkshire.—D. H. Ash, M.A., Walston School-house, Elsrickle, Biggar.
WAMPHRAY, Dumfries.—D. McJerrow, Town Hall, Lockerbie.
WANDELL AND LAMINGTON, Lanark.—W. White, Brookside, Lamington.
WATTEN, Caithness.—W. Alexander, Ruther, W., Caithness.
WEEM, Perth.—J. Fergusson, Bank of Scotland, Pitlochrie.
WEMYSS, Fife.—A. W. Taylor, Wellesley Road, Buckhaven.
WEST CALDER, Edinburgh.—J. T. Mungle, Bank House, W.C.
WESTERKIRK, Dumfries.—R. McGeorge, National Bank Buildings, Langholm.
WEST KILBRIDE, Ayr.—G. McNee, 99, Main Street, W.K.
WEST LINTON, Peebles.—J. Sanderson, W.L.
WESTRAY AND PAPA WESTRAY, Orkney.—G. Seatter, Mount Pleasant, W., Kirkwall.
WESTRUTHER, Berwick.—J. McDougal, Bassendean, Gordon.
WHITBURN, Linlithgow.—D. J. Mitchell, Parish Council Office, W.
WHITEKIRK AND TYNINGHAME, Haddington.—G. Ferguson, Tyninghame, Prestonkirk.
WHITHORN, Wigtown.—J. J. Colquhoun, 23, George Street, W.
WHITSOME, Berwick.—G. Tweedie, Duns.
WHITTINGEHAME, Haddington.—J. Hunter, Schoolhouse, W.
WICK BURGH, Caithness.—D. W. Georgeson, 22, Bridge Street, W.
WICK (Landward).—D. W. Georgeson, 22, Bridge Street, W.
WIGTOWN.—J. Clerk, 9, Agnew Crescent, W.
WISTON AND ROBERTON, Lanark.—A. H. Colthart, Abington, Roberton.
YARROW, Selkirk.—W. Hunter, 13, West Port, Selkirk.
YELL, Shetland.—J. N. Barclay, Mid Yell.
YESTER.—R. McNaughtan, Gifford, Haddington.
YETHOLM, Roxburgh.—A. O. Riddell, 40, Bridge Street, Kelso.
YTHAN WELLS, Aberdeen.—J. Stephen, Templand Cottage, Auchterless, Aberdeen.

TEACHERS REGISTRATION COUNCIL

REPRESENTATIVE OF THE TEACHING PROFESSION

(Constituted by Order in Council February 29th, 1912).

THE Teachers Registration Council, constituted by Order in Council of February 29th, 1912, issued the Conditions of Registration in December, 1913, and has now made definite progress towards the establishment of a Register of Teachers. This Register will be maintained by the Council for the purpose of recording the professional qualifications of those engaged in teaching. The official list of Registered Teachers, which will be issued regularly, will provide a means of ascertaining the names of those whose credentials have been tested and approved by the Council, a body representing every branch of the teaching profession. It is provided that during the first few years admission to the Register may be gained, as a rule, on evidence of satisfactory experience alone, but from the beginning of 1921 onwards the Register will be open only to those who are able to satisfy the Council in regard to their academic and other professional qualifications.

Application Forms and all particulars may be obtained from **The Secretary,**
TEACHERS REGISTRATION COUNCIL,
47, BEDFORD SQUARE, LONDON, W.C. 1.

GENERAL INDEX.

PAGE

Accommodation 68, 69
Administration ...99, 100, 107, 109, 115,
    120, 127, 175, 188, 191, 209, 220,
        234, 250, 337, 349, 435, 443
Administrative Counties.........110, 116, 118
Adolescence 143, 157, 167, 178, 180,
        197, 271, 329, 339, 343, 345, 435
Adult Education 125, 244, 271, 326
Adult Schools 268, 330, 337, 377
Africa, British East 380
Age 72, 77
Agnosticism 27, 44
Agriculture...136, 164, 176, 215, 218, 221,
    224, 225, 226, 230, 231, 233, 237,
        312, 313, 314, 318
Agriculture, Department of 120
America 167–173, 176, 187, 206, 212,
        213, 214, 223, 228, 246, 259, 279
Ambition 162, 258
Anarchists 26
Anatomy 276
Anglican 25, 66, 165, 195, 298
Annuities....................................... 106
Apathy 328, 370, 373
Apparatus 112
Apprentices 177
Aptitude 51
Arabic 229
Architecture 242, 317
Arithmetic..............131, 134, 161, 197, 224
Art 24, 122, 190, 260, 279, 280, 286, 380
Artisan 60, 263
Artists 178, 202, 242, 243
Aspirations.................................... 377
Astronomy 214
Atheists 26
Atmosphere 330, 331, 333, 345
Australia 40, 176, 254, 256, 259, 328,
        335, 336, 353, 440

Baccalaureat 222
Backward Children........................... 90
Backward Races 135
Baptist 165
Barristers 265
Baths 64, 441
Beating 16
Beauty 242
Belgium 175, 212, 234, 235
Bible Lesson 377
Biology 135, 242, 260, 301, 352, 380
Blend 68, 187, 437
Board of Education...132, 212, 253, 269–
    273, 281, 286, 291, 292, 294, 296,
    310, 311, 322, 345, 348, 381, 433,
        440, 441, 443–464
Boarding School 175
Books...157, 183, 195, 205, 208, 109, 227,
    258, 268, 289, 294, 306, 309, 315,
        323, 351, 372, 381
Book-keeping................................... 185
Boroughs and Borough Councillors ...
        110, 112, 116, 118, 268, 464
Botany 214
Brahmans 229

PAGE

Brotherhood 164
Brutality 173
Buddhist 224
Buildings 64, 109, 112, 117–119, 146,
        159, 160, 169, 172, 183, 232, 346
Bursaries (see Scholarships)

Calvinist 26, 30
Camp School 153
Canada...................187, 237, 255, 440
Cape Colony 238
Capital 49, 50, 60, 61, 62, 336, 390
Catholicism 20, 26, 39, 120, 127
Celtic Studies 317
Census of 1911 77
Central Empires.............................. 164
    ,,   Authority...............131, 138, 220
Certificated Teachers 103
    ,,   ,,   in Ireland........ 123
Chamber of Commerce 250
Chapel 64
Character 43, 45, 49, 59, 344, 374
Charity Schools............................... 184
Chemists 42
Chemistry 136, 214, 224, 225, 276
China 212, 233, 226, 227, 228, 250
Chinese Classics 224
Child Labour 370
    ,,   Study 310
Children under 14............................ 349
Children abnormally employed during
        the War 349
Choice of Subject............................. 256
Christians and Christianity...19, 30, 34,
        54, 121, 166
Church ...20, 64, 165, 192, 193, 195, 211,
        212, 220, 236, 278
Citizenship.................146, 179, 200, 375
Civics and Civic Education 28, 62,
    122, 126, 161, 166,170, 176, 221,
        240, 273
Class Consciousness........................ 278
Class Struggle 38, 372, 390
Classics 59, 208
Clay Modelling................................ 145
Clinics 82, 88, 121, 149, 151
Code, School and Christian 73, 162
Co-educational 215
Colonies, The 22
Commerce and Commercial ...49, 128,
    129, 175, 176, 177, 210, 221, 224,
    230, 231, 233, 235, 236, 239, 255,
        286, 302, 311, 312, 317, 318, 333, 337
Competitive Spirit 41
Compulsory Education, etc. 19, 20,
        121, 343, 344, 345
Comradeship 43, 258, 282, 351, 440
Conference 265, 324, 331, 334, 337,
        350, 354, 356, 389
Conscience, Liberty of 28
Conscription 338
Constitution, etc. 260, 263, 375
Consultative Committee to the Board
        of Education 166

R

PAGE

Continuation Schools, etc. 125, 127, 129, 185, 186, 197, 198, 221, 235, 239, 271, 273, 339, 349, 435
Control 55, 60, 61, 238, 245, 249
Controversy 24, 26, 27, 328, 331, 332
Convocation 249, 300, 301, 305, 317, 318
Co-operation 164, 176, 328, 375
Co-operative Movement.........218, 251, 253, 268, 309, 319, 329–331, 334, 341, 374, 375, 388
Co-opted Members 128
Cookery 74, 169
Corporal Punishment 19
Corporate Life 346
Correspondence, Tuition by...371, 375, 389
Council Schools............69, 79, 80, 81, 99
County Boroughs......110, 112, 116, 118, 464
County Councils ....:..110, 112, 132, 464
Cramming 155, 229, 300
Creative Evolution 20, 26, 30
Criminal 179
Culture.51, 53, 59, 166, 227, 248, 260, 301, 325
Curriculum...........................14, 76, 328
Custom....................................... 248

Dairy Work.................................74, 312
Dancing 185, 203, 437
Dangerous 52
Dead-hand 245
Deaf..................................68, 437
Defectives 83, 84
Delinquent 172, 173
Demobilisation 45, 50, 331
Democracy and Democratic .20, 21, 35, 52, 55, 57, 120, 130, 131, 155–158, 164, 170, 175, 185–189, 200, 216, 227, 240, 244, 252, 256, 307, 325, 334, 339, 340, 349, 372, 373
Denmark....................174, 193, 212, 217
Denominational 121, 211, 212, 234, 235, 238, 332
Dental Work 149
Diplomas 256
Discipline......39, 160–162, 179, 223, 277, 293, 329
Discontent 36
Discussions.................................... 237
Dissenters and Dissenting Schools ... 165, 195
Divinity 313, 314, 321
Dogmatic.................................... 156
Domestic Science and Domestics...74, 128, 136, 213, 221, 263, 267, 354, 437
Dramatic Sense................................ 19
Drawing 24, 129, 135, 145, 185, 224, 437
Dressmaking 352
Dumb 437
Duty 371

Ear Strain.................................... 161
Economics... 55, 126, 168, 172–177, 206, 223, 246, 256, 257, 260, 263, 267, 269, 271. 276, 280, 281, 287, 289, 294, 300, 301, 316, 319, 326, 329, 330–333, 337, 345, 350–354, 359, 374, 375, 386, 390, 391, 448
Economy 18, 159, 160, 209
Education Bill No. 2....72, 341, 343–349, 356, 358, 443, 447

PAGE

Educational Committees, Constitution of...... 349
Educational Institutions 348
Egypt.. ....379, 380
Electricity 176, 257
Elementary Schools 64, 67, 68, 76, 107, 109, 131, 134, 157, 159, 162, 164, 180–187, 192, 193, 201, 224, 237, 238, 270, 273, 288, 333, 340, 377, 434, 443
Embroidery 352
Empire Day 164
Employers 346, 390
Employment, Juvenile.. ... 72, 92, 343, 435
Endowments 80, 99, 111, 120, 122, 183, 184, 189, 190–195, 239, 245, 246, 251, 290, 310, 348, 370
Endowed School Commissioners 196
Engineering...... 214, 225, 229, 231, 267, 288, 289, 300, 308, 311–313, 317, 318, 337
English (see Literature)
Epileptic Children 68
Episcopalians 127
Equality 155, 156, 158, 181, 225, 322
Essay Work 257, 262, 289
Esteem (Social)................................ 15
Ethics 137, 138, 139, 260, 267, 325
Europe........................... 223, 259
European History............................ 260
Eurhythmics.......................... 24, 201–204
Evolution 20, 25, 26, 136
Evening Classes, etc............ 107, 124, 337
Examinations 21, 162, 256
Exceptional Children 88
Exemption 344
Exhibitions 139, 153
Expenditure 107, 233
Experiment 159, 168, 169, 213
Experts 328
External Examinations, etc..........233, 298
Extra-mural Teaching...........266, 271, 289
Eye Strain 161

Failures.................................... 328
Far East 212, 223
Fear 162
Fees 99, 108–117, 122, 123, 129, 130, 181–188, 235–238, 242, 264, 275, 290, 310, 315
Feeble-minded 83
Fellowship 339, 377, 379, 387
Feudal 227
Finance 107, 182, 245
First Aid 280, 352
Foreign 211, 212
Forestry 215, 305
Foundations and Other Schools.79, 81, 99
Fraternity....................................155, 158
France...140, 178, 193, 212, 221, 222, 228, 352, 379, 380
Freedom 329
Freethinker.................................... 39
Froebel....................................... 235
Full Time Education 343

Games 14, 222, 233, 344, 347
Gardening 74, 354
Gary Schools, U.S.A....................... 160
Geology....................................206, 225

PAGE

Geography......52, 54, 129, 135, 137, 161,
177, 224 239, 276, 319
Germany 18, 130, 174-178, 193, 211,
212, 223, 224, 228, 241
Girls' Club 290
Governing Class 53
Graduates.........................81, 124, 128
Grammar Schools......63, 127, 192-196,
216, 245, 441
Grants in Aid ..78, 99, 101, 107, 108, 114,
123, 147, 183, 191, 199, 229, 236,
250, 255, 256, 271, 272, 281, 286,
294, 311, 332, 333, 336, 345, 348, 349
Greek 214, 236, 249, 250, 276, 293
Guardians, Boards of 110
Gymnastics 200, 201, 202, 224, 236,
237, 280, 437

HALF-TIME 64, 77, 356, 370
Handwork 74, 237
Headmaster 16, 136
Health 149, 161, 162
Hereditary 139, 143
Higher Education 66, 96, 100, 126,
127, 174, 175, 220, 273, 292, 344
Higher Elementary and Higher Grade
Schools 68, 70, 104, 109, 129
Highway," "The........................... 353
Highway of Education 63, 188
Hindu 229
History and Historians 52, 54, 120,
129, 131, 135, 137, 161, 177, 201,
203, 213-218, 224, 228, 239, 242,
254, 256, 267, 269, 280, 287, 289,
291, 294, 301, 303, 316, 319, 337,
350, 352, 354, 380, 386
Holiday School................................. 358
Holland..212, 235
Holy Orders... 17
Home.................................146, 172
Home Nursing................................. 352
Home Students................................. 305
Horticulture 221, 312
Hostels 101, 175, 233
Hours of Labour 344
Housewifery 74
Humane 256, 342
Human Nature 44, 159, 164
Humanities ...33, 34, 36, 53, 60, 62, 197, 215
Hygiene 122, 137, 235, 280, 297, 352

IDEALS 160, 228, 245, 258, 324, 329, 342,
371, 372
Illiterates 239
Imagination 24, 138, 278
Impartiality.........................371, 372, 390
Imperialism 135
Independence of Teachers 248
India.......................157, 212, 229, 379
Individual Tuition 307
Individualistic 169
Industrial History ... 260, 263, 268, 294,
300, 303, 337, 375, 386
Industrial Questions 409, 132, 197,
330, 333, 337
Industrial Schools.....................109, 111
Industry ... 51, 56, 57, 60, 175, 221, 231,
242, 269, 313, 325, 331, 345, 348
Infantile Mortality................65, 141, 142
Infants' Schools 146

PAGE

Inspection 107, 121, 232, 328
Intermediate Board........................... 120
Intermediate Certificate 129
Intermediate Education.................... 121
International 259
Interpretation 241, 242, 244, 326
Intra-mural 266, 269-271
Ireland 120, 244, 275

JAPAN 212, 223, 226, 227, 228
Jewish Schools........ 165
Junior Republics 173
Juvenile Labour 174

KINDERGARTENS 145, 147, 148, 211,
213, 221, 237, 437
Knowledge, Meaning of 325

LABOUR MOVEMENT...50, 57, 62, 63, 257,
266, 295, 320, 324, 325, 330, 331,
334, 358, 370, 390
Ladder of Education 33, 63, 270
Languages...131, 177, 214, 224, 225, 276,
280, 339, 381
Latin..............................236, 249, 276, 293
Laundry Work 74
Law......15, 171, 214, 215, 225, 228, 229,
231, 247, 275, 300, 302, 305, 314,
317, 318, 321, 337
Layman 328
Leaving Age 64, 127
Leaving Certificate 230
Leisure 157, 165, 179, 200, 244, 270,
279, 307, 328, 339
Liberal Education 19, 30, 344
Liberty 155, 156, 157, 325, 329
Libraries.................188, 205-210, 258, 348
Literary Societies............................ 341
Literature......19, 24, 129, 131, 132, 137,
161, 176, 179, 198, 203, 205, 214,
218, 221, 225, 229, 256, 260, 263,
267, 271, 275, 280, 287, 289, 294,
301, 303, 352, 353, 354, 359, 386, 391
Liturgy 164, 166
Loans......................................108, 183
Local Education Authorities...183, 236,
269, 464
Local Education Authorities, Accounts
of 108-112
Logic 137, 138, 193, 214

MAINTENANCE GRANTS (see Scholar-
ships)
Malnutrition 141, 142, 347
Managers.................................165, 267
Manual Training 135, 161, 213, 214
224, 437
Maps....................................... 183
Marxian 371
Mathematics...20, 136, 137, 218, 225, 298 381
Matriculation 230, 233, 242, 275, 313
Meals, School 64, 91, 344, 346, 347
Mediæval Tradition......................... 130
Mediation 243, 244
Medical and Dental Service...64, 85, 86,
109, 151, 181, 317, 318, 343, 347
Medical Inspections 86, 121, 128, 348
Medical Treatment............82, 85, 149, 187

PAGE

Medicine......214, 215, 225, 228, 230, 236,
    275, 286, 288, 295, 300, 301, 305,
            313, 314, 321, 337
Mendicant Friars 304
Mentally Defective Children ...68, 187,
                  191, 347, 437
Merchant Venturers 288
Merit Certificate 128
Metallurgy 250
Method of Education 19
Methods 228, 264, 328
Middle Class 59
Military Service Acts 73
Military Training ...39, 41, 54, 58, 178,
                    223, 349
Millinery 352
Mining 309
Minor Ailments 150, 151
Missionary Schools 229, 238
Monotonous 339
Montessori.............145, 158, 167, 172, 213
Morals ...19, 42, 161, 164, 166, 170, 176,
         221, 224, 226, 235, 269
Mothers 64, 45, 147, 148, 158,
                    352, 379
Municipalities 192, 205, 207, 232
Munition Areas 381
Music and Musicians...24, 35, 122, 185,
     190, 200, 201, 202, 242, 256, 257,
     260, 267, 275, 279, 280, 300, 302,
        305, 312, 314, 321, 380, 437

NATAL 238, 239
Natural Selection 26
Nature and Natural Science...14, 24,
    137, 141, 161, 164, 206, 218, 224,
     239, 267, 303, 305, 352, 354
Nautical College 129
Needlework 161
Nerve Strain 161
New Age.. 61
New Schools 69
New South Wales...........239, 254, 335-337
Newspapers 243
New Zealand ...187, 239, 336, 338, 353, 440
Nonconformity 25
Non-Provided Schools 64
Norway..................................174, 212, 236
Nurses and Nursery Schools ...64, 72,
    87, 90, 145, 146, 147, 150, 182

OLEGARCHIC 170
One-Year Classes 332, 340-350, 354
Open-Air Schools.........64, 90, 140, 151, 343
Opinion 374
Orange Free State 238
Organisation 162, 234, 269, 330, 342,
          349, 357, 430, 433
Orthodox 53, 326, 370, 379
Oxford and Working-Class Education
                  253, 324
Oxford Home Students 277

PAGEANTRY...................................... 164
Painting 24
Parents ...13, 19, 25, 33, 36, 59, 65, 110,
    142, 145, 147, 153, 165, 171, 173,
        174, 180-187, 343, 370
Parish Schools 127
Partisan 331

PAGE

Part-Time Teachers 71
Passion................................ 59
Patriotism 44, 54, 177, 200, 237
Pensions 64, 99-102, 106, 345
People's High Schools 212, 217, 237
Personality 146, 279, 325, 326
Philologists.................................... 204
Philosophy......26, 53, 165, 189, 229, 242,
     244, 256, 260, 303, 317, 359, 391
Photography 169
Physical Training...40, 64, 129, 222, 237, 347
Physical Defectives 68, 161, 347, 437
Physics 224, 225
Physiology 276
Play-writing 169
Playing Fields and Play Centres ...64,
        121, 160, 343, 346
Poetry 166, 176, 178
Political Science and Politics...20, 26,
    30, 39, 41, 51, 56, 57, 179, 211,
    240, 242, 243, 260, 267, 269, 303,
               354, 375
Poor Law Schools 75
Post-graduate Training 233
Potteries 386
Prefects 170
Preparatory Classes.......................... 356
Preparatory Schools 14, 184
Presbyterians.................................. 127
Priests 189, 192, 193
Primary Education 220, 221, 232-239
Private Study ...160, 184, 212, 220, 234, 239
Prizes 210
Problems 233, 245, 353
Professions..................175, 232, 345, 435
Progress , ... 340
Promotion of Teachers 347
Propaganda...229, 328, 330, 334, 349, 372, 391
Psychology...137, 138, 159, 163, 166, 170,
    172, 202, 214, 241, 256, 260, 263,
             267, 301, 303
Public Opinion........................15, 331
Punishments 21
Pupil Teachers 77, 96, 107

QUEENSLAND 336, 338

RAGGED SCHOOLS.............................. 188
Rates...108, 114, 116, 123, 183-190, 210,
                  238, 348
Reconstruction...57, 63, 66, 130, 228, 254,
    267, 301, 308, 327, 340, 350-358,
                374, 381
Reform Schools............................... 173
Register of Teachers 136
Regulations................................... 255
Religion...22, 27, 30, 166, 179, 180, 211,
    212, 220, 221, 234, 235, 325, 328,
        333, 337, 379, 433, 447
Remodelled Schools 347
Research ...182, 188, 190, 197-199, 207,
        226, 233, 243, 275, 345
Revolution ...19, 49, 53, 56, 58, 63, 66,
       186, 200, 244, 325, 372
Rhetoric 193
Rhythm..............................200, 201, 204
Rochdale Pioneers 374
Roman Catholics......17, 79-81, 99, 165, 277
Royal Commission on Welsh Univer-
    sity Education 323

PAGE

Rural...125, 128, 183, 210, 237, 305, 323, 352
Russia 178

SALARIES...64, 99-105, 112, 118, 122, 123,
131, 182, 183, 271, 347
Sanskrit 229
Scepticism 53
Schleswig-Holstein 218
Scholarships...76, 96, 107, 128, 139, 175,
177, 183, 187, 190, 191, 198, 218,
221, 232, 235, 264, 275, 289, 295,
310, 311, 322, 343-346, 371, 375, 384
School Board 59, 127, 314, 475
Schoolboy 59
Schoolmaster and Schoolmistresses ...
13, 19, 265
School Population 348
School for Mothers 90
Schools of Art 77
Science...20, 37, 53, 129, 164, 175, 176,
181, 192, 197, 214, 224-229, 236,
246-250, 275, 276, 286, 288, 292,
295, 300, 302, 309-318, 321 380
Scotch Education Department......123,
127, 130, 475
Scotland...20, 122, 174, 186, 255-257, 439, 440
Scripture 17, 52
Sculpture 24
Seasonal Industries........................... 344
Secondary Education and Schools, 23,
65, 70, 76, 77, 107, 115, 121, 122,
125, 126, 127, 130-136, 159, 174,
177, 183, 187, 192, 211, 221, 224,
230-242, 245, 269, 270, 276, 344,
345, 375, 434, 441
Secondary Education Committee 128
Secondary School Teachers 436, 438
Secular 26, 157, 166, 212, 238, 239
Self-Education 23, 31
Seminar 259, 264
Sewing.. 224
Sex 170, 178, 179, 337
Shift System 386
Singing 135, 145, 163, 224, 352
Size of Classes 64, 347, 348
Snobbery 18, 185, 298
Social Science, Problems and Ideals
33, 49, 56, 126, 135, 140, 158, 161,
163, 164, 168, 170, 172, 173, 175,
180, 223, 226, 242, 246, 248, 251,
260, 262, 267, 268, 278, 280, 282,
294, 301, 317, 319, 328-330, 332,
333, 337, 375, 386, 390, 391, 447, 448
Socialism 15, 20, 25, 66, 320, 330, 372
Society.....................................35, 53, 57
Soldiers (Disabled) 589
South Africa 238, 255, 353, 440
Special Qualifications....................... 343
Special Trades 346
Special Schools 89, 109, 110, 232
Special Subjects 74, 436
Spiritual ...37, 42, 45, 164, 165, 174, 180,
200, 201, 217, 259, 279, 325, 333,
342, 378
State Control, etc. ...211, 212, 218, 220,
223, 235-239
Status of Teachers 14, 57, 344
Stimulus 329, 371
Street Trading 435
Student-Teachers....................73, 77, 96

PAGE

Student's Point of View..................... 262
Study Circles..................330, 341, 350, 377
Submissive 19
Subsidies....................................... 370
Summer Schools...23, 125, 254, 259, 262,
264, 269, 301, 303, 306, 307, 311,
323, 331, 351, 356, 371, 376, 377, 384
Supplementary Teachers 73
Sweden..........................212, 236, 337
Swimming 64
Switzerland..................174, 176, 212, 234
Syndicalism..................................248, 330

TALE-BEARING 170
Tasmania.....................254, 255, 335, 336
Taste 242
Taxes 47, 48, 184, 185, 189, 190
Teachers, Number of..............73, 176, 433
Teachers' Associations 334
Teachers in Tutorial Classes 267
Teachers' Outlook 442
Teachers, Uncertificated...73, 101, 102, 347
Technical Schools......61, 77, 107, 115,
120, 129, 183-188, 215, 226, 231,
239, 241, 346, 437
Technical Schools Regulations 255
Technical Training.. 52, 60-62, 124, 132,
197, 198, 218, 227, 230, 233, 235-
237, 295, 300, 333, 345, 380
Temperament 39, 44, 202
Text Books....................................... 336
Theology 54, 165, 275, 302, 305, 320, 333
Theory, Educational..................33, 137, 138
Toleration 28, 333
Tolstoyan 28
Town Workers................................... 40
Trade Schools 236
Trade Unions 251, 268, 288, 307, 308
317, 328, 330, 331, 334, 341, 370-
373, 375, 388, 391, 438, 441
Trade Unionism 370, 375
Trades Councils 268, 288, 309, 330,
336, 341, 373, 391
Training of Teachers 101, 115, 118,
119, 129-138, 149, 182, 187, 191,
225, 229, 231, 241, 311, 312, 347, 353
Transvaal 238
Travelling Expenses 358
Treasury 122, 123, 199
Tuition Fees 79
Turks 9
Tutorial Class Movement......217, 253,
255, 256, 266, 270-273, 287, 305,
322, 335, 345, 349, 350, 354, 356,
358, 370, 377
Tutorial Classes, Composition of 267
     ,,   ,,   Growth of... 253
     ,,   ,,   Joint Committees ...
255, 258, 263, 266,
274, 286, 300
     ,,   ,,   Finance.................. 255
     ,,   ,,   Management of..255,
257, 332
     ,,   ,,   Method 257
     ,,   ,,   Member of 305
     ,,   ,,   Standard of Work ... 268
     ,,   ,,   Students.....259, 263,
269, 273
     ,,   ,,   Women in...260, 261, 308

PAGE

Tutors 126, 257, 262, 264, 267, 273,
     275, 306, 307, 323, 330, 351
Tutors' Salaries 269
,,   Status of :........................265, 266

ULSTER 20
Undenominational 378
Unemployment 260
University Extension...126,241,274,291, 308
University Government..................... 248
University Settlements 289
Urban Districts 110, 112, 116, 118, 464

VETERINARY 231
Victoria.......................................336, 338
Vocational....................................33, 34
Voluntary Associations............37, 278, 337
Voluntary Contributions 245
Voluntary Education....................30, 69
Voluntary Work 268, 351

PAGE

WALES................................. 174, 255, 263
War, The...... 17, 37, 39, 60, 61, 69, 149,
    160, 164, 174, 176, 183, 242, 255,
    256, 263, 273, 275, 276, 288, 306,
    308, 309, 316, 323, 326, 330, 338,
    340, 349, 350, 356, 357, 359, 376, 380
Weismannism 20
Welsh Intermediate.................. 79–81, 99
Western Civilisation 260, 359
Will 179
Women, University Education of...226
                249, 298, 305
Women Workers 320
Women's Classes 352
Woodwork 74
Working Men's Clubs.................341, 388
Works Schools 344

YELLOW RACES 223
Young Children................................. 342

ZOOLOGY... 342

INDEX OF NAMES.

ABLETT, NOAH 391
Adams, Miss Jane............................ 282
Andrews, Professor A. W. 380
Aristotle 27
Arnold, Thomas 167
Atkinson, Meredith 255, 294, 335 336

BACON, ROBERT............................... 304
Ballantyne, Dr. 143, 144
Barnett, Canon 278, 282
Bateson, Prof. W. 380
Beaton, Miss Winifred 253
Bell, Andrew................................14, 160
Bentham, Jeremy 298
Bergson, H.......................24, 26, 27
Birrell, A. 124
Bland, F. A.........................254, 335, 353
Bowerman, The Rt. Hon. C. W......... 388
Boyd, Dr. W. 127, 317
Branford, V. 282
Brougham, Lord 383
Brown, Dr. F. B. 353
Brown, P. A. 294
Browne, Miss T. M.................211, 220
Bryce, Lord 174
Burke, Dr. 359
Butler, S.. 26

CALVIN 20, 26, 27
Campbell, Dr. Janet 148
Carnegie, A.................186, 187, 188, 199
Cartwright, E. S. 387
Cashmore, Miss H. 278
Clarke, Sir Ed. 383
Clodd, E.. 26
Clutton Brock, A............................. 33
Cole, G. D. H.............................56, 370
Comte Auguste 181
Copeland, D. B................................ 337
Cranage, Dr. C................................ 292
Curzon, Lord.................................... 229

DAINTON, A. H................................. 294
Dalcroze, Jaques 200, 204
Dale, Professor J. A. 353
Dante 26
Darroch, Professor 316
Darwin, Charles 26, 27
Darwin, Major Leonard..................... 140
Dent, J. J.. 385
Descartes.. 197
Dewey, Professor J. 247
Dicey, A. V. 268

ELIOT, C. W..................................... 214
Erasmus 193
Euripides 24

FALLOWS, J. A. 192, 196
Farquhar, Professor J. N................... 380
Fels, Joseph 149
Finlay, Professor A. 380
Fisher, The Right Hon. H. A. L. ...26,
             166, 464
Fleming, A. P. 177
Foster-Watson, Professor 193, 196
Freeman, A. 56, 180

GALSWORTHY, JOHN.......................... 39
Galton, Sir Frances......................... 139
Geddes, Professor P. 300
Gladstone, W. E. 383
Goethe 24
Gooch, G. P. 301
Greenwood, Arthur 267
Gregory, Prof. R. A......................... 380
Grimshaw, H. A. 245
Grundtvig, Bishop.....................217, 218

HALDANE, VISCOUNT...........15, 19, 21, 197
Hall, Duncan 254
Hall, Fred 374
Hallsworth, Professor..................293, 294

	PAGE
Hammond, J. L.	380
Haywood, Dr.	164, 165, 180
Headicar, B. M.	205
Heath, Miss A. C.	217
Heath, Dr.	199
Heaton, Herbert	255, 337
Hobson, J. A.	51
Hobson, S. G.	19, 59
Holmes, E.	15, 19, 155, 158, 167
Horrabin, Mr. and Mrs. J. F.	391
Hughes, Miss	15, 19, 158, 159, 163

IBSEN ... 24

JEVONS, Dr. F. B.	443
Jones, Professor Thomas	380
Joshi, R. M.	229

KEATINGS, DR.	19
Keatinge, M. W.	131
Kerschensteiner	198
Kidd, Benjamin	76
Knox, John	128
Kold, Kristen	217, 218

LANCASTER, JOSEPH	14, 134, 160
Latimer	192
Laud, Archbishop	305
Leach, A. F.	193, 194, 196
Leach, William	63
Lee, J. W.	293, 355
Leonard, Professor G. H.	288
Ling	237
Lodge, Professor Sir Richard	315, 380
Lowe, R.	52, 240, 241
Louth, T.	391

McCORMICK, SIR W.	199
Macgregor, Dr. Lilias	294
MacMillan, Miss Margaret	19, 146, 148, 149
Mactavish, J. M.	24, 328, 342
Maitland, F. W.	368
Mansbridge, Albert	253, 254, 308, 315, 322–324, 335
Marriott, J. A. R.	309
Marshall, Alfred	230, 332
Marx, Karl	330, 332
Masterman, Canon J. H. B.	381
Medley, Prof. D. L.	380
Mendel, F. W.	140, 141
Moles, T. W.	294
Molesworth, B. H.	254
Montessori, Dr.	151
Morant, Sir Robert	17
Morgan, Dr. C. Lloyd	288
Morris, Wm.	181
Muir, Prof. Ramsay	380
Murray, Prof. Gilbert	381

NIETZCHE ... 24

OSBORNE, C. H. C.	15, 19, 21, 167
Owen, Miss Grace	145
Owen, Sir Isambard	380
Owen, Robert	374
Owens, John	301
Oxford, Bishop of	325

PATON, J. L.	19, 23, 174
Pattison, Professor Pringle	198

	PAGE
Pearse, P. H.	28
Pease, J. A.	443
Pincombe, W. J.	438
Plato	24, 200, 201, 203, 244, 260
Pollen, A. H.	380
Poulsen	277
Poulton, Professor E. B.	380
Price, T. W.	287
Priestley, J. H.	288
Pullein, Robert	304

RAE, W. R.	375
Rahilly, Professor A	120, 318
Ramsbottom, J. W.	294
Ratcliffe, S. K.	381
Ripon, Lord	229
Roberts, Professor T. Stanley	380
Robieson, M. W.	318
Robinson, W. H.	447
Rogers, Miss A. M. A. H.	275
Rousseau	159
Roxby, Professor P. M.	223
Ruskin, John	23

SADLER, DR.	218, 271
St. David	164
St. Thomas Aquinas	27
Saleeby, C. W.	139
Sandwich, Earl	171
Scholes, P. A.	380
Schopenhauer	24
Scott, C. A.	169, 170
Scruton, Miss N.	262
Seldes, Professor G. V.	213
Shakespeare	24, 164, 191
Shaw, Bernard	13, 27, 246
Shaw, Rev. J. Hudson	381
Shimmin, A. N.	263
Simnett, W. E.	339
Simpson, Professor J. Y.	380
Simpson, J. H.	169
Smith, Adam	313
Smith, Sharwood	168
Snowball, F. G.	168
Stanton, G.	374
Stevenson, Miss	293
Stewart, D.	336
Strong, John	130
Struthers, Sir John	128, 475
Stuart, James	291

TAWNEY, R. H.	301, 305, 386
Temple, A.	383
Temple, Rev. W.	324, 380
Thomas, D. Lleufer	323
Thorndyke, E. L.	163
Thornton, —.	217, 219
Toynbee, Arnold	278
Trevelyan, G. M.	301
Trevena, J. G.	293, 355
Turner, Professor H. H.	380

VICKERS, PROFESSOR	294
Vinogradoff	268
Vrooman, Mr. and Mrs.	388

WAGNER	20
Wallace, Sir Whitworth	380
Warner, Townsend	268
Waugh, A.	14

	PAGE
Webb, Sidney 23, 181, 241, 268	
Webb, Mrs. S. 433, 438	
Weismann 27	
Wells, H. G......66, 178	
Whitehouse, Professor W. E....... 380	
Wilkins, H. T. 196	
Wilson, President 214	
Wilson, R....... 294	

	PAGE
Wirt, — 160	
Wykeham, Wm. J. 192	
Yeaxlee, Rev. Basil...... 380	
Zimmern, A. E....... 240	
Zoete, Miss Beryl de......24, 200	

INDEX OF ORGANISATIONS.

Aberdeen County Schoolmasters' Association 449
Accountant Lecturers' Association ... 449
Adult School Union...... 288, 293, 392, 448
Animal Brothers' Guild, Our 392
Art for Schools Association, The 392
Art Masters, The National Society of.. 460
Art Teachers' Guild 450
Arts, Royal Society of...... 392
Assistant Masters in Secondary Schools, The Incorporated Association of 455
Assistant Mistresses in Public Secondary Schools, The Association of 450
Assistant Mistresses in Public Secondary Schools, The Incorporated Association of...... 455
Assistants in Central Schools, London, The Association of 450

Bakers, Amalgamated Union of Operative 448
Barnett House 281
Birds, Royal Society for the Protection of 393
Birmingham Council and Voluntary School Head Teachers' Association 452
Book-keeping Teachers, The Association of 450
Boy Scout Movement, The 393
British and Foreign School Society ... 394
British Association, The Educational Section of the...... 394
British Museum 209
Brotherhood Council, The National ... 395

Carnegie United KingdomTrustees 258
Catholic Colleges, Conference of 395
Catholic Headmasters' Association ... 452
Catholic Teachers' Association, The National Federation of 459
Catholic Working Boys' Technical Aid Association 125
Central Joint Advisory Committee on Tutorial Classes......253, 255, 265, 324, 325
Central Library for Students ... 208, 258, 294, 352, 382
Child Study Society, The...... 395
Children's Aid Association 172
Church School Managers & Teachers, The General Association of ... 396

Church Schoolmasters and Schoolmistresses' Benevolent Institution, The 397
Class Teachers, The National Federation of 460
Club and Institute Union 383, 398
College of Preceptors......311, 433, 436, 452
Commercial and Specialist Teachers, The Institute of...... 456
Commercial Institutes, The London Union of 457
Commercial Teachers, The Incorporated Society of...... 456
Commercial Teachers Union, The Sheffield 461
Conservative Party 441
Consultative Committee of the Board of Education 435
Co-operators' Educational League...... 376
Co-operative Union......293, 302, 374
Co-operative Union Educational Committee, The...... 398
County Councils' Association 398
County Schools' Association, Welsh... 463

Dalcroze Society of Great Britain and Ireland 399
Dalcroze Teachers'Union,The London 456
Dance Teachers, The Imperial Society of 399
Decimal Association, The...... 399
Dentists' Society, School 399
Deptford Health Centre...... 149
Design and Industries Association ... 399
Directors and Secretaries for Education, Association of 399
Drawing Society, The Royal......400, 437
Duty and Discipline Movement 400

Educational Colonies of Self-supporting SchoolsAssociation 403
Education Committees, Association of 401
Educational Institute of Scotland 454
„ Institutions, The Union of 403
„ as National Service 400
„ Officers, The National Association of 401
„ Reform Council 163, 401
Empire Education League 404
„ League of the 404
English Association, The 404
Esperanto Association, British......404, 448
Ethical Society 448
Evening Institutes Association, The Metropolitan 458

PAGE

FABIAN RESEARCH DEPARTMENT 404
Federation of Education Committees
(Wales and Monmouthshire)... 405
Fircroft... 217
Free Church Council 448
Friendly Societies Council 448
Friends' Guild of Teachers 454
Froebel Educational Institute, The ... 405
„ Society, The.............................. 406
„ Union, The National................... 406

GAELIC LEAGUE 125
General Federation of Trade Unions 388
Geographical Association 406
„ Society, Royal.......................... 406
Gilchrist Educational Trust...253, 255,
264, 407
Girls' Clubs, Liverpool Union of 407
Girls' Clubs, National Organisation of 407
Girls' Public Day School Trust 80
Guild of the Epiphany 407
Guild of Graduates.......................... 428
Guilds League, National.................... 61
Guildhall School of Music 437
Gymnastic Teachers' Institute, The
Incorporated 456

HANDWORK ASSOCIATION, EDUCA-
TIONAL 408, 437
Headmasters of the Endowed Schools
in the Midland Counties, The
Association of the 450
Headmasters' Conference 454
Headmasters, The Incorporated Asso-
ciation of.............................. 455
Headmistresses,The Association of..... 450
Headmistresses' Association, The
Yorkshire 463
Headmistresses of Public Secondary
Schools in the Administrative
County of London, The Con-
ference of 453
Head Teachers' Association 438
Head Teachers' Association, The
London................................ 456
Head Teachers, The National Associa-
tion of 458
Historical Association, The 408
Historical Society, Royal... 409
Home Reading Union, National ...381, 409

IMPERIAL UNION OF TEACHERS, THE... 455
Incorporated Union of Graduates in
Music 437
Independent Labour Party 319, 448
Irish Agricultural Organisation Society 320
Irish Schoolmistresses, The Central
Association of....................... 452

JUNIOR REPUBLIC, THE GEORGE 15

KINEMATOGRAPH INTERNATIONAL
COUNCIL, EDUCATIONAL 409

LABOUR COLLEGE............332, 371, 390 469
Labour College, Scottish 409
Labour Party 65, 284, 370, 440, 441
Lancashire and Cheshire Institutes,
Union of 410
Liberal Party..................................... 441

Ling Association, The 410
Little Commonwealth, The 15, 168-173
London Teachers' Association......435,
438, 457
London Schools' Dinner Association.. 410

MANCHESTER AND SALFORD DISTRICT
EDUCATIONAL ASSOCIATION... 411
Manual Training of Teachers, The
National Association of 459
Married Women's Teachers' Associa-
tion, The London.................. 457
Mathematical Association................. 411
Medical Association, British 371
Medical Officers of Schools, Associa-
tion of 411
Miners' Federation 302
Miners' Association, Durham 293
Miners' Association, Northumberland. 293
Miners' Higher Education Movement
(North Staffordshire) 410
Miners' Federation, South Wales...371, 391
Modern Language Association 411
Montessori Society, London 411
Music in Secondary Schools, The
Union of Directors of........... 463
Music Teachers' Association 458
Music, Union of Graduates in............ 412
Music Union, Girls' School 412
Musicians, Incorporated Society of ... 412

NATIONAL AMALGAMATED UNION OF
LABOURERS............................ 293
National Association for the Preven-
tion of Infant Mortality 142
National Education Association 412
National Federation of Class Teachers 438
National Society 413
National Union of Clerks 448
National Union of Teachers 288,
435-436, 438, 439, 445
National Union of Teachers, The
Irish Protestant..................... 456
Naturalists' League, Young 414
Nature Study Society........................ 414
Nature Study Union, The School 414
New Ideals in Education 415
Non-Collegiate Certificated Teachers,
The National Association of... 450
Northern Counties' Education League,
The 410
Nursery Schools Association, Bir-
mingham,............................. 416
„ Schools, Manchester and Salford
Association, for Day Nurseries
and Nursery Schools 417

OLD SCHOLARS' ASSOCIATION 340
Oral Instruction of the Deaf, The
National Association for the... 417
Organising Masters and Secretaries for
Technical Education, The
West Riding Association of ... 463
Oxford and Cambridge Schools Exten-
sion Board, The..................... 418
„ University Extension Delegacy... 418

PARENTS'NATIONAL EDUCATION UNION 419
Pearse's Sgoil Eanna, President......... 15

PAGE

Physical Education, The Incorporated
British College of 419
,, Education and Improvement,
National League 420
,, Education, National Society of... 437
Pitman's Certificated Teachers of
Shorthand, The Society of...... 462
Play Centres Committee, Evening...... 420
The Plebs League 332, 371, 390, 420
Preparatory Schools, The Association
of 420, 451
Private Schools Association 420, 461
Professeurs de Francais en Angleterre,
Le Société des 462
ProgressiveEducationCouncil,London 420
Public School Science Masters, Asso-
ciation of 451

RAILWAYMEN, NATIONAL UNION...371,
391, 448
Representative Managers of L.C.C.
Elementary Schools............... 421
Ruskin College ...18, 332, 371, 384, 388,
390, 421

SANITARY INSTITUTE, ROYAL 421
Scholarships Board, Joint................... 421
School Attendance Officers' National
Association 393
School Board Clerks and Treasurers
in Scotland, Association of ... 422
Schoolmasters' Association 461
Schoolmasters, The Society of 421
Schoolmasters' Widows' Fund, Boro'
and Parochial...................... 421
Schools and Institutions for the Deaf,
The Council of Principals of... 453
Schools Mutual Aid Society............... 422
Scottish Education Reform Committee 439
Scottish School Boards Association ... 422
Science Guild, British 422
Secondary Education, Association of
Scotland 422, 451
Secondary Schools' Association 422
Secondary School Associations, The
Federal Council of 454
Secondary Teachers in Ireland,
Association of........................ 451
Secondary Schools'Scripture Teaching
Conference, The 422
Secondary School Teachers' War
Relief Fund.......................... 461
Sesame House Association, The........ 423
Shaftesbury Ragged School Union ... 423
Simplified Spelling Society, The...... 423
Smith Training College of the Royal
Normal College for the Blind,
The 424
Social Studies Committee, Joint......... 424
Society of Friends 378
Sowerby Division Conference of Youth 424
State Children's Association, The...... 424
Student Christian Union of Great
Britain and Ireland, The 396

TEACHERS OF THE BLIND, THE
COLLEGE OF 453
,, Christian Association, The 425
,, in Commerce, The Faculty of...... 454

PAGE

Teachers of the Deaf, The National
Association of...................... 459
,, of the Deaf on the Pure Oral
System, The Union 463
,, of Domestic Subjects, Associa-
tion of 451
,, Guild of Great Britain and Ire-
land 436
,, Guild 462
,, Insurance Society, Secondary,
Technical, and University...... 461
,, League of the South London
Hospital for Women, The...... 425
,, Registration Council 17, 435,
437, 440, 443
,, in Technical Institutions, Asso-
ciation of 451
,, Training Association................... 462
Technical Institutions, Association of
425, 437
Theosophical Education Trust 425
,, Fraternity in Education, The ... 426
Toolmakers' Society 447
Toynbee Hall.............................. 258
Trade Unions............................... 319
Trades Union Congress...370, 388, 462, 463
Trades Council, Federated 448
Training Colleges under Government
Inspection, The Council of
Principals of 453
Tutorial Class Tutors under the
University of London, The
Association of...................... 452
Tutors' Conference : Constitution...... 265

UNIVERSITY TUTORIAL CLASS
TUTORS, THE CONFERENCE OF 453
Uncertificated Teachers, The National
Union of 460
University Extension Guild............... 427
,, Extension Lecturers' Associa-
tion, The London.................. 458
,, Extension, Manchester 427
,, Lecturers, The Association of ... 452
,, of London, Board to Promote
the Extension of University
Teachers 428
,, of London Graduates' Association 428
,, Settlement Association in East
London 429
,, Women Teachers, The Associa-
tion of 452
Uplands Association, The 429
Urban District Councils' Association.. 430

VICTORIA LEAGUE 430

WAGE-EARNING CHILDREN, COMMIS-
SION ON..................................... 431
Women's Co-operative Guilds............ 352
Women's Gardening Association 432
Women Graduates and Candidate
Graduates, Irish Association of 431
Women's Industrial Council 430
Women in Oxford, The Association
for the Education of 277, 431

PAGE		PAGE

Women's Labour League.................. 352

Women Teachers, The National Federation of 460

Women Workers of Great Britain and Ireland, The National Union of 431

Workers' Educational Association, 324–369, 432

,, Activities of, 350; Affiliations, 334, 350; Branches, 308, 330, 334, 350, 357, 359, 362–69; Central Council, 334, 342, 353; Colleges, 259, 333, 351; Constitution, 315, 325, 327, 350

Workers' Educational Association— Districts, 327, 334, 350, 362–69; Eastern, 354, 362; London, 354, 362; Midland, 355, 363; North-Eastern, 355, 364; North-Western, 356, 364; South-Eastern, 356, 365; Welsh, 357, 366; Western, 357, 367; Yorkshire, 358, 368; Scotland, 359, 369; Ireland, 359, 369

,, Formation of, 324; Overseas, 353; Publications, 360; Spirit, 259

Working Men's College 253; 337

Y.M.C.A 25, 42, 379, 432, 352

Y.W.C.A. 432

Shaftesbury Society and Ragged School Union.

ESTABLISHED 1844.

HELPS TO MAINTAIN through 50 Branches and 90 Affiliated Missions a wide and varied network of social, moral and religious agencies in London and District.

PROVIDES Surgical Instruments and Spinal Carriages, Home Comforts and Country Holidays for thousands of cripple children.

SUPPLIES Clothes and Boots, Toys and Good Cheer for tens of thousands of poor children.

SPECIALLY HELPS children of families hit by the War.

Donations in money and materials are earnestly invited, and should be addressed to SIR JOHN KIRK, *J.P.,* Director, Shaftesbury Society and R.S.U., *32, John Street, Theobald's Road, London, W.C. 1. Gifts of War Loan Stock and Memorial Gifts are respectfully invited. Seventy-third Annual Report sent on application.*

Bird and Tree (Arbor Day)
CHALLENGE SHIELD COMPETITIONS.

ALL INTERESTED IN MODERN METHODS OF EDUCA-
TION AND NATURE - STUDY SHOULD PROMOTE THIS
SCHEME, ORGANISED AND CONDUCTED IN ELE-
MENTARY SCHOOLS BY THE ROYAL SOCIETY FOR THE
PROTECTION OF BIRDS.

It leads children to observe and think for
themselves and to find pleasure in out-door
life; it trains eye and ear and quickens
general intelligence; it affords invaluable
first-hand knowledge of Birds and Trees,
promoting Bird-Protection on a reasonable
basis and encouraging Tree-planting. The
War has emphasised the national need for
such knowledge.

Teachers, members of Education Committees, and others are invited
to send for particulars to the Secretary, Royal Society for the Protection
of Birds, 23, Queen Anne's Gate, S.W. 1.

THE BERGMAN ÖSTERBERG ... PHYSICAL TRAINING COLLEGE,

DARTFORD HEATH, KENT.

Trustees :—

Sir GEORGE NEWMAN, M.D. (Chairman).
Major the Hon. WALDORF ASTOR, M.P.
The MARCHIONESS OF SALISBURY.
The Rt. Hon. Dr. CHRISTOPHER ADDISON, M.P.
The Rt. Hon. LORD SHAW OF DUNFERMLINE.

Principal : Miss H. C. GREENE.

Vice-Principal :—

Miss A. WIKNER (Royal Cent. Inst. of Gymnastics, Stockholm).

THE College was opened in 1885 and was the first of its kind in England. ¶ Students are prepared as teachers of Scientific Physical Education on Ling's Swedish System. ¶ The course extends over two years. ¶ It includes the study of Anatomy, Physiology, Theory of Education; the Theory and Practice of Gymnastics, Massage, and Medical Gymnastics, Dancing, and Outdoor Games. ¶ Students practise teaching in schools in the neighbourhood. ¶ The College stands in its own grounds of Fifteen acres, in a beautiful and healthy locality, close to Dartford Heath. ¶ The course begins in September.

FURTHER PARTICULARS ON APPLICATION to the SECRETARY.

BEDFORD PHYSICAL TRAINING COLLEGE

LANSDOWNE ROAD, BEDFORD.

Principal : - - - - MISS STANSFELD.

Students are trained to become Teachers of Gymnastics and Games in Colleges and Schools.

THE CURRICULUM INCLUDES :—

The Theory and Practice of Educational Gymnastics, and Massage and Remedial Gymnastics (Swedish System) ; Dancing ; Anatomy, Physiology, Hygiene, Psychology.

Games :—

Hockey, Lacrosse, Cricket, Lawn Tennis, Net Ball.

An educational centre like Bedford affords special facilities for practice in Teaching and Remedial Work, and for professional coaching in Games. Swimming and Boating in the Summer.

FEES : - - £105 A YEAR.

FOR PROSPECTUS APPLY

THE SECRETARY, *37, Lansdowne Road, Bedford.*

Church Education Corporation

At each School Pupils are prepared for any of the usual Public Examinations, and for the Entrance and Scholarship Examinations at Oxford or Cambridge.

Offices: 34, Denison House, Westminster, London, S.W. 1.

Chairman: Sir W. MACKWORTH YOUNG, K.C.S.I.
Secretary : C. C. OSBORNE, Esq.

SANDECOTES SCHOOL, Parkstone, Dorset.

Head Mistress: Miss A. GRAINGER GRAY.

Board and Tuition, £100.

A School for the daughters of Gentlemen. There are two large Residences, a School-house, and a Sanatorium. The buildings stand in over ten acres of ground— on gravel soil, high and well-drained. There are grass and gravel Lawn Tennis Courts, a Fives Court, and a large Playing Field. Parkstone is one of the healthiest and most beautiful places on the South Coast.

UPLANDS SCHOOL, St. Leonards-on-Sea.

Head Mistress: Miss MARY V. HILL, M.A., London.

Board and Tuition, £60.

This School is specially intended for the daughters of Gentlemen. It provides a thoroughly efficient modern education. Special Department for Housewifery and Domestic Science for elder girls. There is a Laboratory for practical science work, a well-equipped Gymnasium, a Swimming Bath, Tennis and Fives Courts, and a large Playing Field.

MILHAM FORD SCHOOL, Oxford.

Head Mistress: Miss J. S. H. McCABE

(late of Ladies' College, Cheltenham).

Board and Tuition, 40 to 50 guineas a year.

A well-equipped Modern School for Girls, fitted with every convenience. Science Laboratory, School Garden, Playing Field. There are special advantages for girls preparing for the University.

DE NOAILLES TRUST.

This Trust is for the benefit of daughters of the Clergy of the Church of England who have lost one or both parents. No girl under eight or more than 16 years of age is eligible. The minimum value of a Bursary is £35 per annum; the Board and Tuition fees are £60. A higher bursary may be awarded. Bursars reside under the care of a Headmistress in Oxford, and attend Milham Ford School as day pupils. Holders of Bursaries, on reaching 18 years of age, may be awarded a further Bursary to cover a portion or the whole of the cost of University, or other special training. Applications should be made to the Secretary, Church Education Corporation.

CHERWELL HALL, Oxford.

Training College for Women Secondary Teachers.
Recognised by the Board of Education, by the Oxford Delegacy, and by the Cambridge University Syndicate for Secondary Training.

Principal: Miss CATHERINE I. DODD, M.A.

Students are prepared for the Oxford Teachers' Diploma; the Cambridge Teachers' Certificate; the London Teachers' Diploma; the Oxford Geography Diploma; and for the Cherwell Hall Teachers' Certificate for Junior Form Mistresses.

Fees for the three Terms, from 66 guineas.

THE GIPSY HILL TRAINING COLLEGE FOR TEACHERS OF YOUNG CHILDREN,

GIPSY HILL, LONDON, S.E. 19.

PRINCIPAL: Miss LILLIAN de LISSA (Montessori Diploma, late Principal, Kindergarten Training College, Adelaide, South Australia.

VICE-PRINCIPAL: Miss ISABEL STEPHENS, M.A. (Late English Tutor, City of Leeds Training College).

The College has been founded for the purpose of providing training, both for Resident and Day Students, in the principles and practice of education advocated by Dr. Maria Montessori, and other modern educationalists.

Two classes of students will be received :—

(I) Students taking a Two Years' Course under the Regulations of the Board of Education for the Training of Teachers for Elementary Schools.

These Students will be eligible for the usual grants and to receive the Board's Certificate, under certain conditions, on the satisfactory completion of the Course. A prospectus stating these conditions may be obtained on application.

(II) Private Students taking a Two Years' Course with a view to work in Nursevy Schools, Secondary Schools or as Governesses.

A One Year Course is open to Certificated Teachers.

Students are admitted yearly in September.

EXPERT TUITION BY CORRESPONDENCE.

FOR MATRICULATION, B.A., and other **University** and **Professional Examinations;** and for independent study.

SINGLE SUBJECTS MAY BE TAKEN :—

LATIN	FRENCH	MATHS.	HISTORY	PHYSICS	PSYCHOLOGY
GREEK	GERMAN	ENGLISH	CHEMISTRY	LOGIC	ECONOMICS, etc.

The System is thoroughly individual and ensures to each student the closest attention.

The Staff consists of Graduates of Oxford, Cambridge and London Universities.

For terms, etc., address :—**Mr. J. CHARLESTON, B.A.** (Hons. Oxon, and Lond.), **Burlington Correspondence College, 14, Elsham Road, Kensington, W. 14.**

The London School of Dalcroze Eurhythmics

23 STORE STREET W.C. 1.

(THE DALCROZE SCHOOL OF EURHYTHMICS, LTD.)

Under the personal inspection of Monsieur JAQUES-DALCROZE, of Geneva.

Director : PERCY B. INGHAM B.A.   *Telephone :* MUSEUM 2294.

The BRITISH WOMEN'S EMIGRATION ASSOCIATION. *Canada, Australia, New Zealand*
Information and advice given gratis to all classes of women and girls, Professional, Business, and Domestic. Frequent protected Parties to Canada, Second-class and Third-class. Reserved Car Inland Rail. Special Departments for Teachers and Nurses. TEACHERS MUCH NEEDED FOR GOVERNMENT SCHOOLS IN CANADA. Openings for Trained Nurses in Australia, New Zealand, and Canada. Escort offered to young women joining friends or relatives. HOSTELS IN LONDON AND BRITISH COLUMBIA for the accommodation of those travelling under the auspices of the Association. Full particulars from :—
MISS LEFROY, HON. SEC., B.W.E.A. OFFICE, IMPERIAL INSTITUTE, S.W. 7.